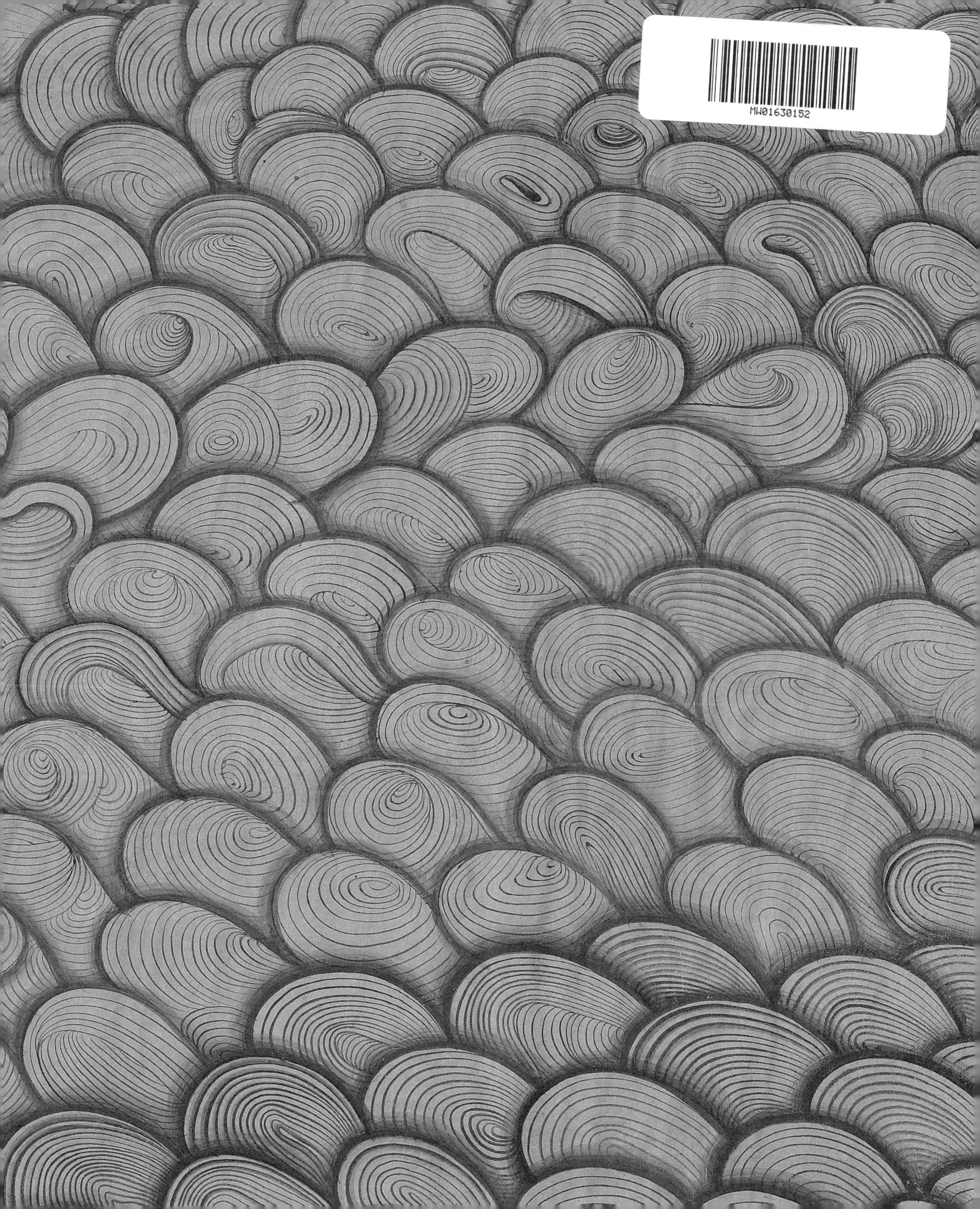

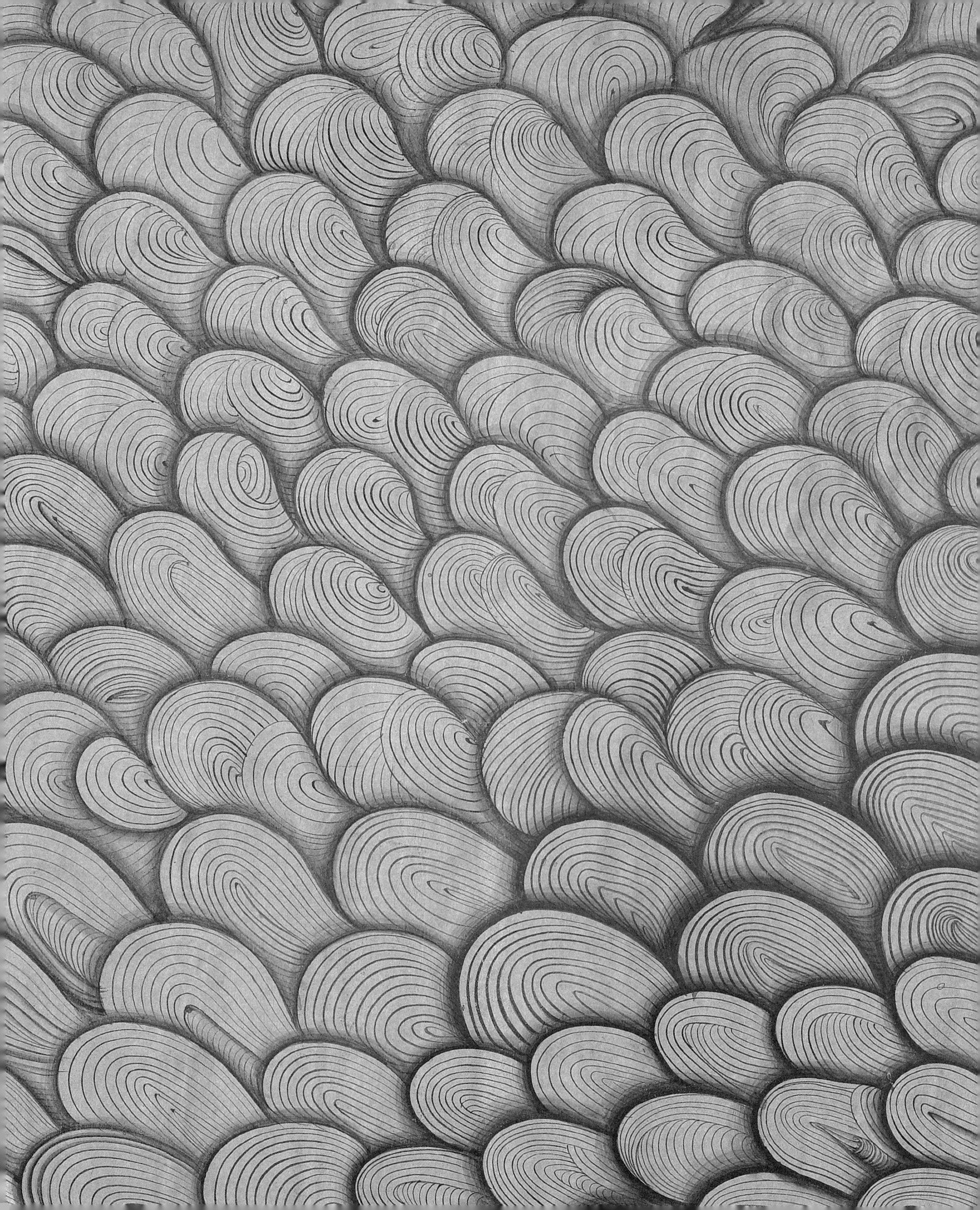

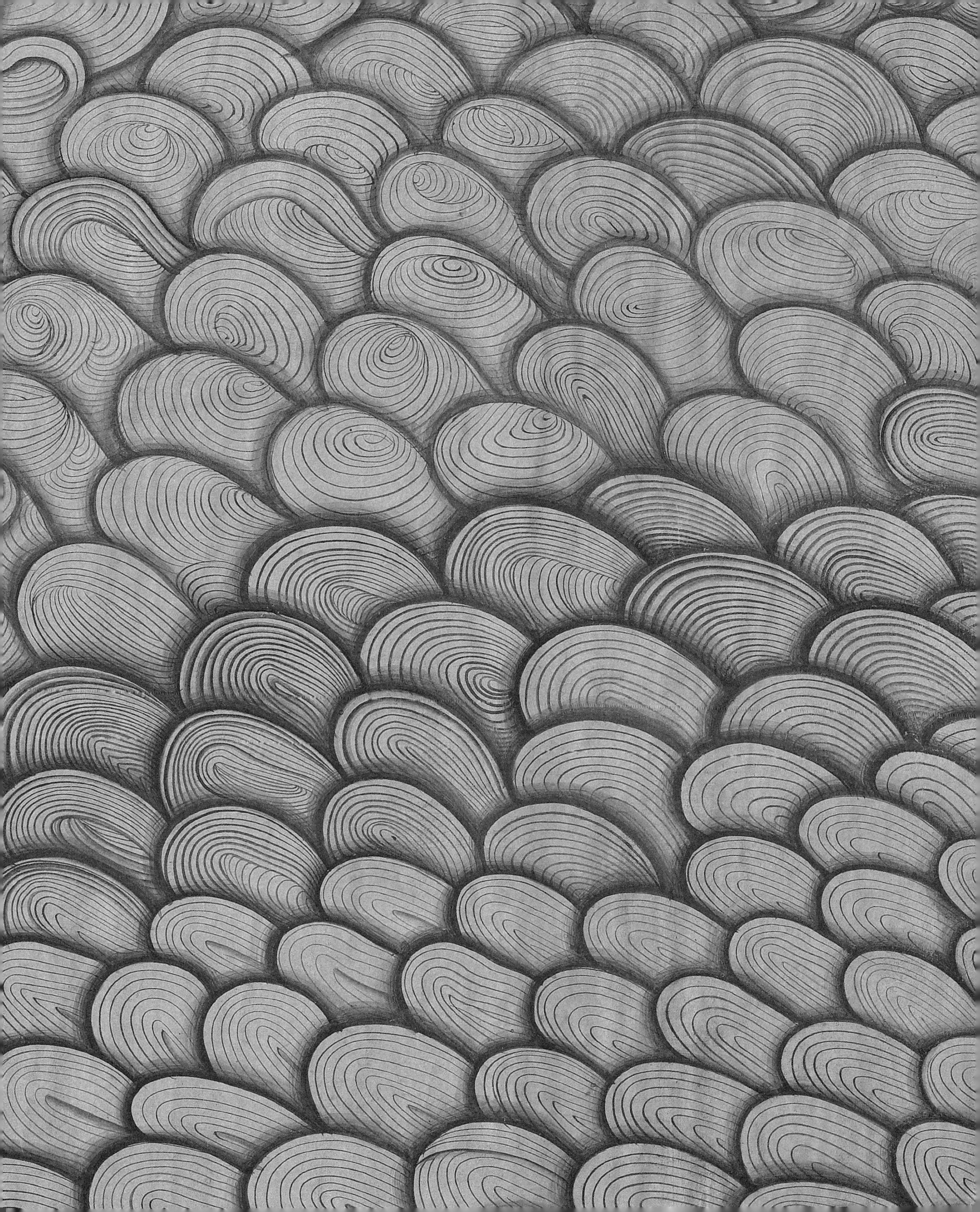

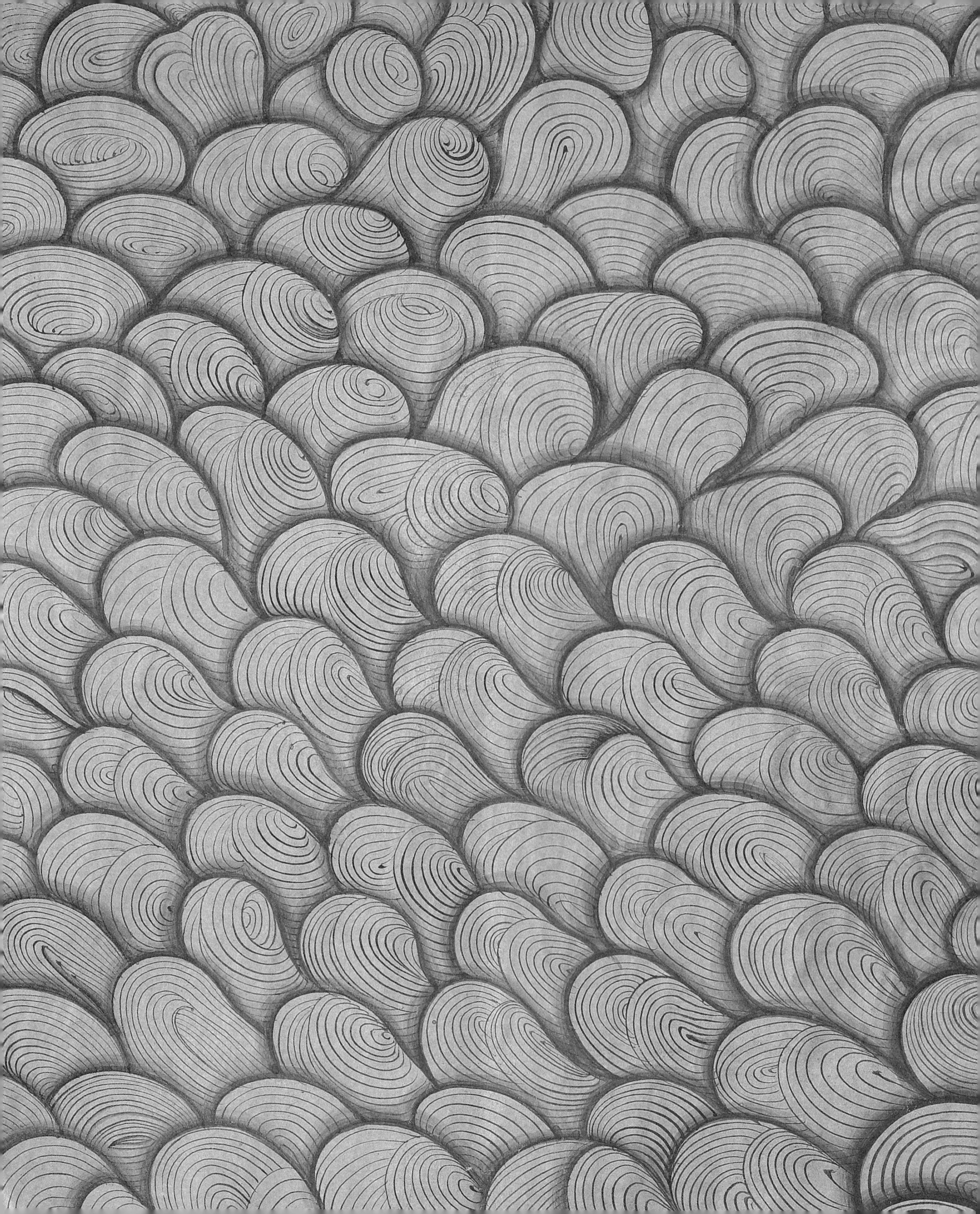

GARDEN&COSMOS

The Royal Paintings of Jodhpur

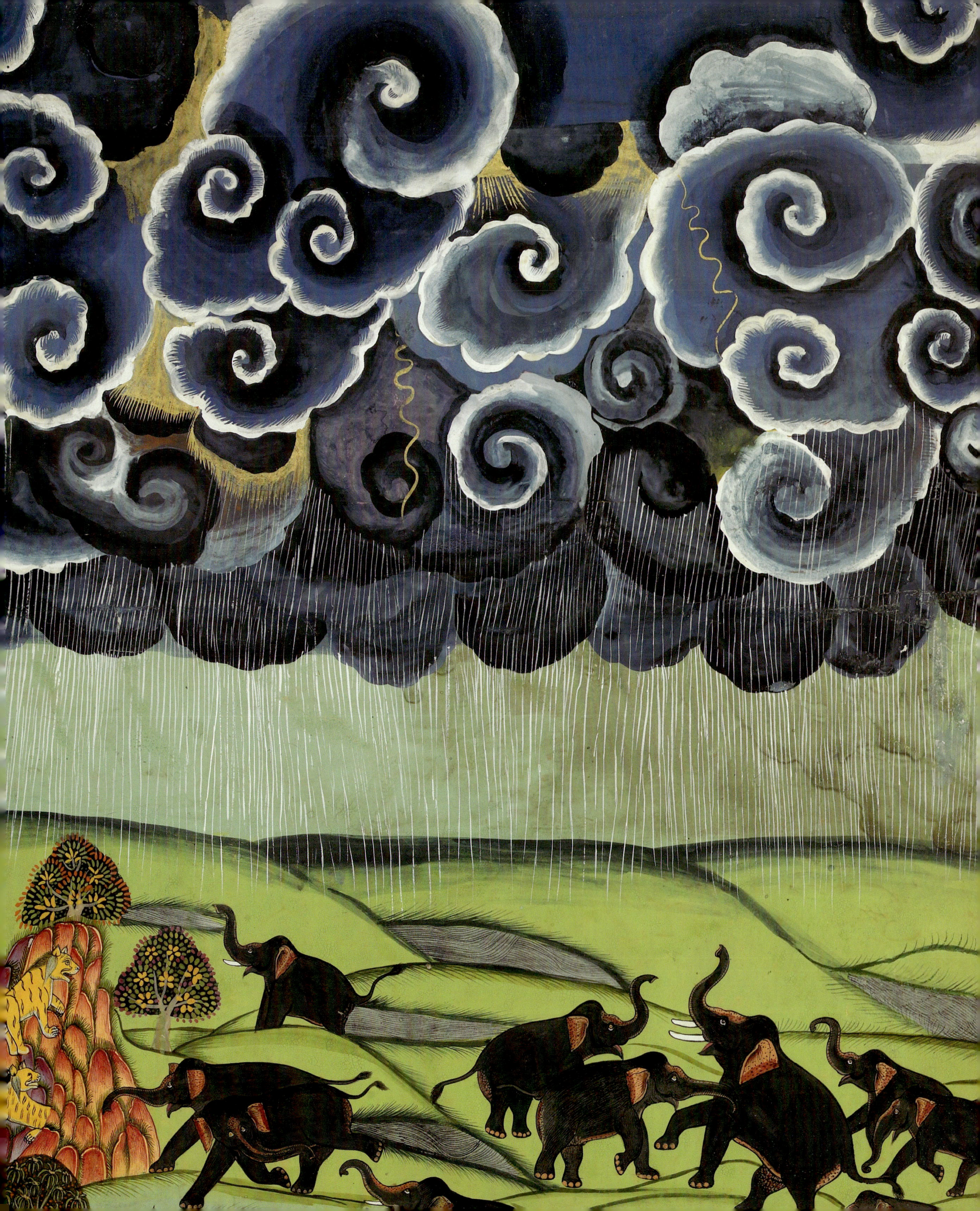

GARDEN&COSMOS

The Royal Paintings of Jodhpur

DEBRA DIAMOND, CATHERINE GLYNN, AND KARNI SINGH JASOL
WITH CONTRIBUTIONS BY JASON FREITAG AND RAHUL JAIN

ARTHUR M. SACKLER GALLERY
SMITHSONIAN INSTITUTION, WASHINGTON, D.C.

Published by the Freer Gallery of Art and the Arthur M. Sackler Gallery on the occasion of the exhibition *Garden and Cosmos: The Royal Paintings of Jodhpur,* October 11, 2008–January 4, 2009. Organized by the Arthur M. Sackler Gallery, the exhibition travels to the Seattle Art Museum, January 29–April 26, 2009, British Museum, May 28–August 23, 2009, and National Museum of India, opening November 2009.

Publisher's note Color reproductions and information about each painting can be found in the catalogue section beginning on p. 51; additional scholarly information and comparative works appear in the reference catalogue beginning on p. 257. The initials listed after each entry refer to the contributors listed on p. 333. Dimensions throughout the book are given in centimeters in this order: height by width.

On the cover and title page: *Death of Vali; Rama and Lakshmana Wait out the Monsoon,* cat. 27, detail

Head of Design and Production: Karen Sasaki
Editors: Jane Lusaka, Nancy Eickel
Catalogue Design and Production: Kelly Webb
Photographer: Neil Greentree
Image and Photo Services: John Tsantes, Neil Greentree
Rights and Reproduction: Cory Grace
Exhibition Design: Nancy Hacskaylo
Exhibition Coordinators: Cheryl Sobas, Kelly Swain

Typeset in Caecilia and Nimbus Sans Novus
Printed in Singapore by CS Graphics

Library of Congress Cataloging-in-Publication Data
Diamond, Debra.
  Garden and cosmos : the royal paintings of Jodhpur / Debra Diamond, Catherine Glynn, and Karni Singh Jasol ; with contributions by Jason Freitag and Rahul Jain.
    p. cm.
  Issued in connection with an exhibition held Oct. 11, 2008–Jan. 4, 2009, Arthur M. Sackler Gallery, Washington, D.C., and at three other institutions at later dates.
  Includes bibliographical references and index.
  ISBN 978-0-934686-08-2 (pbk.)
  ISBN 978-1-58834-257-7 (cloth)
  1. Marwar painting–Exhibitions. 2. Rajput painting–India–Jodhpur–Exhibitions. I. Glynn, Catherine Ann, 1946- II. Jasol, Kr. Fateh Singh, 1942- III. Arthur M. Sackler Gallery (Smithsonian Institution) IV. Title.

ND1337.I4D53 2008
759.954'4–dc22
                        2008024611

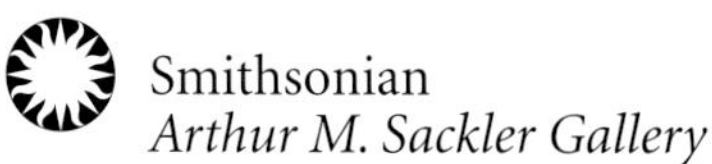

Contents

Foreword

JULIAN RABY

DIRECTOR, FREER GALLERY OF ART AND ARTHUR M. SACKLER GALLERY

Garden and Cosmos: The Royal Paintings of Jodhpur sheds light on an unknown aspect of India's artistic achievements. The exhibition is centered on fifty-five extraordinary paintings, almost all of which are unpublished, from a corpus of some three thousand in the royal collection of the Mehrangarh Museum Trust. Many of these oversized works overturn our expectations regarding Rajput painting, i.e., of miniatures that express a conservative court culture. Glorious gardens in desert palaces, shimmering expanses of gold and silver, and hallucinatory juxtapositions of color reveal that Jodhpur artists repeatedly developed unique styles and imagery. The paintings depict the political and cultural vitality of Jodhpur–Marwar between the seventeenth and nineteenth centuries, and reflect how painters conveyed profound metaphysical conceptions with sophistication and creative genius.

The Indian government has been crucial to the exhibition's success. We gratefully acknowledge the support of Ambassador to the United States Ronen Sen; Minister Ambika Soni and Joint Secretary R. C. Mishra, Ministry of Culture; Vijay S. Madan, director general, National Museum of India; and Rahul Chhabra, minister at the Indian Embassy.

We also sincerely thank the National Museum of India, National Gallery, Victoria, and the British Library for lending important works that elucidate the origins of Marwar court painting. But an exhibition of such import would not have been possible without the Mehrangarh Museum Trust, whose commitment to international museum standards and friendship is a model. His Highness Gaj Singh II, maharaja of Jodhpur–Marwar, and Maharani Hemlata Rajye, whose ancestral collections are represented in the show, have shown a boundless generosity of spirit and remarkable hospitality. Mahendra Singh, CEO of the Trust, and Karni Singh Jasol, curator of the Mehrangarh Museum, have been indispensable to all aspects of this endeavor. They have made this project a delight from the outset.

Garden and Cosmos is part of both a year-long Celebration of India at the Freer Gallery of Art and the Arthur M. Sackler Gallery and a world tour that will take it to Seattle, London, and Delhi. Congressmen Joe Wilson and Jim McDermott, co-chairs of the India Caucus of the U.S. House of Representatives, have shown a keen and active interest in this project, as has Dino Teppara, Rep. Wilson's chief of staff. We received valuable support from the U.S.-India Business Council, in particular its President Ron Somers and staff members Tara Dhawan, Aditi Mody, and Nivedita Mehra.

Ambassador Frank G. and Christine Wisner have been trusted advisors to the Celebration of India. Early financial and in-kind support came through the good offices of David Good of Tata North America, Ian Thomas of Boeing India, and Andrew Steele of the Shangri La Hotel in Delhi. I also warmly thank Grace Bender and the 2008 Gala Committee, who worked tirelessly to coordinate our spectacular events. We further thank Kiran Pasricha of the Confederation of Indian Industry and Ingrid B. Henick of the Cohen Group.

Finally, I most gratefully acknowledge the Friends of the Freer and the Sackler Galleries, whose ongoing support and personal interest in the museums is invaluable and inspiring.

Foreword

HIS HIGHNESS GAJ SINGH II, MAHARAJA OF JODHPUR–MARWAR

Huts of Aak,

Barriers of Thorn,

Bread of Maize,

Lentils of Vetch.

Behold Raja, your Marwar!

In 1226, Rao Sheoji, founder of the Rathore clan, of whom I am the thirty-eighth in line, rode out into the wilderness known as Marwar, an arid but beautiful land inhabited by the proud and courageous, rich in culture and ritual. Rao Sheoji left behind the ruins of the imperial capital of Kanauj, seeking glory and a patrimony of his own. In 1459, Rao Jodha, fifteenth of his dynasty, laid the foundations of Mehrangarh Fort and the seeds of the city named after him—Jodhpur. Five hundred fifty years later, Mehrangarh remains a strong symbol of the clan, my family, and the city—its culture, traditions, festivals, and history.

In 1972, I established the Mehrangarh Museum Trust, housing the museum within the fort's hallowed walls, to ensure that the fort endures as the cultural soul of Jodhpur. Today, the Trust is at the forefront of heritage conservation, a patron of the living arts, and a center of academic study, and the museum displays fine and applied arts of the Rajput–Mughal period.

The paintings handed down by my ancestors are perhaps the most important of the Jodhpur royal collections. During the eighteenth and nineteenth centuries, the Jodhpur atelier developed individual styles that artists interpreted in a host of different ways. Artists trained at the Mughal court introduced sophisticated concepts of portraiture and composition to Jodhpur in the seventeenth and eighteenth centuries, and these ideas were combined with distinctive local styles and bold colors to form a uniquely lively school of painting. The Mughal–Rajput counterpoint is best illustrated by the court and garden paintings produced during Maharaja Bakhat Singh's twenty-five-year custodianship of the Nagaur fort, Ahhichatragarh. The Nagaur artworks represent unusual and sophisticated innovations, juxtaposing contemporary life with architectural representations.

Jodhpur painting took an exuberant turn around the devout Maharaja Vijai Singh (reigned 1752–93), whose artists produced uniquely large manuscripts related to Krishna, Rama, and the Goddess. His grandson, Maharaja Man Singh (reigned 1803–43), continued the Jodhpur tradition of monumental painting. His atelier transformed obscure texts dealing with Nath philosophies into opulent and glowing images of cosmic origins and mandalas.

I am delighted that the first major international exposition of Marwar paintings is opening at the Sackler Gallery, with which we have had a long-standing relationship. I thank Julian Raby for his consistent support and leadership; curators Debra Diamond, Catherine Glynn, and Karni Singh Jasol for their diligent scholarship; and the trustees of the Sackler, Seattle Art Museum, The British Museum, and the National Museum of India for graciously hosting the exhibition at their distinguished galleries. While I cannot name everyone involved with the exhibition, I thank each of them profusely; without their hard work, *Garden and Cosmos* would not have reached the heights it has achieved. Finally, I thank the trustees of the Mehrangarh Museum Trust, whose guidance and support has established our museum as an important entity among its counterparts in the world.

Sponsors

This publication is made possible with the generous support of

LEON LEVY
FOUNDATION

Dr. and Mrs. Kenneth X. Robbins, Mrs. Nunda and Dr. Prakash Ambegaonkar,
and Dr. Susan L. Beningson

Garden & Cosmos is organized by the Arthur M. Sackler Gallery in collaboration with
the Mehrangarh Museum Trust, India. It has received support from:

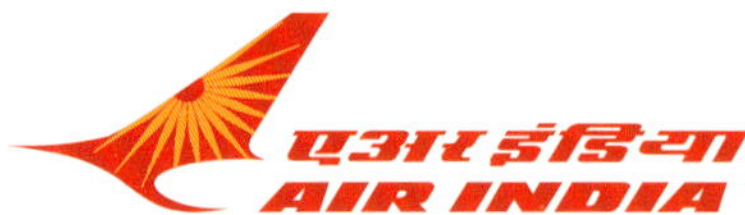

Friends of the Freer and Sackler Galleries
The Embassy of India to the United States
Boeing International Corporation India
The Honorable Max N. Berry and Mrs. Berry
Roger S. Firestone Foundation
Sulzberger Foundation
Elsa Faria Santos and Luis Bento dos Santos
Mr. Robert Rea and Mr. James Mathews
Mr. and Mrs. Jere Broh-Kahn
Ines Farrajota
Dickinson Miller
Caroline C. Stewart
Murray B. Woldman
Sanjay Umashankar, Taj Hotels Resorts and Palaces
Edgar M. Masinter
Susan W. Dryfoos

Honorary Committee

CHAIR

His Excellency, Ronen Sen, Ambassador of India to the United States

Mrs. Laura Bush

His Excellency, Michael Collins, Ambassador of the Republic of Ireland to the United States

The Honorable Hillary Rodham Clinton, United States Senator

The Honorable John Cornyn, United States Senator

The Honorable Jim McDermott, United States Representative, Co-Chair India Caucus

The Honorable Joe Wilson, United States Representative, Co-Chair India Caucus

The Honorable Nick Rahall, United States Representative

The Honorable Howard L. Berman, United States Representative

The Honorable John Lewis, United States Representative

The Honorable Michael R. McNulty, United States Representative

The Honorable Edward Royce, United States Representative

The Honorable Michael Doyle, United States Representative

The Honorable Sheila Jackson Lee, United States Representative

The Honorable Loretta Sanchez, United States Representative

The Honorable Barbara Lee, United States Representative

The Honorable Joe Baca, United States Representative

The Honorable Jan Schakowsky, United States Representative

The Honorable Shelley Berkley, United States Representative

The Honorable Joseph Crowley, United States Representative

The Honorable Linda Sanchez, United States Representative

The Honorable Chris Van Hollen, United States Representative

The Honorable Henry Kissinger, former Secretary of State

The Honorable Frank Wisner, former Ambassador of the United States, and Mrs. Wisner

The Honorable Richard Celeste, former Ambassador of the United States,
    and Ms. Lundquist

The Honorable Robert D. Blackwill, former Ambassador of the United States

Dr. Milo Cleveland Beach, former Director of the Freer Gallery of Art
    and Arthur M. Sackler Gallery

Bim Bissell, New Delhi

Sant and Pardaman Chatwal, New York, NY

Cynthia R. Helms, Washington, DC

Indira Mansingh, New Delhi

Kiran Pasricha, Confederation of Indian Industry

Dame Jillian Sackler, New York, NY

Mahendra Singh, Mehrangarh Museum Trust

Ron Somers, U.S.-India Business Council

Dr. Mahinder Tak, Bethesda, MD

Acknowledgments

The idea for this catalogue and exhibition occurred simultaneously to several different people. Debra Diamond and Karni Singh Jasol were discussing an exhibition of Jodhpur's monumental manuscripts when Catherine Glynn suggested a broader exhibition that included Nagaur court painting as well. From the very beginning, we have received energetic support from our two institutions, particularly Julian Raby, director of the Freer and Sackler, and Maharaja Gaj Singh II of the Mehrangarh Museum Trust.

We could not have organized an exhibition of this complexity without the generous cooperation of many individuals. One of our principal objectives has been to introduce unknown aspects of Jodhpur painting to American, Indian, and international audiences. Special gratitude is due to Ambika Soni, minister of tourism and culture, India, Ronen Sen, U.S. ambassador to India, and Rao Raja Mahendra Singh, CEO of the Mehrangarh Museum Trust, for making this possible. The exhibition in New Delhi would have been impossible without the support of the National Museum of India, including Madan Rajan, director, Raghuraj Chauhan, director of exhibitions, and Dr. Daljeet Kaur, chief curator of painting. We wish to thank Neil MacGregor, Jan Stuart, and Richard Blurton of the British Museum, and Mimi Gates, Chio Ishekawa, and Josh Yiu of the Seattle Art Museum for joining with us to bring this exhibition to London and Seattle.

With their superb expertise and commitment, the Freer and Sackler staff have created a spectacular exhibition and insightful programming, for which we are all sincerely grateful. We express gratitude to all who made the catalogue possible, including authors Jason Freitag and Rahul Jain, Molly Emma Aitken, who carefully read the text, and Neil Greentree, who beautifully photographed the Marwar forts and paintings. The Smithsonian Institution Scholarly Studies program, American Institute for Indian Studies, Columbia University, and The Sterling and Francine Clark Art Institute provided research support.

We received generous assistance from scholars Milo Beach, Rosemary Crill, Vidya Dehejia, Massumeh Farhad, Annapurna Garimella, John Stratton Hawley, Nahar Singh Jasol, the late Rajendra Joshi, the late Komal Kothari, Terence McInerney, Keith Moxey, Mahendra Singh Naggar, Robert Skelton, Andrew Topsfield, and David Gordon White. Other individuals also gave their time and expertise: Pandit Krishna Mohan Bhatt, the late Thakur Raju Singh Bhatti, Dr. Gita Raman, Dr. Kenneth X. Robbins, and the late Thakur Anand Singh. Jessica Farquhar, Marianne Henein, Kathryn Phillips, Roshna Kapadia, Stephanie Rozman, Bhanwar Singh, Nilanjana Som, Rajeshwari Shah Orchha, Mahendra Tanwar, and Pushpinder Ujjwal provided valued research assistance.

We give warm thanks also to the following for their generosity, advice, and support: Maharani Hemlata Rajye, Shobha Kanwar Baiji of Marwar; Bim Bissell; Ambassador Rabinder and Dr. Smita Jassal; Ann Kumar; Maureen Liebl; S. K. Misra, chairman, INTACH; Ambassador Lalit and Indira Mansingh, Elizabeth Moynihan; Diane Schafer; Martand Singh, chairman, INTACH U.K., and Mehrangarh Museum trustee; Catherine Asher, Dan Ehnbom, Baiji Lal Rajeshwari Shahiba, and Barbara Timmer. Finally, we thank those dear friends and perspicacious scholars who visited us in the storerooms of the Mehrangarh Museum Trust, shared our enthusiasm for these incredible paintings, and encouraged us to create this exhibition and publication.

A Note on the Inscriptions and Transliteration

INSCRIPTIONS

Unless otherwise indicated, all painting inscriptions are written in Marwari, a dialect of Rajasthani, in a regional Devanagari script.

Many painting inscriptions refer to the *dholiya* storeroom. During Man Singh's reign (1804–43), the *dholiya* storeroom was established for correspondence and paintings. The room must have been used earlier for drums (*dhol*) or cots (*dholiya*); it is currently the Turban Gallery of the Mehrangarh Fort Museum.

TRANSLITERATION, TRANSLATIONS, AND DATES

For readability, we have avoided diacritics. Since this work reproduces Marwari, Hindi, and Sanskrit texts, any of which may vary from contemporary pronunciation in India, we have opted for the following rules of transliteration.

To approximate the sounds of certain consonants, *sh* is used for both श and ष; *ch* for च and छ; *v* for व; *ri* for ऋ and *m* or *n* for nasalization in the middle of words (e.g., Krishna, samvat). Two exceptions, Marwar and Diwali, reflect common usage. The nasalization of a final vowel is represented by *n*; both long and short vowels are represented by their short vowel equivalents.

We have retained the final vowel of Sanskrit-derived transliterations that are familiar to English readers (e.g., Rama, Shiva, yoga), except in cases that conflict with usage in India and the United States. Marwari and Hindi terms (including the months of the year) are rendered with their final consonant, reflecting common pronunciation.

We have followed Merriam Webster's Third New International Dictionary (unabridged) for anglicization (e.g., ashram, Singh) and use the accepted English spelling for place names.

Several of the names present special challenges. We chose to render the name of Maharaja Vijai Singh in the way that most directly transliterates the archivist's inscriptions on the versos of the paintings, rather than the usual alternatives Bijai or Bijay. We also directly transliterated the other names rendered in Marwari in the paintings' inscriptions, but provide their Hindi equivalents in the translations.

Dated paintings from Marwar bear the Vikram Samvat year; therefore, the transliteration of inscriptions includes the samvat year; the translation subtracts fifty-seven to determine the Gregorian calendar year.

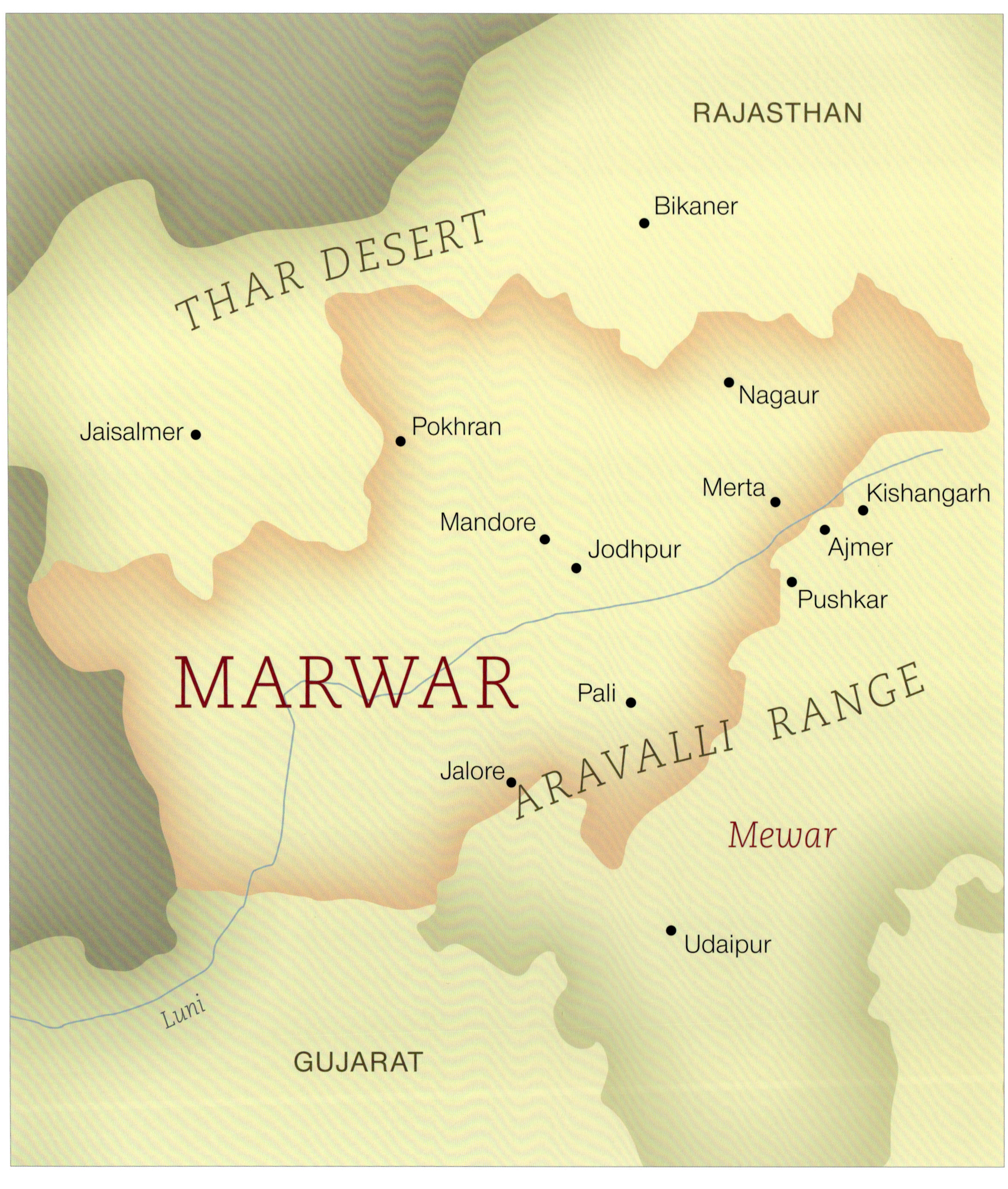

RAJASTHAN
THAR DESERT
Bikaner
Nagaur
Jaisalmer
Pokhran
Merta
Kishangarh
Mandore
Ajmer
Jodhpur
Pushkar
MARWAR
Pali
ARAVALLI RANGE
Jalore
Mewar
Udaipur
Luni
GUJARAT

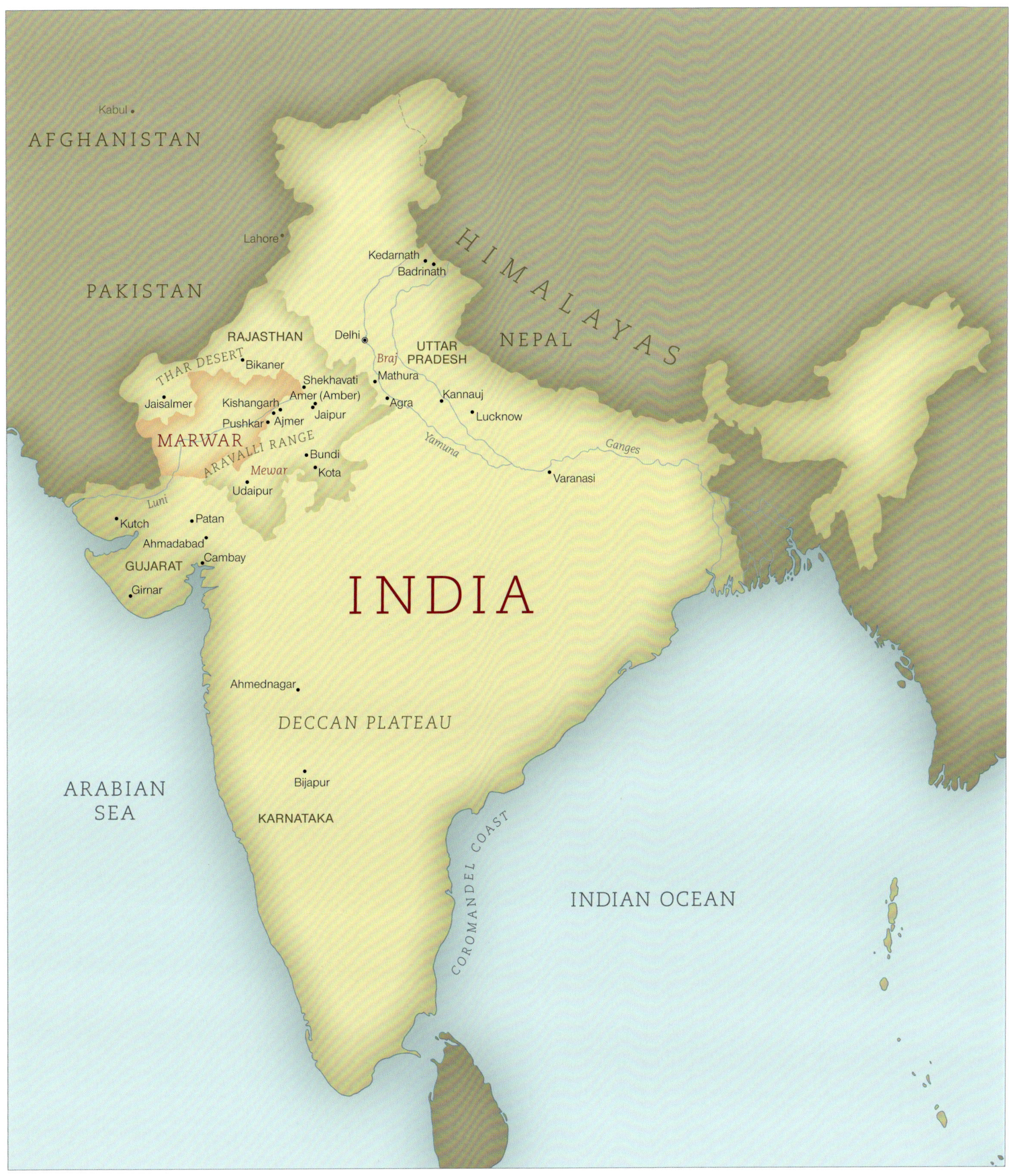

AFGHANISTAN
Kabul
PAKISTAN
Lahore
HIMALAYAS
Kedarnath
Badrinath
NEPAL
RAJASTHAN
Delhi
THAR DESERT
Bikaner
UTTAR
PRADESH
Braj
Shekhavati
Mathura
Amer (Amber)
Jaisalmer
Kishangarh
Kannauj
Pushkar
Ajmer
Jaipur
Agra
Lucknow
MARWAR
ARAVALLI RANGE
Yamuna
Ganges
Mewar
Bundi
Udaipur
Kota
Varanasi
Luni
Kutch
Patan
Ahmadabad
Cambay
INDIA
GUJARAT
Girnar
Ahmednagar
DECCAN PLATEAU
ARABIAN
SEA
Bijapur
KARNATAKA
COROMANDEL COAST
INDIAN OCEAN

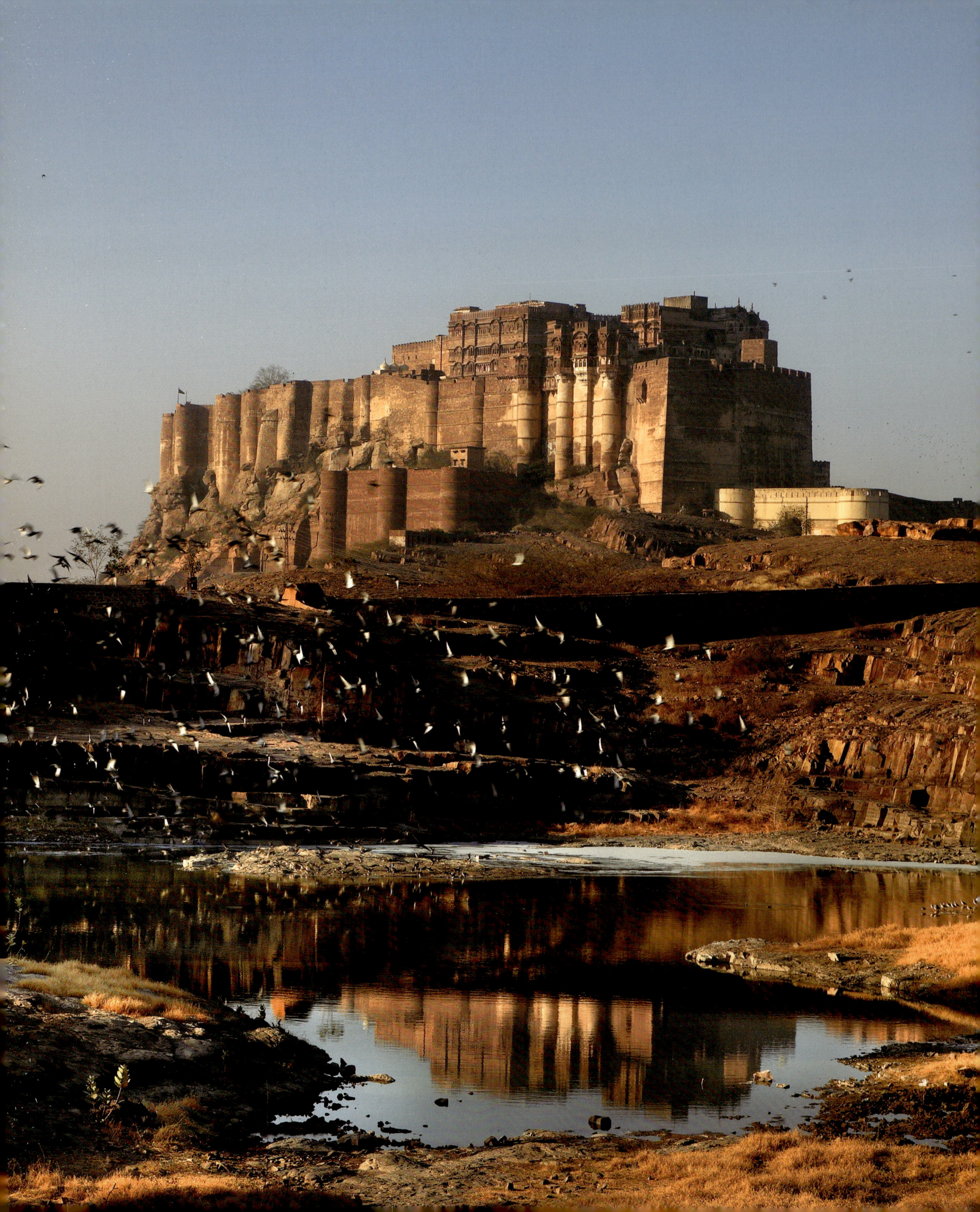

The Rathores of Jodhpur–Marwar

KARNI SINGH JASOL

Once the capital of Marwar—a kingdom located in northwest India at the edge of the Great Indian or Thar Desert—Jodhpur is today part of the state of Rajasthan. Maharaja Gaj Singh II, the thirty-sixth dynastic head of Jodhpur–Marwar, is a private citizen of the world's largest democracy. For him, almost every day is a remarkable negotiation of the past with the present. His dual focus on preserving the cultural heritage of Marwar takes on life in his charitable pursuits,[1] part of his continuing commitment to the ideals of service and learning held by his ancestors.

Before it merged into the nation of India in 1947, Jodhpur–Marwar was the third largest Indian state, after Kashmir and Hyderabad, with an area of over 36,000 square miles. The kingdom was established in 1459 by Rao Jodha, the head of the Rathore clan of Rajputs[2] (literally, "sons of kings"), who claim their descent from the *Kshatriyas*, the hereditary Hindu social class (or caste) of warriors and rulers. Their sense of duty is exemplified in the following verse.

Shauryam tejo dhritir dakshyam, yuddhe chapy-apalayanam,
Danam ishvara bhavashcha, kshatram karma savabhava jam
Valor, brilliance, determination, skillfulness, steadfastness in battle,
generosity and authority are the natural qualities of work for the Kshatriya[3]

Rajputs, particularly Rathores, consistently identify themselves with the quality of valor (Sanskrit: *shauryam*; Marwari: *rajputai*).[4] They are the *kshetrapal*, or the protectors of the domain. This sense of responsibility has informed their behavior over time and was expressed in a verse by a Rathore bard[5]:

In perpetual battles so furious that dust covers the sun,
The Rajput is cut into pieces,
His blood soaks the soil,
But he does not give an inch of the motherland to the enemy.

They sought the blessing of the Goddess Devi (bottom center), to maintain order (dharma), destroy their enemies, and protect their subjects (see p. 3).[6] Rathores continue to honor the great goddess today.[7] Every year in the month of Chaitra (March–April), Maharaja Gaj Singh (top right), like his ancestors, celebrates Navratri—the nine-night festival celebrating Devi—at the Chamunda temple in Jodhpur's Mehrangarh Fort. (See bottom left.)

While goddess worship was and remains a central component of Rathore devotion, each ruler also honored other deities with whom they felt a personal attachment.[8] These devotional affinities legitimated their sacred authority and shaped their individual expressions of kingship.[9] A well-known Marwari verse reveals how the respective devotional inclinations of Maharaja Vijai Singh and Maharaja Man Singh shaped Marwar and encapsulates how these two great kings stamped their sovereign ideals upon their periods:

jodh basayo jodhpur, vijai kino vrajpal.
lakhnau, kashi, dili, man kiyo nepal
Rao Jodha founded Jodhpur,
Vijai Singh made it like Braj [the land of Krishna]
Man Singh made Jodhpur equal to Lucknow [for its refined court culture],
Kashi (for its devotion to Shiva), Delhi [for its concentration of power],
and Nepal [where Nath grace had established dynastic power].[10]

Brilliant generals and true devotees though they may have been, the rajas of Jodhpur–Marwar were also often men of formidable intellect. Many were ardent connoisseurs; several were also respected poets and authors. Within their forts and palaces, they surrounded themselves with highly skilled and talented scholars, artists and musicians. "Garden" and "cosmos" are the metaphors that reveal how Marwari artists evoked the beauty of this world and the power of the gods to express Rathore ideals as they evolved over two centuries.

MEHRANGARH AND AHHICHATRAGARH FORTS

Rathore court culture was centered within two great forts, Mehrangarh, in the capital city of Jodhpur (top left), and Ahhichatragarh, in the northern city of Nagaur (pp. 4–5). To the kings of India, forts like these were objects of great power and prestige. They served not only as military bases, bulwarks against invaders, and sites of devotion with their many temples and shrines, but also as palaces for rulers and their wives and centers for the arts, music, and literature. In Mehrangarh and Ahhichatragarh, architecture, textiles, wall paintings, music, poetry, and court rituals worked together to express an aestheticized ethos of rule. The paintings in the exhibition, created primarily in the two forts, are distillations of this vision.

Previous page Mehrangarh Fort, Jodhpur. **Clockwise from top right,** Maharaja Gaj Singh II in 2006; Throne, Sringar Chauk, Mehrangarh Fort; *Maharaja Ajit Singh Worshipping the Goddess,* Jodhpur, ca. 1720. Mehrangarh Museum Trust, RJS 1972; Chamunda Temple, Mehrangarh Fort; the fort and the city of Jodhpur.

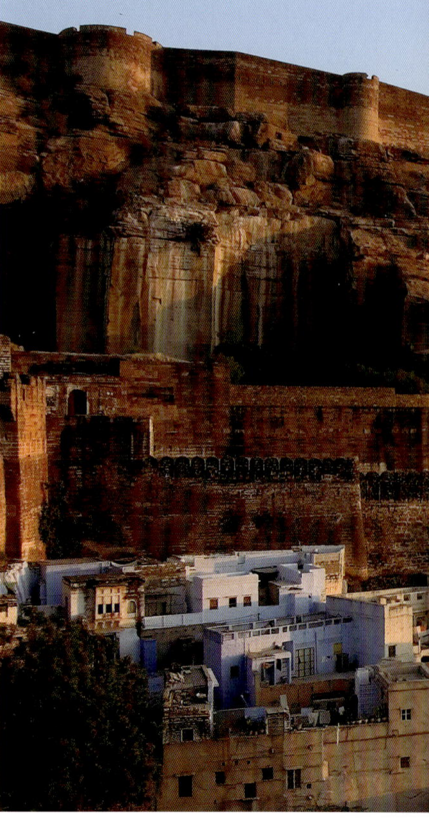

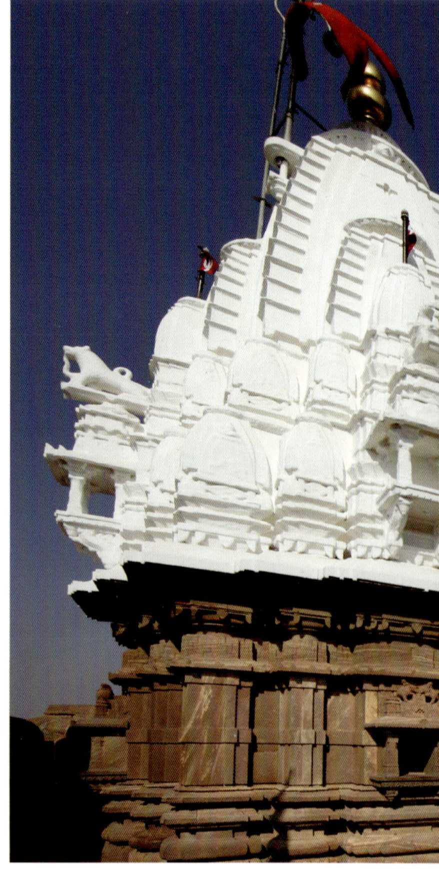

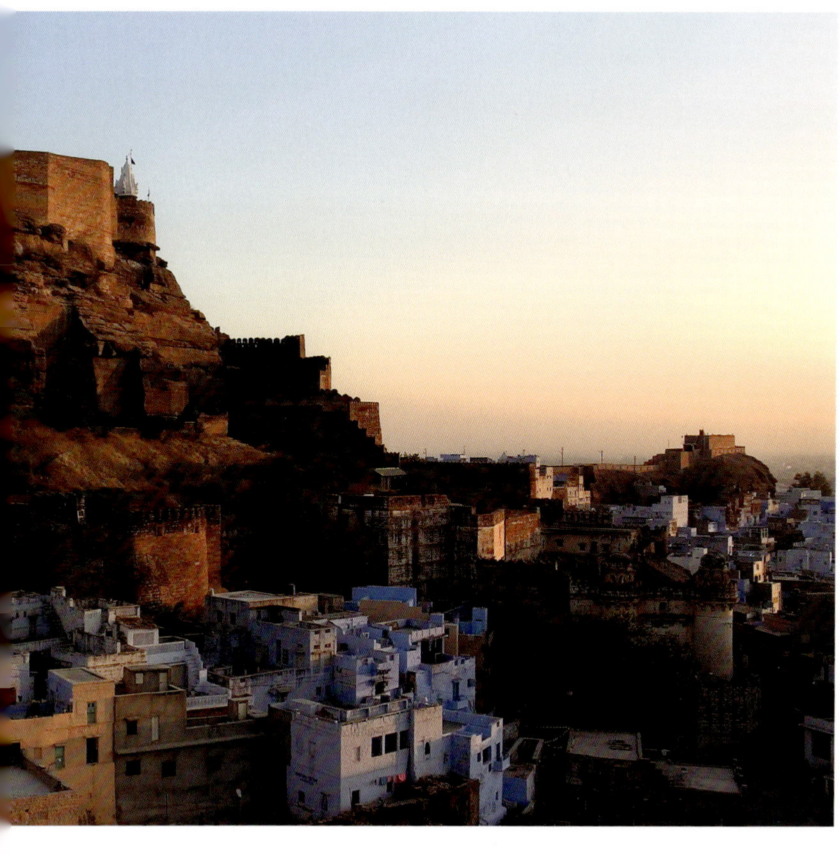

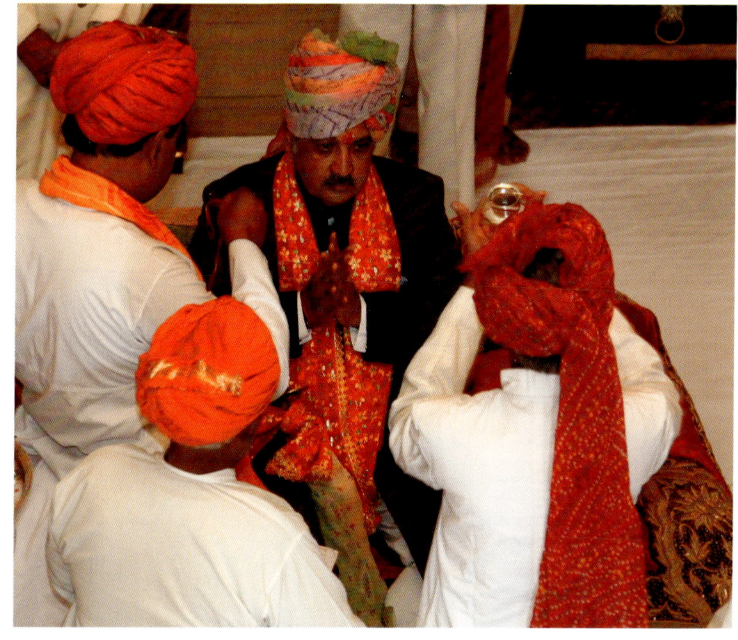

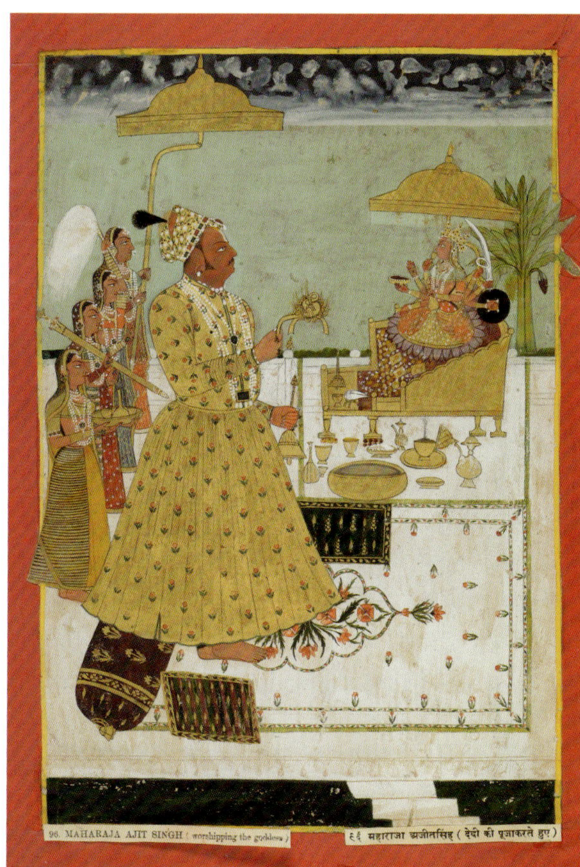
96. MAHARAJA AJIT SINGH : worshipping the goddess
६६ महाराजा अजीतसिंह (देवी की पूजा करते हुए)

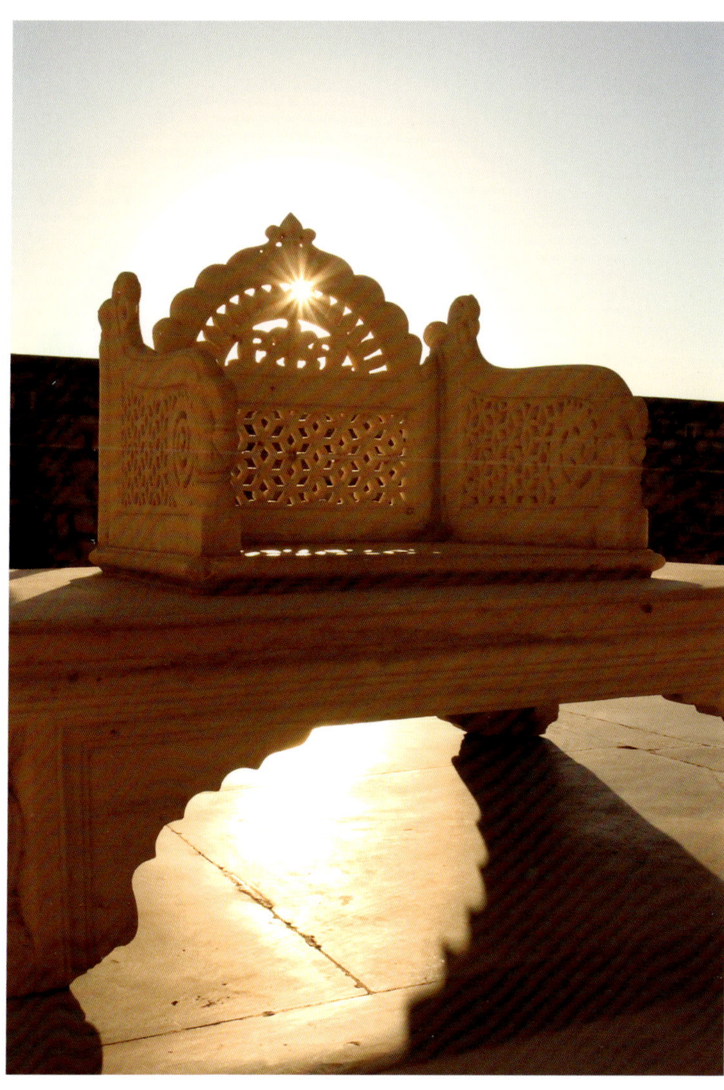

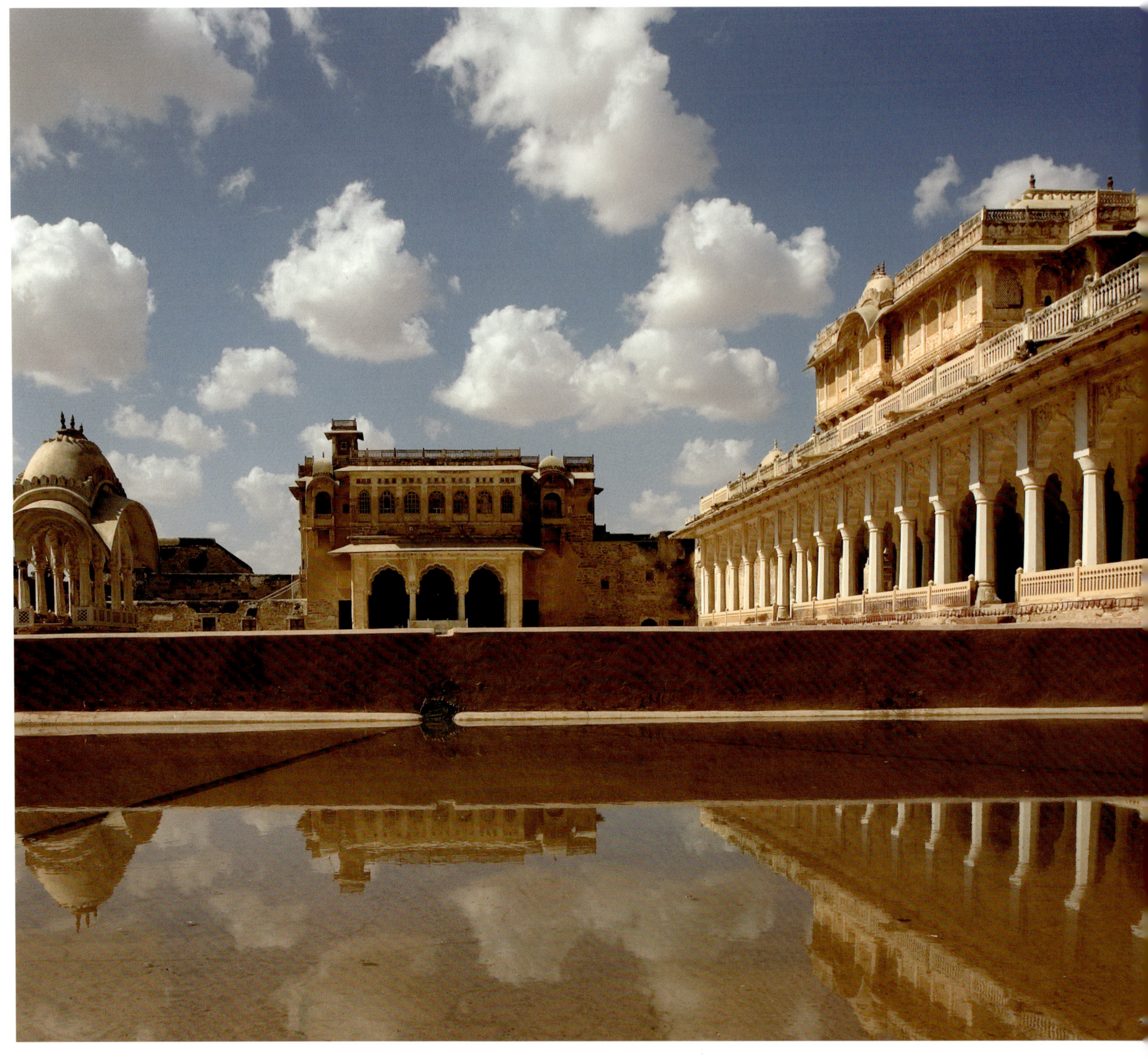

Ahhichatragarh Fort, Nagaur

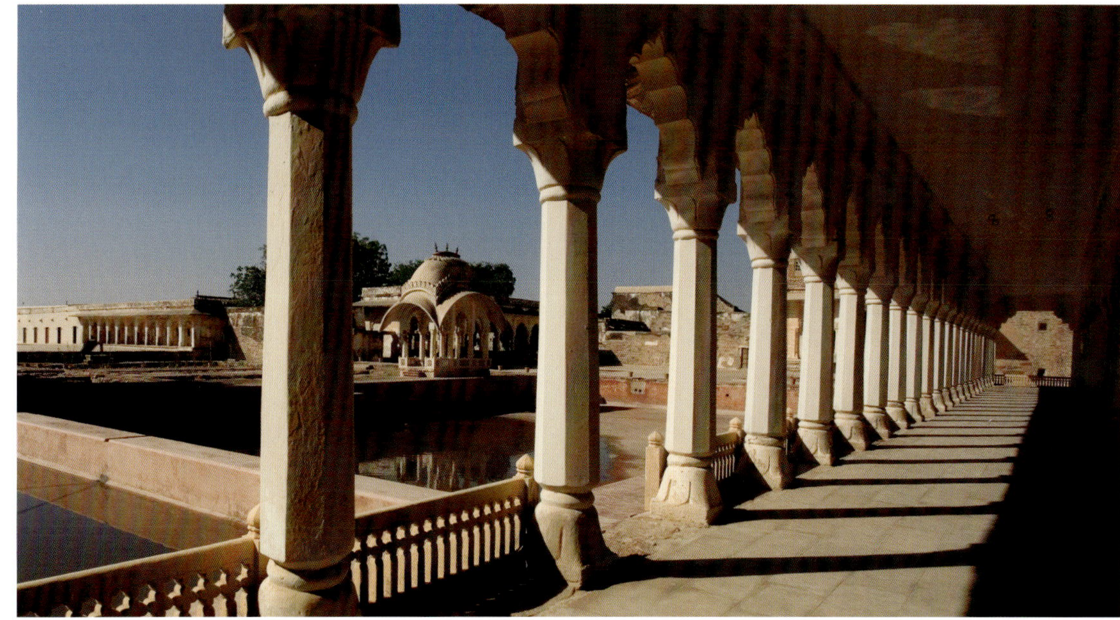

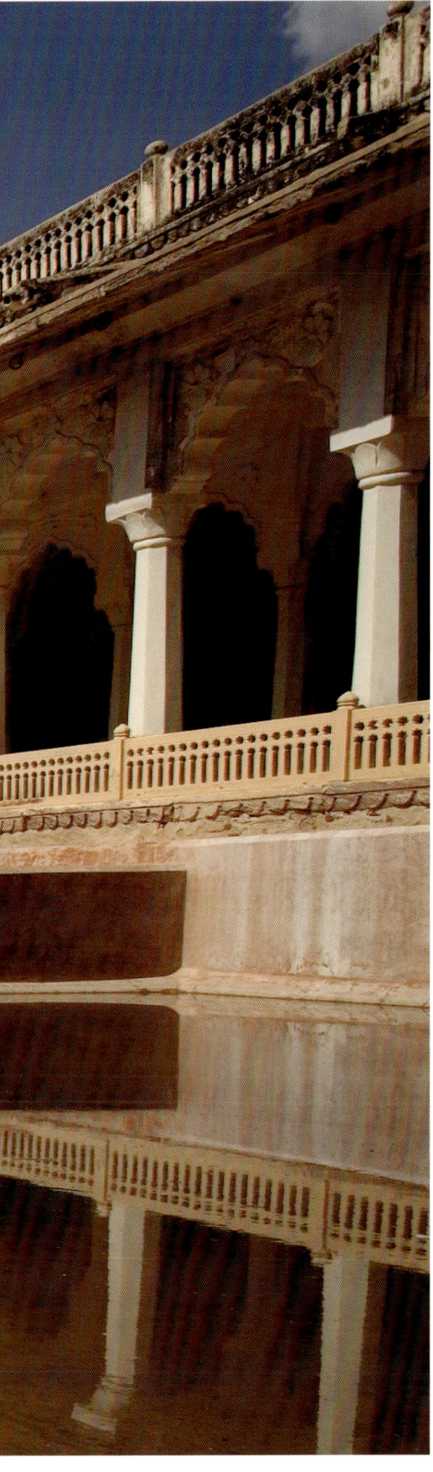

The differences between the forts attest to the interaction of geographic, political, and cultural forces that shaped Rathore identity. In the fifteenth century, Rao Jodha (reigned 1438–89), the fourteenth Rathore to rule in Marwar, began the construction of Mehrangarh (fort of the sun).[11] (See pp. xiv, 3.) It is located on a rocky hill that rises four hundred feet above the surrounding plain and has a commanding presence in the landscape.[12] Mehrangarh's walls are more than five hundred yards long; in places, they rise as high as one hundred twenty feet and are seventy feet thick. One of the largest forts in Rajasthan, it contains some of the world's finest palaces, and its museum preserves many priceless relics of Indian courtly life, including the paintings that form the core of the *Garden and Cosmos* exhibition. Seventeen generations of Rathore rulers have added temples, palaces, and courtyards to the original fort, yet no building seems out of place, for the blending has been skillfully done, and each addition is true in spirit to the original architecture. The rugged impregnable walls belie the delicate beauty of the intricately carved palaces within, whose latticed windows give Mehrangarh a charm unlike any other fort.

In the early eighteenth century, Maharaja Bakhat Singh rebuilt the palaces in Nagaur and established an important painting atelier at Ahhichatragarh Fort, located on a flat desert plain in an Indo-Islamic cultural region north of Jodhpur. Its architecture, with white palaces that open onto gardens, is markedly different from Mehrangarh's. Laid out on a geometric plan that unites gardens, water features, and architectural structures, it evinces Bakhat Singh's close political and cultural ties with the Mughal court of Muhammad Shah (reigned 1719–48). In contrast to Mehrangarh's vertical mass, Ahhichatragarh is horizontal, elegant, and refined. While both palaces have carved facades of great delicacy that enclose areas with similar functions (such as assembly halls and zenana spaces), their differences reflect the historical and geographic diversity of the Rathores in Marwar.

AUTHOR: JASON FREITAG

Becoming Rajput

A Historical Perspective

JASON FREITAG

From the fifteenth to the nineteenth century, the kingdom of Marwar was the center of a web of political and cultural interactions that both defined the imperial climate of north India and helped negotiate the political, social, and cultural position of the Rajput princes who ruled the area. Over the course of this three-century period, the Rathore clan of Rajputs emerged as one of the major Rajput kingdoms and lineages.[1] Throughout, the Rathores were engaged in dynamic processes of identity formation that relied on complex webs of political and social relationships to legitimate their positions. These webs of relationships were central to Rajput identity and a crucial part of the Rathore's ability to negotiate a changing political landscape.

THE "CIRCLE OF STATES"

The very term Rajput, from the Sanskrit *rajaputra* or "son of a king," is a relationship term. While indicating royal status, it clearly also denotes familial connection to a king.[2] This etymological analysis opens up the discussion of the lineage and service linkages that form the Rajput caste.

The classic Indian text on statecraft, the *Arthashastra*, notes that a king rules, or that the essence of political life is, within a *rajamandala* (Sanskrit: circle of states), which exists in a world of "confrontation and alliance, battle and marriage."[3] Within this *mandala* idea fits a Rajput discourse of *naukari* (austere service) to a just king and a committed role as warriors.[4] They derived their historical identity and status from relationships of service between kings, their families, and their clients as well as among the various kingly states themselves.

Rajputs understand their identity as pure *kshatriya* (warrior caste). Traditional historical narratives of the major Rajput houses present a series of genealogical lineages of the "thirty six royal races of Rajasthan"[5] that tie modern Rajputs into this heritage. They share a monolithic view of the development of the Rajput houses: that they arrived on the social and political scene fully formed and then continued over time in a linear fashion.[6] These visions of Rajput history, however, overlook its defining nature, namely, that Rajput is a social identity that is relational.

MARRIAGE

Evidence locates the earliest Rajput kingdoms in a set of inter-clan relationships. Ninth-century inscriptions from Jodhpur and Jaisalmer clearly indicate networks of marriage alliance between (pre-Rathore) Rajput ruling clans and both Rajput and non-Rajput groups.[7] While some Rajput groups were favored partners, the possibility of marriages with other groups shows the openness of a system in the process of consolidation.

From the thirteenth to the fifteenth centuries, mobile groups with martial prowess—like the Rathores who had migrated west to Marwar from central India—became critical players in north Indian state formation.[8] Making themselves available to politically powerful or ambitious elites, some Rathore fighters became prominent figures in their own right. They accumulated landed estates and passed the land onto their heirs. Once established, they sought relationships with kingly families, both to further legitimate their status and to insinuate themselves into increasingly large webs of political power.[9] By the late fifteenth century, the Rathore clan leaders had become kings.

Marriage, therefore, was one currency in the political economy of medieval Rajasthan. The transformative act that brought women into their husband's lineage group, marriage was a key element in a developing web of relationships between emerging groups seeking the title Rajput. During the fifteenth century, for example, Rathore marriages with the Mewar dynasts, the major Rajput court of the time, increased Rathore prestige and influence, but also brought conflict between the courts over issues of succession and political influence.[10] While the marriage alliance cemented the relationship between the two royal houses—and this branch of the Rathore line produced one of the mightiest of the Mewari ranas, Rana Kumbha—the complex web of interrelationships that developed led to future tensions.

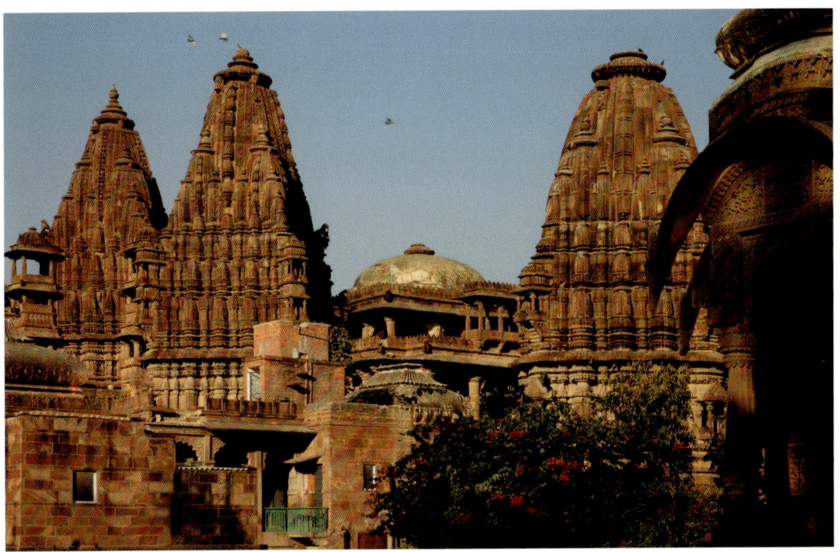

Rathore cenotaphs at Mandore

BROTHERHOOD

Pre-Mughal north India clearly functioned in the idiom of relationship, not simply hierarchy. The signature element of inter-Rajput relationships was the construct of *bhaibandh* (brother's bond). These brotherhood arrangements referred not just to strictly defined groups sharing a male ancestor but expanded to encompass the universe of marriage relationships as well.[11] Under the umbrella of *bhaibandh,* political leadership took on a dynamic character. Early scholars described the system in the European feudal idiom *primer inter pares,* or "first among equals."[12] This phrase illustrates the tension between vertical hierarchy and horizontal relationships of power that mark the development of Rajput identity in this period. The emphasis on equality here shows the internal dynamism of intra- and intergroup relationships, while the clear evocation of the raja as "first" points to the power processes that were at play among individuals and clans.

In 1459, for instance, Rao Jodha founded Jodhpur and made it the new capital of Marwar.[13] To secure the boundaries of his capital, and to provide territory to soothe the ambitions of his brothers, fourteen sons, and other relations, Rao Jodha assigned land to them on the outskirts of Jodhpur in return for loyalty and service. These *bhaibandh* relationships brought about solidarity in the work of the clan. The ideal was cooperation through connection. The inherent tensions in this structure of semi-independent landed members of the family soon became apparent. Even in Jodha's time, independence-minded princes began to challenge the raja's authority, undermining Rathore leadership in general, straining the order of the state, and showing that the alliances with and obligations to the raja were only as strong as the raja himself.[14] After a period of decline, Rao Jodha was able to recapture his rule, and he immediately reinstated his sons and brothers, regardless of their previous disloyalty. The expectations of the *bhaibandh* relationship, therefore, include not only an inherent element of connection but also tension and power play in relationships as well.

SERVICE

As the Mughal Empire (Muslim rulers who reigned 1526–1858) spread in power throughout India, Rajputs engaged a new political dynamic of status, measured in relationship to the Mughal imperial court and military prowess within this hierarchy. Rathore Rajputs took up positions of nobility within the Mughal system, achieving an external legitimation of their political power.[15] In the same period, Rajputs further increased their status through the patronage of Brahmin priests who sanctified their rule. The new priestly advisors emphasized a heightened sense of hierarchy and status differentials based on a perceived purity and ritual differences.[16] More clearly defined visions of Rajput kingliness and caste honor ensued.

Fully formed by the seventeenth and eighteenth centuries, the Mughal political economy revolved around gifting and service in its various forms.[17] It is clear that the very relationships of service that brought the Rajput groups into Mughal employ were part of a much larger cultural logic of interaction and exchange that had been present in north India centuries before the Mughal presence. If relations with the Mughals cemented Rajput polity in the seventeenth and eighteenth centuries, the fluid nature of succession in both Mughal and Rajput courts led to constant negotiations over power, shifting alliances, and military conflicts.

The life of Maharaja Jaswant Singh (cat. 6) illustrates this dynamic between the Mughals and the Rathore court.[18] Maharaja Gaj Singh (reigned 1619–38) (cat. 5) chose as his successor his eleven-year-old son Jaswant Singh (reigned 1638–78) over his older but more reckless brother Amar Singh. Mughal Emperor Shah Jahan (fig. 2, p. 15) chose a *diwan* for the state to act as regent for the young ruler, and Jaswant Singh was brought into Mughal service. Jaswant Singh spent thirteen of his first twenty regnal years outside of Jodhpur in imperial service to the emperor.[19] His multi-layered relationship to Shah Jahan is revealing. The power and support of the Mughal emperor was certainly a factor in Jaswant Singh's easy acquiescence to Shah Jahan's instructions. However, the two men were also blood relatives.[20] The twin ties of political and kinship alliances produced a subtly inscribed relationship of power between the Rajput and the Mughal.

When a succession struggle erupted between the Mughal aspirants Dara Shikoh and Aurangzeb, Jaswant Singh supported Dara Shikoh, who was, in the end, unsuccessful in his bid to become emperor. Jaswant Singh was stripped of his *mansabs* as a result. The ramifications of his unfortunate choice, however, were short lived, as his rank was restored and expanded once he pledged allegiance to Aurangzeb.

Within the Jodhpur court as well, the allegiance of the Rathore nobility (*bhaibandh*) to the maharaja ebbed or increased according to the support of the Mughal emperor. During the period of Jaswant Singh's demotion, the Jodhpur nobles accepted the installation of his nephew Rai Singh as the raja of the state.[21] One widely told story in Marwar relates how Jaswant Singh's queen refused to allow her defeated husband back into the fort, claiming not to recognize someone who could so besmirch the Rajput value of valor. She was even said to serve his food on pottery instead of the traditional metal, so as not to produce any clanging sounds that might frighten him by reminding him of the battlefield.[22] Clearly, Jaswant Singh's defeat, and disfavor with the Mughals, had ramifications for his status at home.

Just as clearly, Jaswant Singh's status within the Mughal empire also fluctuated with the strength of his bonds of service to the emperor. His rank rose steadily under Shah Jahan, was taken away completely during the period of struggle between Aurangzeb and Dara Shikoh, and then was restored and expanded once he pledged his allegiance to the new ruler. The currency in circulation, both within the court in Jodhpur and between the Jodhpur court and the Mughal court, was the relationship between the raja and the emperor.

After Mughal authority waned in the second quarter of the eighteenth century, Rajput kings developed relationships with other nodes of power and authority. As Debra Diamond discusses in "Maharaja Vijai Singh and the Epic Landscape," for Vijai Singh, these were trans-regional Vaishnava connections and alliances with Rajput kings. "Painting, Politics, and Devotion under Maharaja Man Singh" elucidates the relationship between Man Singh and the Naths, a heterodox group of yogins whom he raised to the status of an administrative polity. The alliance with the Naths countered the increased autonomy of the Rathore nobility as well as the ascendancy of the British East India Company, which by 1818 had become the dominant force on the subcontinent.

CONCLUSION

This interplay between local dynamics of the Rathore courts and the global political situation in India played out in patterns of patronage and reference, as the paintings in this catalogue illustrate. The various networks and the legitimating forces they represent are extensions of the long-standing processes of Rajput political development itself and political consolidation in Jodhpur and other states in Rajasthan. To be a Rajput was to be in the center of a series of overlapping service and alliance relationships that provided internal legitimation within the local clan and caste environment and external legitimation within the larger political/cultural world of north Indian politics.

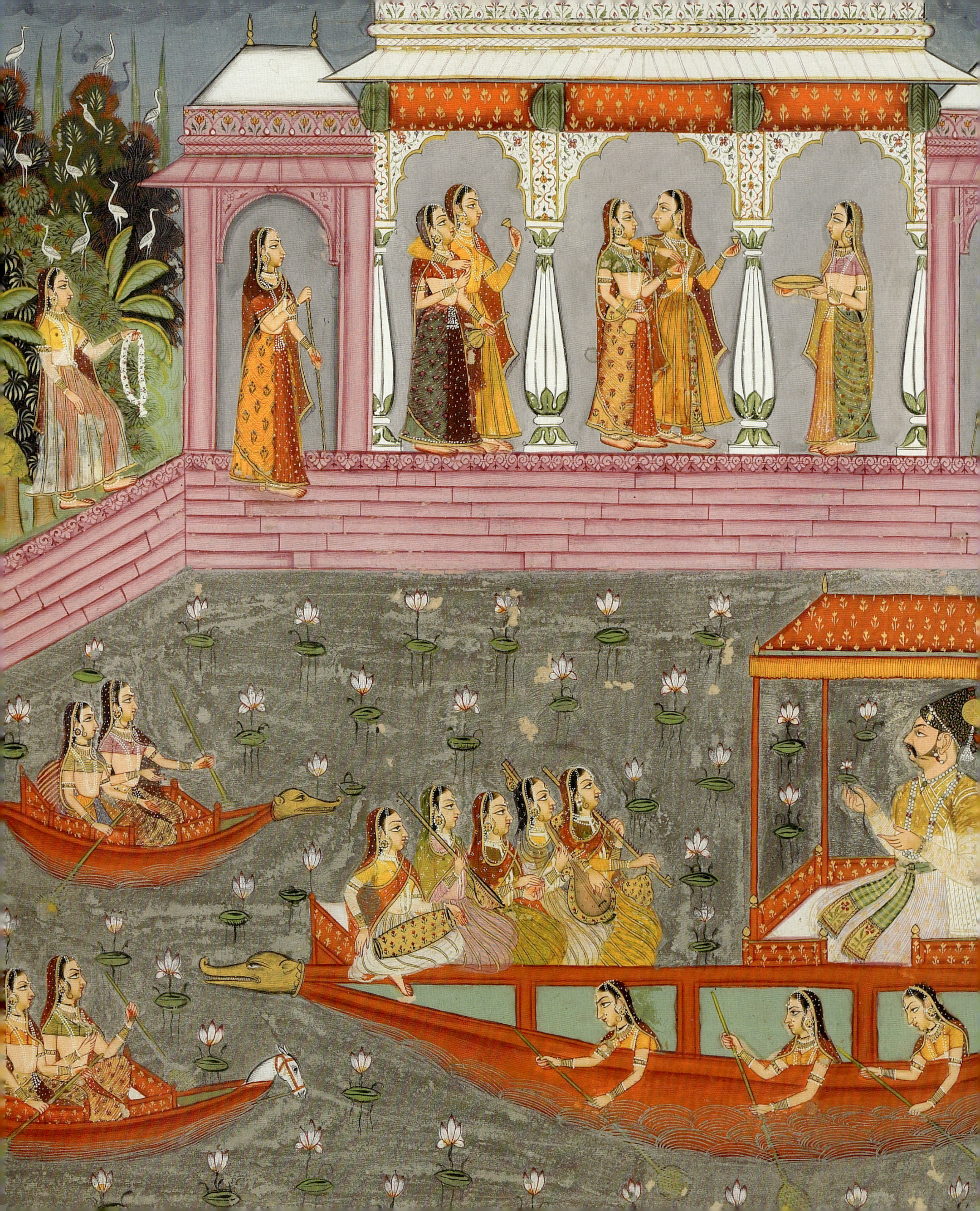

Rathore and Mughal Interactions

Artistic Development at the Nagaur Court, 1600–1751

CATHERINE GLYNN

Under the patronage of Maharaja Bakhat Singh (reigned 1725–51), the atelier at Nagaur, a regional court in Marwar, produced paintings that combine a singular concentration on courtly pleasures with unusual artistic innovation (cats. 10–20).

During the preceding century, two distinct styles flourished in Marwar's capital, Jodhpur: the first, a local genre, had antecedents in the Rajasthani folk idiom of bold colors, simplified figures and vegetation, and a direct point of view. The second style, which appeared later in the century, was modeled upon Mughal court paintings, using a broader color palette, more shading, and multiple perspectives. These two styles set the stage for the exceptional Nagaur paintings created just a generation later.

The predominant subject matter of the Nagaur paintings, the life of pleasure experienced by the maharaja in his palace, is not unusual in north Indian court painting; fig. 1 is a zenana scene painted one hundred years earlier in the Mughal workshop.[1] The Bakhat Singh Nagaur paintings, however, combine large figures within a format that is bigger than the typical Rajasthani painting, use fluid lines that show technical mastery of space and depth, introduce a striking pastel pink, and incorporate accurate representation of intricate textile patterns and architectural motifs. Taken together, the portable paintings and the contemporary wall paintings present a sophisticated vision of the luxurious life at the Nagaur court.

THE MARWAR–MUGHAL ALLIANCE

The Rathores, a Hindu dynasty, had been in Marwar's western desert since the mid-thirteenth century and had ruled much of the area since the 1450s. They were exposed to the Mughal military system, cultural patterns, and practices as early as 1558 after the Mughal emperor Akbar (reigned 1556–1605) conquered Nagaur, a territory in Rajasthan near Marwar's northeastern border. In 1562–63, Jodhpur's Mehrangarh Fort was subdued by Mughal forces,[2] and from that time forward, Jodhpur rajas appeared regularly at the Mughal court and often led military campaigns on behalf of the emperors. Rathore princesses married

Mughal princes, and Rathore nobles introduced Mughal architecture, painting, and textile production to the Marwar lands under their control. Until the death of Raja Jaswant Singh (cat. 6) in 1678, the Rathore rulers of Jodhpur were among the most important Rajput rulers serving the Mughal emperors. The late sixteenth- and early seventeenth-century alliance with the Mughals led to long-term security and stability within the Marwar kingdom, which in turn fostered a flourishing cultural court life. Just as the Rathore nobles were affected by their contact with the imperial styles, Marwar painters were exposed to Mughal paintings (cats. 4, 5) and perhaps to Mughal artists as well. By the middle of the seventeenth century, Marwar paintings had become technically more refined. Color preferences changed from a limited palette of pure colors to more nuanced hues.[3] The progression is visible in cats. 1, 2, 3, 6. The active exchange between the Marwar court and the Mughal court, among rulers and their artists, eventually produced a new idiom, Mughalized Rajasthani painting.

NAGAUR CITY AND FORT

Throughout its history, Nagaur was an area in constant flux between Hindu and Muslim rulers,[4] and was an important site in the pre-Mughal sultanate period. The Muslim presence began with the construction of the Nagaur Fort, called Ahhichatragarh (fort of the hooded cobra), in the year 1111 by Muhammed Bahalim, the agent of Sultan Bahram Shah of Ghazni, which established the site as politically, religiously, and culturally significant.[5] Other sultanate architectural projects included the Atarkin-ka-Darwaza, a massive gateway dating from the first half of the thirteenth century,[6] which was restored during the reign of Muhammad bin Tughluq (1325–51) and again in the sixteenth century, testifying to its continuing importance. Governor Shams Khan Dandani built a noteworthy mosque, the Shams Masjid, in the early fifteenth century.[7] The Jami Mosque was built by the Mughal appointee Khan-i-Jahan (Husain Quli Khan) in 1564–65 and is still the principal mosque in the city.[8] The Mughal emperor Akbar visited Ahhichatragarh Fort twice, in 1570 and 1572.[9] He likely was encouraged to explore the area by Abu'l Fazl, his best friend and biographer, who spent time in Nagaur studying with his father, the eminent Shaykh Mubarak Nagawri.[10]

Unlike Jodhpur, which was an ancestral capital of the Marwar rulers, Nagaur was under direct Mughal ownership (*khalsa*). The Marwar rulers were allowed to govern the city only at the discretion of the emperor. The Mughals used the granting of land—including whether a Marwar ruler could use his ancestral land as an effective tool for managing the empire—to keep the Rathores and other Rajput rulers aware of their subordinate position. In 1626, during the reign of the Mughal emperor Jahangir (1605–27), Nagaur was given to the elder son of Raja Gaj Singh, Amar Singh (reigned 1626–27, 1634–44). (See entries for cat. 5.) Nagaur was taken away from Amar Singh in 1627, but restored to him seven years later by Jahangir's son, Shah Jahan (reigned 1627–78).[11]

There is evidence that paintings at the regional court in Nagaur in the late sixteenth century paralleled the traditional folk idiom prevalent at the central court in Jodhpur.[12] Both schools used a limited palette and figures contained within a bold outline on plain backgrounds. Artists in Jodhpur and Nagaur also employed minimal perspective, primarily by using diagonal lines.

We know that Mughal painters visited Nagaur during the second quarter of the seventeenth century; two paintings (figs. 2 and 3)—probably painted by a Mughal artist, or artists, who visited Nagaur during Amar Singh's second reign—help document this dynamic exchange. Both works are inscribed on the reverse with the words "Nagaur men bani che" (was made in Nagaur).[13] The oval portrait of Shah Jahan (fig. 2) is framed by a buff-colored border featuring

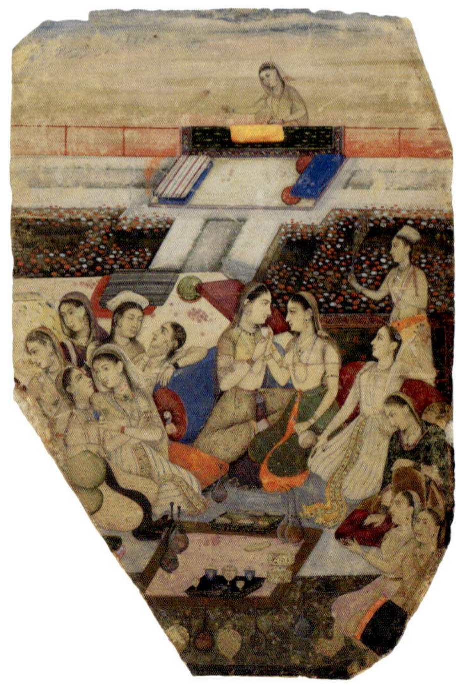

Previous page Cat. 18, detail

Fig. 1. Zenana scene (*The Women of the Harem*), Mughal, ca. 1625–30, 23.5 x 15.8 cm, Museum of Fine Arts, Boston, 66.149

gold washes of vegetation, a popular design during this period.[14] The other painting (fig. 3) depicts an important noble from the Deccan, the Bijapuri ruler Muhammad Adil Shah (reigned 1627–56), also within an oval format but with a border decorated with Deccan landscape elements.[15] Both portraits can be dated to 1635–45, based on comparisons with other Mughal portraits of these individuals.[16] Further research may expand our knowledge about this Mughal–Nagaur artistic connection.

Just as there are Jodhpur and Nagaur paintings from the late sixteenth and first half of the seventeenth century produced in the traditional style (cats. 1–3),[17] these two Nagaur Mughal paintings (figs. 2, 3) are stylistically related to Mughalized works painted in Jodhpur around the same time (cat. 6).[18] This demonstrates that though the two cities were ruled by different administrators, their artists worked in similar styles with similar subject matter. It was not until the eighteenth century that painting in Nagaur changed significantly, abandoning the traditional folk style for the Mughalized style that featured pastel colors, complex architectural backgrounds, and comparatively naturalistic portraiture.

RULING NAGAUR

After Rao Amar Singh's death in 1644,[19] Nagaur was assigned to his eldest son, Rai Singh (reigned 1644–76), an act that was formalized in a grant from Shah Jahan.[20] Aurangzeb (reigned 1658–1707), Shah Jahan's son and successor, allowed Rai Singh to continue governing Nagaur until the latter's death in 1676,[21] when the right to rule the city was given to Rai Singh's son, Indar Singh (reigned Nagaur 1676–1716, 1723–25). Like other Rathore nobles, Indar Singh was an active participant in the Mughal army, serving Aurangzeb with distinction in the emperor's ongoing wars in the Deccan.[22] Until 1707, the year of Aurangzeb's death, Indar Singh remained loyal to the emperor, even fighting against other Marwar nobles during the tumultuous Thirty-Year Rathore War of Independence, 1678–1707. (For more on Amar Singh and the war, see entries for cats. 5 and 6.)

During the years that Rai Singh ruled Nagaur, Raja Jaswant Singh (reigned 1638–78) ruled Marwar from Jodhpur (see entries for cat. 6). Jaswant Singh died in 1678 without a male heir, and Aurangzeb saw an opportunity to extend his power by placing Jodhpur under direct Mughal rule.[23] Much to the displeasure of the Rathore princes, he established a requirement that they convert to Islam.[24] He also placed his loyal ally, Indar Singh of Nagaur, on the Jodhpur throne, although he was only a grandnephew of Jaswant Singh and therefore not entitled to rule Jodhpur, according to Rathore custom.[25]

Indar Singh's reign in Jodhpur, however, lasted only two months. The Rathore nobles rebelled against him and the imperial control imposed by the Mughals, beginning the war of independence. Aurangzeb was ready for the insurgents; his forces attacked Mehrangarh Fort and destroyed the Hindu temples in Jodhpur, dealing the capital a decisive military blow.[26] This short but vivid description from a Mughal text celebrates what must have been the utter destruction of Jodhpur's temples at that time:

> On the 24 Rabi'ulAkhir [April 1679] Khan Jahan Bahadur arrived [in Delhi] from Jodhpur, bringing with him several cartloads of idols, taken from the Hindu temples that had been razed. His Majesty gave him great praise. Most of these idols were adorned with precious stones, or made of gold, silver, brass, copper or stone; it was ordered that some of them should be cast away in the out-offices, and the remainder placed beneath the steps of the grand mosque, there to be trampled under foot. There they lay a long time, until, at last, not a vestige of them was left.[27]

A Mughal administration with little regard for Rajput and Hindu cultural treasures now occupied Jodhpur and Mehrangarh Fort. As a result of the war and Mughal dominance, only a small amount of seventeenth-century material—paintings, textiles, jade, silver, lacquer, and other decorative items—remains in the royal storerooms today.

The Rathore–Mughal war ended when Aurangzeb died in 1707. Jaswant Singh's son Ajit Singh, born in 1679 after his father's death, was acknowledged by the Mughals as the ruler of Marwar (see entries for cats. 7 and 8). Nine years later, on July 20, 1716, the Jodhpur military defeated Indar Singh, who was still ruler of Nagaur, and the victorious Ajit Singh annexed that city and its fort.[28] His hold on Naguar was short, however; by June 1723, Ajit Singh had surrendered the fort and its surroundings to the Mughal emperor Muhammad Shah, who gave Nagaur back to Indar Singh, although he would reign for less than two years.[29] Unfortunately no paintings can be linked definitively to Nagaur in the early eighteenth century.

In 1723, Ajit Singh, still the raja of Marwar, and his first-born son Abhai Singh were at Muhammad Shah's court in Delhi.[30] When Ajit Singh returned to Mehrangarh Fort, his son chose to remain in Delhi. It was an amazingly prescient (or more possibly deliberate) decision, for on the evening of June 23 or 24, 1724, Ajit Singh was murdered in his bedchamber by his second son, Bakhat Singh.[31]

It is unknown whether Abhai Singh incited the murder so he could gain the throne for himself or, as was rumored at the time, Bakhat Singh was enraged that his father was having an illicit affair with his daugther-in-law, Bakhat Singh's wife. Perhaps, as some historians have speculated, it was a joint effort formulated by the brothers to further their dual political and personal agendas.[32] What is known is that when Abhai Singh returned to Jodhpur in late 1724, he gave Nagaur to Bakhat Singh in what many have interpreted as a reward for the murder.[33] The Rathore nobles, however, never forgave this monstrous act. They found the patricide so abhorrent that no prominent structure was built for Abhai Singh at Mandore, the strikingly picturesque Rathore ancestral site where Marwar rajas' deaths are honored with elaborately carved, red sandstone cenotaphs.[34] (See p. 7.)

In any case, Abhai Singh's relations with the imperial court were good—at least, they were early in his reign. Muhammad Shah himself performed the *tilak* anointing ceremony in 1724 that proclaimed Abhai Singh maharaja,[35] but his twenty-five year rule in Marwar (1724–49) was characterized by conflict with his four brothers (see entries for cat. 8); other Rajput rulers, including the rajas of Bikaner, Jaipur, and Mewar; Maratha warriors from the Deccan; and eventually even with the Mughal emperor himself.[36]

After Abhai Singh's return to Jodhpur in late 1724,[37] two of his brothers, Anand Singh and Rai Singh, revolted against his rule. Bakhat Singh took advantage of this fratricidal turmoil by occupying Nagaur in June–July 1725. Even though Abhai Singh had awarded Nagaur to Bakhat Singh the preceding year, it remained under Indar Singh's control. When Bakhat Singh led his army into the city, Indar Singh withdrew to Delhi, ending the Nagaur dynasty begun by Amar Singh one hundred years earlier in 1626.[38]

According to historical accounts, Bakhat Singh was an exemplary ruler—brave, clever, and an admirable administrator: "But for that foul stain [the killing of his father] Raja Bukhta would have been one of the first princes of his race. It never gave birth to a bolder [person]; and his wisdom was equal to his valour. Before the commission of that act, he was adored by his Rajpoots. He was chiefly instrumental in the conquests made from Guzzerat [Gujarat]; and afterwards, in conjunction with his brother, in defeating the imperial viceroy."[39]

After Abhai Singh's death in 1749, a war of succession between his son Ram Singh and his brother Bakhat Singh was inevitable.[40] Both the Mughal imperial forces and many Marwar nobles supported Bakhat Singh. After a brief interlude of ineffectual rule by Ram Singh,

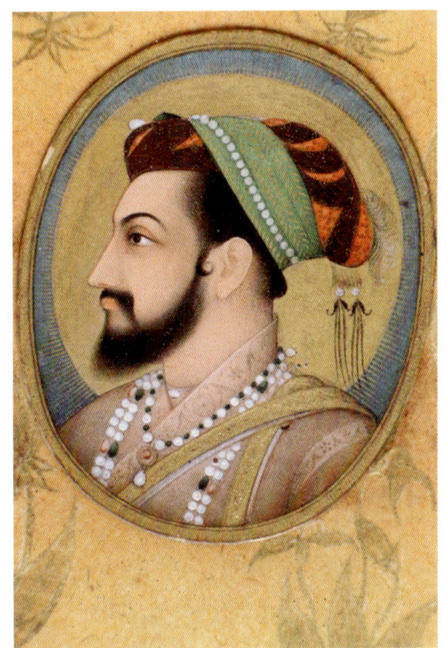

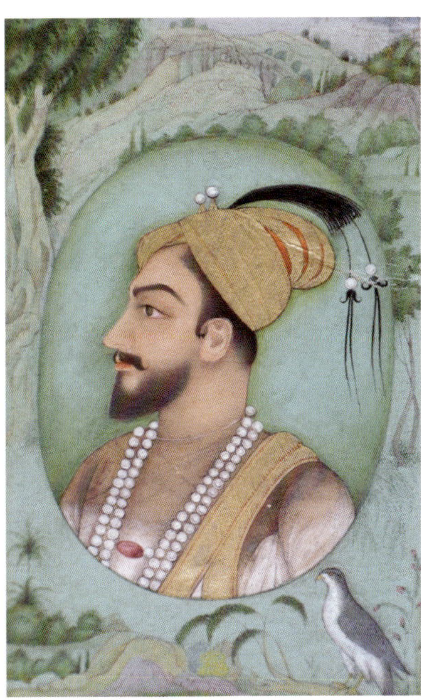

Bakhat Singh was crowned ruler of Marwar in 1751, only to be poisoned the following year.[41] He was away from Nagaur and Jodhpur, near the borders where the Rajasthani states of Mewar, Marwar, and Jaipur meet. Thus he fulfilled the curse—that he would die on foreign soil—supposedly uttered by a sage after Bakhat Singh killed his father in 1724. His niece, a daughter of one of his younger brothers, had arrived at his campgrounds, intending to avenge the murder of her grandfather, Ajit Singh. According to legend, she took a gift for her uncle, a coat she had dipped in poison before her departure from Jaipur. Shortly after Bakhat Singh put on the coat, he succumbed to a fever, never to recover.[42]

DALCHAND'S IMPACT ON MARWAR/NAGAUR PAINTING

In the first quarter of the eighteenth century, the Jodhpur court experienced internal and external discord, but the painting atelier at Mehrangarh was seemingly unaffected, exhibiting a smooth transition from Ajit Singh to Abhai Singh. Just as painters had done for Ajit Singh, Abhai Singh's artists—some of whom likely worked for both maharajas—portrayed the ruler as the main subject in palace settings, riding horseback in the countryside, meeting with his nobles, or with a favorite lover in a garden (cats. 7 and 8). Besides patronizing paintings, Abhai Singh also added buildings to Mehrangarh Fort, including an audience hall, the Phul Mahal (Palace of Flowers).[43]

During Abhai Singh's reign, the Mughalized Rajput painting style evident at Jodhpur while his father was alive (cat. 8) developed an even stronger link to the imperial style favored at the Mughal court in Delhi (see entries for cats. 14 and 19).[44] The inspiration and prominent catalyst for the movement toward the Delhi style was the circa 1724 arrival in Jodhpur of the imperial artist Dalchand.[45] A master of the meticulously detailed, refined, and nuanced Mughal style, Dalchand excelled in the treatment of textiles, decorative objects, and subtly naturalistic facial features (fig. 4).

Abhai Singh may have met Dalchand in Delhi in the early 1720s[46] and perhaps enticed the artist to come to Jodhpur to become the master of the royal atelier. In 1719, Raja Raj Singh (reigned 1706–48) persuaded the artist's father, Bhawani Das, to leave Delhi and become head of the royal studio in Kishangarh, a neighboring Rajput atelier.[47]

Dalchand certainly was aware of royal compositions that had been painted circa 1719–24 for the young Muhammad Shah.[48] This is evidenced by one of the artist's most accomplished works for Abhai Singh (fig. 4), a magnificent palace scene showing the young Rathore seated in front of a striking, lush Mughal or Mughal-style carpet, watching a dance performance. Painted shortly after Abhai Singh's return to Jodhpur in 1724, and exuding pomp and splendor, it may have been intended as a "coronation" statement and clearly is modeled on images of Muhammad Shah at leisure.[49] Dalchand's paintings add elements of the Marwar aesthetic to the Mughal style: heightened color, a flatter space, and a more religiously imbued or iconic view of the temporal ruler. The brilliant white of the buildings and tile floor is juxtaposed with warm tones of red, orange, and brown. The focal point of the composition, in competition with the raja on his gold throne, is the splendid Mughal or Mughal-style carpet, almost alive with scrolling vines, open flowers, and *saz* (serrated-edge) leaves, paralleled by the natural beauty of the garden in the distance.[50]

Dalchand remained in Jodhpur until at least 1727; there are two portraits of Abhai Singh ascribed to him, one of which is dated that year.[51] By 1729, he had moved to Kishangarh, where he worked for Raja Raj Singh (his father's patron), for which he was paid thirty-five rupees a month.[52] His father remained in residence at Kishangarh until either 1743 or the death of Raj Singh in 1748.[53]

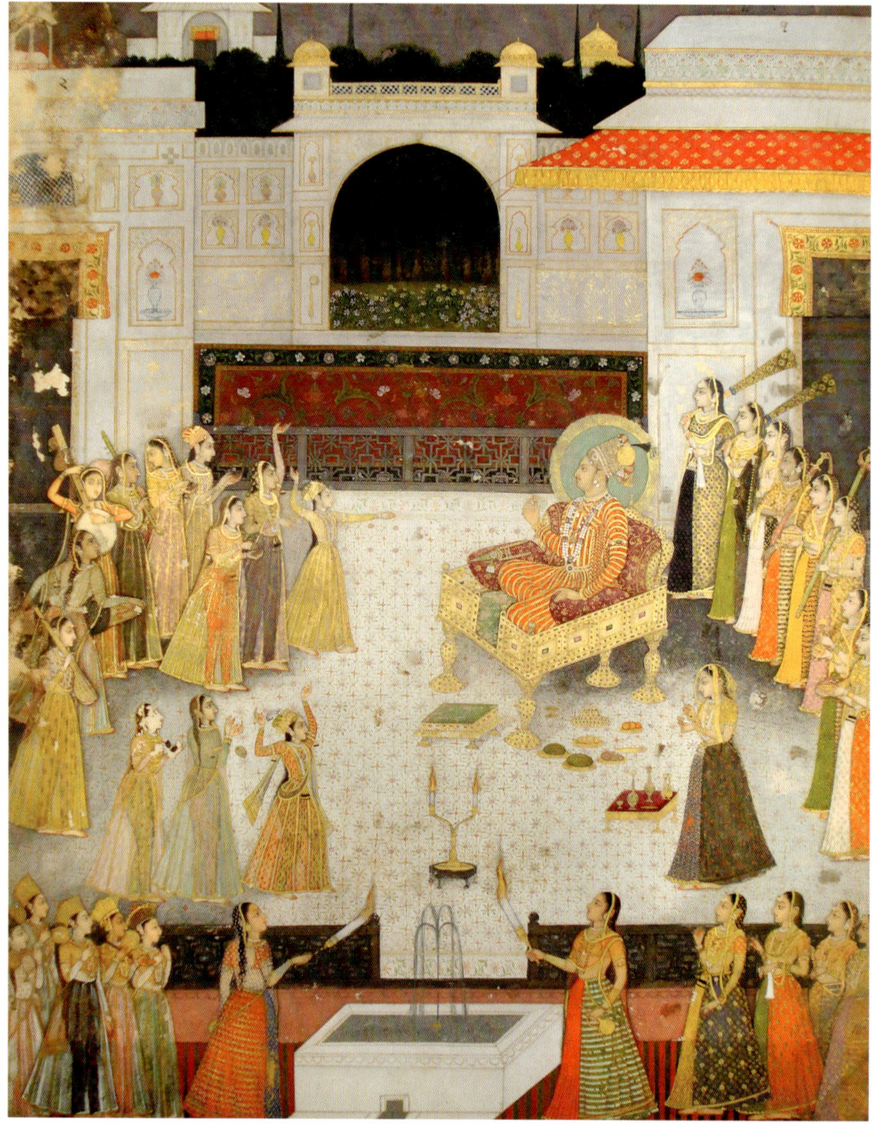

Fig. 4. *Maharaja Abhai Singh Watching a Dance Performance* by Dalchand, Jodhpur, ca. 1725, 43.5 x 34.5 cm, Mehrangarh Museum Trust, RJS 24 (28)

After Dalchand's departure from Jodhpur at the end of the 1720s, painters there and in ateliers in sub-states (*thikanas*) within the Marwar orbit, such as Ghanerao and neighboring Jaisalmer, seem to have abandoned his Mughalized Rajasthani style in a short matter of time, returning to a traditional Rajasthan idiom.[54] It is clear, however, that Dalchand's style, technique, and paintings continued to have an impact on artists working in Nagaur for Bakhat Singh during the 1730s and 1740s (see entry for cat. 16).[55]

WALL PAINTINGS AT NAGAUR

Bakhat Singh reigned in Nagaur for more than twenty-five years, from 1725 until 1751, when he also became the ruler of Jodhpur. (See Bakhat Singh chronology.) He built a pleasure palace at Nagaur on the foundation of the existing fort.[56] The palace at Nagaur, in fact, represents the most successful combination of exterior and interior palace decorative styles in Rajasthan. It was an elegant combination of prevailing Rajput architectural elements, such as the viewing pavilions (*chatris*), along with delicate decorative elements popular at the

Mughal court (see, for example, cats. 13–15, 20), and graceful lines similar to the sultanate buildings in nearby Gujarat. Bakhat Singh spent a portion of his career in Gujarat, whose sultanate buildings are among the most graceful, sophisticated, and visually accomplished examples of pre-Mughal architecture.[57] Gujarat architecture may have influenced him, much as it did Akbar one hundred and fifty years earlier.

All of the exterior surfaces were covered with white stucco, which, although a less-expensive alternative to white marble, achieved the similar effect of glistening under the ever-present desert sun. The stucco was painted with elegant floral patterns, as seen in an artist's rendition from 1737 (see cat. 15), providing a sumptuous visual experience for both residents and visitors and turning walls into virtual garden experiences. Even today the palace buildings show evidence of the patterns and colors documented in contemporary portable paintings.

The embellished interiors were covered with wall paintings that continued the pleasure-garden theme indoors (see cats. 11, p. 264, and 18, p. 272). Wall paintings in the Hadi Rani Mahal, which are the most numerous and best-preserved artworks at the fort, depict women in garden settings, around water elements, dancing, playing musical instruments, and in close friendship. The figures, elegantly and gracefully rendered with elongated proportions and animated gestures that bring the daily activities of the palace women to life, are painted in black outline and filled with blocks of solid color. The artists paid great attention to detail— visible, for example, in the individualized treatment of textiles, clothing, and headgear.

At the same time that Bakhat Singh's artists were painting the interior walls of the Hadi Rani Mahal, the Sheesh Mahal, and the Krishna temple, they also produced a remarkable series of portable paintings. Art historians have been aware of the wall paintings since the mid-twentieth century,[58] but the very recent discovery of the portable artworks provides a wealth of material for scholars in many disciplines.[59] New information is now available on the number of artists under Bakhat Singh's employ, varieties of garden design at Nagaur, architectural modifications after 1751, and the transition of painting styles and artists in the early reign of his son and successor, Vijai Singh. (See entries for cats. 12, 13, 15, 17, 20.)

Bakhat Singh was justly proud of his Nagaur palace and the luxury, comfort, and opulence within its walls. The pleasure he took in his palace inspired his patronage and his artists. This is evident from the fact that many of the buildings he built during his reign were memorialized in the portable paintings. Many seventeenth- and eighteenth-century Rajput paintings from other ateliers depict generalized or idealized buildings.[60] The Bakhat Singh Nagaur paintings, however, present specific buildings in the palace compound as the backdrop for the activities of the raja and the women in the zenana. Intricate textiles augment the scenes, providing additional visual stimuli and contributing to the sensuousness of the setting. There is a direct parallel between the actual buildings (fig. 5 and p. 4) and the structures portrayed in the portable paintings (see cat. 15), which were created "in situ" by artists familiar with the palace and its importance to the culture of the court.[61] The Nagaur paintings provide a distinctly accurate and detailed depiction of contemporary architectural elements.

During the early eighteenth century, the Jodhpur court studio produced paintings in both the more Mughalized Rajasthani style and the Marwar traditional style (see scholarly entry for cat. 8); a unified and distinctly Mughalized Rajasthani style, however, dominated court painting in Nagaur (cat. 9).[62] Nagaur artists introduced a set of artistic innovations that were unique and pioneering: a consistent format that was larger than the typical Rajput painting (ranging from 35.5 x 25.5 cm to 53.5 x 73.5 cm); generous-sized human figures that matched the larger format; exceptional technical mastery of line; significant skill at rendering spatial recession; and a distinctive palette dominated by pastel colors. The painting style presents a sophisticated and encompassing vision.

Almost all of the paintings, permanent and portable, feature pleasurable activities within a desert oasis palace. Gardens abound, complete with large water tanks and fountains operated by a complicated hydraulic system (see cats. 11–13, 16, 18, 20). In most of the portable paintings, Bakhat Singh is depicted in various amorous situations as the definitive paramour (*nayika*); the raja's image is now an icon for the ultimate lover (p. 10).

Most of the Nagaur portable paintings do not illustrate the Rajput pursuits depicted in the majority of paintings from other Rajasthan studios. There are no hunts, battle scenes, equestrian portraits, *darbars*, wrestling matches, or royal visits to revered holy figures.[63] It is especially curious that there are no paintings of horses, either in battles or in equestrian portraits, since Nagaur and Marwar are noted for an outstanding breed of horse, and paintings of rulers on horseback are ubiquitous at other courts.[64] There is an equestrian portrait of an older Bakhat Singh riding a horse, but it was painted not by a Nagaur artist but by a painter from Jodhpur around 1751, the year the ruler married his ninth and tenth wives.[65]

Another curiosity of the portable paintings is the absence of illustrated texts, such as *Bhagavata Puranas*, *Ramayanas*, *Devi Mahatmayas*, and *Ragamalas*.[66] Subjects from these various texts make up a large percentage of the paintings in other Rajput painting ateliers. With the exception of the Krishna temple painting (cat. 12), the portable paintings depict only one subject: Bakhat Singh enjoying life in the palace, usually surrounded by the beautiful buildings, gardens, and waterworks and/or accompanied by the women of the zenana in the nearby verdant countryside. The paintings convey the essence of a pleasurable and successful life, filled with sensual delight, music, flowers, rich textiles, and sumptuous meals— private and personal diversions from his warrior activities outside the palace. Nagaur was Bakhat Singh's place of refuge, a shelter where the gardens filled the air with pleasant aromas, fountains flowed at his feet, and beautifully decorated buildings provided a sanctuary from external discomforts and never-ending warfare.

In many ways, the portable paintings exemplify the diversity and contradictions that remain Rajasthan's allure, as local life continues despite difficult external currents and peaceful personal beauty is juxtaposed with the hard life of the outside world. These paintings depict a truly Rajput vision of life within the palace, cloaked within the stylistic ornament of Mughal inspiration; they emerge from local tradition, incorporate courtly elements from imperial rulers, and capture both the reality and the ideal of royal life at its best. This fusion of styles and vision under Bakhat Singh epitomizes artistic excellence and imagination and the best of Rajput and Mughal aesthetics.

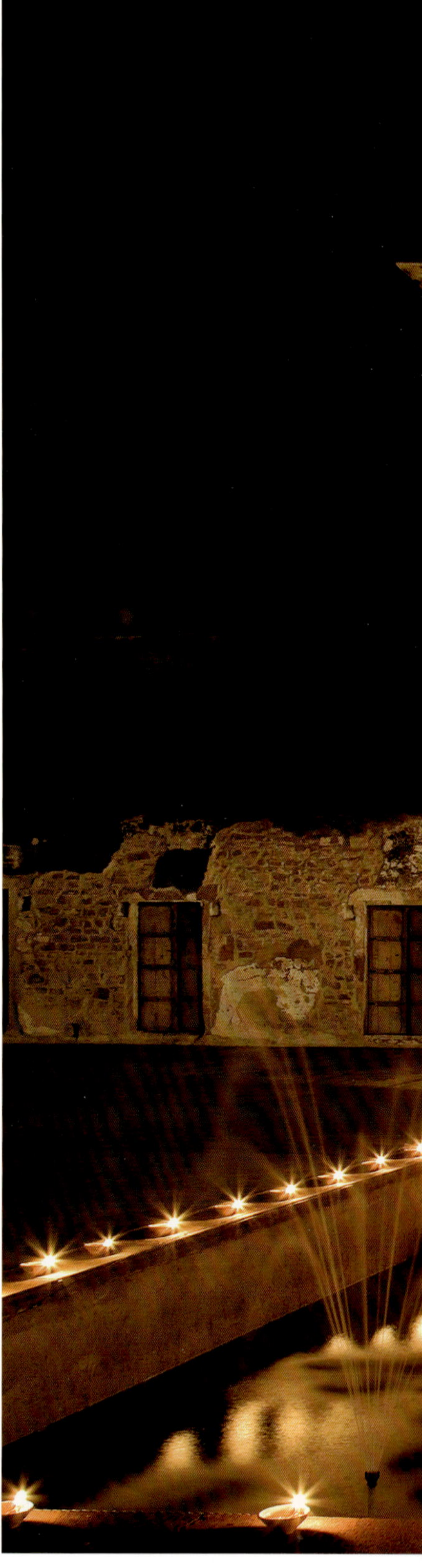

Fig. 5. Bakhat Singh Mahal at night, Ahhichatragarh Fort, Nagaur

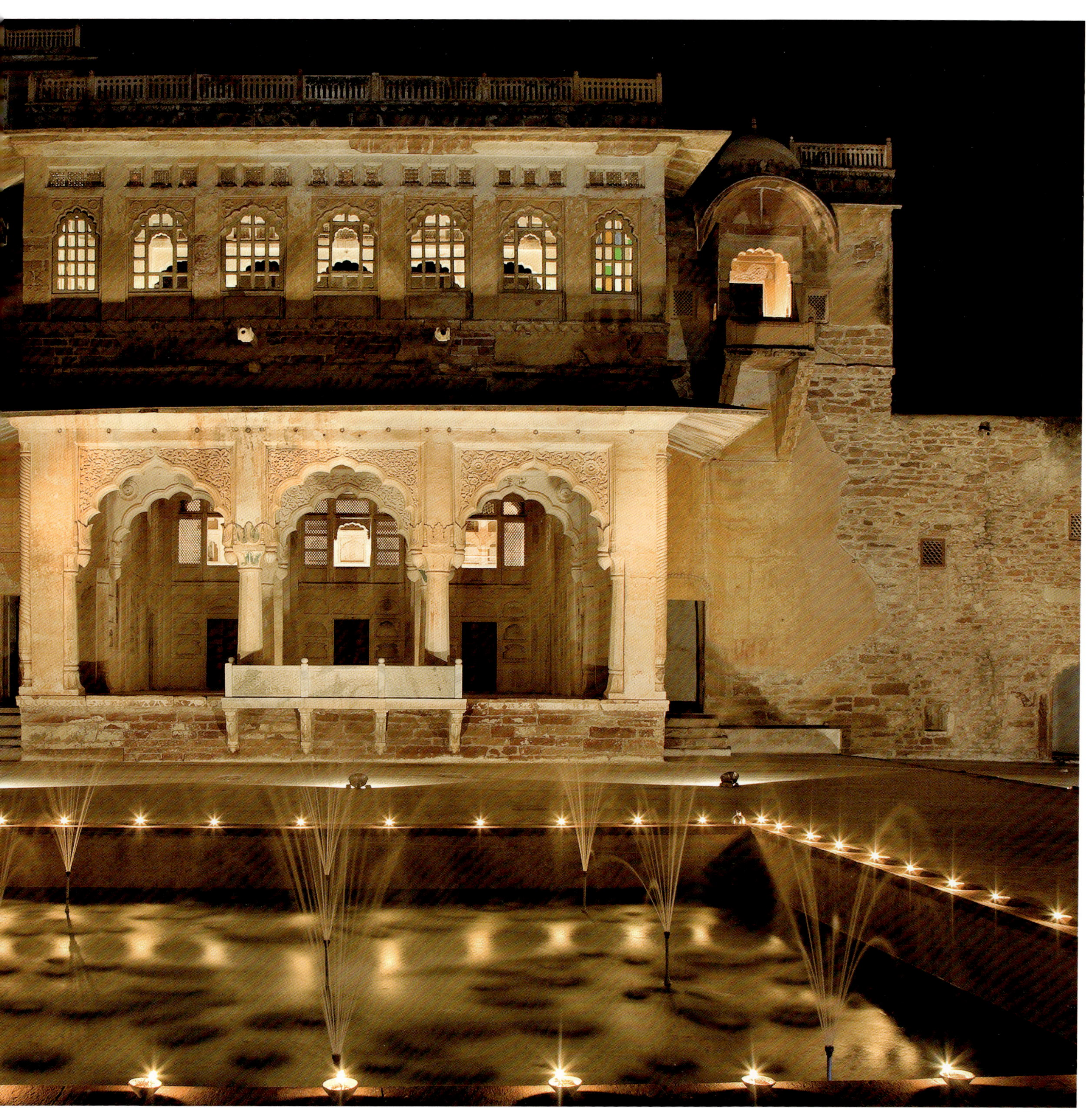

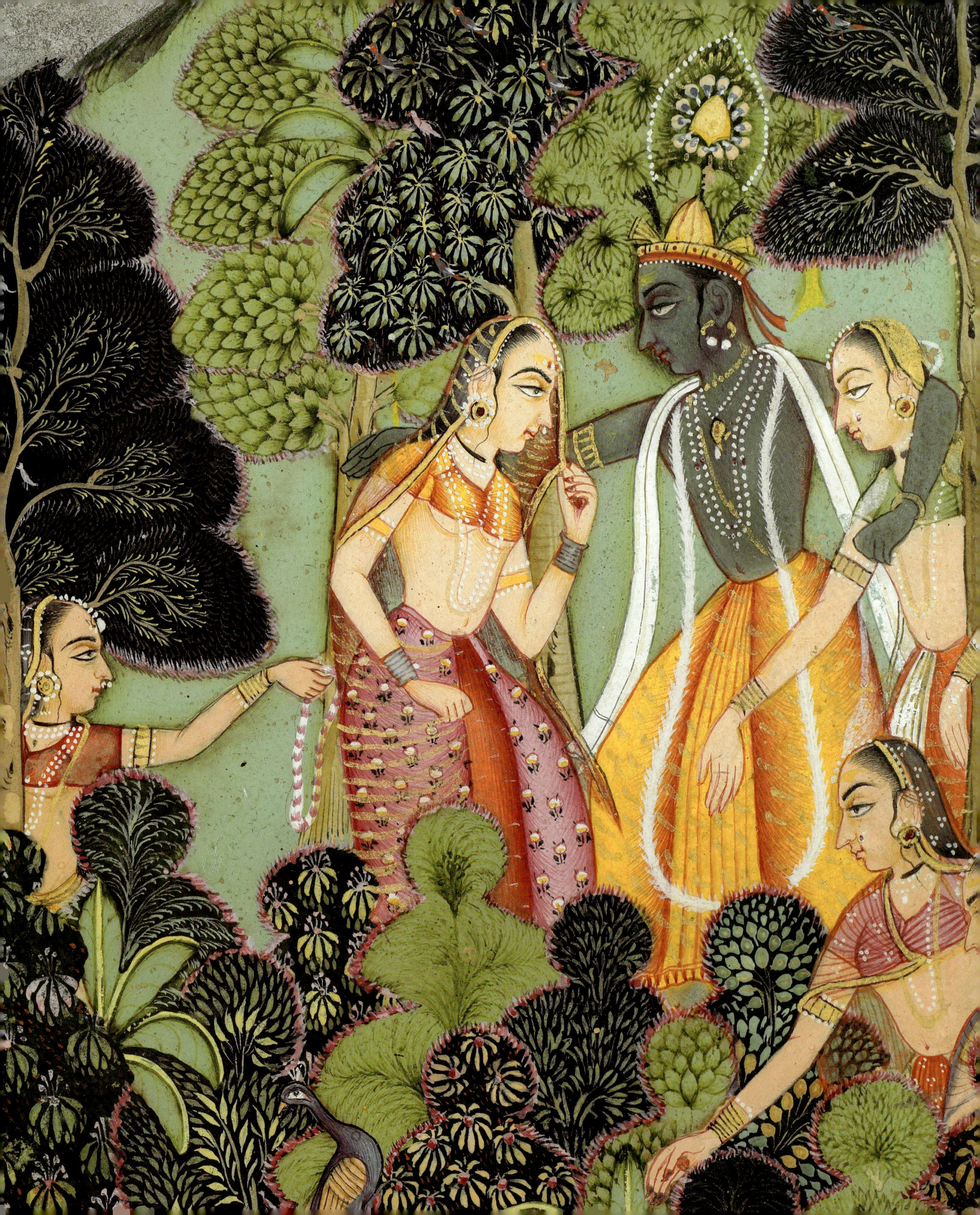

Maharaja Vijai Singh and the Epic Landscape, 1752–93

DEBRA DIAMOND

Over the course of Maharaja Vijai Singh's forty-one-year reign (1752–93),[1] court painters continued to employ the Nagaur palette and its aesthetic of delight, but they transformed intimate depictions of royal pastimes into visions of heavenly palaces and landscapes for divine *lila* (play). The new maharaja's ardent interest in religion was expressed, moreover, in illustrated manuscripts of unprecedented size. These transformations—from human to divine, from intimate to monumental—signal a momentous shift in Jodhpur painting and court culture. The Vijai Singh corpus delineates a quite different cultural landscape from that of Bakhat Singh's Nagaur court. The subjects and scale of the artworks demonstrate Vijai Singh's engagement with Rajput and Vaishnava networks of political and religious authority, which gained currency in the second half of the eighteenth century when the Mughals ceased to be the subcontinent's paramount power.

Until now, art historians have attributed only unadventurous portraits and a single illustrated manuscript of conventional size to the reign of the sixteenth Rathore sovereign. The foundational work of two scholars, B. N. Reu and Hermann Goetz, provided the invaluable first lineaments of the Jodhpur School, but established an unpromising stage for Vijai Singh's atelier. Reu's publications of the 1930s and 1940s erroneously date all but one of the Vijai Singh-period manuscripts to the reign of his grandson Man Singh (1803–43). Goetz apparently was unaware of the many Nagaur-style paintings produced during Vijai Singh's reign and concluded that Bakhat Singh's artists—after their moment of brilliance in early eighteenth-century Nagaur—scattered to other kingdoms.[2] Later art historians accepted both Reu's dates and Goetz's scenario.

The exciting realization that one hundred and fifty-six large folios from four monumental manuscripts were produced for Vijai Singh, however, shows that neither his atelier's engagement with broader cultural shifts nor its creativity have received proper recognition. Vijai Singh's artists created a new genre of manuscripts with folios measuring approximately 46 x 122 cm that required fresh approaches to composition and pictorial narrative; their dimensions also imposed new viewing practices at court (see "Monumental Manuscripts"). Since the paintings draw largely upon motifs and color harmonies from the Nagaur atelier of the maharaja's father, Bakhat Singh, and the Jodhpur workshop of his grandfather, Abhai Singh, the art-historical discussions in this essay focus primarily on stylistic interactions within Marwar borders. This allows for the most succinct identification of the workshop's considerable and distinctive contributions to Indian painting, while outlining its evolution during this period.[3]

THE EARLY YEARS

Vijai Singh (1729–1793) was raised in the delicate white palaces at Ahhichatragarh Fort in Nagaur, the semi-independent state ruled by his father, Maharaja Bakhat Singh. Paintings from the 1730s record the young prince's attendance, alongside his father, at an entertainment and an elephant fight.[4] When Bakhat Singh relocated to Jodhpur, after succeeding to the Rathore throne of Marwar in 1751, Prince Vijai became in effect, if not in name, the new overlord of Nagaur. A portrait, circa 1751–52, with a cartouche inscribed "maharaja kunwar [heir apparent] sri ijai singhji" depicts the young noble in this transitional phase (fig. 1). A discreet halo, almost hidden in the garden leaves surrounding Vijai's head, unusually and adroitly signals the status of the young prince. Densely rolling clouds above the lush foliage convey the hothouse transformation that the yearly monsoon rains bring to the desert region of Nagaur.[5] The painting's exuberantly floral carpet and the terrace railing's foliate tracery accentuate the garden's charm at its peak in late summer.

A second portrait of Vijai Singh, completed shortly after his accession to the Marwar throne in 1752, depicts the young king seated within a *jharokha* window, participating in the ceremony in which rulers are viewed by their courtiers and subjects (see fig. 3).[6] Its rich pastel tones and the graceful balcony adorned with foliate arabesques and polychrome lotus finials are hallmarks of the Nagaur style that emerged under Bakhat Singh. In contrast, the short nervous strokes of the glowing halo, the febrile delicacy of the maharaja's hands, and his green and pink-tinged eyelid are unique to the artist Fazl. A second work by Fazl, which employs the more restrained patterns of the Jodhpur court style, demonstrates that artists in this transition period worked in both the Nagaur and the Jodhpur idioms.[7]

The Nagaur idiom patronized by Bakhat Singh in the second quarter of the eighteenth century continues in a relatively undiluted form throughout the 1750s, as evidenced by a trio of similarly sized paintings depicting three aspects of the great Hindu deity Vishnu. (See fig. 2 opposite, cat. 22, and fig. 22a, p. 277).[8] In each painting, Vishnu holds court within a gleaming palace, attended by maidens and musicians.[9] His wide face, pointed chin, and diminutive smiling mouth recall Bikaner court paintings of the deity from the reign of Karan Singh (1631–69), which likely were given as gifts to rulers of Marwar (fig. 12b, p. 266).[10] But the Nagaur style remains dominant. Vijai Singh's artists retained the garden palace settings, foliage, rich pastel palette, and the three horizontal registers—foreground garden, central palace, and background sky—of the Nagaur atelier.[11] Rajput painting often represents deities with the regalia and palaces of royalty, but here the subject matter, from court entertainments to heavenly palaces (cat. 22 and fig. 12b), also foreshadows the piety that Vijai Singh increasingly demonstrates after 1765.

Style alone cannot tell us whether these early paintings were produced in the capital of Jodhpur or in Nagaur, especially since accomplished artists like Fazl mastered both idioms. Vijai Singh, who often returned to Nagaur during his reign, may have retained an atelier there. At least one Nagaur artist moved to Jodhpur; an inscription on a Vijai Singh portrait (dated circa 1755) identifies him as "Kayam from Nagaur."[12] The considerable production of paintings

Fig. 1 *Prince Vijai Singh Sitting on a Terrace,* Nagaur, ca. 1751, 33.7 x 22.2 cm. Mehrangarh Museum Trust, RJS 2042.

Fig. 2 *Vishnu and Lakshmi,* Jodhpur or Nagaur, ca. 1755, 43.8 x 62.2 cm. Mehrangarh Museum Trust, RJS 1819.

Fig. 3 *Maharaja Vijai Singh Seated in a Jharokha,* by Fazl, Jodhpur or Nagaur, ca. 1752–55, 31 x 23 cm. Mehrangarh Museum Trust, RJS 2045.

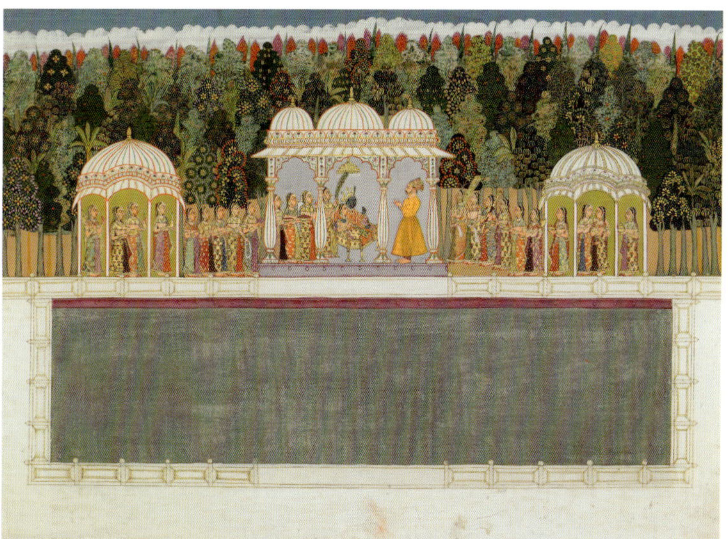

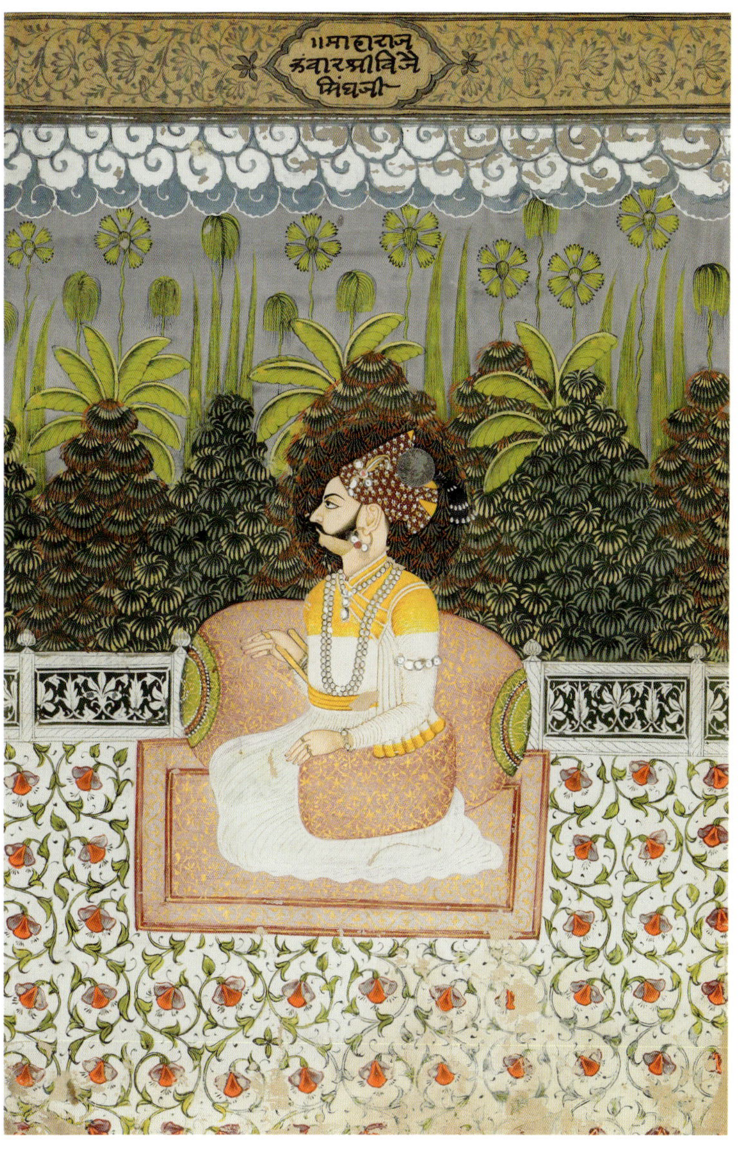

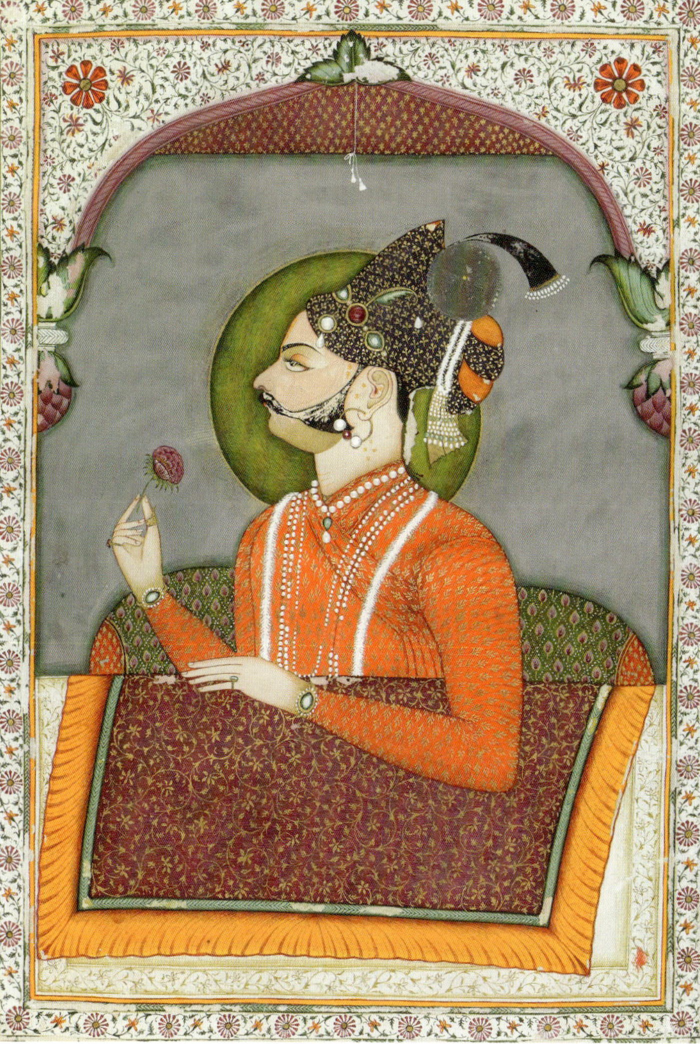

in the Nagaur style or with Nagaur elements over the course of Vijai Singh's long reign strongly suggests that Kayam was not the only artist who relocated to the royal court in Jodhpur. These Nagaur émigrés would have trained younger Jodhpur artists, and their paintings would have been studied and cited by court artists.

In sum, the local Nagaur idiom was deemed appropriate for royal portraits and was flexible enough to adapt to religious subjects in the first decade of Vijai Singh's reign.[13] The prominence of the aesthetic during this period demonstrates the endurance of Vijai Singh's ties to Nagaur. When he inherited the throne after his father's death in 1752, Maharaja Vijai Singh's principal residence, like that of generations of Rathore rulers since 1459, became Mehrangarh Fort in Jodhpur. But he regularly visited, sometimes for extended periods, the strategically located and politically important stronghold of Nagaur.[14] While paintings in the Jodhpur court style continued to be produced (see figs. 4, 7), the marked persistence of the Nagaur idiom suggests that Vijai Singh preferred the floral aesthetic. There may have been political implications. Molly Aitken's work on style in Rajput painting demonstrates how distinctive palettes and profiles were recognized elements of a court's identity.[15] Perhaps Vijai Singh downplayed the Jodhpur court style associated with his uncle, Maharaja Abhai Singh (reigned 1724–49), in favor of the Nagaur idiom fostered by his father. Bakhat Singh had become Marwar's ruler in 1751 only after forcibly ousting Abhai Singh's son, Ram Singh (reigned 1749–51), from the throne. Less than two years later, Bakhat Singh died and was succeeded by his first-born son. Vijai and his cousin Ram Singh squared off in a civil war that lasted until 1756. Ram Singh was politically marginalized, but until his death in 1772 he remained a potential threat to the maharaja. To court audiences, Vijai Singh's patronage of the pastel Nagaur idiom may have emphasized the legitimacy of his succession via Bakhat Singh rather than through the Jodhpur line of Ram Singh's father, Abhai Singh.[16]

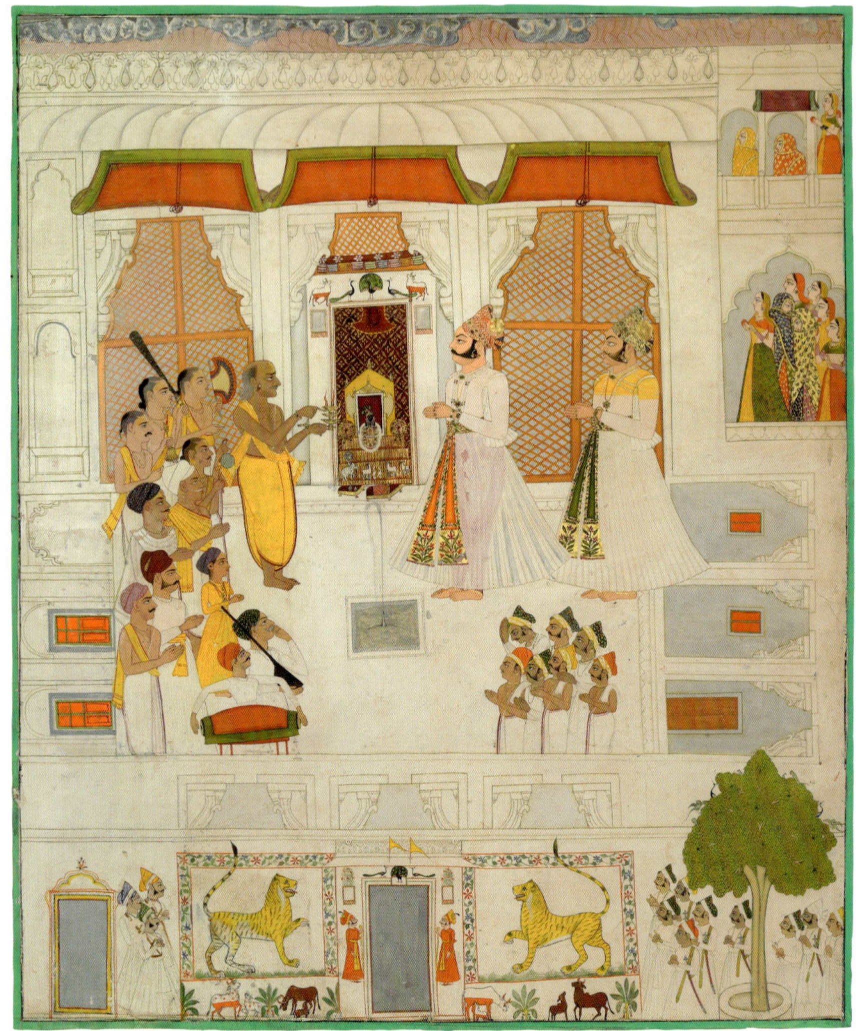

Fig. 4. *Maharaja Vijai Singh Worshiping Krishna*, by Udairam, Jodhpur, ca. 1770, 55 x 48 cm. Mehrangarh Museum Trust, RJS 2049.

THE PATH OF GRACE

In 1765, Vijai Singh was initiated into the Hindu religious community known as the Vallabh Sampraday or Pushtimarg (the path of grace). Founded by the saint Vallabha (1479–1531), the order espouses joyous devotion to an eminently accessible Krishna.[17] Icons of Krishna graced by Vallabha or his direct descendants were highly potent manifestations of the deity, and one was installed at Chopasni, a village not far from Mehrangarh Fort.[18] At the upper border of Udairam's *Maharaja Vijai Singh Worshiping Krishna* (fig. 4), a narrow strip of rocky outcrops (beneath swirling clouds) sites the Chopasni temple's location just outside Jodhpur. At the temple's center, Vijai Singh honors the deity as his religious preceptor, the priest (*gosain*) Giridharji, circles a lamp flame around the Vallabh icon.[19] Male devotees—with the maharaja and *gosain* in the two most important positions closest to the deity—gather in the colonnaded interior courtyard as a singer, lifting his hand to his mouth, raises his voice in a devotional *bhajan* (song). Women of the court and Giridharji's family congregate apart from the men on a shaded terrace and balcony.

Similar to all Vallabh Krishna icons (and their representations in paintings), the deity stares straight ahead in order to engage the gaze of the beholder/devotee. Such paintings were created for a ritual practice among members of the sectarian community in which devotion to the painted image is equivalent to direct interaction with Krishna.[20] The Hindi/Rajasthani terms describing these Vallabh modes of engagement are *chitra darshan* (picture sight), which implies the mutual gaze between devotee and deity, and *chitra seva* (picture service), which refers to the devotional acts (such as circling a lamp or offering food) that a devotee undertakes to interact with and delight Krishna.[21] Thus Udairam's painting both celebrates a particular ritual at the Chopasni temple and gives the viewer access to continuous and profound engagement with the divine.

Vijai Singh publicly expressed his ardent devotion to Krishna throughout his kingdom by outlawing cow slaughter, forbidding the consumption of meat and liquor, and proclaiming that cowherds should be addressed as *jagirdar* (landlord). In Jodhpur, he built two grand Krishna temples, the Gangashyamji and the Balkrishnaji. Between 1765 and the final years of his reign, he made generous donations to the Chopasni shrine, both to the deity on behalf of the temple and to the *gosain* Giridharji. These included money and ornaments for Krishna, food for temple festivals, and gifts for the temple priests. The maharaja's religious patronage also extended beyond Marwar's borders; he was broadly recognized as an ardent supporter of Vallabh temples and festivals across Rajasthan.[22]

Vijai Singh's pious generosity kept him in close contact with a cohort of royal devotees from neighboring Rajput kingdoms, who patronized an extraordinary corpus of devotional paintings in the eighteenth century.[23] Vallabha's teachings, which encourage the arts of music, poetry, painting, and gastronomy in Krishna's service, had found fertile ground in the Rajput courts—where art patronage was an already established royal tradition—and led to astonishing transformations within the Jodhpur painting tradition.[24]

EPIC LANDSCAPES

Vijai Singh's devotion to Krishna surfaces spectacularly in seven large paintings of the deity sporting with *gopis* (female cowherds; see p. 20 and cats. 23–25). Subject, style, and compositional logic date the unbound manuscript to 1765 or shortly thereafter.[25] The paintings illustrate the Sanskrit verses of the *Raslila*, which to Vallabh devotees of Krishna epitomize the love between deity and devotee. As the verso inscriptions indicate, in Jodhpur the *Raslila* chapters in the *Bhagavata Purana* were known more colloquially as the *Krishna Lila* (divine play of Krishna). The paintings' dreamlike foliage and elongated figures of women garbed in sherbet colors suggest that they were painted by artists who began their careers in Bakhat Singh's atelier at Nagaur. The folios measure an extraordinarily large 148 x 47 cm but retain the pictorial logic of a miniature, suggesting that the artists were dealing with this expansive scale for the first time. Scores of small figures, trees, birds, fish, and stars—the same size as those in more intimately scaled paintings—are depicted across the horizontal expanse of each folio. The proliferation of small figures sensitively conveys the sacred narrative of the *Raslila*, evoking the crush of *gopis* who join Krishna in the enchanting landscape (cat. 23), the expanse of the forest where they search for Krishna after his mischievous disappearance

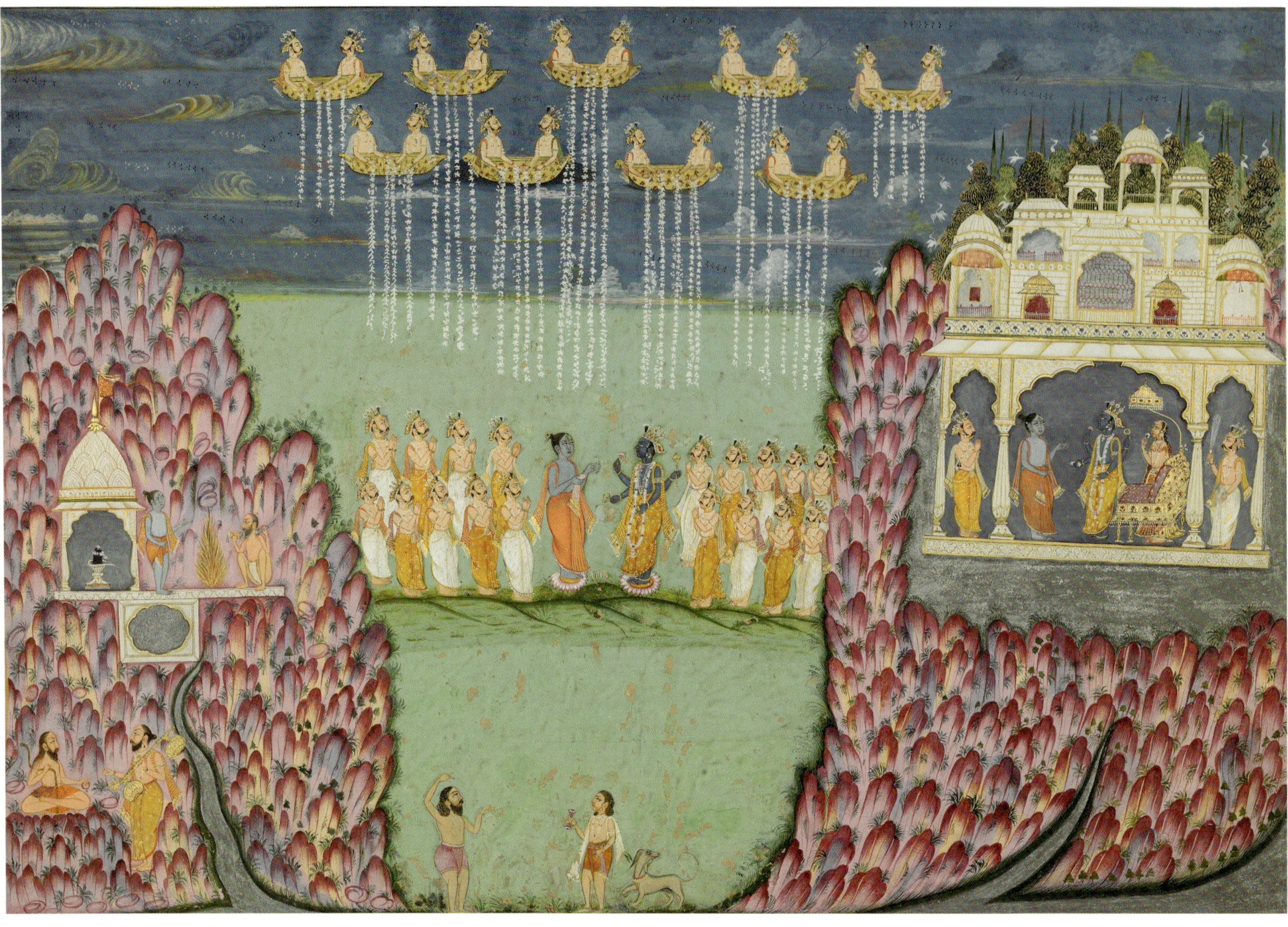

Fig. 5. *The Story of Vikrasura*, folio 63 from the *Bhagavata Purana*, Jodhpur, ca. 1775, 31 x 44 cm. Mehrangarh Museum Trust, RJS 1814.

(cat. 24), and the magically generous way that Krishna ultimately multiplies himself to satisfy their longing (cat. 25).

At the same time, the long, silvery streak of the river—across which light skips when the images are viewed—and the horizontal unfurling of the forest invite an immersive experience into Krishna's enchanting world. Although Vijai Singh's Vallabh community was part of the larger devotional movement known as *bhakti*, which promoted a direct engagement with an accessible god, the Vallabhans were unique in their emphasis upon aesthetic envelopment. In Vallabh temples, multiple art forms (including large paintings on cloth) were layered to enhance the devotee's passionate interaction with the deity.[26] The unprecedented scale of the illustrated folios may have developed from this tendency toward dramatically engaging devotees, for those who mentally entered Krishna's world (in the temple or through the *Bhagavata Purana* verses) were promised the same liberation as those who interacted with the god when he lived on earth.[27] The grand vision of the *Krishna Lila* becomes the central expression of the Vijai Singh atelier. Over the course of his reign, artists would create another one hundred forty-nine equally large folios for three manuscripts: the *Ram Charit* (the *Ramcharitmanas*, the Hindi telling of the *Ramayana*), the *Gajendra Moksha* (an account of

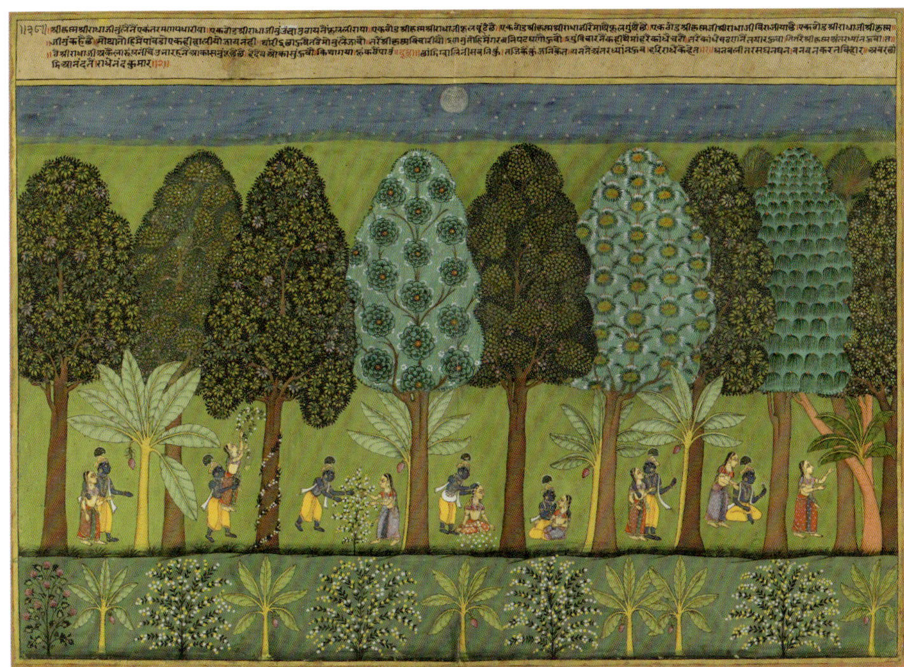

Fig. 6. *Krishna and Radha in the Forest,* folio 17 from the *Bhagavata Purana,* Jodhpur, ca. 1775, 31 x 44 cm. Mehrangarh Museum Trust, RJS1768.

the salvific activity of the deity Vishnu), and the *Durga Charit* (more widely known as the *Devi Mahatmya,* which recounts the heroic victories of the goddess).[28] For workshop practice, see "Monumental Manuscripts at the Jodhpur Court, 1765–1830."

The vernacular *Ramcharitmanas* composed by the poet Tulsidas in the late sixteenth century retains the narrative of the ancient Sanskrit *Ramayana,* but recasts the saga of Rama's exile and quest for his abducted wife, Sita, within the devotional frame of *bhakti.* All of Rama's actions are recounted as *lila,* and all of the epic's characters— whether human, simian, or demon—who recognize Rama's divinity receive his grace. While the Sanskrit *Ramayana* was often illustrated in the Hindu courts of north India, Tulsi's telling rarely entered the court painting tradition. Vijai Singh's unusual patronage of the Hindi epic manifests his spiritual inclinations and expresses a model of ideal kingship that differs markedly from that of his father's.[29]

The looser, less-polished version of the Nagaur aesthetic that dominates the ninety-one folios of the *Ram Charit* suggests a production date of circa 1775 (cats. 26–29).[30] Several folios exhibit delicately painted, elongated ascetics, but the more spontaneous paintings are exuberant landscapes with short, energetic figures. In these folios, artists first laid down patches of thin, flat color, roughly the size and shape of each individual figure, over which they rapidly limned contours, evoked texture, or created a sense of volume. The best folios creatively exploit the monumental scale with delightfully improbable landscape elements or vividly colored vignettes in which the Nagaur palette is pitched to the highest key.

Tulsidas' epic concludes with the establishment of a harmonious kingdom where Rama's *lila* unfolds eternally. The final four folios of the *Ram Charit*—which depict Rama and Sita holding court, enjoying entertainments, pleasure boating (cat. 30), and throwing color during the festival of Holi—translate the *Ramcharitmanas's* description of the divine realm into a significant visual coda.[31] In representing *Ramrajya,* Rama and Sita's just reign over their idyllic kingdom, these paintings encapsulate Vijai Singh's identity as devotee and ruler.[32] For *bhaktas* (devotees) like the maharaja, Rama and Sita's delight in each other and their garden palace was a central focus of worship. It is significant that the representations of the divine court—and these particular royal pastimes—refocus Bakhat Singh's intimately scaled Nagaur paintings. The Nagaur palace is evoked through similarities in architecture, court entertainments, and palette, but it also is transformed through magnification. Bakhat Singh's imperial milieu is rearticulated within the Vaishnava landscape shared by Rajput rulers in the latter half of the eighteenth century. For Hindu kings confronting the decline of Mughal hegemony by engaging in new alliances and enunciating new identities, *Ramrajya* (rather than the imperial court) served as an archetypal model of rule.[33]

Vijai Singh's ardent devotion of Krishna finds continued expression in an illustrated *Bhagavata Purana,* the canonical account of the deity, whose chapters include the *Raslila* (figs. 6, 7).[34] Its stylistically heterogeneous folios are conventionally scaled: nine paintings measure 44 x 62 cm and fifty-nine paintings measure 31 x 44 cm.[35] The larger group of folios is dated circa 1775 because so many of them are exceedingly similar to ones in the illustrated *Ram Charit*. The *Ram Charit's* rich pastel palette and swooping pink mountains reappear in smaller scale, for example, on folio 63, which depicts deities in sky chariots showering strands of white blossoms on Vishnu and Shiva (fig. 6).[36] In contrast, folios by other court painters employ a deep palette, flatly painted forms, and stocky figures. Folio 17 (fig. 7) beautifully conveys the affectionate play of Radha and Krishna and is remarkable both for its emotional charge and its charmingly patterned trees, which recall the woodblock print textiles of Rajasthan.[37] (See also fig. 46a, p. 291.)

The creative vigor of the Vijai Singh atelier finds its final expression in the stylistically diverse folios of the monumental *Durga Charit*. Its broad gamut of style and quality demonstrates that artists were given free reign to express individual sensibilities as the workshop continued to grow. Although numerous folios draw directly on the Nagaur style—and include motifs such as dancing girls copied directly from Bakhat Singh paintings—other folios exhibit the harder-edged abstractions, such as bell-shaped skirts with flaring hems, that became characteristic of Jodhpur portraiture by the last decade of the eighteenth century. The manuscript, therefore, is dated by style to roughly circa 1785.[38]

The finest paintings, by the "Durga Master," are richly colored, selectively burnished (the highest gloss is reserved for depictions of deities), and exhibit a sensitive contour line that convincingly describes relaxed rather than purely schematic figures (fig. 8). A pivotal image exemplifying this master's style depicts a lush hermitage and the cosmic ocean (cat. 32). The idyllic forest ashram reworks the garden palette first developed in Nagaur under Bakhat Singh's patronage, while the undifferentiated space of the cosmic ocean prefigures the aesthetic of early nineteenth-century Man Singh-period painting. The manuscript's next two folios, also by the "Durga Master," are even more radically minimal, eschewing any reference to human landscape, scale, or temporality. Most of the other *Durga Charit* folios stage the goddess's battles against demons on backdrops of rolling hills in muted verdigris, ochre, or olive green.[39] Iconographic details (such as white-flower garland streamers descending from deities' sky-chariots) and compositional similarities reveal that a number of *Ram Charit* and *Bhagavata Purana* artists were engaged in the *Durga Charit's* production. In addition, the depiction of the goddess's many arms, her three-quarter visage, and her deeply colored garments recall contemporaneous and slightly later Bikaner paintings of Durga slaying the buffalo demon.[40] Bikaner artists created these small paintings as *nazar* (offerings) to their maharaja during the annual festival of Dussehra, in which Hindu kings both worship and symbolically reenact Durga's victory for the benefit of their kingdoms. Similarly, the Jodhpur manuscript may have celebrated, albeit on a grander scale, the power of the goddess and the maharaja's desire for her grace.

THE FINAL YEARS OF VIJAI SINGH'S REIGN

Although Vijai Singh patronized a flourishing atelier, his kingdom—like the rest of northern India during the second half of the eighteenth century—was affected by the decline of Mughal hegemony. In Jodhpur, strong imperial support had bolstered the authority of successive maharajas, but as this gave way, the Rathore nobility advanced their own claims for power. In response to challenges from his Rathore kinsmen, who previously had provided the recruits for the kingdom's armies, and territorial bids by several Rajput kings, Vijai Singh hired his own troops, enlisted the military support of Maratha generals from central India, and sought alliances with other Rajput rulers. While diplomatic and military successes resulted in periods of prosperity, the creation of a paid army periodically strained the royal

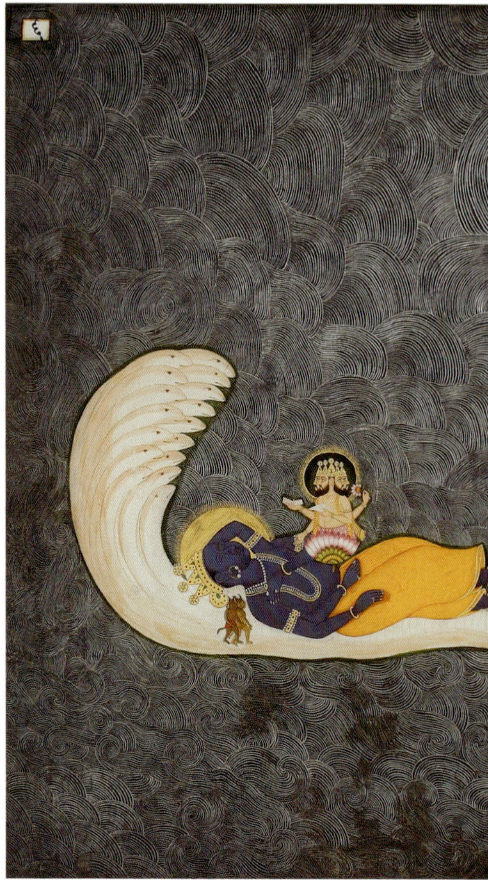

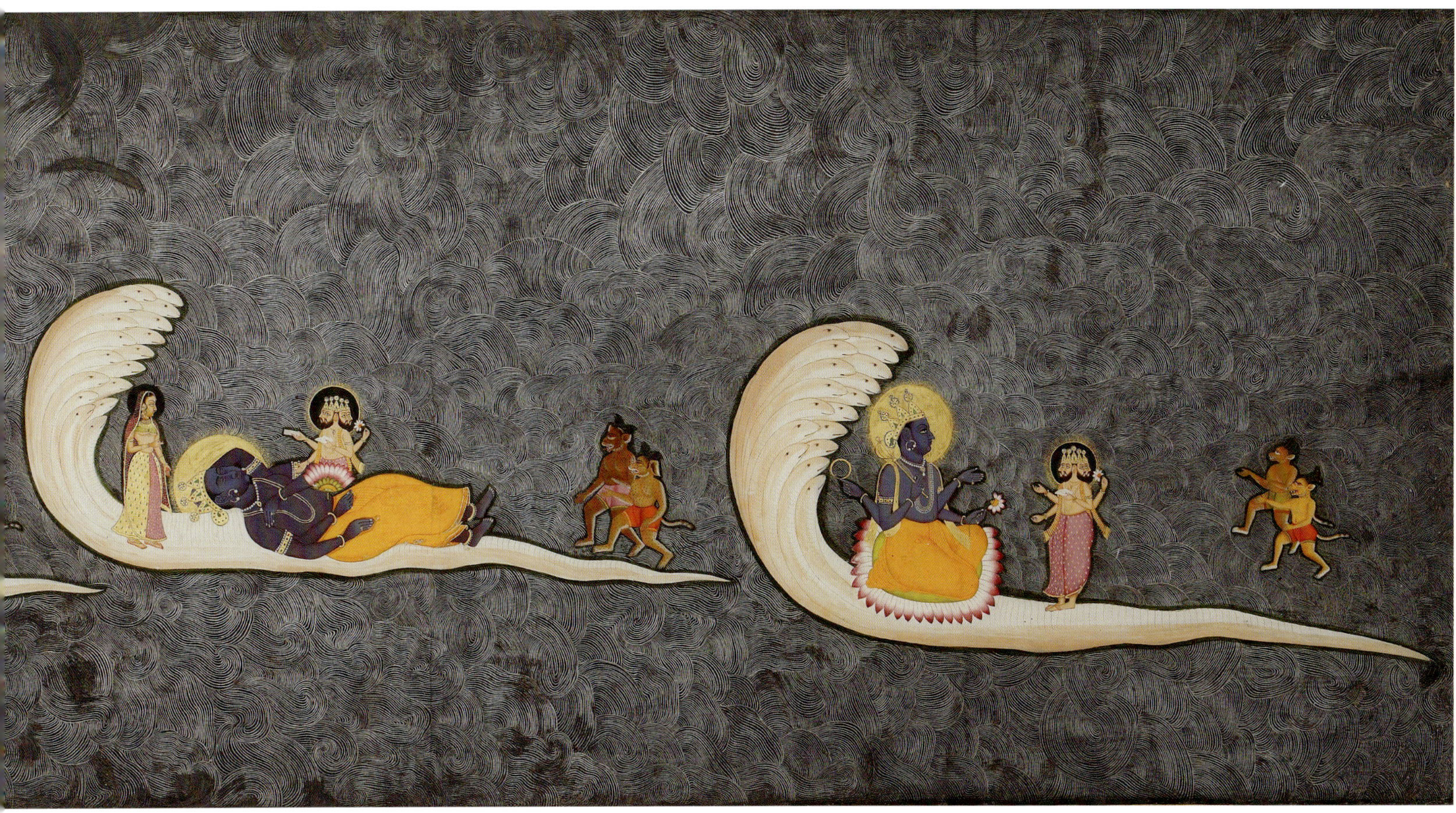

coffers, and the Maratha alliance introduced dangerously independent players, who extorted onerous tributes, into Marwar's political landscape.

Within the kingdom, the nobility's opposition to Vijai Singh crystallized as antipathy toward his non-Rajput consort, Gulab Rai. The maharaja may have met Gulab Rai, a devotee of Krishna, when she was a singer at the Chopasni temple; over the ensuing years, he showered her with gifts, which included the impregnable Jalore Fortress, south of Jodhpur.[41] It is not clear whether she intervened inappropriately into affairs of state or was simply a convenient scapegoat for the restive nobility. But when she adopted the maharaja's young orphaned grandson and heir, she wisely sent the boy to safety in Jalore Fortress. This was a canny move, for in 1791 Gulab Rai was murdered by three Rathore noblemen.[42] A year later, while the distraught Vijai Singh camped outside Jodhpur, his ambitious nephew Bhim Singh seized power. Vijai paid off his scheming nephew and returned to power in 1792, but died shortly thereafter. With the support of the noble faction that had challenged Vijai Singh throughout his reign, Bhim Singh was crowned in 1793. Over the next ten years, this maharaja would murder all but one of the potential claimants to the throne. By 1803, only the young, orphaned Prince Man Singh, the boy Gulab Rai sent off to Jalore, remained as a threat to Bhim Singh's sovereignty.

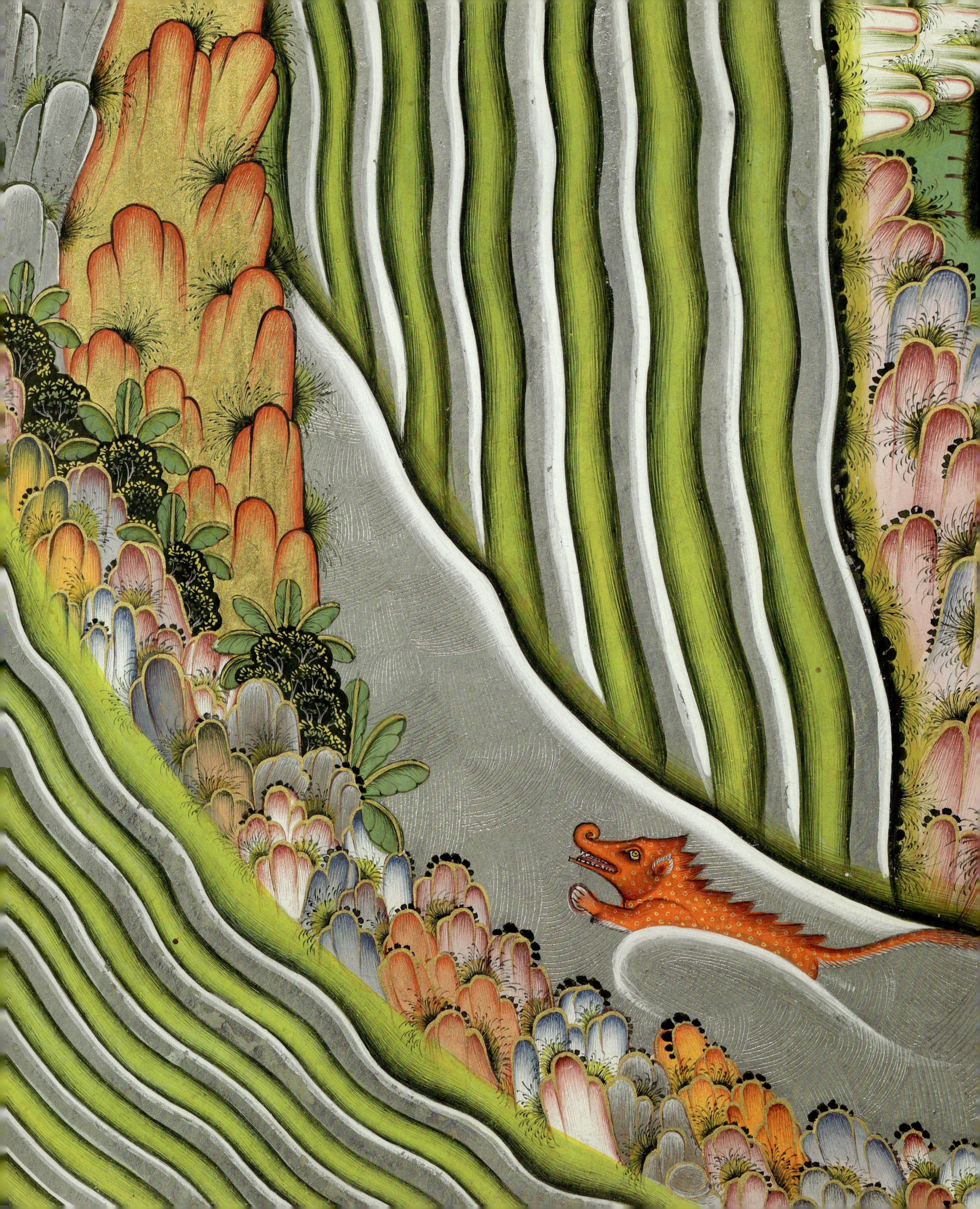

Painting, Politics, and Devotion

Under Maharaja Man Singh, 1803–43

DEBRA DIAMOND

Between 1803 and 1843, Maharaja Man Singh of Marwar radically reconceived sovereignty in Marwar. He devoted his kingdom to an immortal ascetic associated with a heterodox yogic order and transformed his religious preceptors into the kingdom's most powerful ruling elite. His coalition with the Nath sectarian order displaced many of his Rathore kinsmen, the traditional bulwark of the state, and unsettled the Brahmin religious establishment. Man Singh's support of the Naths, who had not figured prominently at court during the reigns of his predecessors, invited severe resistance. But the association between the maharaja and the yogic order was strong enough to withstand forty years of military challenges from within and outside Marwar.[1] The visual arts played no small part in this success. Paintings worked to legitimate Man Singh's conception of sovereignty. They established the divine greatness of immortal Naths and their living representatives and expressed the inevitability and fit of Nath prominence in the court and kingdom.

Court painters responded to the challenge of new Nath subjects—which ranged from metaphysics to hagiographic narratives to portraits of the king's gurus—with daring abstractions, dazzling imagery, and bold juxtapositions of motifs appropriated from diverse visual arenas. Their astounding paintings, along with the political acumen of the state, belie standard art historical assessments of early nineteenth-century painting as derivative reflections of a glorious past.[2] Man Singh, the grandson of Maharaja Vijai Singh (reigned 1752–93), always connected his devotion to the Naths with his miraculous accession to the Marwar throne. In the summer of 1803, the young prince's chances for survival, let alone succession, were bleak. His uncle, Maharaja Bhim Singh (reigned 1793–1803), had assassinated every other claimant for the throne, and his army now besieged Man Singh's fortress in Jalore. By August, the prince's forces, supplies, and money were depleted. Man Singh later described that grim summer[3]:

King Bhim's anger took fierce form…. No senses can apprehend the furious war that raged on and on. All materials and money were gone. Hope of keeping the fort faded. In those times, great worries pressed on Man Singh's heart from morning until night.

Despite such troubles, however, Man Singh also noted that his days were filled with joy due to his worship of the immortal ascetic Jallandharnath (whom he called Nathji):

But his heart was filled with joy at the thought of Nathji. With his heart and breath he continuously worshipped Nathji at the incomparable Nath temple in the fort. He cared neither for himself nor for worldly affairs as the greatness of Nathji enveloped his heart.[4]

In early October 1803, shortly before the Hindu festival of Divali, Man Singh agreed to surrender to Bhim Singh's army. As the prince prepared to vacate the fortress, his spiritual preceptor, the guru Dev Nath, approached him with a divine message: the immortal ascetic Jallandharnath had announced that if Man Singh held out until Divali, he not only would keep Jalore but also rule all of Marwar (see cats. 32 and 33). Within the next few days, Bhim Singh suddenly and unexpectedly died. The maharaja's general, Inderaj, then threw the support of the royal forces behind Man Singh. Together they marched speedily toward the Jodhpur capital. The great nobles of Jodhpur who had supported Bhim Singh's bloodthirsty actions toward his rivals—or, at least, passively encouraged the disputes to further their own consolidation of power—grudgingly accepted the "coup."[5] Man Singh's *abhisheka* (coronation) was celebrated on January 17, 1804 (see cat. 31), and he was formally initiated by his guru Dev Nath into the Nath Sampraday (sectarian order) the following year.

Man Singh reigned for forty years as a devotee of the Nath Sampraday, a once-considerable (but now lesser-known) religious presence in India.[6] The Naths originated hatha yoga in the twelfth–thirteenth century. Over the succeeding centuries, they gained a broad popular base to become India's paradigmatic yogins. They revered and emulated immortal ascetics known as *mahasiddhas* (great perfected beings), who had vast powers that surpassed even those of the Hindu gods. When not meditating in the highest heaven, these *mahasiddhas* roamed earth in the guise of ordinary yogins. Covering their bodies with sacred ash, clad in rough saffron-colored garments and wearing unkempt dreadlocks and large earrings (*kundal*) through holes bored into their ears' inner cartilage, they often presented a fearsome visage. Popular lore and Nath hagiographies alike abound with stories of dramatic encounters with Naths.[7] With their supernatural powers, they punished those who failed to recognize or acknowledge them with fiery conflagrations, devasting droughts, or battlefield massacres. But they conferred grace and wonderful boons upon those who treated them with respect— most famously transforming fledgling princes into powerful kings.[8] Man Singh's reign as Jallandharnath's supreme devotee was thus an extreme but not unprecedented spiritual affiliation for a Hindu ruler.[9]

Nath initiates revered the *mahasiddhas* as teachers who passed on the powerful and esoteric discipline of hatha yoga (the yoga of violent exertion). Far broader than the modern conception of yoga, hatha yoga is a systematic set of meditation and somatic practices that enables mortals to achieve immortality and gain supernormal powers. These include the ability to foretell the future, fly, hear or see over great distances, and achieve blissful awareness of the oneness between the self and the universe. While not all Nath yogins achieve the perfected state needed to become *mahasiddhas*, all Nath disciples are understood to wield at least some of their powers.[10] Outsiders called them, often pejoratively, "*kanphata* jogis" (split-eared yogins) after their *kundal* earrings, but they were more respectfully known as

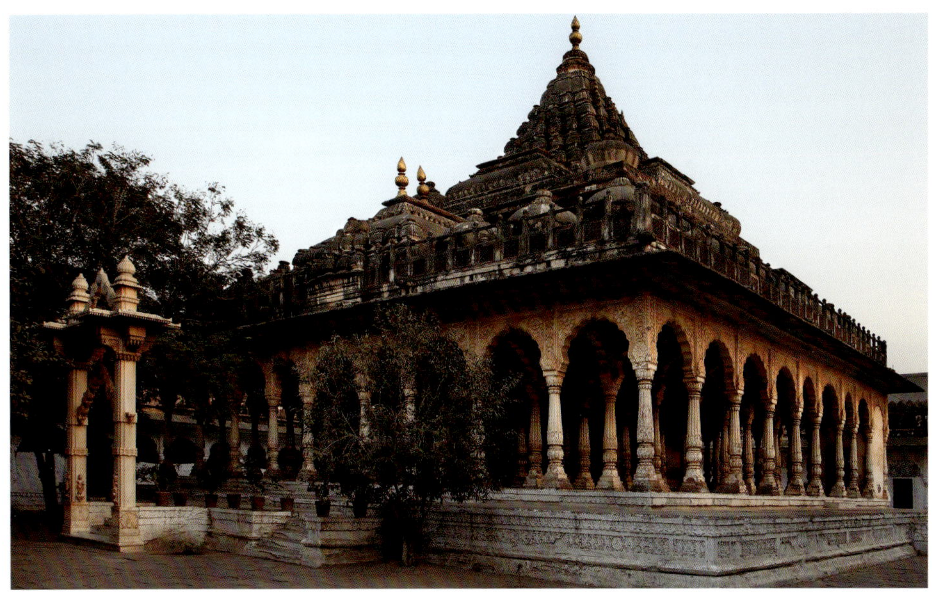 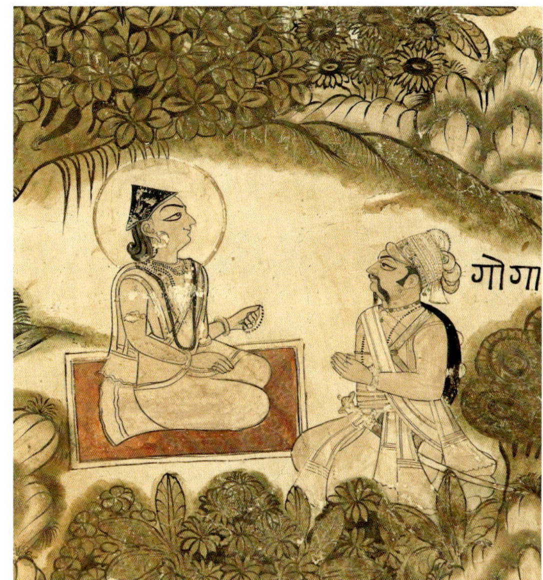
गोगा

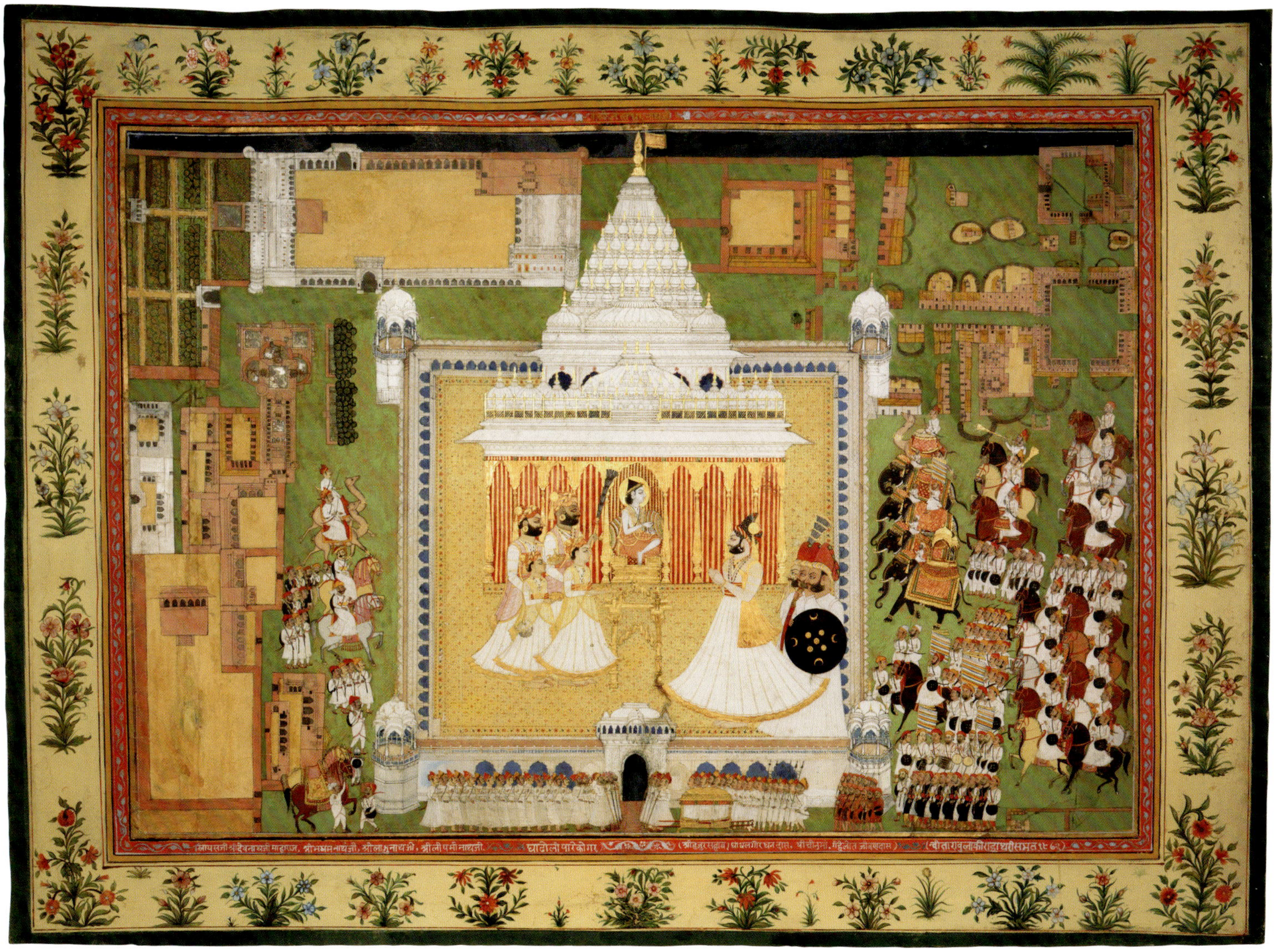

siddhas—accomplished or perfected ones.[11]

Prior to Man Singh's reign, Nath ascetics and householders were just one of Marwar's many religious communities.[12] Throughout the eighteenth century, as Maharaja Bakhat Singh (reigned 1725–51) transformed Nagaur Fort into an earthly paradise and his successor Vijai Singh expressed his devotion to Krishna, Nath yogins and householders led quiet lives in hermitages, villages, and towns across Marwar. In Rajasthan, the Nath monastic order that recognized the *mahasiddha* Jallandharnath as its spiritual founder was centered at Jalore (see cat. 33).[13] Next to the fortress where Prince Man Singh spent his youth, the sacred seat included a monastery and two Jallandharnath temples.

PIETY AND PATRONAGE

Man Singh's cultural patronage, which centered upon the Naths, was intertwined with his elevation of the sectarian order into an honored and powerful polity. In the first year of his reign, Man Singh brought his spiritual preceptor Dev Nath from Jalore to Jodhpur. He bestowed generous land grants upon Dev Nath and his four brothers, who became *jagirdars*, landowners who were lords over their territories. In Jodhpur, the maharaja constructed three temples for his guru's family: Mahamandir, a grand temple within a walled township (figs. 1–3, cats. 36 and 37), Udaimandir (fig. 32a, p. 281), and Nijmandir (cat. 38).[14] Like all royal acts of religious patronage—a sovereign activity as central to Indic state formation as revenue collection—Man Singh's conspicuous piety set in motion a transaction of mutual legitimation that gave authority to his reign

Man Singh's gurus—there were three more after Dev Nath's death in 1815—advised the maharaja on policy and further extended their influence by placing supporters in almost every administrative post within the state.[15] Additional land grants and special taxes increased their income, and the order eventually controlled one-fifth of the kingdom's annual revenues. Dev Nath's family and other newly powerful Naths, hereafter designated as the Nath elite, administered this wealth and functioned as the heads of semi-autonomous polities with their own courts of law, military forces, and *darbars*.[16] (See fig. 6, discussed below.)

PORTRAITS AND POWER

Hindus recognized the spiritual power of Naths but doubted their purity because disciples came from any number of low castes, engaged in polluting practices (such as eating with other castes), and practiced socially unconventional behavior (such as prodigious smoking of hashish).[17] Moreover, because they were householder Naths, Man Singh's gurus had lower status than Nath ascetics. When they arrived in Jodhpur, Dev Nath's family strived to mitigate their dubious standing and establish an identity commensurate with their new authority. Their strategies included a genealogical narrative that announced the family's divinely sanctioned

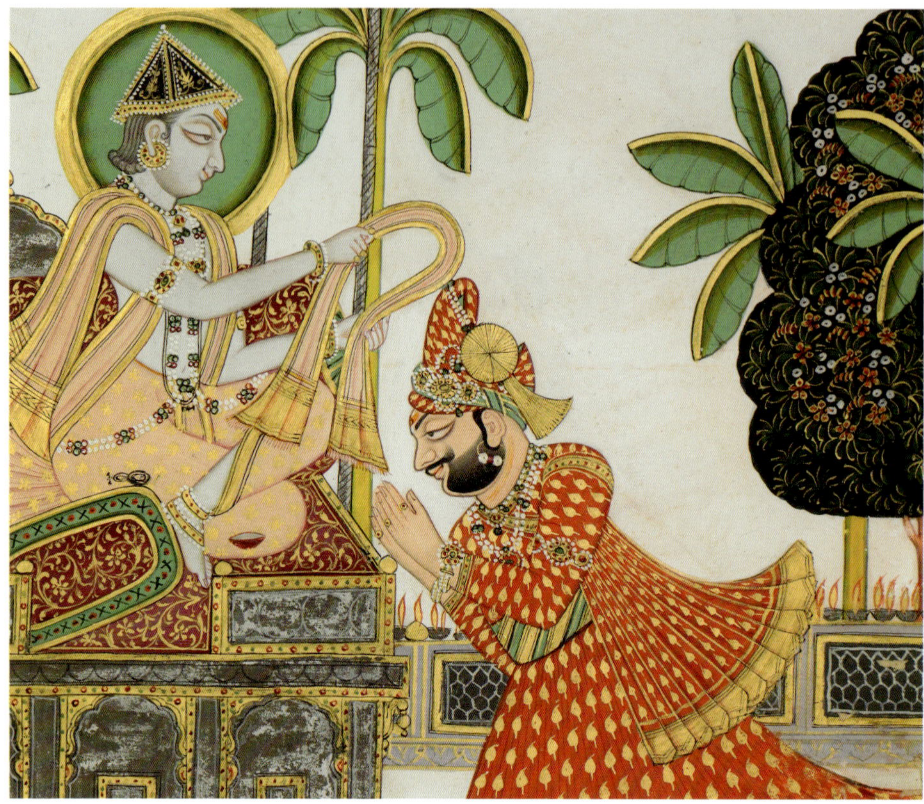

Fig. 4. Cat. 32, detail.

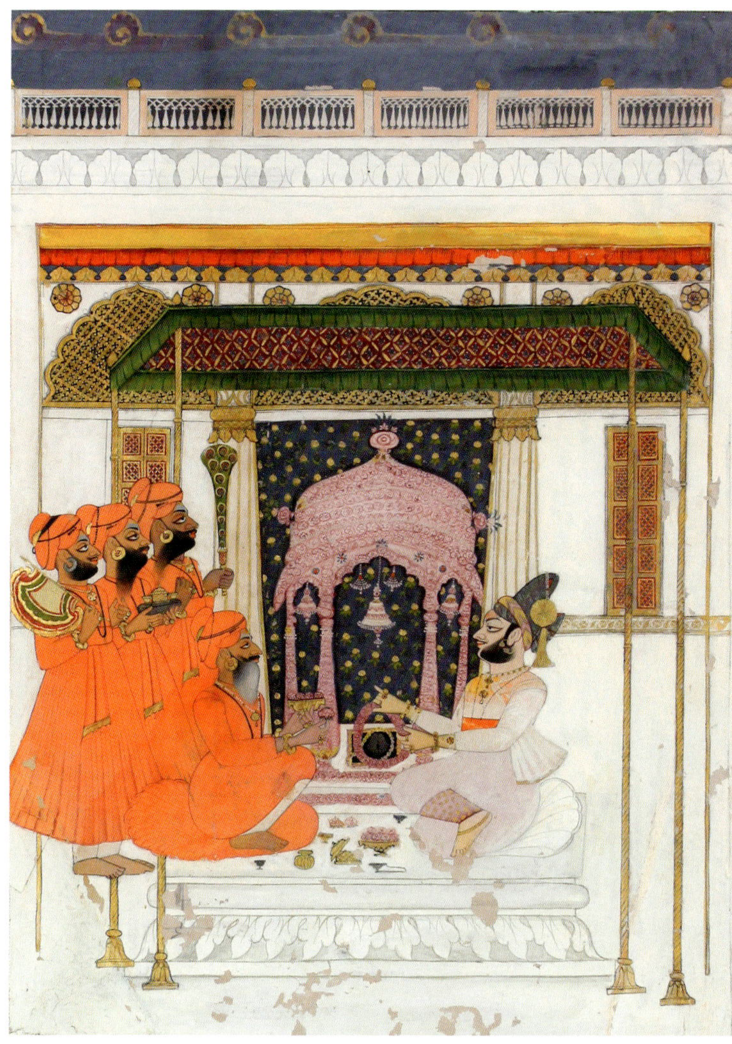

descent from a Rajput; an injunction against widow remarriage (which signaled aspirations towards greater purity); and the patronage of painters and bards attached to the Jodhpur court.[18]

Portraiture—arguably, the central genre of Jodhpur court painting in terms of sheer numbers—played a central role in establishing noble identity by erasing vulgar associations. It is unlikely that the parvenu elite had been depicted in portraits before they moved to Jodhpur, and their adoption of the genre follows a pattern in which state power and portraiture became intertwined.[19] Portraits of Dev Nath's family document a swift rise in aristocratic identity during the course of Man Singh's reign. In the earliest extant Nath portrait produced in the royal atelier, Dev Nath's eldest brother Har Nath and Man Singh worship the footprints of Jallandharnath with offerings of rose garlands and blossoms (see fig. 5).[20] Although gold jewelry marks Har Nath's high status, he is clad in the saffron cloth of a holy man, his demeanor is humble, and he officiates as a priest in a sacred ritual.[21] The quietly intimate painting depicts Har Nath, the abbot of the Jalore Nath temple and a *jagirdar*, as a respected priest—equal to, but essentially different from, the head of state. This distinction became increasingly blurred in subsequent portraits of the Nath elite, which emphasize their resemblance to the king, obscure their identity as holy men, and construct their identity as Rajputs.

In an 1815 double portrait of Man Singh and Dev Nath, the guru's garments and posture, the son by his side, and the attendant by his back mirror those of the maharaja (see cat. 36).[22] Indeed, only his large, round earrings reveal that he is a Nath rather than a Rajput nobleman. Dev Nath, moreover, is positioned as superior to the king. Slightly larger than Man Singh, he leans against pillows and raises his hand in a gesture of explication. Man Singh appears in the less powerful role of supplicant and visitor: his hands are clasped in a gesture of respect and worship, his attendant stands closer to the palace gate (the bell-shaped curve of his *jama* extends into the sand-colored courtyard), and the royal elephant and soldiers wait outside the palace.

If these two portraits reveal how the Nath elite came to look like the king, paintings of Nath *darbars* (formal assemblies) demonstrate that they started to act like him as well (fig. 6). The Rajput *darbar* was the arena in which royal and noble rank was mediated, and *darbar* paintings document the hierarchical relations of service and loyalty that constituted political authority in a kingdom (see cat. 31 and p. 280). Since the Nath elite, like the king and the Rajput nobility, exercised jurisdiction over territories, it is not surprising that they held *darbars* and commissioned paintings of court assemblies, although their *darbar* paintings audaciously look more like royal than noble images.[23] Moreover, these paintings indicate that elite Naths were patrons of Man Singh's court artists.[24]

A vertical painting of a Nath *darbar* appropriates many of the formal elements associated with representations of Rathore assemblies (fig. 6; compare with cat. 31). Dressed in white, Ladu Nath (Dev Nath's son) sits at the center and apex of a formal assembly on the terrace of a gleaming white palace. The courtyard architecture suggests this is the *haveli* (mansion) at Mahamandir, where Ladu Nath presided as abbot (*mahant*) in the 1820s. The young Nath raises his hand in a gesture of speech, possibly ordering the distribution of the bags

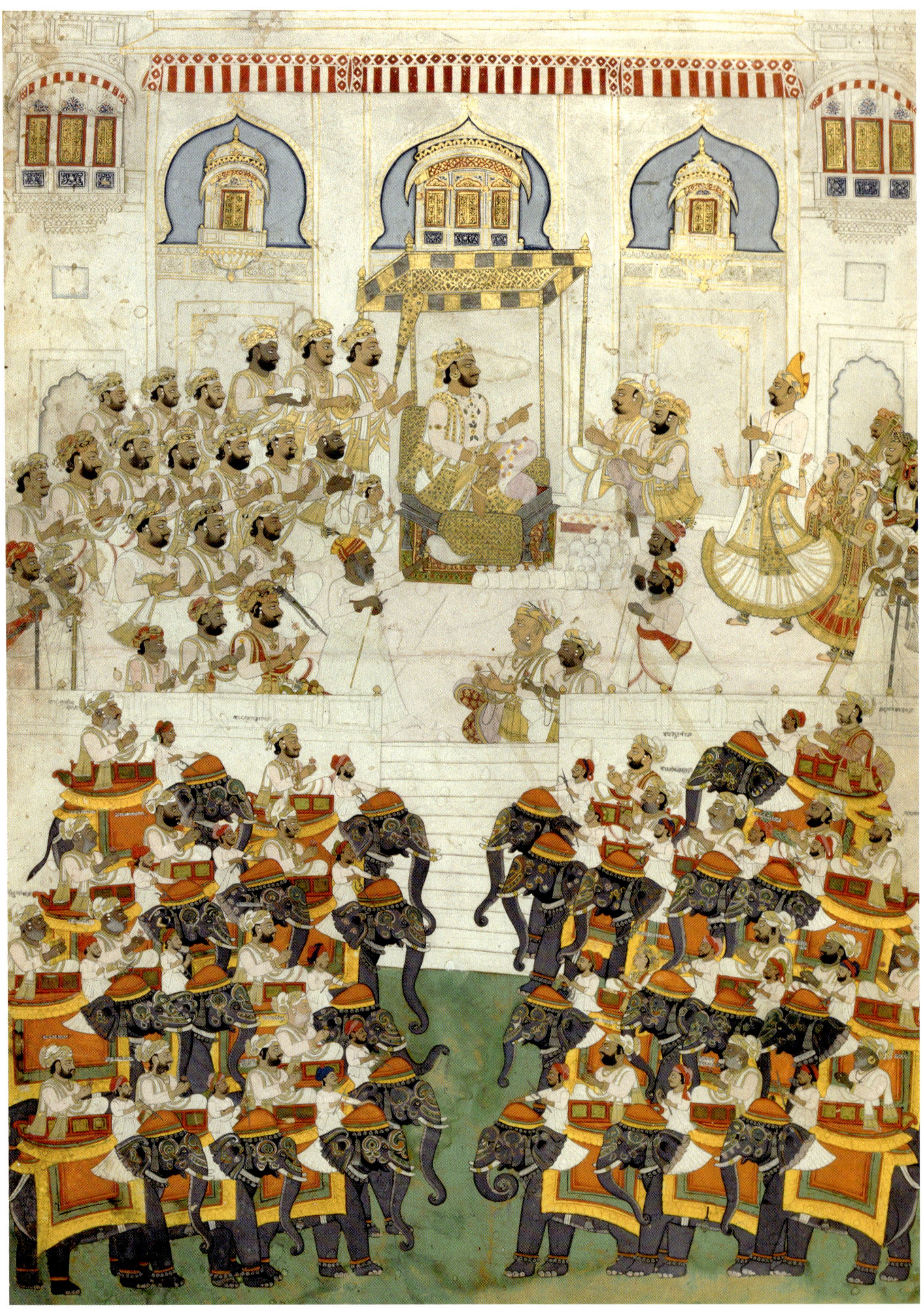

The names of twenty artists were culled from archival ascriptions on the backs of small and monumental paintings in the Mehrangarh Trust Museum collection:

Ali

Amardas Bhatti (son of Narayandas)[31]

Bulaki (*musalman citera*,
    "the Muslim artist")

Dana Bhatti (son of Amardas)

Dhira (son of Khirat/Kivat/Kirat)

Durga (son of Bhana)

Gula Bhatti

Jala Akhavat

Madho

Magni Ram

Mahesh (son of Dana)

Mathenivasu (son of Megha)

Motiram (son of Narayan)

Rai Singh

Raso

Satidas Sasavat (son of Bhana)

Shivdas Bhatti (son of Udairam)

Shivdat Bagsi (son of Ram)

Udairam Bhatti

Vana Akhavat

Fig. 6. *Ladu Nath in Darbar Honoring Bards,* Jodhpur, ca. 1827–28, 61 x 44.5 cm. Kumar Sangram Singh Collection, no. 44.

of gold lying near his throne; the painting commemorates the abbot's generous awards to the forty *charans* assembled in the lower courtyard.[25] The subdued yet rich palette seen in Marwar paintings as early as the 1623 *Pali Ragamala* (cat. 1) dominates the painting's lower section. The contrast between the courtyard's deep earthy tones and the glittering palace above creates a sharp distinction between the poets and the Nath assembly and invokes the imminent gift of coins from the dazzling realm of the Nath court. The pictorial documentation of the ceremony reveals that the Nath elite sought to establish its fame by patronizing the kingdom's most prominent *charans*, who composed the panegyrics (and denouncements in verse) of Rajputs.[26] Through his support of the bards, Ladu Nath assumed one of the traditional patronage roles associated with Rajput status and identity—and effected a savvy act of self-promotion.

PAINTING AT THE COURT OF MAN SINGH

During the first half of the nineteenth century, painters at almost every court in Rajasthan moved towards flatter patterns, bolder colors, and idealized, hierarchically sized figures. This tendency towards bold and decorative abstraction, as Hermann Goetz noted in his seminal study, reached its apogee in the Jodhpur atelier.[27] Paintings by Shivdas Bhatti and Bulaki epitomize the "sparkling, sweeping" style in which bodies and objects are constructed as a sequence of cylindrical forms and placed within emphatically planar settings of glittering opacity.[28] In a detail of a Shivdas painting (fig. 4), the rhythmic contours of Man Singh's shoulders echo the jaunty sweep of his gold-bordered garments, the animated lilt of his upturned mustache, the buoyant plantain leaves, and the crisp arc of the proffered *dupatta* (scarf). The discretely bounded forms are starkly silhouetted against a highly burnished white ground, epitomizing the aesthetic preference for gleaming surfaces.

Extolled in court poetry as desirable in gods, kings, and architecture, shine became one of the most important pictorial qualities sought by Man Singh's painters. Silvery bodies of water had emerged as a motif in Bakhat Singh's Nagaur palace scenes, but early nineteenth-century court paintings are more highly burnished and lavishly gilded.[29] Shading also was often employed because of its potential to create glimmering forms (see cat. 46).

If the formal qualities of rhythmic abstraction and surface dazzle are already familiar to students of Marwar painting, the previously unpublished paintings presented here reveal that Nath subjects spurred Man Singh's artists toward even bolder levels of abstraction. While the pulsating surfaces, multiple perspectives, and hypnotic repetition of monumental manuscript folios often bear an uncanny resemblance to modernist paintings, their aesthetic emerges in relation to Nath metaphysics and cosmography. Representations of transcendent being and matter crystallize the period's tendency towards planarity through large fields of shimmering color or abstract patterns (see "Origins of the Cosmos"). Paintings that depict an immeasurable universe dense with celestial landmarks juxtapose, to dizzying effect, multiple perspectives and scales (see "Mapping the Cosmos"). Pictorial sequences with hundreds of shrines led artists to employ grids to organize the surface of paintings (see "Sacred Sites").

For art historians, the most significant, indeed exciting, development is the atelier's creation of compositions and pictorial cycles for Nath manuscripts that had never been previously illustrated. So often in Indian art, the unique and historically contingent contributions of artists cannot be isolated because subjects and motifs persist over centuries.[30] The *Ramayana*, for example, had been depicted all over the subcontinent for almost two millennia before Vijai Singh's artists took on the subject. In contrast, the Nath conception of a *nirgun* godhead (without qualities, i.e., formless) and the Sampraday's focus, since its inception, on somatic and alchemical practice did not encourage the production of images.[32] Diagrams of esoteric Nath knowledge, sometimes painted, were tightly restricted to initiates.[33] Man Singh collected scores of Nath treatises, commentaries, and hagiographies from all over India and Nepal, and only one included a drawing (see fig. 44a, p. 290). There was little visual material on which to base the new Nath paintings.

Thus the Jodhpur artists in Man Singh's workshop faced unique challenges. Their folios for six Nath-related monumental manuscripts convey cosmological and ontological conceptions as well as narratives that had not entered the court-painting tradition before; some of these concepts never entered Indian visual traditions at all. Artists responded to new texts by adapting, citing, and combining images from various court genres as well as from cartographic and sectarian visual traditions. Their creative accomplishments can be clearly identified because the historical parameters surrounding Man Singh's extraordinary affiliation with the Naths are so clear. The catalogue entries give evidence of interconnections between courtly and vernacular visual cultures and provide a lens onto the broader process by which Rajput painters addressed new subject matter.

Man Singh's atelier was more structured than those of the eighteenth century, and his artists adapted their styles to different genres (devotional images, royal portraits, secular subjects, and monumental manuscripts). Each genre had distinctive if overlapping parameters regulating formal elements. The oeuvre of Amardas, one of the atelier's greatest masters, clearly reveals that the court's important subjects—the maharaja and the Naths—were the most flatly realized. Within Man Singh's atelier, Amardas was the artist who consistently played with spatial illusion (cat. 34). With the exception of an early image of Jallandharnath (cat. 33), however, his paintings of both Nath subjects and the maharaja (cats. 31, 39) are quite consistently bound to the two-dimensional surface. We see this further demonstrated in paintings by Amardas' son, Dana, of Man Singh enjoying singing and dancing. In these works, Dana represents extensive gardens and far-off palaces but deploys a spatial rhetoric that distances these works from the king's portrait.[34] In this example (fig. 8), his rhythmically contoured and flatly painted courtiers and entertainers adhere to the picture plane. Dana introduces some depth in his perspectival rendering of the pavilions. But the parterre garden glimpsed through the central pavilion leads onto another world. Its paths converge at a distant river; on the far shore, tiny buildings are softened by pastel washes of diluted paint. The atmospheric garden forms part of Man Singh's view but, carefully framed by the pavilion walls, it is distinct from the sparkling two-dimensional plane of the court.

Increased workshop centralization is revealed not only by generic parameters, but also by evidence that artists from different families occasionally shared stencils and worked together on paintings.[35] Nonetheless, the leading artists—the Hindu painters Amardas Bhatti, his son Dana, Shivdas Bhatti (no relation), and the Muslim artist Bulaki—have distinctive styles or "signature characteristics" that enable us to identify their paintings with a fair degree of confidence. Amardas' signature is a heavily shaded profile face with a small eye (cats. 31, 34, 35, 39), and Dana's tell-tale mark is Man Singh's springy checkmark sideburn (fig. 8 and fig. 31a, p. 280). Examination of small devotional paintings with images of Jallandharnath that bear Bulaki's name reveals his idiosyncratic inflection of the *mahasiddha* archetype, which includes:

Very long, narrow, sickle-shaped eye tinged deep pink or crimson

Pointy, sharp-tipped, nose

Pale, cool complexion—white, light blue, or light gray

Air-brush smooth shading on face, often in a pale gray

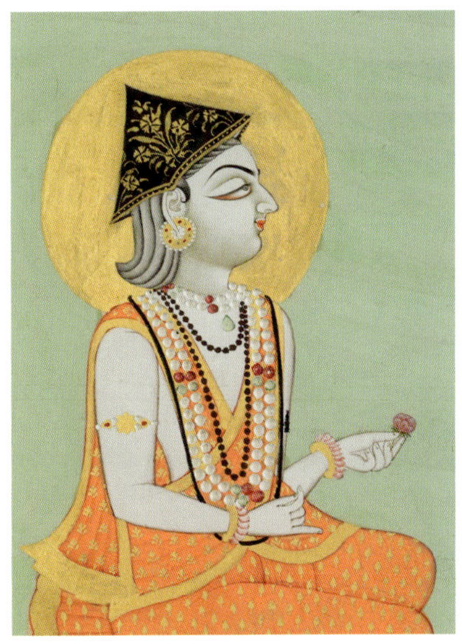

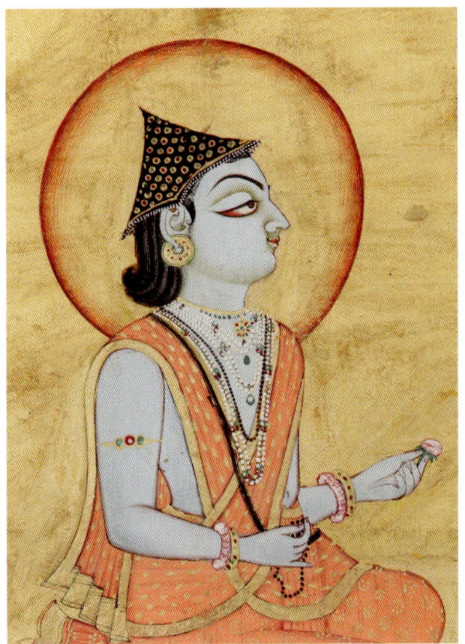

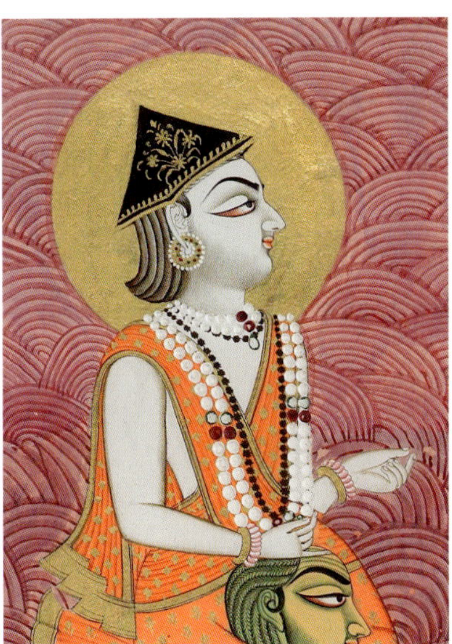

Hair often as pale as the face, leading to a bleached appearance
Thick "page-boy" dreadlocks ending in a tight curl[36]
Short, striated bangs (often)
Gold flowers or decoration on triangular black hat
Large flat bolsters in stripe or floral patterns
Banyon trees with hanging roots
Two-dimensional compositions; avoidance of overlapping motifs
Flat, often strident, colors, particularly in his more hastily painted works

Bulaki's distinctive *mahasiddha* face—along with his penchant for large color fields—appear on the monumental folios inscribed to "the Muslim artist" (fig. 7a).[37] Judging by their names, Bulaki and Ali were the only Muslim artists in the atelier. Ali works in a somewhat less-accomplished variation on the Bulaki style, which suggests that he is a younger relative of the artist, perhaps his son. Therefore, it is with some confidence that I identify the "Muslim artist" as Bulaki (see cats. 40, 44, 47, 48, 53, 56a–g).

"NATHJI, YOUR GLANCE IS POISON"

Nath wealth, power, and status—localized in the numerous temples and monasteries constructed by Man Singh—attracted new recruits and linked those Naths previously scattered around Marwar's villages and towns into a network of state-sanctioned holy men. They were now feared and respected both because they were backed by state force and because of their supernatural powers.

The Naths were Man Singh's loyal allies during his severely contested reign. In exchange for the maharaja's recognition and gifts, the Naths offered Man Singh spiritual succor, divine legitimation, and political service to the state. The maharaja's gifts of land and honors gave the Nath elite and their followers a status like that of the nobility, although their involvement with the central administration and the honors they received far exceeded those of Man Singh's Rathore kinsmen.

Such wealth, status, and influence undoubtedly added to their reputation as potent holy men, but Nath power and abuse of power also engendered concerted opposition.[38] For much of Man Singh's reign, most of the maharaja's Rathore kinsmen challenged his sovereignty. From the safety of their fortresses or while in exile, they negotiated or fought for the resumption of their hereditary rights (land, wealth, and status), sometimes united under the pretender's banner.[39] In 1815, a faction of refractory nobles assassinated Dev Nath and Inderaj, who later became Man Singh's top administrator.[40] During the 1820s and 1830s, they petitioned the British, who were increasingly inserting themselves into the kingdom, to repress the Naths,[41] and accounts suggest that all through Man Singh's reign, they skirmished with Nath forces to protect their prerogatives.

In the later years of the reign, both internal dissension within the Nath elite and outward abuses increased dramatically. The Nath gurus vied for supremacy (on occasion with force), backed by the powerful Jain families in the upper echelons of the state administration.[42] Without fear of reprisal, roaming bands of Naths abducted women and girls, kidnapped "boys of good family" (cutting their ears to transform them into Naths), and seized the property of merchants.[43] A folk song from this period, which begins "Nathji, your glance is poison," expresses the growing anger of the populace.[44]

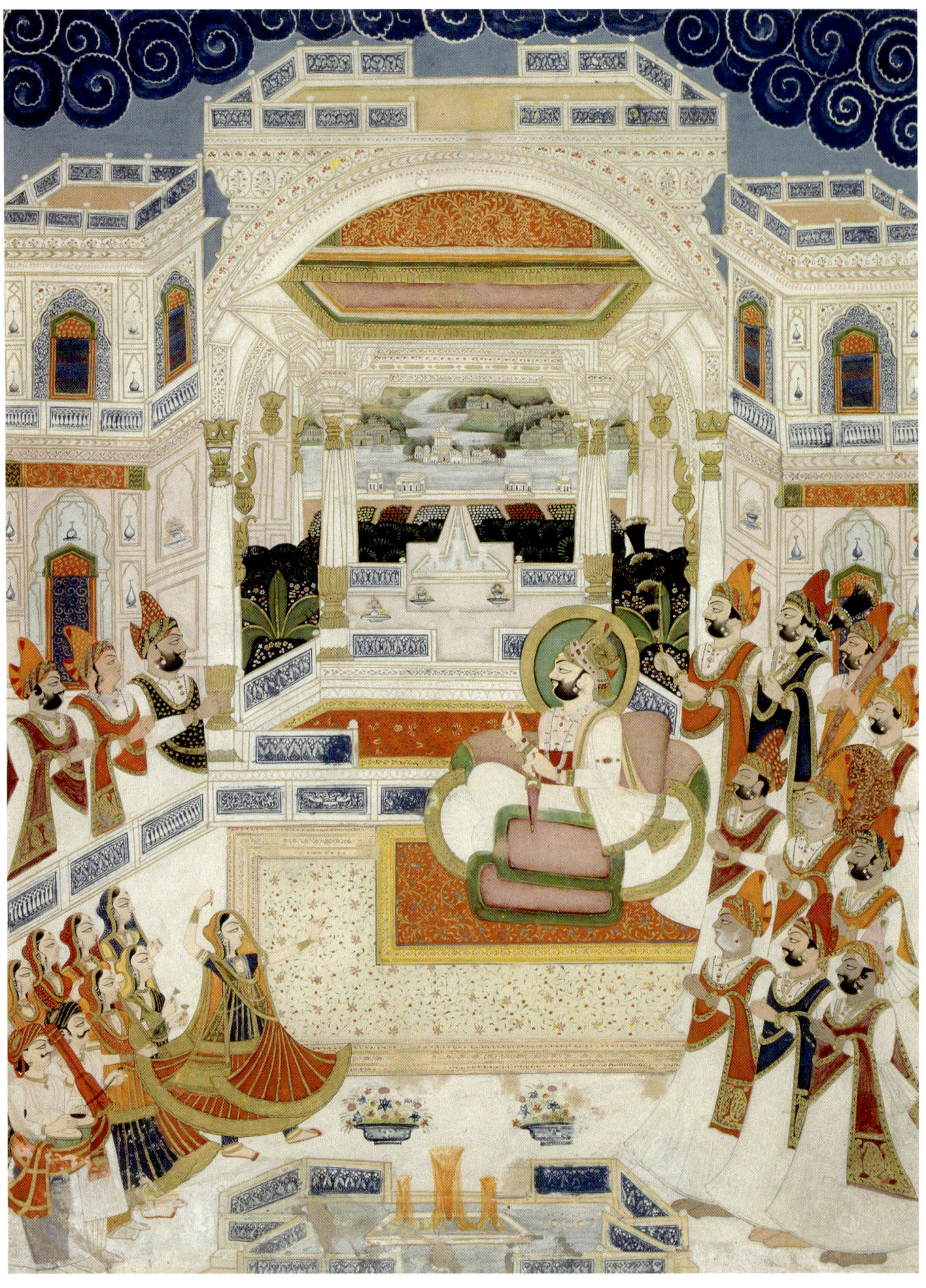

"THE LAST OF THE OLD SOVEREIGNS"

The Naths most severe challenge ultimately came from the British East India Company, which signed a treaty of protection with Jodhpur in 1818.[45] Company officials and political agents saw the Naths as a serious impediment to a compliant, peaceful, and solvent kingdom that would render regular tribute payments into their coffers. For two decades, Man Singh protected the Naths while simultaneously using them to deflect British penetration into the kingdom's affairs.[46] The maharaja was able to sustain this double maneuver for years because the British were reluctant to act against a king whose subjects regarded him "with reverence… as the last of the old sovereigns." This "deference, respect and homage," grumbled Colonel Sutherland, "deprived us of the exercise of that legitimate influence which we had a right to expect on the part of the Chiefs and Ministers, who were originally, and are still, as much opposed to the Naths as we were and are…."[47]

Despite the nobility's refusal to unite with a foreign power against the maharaja, the British stepped up efforts to contain the Naths in 1839.[48] Acting upon the nobility's complaints of Nath abuse, Colonel Sutherland marched upon Jodhpur with an army and formed a governing council of Rathore noblemen.[49] But Man Singh, who believed his salvation would be compromised by alienating the Naths, pawned his jewels to provide the order with continued financial support.[50] In 1841, a British plan to place a more amenable Nath in Mahamandir was foiled by its abbot Lakshminath.[51] Then in 1843, the British arrested two prominent Naths for kidnapping a Brahmin girl for ransom.[52]

In response to the arrest, Man Singh left the fort, removed his royal raiment, covered his body in ash, began a fast, and made plans to go on a pilgrimage to Girnar.[53] When the political agent Colonel Ludlow informed the maharaja that if he left Marwar, the British would place Dhonkal Singh on the throne, Man Singh moved on June 30 to a "wretched" tent in a Jodhpur garden, where he lived as a humble ash-smeared yogin.[54] On July 29, Man Singh went to Mandore, the old Rathore capital five miles outside Jodhpur, where the grand cenotaphs of past Marwar kings are located (see fig. 1, p. 7). He died five weeks later from summer fever. It was said that Man Singh, like an advanced adept, predicted his own passing: on September 5, he covered himself with a white *dupatta* (unstitched garment), saying that only Brahmins should enter the next morning (to take care of his body).[55]

In concert with the nobility, the British placed Takhat Singh, Man Singh's closest relative and designated heir, on the throne. Nath revenues were drastically reduced and their leaders were exiled. Denied state support, many Naths left and the others faded back into the heterogeneous religious landscape of Marwar. Nath temples fell into disrepair, and the court's Nath paintings were stored away.

Fig. 8 Maharaja Man Singh in a *Mehfil,* by Dana, Jodhpur, ca. 1829, 50.8 x 38.1 cm. Kumar Sangram Singh Collection, no. 99.

Monumental Manuscripts at the Jodhpur Court

DEBRA DIAMOND

"North Indian court painting" usually calls to mind small works on paper that can be held in the hand and viewed from an intimate distance. But more than five hundred large paintings, each measuring approximately 45 x 122 cm, are extant in the Mehrangarh Museum Trust collection.[1] Created between 1765 and 1830, the paintings are the folios of ten illustrated manuscripts. Like many Rajput and Pahari pictorial narratives, the manuscripts are unbound; the sheets of handmade paper (*wasli*) are painted in opaque watercolor; red or yellow borders protect the pages when they are lifted for viewing; and they do not contain text (except for glosses on the verso of a few folios).

Large paintings were produced in a number of Rajput ateliers, but oversize manuscripts are an innovation of the Jodhpur atelier.[2] Due to their unprecedented scale, they stand out among the many illustrated texts from the Rajput courts of north India. The large format prompted artists to approach visual narratives in new ways, advanced the centralization of the Jodhpur atelier, and transformed the viewing of paintings at court. Thus, they constitute a distinctive corpus and are henceforth called "monumental manuscripts." Between 1924 and 1947, scholar B. N. Reu took on the massive task of cataloguing the monumental manuscripts. My subsequent research builds upon his impressive contribution, while correcting some of its errors. Reu assigned all ten monumental manuscripts to Man Singh's reign, but because of their style and subject (discussed above) four of them are redated here to the period of Vijai Singh.[3]

MONUMENTAL MANUSCRIPTS AND WORKSHOP ORGANIZATION UNDER VIJAI SINGH

The atelier of Vijai Singh (reigned 1752–93) produced four monumental manuscripts—the *Krishna Lila*, *Gajendra Moksha*, *Ram Charit*, and *Durga Charit*—with a total of one hundred fifty-six folios. The unbound, horizontal format (*pothi*) is characteristic of Hindu manuscripts, and all the narrative subjects are familiar from other Rajput courts. None of the Jodhpur monumental manuscripts, however, relies strongly on extant archetypes. The large scale of the folios simply demanded new compositions. The markedly diverse solutions and range of styles that resulted reveal that the royal workshop expanded in this period to include artists from outside the capital city of Jodhpur. Workshop centralization undoubtedly also increased: many custom-made sheets of oversize paper and a significant volume of pigments were required for the longer manuscripts.

By 1765, the first monumental manuscript—the seven-folio *Krishna Lila*—was created in the Nagaur idiom (cats. 23–25). A master artist with a unified vision conceived the compositions with figures and landscape elements of consistent scale and proportion. Although at least three different artists completed the folios, their relatively uniform style suggests that they were members of a single artist family.[4]

In contrast, the far more massive undertaking of a ninety-one-folio *Ramcharitmanas* (referred to as the *Ram Charit* in the archival inscriptions; cats. 26–28), circa 1775, required greater centralized coordination to obtain consistent paper and pigments. The vivid palette is notably constant throughout the manuscript.[5] Manuscripts produced at other Rajput courts were coordinated by atelier supervisors, and this system probably also was employed in Vijai Singh's atelier.[6] The supervisor would have worked with a scholar or priest to transform the lengthy epic into pictorial sequences.[7] The inconsistency of visual narrative modes and several duplicated episodes, however, suggest that the supervisor provided artists with verbal instructions, rather than actual sketches.

The loose workshop supervision of the *Ramcharitmanas* continued into the final years of Vijai Singh's reign, when the fifty-six-folio *Durga Charit* (fig. 7, p. 29, and cat. 30), circa 1785, was produced. A preliminary study of the manuscript reveals that sequences of paintings were distributed among artists with markedly diverse palettes, burnishing methods, compositional sensibilities, and iconography. Some folios include passages adapted or even directly copied from Bakhat Singh palace paintings. Others employ the exaggerated curves and sweeping rhythms that came to dominate Jodhpur court painting in subsequent decades. The goddess iconography and muted palette of contemporaneous Bikaner paintings appear in a number of folios, and several paintings anticipate the minimal aesthetic of monumental manuscripts produced in the 1820s.

DEVELOPMENT AND IMPORT OF MAHARAJA MAN SINGH'S MONUMENTAL MANUSCRIPTS

Man Singh's spiritual attachment to Jallandharnath, his ardent interest in Nath knowledge and lore, and his always magnanimous patronage of the arts underlie the production of six monumental manuscripts: the *Siddha Siddhanta Paddhati*, *Nath Purana*, *Nath Charit*, *Meghmala*, *Shiva Rahasya*, and *Shiva Purana*.[8] The rhythmic planarity, glossy surfaces, and saturated hues of paintings in the three dated (1823, 1824, and 1827) manuscripts are stylistically consistent with the folios from the three non-dated manuscripts. Production of the corpus therefore can be assigned to the second decade of the nineteenth century.

The Jodhpur workshop expanded considerably under Man Singh's aegis, completing perhaps a thousand smaller paintings and more than three hundred forty monumental folios (more than double the number produced in Vijai Singh's reign).[9] A cataloguing system and textual glosses in a fine hand on the verso of some folios indicate that the workshop further grew to include an archivist and a calligrapher. In verso inscriptions, the archivist entered every folio into the *dholiya* storeroom, usually wrote the manuscript title, and occasionally noted the date of the manuscript or the name of an artist.[10] Twenty artists (see p. 37), two of whom are also identified as manuscript supervisors, appear in the inscriptions.[11]

My correlation of the twenty-five numbered folios of the illustrated *Siddha Siddhanta Paddhati* with the critical edition of the Sanskrit text confirms Reu's cataloguing of this manuscript. However, the folios assigned by Reu to the *Shiva Purana*, the *Nath Purana*, and the *Nath Charit* raise questions. The *Shiva Purana's* folios bear verso inscriptions naming its title, but duplicated episodes may indicate interspersed folios from another copy of the manuscript. The *Nath Purana* and the *Nath Charit* pose different challenges to the cataloguer. Man Singh's archivist only partially inscribed manuscript titles on the folios. The recto numerals, painted by the artists in several styles, that appear on many but not all of the folios do not form any consistent relationship to the titled paintings.[12] Moreover, Reu found that the numbered paintings did not correspond with the order of episodes in the texts he consulted and that some folios ascribed to one manuscript actually related to episodes from the other text. Since both the *Nath Purana* and *Nath Charit* are compilations of Nath lore collected from all over the subcontinent and then anthologized at Man Singh's court, it seems plausible that the paintings and texts were produced simultaneously. Artists may have developed their compositions at a time when the episodes themselves had not been placed in a definitive order. Further study of these paintings and the numerous related texts and text fragments preserved in the Pustak Prakash Library is urgently required. Of the two remaining manuscripts, the one hundred and one-folio *Shiva Rahasya* appears complete, while four folios tentatively connected by Reu to the *Meghmala* are clearly partial.

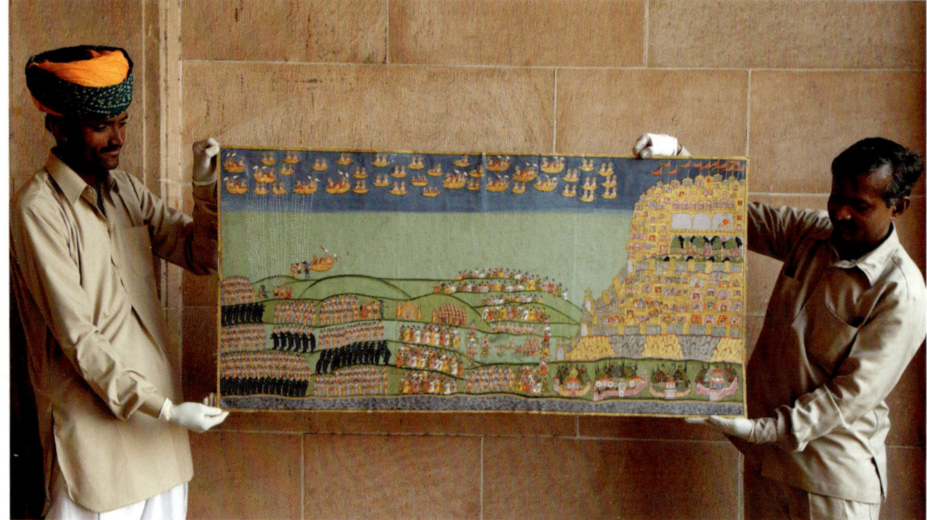

Fig. 1. Lifting a monumental *Ramcharitmanas* folio, 2006.

The production scenario for the Man Singh monumental manuscripts can be partially reconstructed by considering the novelty of the texts. The three Nath texts composed in Marwari during Man Singh's reign, the *Nath Charit, Nath Purana*, and the *Meghamala*, could not have been illustrated earlier; nor is there any evidence that any of the other manuscripts, with the exception of the *Shiva Purana*, had previously entered the realm of the visual.[13] Historically, Naths had little impetus to commission paintings other than yogic diagrams.[14] Adepts were focused on yogic practice, and Nath shrines contained aniconic images (such as mounds) or traces of *siddhas* (such as sandals). Popular, sectarian, and royal legends of the great Naths circulated in oral and written but not visual genres.

Because Nath legends incorporate canonical myths, some of the images in the monumental manuscripts draw upon motifs that were already within the visual repertoire of Jodhpur court painting (note, for example, how Man Singh's artists drew upon the figure of the sleeping Vishnu, dated circa 1785, to compose a *Shiva Purana* folio; see cats. 30 and 41). The atelier's artists, however, created most of the manuscripts' narrative cycles and the folios' compositions *ex nihilo*. This is particularly intriguing. Dramatic breaks within Rajput painting traditions only rarely can be historicized because court artists generally created paintings by drawing upon (i.e., tracing, copying, or adapting) already existing elements from older court paintings. For example, Jodhpur artists drew upon an archetype of the holy man that circulated broadly in north Indian painting to create a fixed iconography for the depiction of *mahasiddhas* early in Man Singh's reign.[15] But the manuscripts provided more complex challenges. How did Man Singh's artists develop images for narratives and concepts that had not been the previous subjects of court painting?

Production of the manuscripts must have begun with a learned Nath explicating the unfamiliar texts to the workshop supervisor.[16] Nath pandits also provided both supervisor and artists with esoteric diagrams, which undoubtedly came from collections in monasteries (*akharas*).[17] Artists developed compositions that referenced not only Nath images but also court paintings and maps in the royal collection, and possibly also Jain images from an unspecified local source (see especially cats. 44 and 48).[18] They freely juxtaposed motifs from these diverse sources to create unique works.

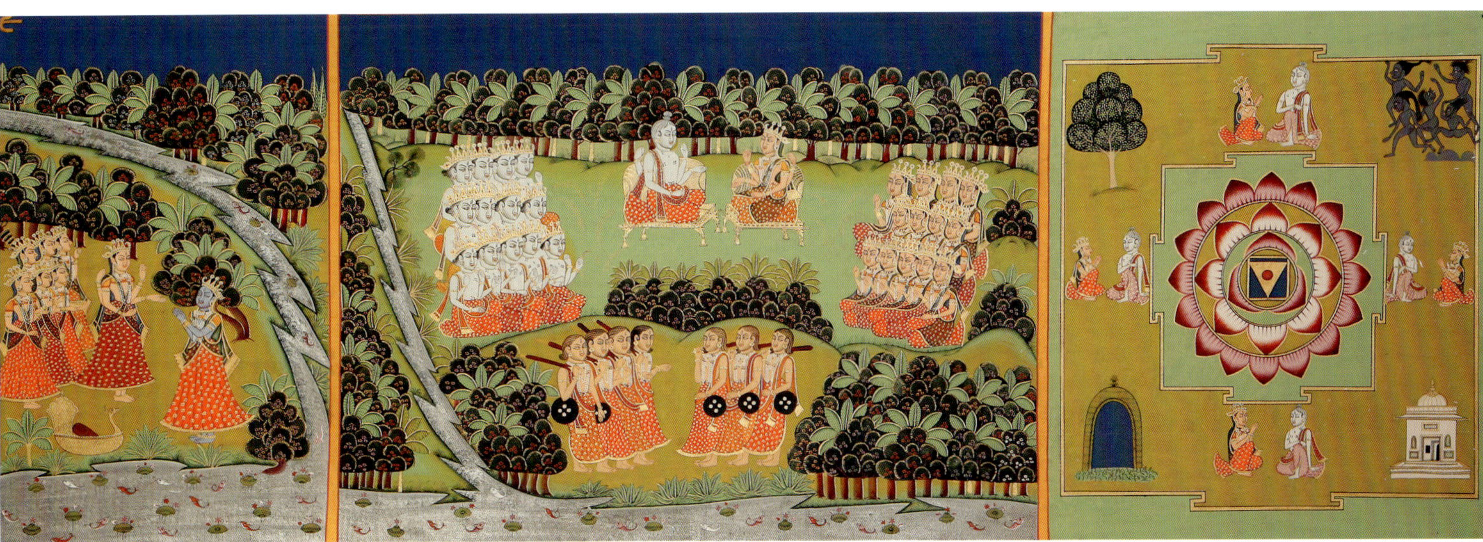

Fig. 2. Yantra from the *Meghmala*, ca. 1825, 41.4 x 199.4 cm. Mehrangarh Museum Trust, RJS 2506.

The extraordinary compositional and conceptual diversity of the corpus is specifically addressed in the entries for cats. 39–55. The range suggests that various artists, rather than the workshop supervisor, had the responsibility of creating master drawings for any given manuscript. However, the monumental folios as a group are more two-dimensional, glossier, and often more spatially complex than smaller paintings of secular subjects.

Inscriptions provide additional information on production and workshop organization. Roughly eight percent of the folios bear ascriptions that reveal that both Hindu and Muslim artists contributed to the Nath manuscripts. *Vagera* (et cetera) appears after some artists' names, indicating that multiple painters worked on the same folio; other folios name two artists.[19] The *Siddha Siddhanta Paddhati*, *Nath Charit*, and *Nath Purana* colophons name "the Muslim artist" as workshop supervisor.[20] *Shiva Purana* folios name eleven artists, several of whom are mentioned here for the first time during Man Singh's reign; it is possible that these were younger painters brought into the atelier during a period of expanded production.

Only one preparatory drawing (*khaka*) exists today. Its smudged contours indicate that it was created by pouncing charcoal through a master drawing (*charba*) pricked with holes.[21] However, compositionally identical folios by Amardas and Bulaki, two artists from different families, confirm that master drawings were housed in the royal atelier at the time of production.[22] (See cats. 39 and fig. 39a, p. 286.)

All of the manuscripts include folios that are exquisitely detailed with rich and gleaming colors indicating finely milled pigments and extensive burnishing, but others are hastily painted and awkwardly composed. Content does not provide an explanation for the varying quality as narrative sequences extending over several folios contain both refined and crude paintings.

VIEWING THE MONUMENTAL MANUSCRIPTS

The large-format folios necessitated a shift in the mode of viewing paintings at the Jodhpur court. Small paintings were designed to be held in the hand for individual delectation, but the outsize folios must be held aloft by two persons (or the paintings buckle) and viewed by others from a distance (fig. 1).[23] No archival material concerning their presentation has yet been located. However, if the maharajas viewed the manuscripts (as opposed to patronizing them purely for religious merit), it is more than plausible that they experienced them in collective and performative contexts.

Several cultural factors support the contention that recitation accompanied the viewing of monumental manuscripts during Vijai Singh's reign. These include the performative traditions surrounding the *Raslila* and the *Ramcharitmanas*, the promise of salvation for those who heard sacred verses, a fervently devout maharaja, and popular traditions of picture-storytelling. The Vaishnava devotional texts related to the monumental paintings circulated primarily, even in literate circles, as spoken and heard verse.[24] Indeed, the monumental-manuscript genre begins with two texts that were most widely transmitted in performative contexts that combined the visual and the aural. Audiences listened to the verses of the *Raslila* and the *Ramcharitmanas* (sung or chanted from memory by specialists) while viewing temple sculptures, devotional paintings, or enactments of their content. The *Raslila* verses were sung in Vallbha temples in front of shrines typically adorned with a large painting on cloth (*picchwai*); the *Ramcharitmanas* was chanted and sung by *kathakaras* (professional reciters) and staged in reenactments each autumn during the Hindu festival of Dussehra.

While the format of the unbound manuscripts is that of smaller court manuscripts, their substantial scale recalls the large images employed within the picture-storytelling traditions that flourished within contemporaneous popular contexts.[25] Instances of picture-storytelling employing oversize paintings on cloth and paper in northern Indian courts are less well-documented but not unknown. The imperial Mughal *Hamzanama* folios, unbound and painted on cloth, were presented along with recitation at the court of Akbar (reigned 1556–1605).[26] In addition, Karl Khandalavala convincingly proposed that the oversize *Siege of Lanka* folios were viewed as a storyteller relayed their content at a Punjab Hills court in the first half of the eighteenth century.[27]

A marked shift in the type of manuscript occurred during Man Singh's reign. Esoteric texts, like the twelfth-century Sanskrit *Siddha Siddhanta Paddhati*, were transmitted primarily as oral teachings, but only privately between gurus and their disciples. Others, such as the Marwari *Nath Charit,* were composed during Man Singh's reign. However, all the texts would have been incomprehensible to court audiences without some form of explanation. Not only were many narratives unfamiliar but many of their images would have been opaque. In other words, Rajput courtiers would have recognized canonical narratives of Rama or the goddess, but not Nath hagiographies or cosmologies, without an established iconography. It seems possible that Man Singh's court built upon the Vijai Singh-period practice of displaying Vaishnava paintings with oral narratives. We know that Man Singh made his courtiers listen to Nath teachings. The monumental manuscripts might have served those pedagogical interests as well as satisfied Man Singh's ardent devotion and voracious appetite for philosophical and hagiographic accounts of the Naths.

CODICOLOGY OF MONUMENTAL MANUSCRIPTS FROM THE MAN SINGH PERIOD

Siddha Siddhanta Paddhati

	Cats. 48, 53
Codicology	23 horizontal folios, 46 x 122 cm[28]; 2 vertical folios, 46 x 122 cm; 1824 (Samvat 1881).
Recto	nagari numerals in gold, upper left corner.
Verso	*sri sidh sidhant padhati* and *da[khal] dholiya re kothar* on all folios; colophons on folio 1: In 1824 the Muslim Artist prepared the *Siddha Siddhanta Paddhati's* 25 folios (*sri sidh sidhant padhati 1881 men citara musalmanan kane tyar karai su pana 25*); and folio 24: In 1824, the Muslim artist prepared the *Siddha Siddhanta Paddhati* (*sri sidh sidhant padhati 1881me citaran musalmanan tyar kino*).
Text	Sanskrit, twelfth–thirteenth century; attributed to Gorakhnath, a *mahasiddha* and the historical founder of the Nath Sampraday; regarded as the most clear and systematic exposition of Nath metaphysics.
Notes	The Muslim artist/Bulaki was the workshop supervisor as well as painter of the first six folios, which depict the creation of the cosmos, the subtle body, yogic postures, and ultimate realization. Most of the remaining folios are painted less finely by other artists and depict ascetic groups mentioned in the Sanskrit text as well as scenes of Muslim, Jaganath, and Vallabha worship that do not appear in the text.

Nath Purana and Nath Charit

Nath Purana	Cats. 39, 45, 47
	27 horizontal folios, 47 x 126 cm; 1 vertical folio, 122 x 45 cm; undated.
Recto	often nagari numerals in gold, upper left corner.
Verso	colophon on folio 1: Bulaki and others made this (*citara bulaki bagera ra kiyo*); on folio 18: prepared by the Muslim artist (*citara musulman tiyar kiya*); textual synopses in Marwari in a fine nagari script on some folios; *sri nath purana* or *sri nath charit* on many folios; *da[khal] dholiya re kothar* on all folios.
Nath Charit	Cats. 40, 43, 44, 50, 56a–g
	70 folios, 122 x 46 cm; 1823 (Samvat 1880).
Recto	nagari numerals in red in the upper left corner by Reu.
Verso	Colophons on folio 15: the Muslim artist prepared in 1823 (*citara musalmanan tyar kino 1880 me*); folio 18: the Muslim artist placed in an orderly way in the box (*citara musalmanan tyar kiyo jojdan pavoi*); and folio 65: the Muslim artist...prepared the book (*citara musalmanon... tyar kiyo granth*); *sri nath carit* on most folios; *da[khal] dholiya re kothar* on all folios.[29]

| Texts | Both Marwari texts were compiled during the reign of Maharaja Man Singh. Each includes a cosmology, puranic narratives, and earthy folktales that extol the greatness of legendary Naths and the deity Shiva. Some episodes recount the stories of Rajasthani folk heroes who were *siddhas* or the disciples of *mahasiddhas*, such as Bhartrihari and Gogade Rathore (see fig. 2, p. 33). Major Hindu deities and the heroes of the *Mahabharata* and the *Ramayana* are positioned within accounts of Nath supremacy. |

Texts — Both Marwari texts were compiled during the reign of Maharaja Man Singh. Each includes a cosmology, puranic narratives, and earthy folktales that extol the greatness of legendary Naths and the deity Shiva. Some episodes recount the stories of Rajasthani folk heroes who were *siddhas* or the disciples of *mahasiddhas*, such as Bhartrihari and Gogade Rathore (see fig. 2, p. 33). Major Hindu deities and the heroes of the *Mahabharata* and the *Ramayana* are positioned within accounts of Nath supremacy.

Notes — The Muslim artist was the workshop supervisor of both the *Nath Charit* and the *Nath Purana*. The illustrated *Nath Purana* is dated by style to circa 1825. Reu's assignation of folios to the two manuscripts is imperfect; see the reference catalogue entry for cat. 42 for reattribution of three folios (p. 288).

Shiva Rahasya

Cats. 46, 50, 51, 54

Codicology — 101 paintings; 42 x 116 cm; 1827 (Samvat 1884).

Verso — *sri siv rahasya sa[mvat] 1884* on several folios; the folio number and its location in the first, second, or third *amsh* (section), and *da[khal] dholiya re kothar,* appears on each folio.[30]

Text — Sanskrit; the revelation of Shiva's son Skanda to the sage Jaigishavya forms the third chapter of the *Himvat Khanda* (a book of the *Skanda Purana*). The *Shiva Rahasya* relates exploits of Shiva.

Shiva Purana

Cats. 41, 42, 55

Codicology — 109 paintings, 47 x 126 cm; undated.

Recto — nagari numerals in gold, upper left corner of most folios.

Verso — 11 artists are named: Dana, son of Amar[das] (f. 69); Dhira, son of Kirat/Kivat (ff. 16, 30, 44); Durga, son of Bhana (f. 6); Jala Akhavat (ff. 29, 68); Madho, son of Vana (ff. 34, 66); Mahesh, son of Dana (ff. 21, 74); Mathenavivai, son of Megha (ff. 4, 71); Motiram, son of Naran (ff. 22, 27, 70, 72, 73, 77); Satidas Sasavat (f. 20), probably also known as Satidas, son of Bhana (f. 85); Shivdat Vagsi/Bagsi, son of Ram (ff. 5, 75); Vana Akhavat (ff. 31, 76); Vana and others (f. 64); textual synopses in Marwari in a fine nagari script on some folios; *sri siv puran* and *da[khal] dholiya re kothar* on all folios.

Text — Sanskrit; the text includes a cosmogony, descriptions of the ages of Manu and rituals, royal genealogies and deeds, and divine narratives. It is sometimes, but not always, included in the list of the eighteen *Mahapuranas* (great Puranas).

Notes — The illustrated manuscript is dated circa 1828 because the appearance of many new artist's names, which don't appear on any other paintings, suggests the workshop was expanded toward the end of the monumental-manuscript production. The appearance of patronymics is unusual, but not unprecedented, in Jodhpur painting.[31]

Meghmala

	Fig. 2 and cat. 49a–c
Codicology	4 folios, 47 x 123 cm; undated.
Recto	nagari numerals 6–9 in gold, upper left corner.
Text	Written by Sri Paramadvaita Nath in 1818 in Sanskrit for Man Singh. Framed as the revelation of Shiva to the sage Narada on Mount Kailash, it begins with a cosmogony and includes stories within stories, including the *Ramayana,* dated by style to ca. 1825.[32]

Dispersed Folios

Folio 5 from a *Siddha Siddhanta Paddhati*, ascribed to Amardas. Collection of Vyakul Acharya, Jaipur.

Drawing for a monumental subtle body with *nadis*, possibly for a second *Sidhha Siddhanta Paddhati*. Ajit Mookerjee Collection, National Museum of India, New Delhi. Ajit Mookerjee and Madhu Khanna, *The Tantric Way: Art, Science, and Ritual* (Boston: New York Graphic Society, 1977), 151.

Folio (cut into three sections along its internal borders), probably from a *Shiva Purana*. Collection of Vittorio Ducrot, Italy.

Fragment (1/3 folio) depicting Brahma and Vishnu worshiping Shiva's fiery lingam, inscribed *Sri siv puran*. Virginia Museum of Fine Arts. Joseph M. Dye II, *The Arts of India* (Richmond: Virginia Museum of Fine Arts, 2001), fig. 114.

Fragment (1/2 folio) depicting Sati burning, probably from a *Shiva Purana*. Collection of Kenneth X. Robbins, Maryland.

Fragment (1/2 folio) depicting Dakshina's sacrifice, probably from a *Shiva Purana*. *Indo-Asian Art from the John Gilmore Ford Collection* (Baltimore: Walters Art Gallery, 1971), fig. 44.

ORIGINS OF JODHPUR COURT PAINTING

During the early seventeenth century, painting in Jodhpur, the royal capital of Marwar, reflected the indigenous Rajput tradition in both style and subject matter. Jodhpur artists painted scenes from the musical series called *Ragamalas* and illustrated the popular romance of *Dhola and Maru* using primary colors and the predominantly horizontal format of medieval palm-leaf painting.

By the middle of the seventeenth century, Jodhpur's royal patrons had become exposed to the painting styles of the Mughal court. They encouraged the artists in their palace ateliers to implement a novel style that combined elements of the earlier tradition with a new interest in a vertical format and a broader color palette. Paintings depicted the raja as a Rajput hero, hunting, on horseback, enjoying dance performances, or with his nobles in assemblies. This "Mughalized Rajasthani" style of painting became the basis for the innovative artworks produced at Nagaur in the following century under the patronage of Maharaja Bakhat Singh.

Page from a Ragamala Series: Gujari Ragini
Pali, Marwar, 1623 (Samvat 1680); 15.9 x 20.3 cm
National Museum of India

A young maiden, personifying Gujari Ragini, sits in a forest meadow holding a musical instrument, the double-gourd stringed *vina*. She sings and gestures to a peacock hidden nearby, a symbol of love and longing, while she waits on a bed of leaves to receive her expected lover. A charming design element is the repetition of the flowers on the tree on the left, which become the feathers of the peacock sitting in the tree on the right.[1]

Ragamala, literally translated, means a garland (*mala*) of melodies (*raga*). Male songs are called *ragas*, their female aspects are *raginis*, and some elaborate series feature songs called *putras* (sons). A *Ragamala* series is a set of paintings, usually thirty-six but sometimes more, that visually interprets Indian musical modes, each of which expresses a specific mood appropriate to a time of day and time of year. Poets later connected the various moods to the seasons and phases of love. The paintings comprising a *Ragamala* series represent human situations that have the same "emotional content" as the musical modes and poetry, so that "the burden of the music, the flavor of the poem and the theme of the picture are identical."[2] *Gujari Ragini* takes its name from the Gujara tribe in the Gujarat state.

This *Gujari Ragini* belongs to a *Ragamala* series from Pali, a town in the Marwar region of western Rajasthan that lies thirty miles southeast of Jodhpur. Pali occupies a strategic position on trade roads from Gujarat, whose ports were active commercial centers along the Arabian Sea, to Jodhpur and Delhi.[3] Dated 1623, this *Ragamala* series is the earliest painted manuscript that we can securely place in Marwar.[4] Two of the aristocratic patrons of the series, Gopal Das and Bithal Das, had illustrious careers, not only aiding the Jodhpur rulers Udai Singh, Suraj Singh, Gaj Singh, and Jaswant Singh (see cats. 4–6) but also serving as warriors for the imperial Mughal forces.

Despite the patrons' diplomatic alliances with the Jodhpur and Mughal courts, the *Ragamala* is painted in a style that relates it to Gujarat and western Rajasthan. In those regions during the sixteenth century, painters used blocks of restricted colors, such as red, blue, and white. This was true even in works—commissioned by aristocrats, royalty, and wealthy merchants—with more costly pigments, such as lapis lazuli and gold. Artists from Marwar seemed to have had little desire to show either spatial depth or the shading or modeling of the figure that appear in Mughal paintings of this period. The bold, linear outlines in this work accentuate the oversize faces and pointed noses; the pattern, mood, and subject are more important than spatial recession. Architecture, individuals, and vegetation are placed against a flat backdrop, as if they are on a stage. In fact, village-theater was and remains a vital and integral part of festivals and celebrations in Rajasthan.

The paintings presented here were produced in a horizontal format, replicating the proportions of palm leaves, the earliest support material used in Buddhist, Hindu, and Jain religious manuscripts. While the vertical page format was used in many Rajasthan ateliers by the beginning of the seventeenth century, painting in Marwar, of which this Pali series is an excellent example, retained the classic, older horizontal format. CG

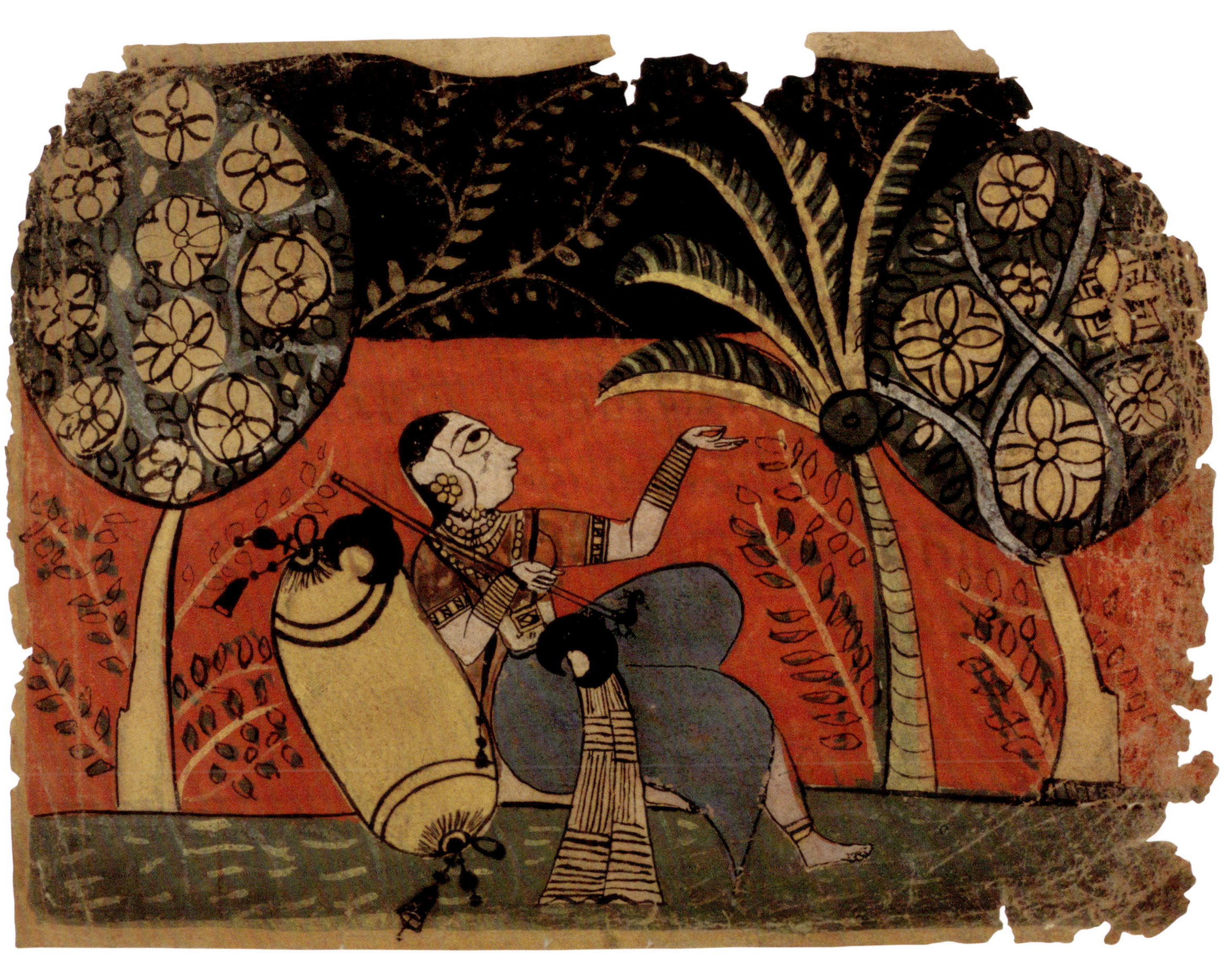

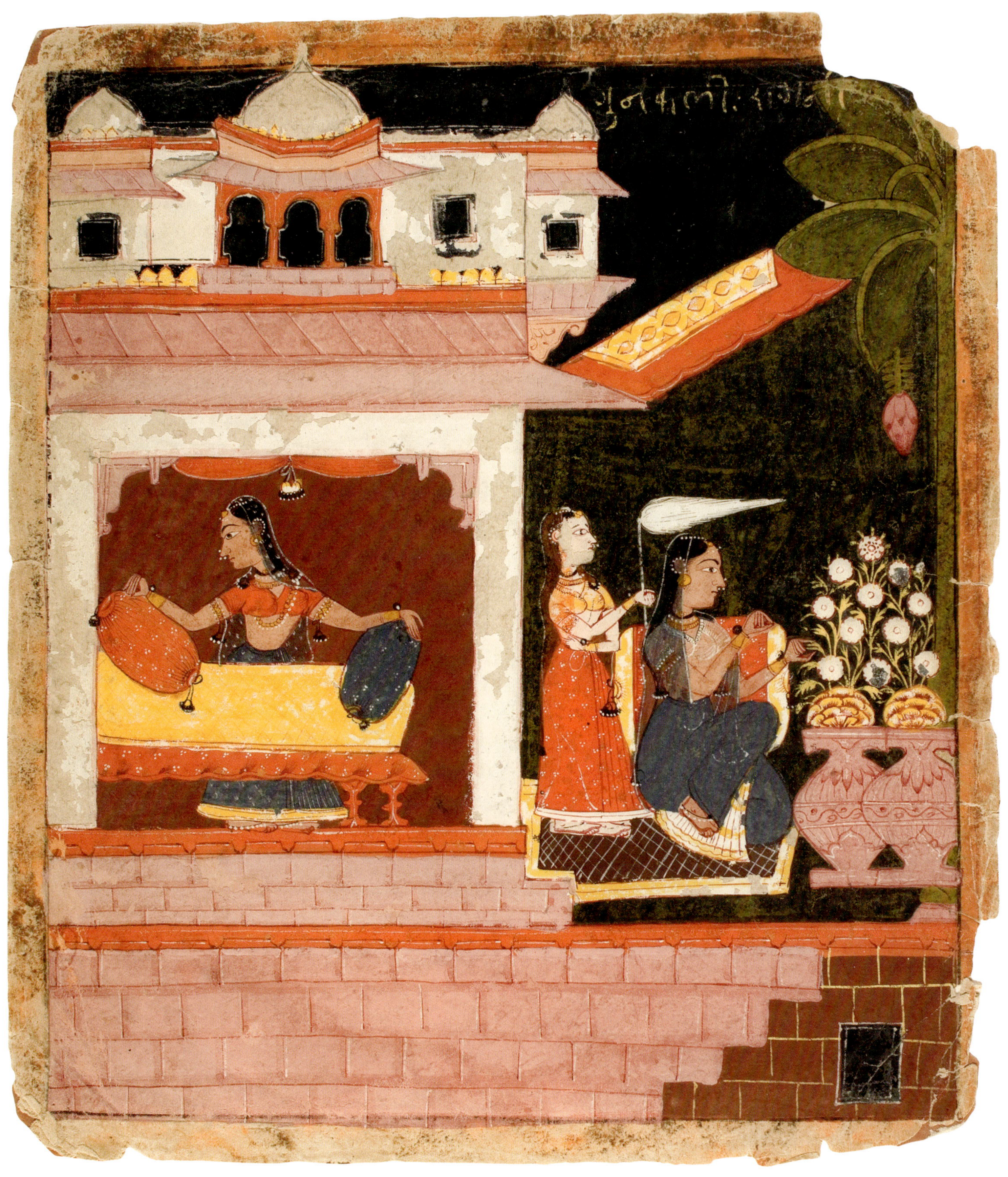
गुनकली रागिनी

2

Page from a Ragamala Series: Gunakali Ragini

Jodhpur, ca. 1640–50; 31.5 x 28.3 cm
San Diego Museum of Art

In this page from a different and later *Ragamala* series than cat. 1,[5] a woman waits for her lover who has taken advantage of the cool months to travel on business. To pass the lonely hours, she arranges flowers in two large pots, symbols for the two lovers. The pots are separate but the flowers are intertwined and their scents intermingle. The song associated with *Gunakali Ragini* comes from a poem sung during the winter months, accompanied by music that evokes the season. *Ragamala* paintings capture various emotions and sensations of a particular moment in time.

One of the identifying characteristics of this *Ragamala* series is a somber background palette, usually blue or black.[6] The dark color effectively sets off the vivid architectural and vegetative elements. Pulsating pink, yellow, and white colors characterize many Marwar paintings of this period, including cat. 3. A similarly restrained background with a palette of earth tones appears in the earlier Pali *Ragmala* series (see cat. 1). With their pointed noses and oversize heads, the figures in the *Gunakali Ragini* are clearly Pali types.

Many of the same elements found in this work—dark background, flat perspective, accentuated facial features, and architectural details—are also found in a circa 1650 manuscript from neighboring Nagaur that depicts the romance of Dhola and Maru, the mythical couple from Marwar.[7] These works illustrate the stylistic similarities between the two Rathore ateliers, Marwar and Nagaur, at the time.

During the first half of the seventeenth century, Marwar painting retained a confident folk charm and vibrant aesthetic that was different from the style of the imperial Mughal court in Delhi, which had been adopted by some of the other Rajput courts.[8] The traditional, popular style of painting is known for its straightforwardness, emotional impact, and visual directness. It was a long-established, informal style, not complex in either compositional structure or in the rendering of figures; it was the successor and continuation of the Chaurapanchasika and other pre-Mughal styles established one hundred years earlier in north India.[9]

A new subject matter, portraiture, became part of Marwar painters' repertoire after the middle of the seventeenth century, when Mughal portraits of Marwar rulers (see cats. 4 and 5) became available to the artists in local and royal Marwar workshops (see fig. 5b on p. 260 and cat. 6). At the end of the seventeenth century and throughout the eighteenth century, court artists in Jodhpur and Nagaur employed a variation of the Mughal style, with faces that capture individual appearance or physiognomy and muted colors, reflecting the new taste in actual representation. In Jodhpur, the traditional Rajput style was reserved primarily for manuscripts illustrating musical modes or romances. CG

3

Page from a Ragamala Series
Jodhpur, ca. 1660; 29.3 x 18.4 cm
National Museum of India

Desavarati is a forlorn woman who longs for her absent lover. Her hands are joined in a tight clasp over her head in a gesture known as "crab-claw" (*karkata-hasta*).[10] Her outstretched arms express her yearning and desire to embrace a lover who is far away. She leans back against the wide cushion, waiting for his return: "at ease and in silence, her body twisted as the creeper [vine], arms up stretched, and rolling eyes—such shall be Desavarati, the fair one."[11] While this verse is inscribed at the top of an earlier (circa 1650) Desavarati painting—part of a *Ragamala* series from the neighboring state of Mewar—it is applicable here as well.

The inscription on the top border identifies the image as Sorath Ragini, but as is the case with many *Ragamala* paintings, the scribe has written the incorrect name. While Desavarati always is associated with a woman with joined arms over her head,[12] Sorath's iconography is quite varied and can be illustrated by a lady making a garland of flowers or offering a savory to her husband, or by an equestrian warrior.

"Desavarati" is one of the songs that belong to the hot, dry summer months, a time before the cooling monsoon rains, when the skies become dark with stormy clouds. The luminous palette of vibrant yellow, dazzling white, and "hot" pink reflects this blistering season.

The style of cats. 1, 2, and 3 is characteristic of an indigenous Rajput folk or "village" style, in which color and form are used to convey strong emotion and dramatic impact. However, the artist of this work has employed a brighter than usual palette. The oranges and pinks may be the result of the artist's familiarity with Deccan painting of the first half of the seventeenth century, which was known to the painting workshops, both princely and non-royal, in Marwar.[13] Raja Jaswant Singh (cat. 6) could have become the conduit for these influences from the south as a result of his military assignments in the Deccan.[14]

With its bright oranges, pinks, and yellows, cat. 7, produced much later in a royal workshop in Marwar, represents the continuation of this "candy-colored" style into the early decades of the eighteenth century. These pastel shades became the color foundation for the Nagaur Bakhat Singh portraits (cats. 10–20) in the second quarter of the eighteenth century. CG

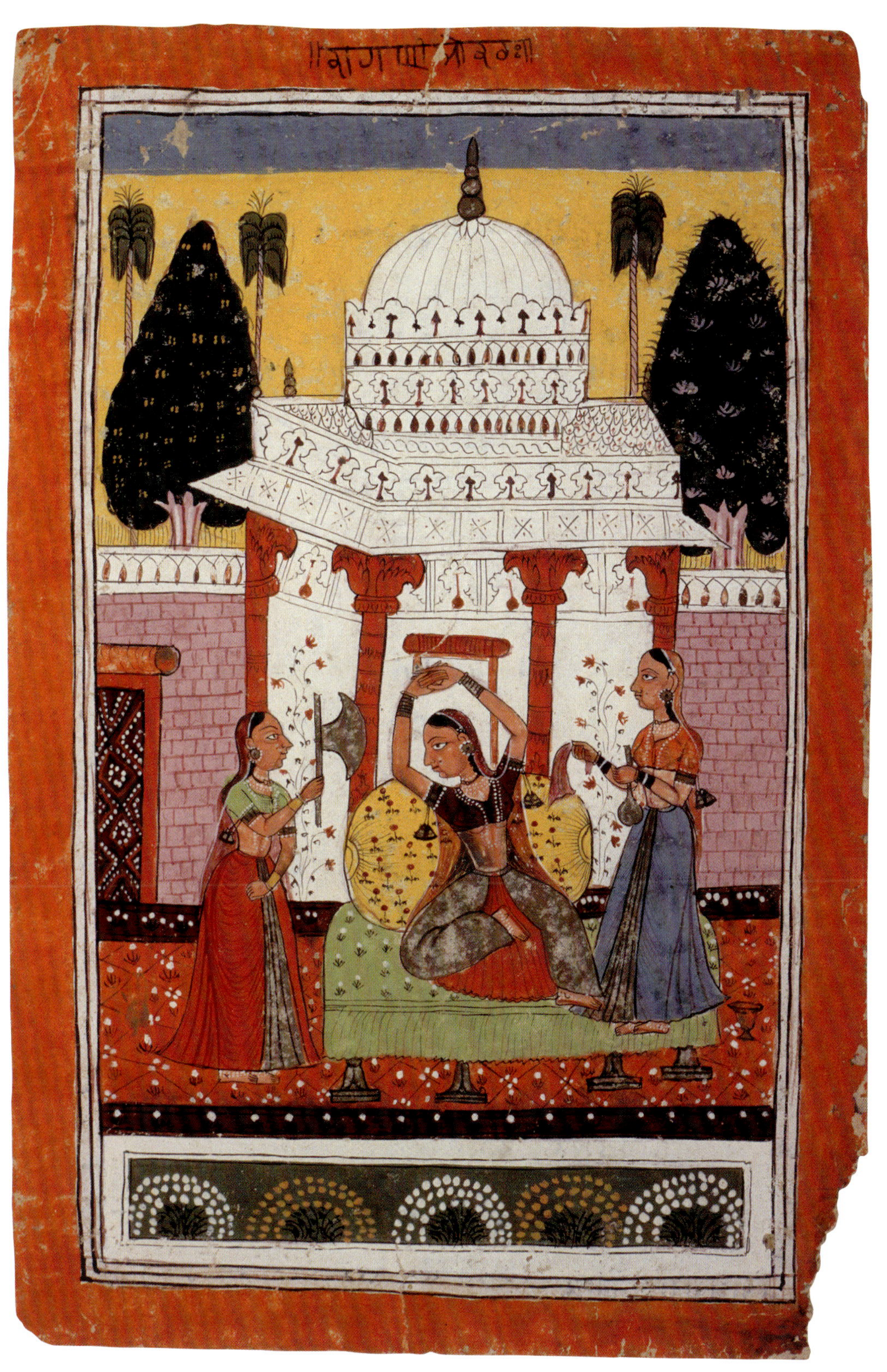

रागपथोरवशी

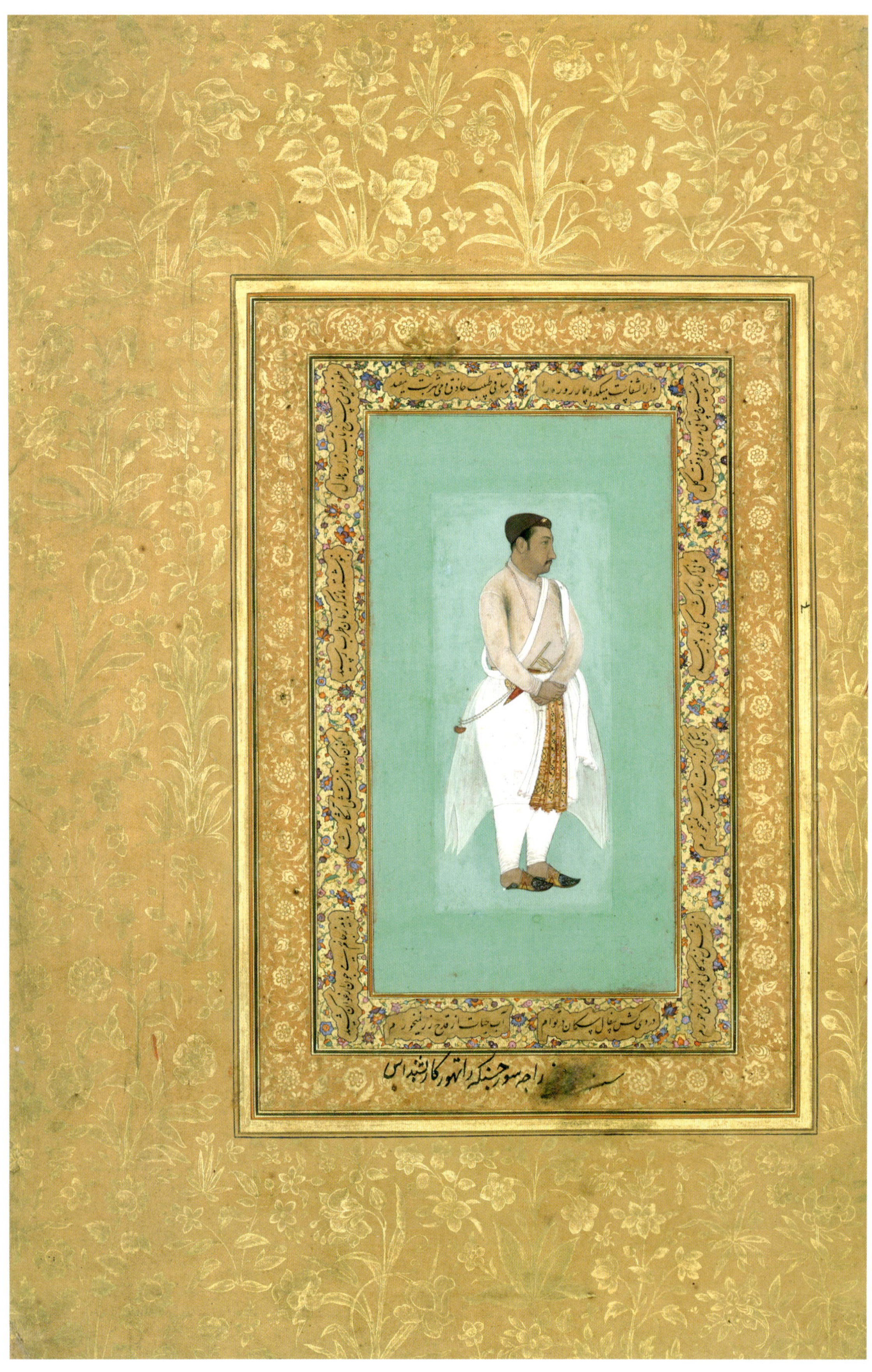

4

Raja Sur (Suraj) Singh of Marwar

Bishan Das
Mughal, ca. 1595; 38.7 x 25.6 cm
The Metropolitan Museum of Art

shabih-i...raja surajsingh rathor, kar-i bishandas (Persian)
a portrait of the Rathore Raja Suraj Singh, painted by Bishan Das

The house of Rathore had been allied politically and culturally with the Mughals
for a generation when Suraj Singh (1571–1619, reigned 1595–1619) inherited
the Marwar throne from his father, Udai Singh. With his distinct headgear, darker
skin, and humble stance, Suraj Singh can be identified in numerous imperial
Mughal paintings recording significant political events in the first two decades of
the seventeenth century.[15] During his reign, many Mughal administrative policies,
practices, and customs were adopted by the Marwar court. *Darbar* protocol
changed to include precise positioning of the nobles based on rank, similar to the
Mughal manner,[16] and a separate room at Mehrangarh Fort, the Moti Mahal, was
designated just to accommodate these royal assemblies. State administration was
reorganized into districts and departments associated with the Mughal system.[17]

Portraits of Suraj Singh in three imperial albums—one made for Jahangir, a
second for Shah Jahan when he was a prince (the Prince Khurram album), and
a third for Shah Jahan when he was emperor—confirm his position within the
greater Mughal extended family. In 1586 his father married Suraj Singh's sister,
Jagat Gosain Manmati (also known as Jodh Bai), to Prince Salim, who became
Emperor Jahangir upon the death of the great Mughal emperor, Akbar, in 1605.
The child of that union, born in 1592, became Shah Jahan, the fifth Mughal
emperor, builder of the Taj Mahal, and commissioner of the album that includes
this painting. Thus, Suraj Singh had a familial connection to all three Mughal
emperors. He was the brother of Akbar's daughter-in-law, Jahangir's brother-in-law,
and Shah Jahan's maternal uncle.

Suraj Singh spent most of his reign away from Jodhpur, performing military and
administrative tasks for Akbar and Jahangir in Gujarat and the Deccan.[18] Akbar
bestowed the exalted title "sawai" on Suraj Singh after a series of particularly
successful military campaigns. Meaning "one and a quarter," sawai distinguished
the holder as superior to the average noble. Suraj Singh was so loyal to the
imperial forces that in 1614, during Jahangir's reign, he participated in the Mughal
campaign against his fellow Rajputs that subdued Mewar, the Rajasthan state
just south of Marwar.

Marwar became the largest kingdom in Rajasthan, and developed
geographically, economically, and politically because of Raja Suraj Singh's
powerful personality, his familial connections, and his value as a successful ally
of the Mughals.[19] CG

5

Maharaja Gaj Singh I

Mughal, ca. 1630–38; 26.5 x 16.5 cm
The British Museum

Gaj Singh I (1595–1638, reigned 1619–38) was born the year his father, Raja
Suraj Singh, became ruler of Marwar. Like his father, Gaj Singh spent a considerable part of his rule away from Jodhpur, in service to the Mughal emperors
Jahangir and Shah Jahan.[20] His greatest military achievement was against Malik
Ambar,[21] the Abyssinian prime minister of the Deccan state, Ahmadnagar, who
had led a surprise attack against a Mughal garrison stationed on the banks of
the Narmada River in spring 1621. Gaj Singh defeated the Ahmadnagar forces
and carried away the enemy's scarlet flag. The red stripe on the current
Jodhpur flag immortalizes Gaj Singh's victory and the pennant trophy.[22]

Marwar's geographical, political, economic, and cultural progress under Suraj
Singh continued during Gaj Singh's stewardship of Marwar, resulting in a period
of unprecedented affluence and influence. Emperor Shah Jahan, Gaj Singh's
cousin by marriage, gave him the title "maharaja," one of the first Rajput princes
to be so honored by the Mughal court.[23] Many awards and gifts were bestowed
upon the new maharaja: elephants, Arabian horses, diamond *sarpeches* (turban
ornaments), emerald brooches, swords and daggers, and robes woven with
gold thread (*zari*).[24] So privileged was his position that his horses did not have
to be branded with the imperial marker, and Gaj Singh was allowed to beat his
own kettle-drums in the imperial capital, an honor given by the emperor and
usually reserved for members of the Mughal court.[25]

While painted by an unknown artist (and later placed within an early eighteenth-
century album border),[26] Gaj Singh's likeness resembles other representations of
the Marwar maharaja produced during his lifetime by identified Mughal artists.[27]

A solitary figure placed against a blue-green background was a typical
composition in Mughal portraiture during the late sixteenth century. Most of the
individuals depicted in albums made for Mughal emperors were grandees of the
realm: the emperor's male relatives and Mughal empire officers and administrators, including prominent Rajput rulers and nobles. Gaj Singh wears the apparatus
of his military profession: a sword with a gem-encrusted hilt, a black leather
shield, and a two-handled dagger encased in a diamond-encrusted sheath. The
artist depicts Gaj Singh's high-ranking status not only by including the jeweled
weapons, but by meticulously recording his other precious ornaments: a turban
bordered with pearls, large double-pearl earrings, an enormous red gem hanging
from a double string of pearls, and a longer string of pearls. His coat and waist
sash are decorated with gold thread, confirming Gaj Singh's position as a man
of considerable importance and stature. CG

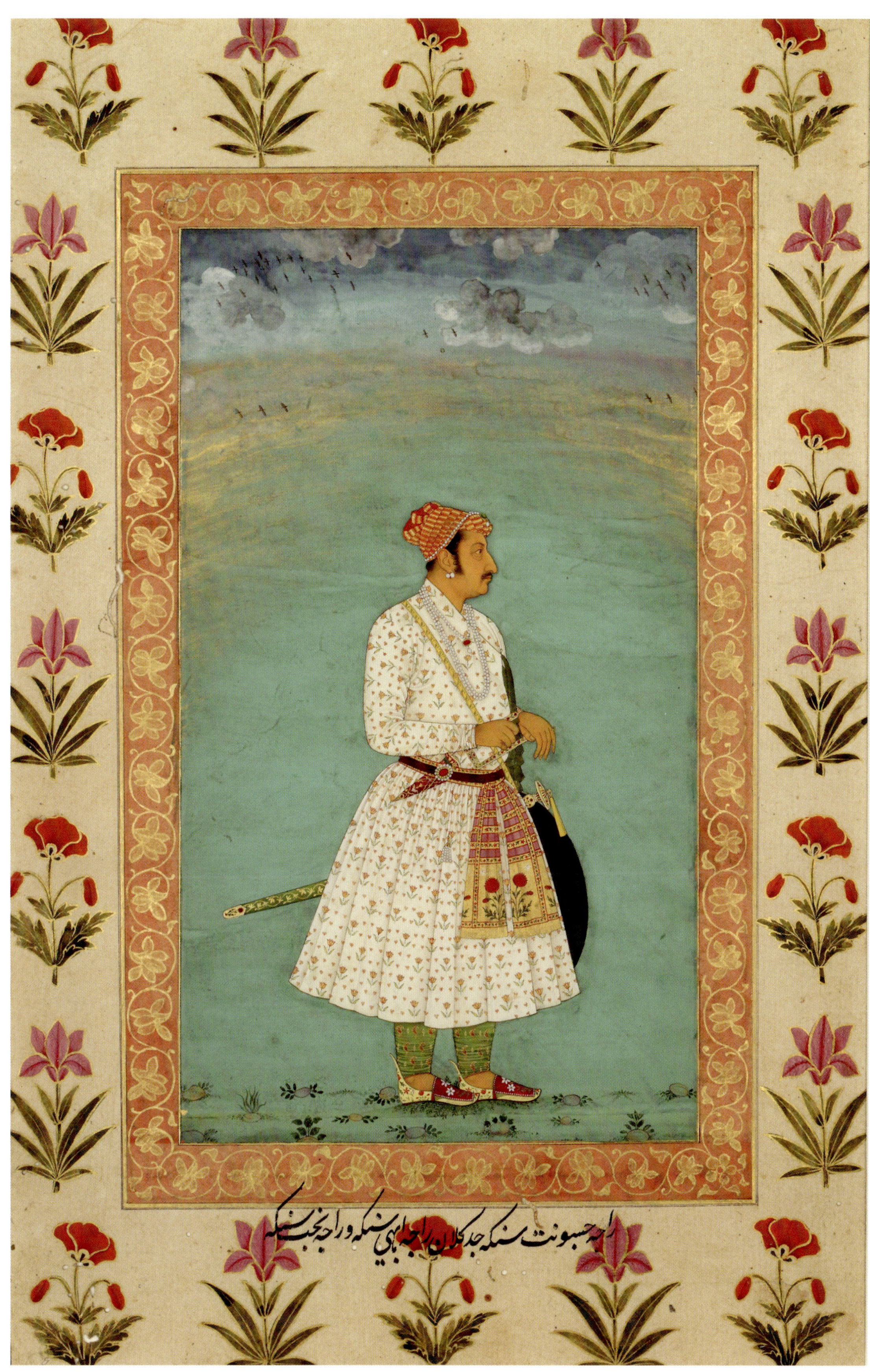

6

Maharaja Jaswant Singh I at a Music Performance during a Monsoon

Jodhpur, ca. 1670; 26.8 x 17.4 cm
National Gallery of Victoria

bahadur jaswant sang (Persian)
the noble man Jaswant Singh

jasut sihaji raja bikaner ka ri chabi majal ki (Rajasthani)
Raja Jaswant Singh of Bikaner[28]

Jaswant Singh (1626–1678, reigned 1638–78) succeeded to the throne of Marwar at the death of his father, Gaj Singh, even though his older brother, Amar Singh, traditionally would have been designated the next ruler. In 1634 Gaj Singh had banished Amar Singh (see the reference catalogue entry for cat. 5 on p. 259) from the court because of his bad temper, and in addition, the chief Rathore nobles considered him unfit to rule.[29]

Jaswant Singh, however, was politically astute. Not only was he able to wrest power from his older brother, he also formed a series of successful coalitions with competing external Mughal factions. In fact, during the war of succession that took place after the death of Shah Jahan in 1657, Jaswant Singh sided in turn with each of the late Mughal emperor's four sons during their struggles to gain supremacy. He ultimately supported the victor, Aurangzeb, in the battles for the throne.

This painting of Maharaja Jaswant Singh depicts him at the height of his military career and political influence.[30] Like his father and his grandfather Suraj Singh, Jaswant Singh served the Mughals as a military commander. He was rewarded for his military triumphs and allegiance with the title of maharaja and was given the prominent political position of viceroy over three distinct regions: Malwa, Gujarat, and the Deccan.[31]

Jaswant Singh's reign coincided with the completion of two major imperial Mughal garden projects: the planned geometric design surrounding the Taj Mahal at Agra (1632–48), which he would have seen, and the Shalimar gardens in Lahore (1641–42), which he also visited.[32] They perhaps stirred Jaswant Singh's interest in building a garden and pleasure palace by the Sur Sagar Lake, two miles north of Mehrangarh Fort. It is possible that this Sur Sagar garden palace, built in 1672, is the garden depicted in cat. 6. The magnificent painting is a visual garden, with densely packed, blossoming trees in the background that echo the floral aspects of the carpet in the middle and the flower beds at the bottom, perhaps all inspired by Jaswant Singh's awareness of the emperors' cosmopolitan tastes in gardens.

Yet the heightened color scheme of vibrant purples, pinks, and oranges, which contributes to the intensity and almost shimmering quality of the work, is markedly Rajput. These colors also are familiar in paintings that Jaswant Singh may have seen while he was stationed in the Deccan.[33] During the rule of his grandson Bakhat Singh some seventy years later, pinks, purples, and oranges would reappear in Nagaur painting, though in pastel hues rather than the deeper shades we see here (see cats. 10–20). CG

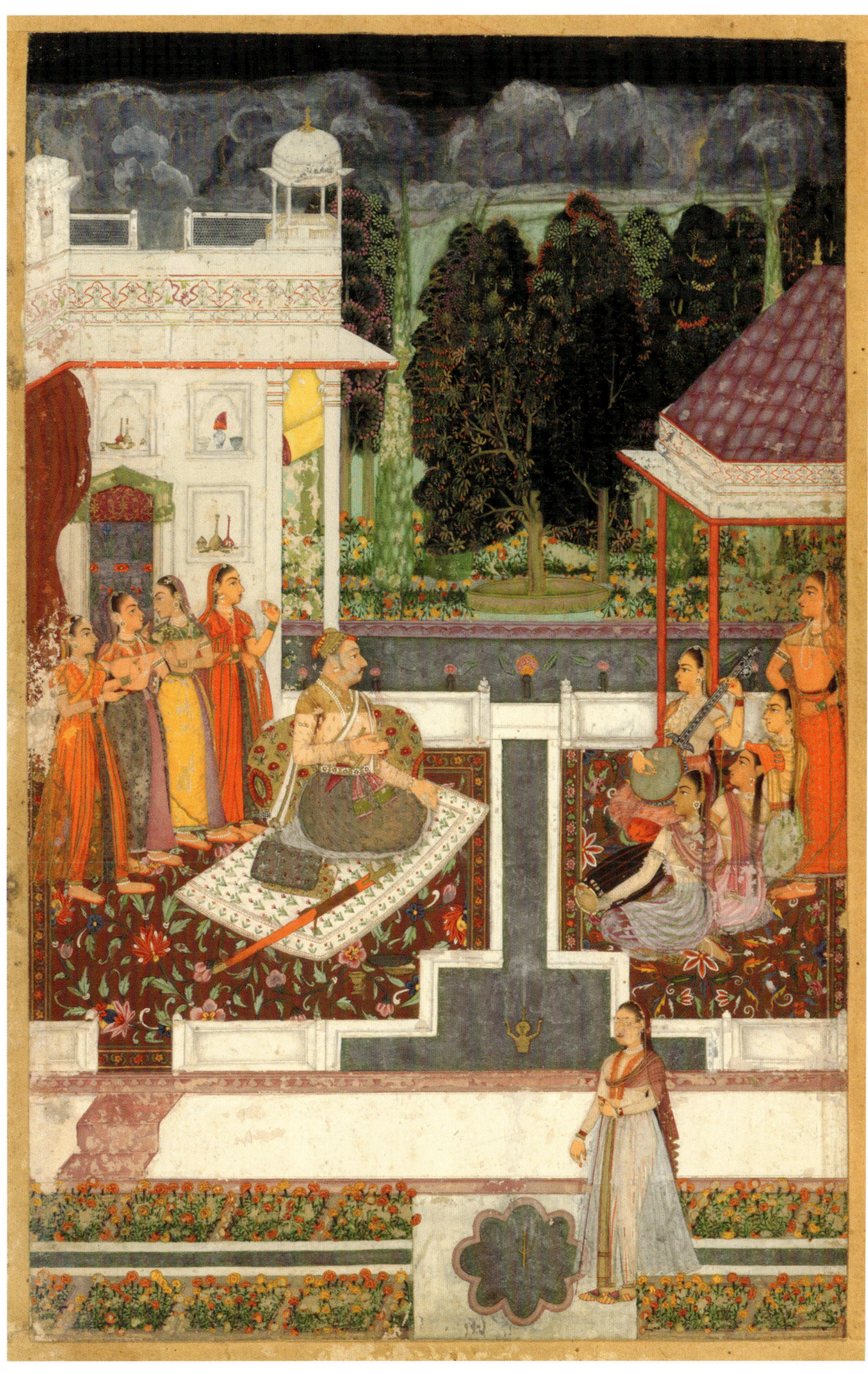

7

Evening Musical Festivities within a Garden
Jodhpur, ca. 1715; 40.6 x 30.5 cm
Mehrangarh Museum Trust

Rajrajeshvar maharaj sri ajit singhji ri sabi
Portrait of lord of king of kings, supreme king, glorious Ajit Singh

Da [khal] dholiya re kothar
Entered in the *dholiya* storeroom

This bucolic portrait of Maharaja Ajit Singh (1679–1725, reigned 1707–24) carries on the tradition of Marwar paintings depicting royal gardens established during the reign of his father, Jaswant Singh (cat. 6).[34] "Royal gardens in India united visual, acoustic and aromatic elements in an effort to create ultimate sensual pleasure. Water, trees, flowers, birds, animals, wind, and light combined to enhance the seductive experience."[35] A painter who depicted a perfect garden conveyed a courtly ideal; similarly, the garden landscape inspired and stimulated an artist's imagination, providing a colorful convention for poetic and sensitive expression. Bakhat Singh, Ajit Singh's second son, grew up surrounded by garden paintings and later took the tradition to Nagaur, which he ruled from 1725 until 1751 (see cats. 12, 13, and 16).

Like the scene of Ajit Singh's family in the Philadelphia Museum of Art (see fig. 8a, p. 262), cat. 7 is clearly Rajput in style—with bold and vivid primary colors, idealized treatment of figures and landscape, and schematic composition.[36] The candlestick and women holding devices with flames indicate that the occasion takes place in the evening, although the palette maintains the vibrancy of a daylight scene. Cats. 7 and 8 demonstrate that during Ajit Singh's reign, artists in Jodhpur worked in two styles: the established Rajput style (cat. 7) and a Mughalized style (see entries for cat. 8).

Prior to Ajit Singh's reign, the rulers of Marwar used the titles of raja or maharaja. The ninth Mughal emperor, Muhammad Farrukh Siyar (1683–1719, reigned 1713–19), bestowed an additional title on Ajit Singh[37]—*rajrajeshwar*— perhaps because Ajit Singh's daughter, and Bakhat Singh's sister, Indra Kunwar, had married Farrukh Siyar in Delhi on December 11, 1715, making the Mughal emperor Ajit Singh's father-in-law.[38] Subsequent Marwar rulers also would use this new title. Bakhat Singh was called *rajrajeshwar* after he received Nagaur as a reward for killing his father, confirming both that Nagaur had achieved semi-independence from Jodhpur and that the Mughal rulers recognized his legitimacy. CG

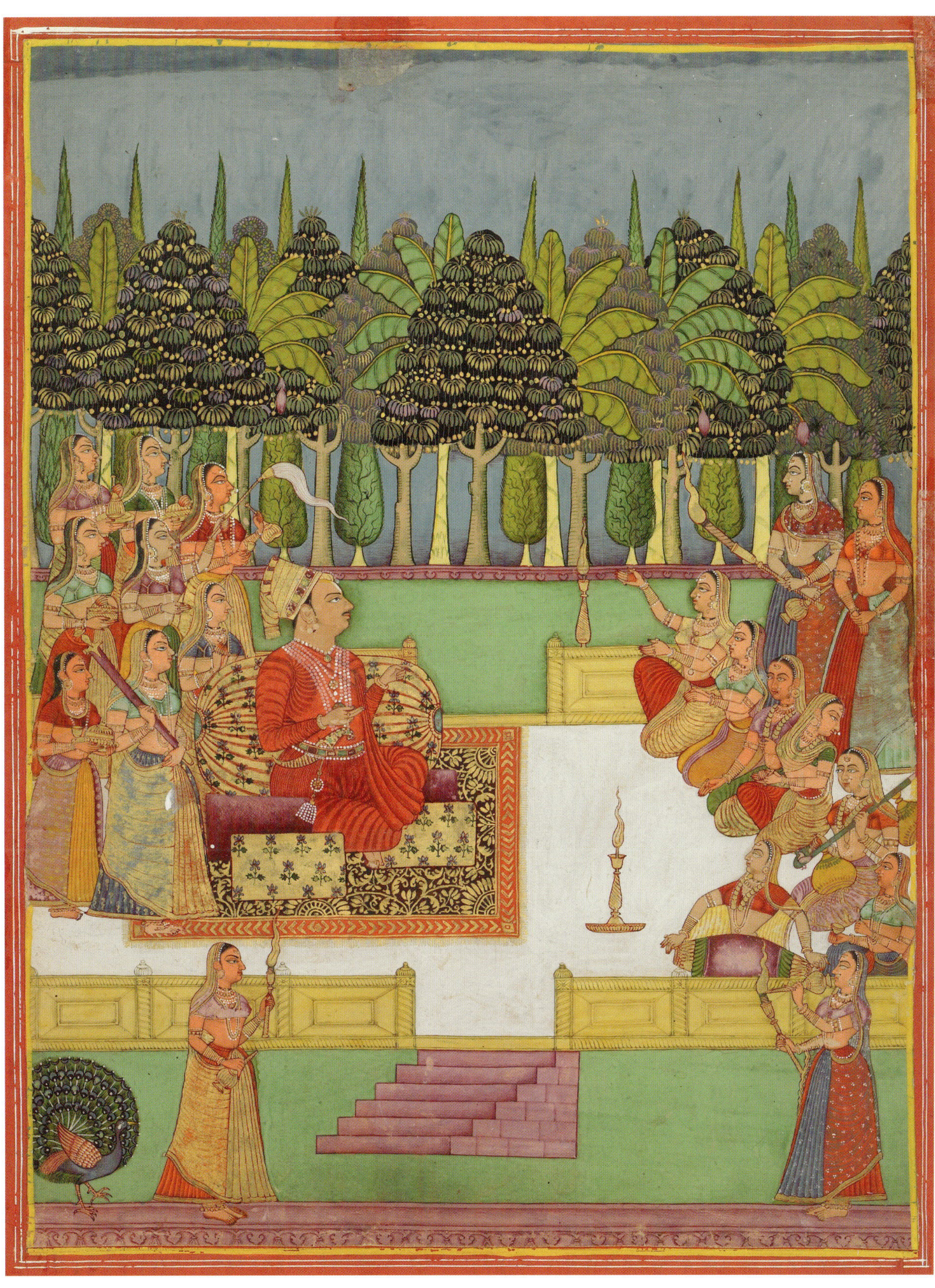

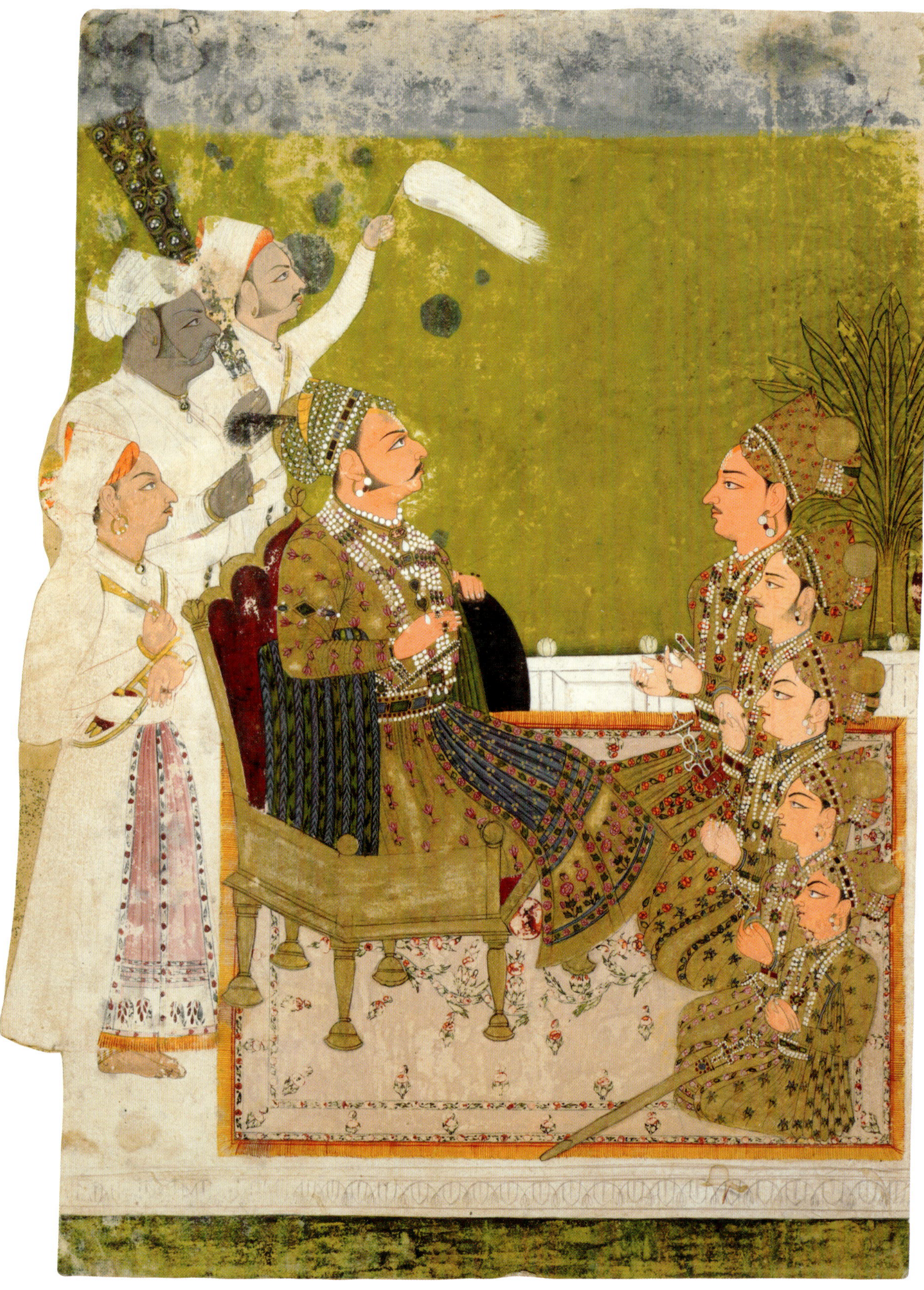

8

Maharaha Ajit Singh and Sons during the Festival of Diwali
Jodhpur, 1721 (Samvat 1778); 33.8 x 25.3 cm
Harvard University Art Museums

The complete inscription appears in the reference catalogue.

After ruling Marwar for forty years, Maharaja Jaswant Singh (cat. 6) died in November 1678 in Jamrud, near Peshawar in present-day Pakistan, without a male heir.[39] Fortunately, however, two of his wives were pregnant at the time. On the journey back to Rajasthan, each rani gave birth to a son in Lahore, but only one of the boys, Ajit Singh, born February 1679, survived the hardship of birth away from home.

Marwar and the Mehrangarh Fort were vulnerable after Jaswant Singh's death.[40] A war known in Marwar as the Thirty-Year Rathore War of Independence ensued between Aurangzeb's imperial forces and the nobles of Marwar. The nobles were led by Durga Das, one of the young Ajit Singh's primary guardians and a principal foe of Aurangzeb. Prince Ajit Singh and his supporters became refugees, forced to find asylum in various Rajput principalities, including Amber and Udaipur. Only after Aurangzeb's death in 1707 did Ajit Singh claim his rightful position as ruler of Marwar.[41] On March 12, 1707, after Mehrangarh Fort had been purified with water from the Ganges, twenty-eight-year-old Ajit Singh proudly entered the stronghold, the twenty-fifth in the long line of Rathore rulers of Marwar.[42] Ajit Singh built the Fateh Pol (Gate of Victory), the ceremonial gateway at Mehrangarh that leads out from the fort into the city below, to commemorate his successful return.

Ajit Singh was not in a position to patronize the arts during the chaotic period before he assumed the Marwar throne. However, once there was stability, he did support the royal painting ateliers.[43] This documentary painting depicts the Marwar raja and five of his sons in Ajmer during the grand Diwali festivities of 1721.[44] It is balanced in composition: four figures on the left, five figures on the right. Still, the painting reflects a trend often encountered in Marwar royal portraits: a combination of sensibilities, creating what might best be described as a Mughalized Rajasthani painting. The stacked figures, strongly sculptural presentation, and oversize heads are Rajput; and the physically powerful figures reflect the Rajput ideal of kingship. The golden decorative textiles, individualized profile portraits, and subdued palette are all elements that were adopted earlier from Mughal portraiture.

All of the royals wear similarly patterned textiles, though Ajit Singh's turban and entire upper torso are distinguished by the addition of scores of pearls and colored gems, appropriate for the patron of the painting.[45] Father and sons have individually distinguished facial features; the raja sits on a gold throne before the young princes, arranged in chronological order: Kumar (heir apparent) Abhai, Bakhat (later to rule Nagaur and Marwar), Anand, Kesor, and Rai. The sons appear to offer obeisance submissively to their father. In 1724, however, three years after this painting was completed, the two oldest sons plotted the successful assassination of their father, and the three younger siblings then fought unsuccessfully to overthrow their older brothers. cg

9

Maharaja Bakhat Singh

Nagaur, ca. 1740; 43.1 x 30.4 cm
National Gallery of Canada

raja sri bakhat singhji
glorious king Bakhat Singh

Bakhat Singh (1706–1752, ruled Nagaur 1724–50, ruled Marwar 1751–52) was the second of Ajit Singh's sons, and often is described as an outstanding military general. One Marwar historian has noted that he was "tall and powerfully built, with an impressive moustache, he was—in appearance at least—the quintessential Rathore warrior and counted among his lady admirers the wife of the fifteenth Mughal Emperor Ahmad Shah. As the chronicles loyally record, the empress even urged her husband to follow the same diet as the Rathore."[46]

Here, he appears almost as an icon within a *jharokha* window.[47] His fingers are posed to hold either a flower or a jewel, though there is nothing visible in his hand.[48] Three pearls hang next to his ear, pearls supporting a dangling red gem adorn his neck, and two more pearl strands drape luxuriously over his shoulders. The floral embellishment of his turban and the flowered arch above his head contrast with his rigorously striped *jama* and the plain window textile on which he rests his hand.[49]

The concept of a window from which the populace could observe and pay homage to royalty arose from Hindu tradition, in which sanctity was associated with being in the presence of a deity and viewing a deity's image. This idea was gradually extended to the temporal sphere, i.e., the Mughal and Rajput courts. When a ruler appeared in the *jharokha* window, many objectives were satisfied: it was clear that the ruler was still alive and able to exercise his rule; his subjects were able (theoretically, at least) to approach him personally with grievances or injustices; and the public benefited by being in close proximity to the ruler, who represented the deity's presence on earth.[50]

Unique among Rajput portraiture because of their generous size and composition, these *jharokha* paintings may have been commissioned by Bakhat Singh as rewards to clansmen in recognition of exemplary service or as gifts to other Rajput nobles. We know that at least four were painted;[51] however, no paintings of this type are currently in the Jodhpur royal collection, which suggests that they were given away. In addition, none of the late eighteenth- and early nineteenth-century posthumous portraits of Bakhat Singh in the royal Jodhpur collection and elsewhere follows this unique *jharokha* compositional format.[52] CG

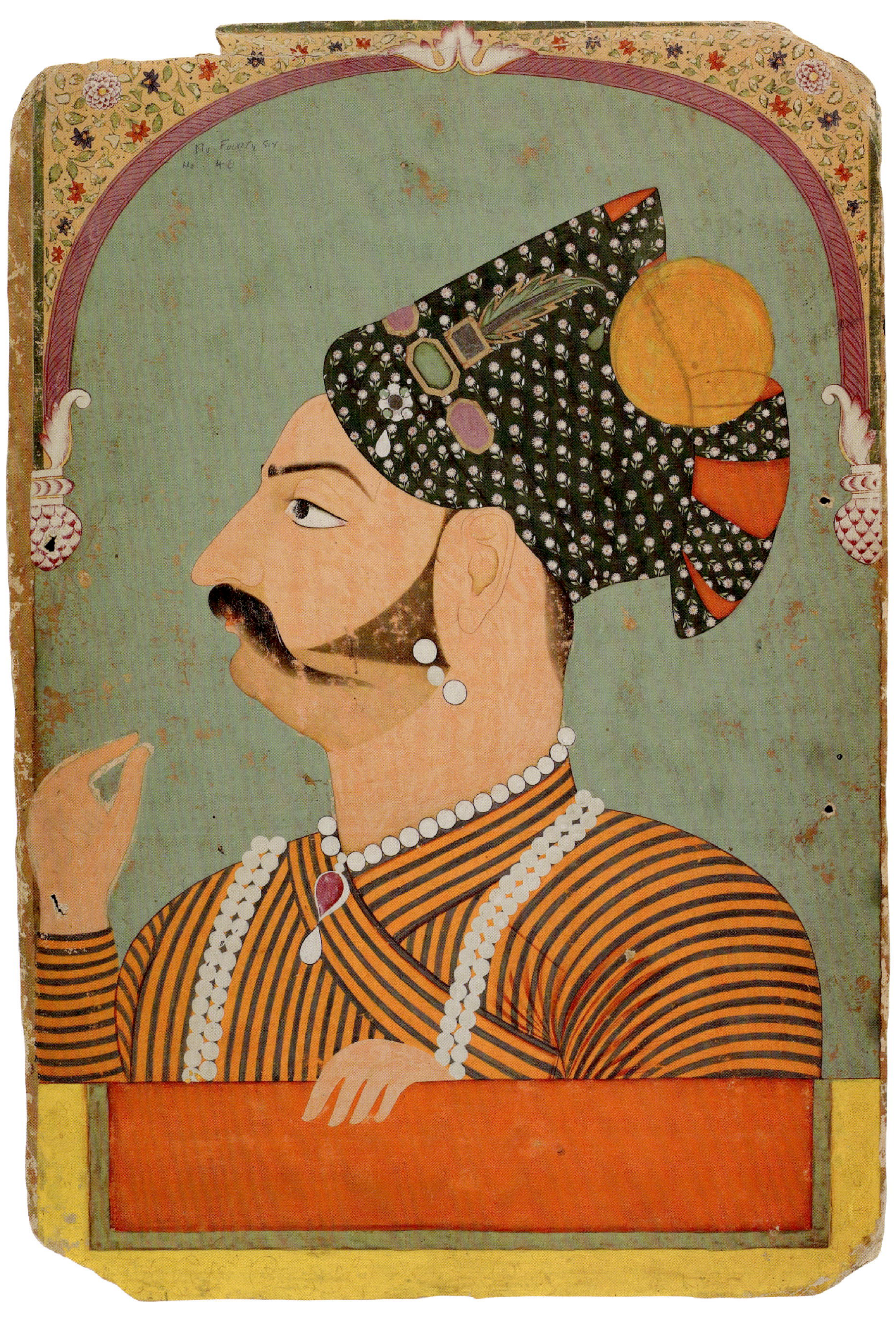

ROYAL PASTIMES IN THE GARDENS

AT NAGAUR PALACE

During a brief quarter-century reign at Nagaur (1725–51), Maharaja Bakhat Singh created a pleasure palace oasis just eighty-five miles northeast of Jodhpur. He built elegant zenana quarters for the women of the palace, stylish assembly halls, a graceful multi-pillared verandah, and an elaborate hydraulic system to irrigate his numerous gardens. At Nagaur, Bakhat Singh focused his creative sensibilities on making his palace a center of luxurious splendor, in stark contrast to the surrounding desert.

Through his patronage of permanent wall paintings and portable paintings, Bakhat Singh preserved his vision of intimate home life and treated the viewer to a personal reflection of royal life at Nagaur. The paintings exhibit an unusual veracity, showing the gradual aging of the patron as they document his enjoyment of palace life, and accurately portraying his architectural achievements.

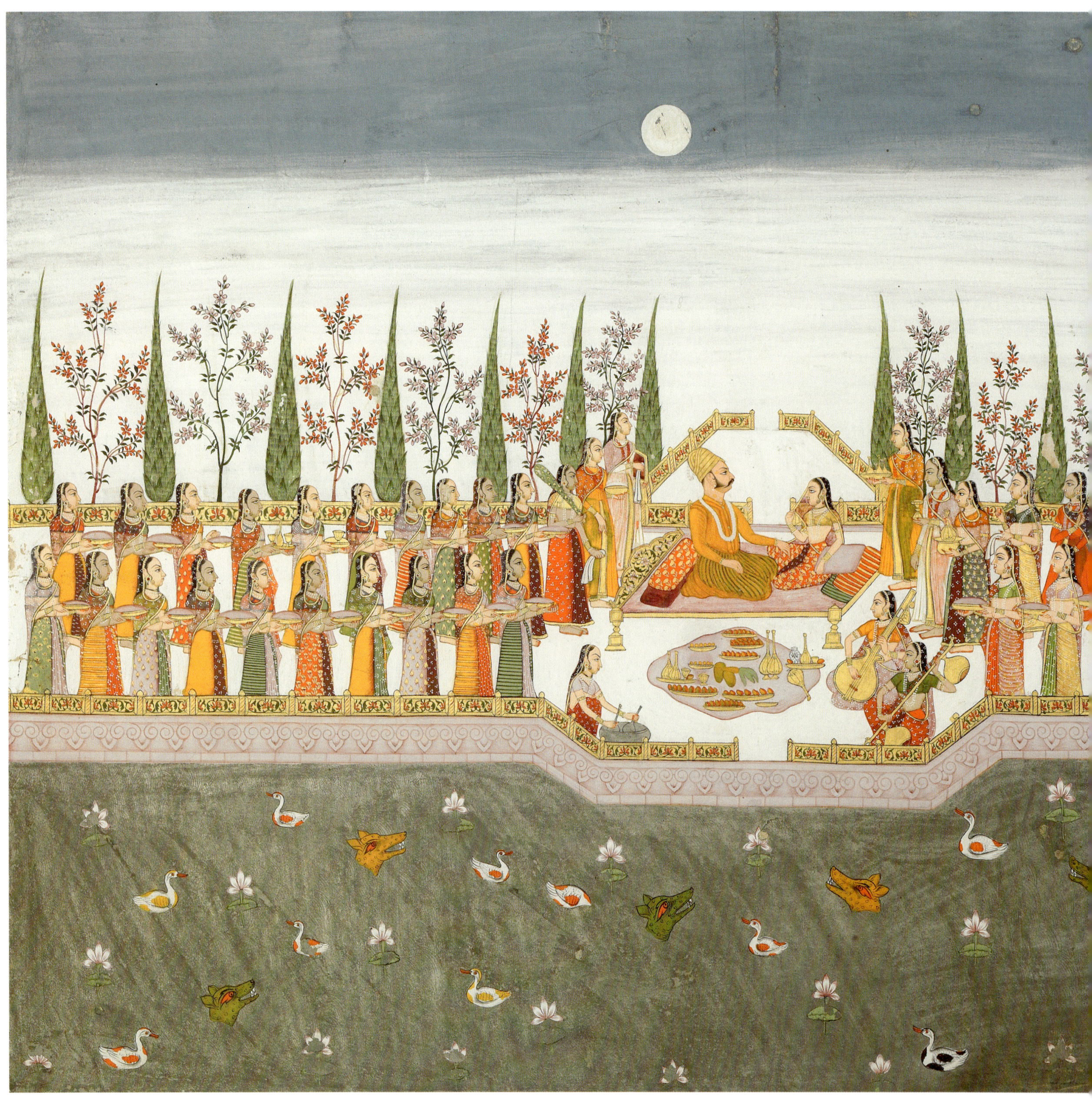

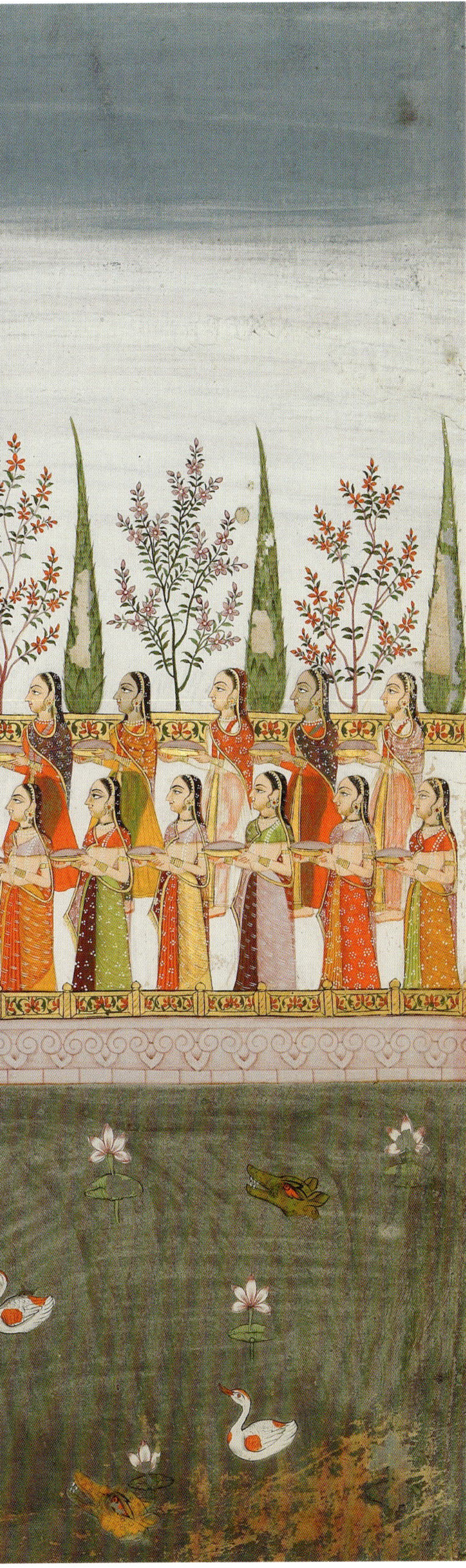

Amusements on a Moonlit Water Terrace
Nagaur, ca. 1729–32; 45.1 x 65 cm
Mehrangarh Museum Trust

Rajrajeshwar maharajadhiraj maharaja sri bakhat singhji ri tasbir
Picture of lord of king of kings, supreme king of great kings, great king,
glorious Bakhat Singhji

As the full moon rises, Bakhat Singh (1706–1752, reigned Nagaur, 1725–50;
reigned Marwar, 1751–52) enjoys the pleasures of women, wine, food, and music.
A garden scene under the moon was a popular Mughal subject and a natural
scene for the Rajput courts, which had celebrated moonlit evenings well before
the Mughal era;[1] a similar moonlight scene is depicted in cat. 19. The raja and a
female favorite sit on a low floral-decorated charpoy that has cushions at either
end for support. The reserved young woman who receives the raja's attention
modestly draws her veil before her face, discreetly and coyly engaging her lover,
who has a garland of flowers dangling from his turban as a fragrant enticement.[2]

The setting is a long, rectangular terrace bordering a waterway. A woman on
the right carries a gold-colored (though probably brass), long-necked vessel of the
type used to pour water for washing one's hands before eating, and a matching
basin for catching the water. Another female servant keeps the liquid contained in
the *surahi* (vessels) cool by placing them in a large silver tub. Gold dishes nearby
hold *pan* (a savory wrapped in betel leaf) and mangoes. Green-leafed carrots
and small fruits on a fabric square create a visually attractive still life. Next to one
of the wine vessels is a small blue-and-white container shaped like a ginger jar,
which could be either Chinese or Dutch in origin, a prized object used to hold
something special.[3] Although Chinese ware appears more frequently than Dutch
delft in Rajput paintings of the eighteenth century, it is interesting to note that
blue-and-white pottery became all the rage in Rajasthan after it was introduced
by traders from the Dutch East India Corporation. In fact, in 1711 Dutch envoy
J. J. Ketelaar paid a visit to the court of Udaipur, bringing with him delft tiles that
are still on the walls of some palace rooms.[4]

Behind the two lovers is a small terrace, a perfect venue for viewing the moon
and the garden beyond. When the composition is viewed from a distance, the
shape of the arched terrace railing resembles a palanquin that, along with the rows
of women and trees on either side, conveys the idea of the king in procession,
a common theme of Rajput portraiture.[5] The arch also may have had a symbolic
purpose: to resemble a *torana* (gateway)—differentiating this garden scene from
a purely Mughal design. Mythical dragons, symbols of good fortune, and water
birds populate the silvery water. CG

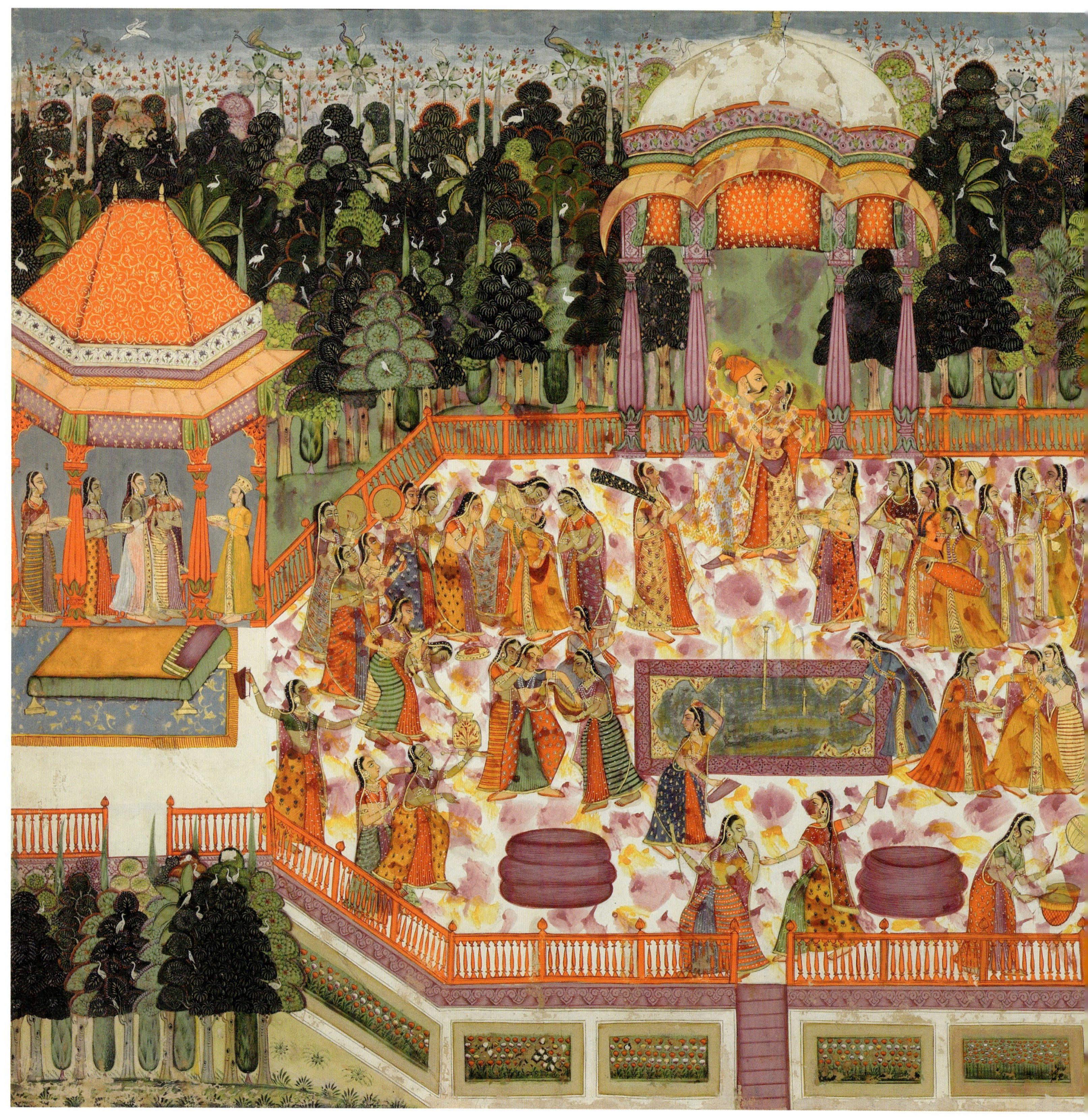

11

Celebration of Holi in a Garden Pavilion
Attributed here to the "Nagaur Master"
Nagaur, ca. 1729–32; 45.1 x 62.2 cm (image)
Mehrangarh Museum Trust

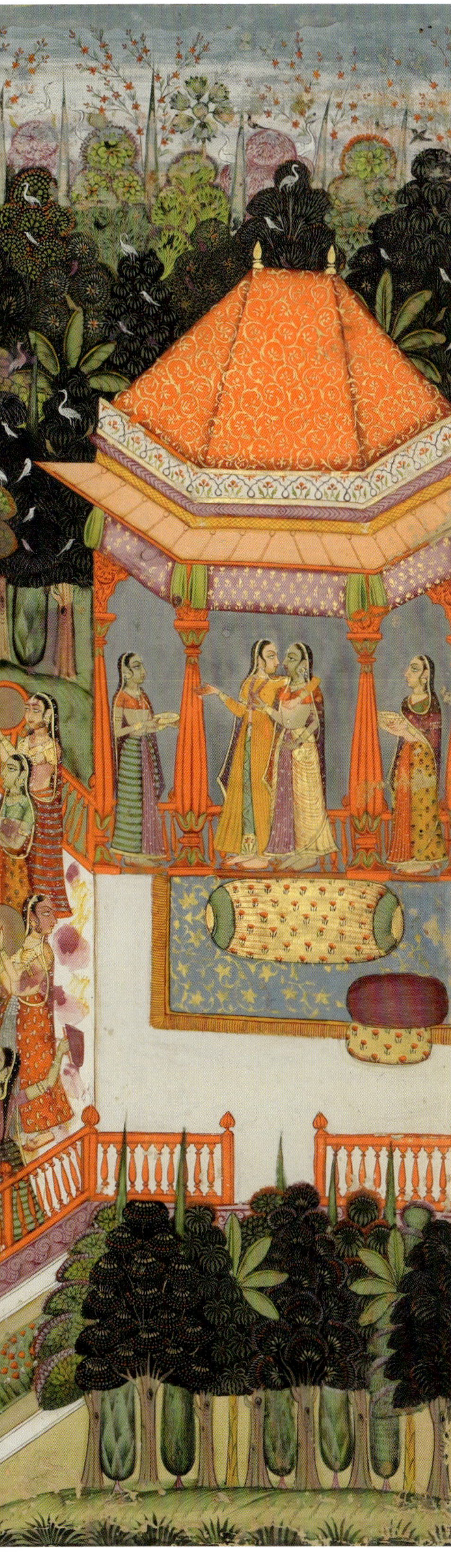

Rajrajeshvar maharajadhiraj maharaja sri bakhat singhji ri tasbir
Painting of the lord of king of kings, supreme king of great kings,
supreme king, glorious Bakhat Singhji

Dakhal dholiya re kothar hajri sam[vat] 1885 ra savan sud 12 mandi
Entered in the *dholiya* storeroom and inventory on the twelfth day
of the light half of Shravan (July–August), 1828

The Hindu festival of Holi, a boisterous expression of happiness and prosperity,
takes place in late February or early March. The Holi play of Krishna and Radha—
in particular the story of the extreme delight that Krishna took in splashing dye
on Radha and the other female cowherds—is a feature of *bhakti* devotionalism in
north India. Recreating Krishna's prank became one of the essential Holi activities;
during the festival, participants spray saffron- or red-colored water on each other
with *pichkaris* (syringes) or simply throw buckets of the colored liquid at one another.

Containers for the colored water, large clay pots and smaller vessels, such
as the glass container decorated with red flowers held by a woman at the lower
left, are ready for the festivities. A woman has inserted her syringe into the glass
bottle, preparing to spray color on her companions. Palace women surround
Bakhat Singh, who seems to be playing the role of Krishna, as he and the women
reenact the Holi gaiety. The possibility that some kind of sexual encounter will
follow the festivities is suggested by the bed and an oversized cushion and pillow
footrest in front of the left and right pavilions, respectively. The garden is flourishing
as if in early spring (when Holi occurs): new growth promises abundance, and
although the weather may have been cool, the merriment extended to the outdoors.

The once-white terrace is now a riot of color, dominated by the particular pink
so prevalent in Nagaur paintings of the period. In his final step, the artist applied
the color as a transparent wash, partially covering the faces of some of the figures.
Singing and music—including drums of different sizes and types, played by women
rather than men because the maharaja is the only male who participates in festivals
or celebrations with zenana women—add to the cacophony and raucous revelry.
At the lower right, one woman plays a pair of *naqqara* (small kettle-drums). Standing
closer to Bakhat Singh, another woman holds an orange double-headed barrel
drum. Usually, this type of drum had strings on the sides to control the sound;
here, however, instead of the strings the artist has chosen to highlight the gold
decoration. On both the left and the right, women play flat, round frame drums.

The festivities take place on a platform surrounded by an octagonal fence.
Other Bakhat Singh paintings from Nagaur also have an octagonal shape as a
central feature (see cats. 16, 18, 20).[6] This painting, produced early in his reign
at Nagaur, reveals how the palace looked before Bakhat Singh renovated the
complex to suit his needs and tastes. CG

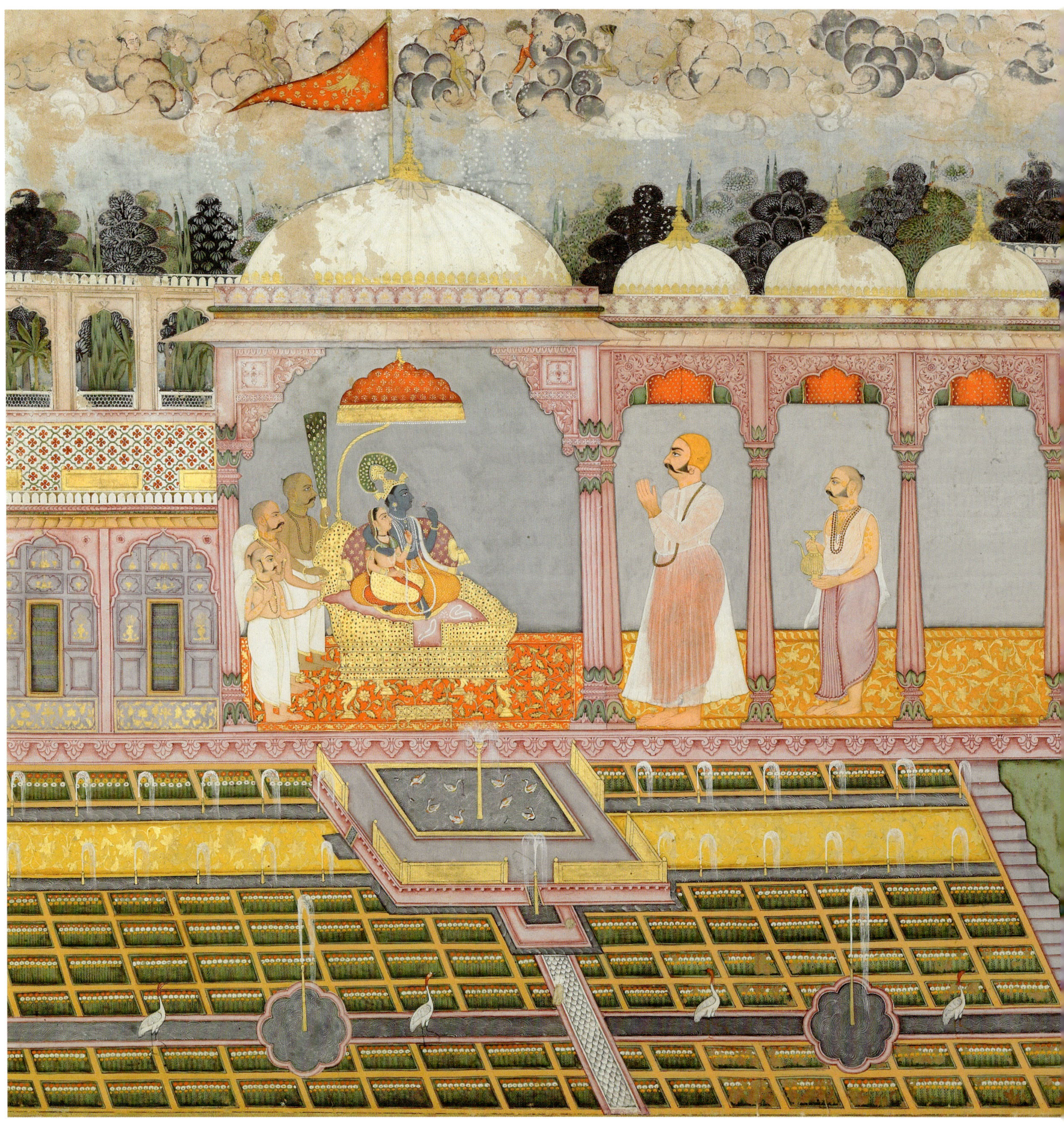

12

Maharaja Bakhat Singh Worshiping Krishna
Attributed here to the "Nagaur Master"
Nagaur, ca. 1730–35; 23 x 34 cm
Mehrangarh Museum Trust

Maharajadhiraj maharaj sri bakhat singhji
Lord of king of kings, supreme king, glorious Bakhat Singhji

Dakhal dholiya re kothar hajri sam[vat] 1885 ra sravan sud 12 budhvar
Entered in the *dholiya* storeroom and inventory on Wednesday, the twelfth day
of the light half of Shravan (July–August), 1828

Under the clouds of an imminent monsoon, a young Bakhat Singh, raja of Nagaur,
pays obeisance before Krishna.[7] The deity and his confidant, Radha, are under
a canopy on a large, golden throne encrusted with semi-precious stones. Radha
is seated on Krishna's lap and accepts his loving embrace. The celebration
documented by this painting is a special *puja* conducted for Krishna's birthday,
Janmashtami, held on the eighth day of the second half of the month of Shravan
(July–August). It is also the time of the monsoon, clearly depicted here by the
swirling storm clouds overhead and threatening skyline.

Behind Krishna are three priests holding symbols of honor: a *morchal* (peacock-
feather fan) and horsetail flywhisks. A fourth priest carries a brass pot filled with
sanctified water, integral to the religious ceremony. No women are present; they
worshiped at a private temple that still exists within the zenana at Nagaur. Of
course, none of the participants carry any weaponry, which were the ubiquitous
accompaniments of Rajput warriors during secular events. Considered offensive
to the sanctity of most religious ceremonies, weapons were permitted only during
Durga puja and Dusserha, both of which are martial ceremonies.[8] Adding sanctity
and royal ratification to this occasion are four angelic figures in the clouds near
the flag of the red temple. Clearly adopted from Mughal paintings, one angel
even wears a Chaghatay Turkish hat.[9]

A sumptuous red carpet, ornamented by a floral pattern of golden silk threads,
completes the lavish decorative elements surrounding the deities.[10] According
to his prescribed iconography, Krishna is dark-skinned and wears a *mor mukut*
(crown of peacock feathers) and a yellow lower garment. The peacock-feather
headdress associates this form of the deity with Braj, the geographical center for
bhakti (devotion) among Krishna followers who long to take part in his childhood
lila (play); see cats. 23–25 for more on *lila*.[11]

Bakhat Singh, who looks to be in his mid- to late twenties, wears a prayer cap
tightly on his head and a sacred thread across his body. He wears an earring
composed of rustic beads usually associated with Hindu holy ascetics, a marked
difference from the opulent pearl and precious-stone earrings he wears in other
Nagaur portraits (cats. 10, 11, 13–20). On his forehead is the yellow U-shaped *tilak*
mark, which denotes that he is a worshiper of Vishnu.[12] Bakhat Singh's presence
before the family deities, attended by the Brahmin establishment, links his relatively
recent temporal rule—he was given Nagaur in 1725—to a spiritual source and
confirms the grace and blessing inherent in his devotion to Krishna. CG

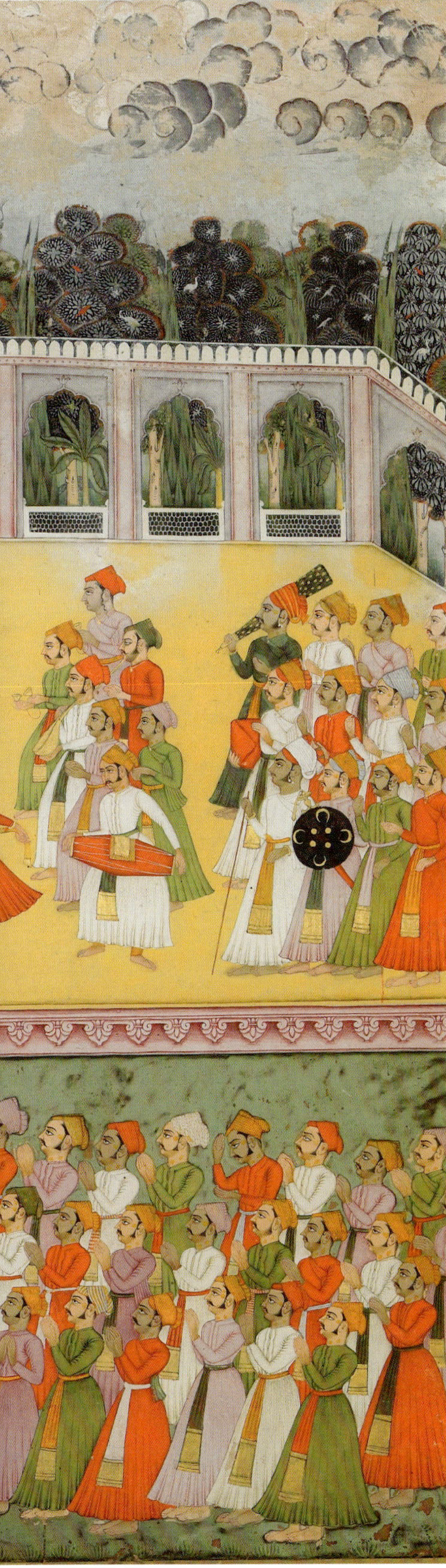

Musical Merriment for Maharaja Bakhat Singh
and Prince Vijai Singh
Attributed here to the "Nagaur Master"
Nagaur, ca. 1736; 43.5 x 61.3 cm
Mehrangarh Museum Trust

Rajrajeshvar maharajadhiraj maharaja sri bakhat singhji ri tasbir
Painting of the lord of king of kings, supreme king of great kings,
supreme king, glorious Bakhat Singhji

Maharaj kanvar sri vijai singh
Heir apparent Prince Vijai Singh

Dancers and musicians fill the central courtyard at Nagaur as the cooling clouds of a monsoon appear on the horizon.[13] Musicians were essential to court life; they provided regular entertainment, led processions on ceremonial occasions, and were responsible for the pageantry that accompanied the arrival and departure of the raja and his distinguished guests. Their musical messages could be heard throughout the palace; the music at the fort would tell all at Nagaur that a gala was in progress. Mughal paintings of outdoor dance performances on vast marble terraces date from the early eighteenth century, but they became particularly popular during the reign (1719–48) of Mughal Emperor Muhammad Shah (see fig. 19a, p. 273), and no doubt that kind of "zenana painting" was an inspiration for this work.[14]

Vijai Singh, Bakhat Singh's son and heir apparent, is presented to his father amid the pomp and merriment. Vijai, who appears to be about seven years old, sits facing the raja, but there is no sense of closeness between parent and child, partly because there is no direct eye contact; Bakhat Singh appears to be looking beyond his offspring. Based on the age of the young prince, the painting dates from around 1736.[15]

Standing near the two royal figures are women carrying Bakhat Singh's maces, staffs, and peacock-feather fans—symbols of his leadership, authority, and powerful position. At the left, another group of women brings plates of food and other treats.

A solitary woman sits in *purdah* at the right, behind a *chik* (screen) of painted bamboo slats. A single dancer performs, accompanied by female musicians and singers who provide the rhythm and tempo for her movements. In addition to the percussive beat of *talam* (cymbals) and the double-headed *pakhavaj* (barrel drum), the royal family listens to three musicians playing the melody on stringed instruments. The woman in white plays a *sarangi*, holding the bow in her lower hand. Behind her, dressed in green, is the player of a large stick zither, called a *bin* or *vina*, distinguished by two gourds at the top and bottom. In the middle of the crowd, a woman in orange holds a *tambura* (long-necked lute). Since this scene takes place in the zenana, no male musicians are present.[16] CG

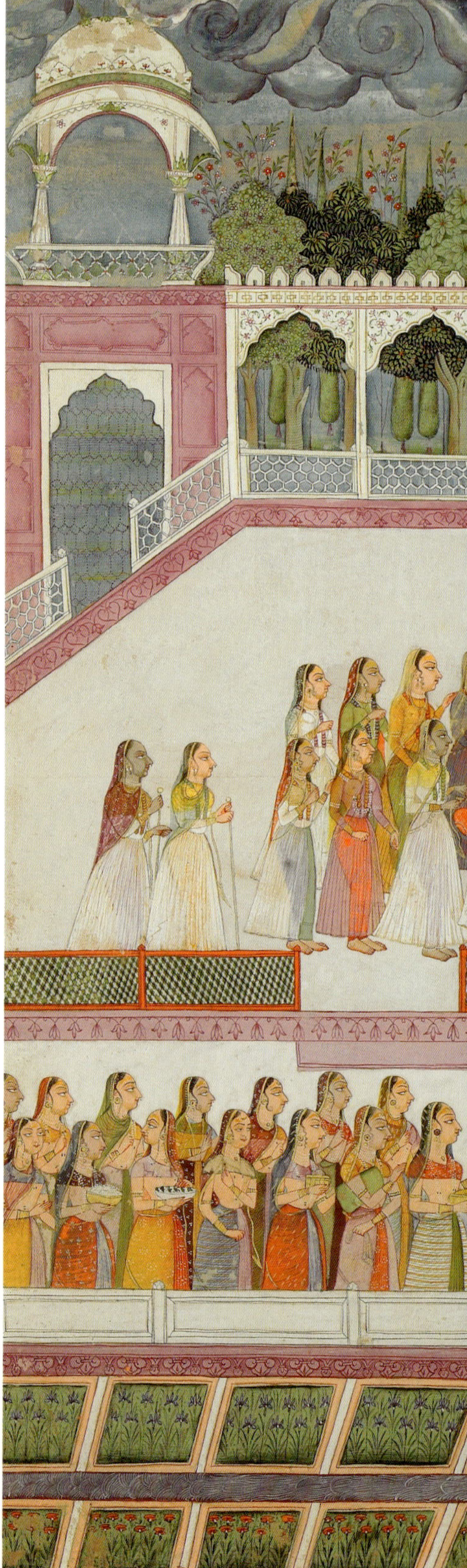

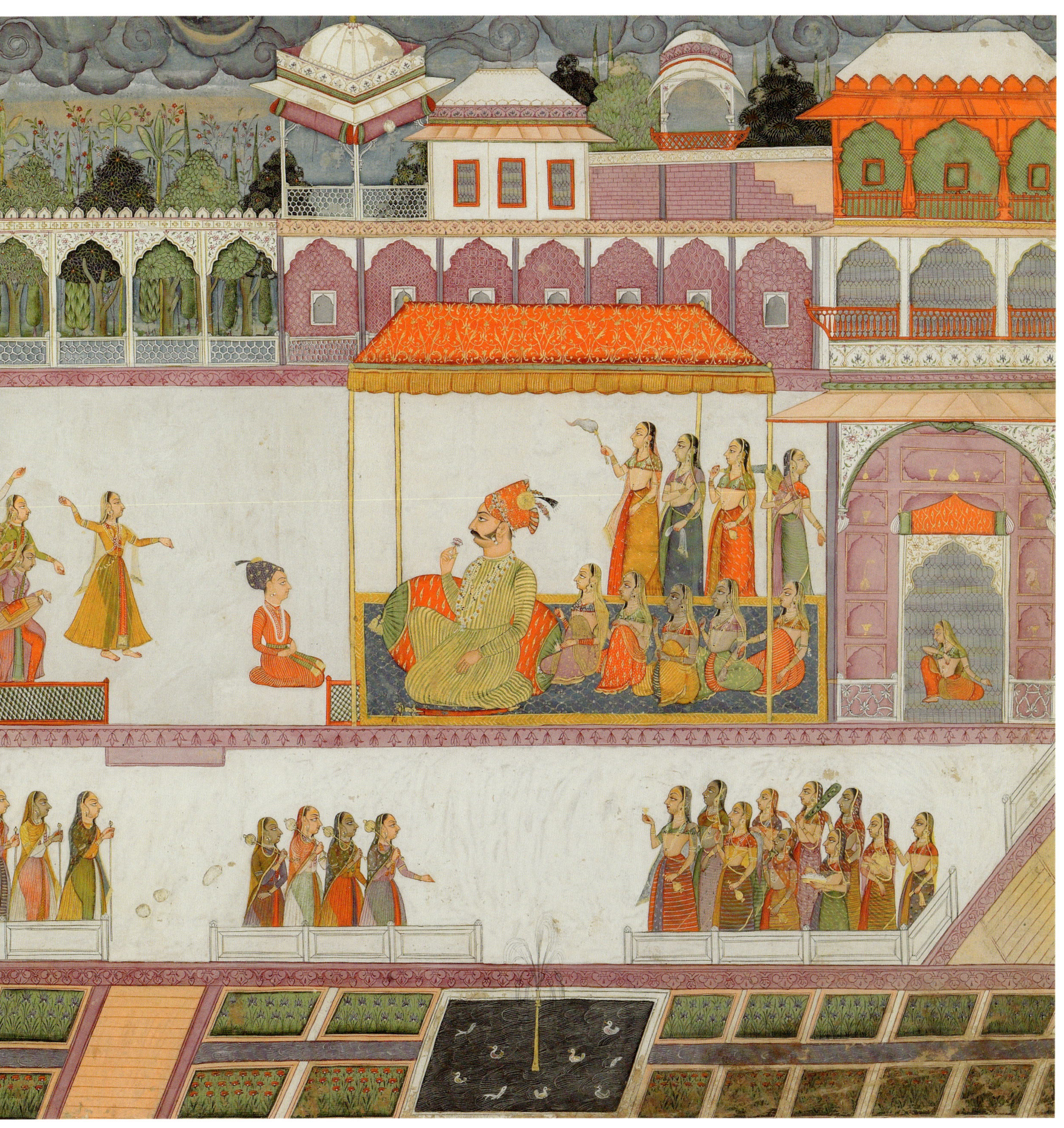

Maharaja Bakhat Singh Watches a Dance Performance
at the Bakhat Singh Mahal
Attributed here to "Artist 2"
Nagaur, ca. 1737; 44.5 x 63.8 cm
Mehrangarh Museum Trust

[numbered] 31
Rajrajeshvar maharajadhiraj maharaja sri bakhat singhji ri tasbir nagare thaka ri
Painting of the lord of king of kings, supreme king of great kings,
great king, glorious Bakhat Singhji when in Nagaur

Da[khal] dholiya re kothar hajri sam[vat] 1887 ra jeth main mandi
Entered in the *dholiya* storeroom and inventory in Jeth (May–June), 1830

Now in the middle of his reign as raja of Nagaur, Bakhat Singh holds a flower
to enhance his senses as he relaxes on a gold throne inlaid with stones or glass.
A slim young girl dressed in yellow moves her feet to the beat of cymbals and
a double-headed drum.

Storm clouds suspended over a grove of various types of trees, including
palms, cypress, and mango, threaten on the left. A lavish red cotton canopy,
decorated with golden flower sprigs that seem to glow, provides shade and
protection and has been carefully positioned to allow for any cooling breezes
that may be present. Whether used in awnings, carpets, or clothing worn by the
raja and his court, textiles brought visual splendor to the desert court of Nagaur.
Here, the large, red fabric—which has a green border to simulate the grassy
ground and a fluttering yellow fringe that might symbolize the sun's rays—
is not simply utilitarian, it is majestic.[17]

This is one of the many Nagaur paintings in which the textiles show the
significance of Gujarat. Positioned southwest of Marwar and bordering the Arabian
Sea, Gujarat was in a perfect location for maritime trade, exporting local manu-
factured items such as brassware, glass, swords, tobacco, sugar cane, and above
all, cotton and silk textiles.[18] After his brother Abhai Singh was appointed governor
of Gujarat by Emperor Muhammad Shah in June 1730, Bakhat Singh frequently
traveled with him to the region. Both brothers were part of the force that conquered
the region for the Mughals later that year.[19] Three years later, in early 1733, Bakaht
Singh was in Gujarat again, this time leading the Nagaur army to quell the advance
of the Marathas.[20]

Many of the paintings in this catalogue reveal Bakhat Singh's love of Gujarati
textiles. The cloth of his turbans in this painting and cats. 9, 16, 18, and 19
appears to be of Gujarati origin, as do the patterned *jamas* (over-garments) he
wears here and in cats. 15 and 17, and fig. 13b, p. 267. The *jama* fabric is probably
mashru, a combination of cotton on the inside and silk on the outside, an indicator
of luxury.[21] The prominent carpet in cat. 16 is a Gujarati adaptation of a Mughal
floral design; the tent depicted in cat. 13 has Gujarati embroidery work; the carpet
in cat. 22 also appears to be of Gujarati design. Of course, a magnificent example
of actual Gujarati textile design and workmanship is cat. 21, the large tent canopy.
The paintings illustrate the central role played by beautiful fabrics in the life of
the court. cg

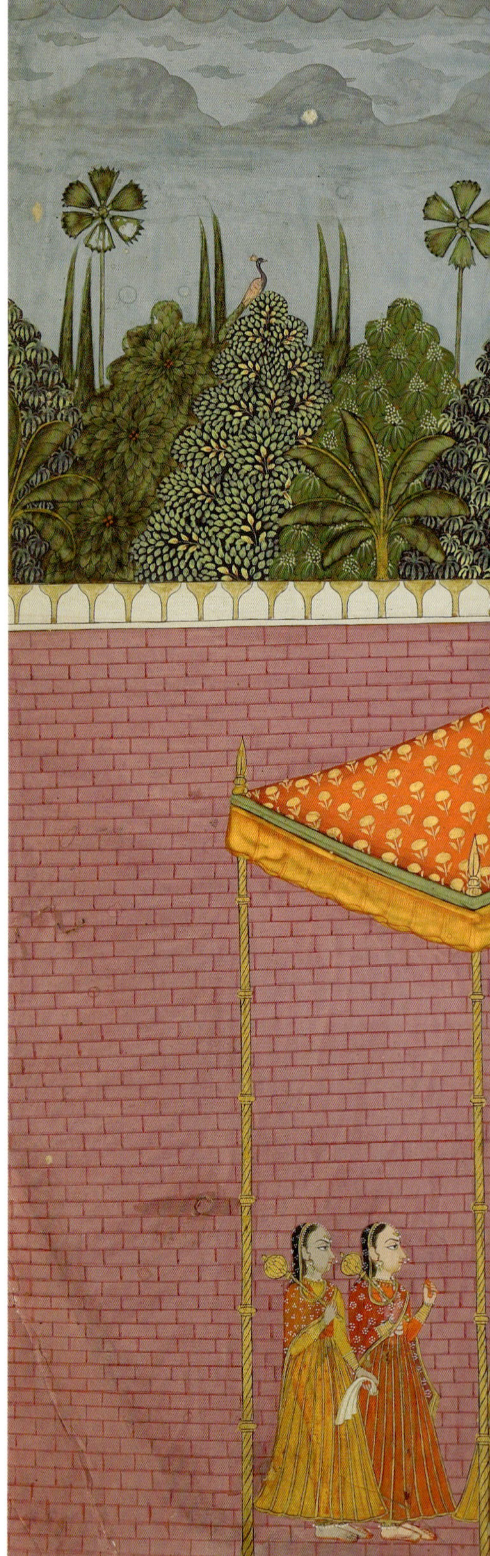

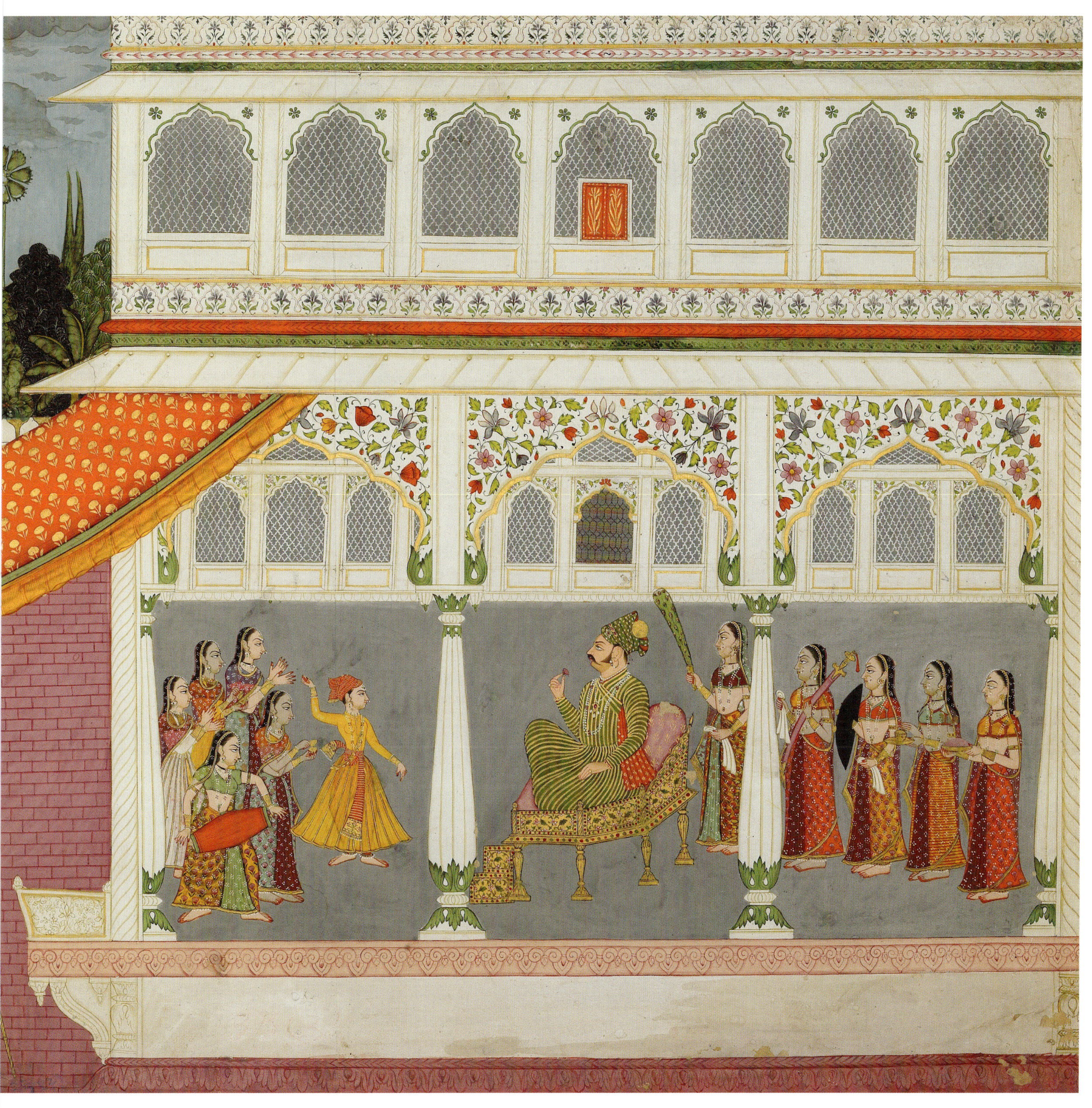

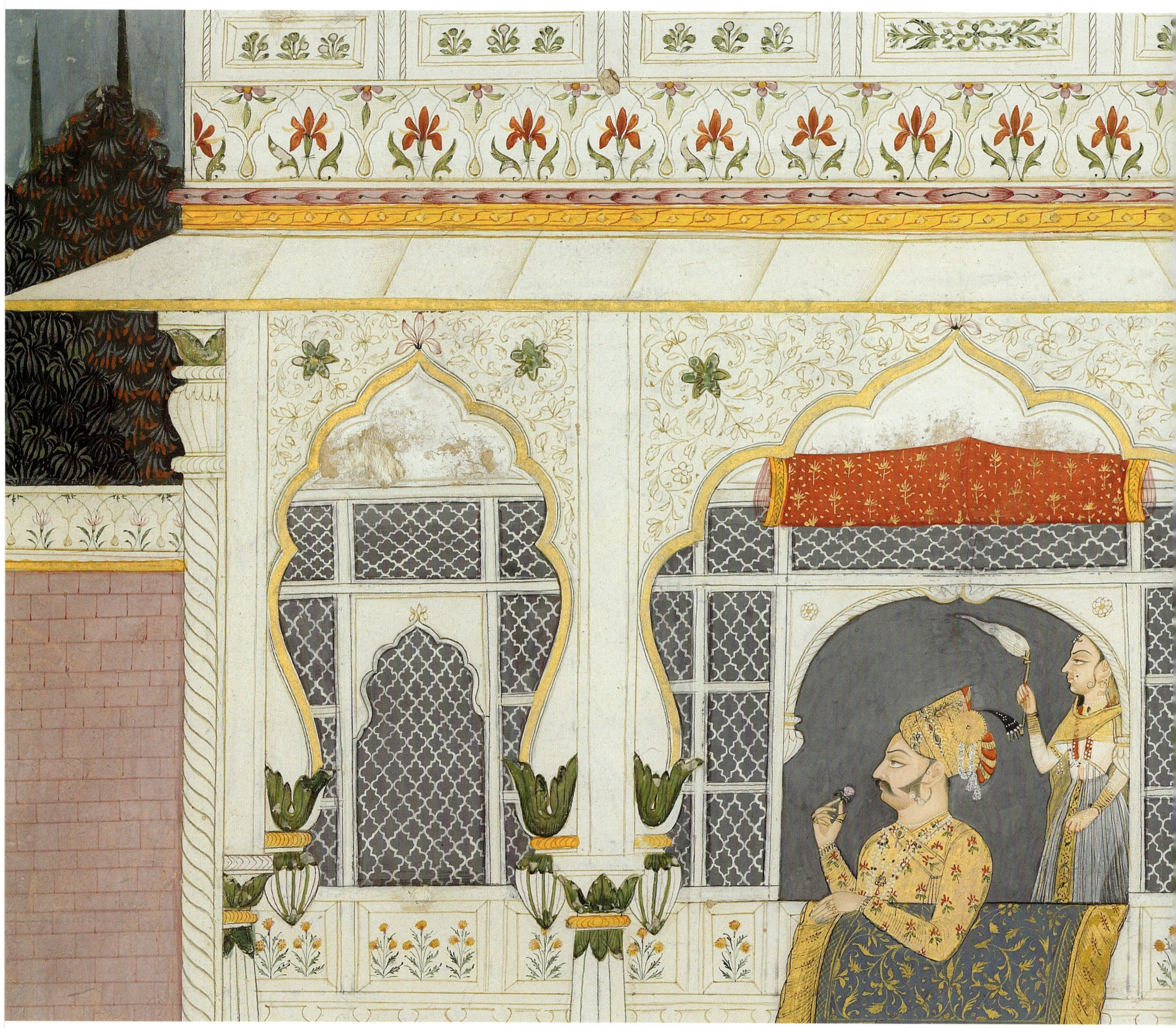

Cat. 15 Detail

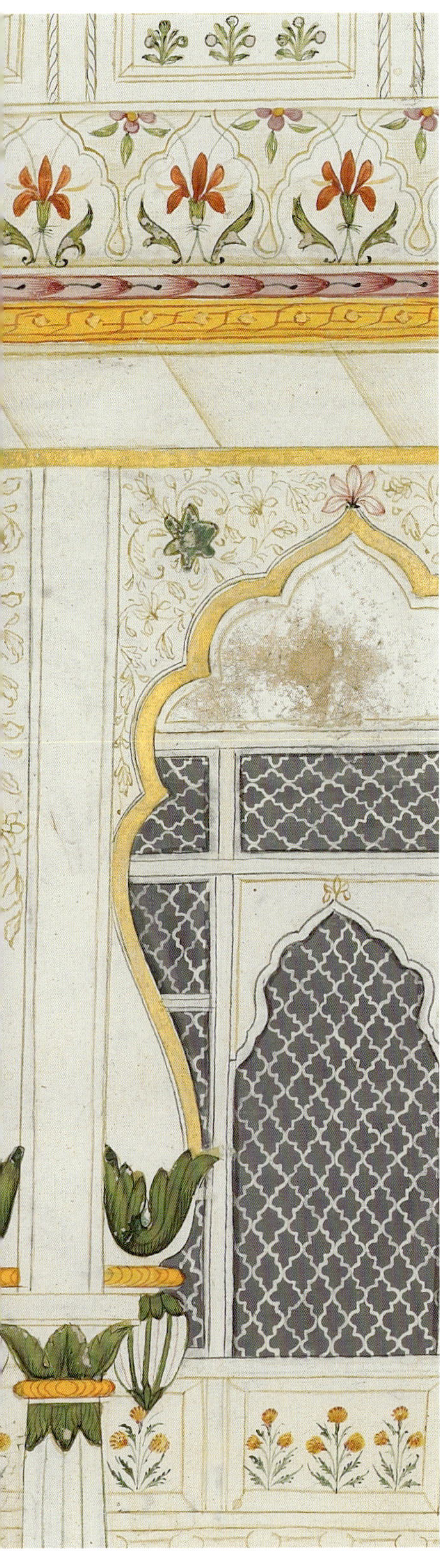

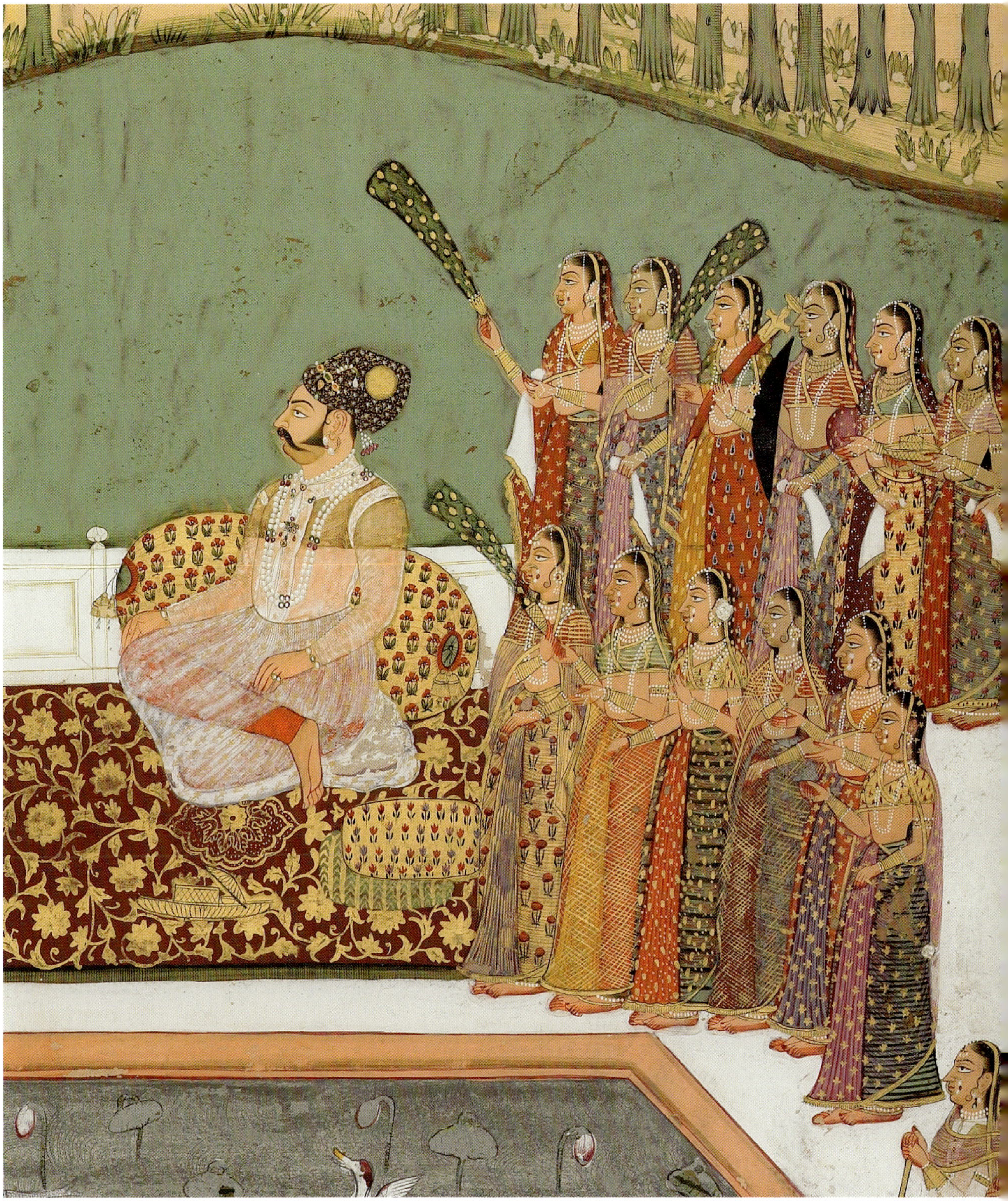

Cat. 16 Detail

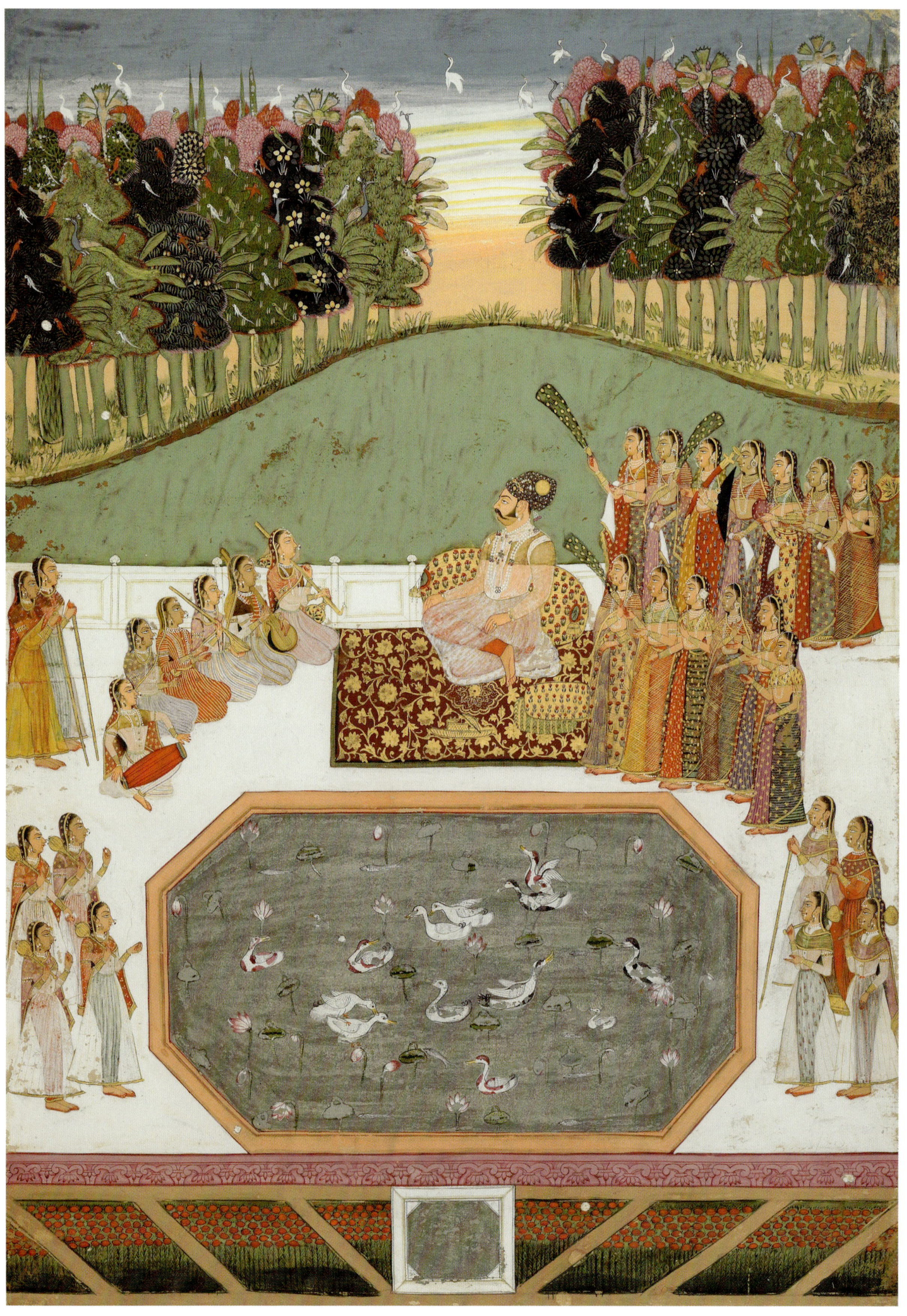

16

Maharaja Bakhat Singh Delights in an Outdoor Musical Performance

Attributed here to the "Nagaur Master"
Nagaur, 1737 (Samvat 1794); 52.1 x 42.5 cm
Mehrangarh Museum Trust

Sri rajadhiraj vakhat singhji ri sabi sammat 1794 ra vaisak
Portrait of glorious, king of great kings Bakhat Singhji;
the month of Vaishakh (April–May), 1737

Dakhal dholiya re kothar hajri sam(vat) 1885 ra savan sud 12
Entered in the *dholiya* storeroom and inventory in Shravan (July–August), 1828

Bakhat Singh and women from the zenana enjoy a musical performance as the sun sets and the cooler evening begins. The setting is probably a delightful, tranquil oasis near the Nagaur complex since any journey away from the fort would require a slow, bumpy ride via palanquins. The raja focuses on the six musicians with rapt attention.

Three pairs of birds in the large pool are mating, perhaps a suggestion that the celebration will conclude with a sexual encounter between the raja and one of the women. This unusual symbolism may indicate the anticipation of a pending conception or birth of a child, hopefully an heir. Fertility and fecundity are echoed here by two lines of flowering trees, almost touching across the grassy bed. The inscription on the reverse mentions the month of Vaishakh (April–May), a hot, dry month in India that may have prompted this excursion to a venue that was cooler than the enclosed palace. Pinned to Bakhat Singh's turban is a festive gold disk resembling those in cat. 8, in which the inscription mentions the Diwali holiday. The inclusion of the disk here suggests that this may be a festive occasion (see p. 85).

The well-tended plants in the border garden, the carefully constructed water pool, and the pathway formed by symmetrical lines of trees all demonstrate the raja's organization of nature.[28] Although this composition is relatively simple and restrained in comparison to other Bakhat Singh paintings in this catalogue, it is also one of the most elegant. This is in part because of its clarity, accessibility, and symmetry, and in part because of the beautiful multi-patterned textiles, which bring opulence and luxury to this lush setting.

The tranquility of the scene belies the external political upheaval of the times; in 1737, the Marathas "plundered the city of Merta in Jodhpur, took some tribute from Bakhat Singh of Nagor and then arrived in Ajmer."[29] Throughout the eighteenth century, Rajasthan lived in fear of the increasingly destructive and ruinous Maratha invaders from the south.

Studies of the similarities and differences among the paintings help identify the artists of certain works. This work is by the hand of the painter I call the "Nagaur Master," whose trademark motifs also appear in cats. 11, 12, 13, and 18: the wispy trees covered with creepers and birds, the orderly garden arrangement, bold textile patterns, large-proportioned figures, and the multiple shades of pink in the architectural elements.[30] CG

17

Maharaja Bakhat Singh Watches Elephants Wreaking Havoc

Nagaur, ca. 1740; 45.1 x 64.1 cm
Mehrangarh Museum Trust

Rajadhi[ra]j sri bakhat singhji nagare
King of great kings, glorious Bakhat Singhji of Nagaur

Dakhal dholiya re kothar hajri sam[vat] 1885 ra savan sud 12
Entered in the *dholiya* storeroom and inventory on the twelfth day
of the light half of Shravan (July–August), 1828

This highly emotional scene—showing the disorderly frenzy caused when two
elephants break away from their handlers—takes place in the expansive Diwan-i-Am
(public audience area) at Nagaur, located within the walls of the fort but outside
the main palace wall. A staged combat between valuable elephants—symbols of
sovereignty, power, and wealth—before nobles assembled below Bakhat Singh on
the *jharokha* platform has been interrupted, and the elephants now are wreaking
havoc in the crowd. In the melee, turbans have been lost, and men carrying lances
and Catherine wheels[31] scurry about; some flee for their own safety, others attempt
to control the massive beasts. Some have vaulted into nearby trees for shelter.[32]
One can almost feel the ground rumble as the panicked elephants thunder across
the expanse amid the high-pitched screaming and wailing of the handlers.

The Diwan-i-Am accommodated the maharaja's public functions: reviewing
the troops, elephant parades and combat, welcoming dignitaries and their retinues,
and other events that that took place outside the personal and private spaces
of the palace, located behind the wall that includes the *jharokha* platform.[33] Two
dodhidars (guards)—identifiable as eunuchs by their lack of facial hair—stand at
doors in the pink wall, guarding the stairway entrances to the private area. One
of their jobs was to restrict male access to the zenana. Hidden behind sixteen
windows lined with *chiks* (woven screens), thirty women observe the chaos taking
place below. The windows allow the women to be part of the event while they
observe *purdah*.

Gazing from each window is a light-skinned and a dark-skinned woman, a
pleasing visual pattern that conveys the diversity of Bakhat Singh's zenana. By
cutting the last window on either end in half, the artist makes clear that the viewer
is seeing only part of the palace wall. He also uses color to increase the sense
of the horizontal. The scene is divided into three obvious rectangles. Each section
has a dominant palette: blue and green at the top, pink in the middle, and earth
tones at the bottom.

White is the unifying element in each register; it forms a triangle, starting with
small shapes on the bottom and culminating in the symmetrical covered platform.
The artist's eye for color and geometric form is apparent: at the top, a large white
square encloses the raja. In the middle, a smaller triangle of attendants in white
breaks up the rectangle of the solid wall. Finally, in the midst of the melee at the
bottom of the painting, the smallest white shapes scatter in motion. CG

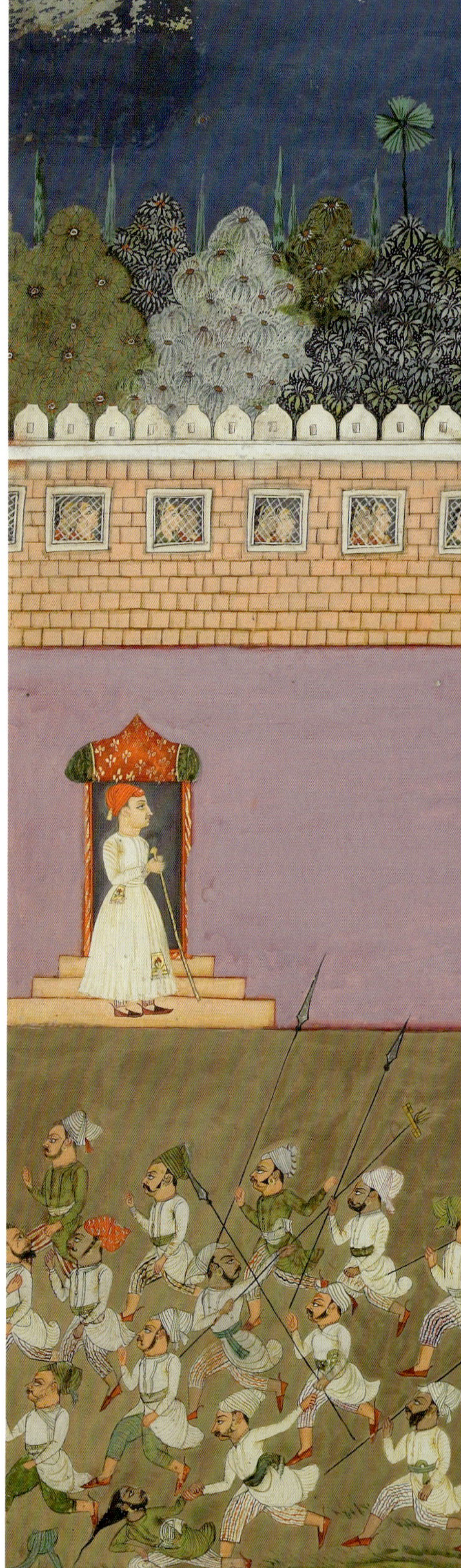

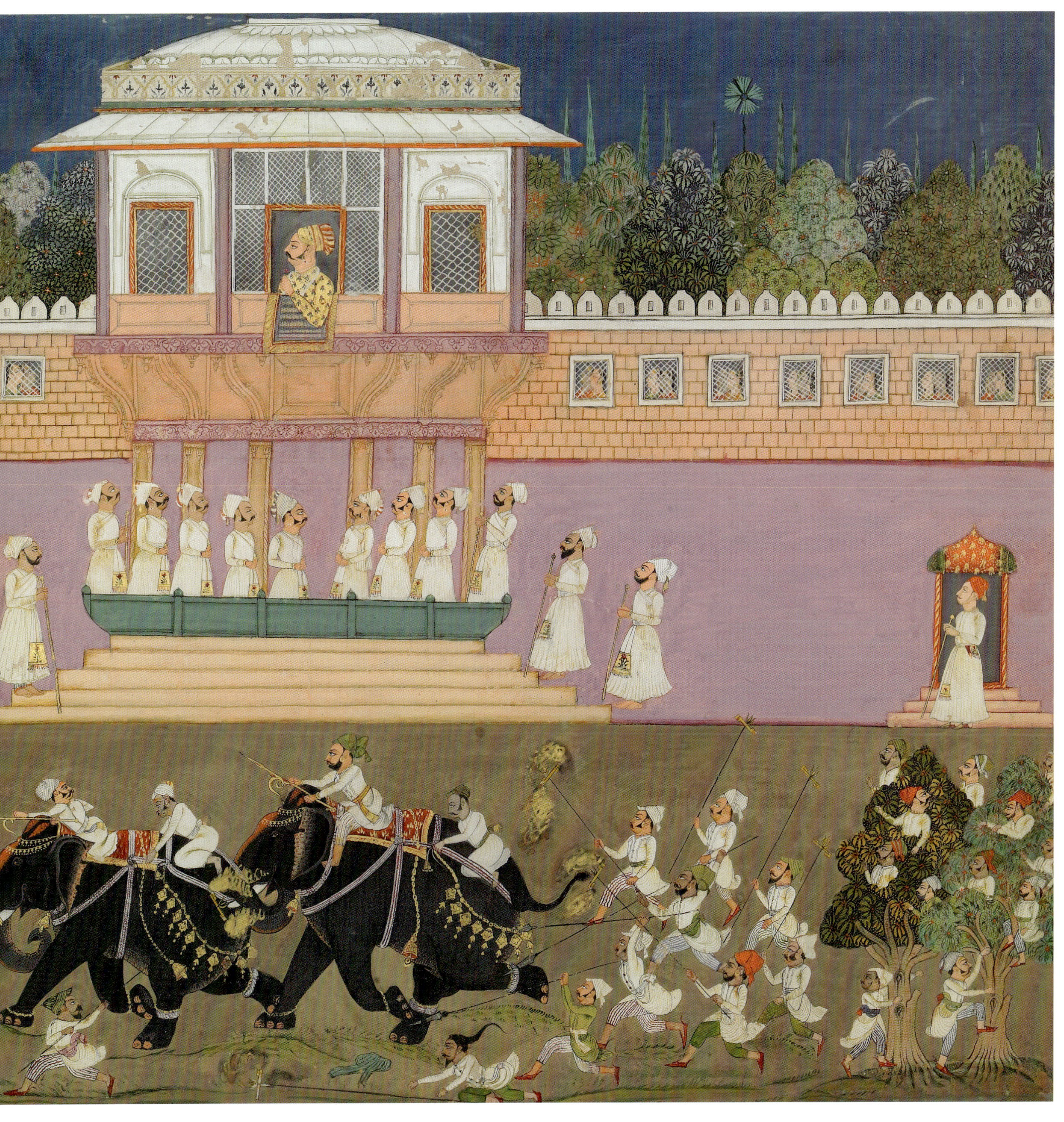

Royal Pastimes in the Gardens at Nagaur Palace

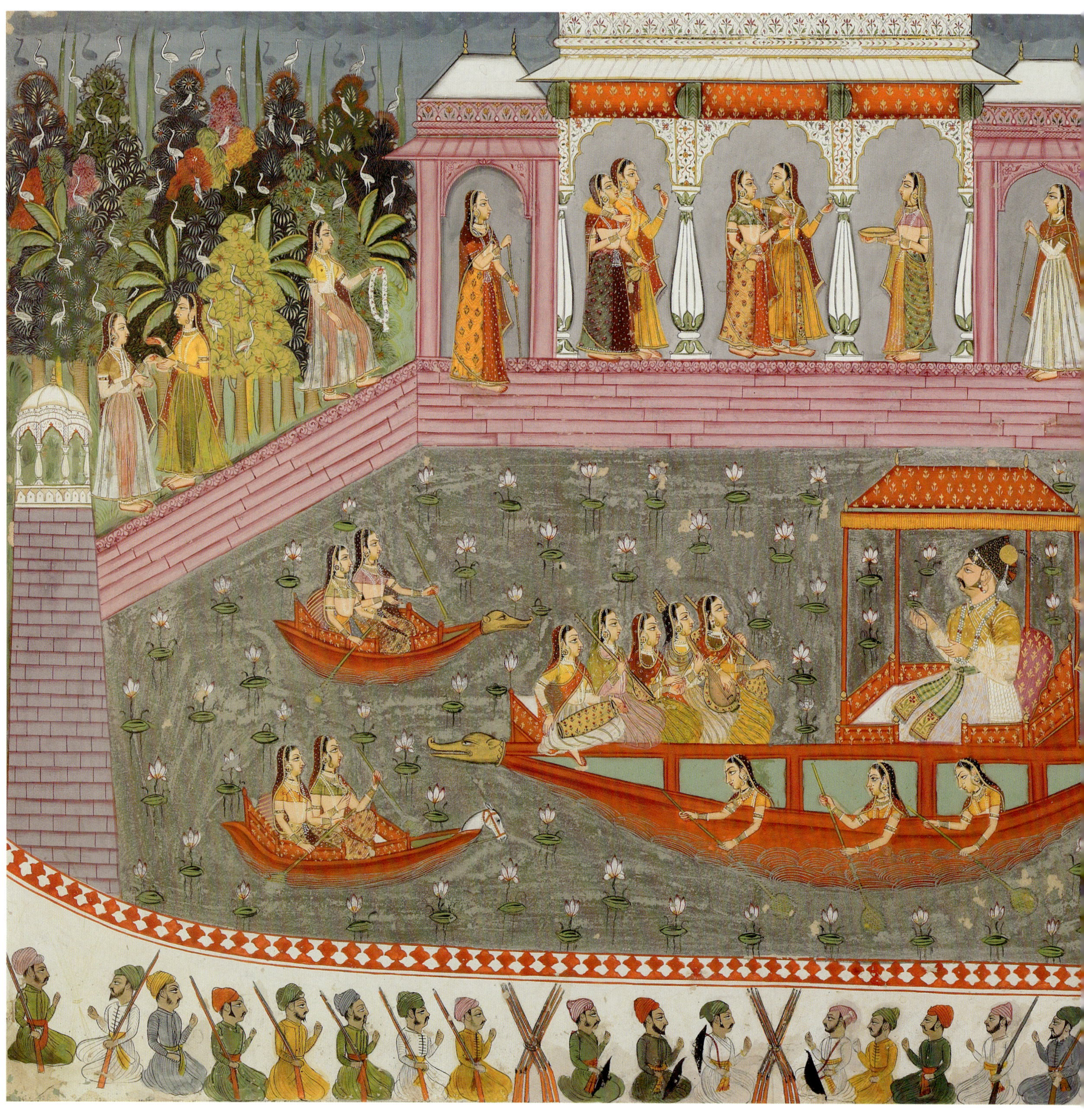

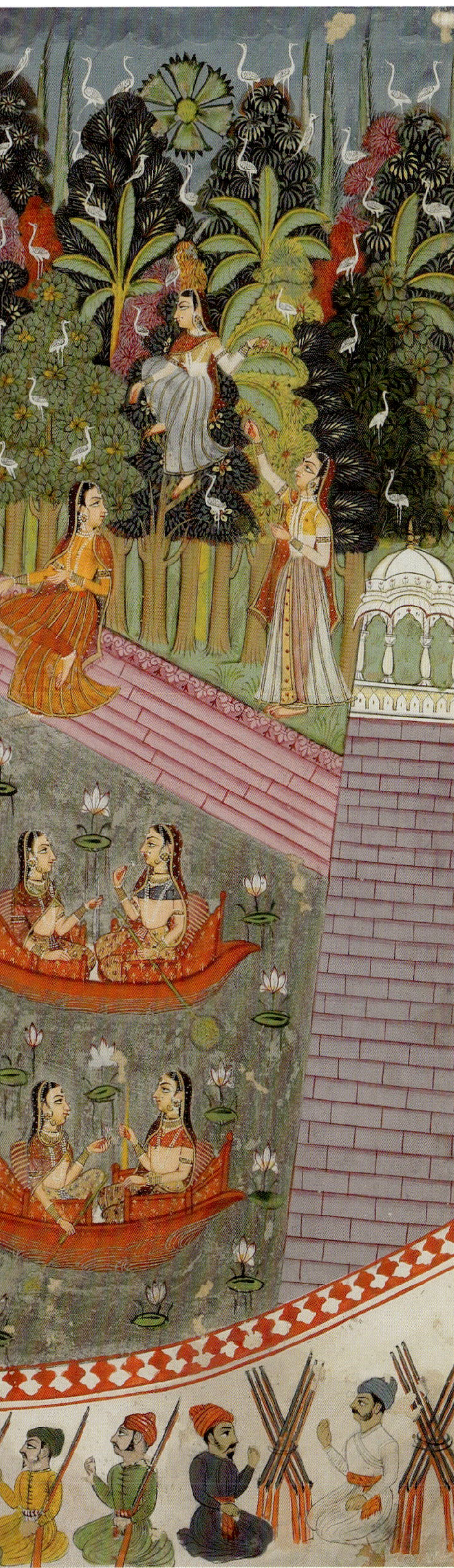

18

Maharaja Bakhat Singh Revels in a Pleasure Boat Ride

Attributed here to the "Nagaur Master"
Nagaur, ca. 1745–48; 43.2 x 61 cm (image)
Mehrangarh Museum Trust

Rajadhiraj sri vakhats Singhji
King of great kings, glorious Bakhat Singhji

Dakhal dholiya re kothar hajri sam[vat] 1885 ra savan sud 12
Entered in the *dholiya* storeroom and inventory on the twelfth day
of the light half of Shravan (July–August), 1828

Bakhat Singh and women of the zenana have ventured from the sultry enclosed area of the Nagaur fort and palace to the nearby countryside. The trees, birds, and, most refreshingly, the water in the enclosed tank provide a reprieve from Nagaur's ever-present heat. Historically, waterworks, water gardens, and structures such as this tank enabled alfresco pleasure in one of the driest regions of India.

During this period, Nagaur and, in fact, the entire state of Marwar suffered from a critical lack of precipitation: "In 1747 an unprecedented severe famine raged throughout Rajputana and western India. There was an utter failure of the seasonal rains; no crop could grow; the watercourses dried up; not a green blade could be seen anywhere; month after month a dusty haze covered the horizon and never a drop of rain or dew. The cattle perished for want of fodder and men from the dearth of grain. As a Maratha observer wrote, 'Men, it seems, cannot get even water for washing their faces.'"[34]

In contrast to this heartbreaking description, the painting suggests a very different environment: a vision of relief from the oppression of a sweltering day. The lush vegetation (see p. 92) and water tank large enough to accommodate numerous boats depict a paradise far different from the western desert region that surrounds the fort, where the water table is watched with rapt attention.

Four smaller boats filled with pairs of women and one larger vessel for the raja and the female musicians float on the lotus-filled water. Tin alloy has been used by the artist to give the water a silvery sheen. Each boat has a distinguishing and charming prow: two are horses, two are *makaras* (crocodiles), and one is an elephant. The "gondoliers" of the raja's vessel are women, since no men would have been allowed inside the carefully guarded enclosure. A white *qanat* (tent wall) provides privacy; soldiers, the only other men at the scene, rest outside, their rifles arranged in a decorative pattern of Xs.[35]

The tank is surrounded by a formidable wall, with a *jal mahal* (water palace) at one end for viewing the activities, and bastion towers on the sides—all designed to protect the miniature lake. There are a number of such tanks in the Nagaur area, at least three of which date to before Akbar's time: "During [Akbar's] ceremonial visit, he observed three water reservoirs in a state of dilapidation. Akbar ordered the reservoirs to be restored and cleaned up."[36] Those reservoirs are still serving the local population.[37]

The hand of the "Nagaur Master" is apparent in the treatment of the trees and birds, the pink architectural elements, and the large-headed female figures.[38] CG

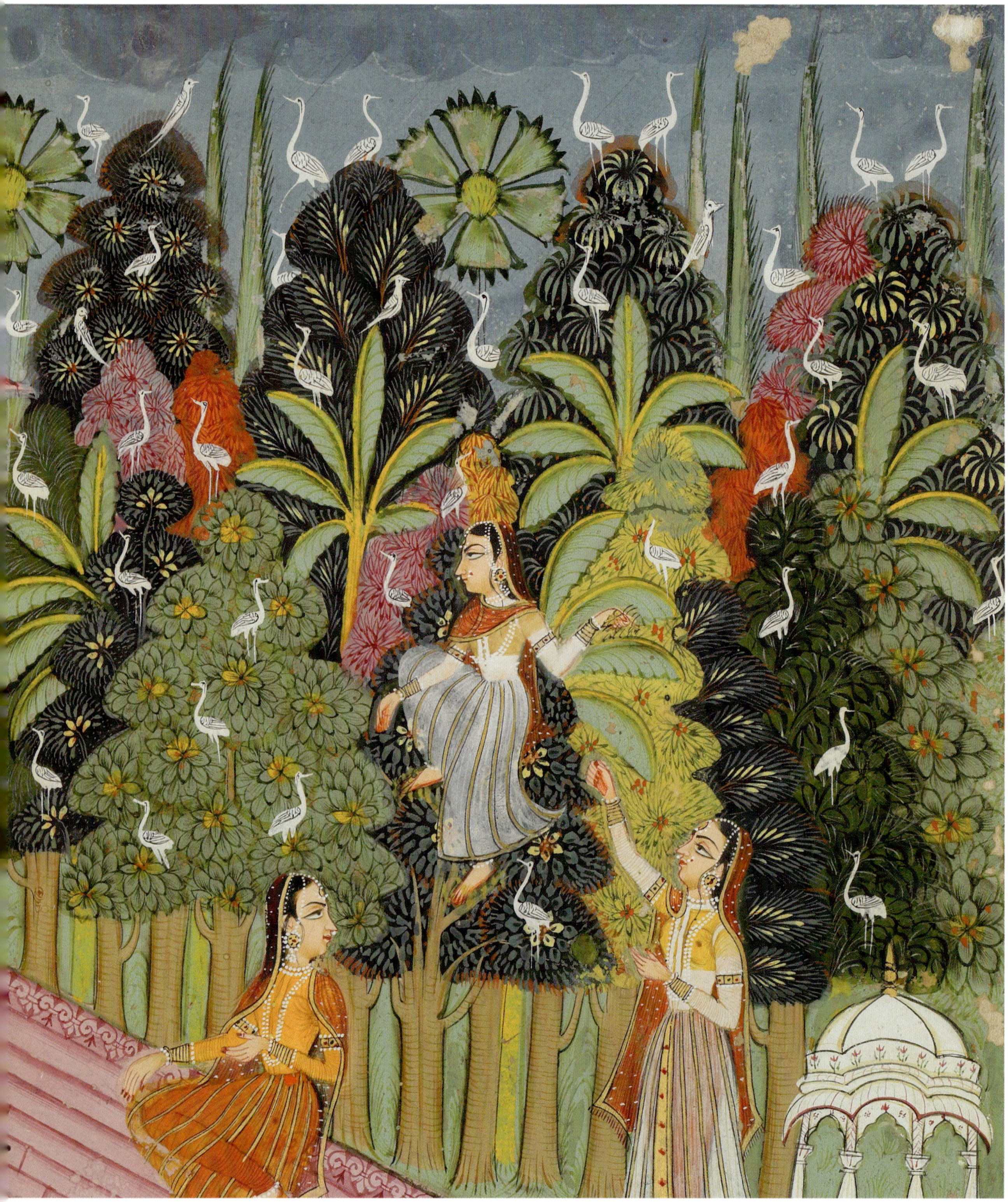

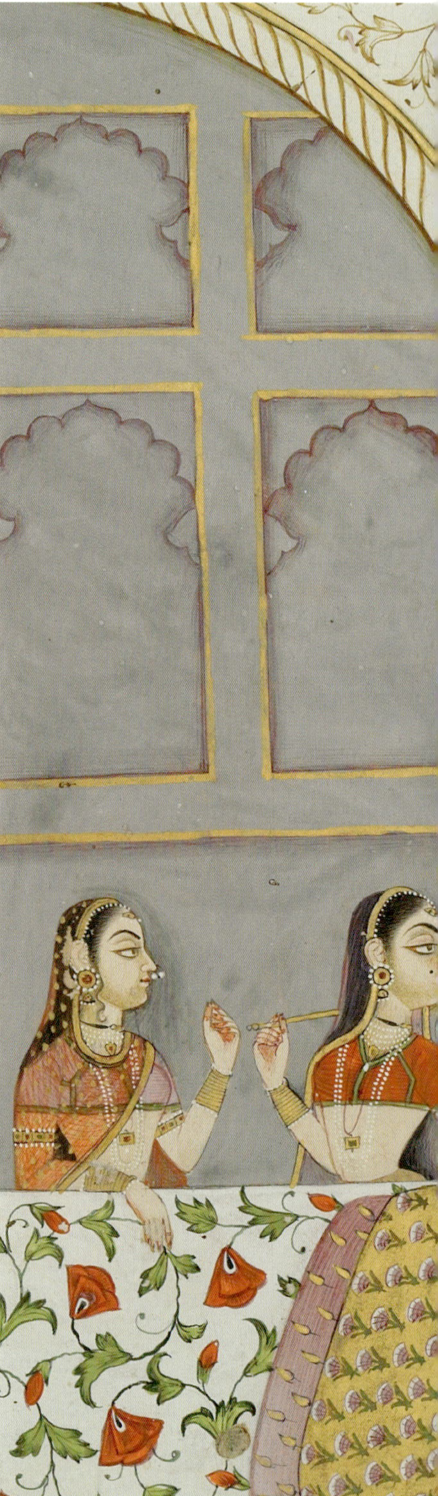

Cat. 18 Detail

Cat. 20 Detail

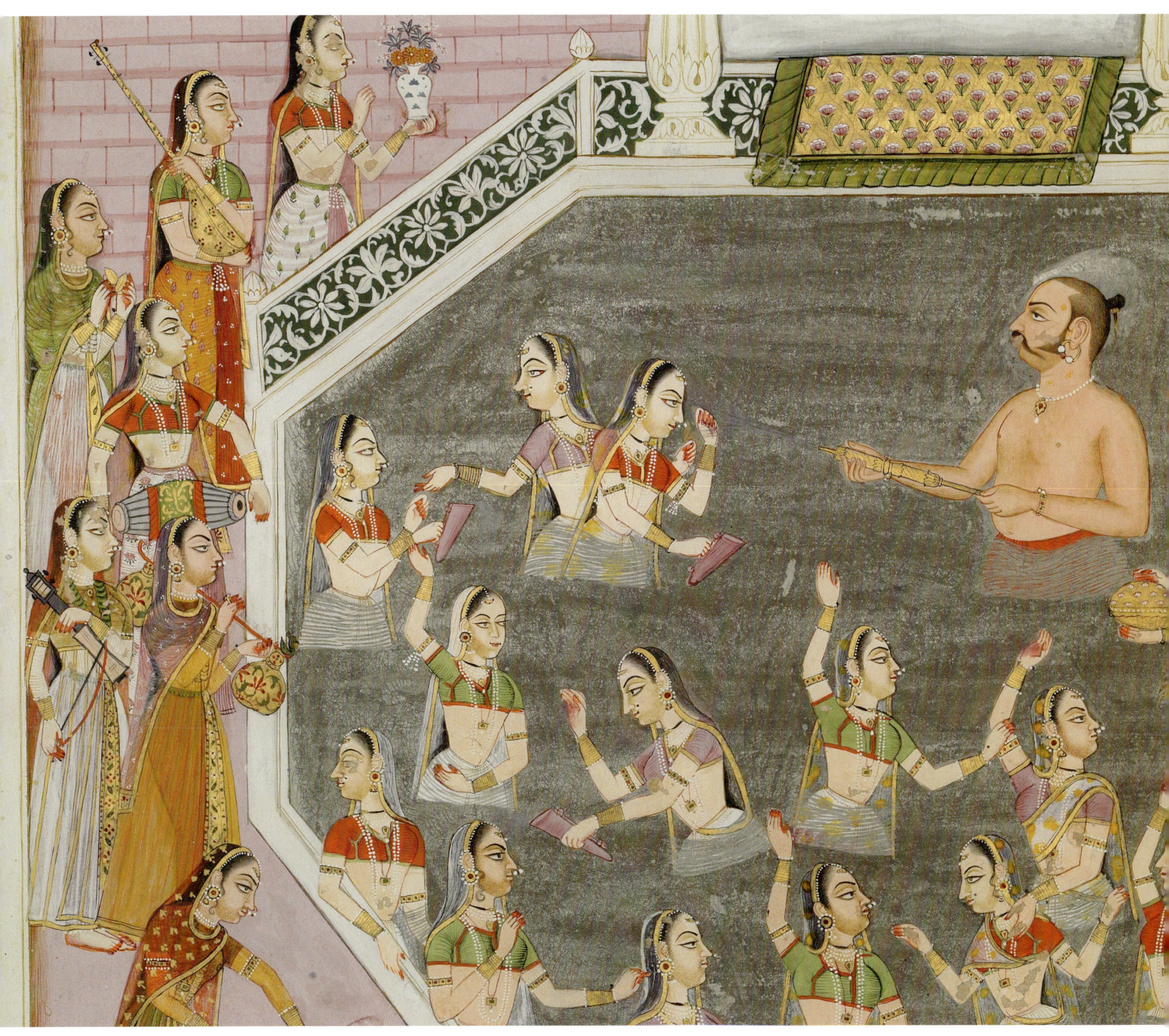

Royal Pastimes in the Gardens at Nagaur Palace

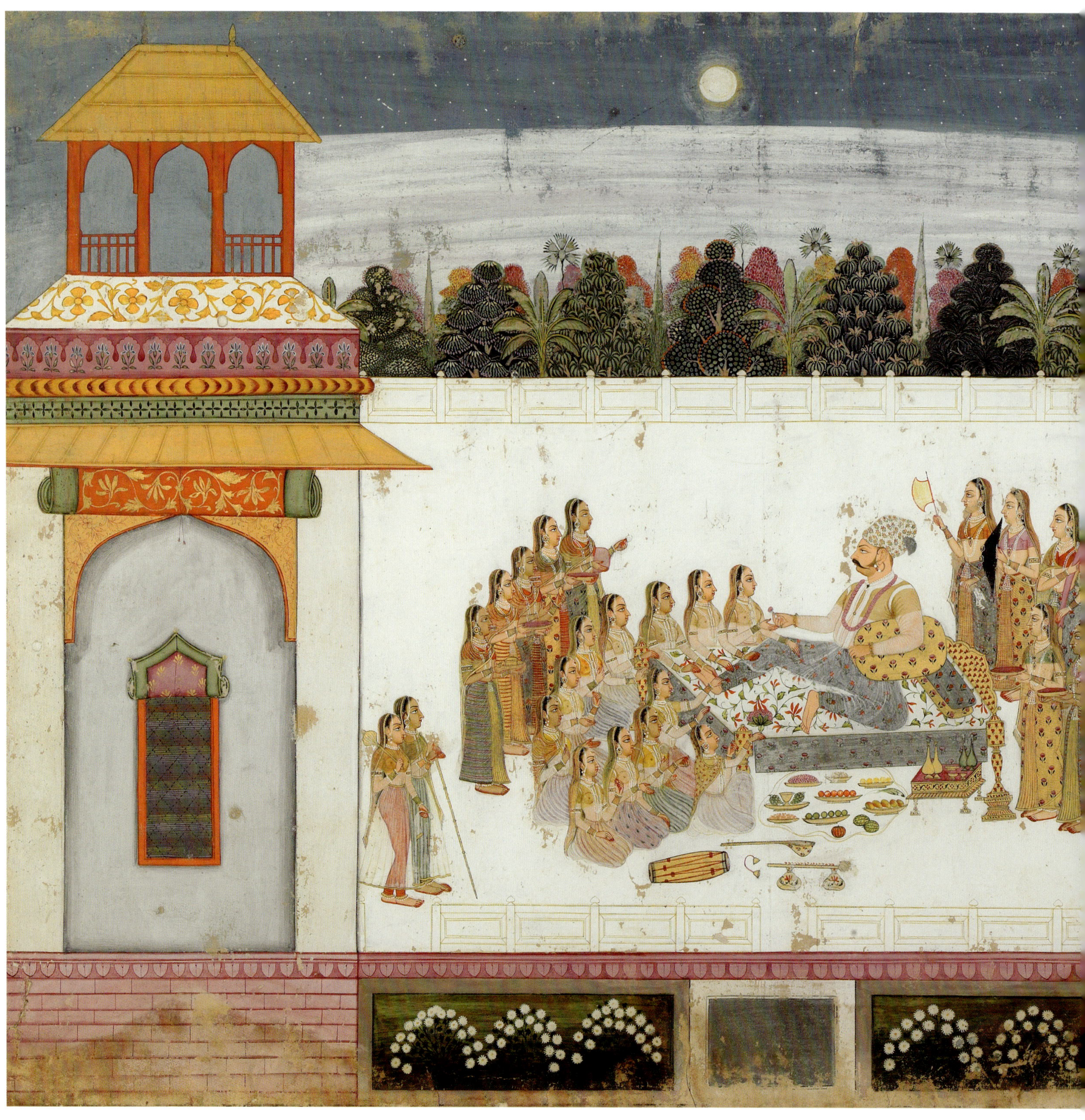

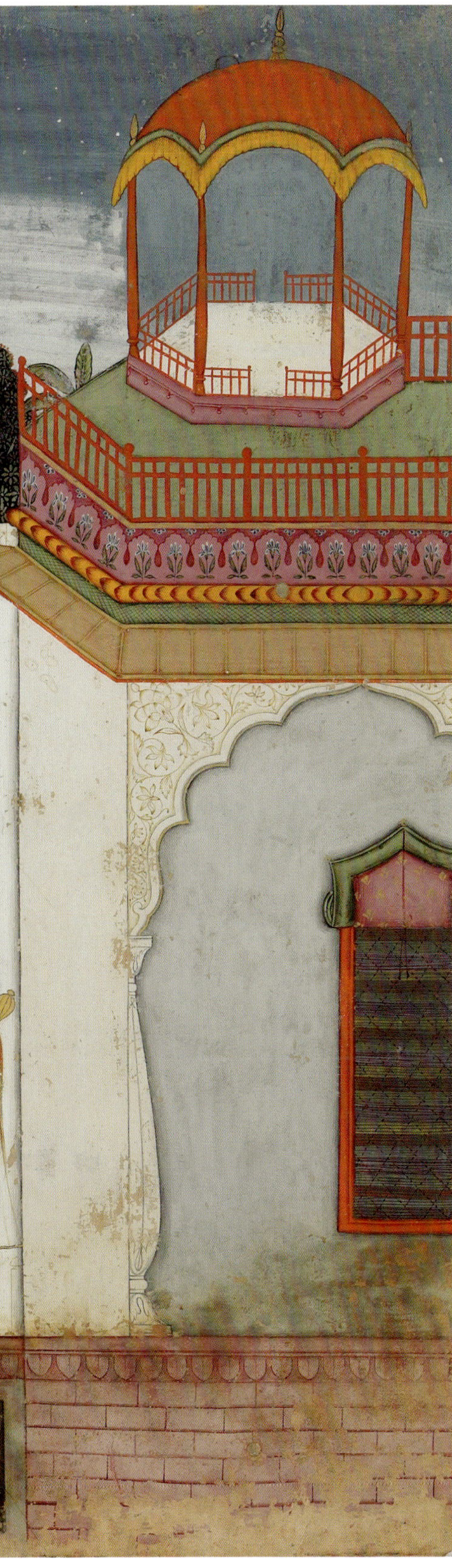

Maharaja Bakhat Singh and Zenana Women
Savor the Moonlight Evening

Attributed here to "Artist 3"
Nagaur, ca. 1748–50; 45.4 x 63.5 cm
Mehrangarh Museum Trust

Rajrajeshvar maharajadhiraj maharaja sri bakhat singhji ri tasbir
Painting of the lord of king of kings, supreme king of great kings,
supreme king, glorious Bakhat Singhji

Dakhal dholiya re kothar hajri sam[vat] 1885 ra savana sud 12 mandi
Entered in the *dholiya* storeroom and inventory in Shravan (July–August), 1828

As the full moon rises, Bakhat Singh sits on an open terrace, attended by several
women from the palace. Much of the life of both the Mughal and Rajput courts
took place primarily during the day, and was recorded in paintings of *darbars*,
hunts, battles, and animal sports such as staged elephant fights. Music and
dance performances, whether large-scale or intimate, generally were reserved
for the evening; nights were set aside for private pleasures. As one scholar has
noted, "moonlight gardens were a tradition enjoyed by the Indians before the
Mughals. After sheltering from the day's heat, they took their ease amid fragrant
white blossoms and flowering trees in the cooler night air"[39]—a perfect description
for this Nagaur evening.

Bakhat Singh had ruled for almost twenty-five years at this point; he clearly
is the focal point of the women who surround him, fanning him, bringing him food
and drink, and most intimately, massaging his feet. Although gardens could be
places for meditation and contemplation, here the context is sensual, even sexual.

The musical instruments—the *vina* with its two gourds, the stringed *tambura*,
cymbals, and drum—on the terrace suggest that a performance has just ended;
perhaps this scene represents an "intermission." Golden wine vessels, green glass
perfume bottles, and small drinking cups sit on an exquisite golden inlaid table.
Plates and bowls of fruits and other delicacies are on a white cloth in front of
the raja.

The parallel and balanced aspects of the painting show how the Nagaur
artists adopted selected Mughal artistic conventions that were transmitted
during the eighteenth-century by paintings from the reign of Mughal Emperor
Muhammmad Shah (1719–48). In this Nagaur painting, the balanced composition
prized by the Mughals is emphasized by two parallel pavilions—each with a fabric-
covered window and crowned with a *chatri* (viewing tower)—and two pairs of
women standing on either side of the terrace, holding royal symbols.

Both this work and cat. 20 have similar architectural arrangements, decorative
motifs, trees, and flowers. For these reasons, I believe the same artist painted
both works. I call him "Artist 3." CG

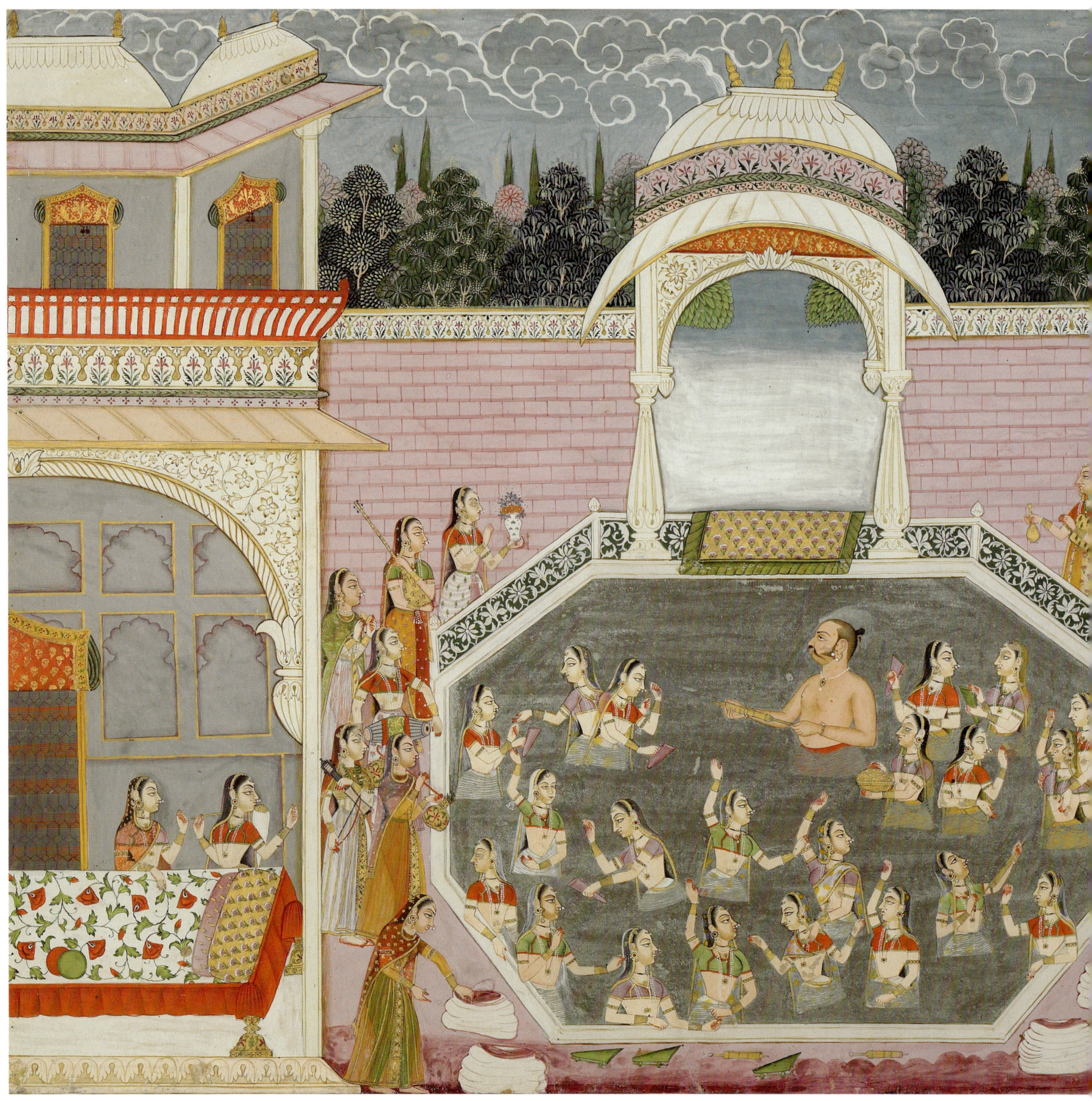

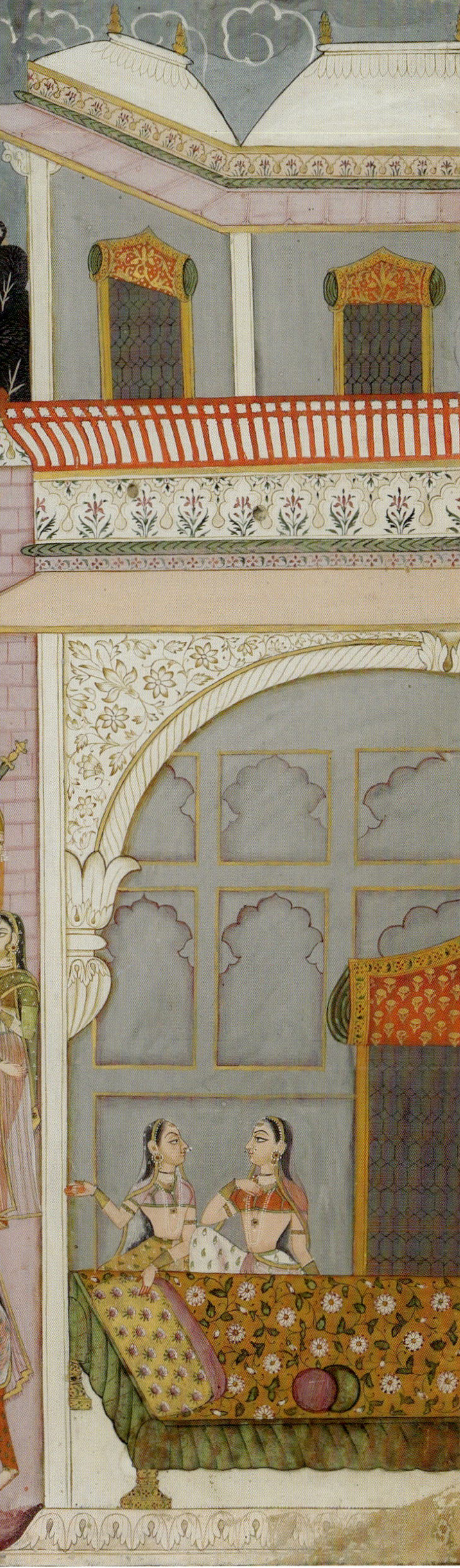

Maharaja Bakhat Singh Rejoices during Holi

Attributed here to "Artist 3"
Nagaur, ca. 1748–50; 44.1 x 65.1 cm
Mehrangarh Museum Trust

Rajrajeshvar maharajadhiraj maharaja sri vakhat singhji ri tasbir
Painting of the lord of king of kings, supreme king, glorious Bakhat Singhji

Da[khal] dholiya re kothar hajri sam[vat] 1885 ra savan sud 12
Entered in the *dholiya* storeroom and inventory in the month of Shravan
(July–August), 1828

The Hindu festival of Holi, the joyful celebration that welcomes spring, takes place during the full moon in the Hindu month of Phalgun (February–March).[40] The watery celebration is a prelude to sexual activity, attested to by the bedchambers on either side of the pool.[41] The conclusion of the celebration—when one is cleansed and is in close physical contact with members of the opposite sex—is an optimal time for arousal and gratification.

Of all the paintings in the Bakhat Singh group, this one has the most explicit erotic overtones. The women frolicking in the octagonal pool are fully clothed, while the raja is bare-chested and without his turban, although he has not abandoned his pearl earrings, pearl necklace, and precious stone-filled gold bracelet (see p. 93). His close-cropped hair is tied in a *choti* (ponytail).

Cat. 11 also depicts this jubilant event, but cat. 20 is more restrained and uses shades of pink rather than yellow and orange. As in other Nagaur court paintings, Bakhat Singh is at the center, once again surrounded by several women who attend to his sense of frivolity. The buckets of scarlet-colored water tell us that Holi is being celebrated. As part of the festivities, participants throw the colored water at one another or spray the water through *pichkaris* (syringes), all of which enhance the sense of merriment and abandon. In the painting, clean green funnels used for scooping up the water are scattered about; the women in the water hold similar funnels that already have been used to splash the red liquid.

Various women hold the raja's sword and shield (right), offer him a gold perfume bottle (top), and entertain him (left) with rhythmic hand clapping and musical instruments, including a long-necked plucked lute, cymbals, double-headed barrel drum, fiddle, and stringed *vina*. An interesting international reference is the graceful blue-and-white vase held by the woman above the musicians, which may be of Dutch or Chinese origin. Another example of a blue-and-white ceramic piece, probably Chinese because of its shape, can be seen in cat. 10. CG

GARDENS FOR DIVINE PLAY

During the reign of Maharaja Vijai Singh (1752–93), the Jodhpur atelier created the unique format of the monumental manuscript, with folios that are full-page paintings measuring approximately 135 cm in width. Depicting the narratives of the Hindu deities Krishna, Rama, and Durga, the manuscripts express the maharaja's ardent religiosity as well as his engagement with the Rajput cultural forms and Vaishnava devotional movements that became increasingly important across Rajasthan in the second half of the eighteenth century.

Whether sensuously lush, charmingly magical, or celestial, the folios exhibit fresh compositional strategies for well-known pictorial cycles. Early works, which transform Bakhat Singh's palaces into heavenly realms, reveal the continued salience of the Nagaur idiom. By the 1770s, stylistic diversity and an increased volume of production were demonstrating the atelier's expansion and the vitality of Jodhpur painting under Vijai Singh.

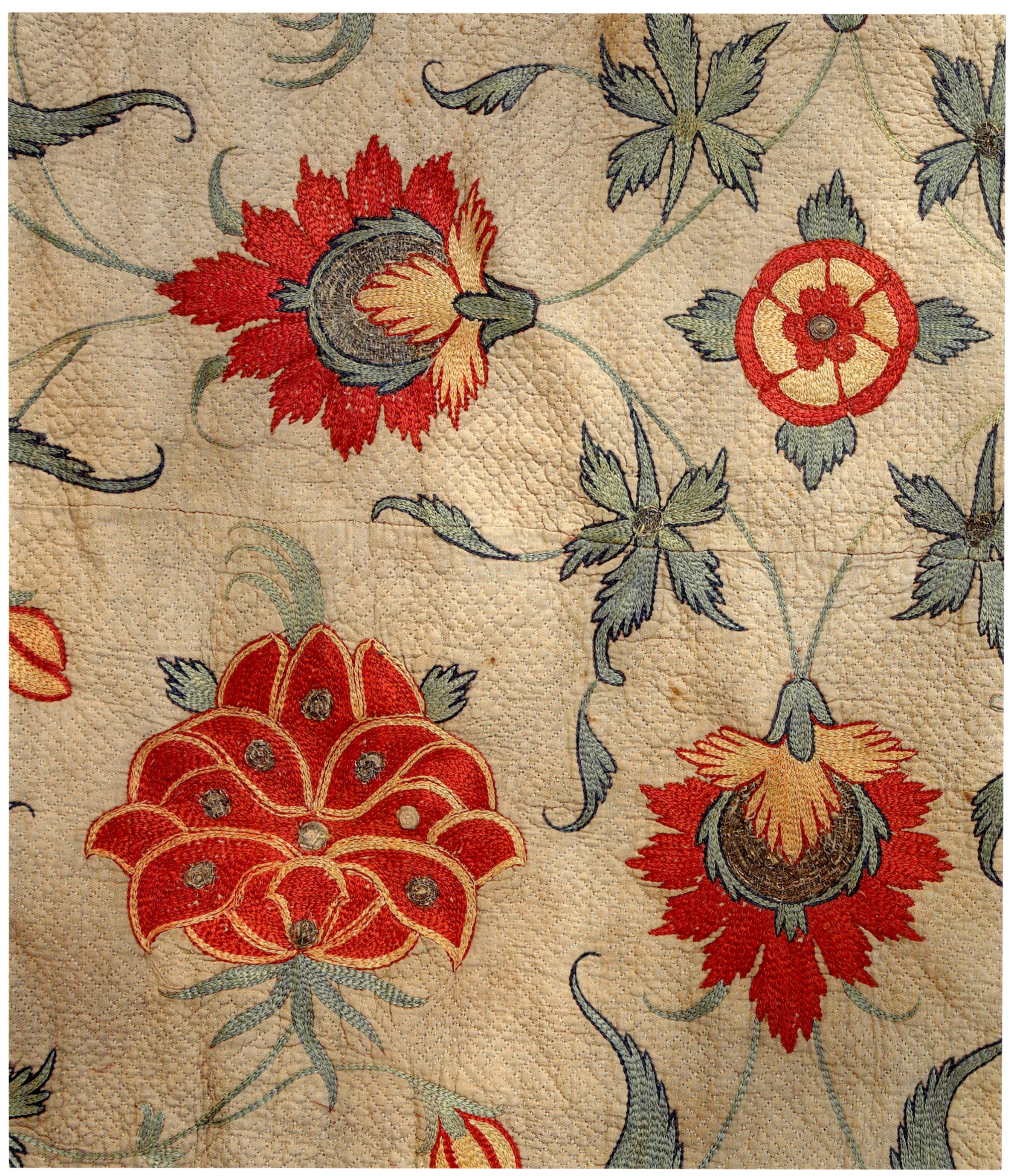

Embroidered Canopy

Gujarat or north India, first quarter of the 18th century
364 x 352 cm (central rectangular panel), 364 x 112 cm (triangular side panels)
Mehrangarh Museum Trust

This embroidered *chatbandi* (canopy) belongs to an important group of late Mughal tents at Mehrangarh Fort. It was constructed from a large, rectangular, central panel attached at both ends to triangular gusset panels, creating an inverted boat-shaped ceiling. It would have been raised above a rectangular enclosure made from similarly embroidered *qanats* (tent wall panels), part of a much larger, more elaborate network of tented rooms in a royal encampment.

Cloth architecture was among the most dramatic and colorful paraphernalia of royal life and material culture in medieval India. Vast tented encampments accompanied the region's rulers and chiefs on their wars, vacations, and pilgrimages. Far more time was spent on those travels than in residence at the royal capitals and citadels. During those long periods, portable, often highly decorative palaces of cloth afforded royal entourages shelter, comfort, and beauty. Precious carpets, colorful chintzes, rich embroideries, brocades, and velvets gave encampments the magic and splendor of imperial residences. In the hot climate of upper India, cloth awnings, partitions, canopies, curtains, and hangings sheltered and extended royal residences and audience halls, courtyards and gardens, mosques and tombs, bazaars and *sarais*. Together with the use of flowing water, this soft architecture offered a viable and attractive means of tempering the micro-climate. It released large private and public spaces for perennial occupation and enjoyment.

The Mehrangarh tents represent one of the world's largest assemblages of late Mughal furnishings.[1] The tents surive only as incomplete ensembles, with miscellaneous tent walls, floorspreads, and canopies related to each other by their generic design, material, and technique. Many were stitched from panels of sturdy white or undyed cotton, wadded with several layers of cotton fiber and fabric, usually quilted in a simple geometric pattern. They were embroidered in a chain stitch with late Mughal flowers, vines, and arabesques in colored silk thread.

This canopy is exceptional for its scrolling rows of fantastic blossoms and palmettes, reminiscent of the exuberant dye-painted chintzes of the Coromandel coast of southern India.[2] Most of the other Mehrangarh tents show an attenuated style of floral pattern that loosely imitates *pietra dura* decoration on seventeenth-century Mughal buildings in northern India. Room furnishings decorated with similarly delicate floral patterns against white or gold backgrounds appear in Mughal and Rajput painting from the first half of the eighteenth century.[3] Cat. 20, for example, features a large bedcover with an elegant scrolling pattern of red poppies on a white background; cats. 19, 20, 22, and fig. 1, p. 23 also depict similar textiles. RJ

Vishnu and Lakshmi in Their Heavenly Palace

Attributed to the "Nagaur Master" or a close follower
Nagaur or Jodhpur, ca. 1755–60; 44.5 x 62.2 (image)
Mehrangarh Museum Trust

Numbered 91 on verso.

This light-infused courtyard is the artist's interpretation of Vaikuntha, the celestial abode of the Hindu god Vishnu and his companion, Lakshmi. The artist uses one of the colonnade arches to frame the holy couple as they sit on a golden throne, covered by a golden umbrella that signifies their divine status. While they are positioned off center, they are clearly the focus of the painting.[4] The atmosphere of this heavenly court—with gardens, buildings, and background trees almost paralleling the architectural elements at Nagaur itself—is one of a joyous celebration.

Painted during the early reign of Vijai Singh, this work is remarkably similar to a painting from Nagaur (cat. 13) produced some two decades earlier, under the patronage of Bakhat Singh. Both paintings feature comparable architectural details[5] and a geometrically groomed and partitioned garden at the bottom, with a fountain as the element that leads the viewer's eye to the activity in the middle of the composition—here, a large carpet medallion in front of Vishnu and Lakshmi, and in cat. 13, Bakhat Singh himself. Clearly, at least one of the artists working under Vijai Singh adopted the style of the atelier of Bakhat Singh.

Either the "Nagaur Master," or a very close follower, painted this work. Not only are the compositional elements here related to cat. 13, but the facial features of the women correlate closely with the female holi participants in cat. 11, and the garments of the women in both paintings are extremely similar, if not identical. The background trees and birds mimic the "Nagaur Master's" signature vision of nature, as seen in cats. 11–13, 16, and 18.

On the right, female attendants offer food and other delicacies on gold trays, while a single female dancer moves to the rhythm of the music played by female musicians on the left. The entertainment recalls the Bakhat Singh zenana paintings, in which the raja is the only male among the women of the palace. The difference is that, here, Vishnu and Lakshmi take the place of the raja.[6]

The substantial white-ground floor spread with its intricate floral patterns is the dominant visual feature, occupying almost half of the painting's surface. Red and orange poppies on green vines flow outward from the central pink-flowered cartouche, simulating the sense of being seated within a field of flowers. There are marked similarities between this particular floral design, those used in a portrait of Vijai Singh completed shortly after his accession in 1752 (fig. 1 on p. 23), the textile designs in cats. 19 and 20,[7] and a silk embroidered tent in the Mehrangarh collection (see cat. 21). CG

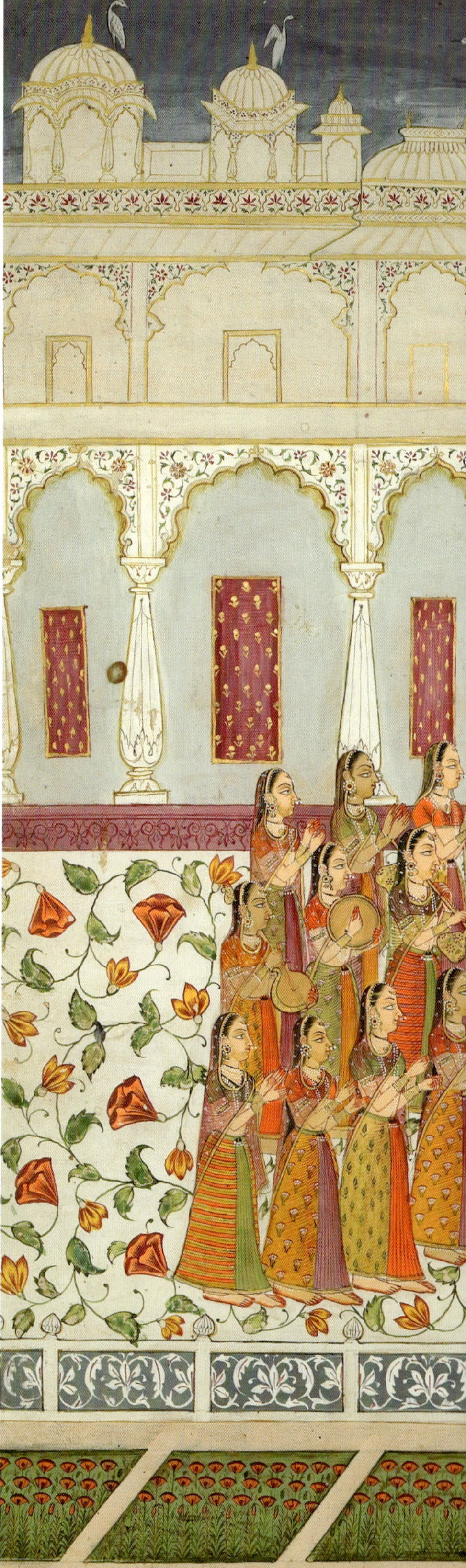

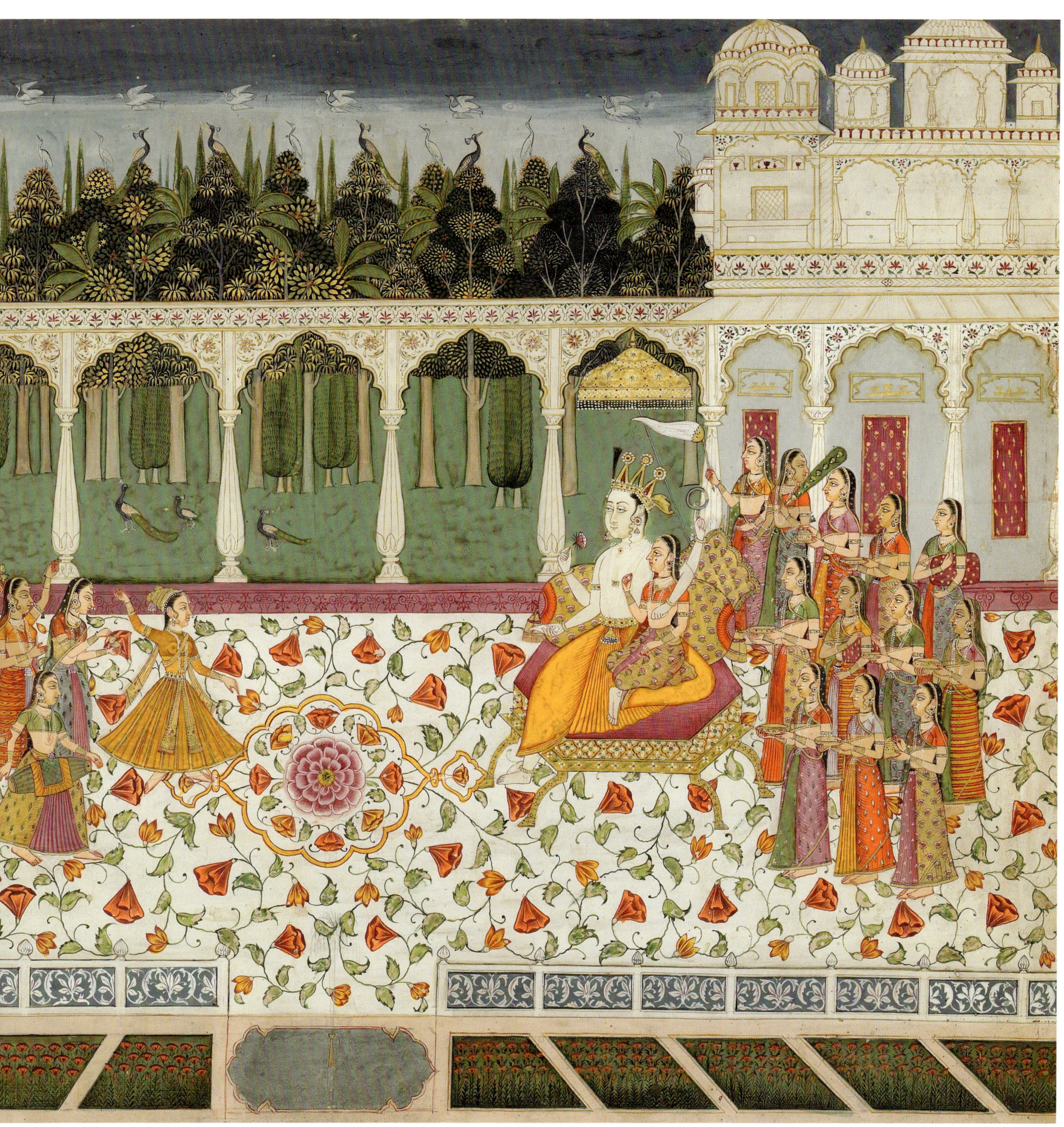

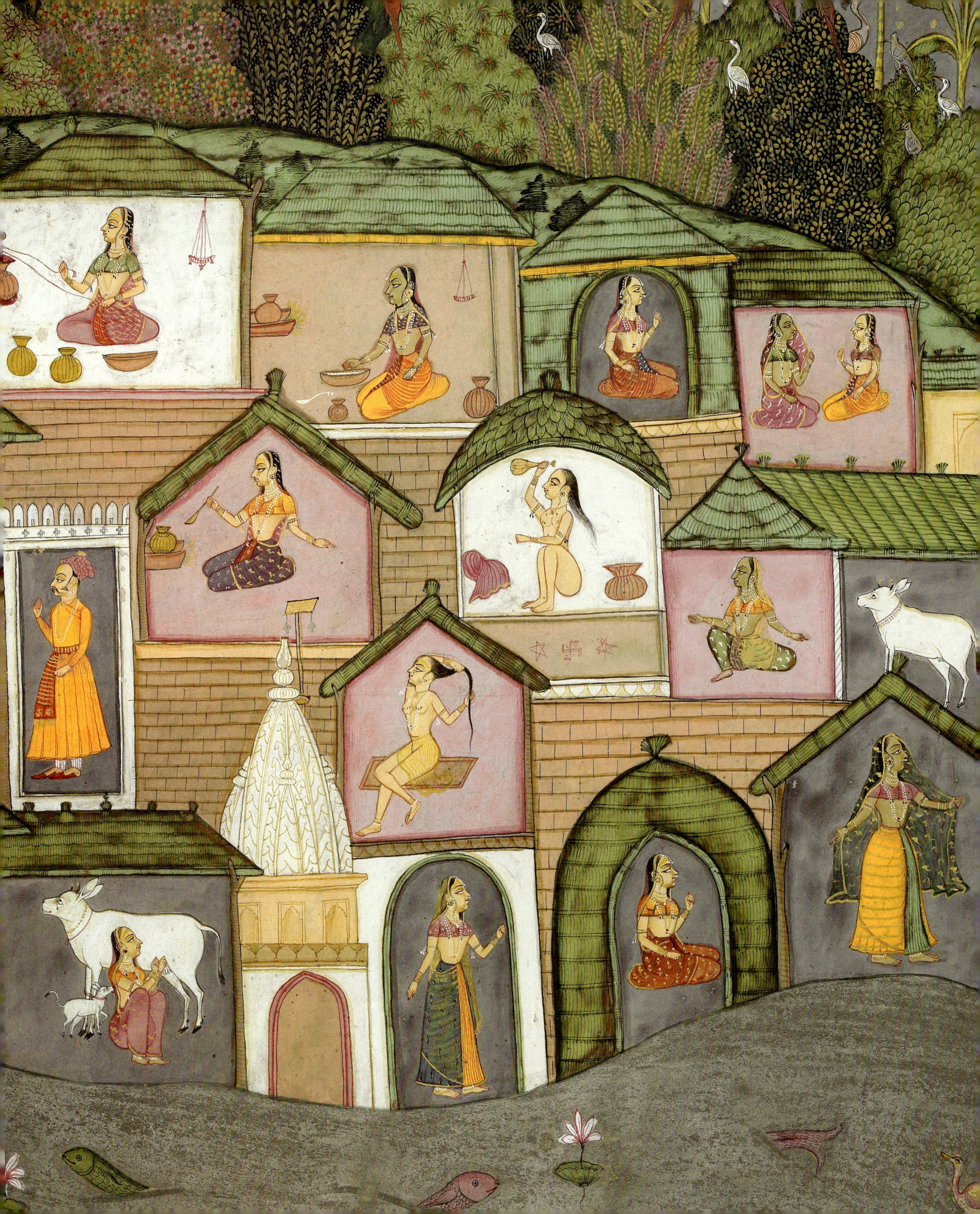

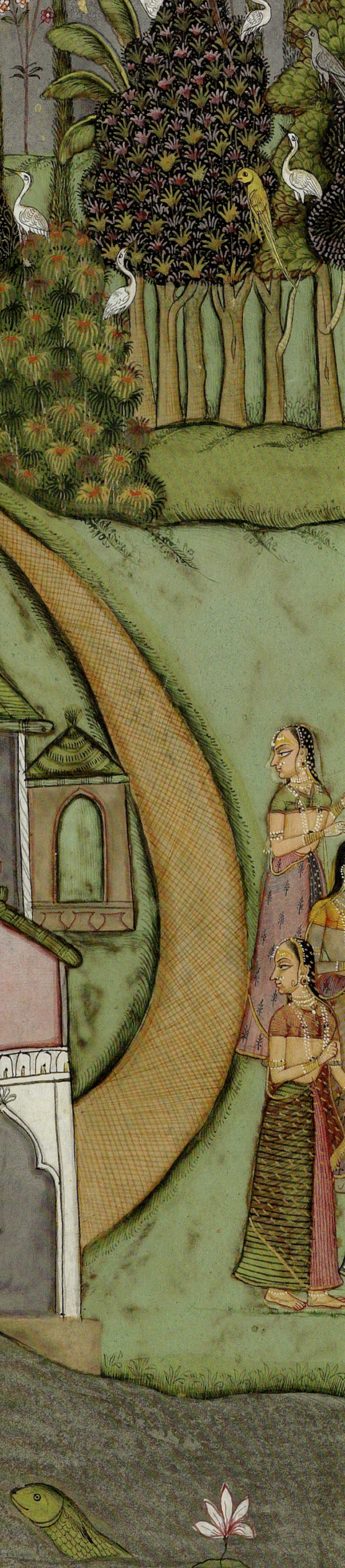

The Gopis Leave the Village to Meet Krishna

folio 1 from the *Krishna Lila*
Jodhpur, ca. 1765; 63.5 x 136.5 cm
Mehrangarh Museum Trust

Sri krishnalila
Da[khal] dholiya rai kothar
Glorious Krishna Lila
Entered in the *dholiya* storeroom

> Seeing that full [moon], heralder of the white night-lilies, reddened with fresh
> vermilion powder, its splendor like the face of Lakshmi, the goddess of fortune,
> and seeing the forest colored by its silky rays, Krishna played [his flute] softly,
> capturing the hearts of the beautiful-eyed women.
>
> The music aroused Kama. When they heard it, the women of Vraj, enchanted
> by Krishna, came to their lover, their earrings swinging in their haste, and
> unknown to one another.
>
> Some, who were milking cows, abandoned the milking and approached eagerly.
> Others had put milk on the fire, but then came without even removing
> [the milk or] the cakes [from the oven].
>
> Others interrupted serving food, feeding their babies milk, and attending to
> their husbands. Still others were eating, but left their food. Others were putting
> on make-up, washing, or applying mascara to their eyes. They all went to be
> near Krishna, their clothes and ornaments in disarray.
>
> Their hearts had been stolen by Govinda [Krishna], so they did not turn back
> when husbands, fathers, brothers and relatives tried to prevent them. They
> were in a state of rapture.
>
> —*Bhagavata Purana*, chapter 29, verses 3–8 [8]

These verses recount the *lila* (spontaneous play) of the deity Krishna with adoring
gopis (female cowherds), whose encounters take place on a moonlit evening in
a village of Braj. Inspired by the moon's beauty, Krishna plays enchanting music
on his flute, which lures the women from their homes into the magically beautiful
forest. The artist's bifurcated composition (see pp. 106–7) juxtaposes the
women's domestic sphere (both the round-walled village and the rows of men
imploring them to stay home) with a dreamlike expanse of foliage thick with parrots
and egrets. The contrast makes vivid the extreme devotion of the gopis, who
rejected social convention in favor of intense engagement with the captivating god.

Devotees of the Vallabh (Pushtimarg) spiritual tradition seek to experience an
intimate relationship with Krishna; the passion of the gopis epitomizes this spiritual
goal. Vijai Singh, who was formally initiated into the Vallabh community in 1765,
undoubtedly commissioned the manuscript as an expression of his piety. DD

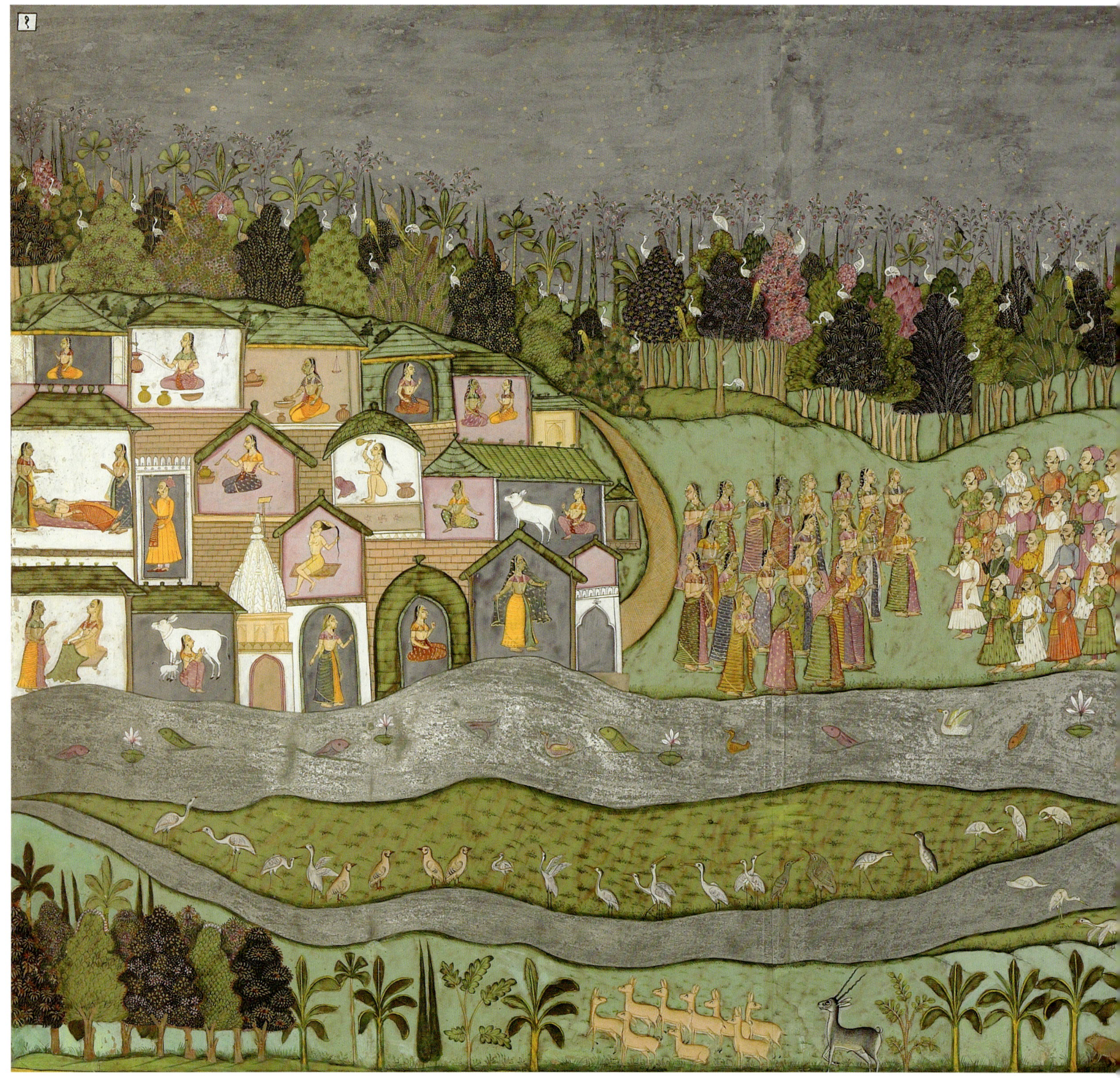

Cat. 23

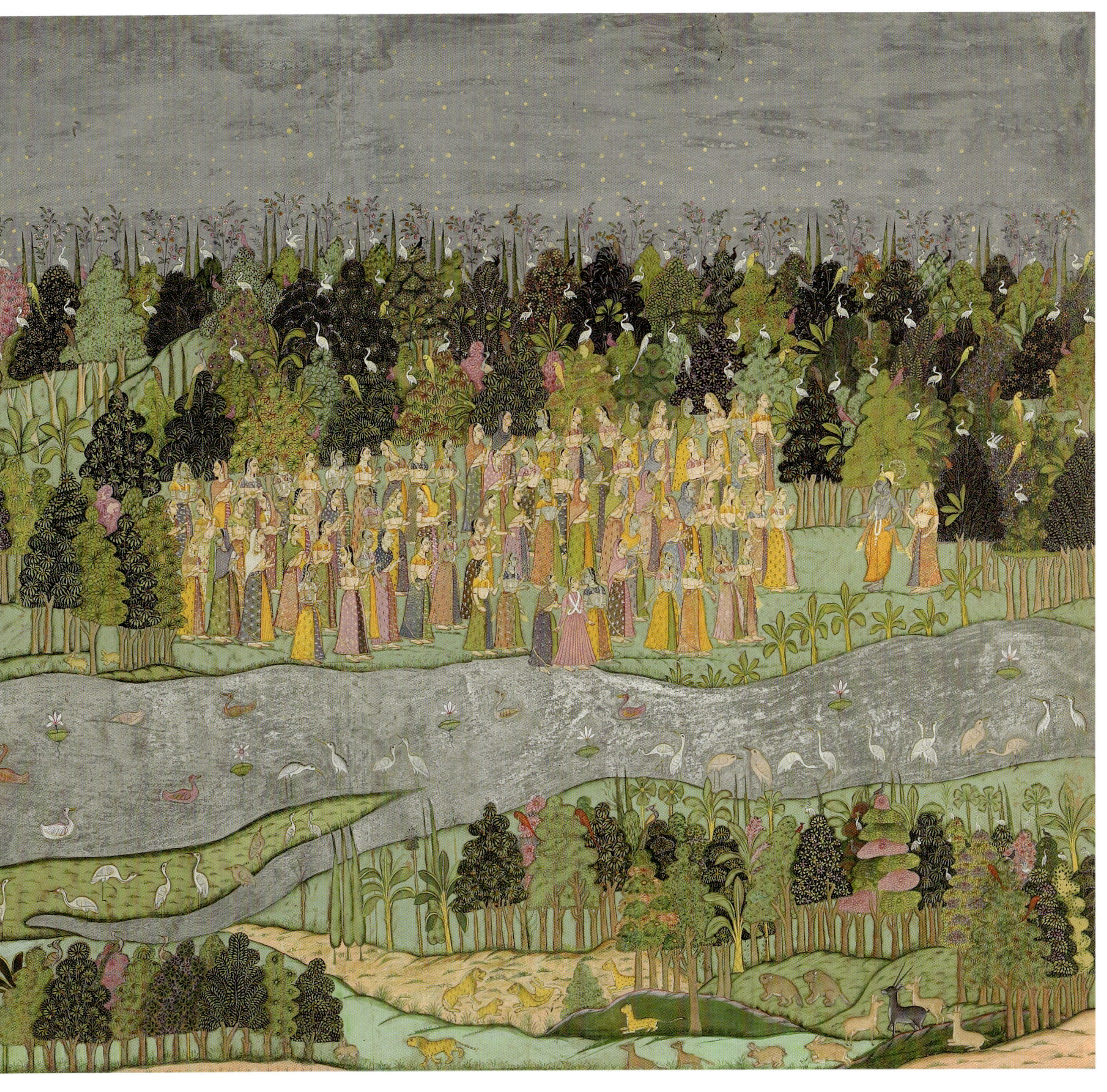

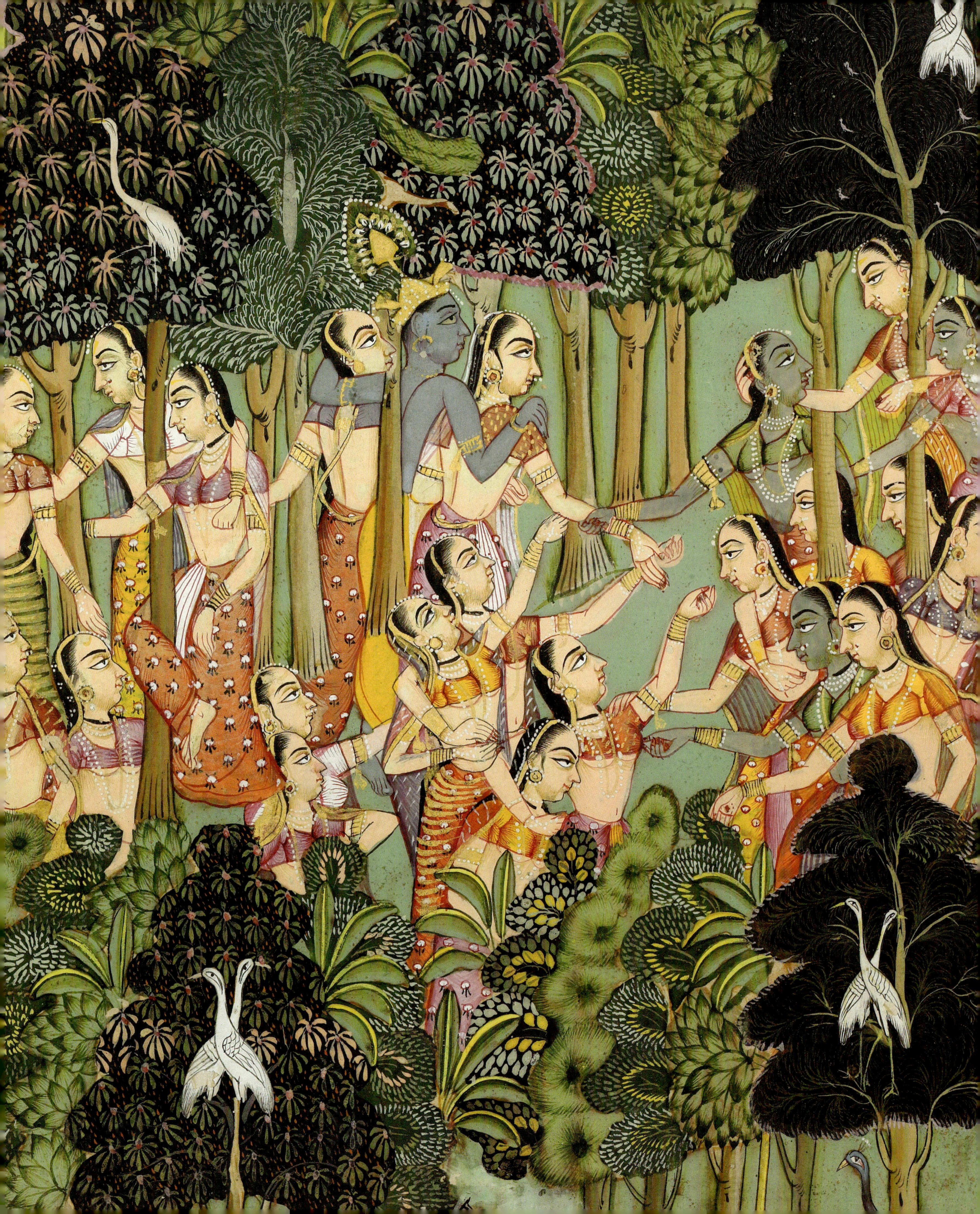

24

Krishna Frolics with the Gopi Girls

folio 2 from the *Krishna Lila*
Jodhpur, ca. 1765; 63.5 x 136.5 cm
Mehrangarh Museum Trust

Sri krishnalila
Da[khal] dholiya rai kothar
Glorious Krishna Lila
Entered in the *dholiya* storeroom

> Krishna, the infallible one, whose conduct is upright, shone forth with the
> assembled gopis, who were dazzling with jasmine flowers and broad smiles.
> As the gopis' faces blossomed from the glances of their beloved, Krishna
> appeared like the moon surrounded by stars.
>
> Praised in song, and singing loudly himself, the Lord of hundreds of women,
> wearing a garland of *vaijayanti* flowers, frolicked in the forest, making it beautiful.
>
> Accompanied by the gopis, Krishna approached the bank of the river. Its cool sand
> was swept by a wind bearing the scent of the *kumunda* flowers and refreshing
> from its contact with the waves. Arousing Kama in the young women of Vraj
> with jokes, smiles, and glances, playfully scratching their breasts, girdles, thighs,
> hair and hands with his nails, and embracing them with outstretched arms,
> he gave them pleasure.
>
> —*Bhagavata Purana,* chapter 29, verses 45–46

This sensitively conceived painting epitomizes the joyous and sensuous nature of
the *Krishna Lila*'s verses. Gentle curves and unhurried movements predominate.
The silver Yamuna River gently winds through softly rolling hills (see pp. 110–11).
Slender women gesture dreamily. The artist has depicted the smiling Krishna
nine times to convey the god's generous act of multiplying himself to convince
each gopi that he is only with her. The maidens languidly entwine their bodies
around tree trunks in a manner that suggests their surrender to both the
enchanted forest and Krishna's charms.

Krishna's tender expression and the soft magenta modeling of his blue
complexion evince the skill of this artist, who began his career as a painter for
Bakhat Singh at Nagaur. His *Krishna Lila* forest (p. 112) is a denser and more
complexly composed rendering of the line of trees that adorns the background
of *Maharaja Bakhat Singh Delights in an Outdoor Musical Performance* (cat. 16).
In both works, leaves with pink edges grow on knot-speckled trunks that termi-
nate in vertical branches, and rosy trees peek out from the forest's distant edge.
Moreover, the artist's elongated women, swan-necked herons, and vivid blue
peacocks remained essentially the same over the twenty years that separated
the production of the two paintings. DD

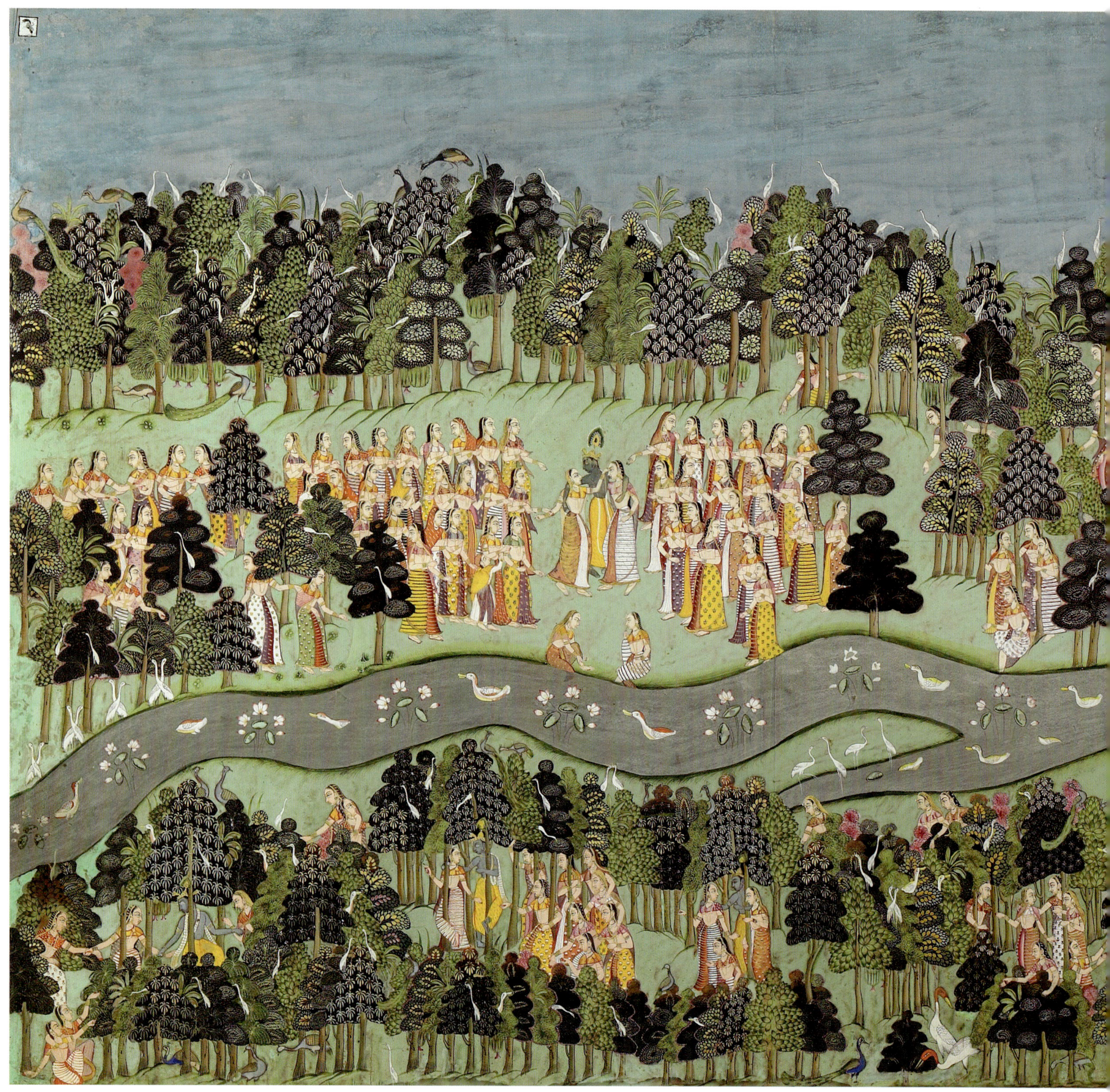

Cat. 24

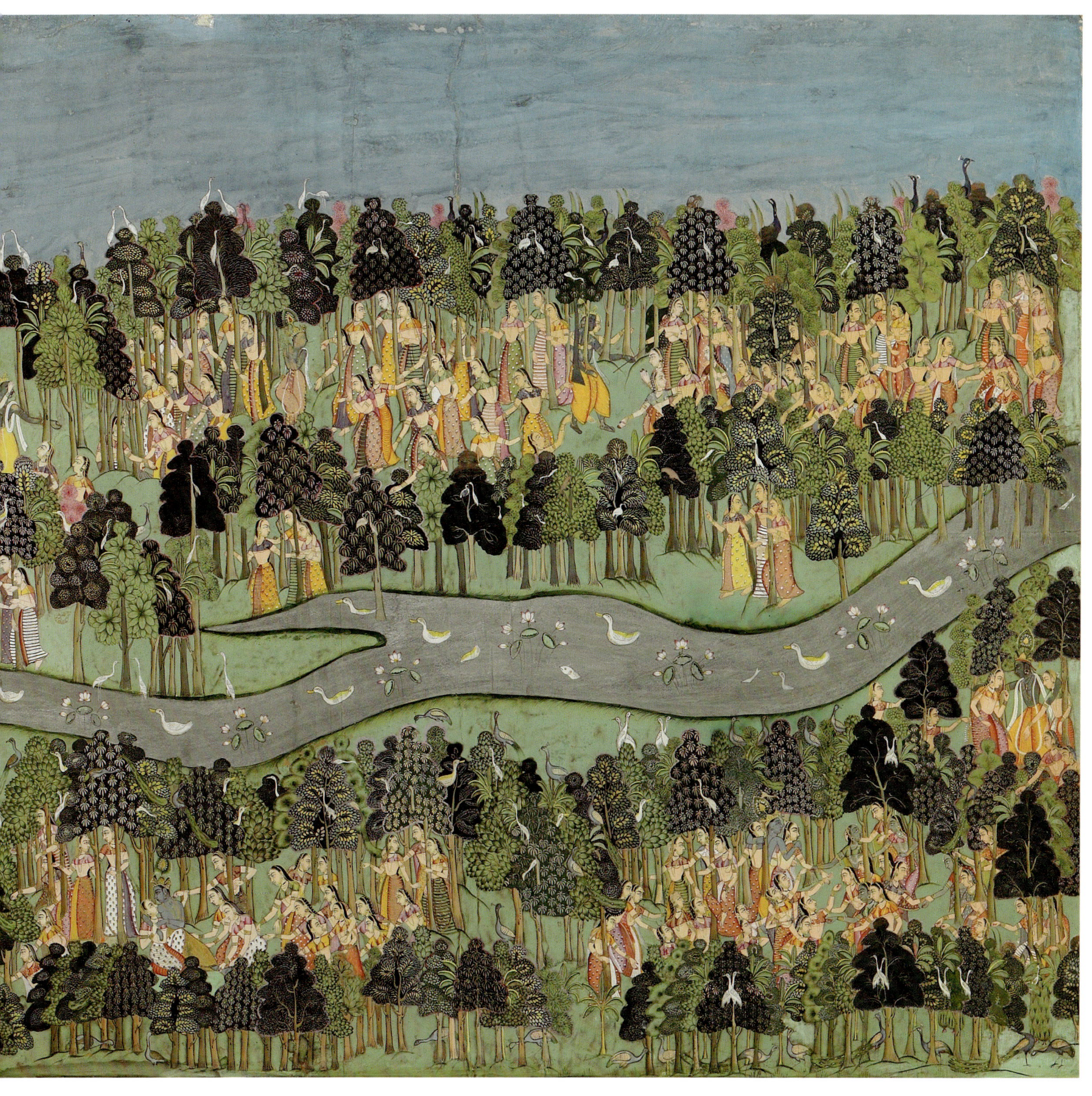

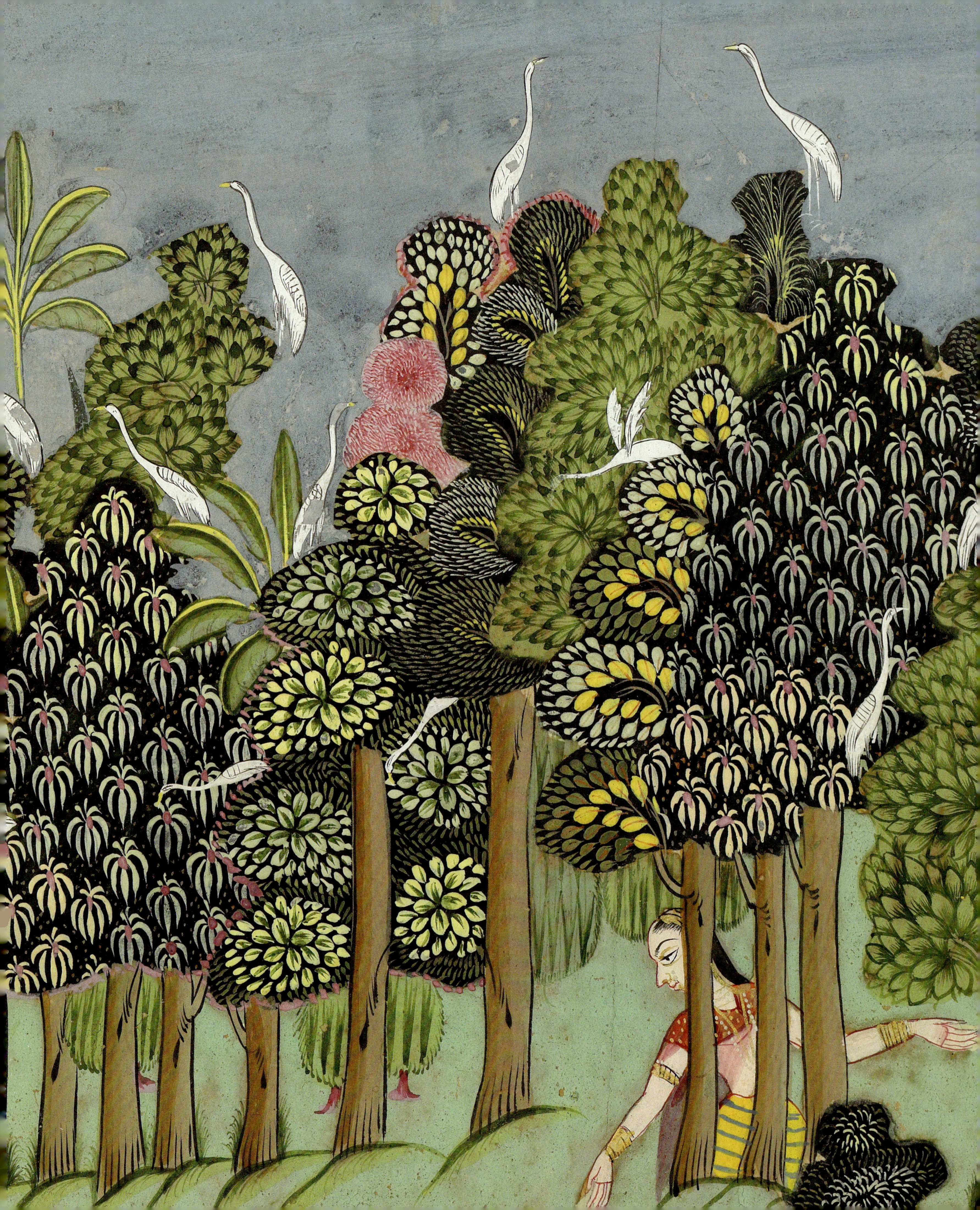

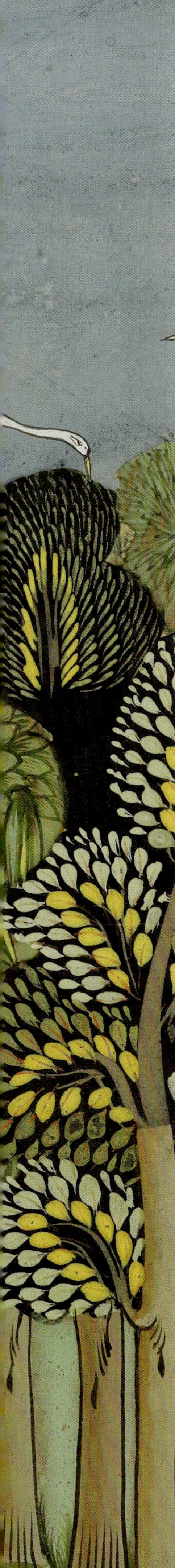

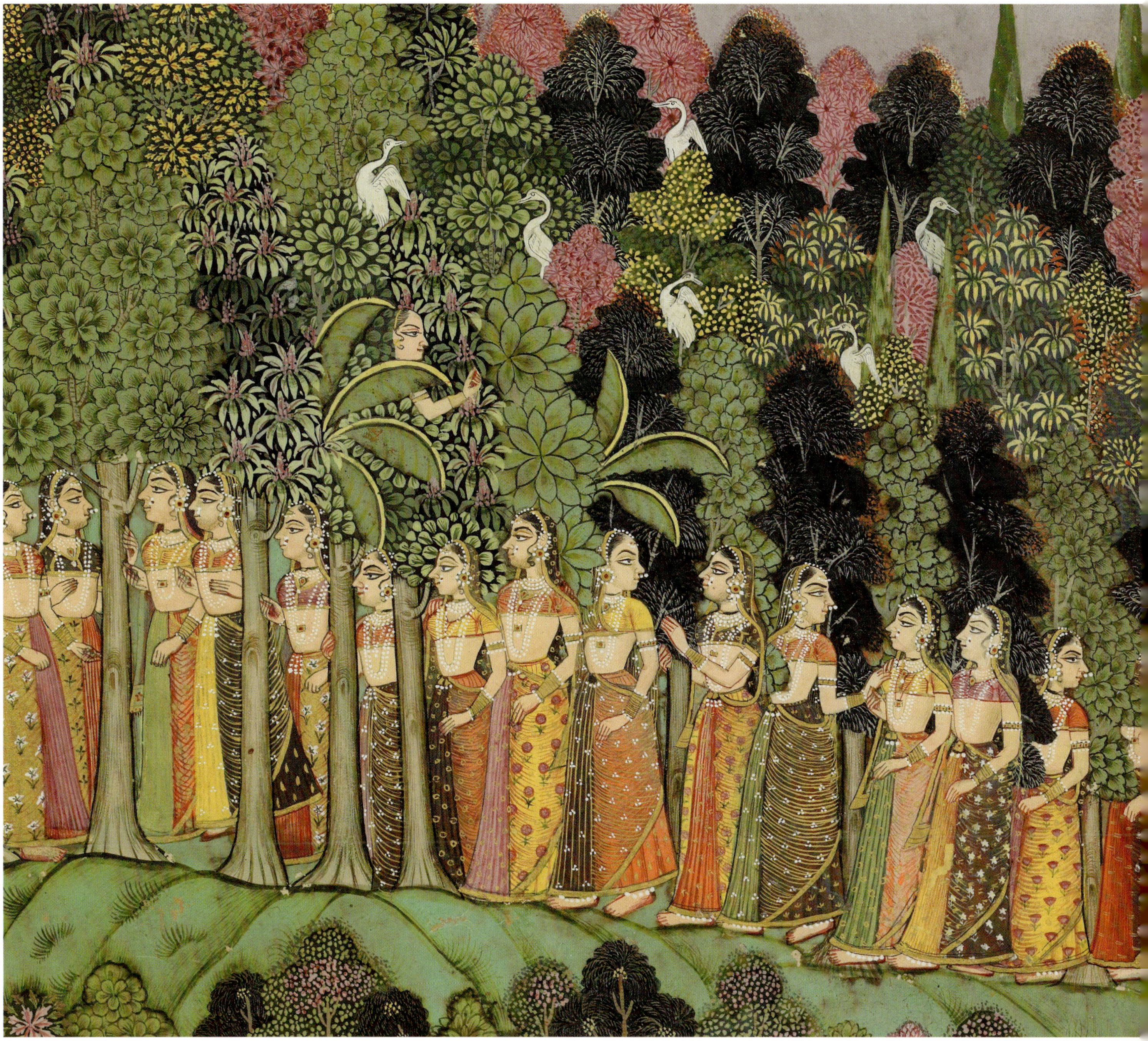

Cat. 25 Detail (above)

Cat. 24 Detail (left)

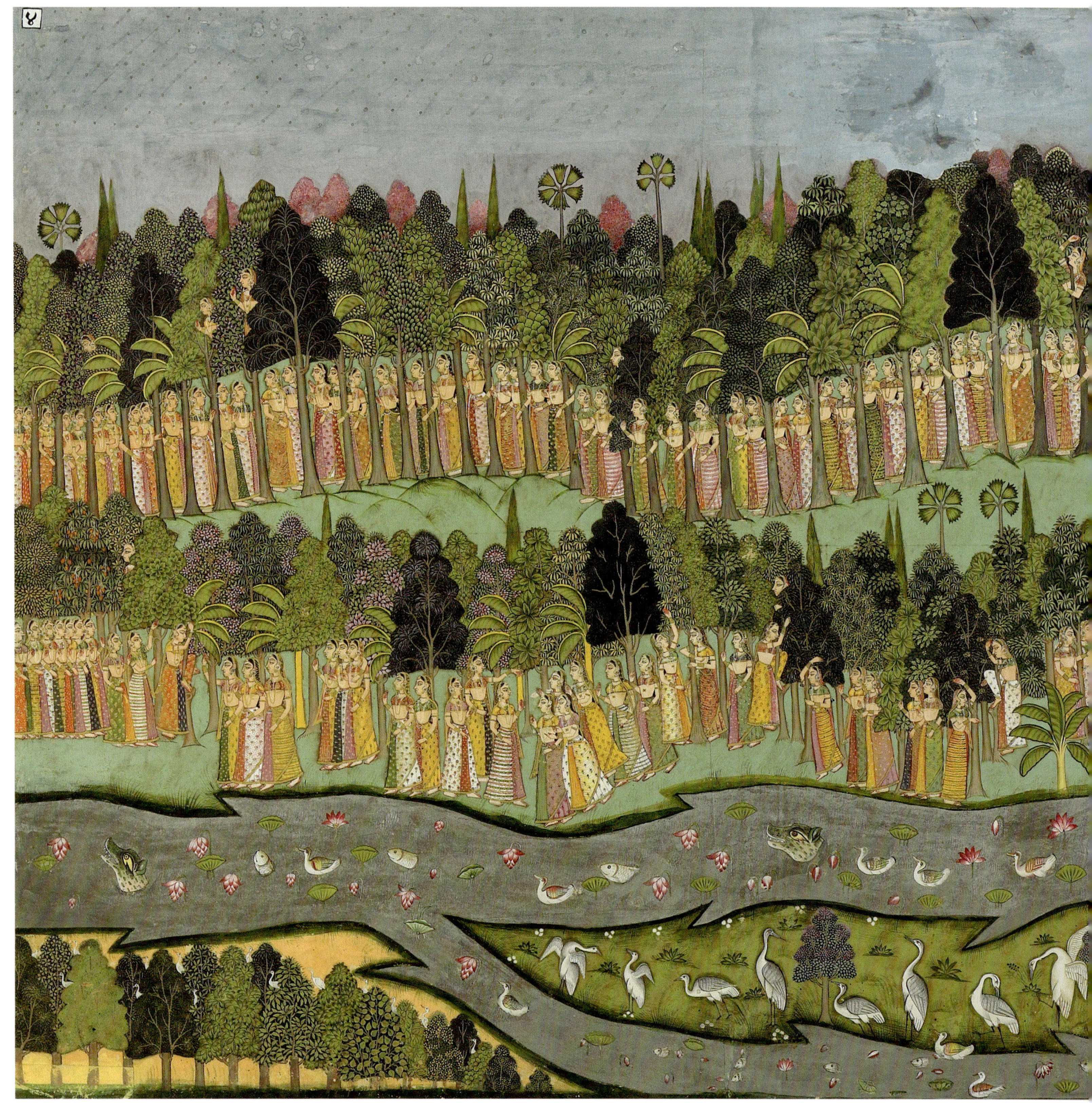

Cat. 25

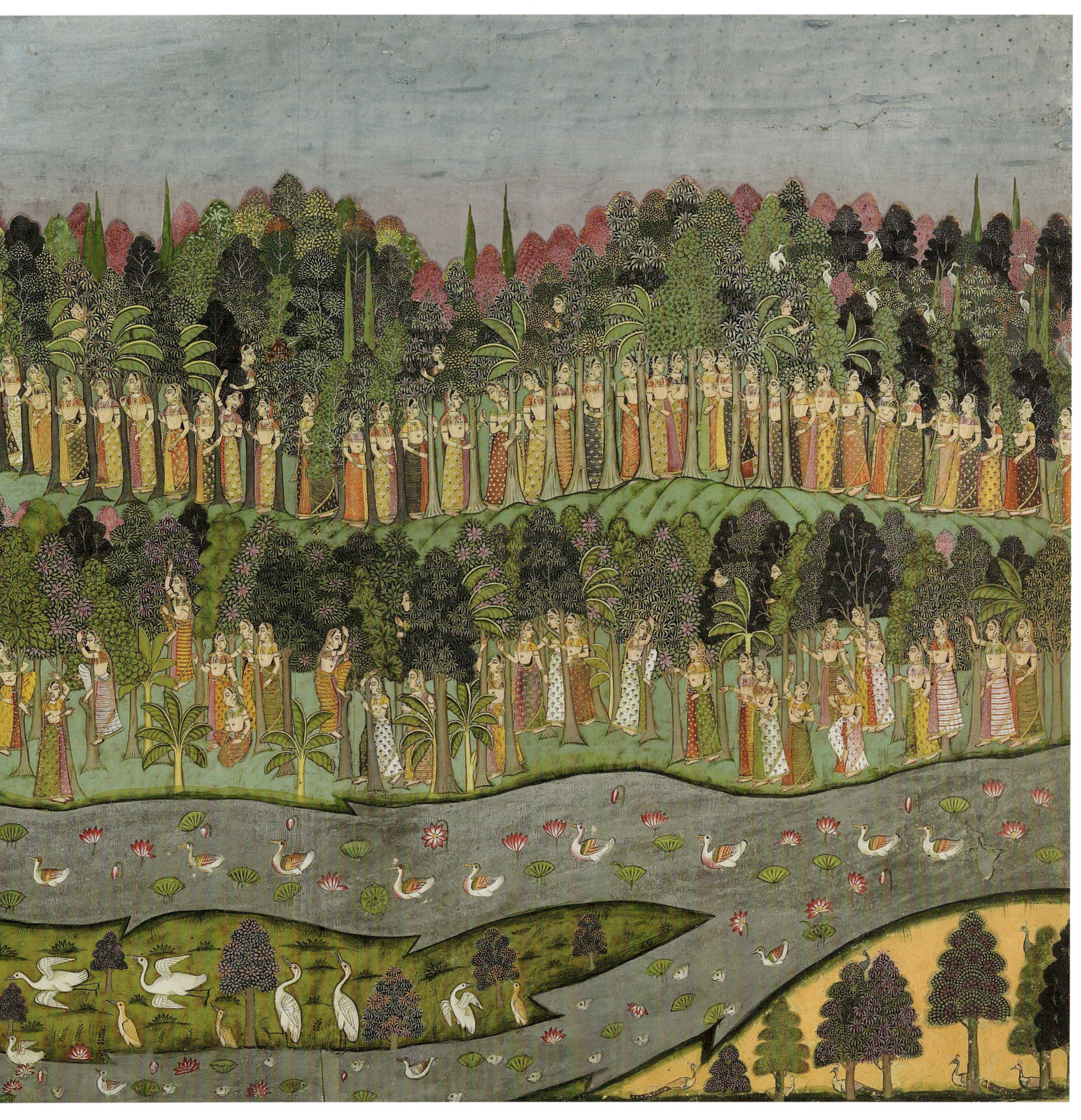

25

The Gopis Search for Krishna

folio 4 from the *Krishna Lila*
Jodhpur, ca. 1765; 63.5 x 136.5 cm
Mehrangarh Museum Trust

Sri krishnalila
Da[khal] dholiya rai kothar
Glorious Krishna Lila
Entered in the *dholiya* storeroom

Singing loudly in unison only about [Krishna], they searched from grove to
grove, like mad women. They asked the trees about the supreme being who,
like space, is inside and outside living creatures:

O *ashvatta* tree! O *plaksa* tree! O *nyagrodha* tree! Have you seen the son of
Nanda at all? He has stolen our minds with his glances and smiles of love,
and has gone.

O *kurabaka, asoka, naga, punnaga,* and *campaka* trees! Has the younger brother of
Balarama [passed] by here? His smile steals away the pride of haughty women.

Their minds absorbed in Krishna, the gopis' conversations focused on him,
their activities centered on him, and they dedicated their hearts to him.
Simply by singing about his qualities, they forgot their own homes.

Meditating on Krishna, they reached the bank of the Kalindi [Yamuna] river
again. Gathering together, they sang about Krishna, longing for his arrival.

—*Bhagavata Purana*, chapter 30, verses 4, 5, 6, 43, 44

When the mischievous Krishna disappears from the forest during the evening
of revelry, the bereft and fretful gopis seek their beloved among the thickets and
groves. The animated preening of the sharp-beaked shore birds between the
river's arms (see pp. 114–15) nicely mirrors the gopis' anxious interrogation of
the forest's trees.

As the village women continue to seek their adored god, they become totally
absorbed in thoughts of Krishna and forget their sorrow. Their transformation
sets an example for devotees who listen to the *Raslila* verses (see cat. 23). Indeed,
the verses are said to purify the listener, alleviate suffering, end lust, and provide
liberation from the cycle of rebirth.[9]

The somewhat stiff, paper-doll quality of the female figures in this painting
(see p. 113) differs from the more fluid postures of the women in the previous
two folios (cats. 23, 24). This difference suggests that another artist painted the
folio. Nonetheless, the similarities in proportions, gestures, and garments indicate
that this painter was a member of the artist family that produced the series. DD

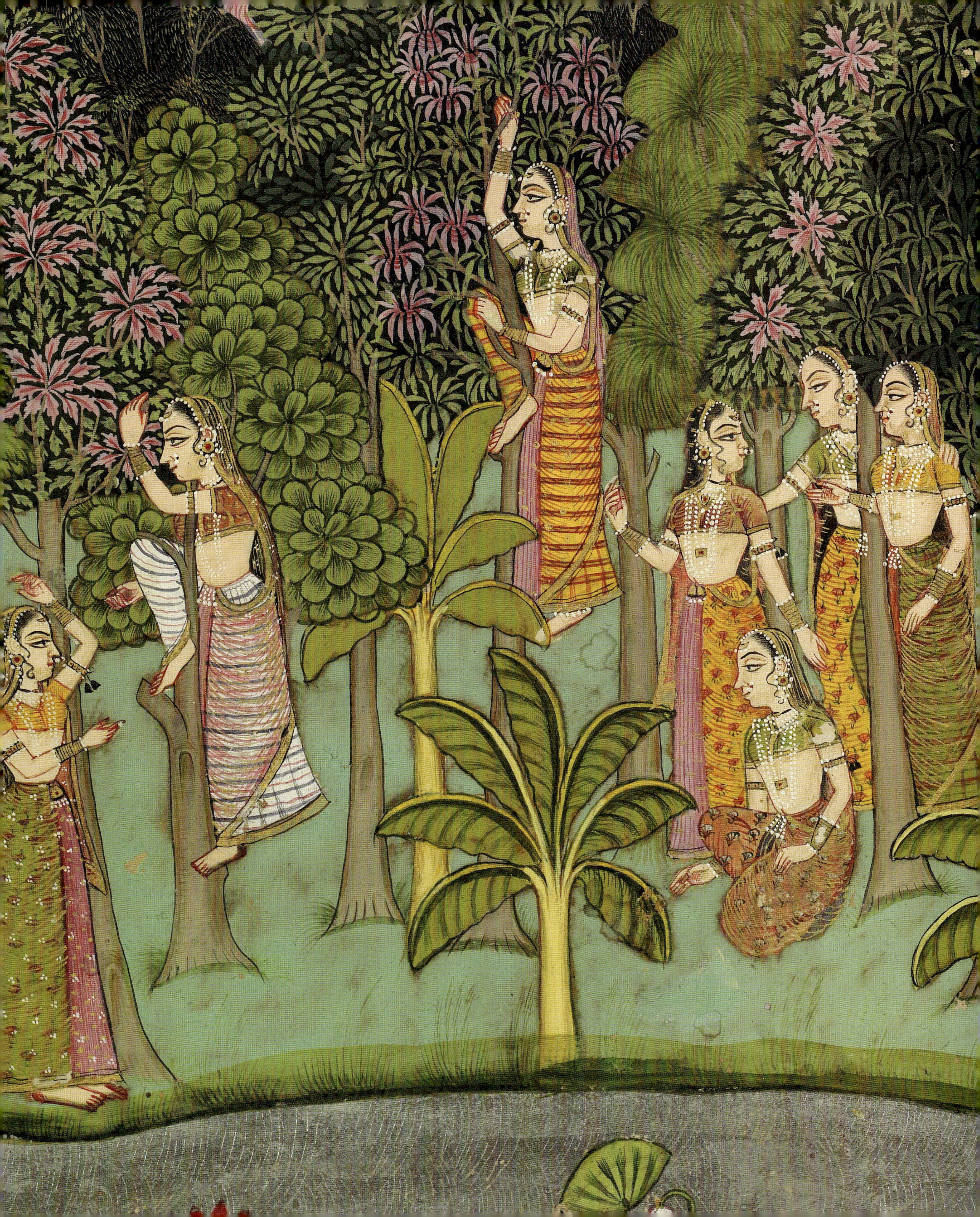

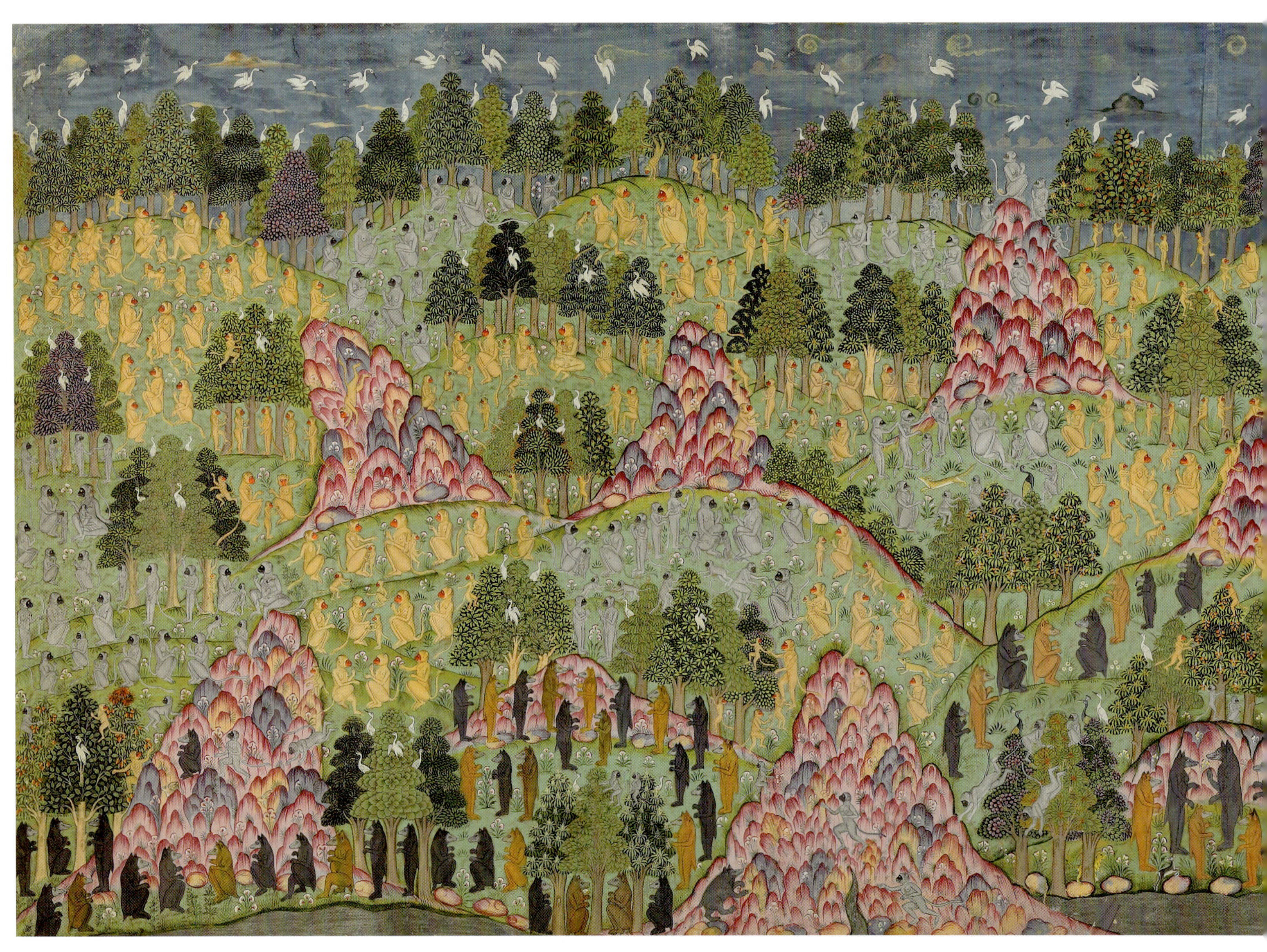

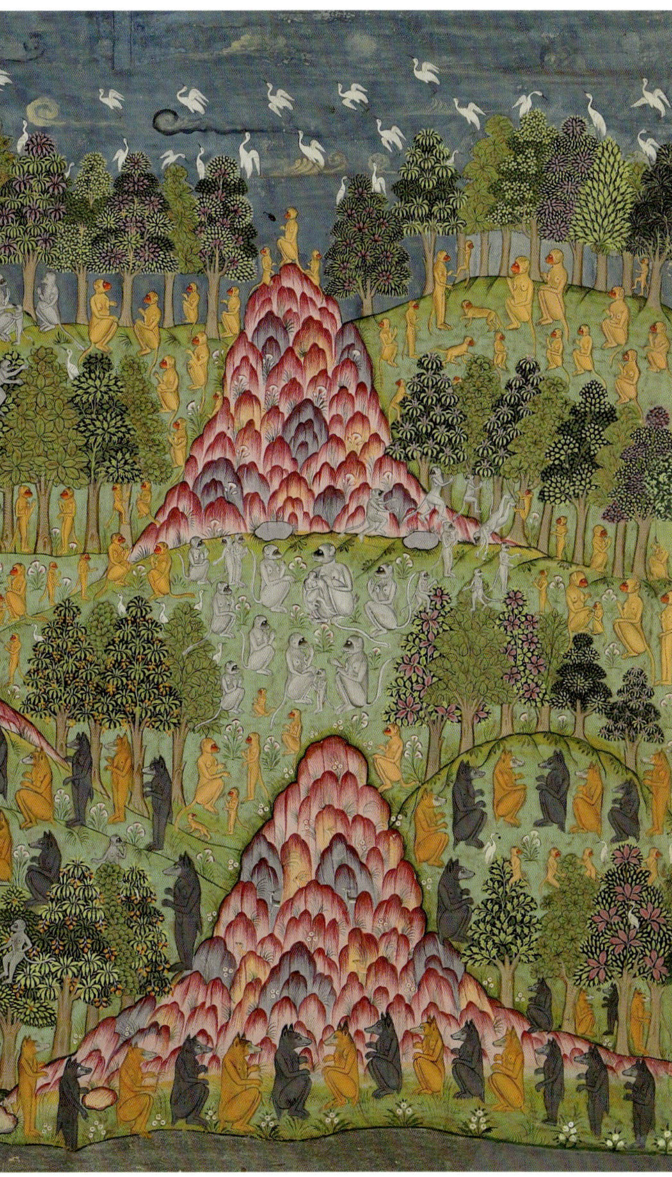

26

Monkeys and Bears in the Kishkindha Forest
from the *Ramcharitmanas* of Tulsidas (1532–1623)
Jodhpur, ca. 1775; 64 x 130 cm
Mehrangarh Museum Trust

Sri ram carit
dakhal dholiya re kothar
Glorious Ramcharitmanas
Entered in the *dholiya* storeroom

Written in vernacular Hindi verse in the late sixteenth century, Tulsidas' *Ramayana* relates the epic of the hero-god Rama.[10] It soon became the most influential and popular telling of the Sanskrit *Ramayana* in northern India. Even during the poet's lifetime, itinerant holy men spread Tulsidas' verses from Varanasi in eastern India, where they were composed, to Rajasthan. By the second half of the eighteenth century, Hindu kings were sponsoring recitations and reenactments and became the epic's most prominent patrons. Maharaja Vijai Singh's atelier produced a monumental illustrated manuscript of Tulsidas' *Ramayana* in this milieu. Its ninety-one folios illustrate the young Prince Rama's exile from Ayodhya, the abduction of his beloved wife Sita, the massive war with the demon Ravana, and the divine couple's glorious return to Ayodhya as its king and queen.

This fanciful landscape, filled with chattering monkey families, conversing bears, and flying herons (see pp. 120, 121), depicts the forest of the monkey kingdom Kishkindha. The artist, who also painted cat. 37, conveys the whimsical quality that pervades the *Ramayana's* descriptions of simian antics (including those of the monkey god Hanuman!). While the painter covered almost every possible surface with animals and foliage, his light touch prevents the painting from seeming labored. With a brush, he loosely drew contours and details over thinly painted areas of color that approximate the shapes of figures and landscape elements. The sprightliness of his line is apparent in the springy tufts of grass and the quick magenta strokes of shaded boulders, but it is his affectionate observation of monkey behavior that truly delights. Silver-gray langurs and tangerine and ochre rhesus macaques clamber up trees, gambol across hills, feed babies, care for their young, and affectionately converse. Herons, with long and variously curved necks, float lightly in a sky adorned with delicate coils and tufts of clouds.

Many of the monumental folios in this series include passages and motifs that suggest the atelier's familiarity with illustrated *Ramayanas* from other north Indian Hindu courts. Several *Ramayana* pictorial cycles, for example, devote entire paintings to depictions of frolicking monkeys in the Kishkindha forest.[11] Rama's leaf garb and the warrior monkeys' red shorts appear in other manuscripts, as does Ravana's gold citadel, placed to a far side of the folios (see cats. 34 and 38).[12] Yet the Jodhpur atelier did not develop the monumental cycle from an existing archetype. While some folios, including this painting, increase the number but retain the size of figures employed in small paintings, subjects not drawn from the Sanskrit *Ramayana* as well as the large size of the folios inspired imaginative compositions that combine several incidents or magnify palace architecture and landscape elements (see cats. 27, 28, and 29). DD

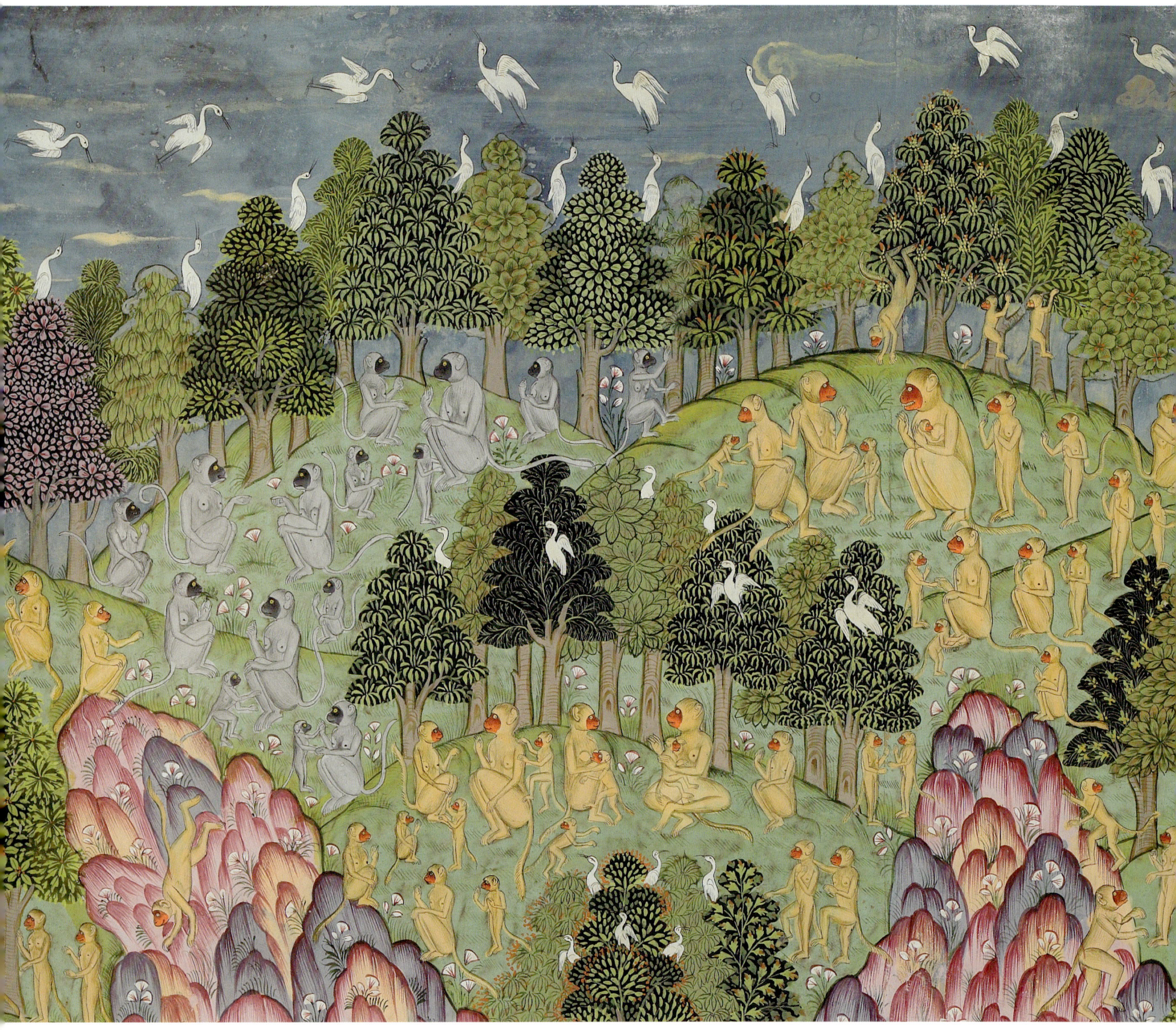

Cat. 26 Details

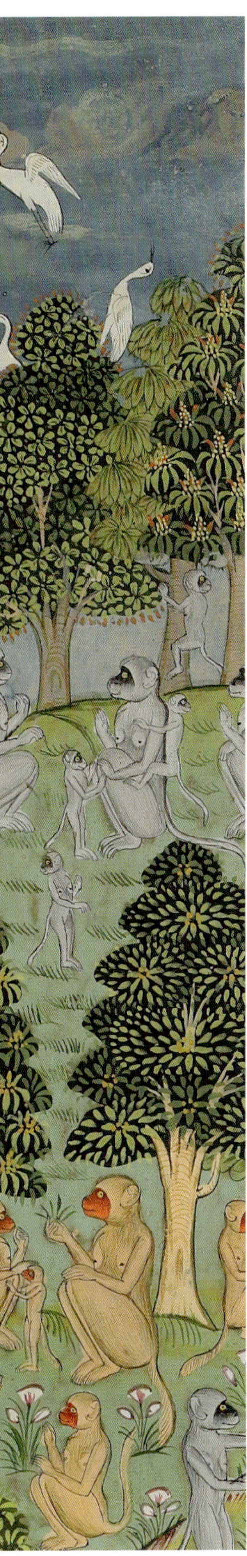

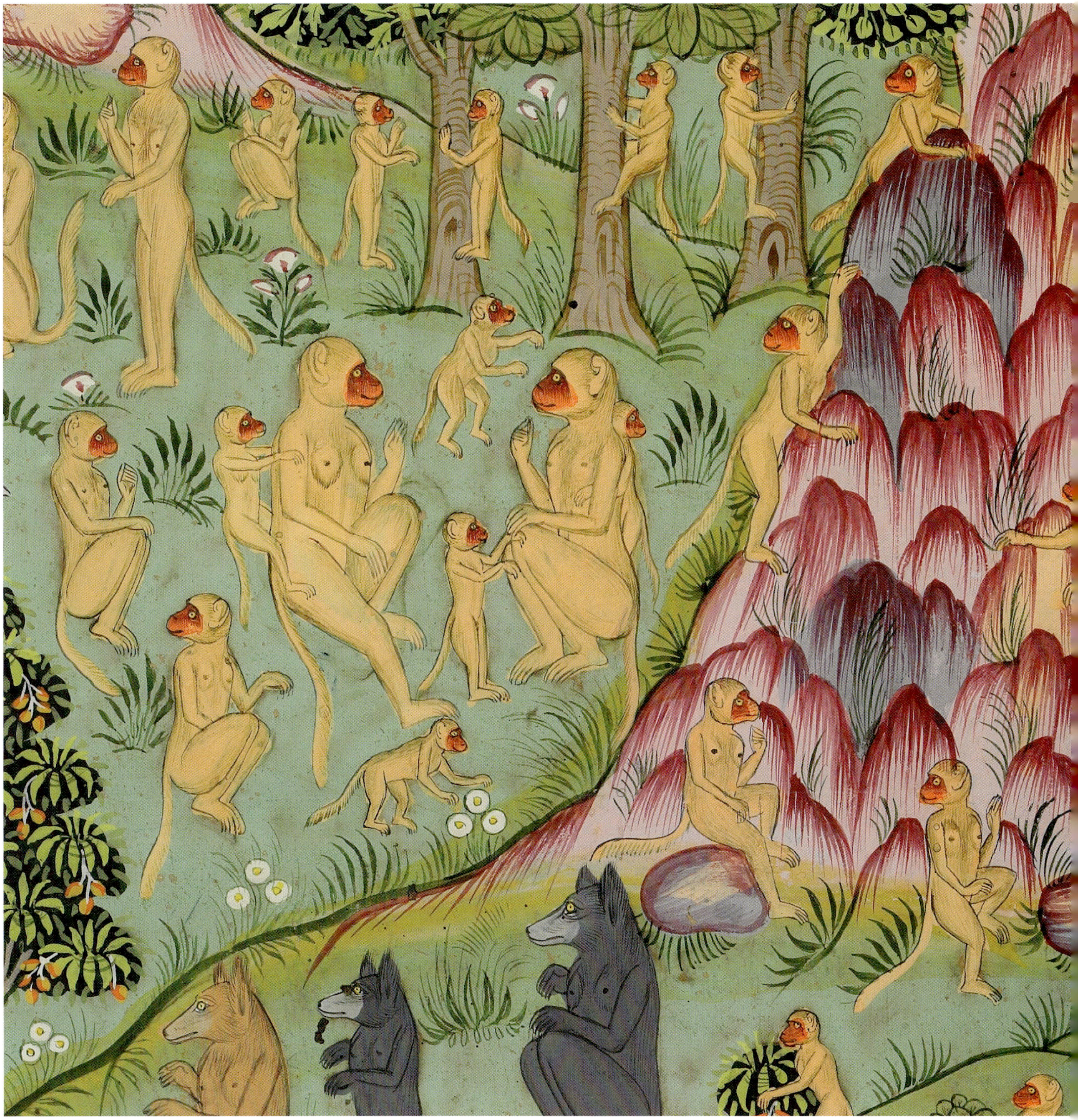

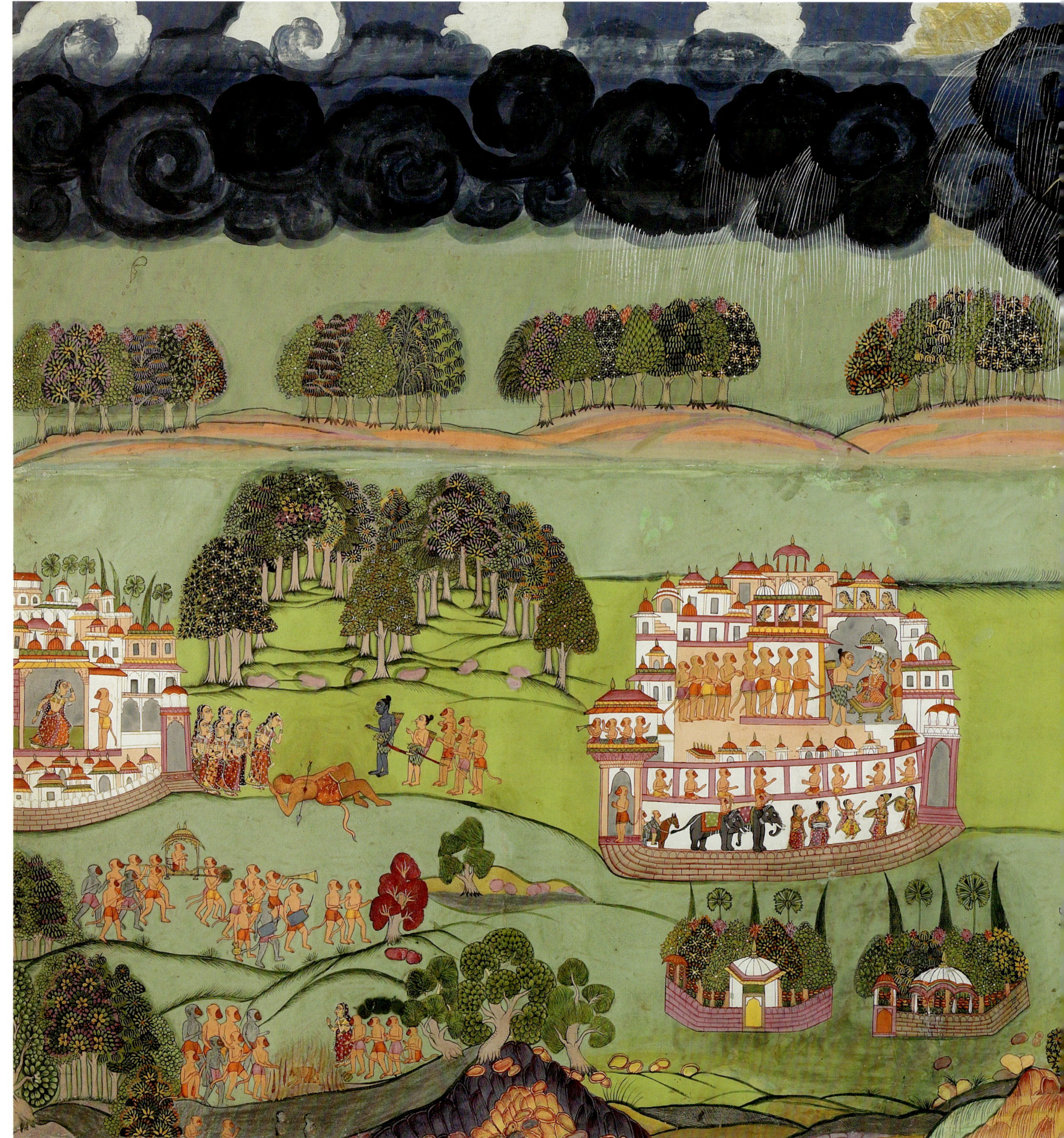

Cat. 27

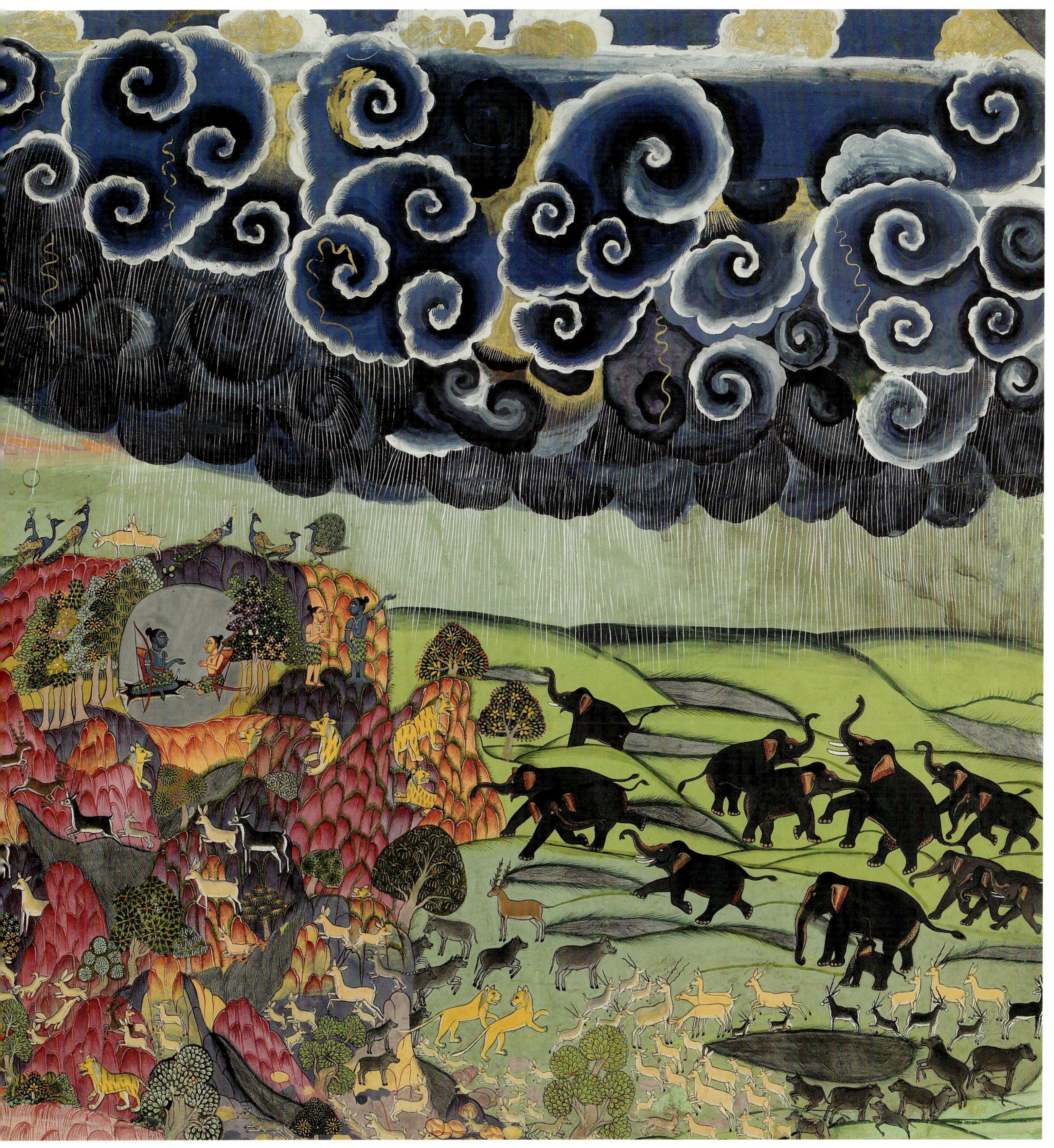

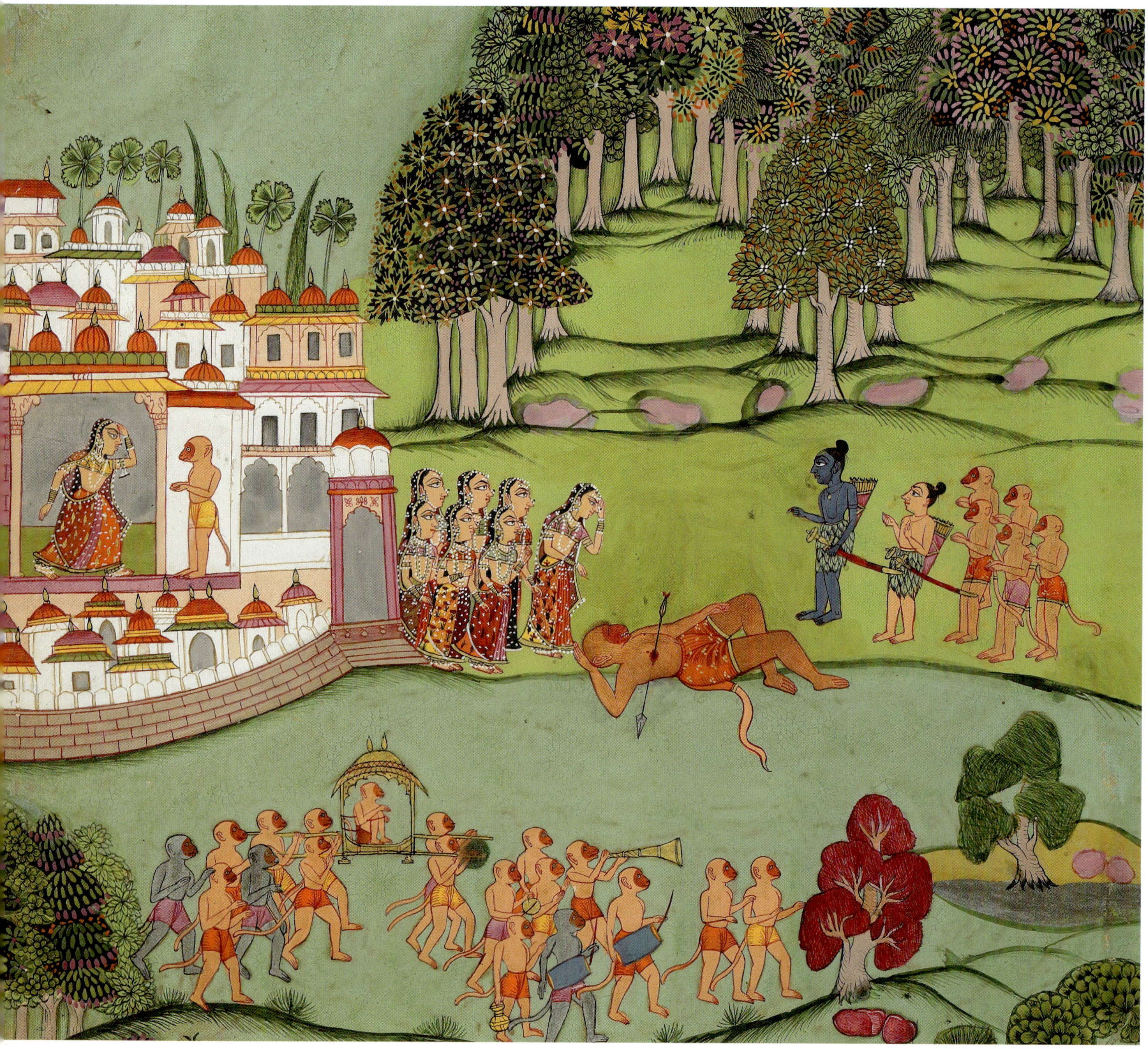

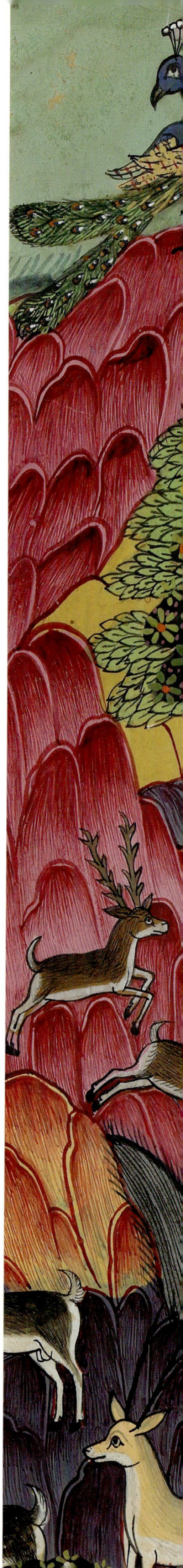

Cat. 27 Details

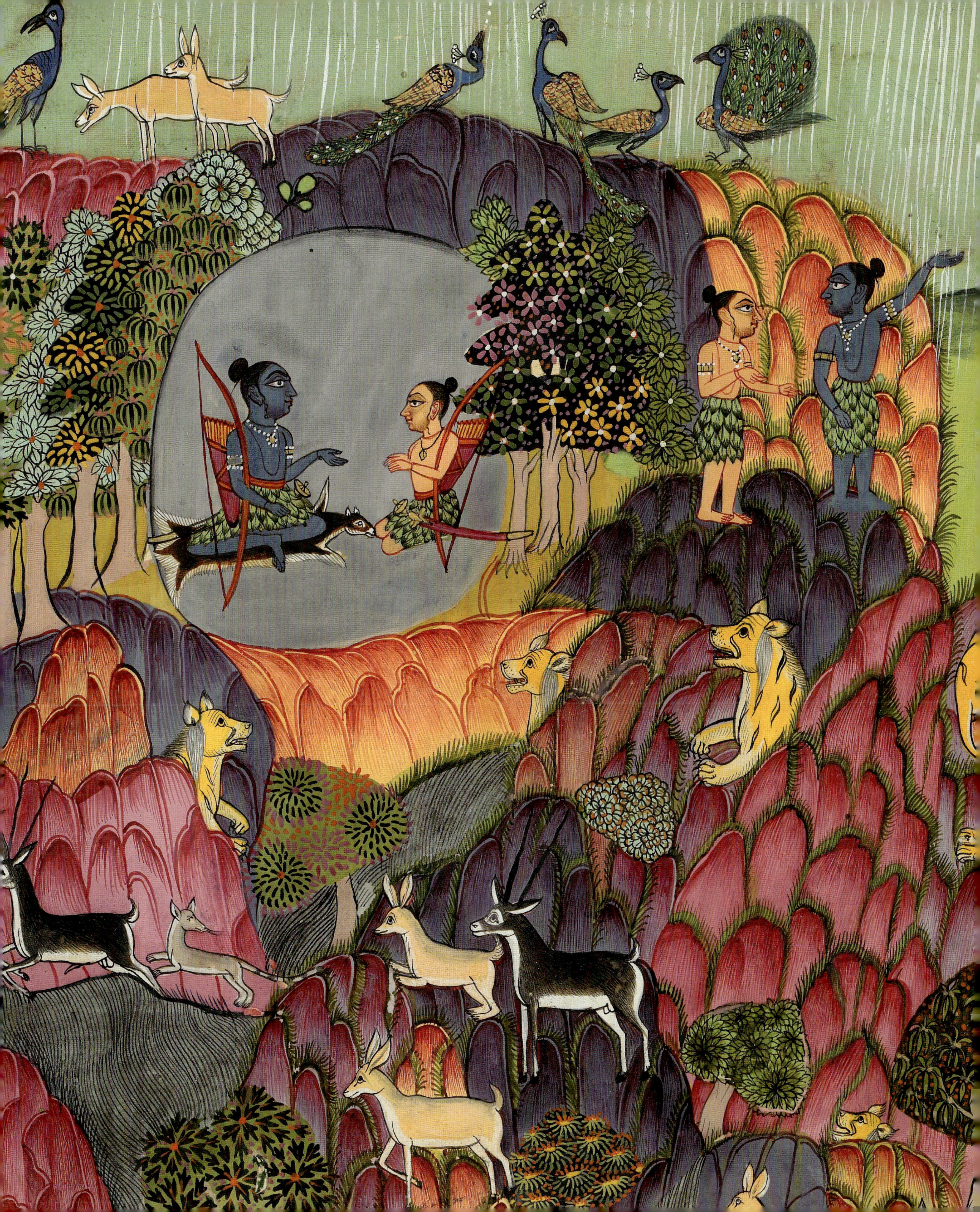

Death of Vali; Rama and Lakshmana Wait Out the Monsoon

from the *Ramcharitmanas* of Tulsidas (1532–1623)
Jodhpur, ca. 1775; 62.7 x 134.5 cm
Mehrangarh Museum Trust

Sri ram carit
Da[khal] dholiya rai kothar
Glorious Ram Charit
Entered in the *dholiya* storeroom

During Prince Rama's fourteen-year exile from his kingdom of Ayodhya, his beloved wife Sita was kidnapped by the powerful demon-king Ravana. Searching for Sita, Rama and his faithful brother Lakshmana arrived at an enchanted kingdom of talking monkeys, where they created an alliance with the deposed monkey-king Sugriva. In exchange for assistance in finding Sita, Rama killed Vali, who had usurped Sugriva's throne.

On the painting's left, the Jodhpur artist depicted the five major episodes that followed Vali's death within a triangular space created by two white palaces and the silver river at bottom (see p. 122). Employing the pictorial mode of synoptic narrative, in which successive incidents can be identified by the repeated appearance of protagonists,[13] the painter interwove the solemn events of Vali's death and cremation with the fanfare of King Sugriva's procession and coronation. The red-skirted Queen Tara can be seen in her palace, raising her hands in grief as she learns of her husband's defeat (see p. 122), then as she laments over Vali's body, and a third time, standing by his funeral pyre at the river's edge. Rama, who is "blue as a blue lotus, blue as an amethyst, blue as a rain-bearing cloud" appears first standing by Vali's body (see p. 124) and later on the multi-colored mountain in the center that divides the composition into two halves.[14]

The flurry of events in the social space of the monkey kingdom on the left are contrasted with the monsoon landscape on the right, which inserts a temporal pause into the flow of the narrative. Rama and Lakshmana settle into a mountain cavern (see p. 125) for the monsoon's duration, much as Indian armies ended their campaigns and travelers returned home when water-logged roads became impassable. Tulsidas' verses describe at length the beauty of the rainy season, with its thundering clouds, refreshing breezes, and gamboling wildlife, but also poignantly relate Rama's anguished longing for Sita.[15] The painting's unusually expansive landscape conveys the poet's emphasis on nature in this passage. Its magnificent rain-laden clouds and the lake-studded plain on which elephants playfully trumpet are atypical of north Indian court painting, in which landscapes typically frame figures and remain as background elements. Indeed, the artist reserved his most virtuoso efforts for the monsoon sky. While many north Indian court artists drew upon the fluid potential of watercolors to depict clouds, their compositions typically restrict freely painted skies to a narrow strip at a painting's upper border (cat. 13). In contrast, this artist dramatically expanded the sky into a glorious passage of painting. Washes of atmospheric color—charcoal, purple, and green—and short spiky lines energize the scallop-edged clouds, while loosely brushed areas of gold hint at the sun's veiled presence. DD

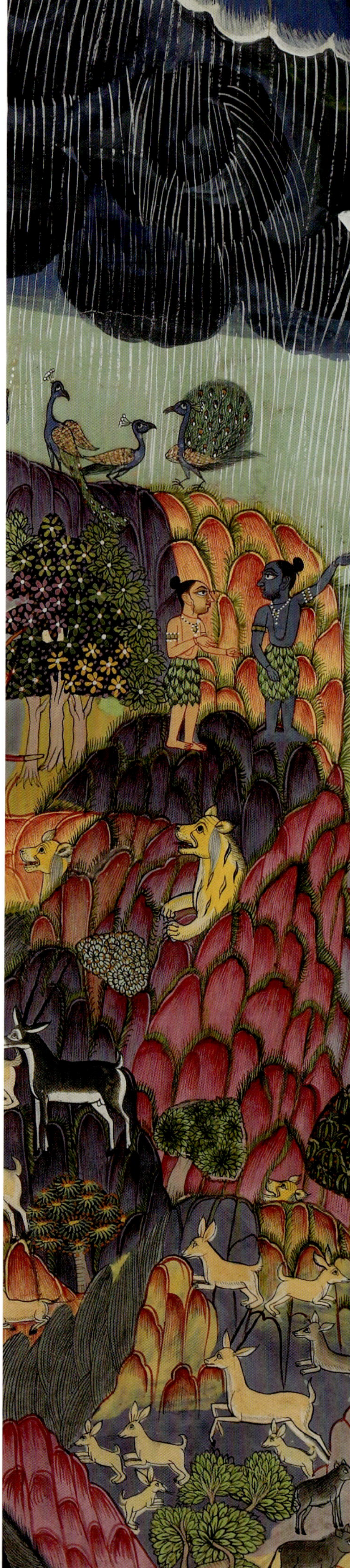

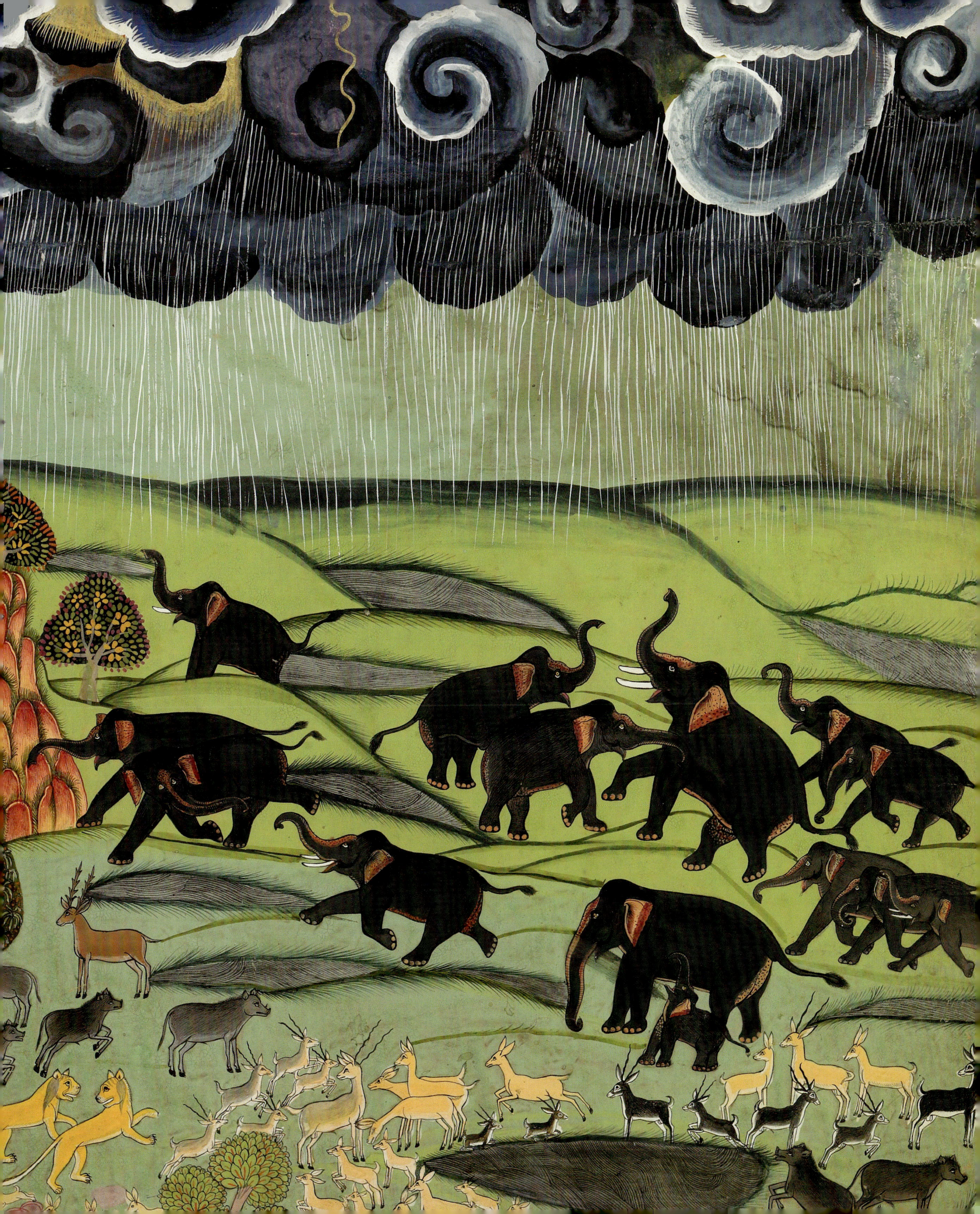

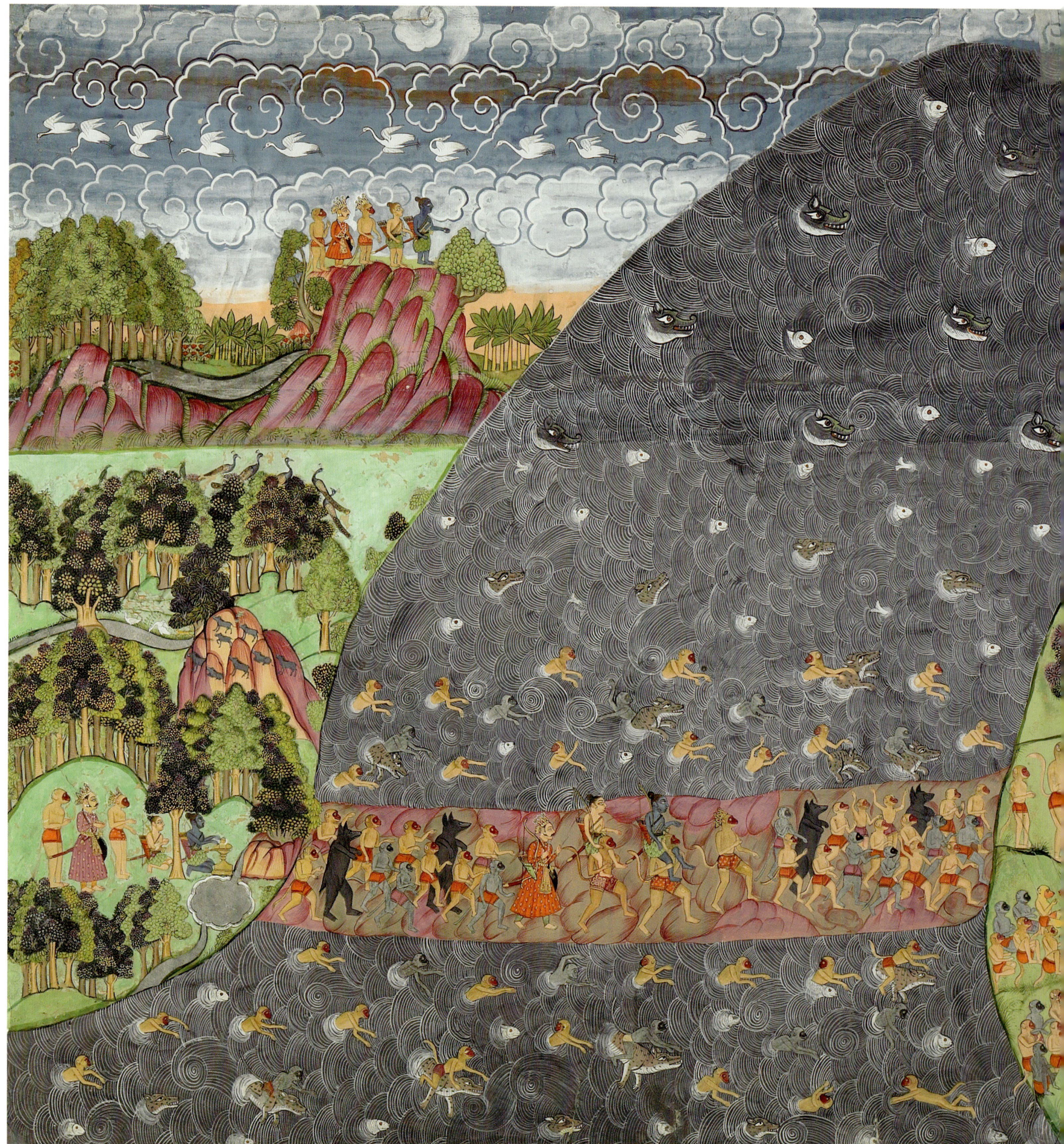

Cat. 28

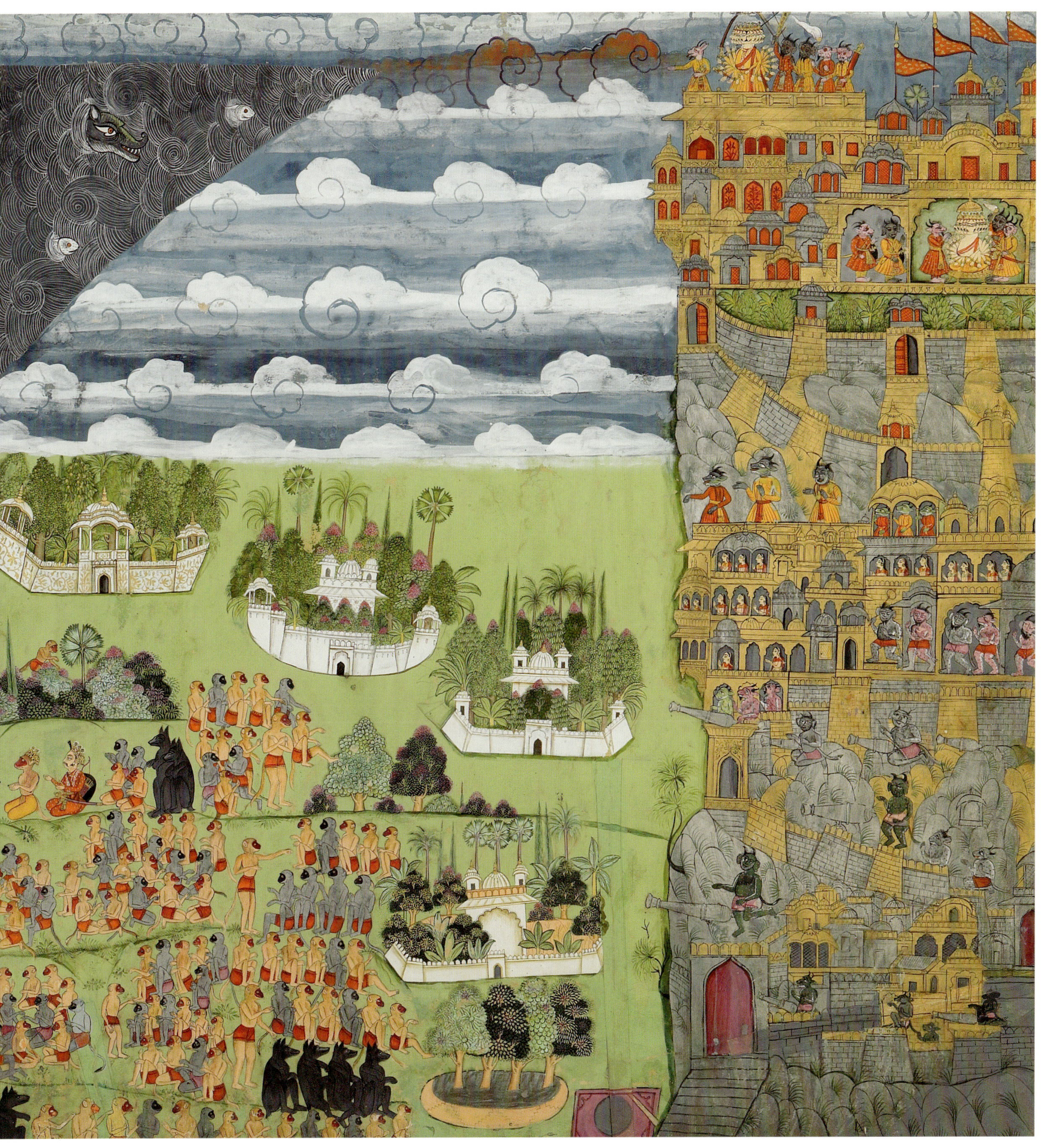

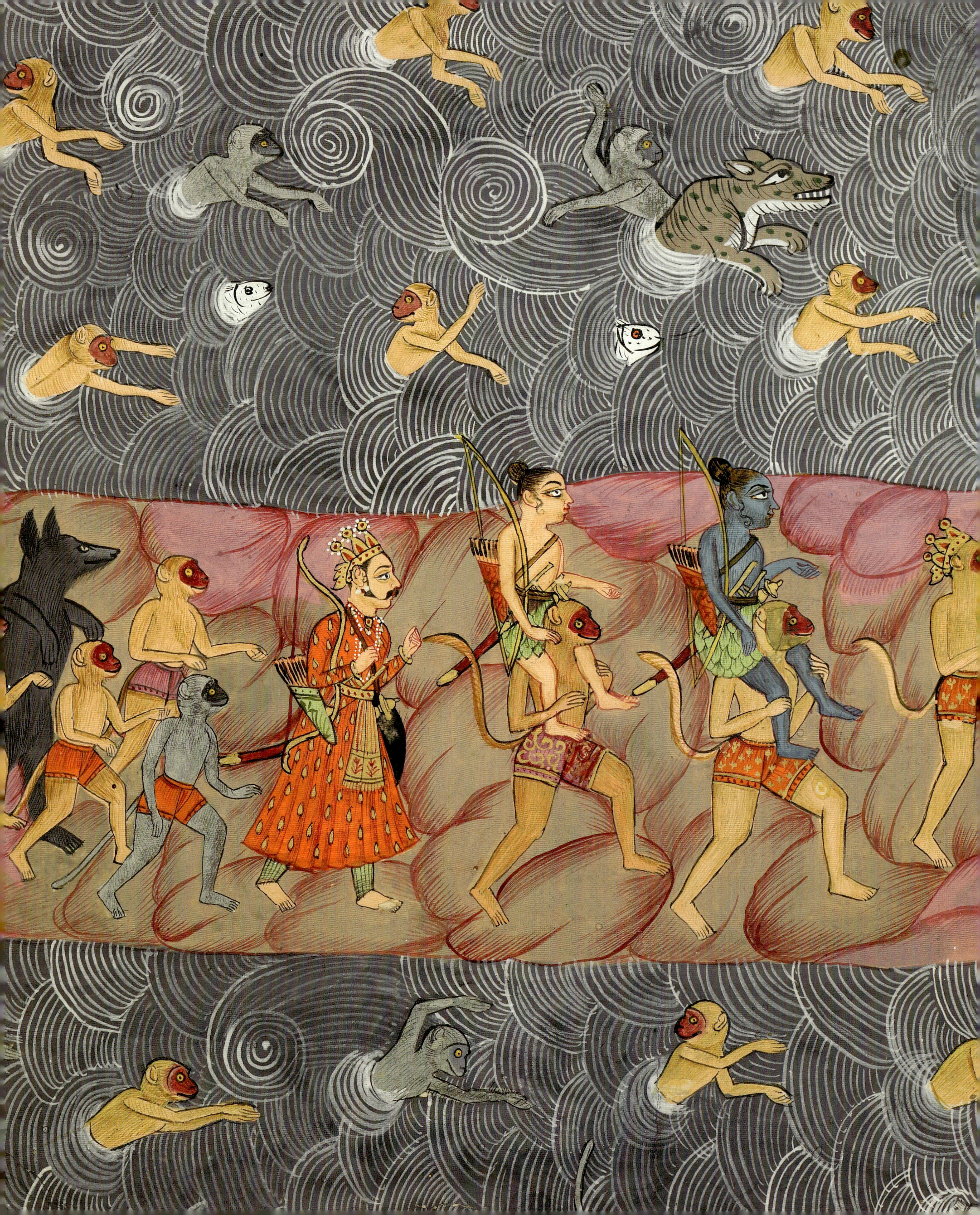

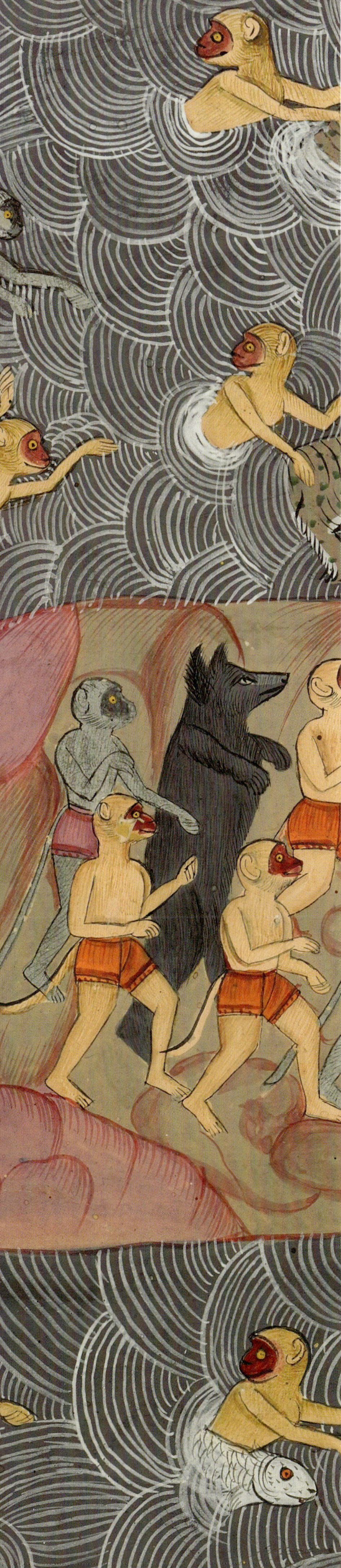

Rama's Army Crosses the Ocean to Lanka

from the *Ramcharitmanas* of Tulsidas (1532–1623)
Jodhpur, ca. 1775; 63 x 125.8 cm
Mehrangarh Museum Trust

Sri ram carit
dakhal dholiya re kothar
Glorious Ram Charit
Entered in the *dholiya* storeroom

This fantastic and energetic landscape anticipates the fierce battle between
the hero-god Rama and the demon Ravana to establish harmony on earth (pp.
128–29). Clouds tumble, banners flap, and flying herons twist their long, sinuous
necks as the two generals observe the scene at different moments. By conflating
successive episodes into a single composition, the artist contrasts the two adver-
saries representing good and evil. At the painting's upper left, Rama and his
entourage, having climbed the magenta peaks (see p. 132), calmly plan their
ocean crossing to the island of Lanka, where Ravana resides. On the right, from
atop the towering fortress bristling with cannons, the demon-king observes Rama's
armies camped outside his castle (see p. 133). Foreshadowing the triumph of virtue
over iniquity, the humbly leaf-clad Rama conveys the self-possession of a god while
the whirling arms of the sword-wielding Ravana and the anxious expression of
his goat-headed lieutenant imply misdirected energies and impending defeat.

The artist, who also painted cat. 27, boldly depicted an ocean that improbably
arches upwards to meet scallop-edged clouds tumbling across a bright sky. The
ocean's strong blue-gray arc divides the Indian subcontinent on the left from Lanka
on the right, and counterbalances the vertical mass of Ravana's golden fortress
(see pp. 128–29). The monkey and bear armies rush to Lanka across the stone
bridge they have constructed. Two prancing monkeys, flanked by the monkey-
prince Angada and Jambhuvan, king of the bears, carry the ever-composed
Rama and his brother Lakshmana on their backs. Other monkeys lean forward
and point enthusiastically in their haste, scamper with arms raised in pure glee,
hitch rides on the backs of friendly *makaras* (alligator-like creatures), or swim
and splash across the water.

Short staccato brushstrokes, which shade and texture objects, contribute to
the painting's fervent pace. The artist's exuberant and varied line describes even
subsidiary landscape elements with great spontaneity. The pink boulders of the
mountain at left lean toward Lanka, lush gardens (stylistically akin to those in the
Krishna Lila folios and Bakhat Singh's Nagaur paintings) almost burst from the
walls of white palace cities, and a spiky, jabbing line describes Ravana's cruel
citadel. Spots of strong color placed across the painting's surface—from tangerine
clusters of monkeys to fuchsia mountains, flowers, and demon hides—further
animate the lively composition. DD

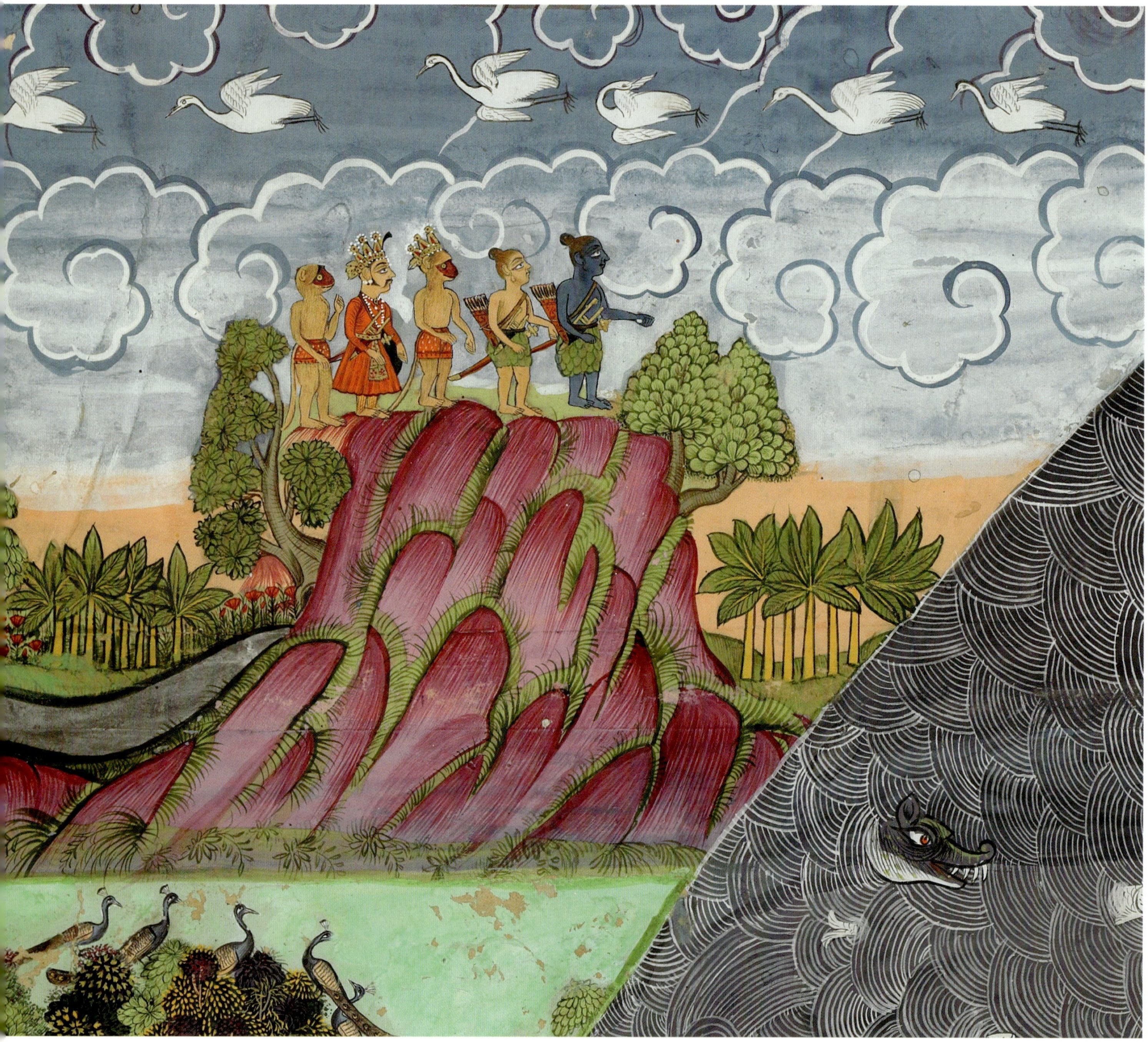

Cat. 28 Details

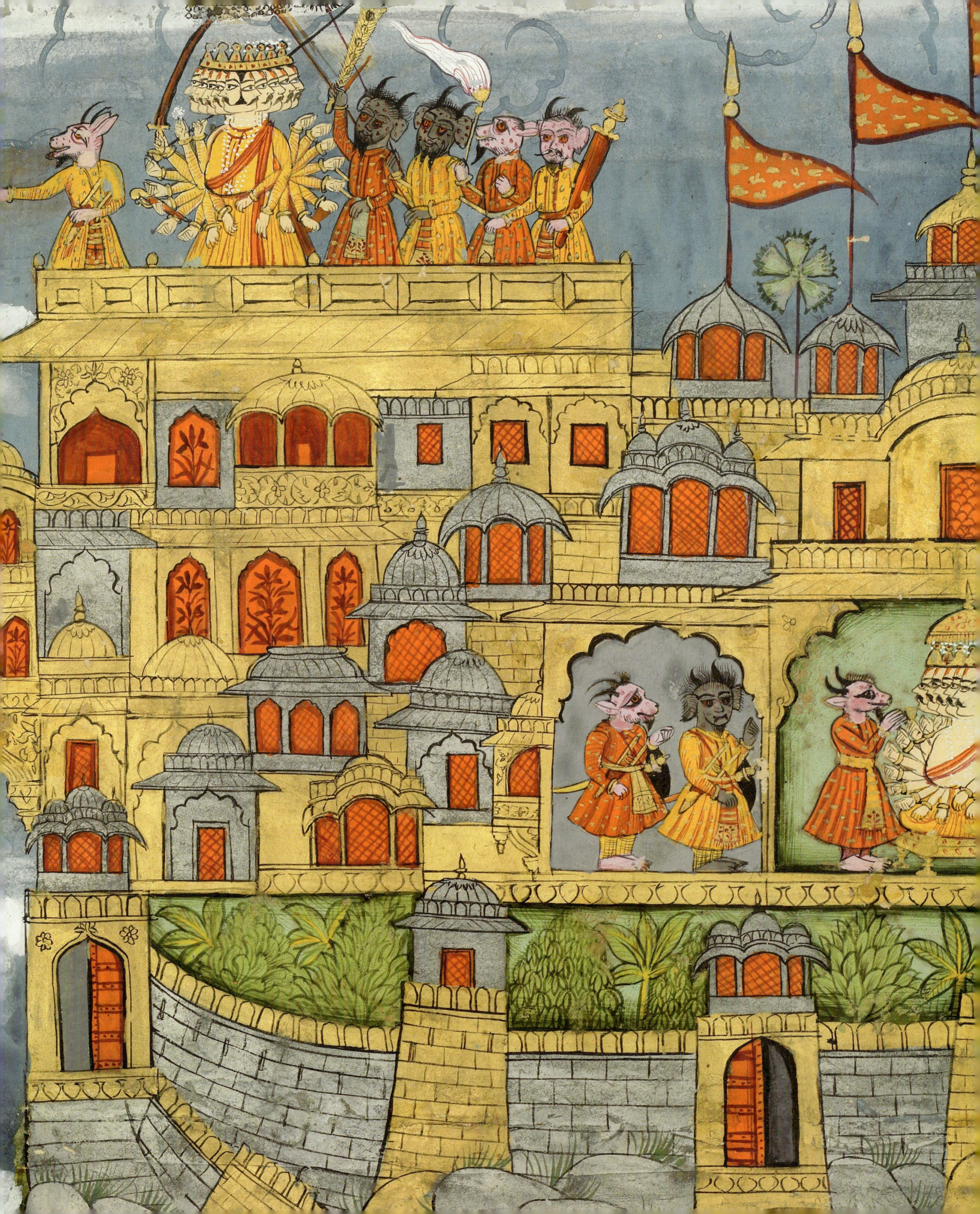

Sarayu Palace
from the *Ramcharitmanas* of Tulsidas (1532–1623)
Jodhpur, ca. 1775; 60.9 x 128.2 cm
Mehrangarh Museum Trust

Sri ram carit
Da[khal] dholiya re kothar
Glorious Ram Charit
Entered in the *dholiya* storeroom

The *Ramcharitmanas* concludes with Rama and Sita's joyous reign in the idyllic realm of Ayodhya, where everyone, including animals, is contented, virtuous, and healthy. Tulsidas' verses further reveal that Ayodhya is an earthly mirror of the celestial realm of Saket, where Rama dwells eternally in a transcendent (but embodied) form with the supreme goddess Sita.[16] This concluding folio from the Jodhpur *Ram Charit* depicts Ayodhya/Saket by expanding upon the Nagaur aesthetic of the water palace. While the architecture and pastel palette are similar to paintings from the workshop of Bakhat Singh (reigned 1725–52), the folio's width allows for multiplication and amplification. Fifteen fanciful pleasure boats floating on a vast silver pool, formal flower gardens opening onto lush groves, a gold-domed water pavilion rising three stories, and hundreds of female attendants adorn Rama and Sita's divine realm. Lovingly reunited after their travails in exile, the deities are depicted three times beneath jeweled and fringed gold umbrellas. Amused and adored by attendants, they enjoy a dance performance beneath the assembly hall's high ceiling as well as cool breezes and music as they are trans-ported in a pleasure boat; from the water pavilion's more intimate surroundings, they watch waterfowl splashing among lotuses.

The ideal social order of Ayodhya/Saket is known as *Ramrajya* (the rule of Rama). In the eighteenth century, as Mughal political and cultural authority declined, *Ramrajya* became an increasingly important paradigm for Hindu rulers across northern India.[17] Hindu kings commissioned recitations and reenactments of Tulsidas' epic, although most court ateliers conservatively continued producing illustrated manuscripts of Valmiki's Sanskrit *Ramayana*.[18] Vijai Singh (reigned 1752–93) took the more unusual route of commissioning a pictorial cycle of the Hindi version.[19] This is strikingly apparent in the manuscript's final four folios depicting Tulsidas' idyllic ending, which differs from the Valmiki conclusion featuring the more troubling events of Sita's fire ordeal and Rama's death. In each folio, the divine couple enjoys royal pastimes also depicted in smaller paintings of Jodhpur rulers, including playing holi and watching elephant fights (see cats. 11, 17, 20), which creates a visual connection to Rajput court culture. The monumental scale and the increase in grandeur befits the great gods Rama and Sita. DD

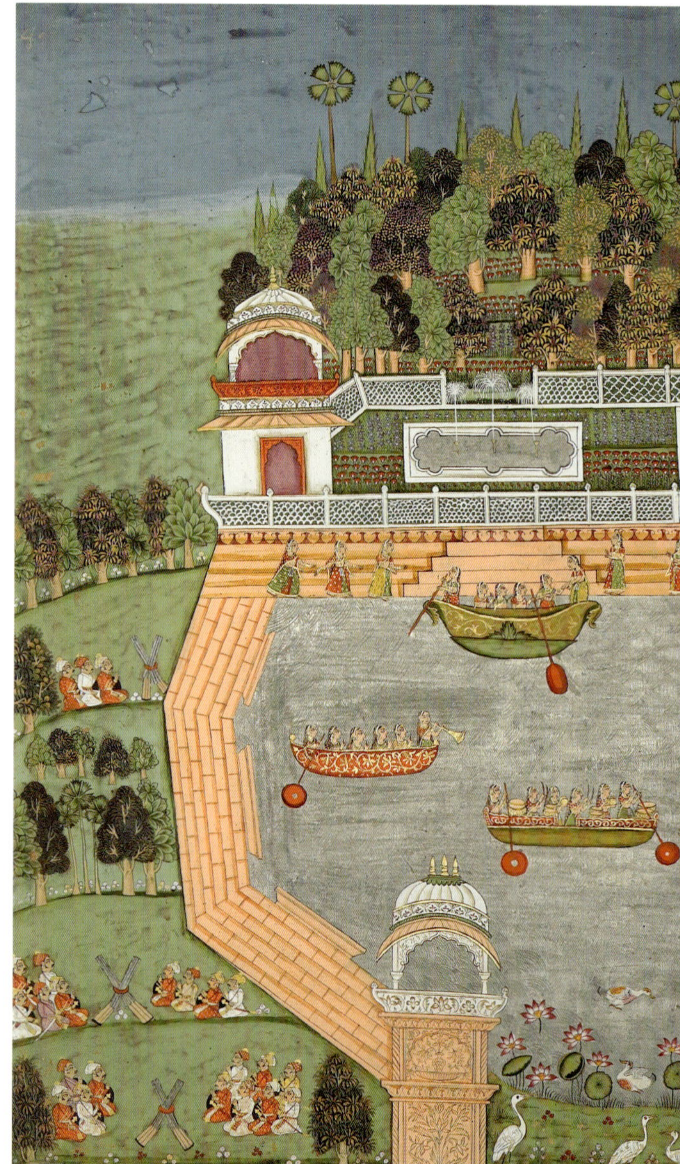

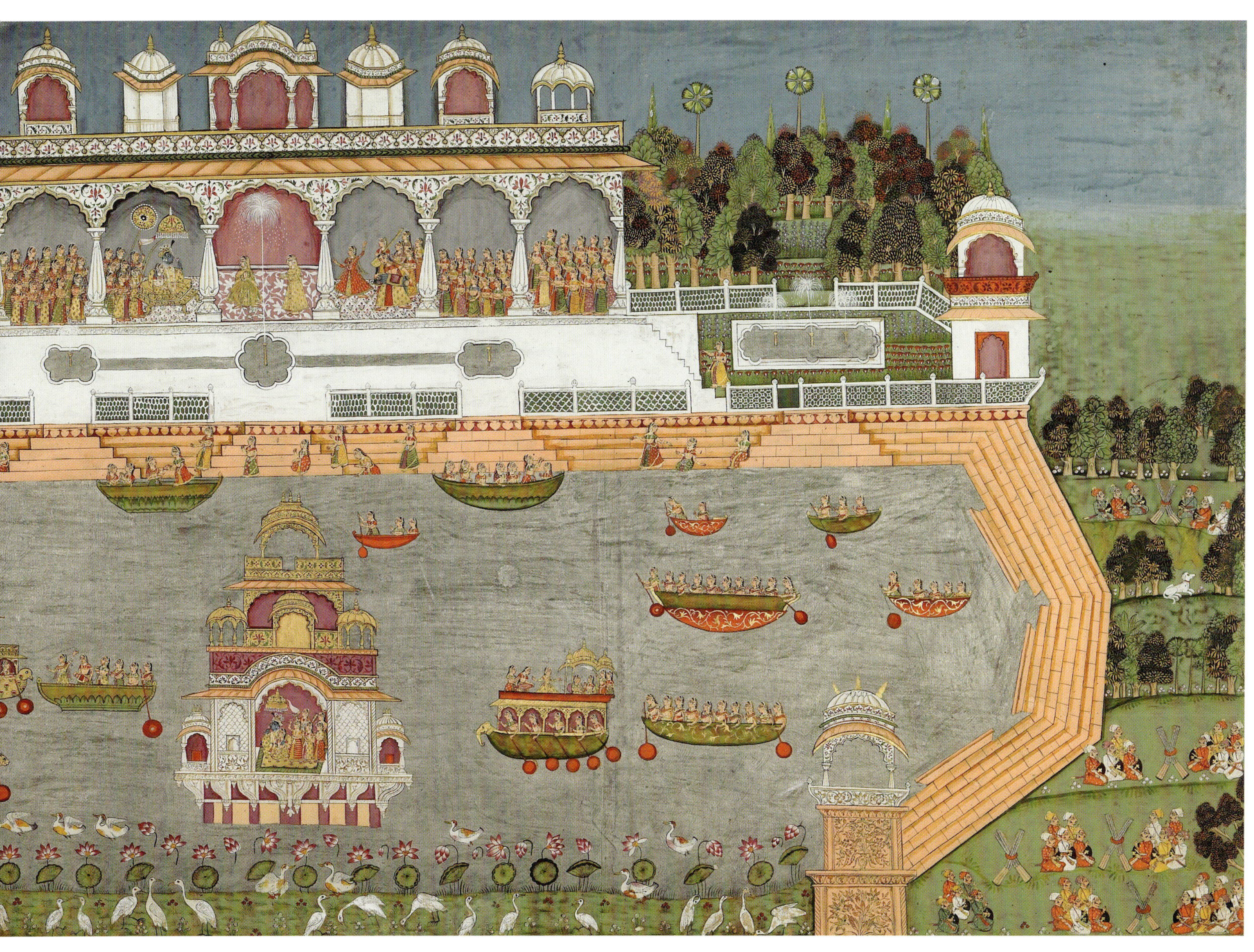

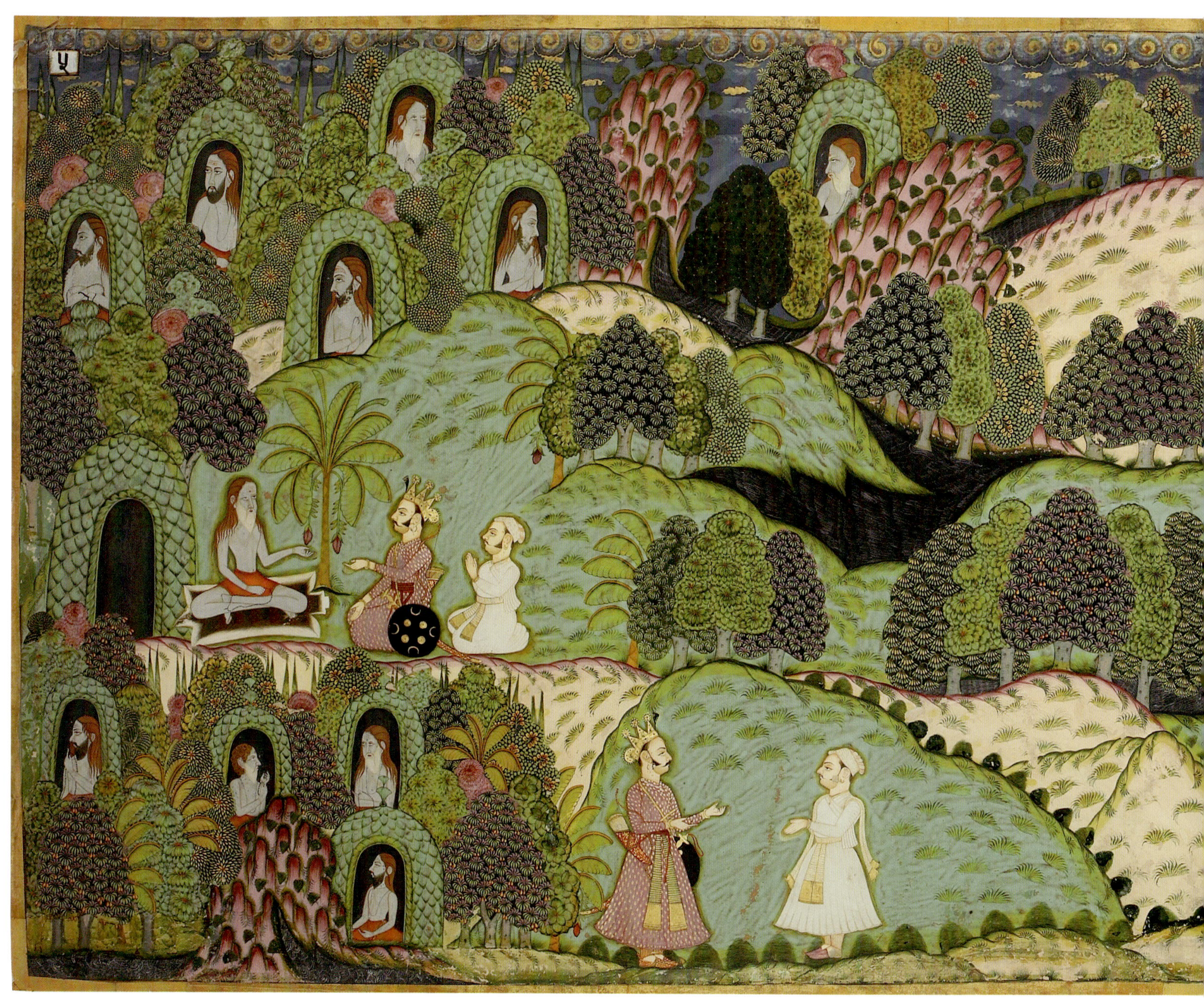

Cat. 30

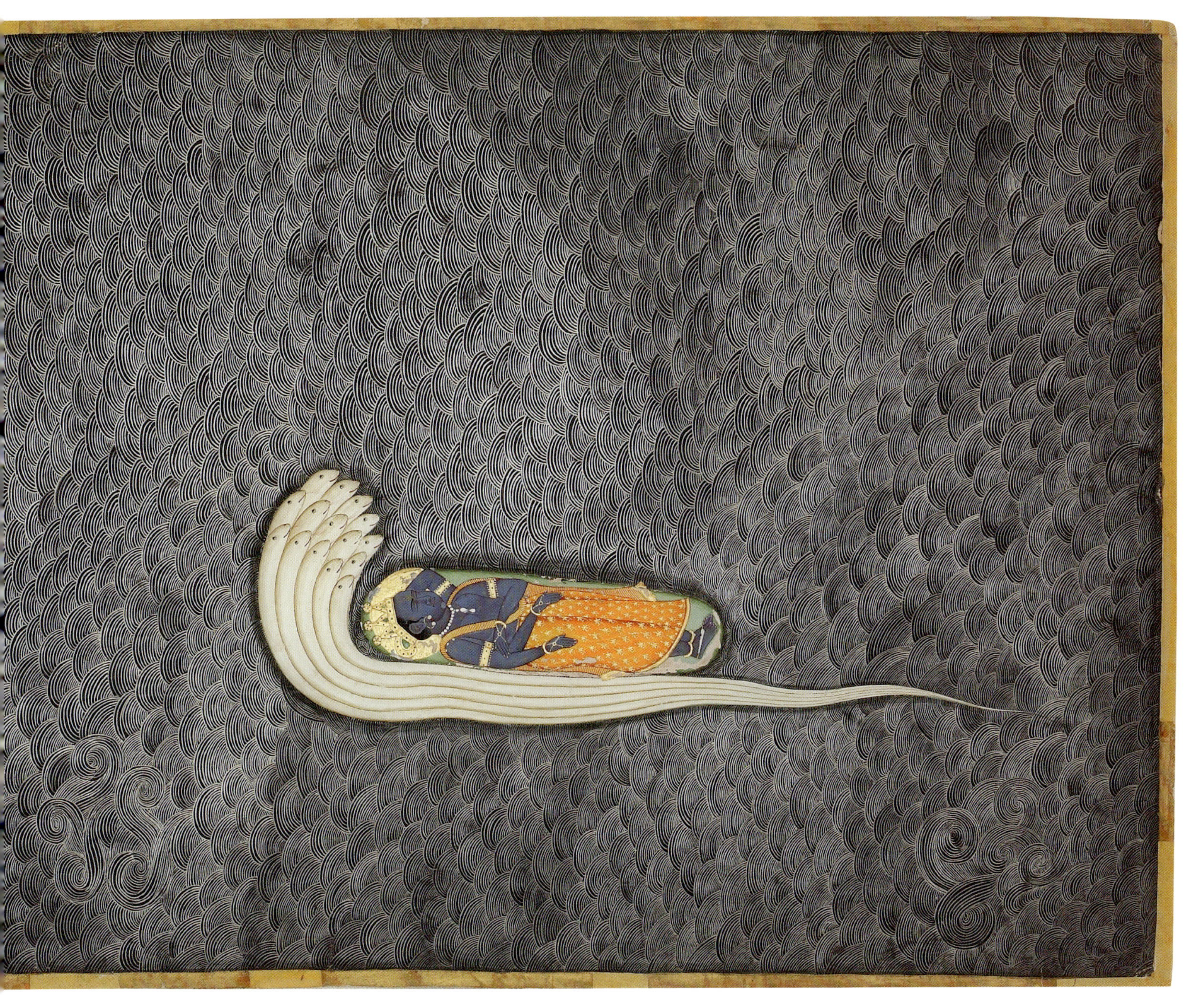

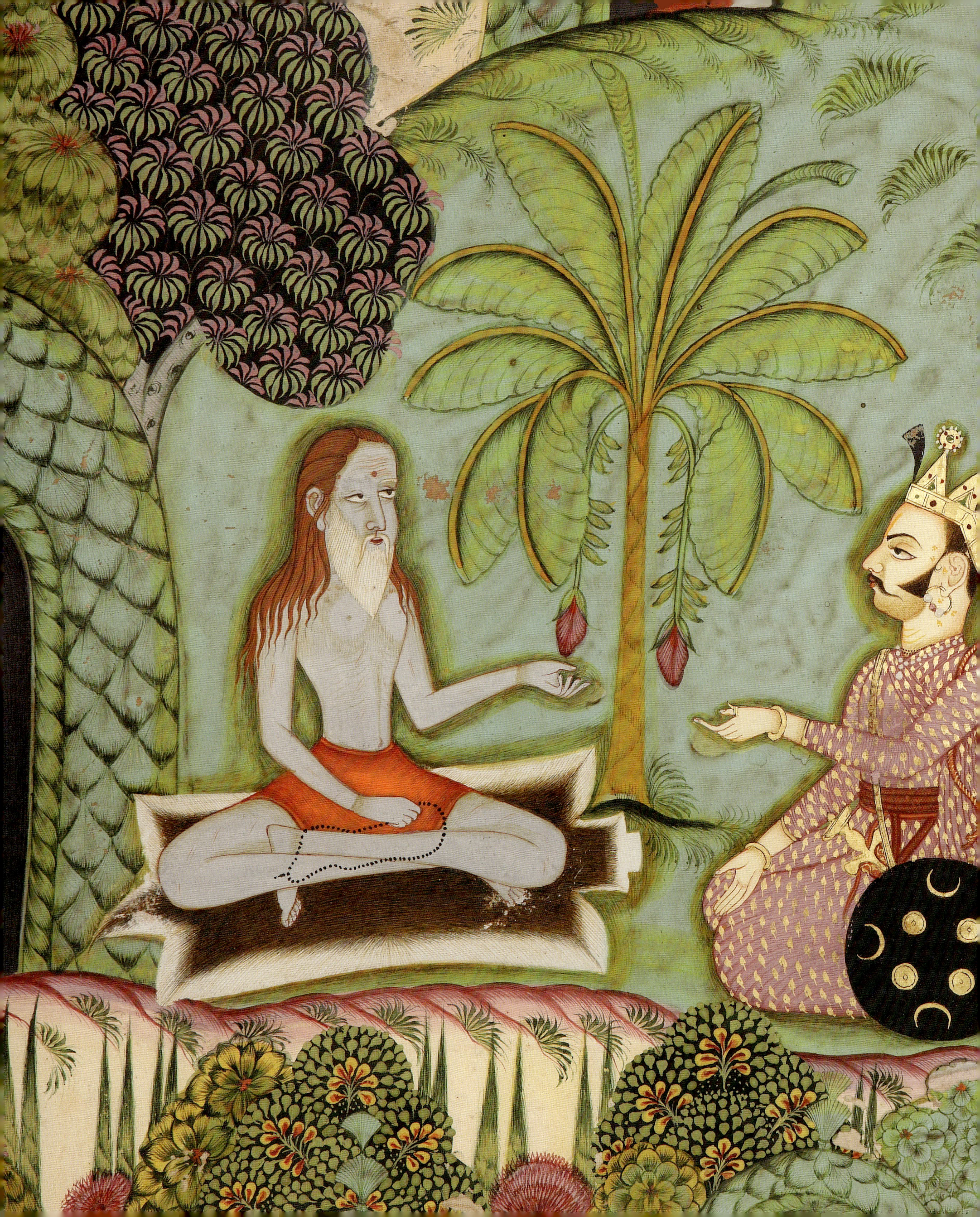

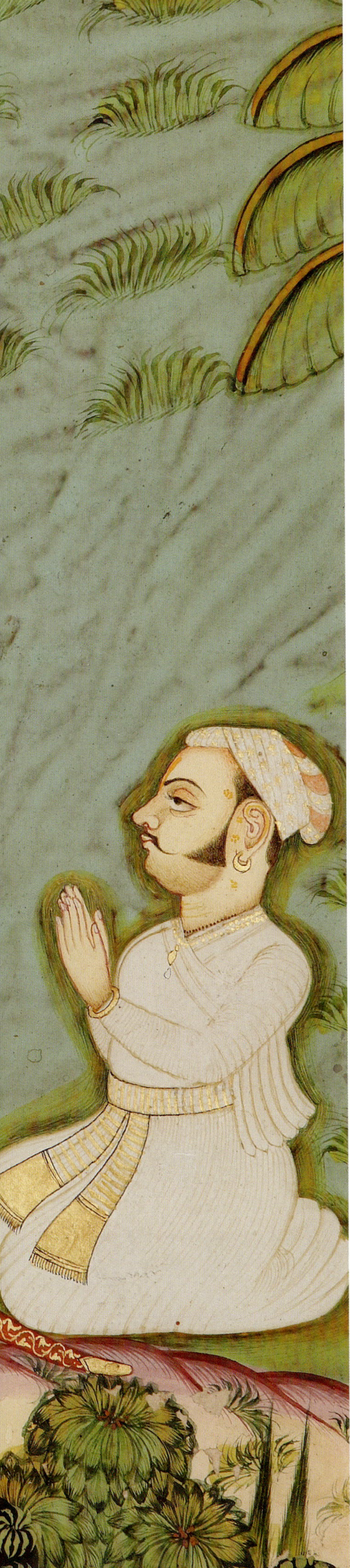

Sage Markandeya's Ashram and the Milky Ocean

folio 5 from the *Durga Charit*
Attributed to the "Durga Master"
Jodhpur, ca. 1780–90; 48.3 x 129.5 cm
Mehrangarh Museum Trust

The complete inscription appears in the reference catalogue.

The *Devi Mahatmya* (Greatness of the Goddess), which recounts Devi's victories over fierce demons, had particular resonance for Rajput rulers, who worshiped the goddess because she provided strength to warriors and kings.[20] This folio, from the last monumental manuscript created during Vijai Singh's reign (1752–93), illustrates the *Devi Mahatmya's* framing story (pp. 136–37). Two distraught souls, a king and a merchant, travel to the peaceful hermitage of the illustrious sage Medha to seek release from their attachment to the material world.[21] To assuage their pain, Medha reveals that the apparent solidity of this world is an illusion (*maya*).[22]

The sylvan landscape on the left draws upon the garden aesthetic of Nagaur paintings from the second quarter of the eighteenth century. Medha's lush forest abode is realized in the Nagaur palette of pale greens and pinks, to which the "Durga Master" harmoniously adds pale gray-blue and peach. While several of the tree types and the slender, elongated figures emerge directly from the Bakhat Singh workshop, the expansive idyllic landscape is the distinctive contribution of his son Vijai Singh's atelier. The painting's shallow depth is characteristic of the workshop's approach; hillocks and leaf huts are essentially stage flats that overlap to create a space for the reenactment of epic events. The "Durga Master" has created a gradual transition between the completely natural landscape toward the right, in which peach-colored hills dominate, and the greener ashram on the left (see p. 136). The "Durga Master's" complete command of the formal elements creates a mood of contemplative quiet. All the elements are gently rounded, subtly shaded, and delicately contoured; even the lake's jagged banks are curved. A particularly delicate line describes the emaciated ascetics, and contour-softening washes of translucent green around the figures of Medha and his visitors integrate them into the verdant landscape.

The sage begins his revelation (on the right) by conjuring a time when the universe was in a state of dissolution and only vast waters existed. The text's leap from the human present to the cosmic stage (see pp. 136–37) is echoed in the dramatic visual contrast between the finely detailed hermitage and a starkly two-dimensional cosmic ocean, where Vishnu sleeps upon his multi-headed serpent Shesha. Highly burnished, Vishnu's body shines against the matte ground of deep indigo blue and dull silver. His three-quarter-view face, with its pointy chin and sweet, small smile, recalls the Vishnu series from circa 1765 and Bikaner paintings of Krishna (cats. 23–25). If the depictions of Vishnu and Medha's ashram demonstrate the continuity of an aesthetic and motifs that emerged earlier in the century, the ocean upon which the god sleeps introduces a new element. The undifferentiated cosmic space, which here fills the right panel, covers the entire surface of the manuscript's next two folios (also painted by the "Durga Master") and becomes a dominant motif in Jodhpur court painting of the early nineteenth century (see fig. 7, p. 29). DD

MAHARAJA MAN SINGH AND THE NATHS

During his reign, Maharaja Man Singh (reigned 1803–43) reconceived sovereign authority in Marwar. He marginalized the hereditary nobility, dedicated his kingdom to the immortal ascetic Jallandharnath, and elevated his guru's family into a sectarian elite. The small and medium-size paintings in this section demonstrate how court artists contributed to Man Singh's project of legitimation.

Paintings of Man Singh with his Nath gurus and kinsmen document the dynamically evolving court. Datable both by the inscriptions and also by the appearance of individuals who were subsequently murdered or exiled, they articulate new landscapes of power with recognizable architectural structures and town plans.

Other paintings demonstrate how Man Singh's devotion to Jallandharnath was fully assimilated into an already-established mode of religious visuality, and how a mythic past that prefigured his accession was articulated, for the first time, through imagery. A folio from a monumental manuscript brings the revelation of an immortal ascetic into the opulent aesthetic of court painting.

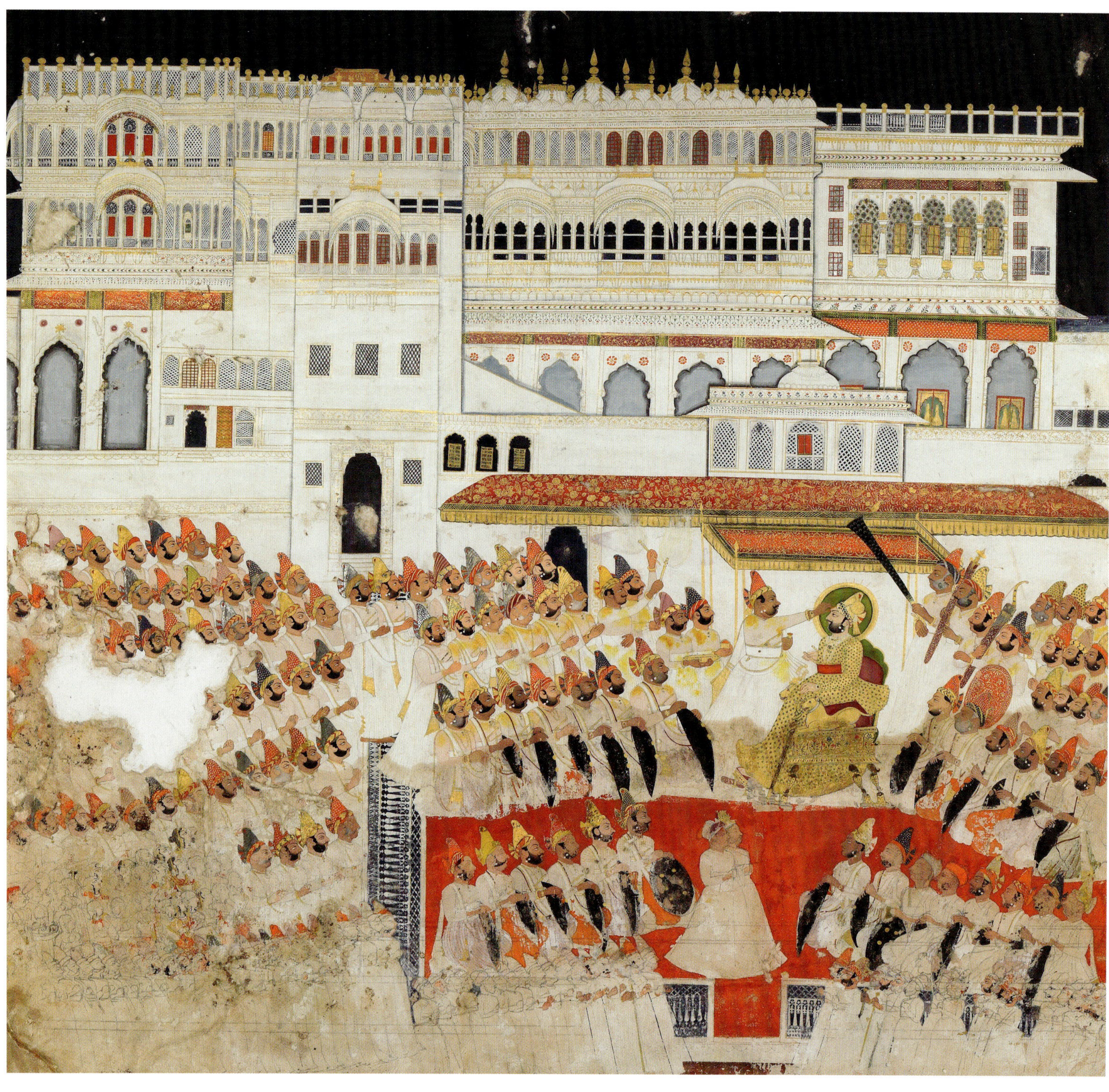

31

The Rajtilak Darbar of Maharaja Man Singh

Amardas Bhatti, ca. 1804; 74 x 80 cm
Mehrangarh Museum Trust

Raj rajeswar maharajadhiraj maharaja man singhji rajtilak
Citara amar das ra hath ri
Da[khal] dholiya re kothar
The coronation of the lord of king of kings, supreme king of great kings,
Maharaja Man Singhji
From the hand of the painter Amardas
Entered into the *dholiya* storeroom

On January 19, 1804, the noblemen of Marwar gathered within Mehrangarh
Fort for the coronation (*rajtilak*) of Man Singh. Amardas, who would become
one of Man Singh's greatest painters, presents the fort's Shringar Courtyard
as a magnificently ornate stage for the important state event. While the opulent
delicacy of the palace backdrop evokes rather than replicates the courtyard's
intricately carved walls, the lower half of the painting carefully records the
assembled courtiers (see p. 144). The thakur of Bagri applies the sandalwood
paste mark (*tilak*) of sovereignty upon Man Singh's forehead (see p. 145); the
most important nobles flank the maharaja; the next tier observes the event from
the raised platform where the new king is enthroned; and the least prominent
participants (including women) stand in the lower courtyard.[1] Man Singh's golden
attire attests to his supreme status, and the nobles express their allegiance by
replicating his appearance on a less-opulent scale, wearing turbans of gold cloth
distributed by the maharaja in acknowledgement of their support.

All Rajput paintings of *darbars* authorize a hierarchy of relations, with the king
at the state's apex and the nobility, by dint of birth and service, as the state's
support. Since every participant's body reveals the *darbar* protocols of dress and
ranked seating, images of court assemblies are compendia of signs indicating
status, as well as documents of historical events. But in Amardas' *rajtilak* painting,
the conviction of the courtyard's massive walls, the calm assurance of the king's
portrait, and the completely rendered nobility on the upper terrace trail off into
faintly limned, almost ghostlike, courtiers and attendees at the lower left border.
The visible underdrawing reveals that the grandly conceived pictorial record of
Man Singh's coronation was never completed. Amardas must have stopped
working on the painting when the fragile truce surrounding Man Singh's accession unraveled late in 1804. The prominent noblemen who had only grudgingly
accepted his "coup" abruptly quit the capital to back the cause of a pretender.[2]
In that political climate, the completion of a painting celebrating the allegiance of
these traitorous Rathore kinsmen would have been, to put it mildly, unwelcome. DD

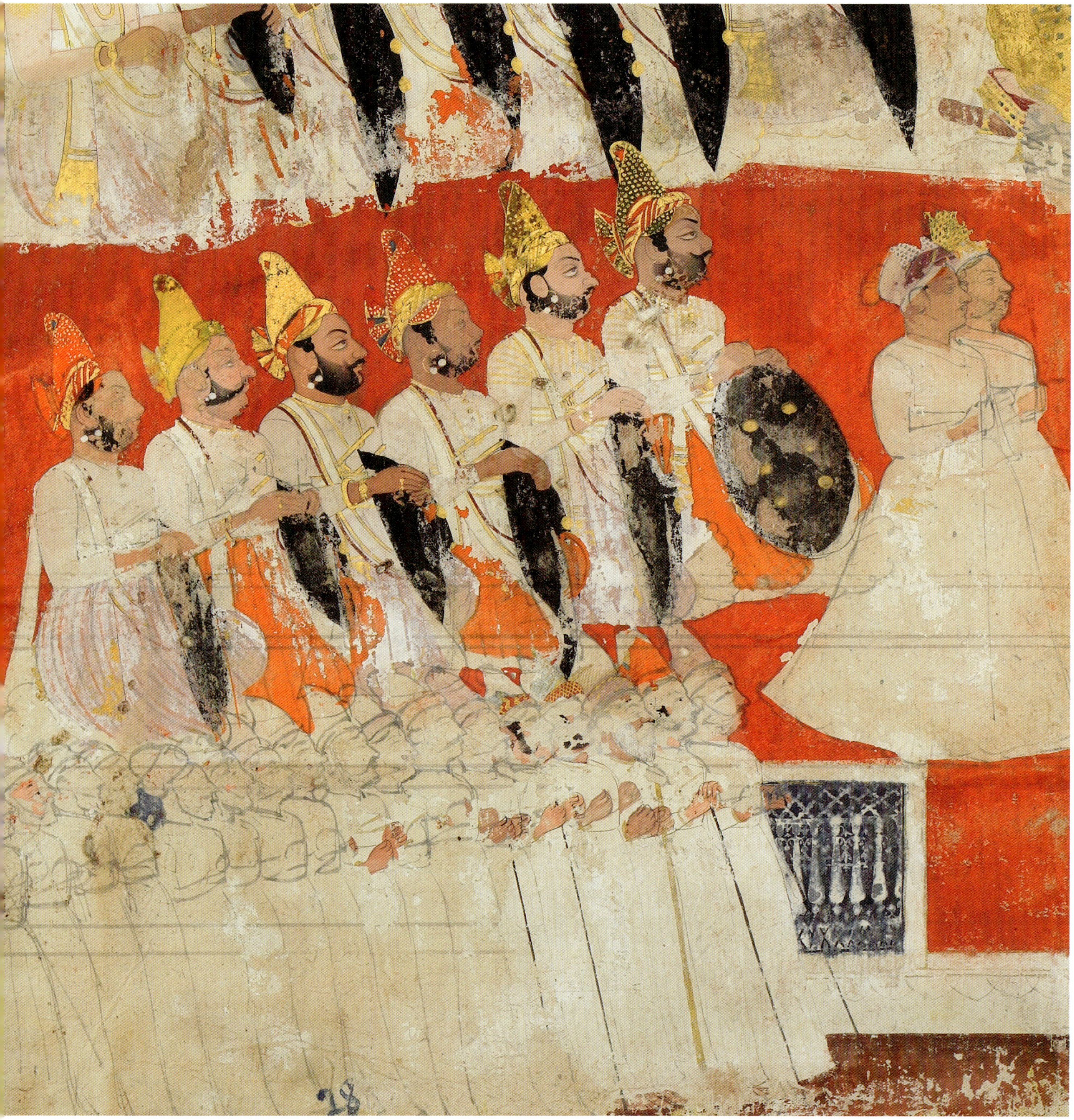

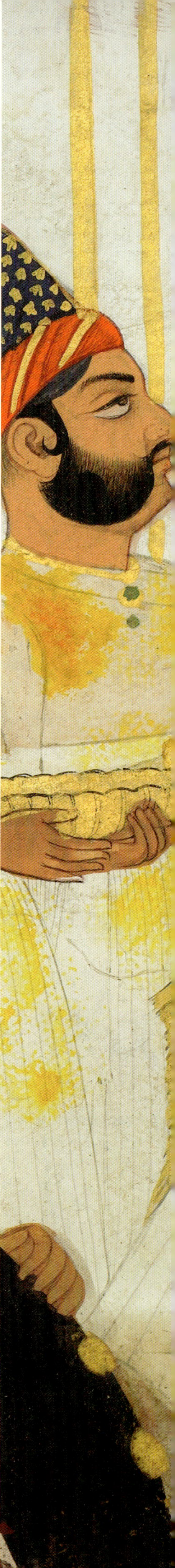

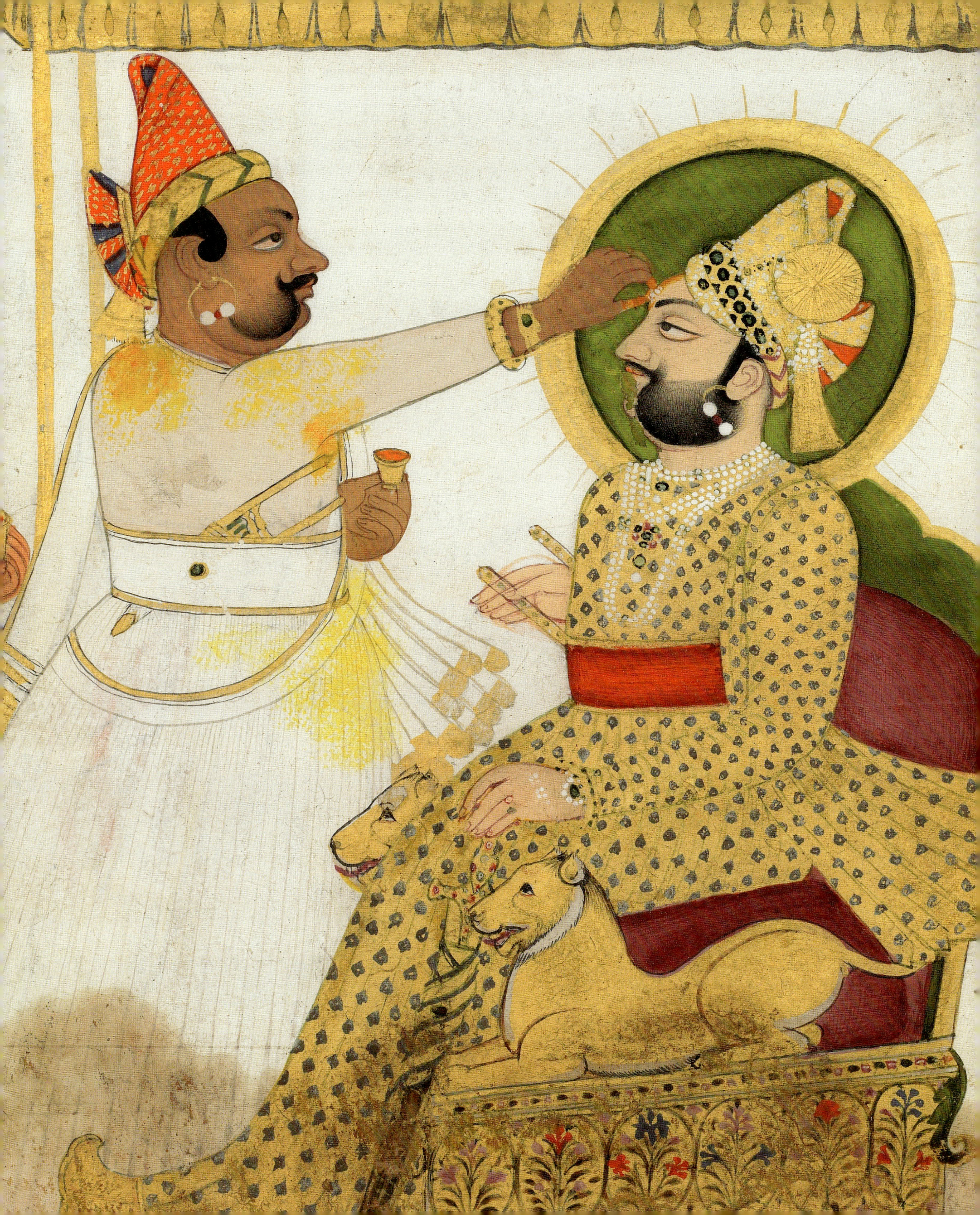

32

Jallandharnath and Maharaja Man Singh on Diwali

Shivdas Bhatti, ca. 1820–before July 1825; 50 x 33 cm

Mehrangarh Museum Trust

Da[khal] dholiya re kothar 1882 savan sud 11
Kalam Citara Shivdas ri
Entered into the *dholiya* storeroom on the eleventh day
of the bright half of Shravan (July–August), 1825
The work of the painter Shivdas

Man Singh commissioned hundreds of paintings that depict him worshiping the immortal ascetic Jallandharnath. These paintings construct Man Singh as Jallandharnath's supreme devotee. In each, the maharaja stands as humble supplicant, with his hands clasped in the gesture of respect and worship, and faces the elevated, enthroned, and haloed Jallandharnath.

After its creation in the early years of Man Singh's reign, the image of Jallandharnath acquired a legibility from its fixed and persistent replication by all the artists in his atelier. Jallandharnath, depicted in profile, has the ash-pale skin, *rudraksha* bead necklace, saffron garment, and *jata* (dreadlocks) of a Shaiva holy man (see fig. 4, p. 34). His large *kundal* earrings (worn through holes bored in the ears' inner cartilage), triangular black hat, and deer-horn whistle identify him specifically as a Nath. His slender body, arched back, and beardless face convey the youthful appearance of the "seventeen-year-old boy" that Man Singh praised in his devotional poetry.[3] Specific to the Jodhpur archetype are his pearl necklaces, gold-decorated garments, jeweled *kundal* earrings, and halo, as well as the large, heavy-lidded eye, pursed smile, heavily shaded jaw, and chin-length dreadlocks terminating in a tight curl. Similar to most Jodhpur paintings of this period, Jallandharnath's body and garments are flat forms demarcated by a prominent contour line, and shading is limited to the face.

Shivdas' painting exceeds the iconography of these devotional images by commemorating not only the maharaja's enduring piety, but also Jallandharnath's original act of grace at Jalore in 1803 during the week of Diwali, the Hindu festival of lights. The artist situates the two upon a palace's gleaming marble terrace, where Jallandharnath places a ceremonial shawl over the maharaja's shoulders, bowed in humility. The golden candelabras and small lamps (*dipas*) lining the terrace, the deep-blue night sky lit by shooting fireworks, and the flame pattern on Man Singh's red garment all refer to the eve of Diwali.

Shivdas' striking palette of bold primary colors is somewhat unusual because most Jallandharnath devotional paintings are dominated by orange and green. With its highly burnished surface, and its crisply curving forms set against rigidly geometric architecture, however, the painting is among the most striking of the Man Singh-period devotional paintings. DD

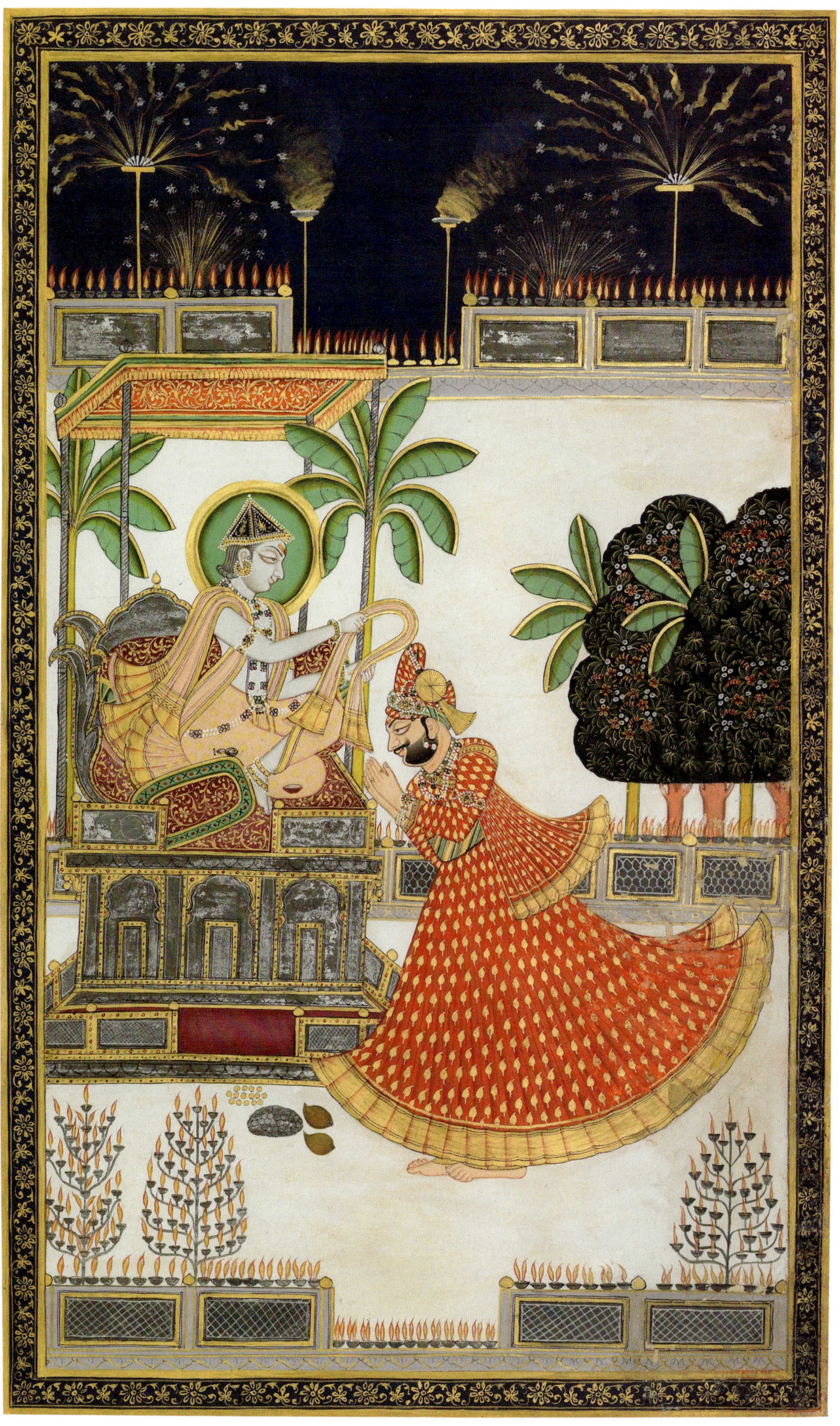

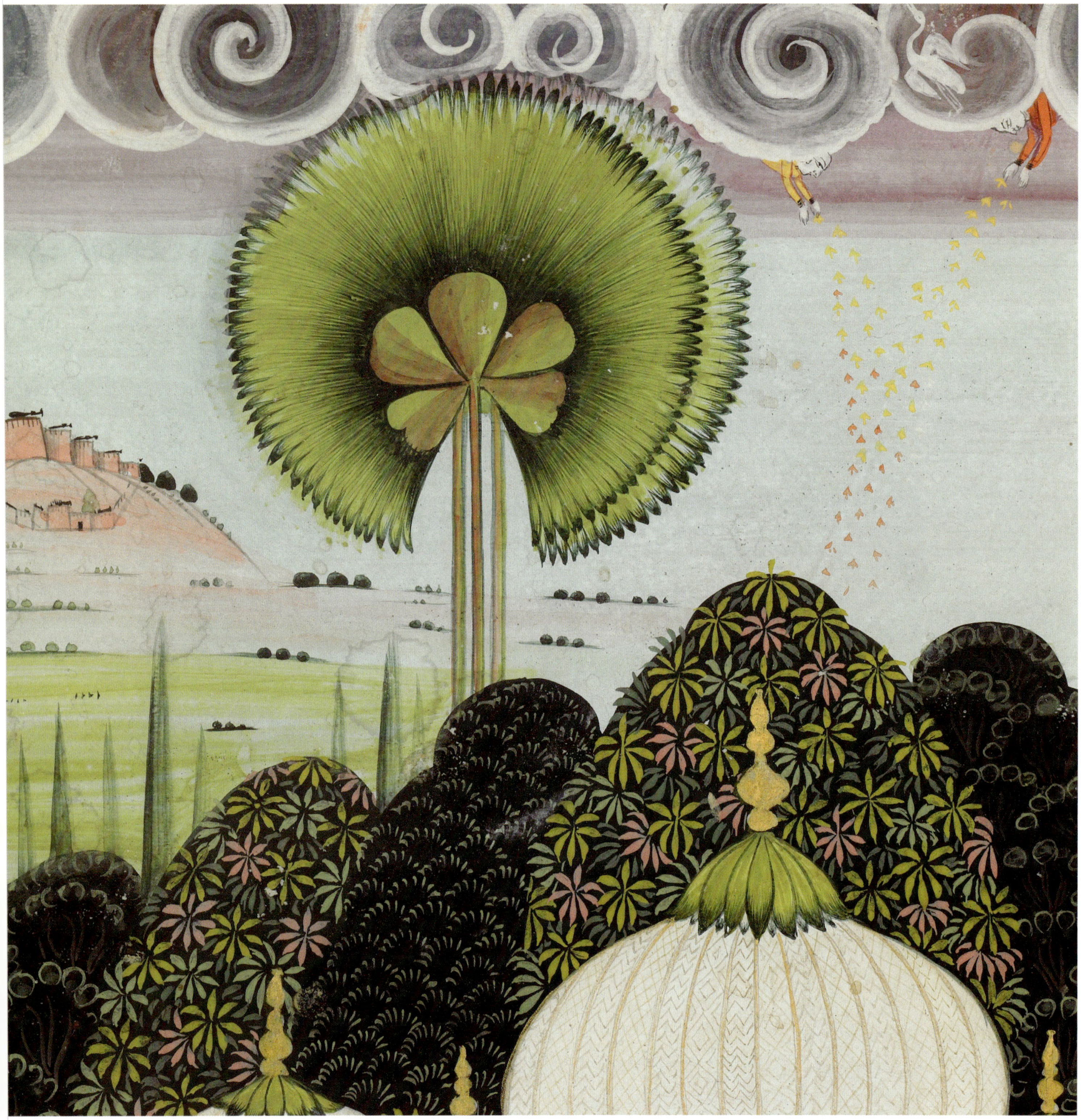

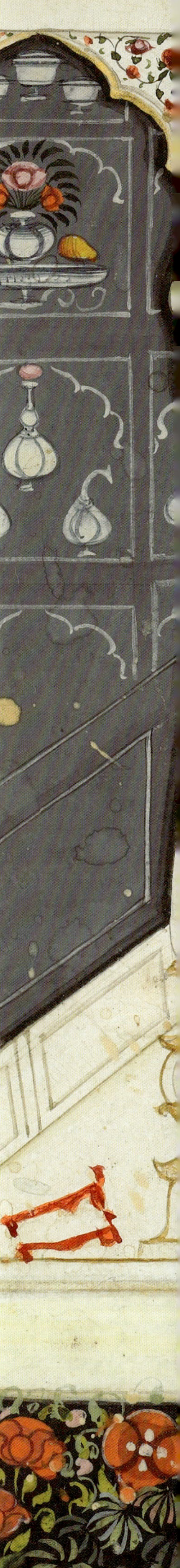

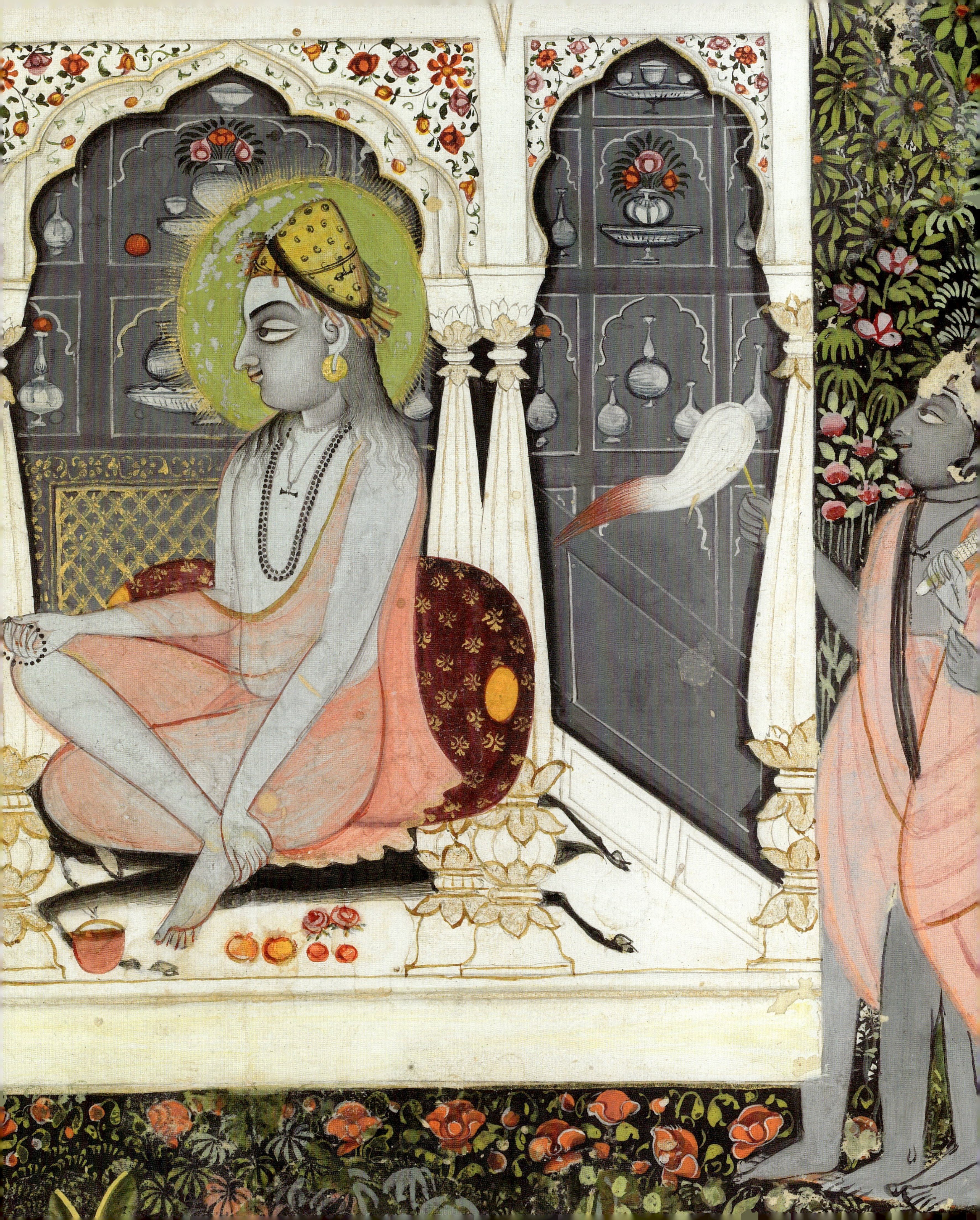

34

Jallandharnath and Princess Padmini Fly over King Padam's Palace
folio 19 from the *Suraj Prakash*
Amardas Bhatti, 1830; 23.3 x 38.6 cm
Mehrangarh Museum Trust

The complete inscription appears in the reference catalogue.

After a truce negotiated by the British in the late 1820s, Maharaja Man Singh, his Nath gurus, and the Rathore nobility again found themselves in an uneasy rapprochement. Within this tense political landscape, Man Singh commissioned an illustrated manuscript of the *Suraj Prakash* (Light of the Sun), the most renowned of the Rathore *vamshavalis* (dynastic narratives).[6] *Vamshavalis* valorized dynastic continuity, kinship bonds, clan loyalty, and proper kingly actions and were central to identity and prestige in the Rajput courts. Bards, whose compositions were accepted as historical truth, recited the genealogies in verse at court assemblies as well as on the battlefield.

The illustrated *Suraj Prakash* (1830) marks the first time that any Jodhpur chronicle entered the realm of manuscript painting.[7] As a visual narrative of dynastic events, the illustrated chronicle breaks with the oral performance tradition. Moreover, its pictorial cycle omits or abbreviates many of the chronicle's regnal histories. Paintings focus on those princes who were transformed into powerful kings and clan founders by divine grace. The conception of sovereignty expressed in its paintings thus prefigures Man Singh's miraculous accession to the throne. Commissioning the illustrated *vamshavali* may have been an attempt to mollify Rathore kinsmen opposed to Man Singh's alliance with the Naths.

This rather charming image depicts an early moment in the narrative of the twelfth-century King Padam, who later will defeat a rival king, win the hand of Princess Padmini, receive grace from a Nath *mahasiddha*, and found a cadet clan. The regnal history begins with the beautiful king sporting with the women of his harem in a lotus-filled pleasure pool. Sheltered by a lush banyan tree, the haloed Padam embraces a favorite while the other women frolic. One woman spits a stream of water at her friend; another is submerged (except for her hennaed hand) in a game of hide-and-seek. The emphatically silver surface of Padam's pleasure pond meets the horizon with a river's jagged edge; its terrace fronts a palace city rendered in vertiginous perspective. Above the palace, the *mahasiddha* Jallandharnath flies through the sky with the Sri Lankan Princess Padmini, whom he has enchanted.[8] The princess spies the handsome king from the sky and drops her golden bracelet to him as a token of love (see pp. 154–55).

The fragmented composition epitomizes Amardas' playful appropriation and juxtaposition of motifs from different sources. The palace rendered in deep perspective is a motif that was popular in this period in the Jaipur, Mewar, and Kutch courts. The bathing scene is adapted from a different painting that depicts the god Krishna frolicking by the Yamuna River with village maidens (see figs. 34a and 34b, p. 282). Although Amardas transforms the deity into an earthly ruler and the rural women into royal consorts, he retains the jagged river bank at the far edge of the palace pool. The reference to a pastoral landscape recalls the play of the irresistibly beautiful Krishna (cats. 23–25), and thus emphasizes King Padam's charm. DD

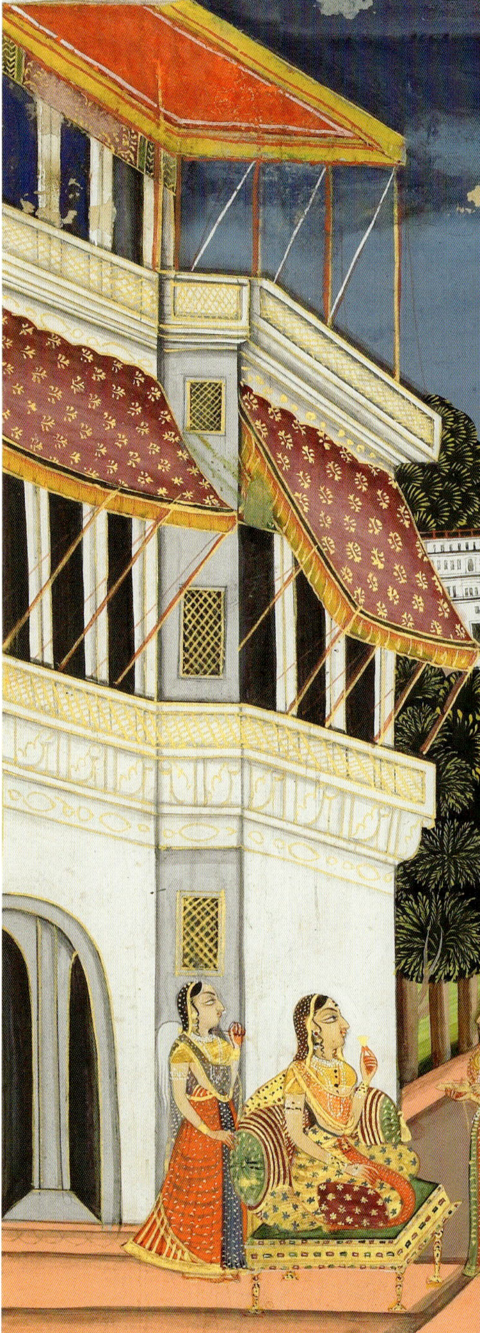

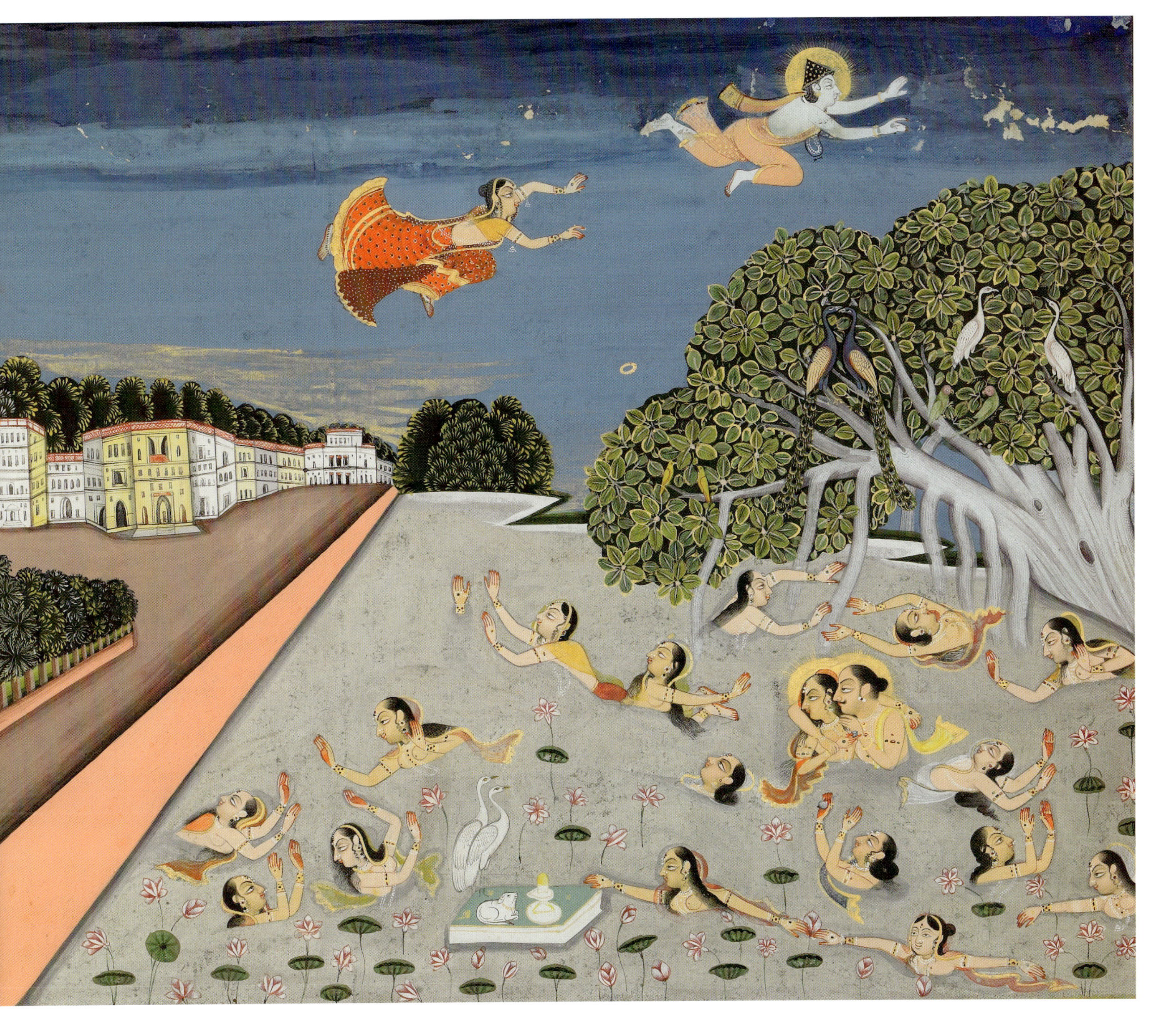

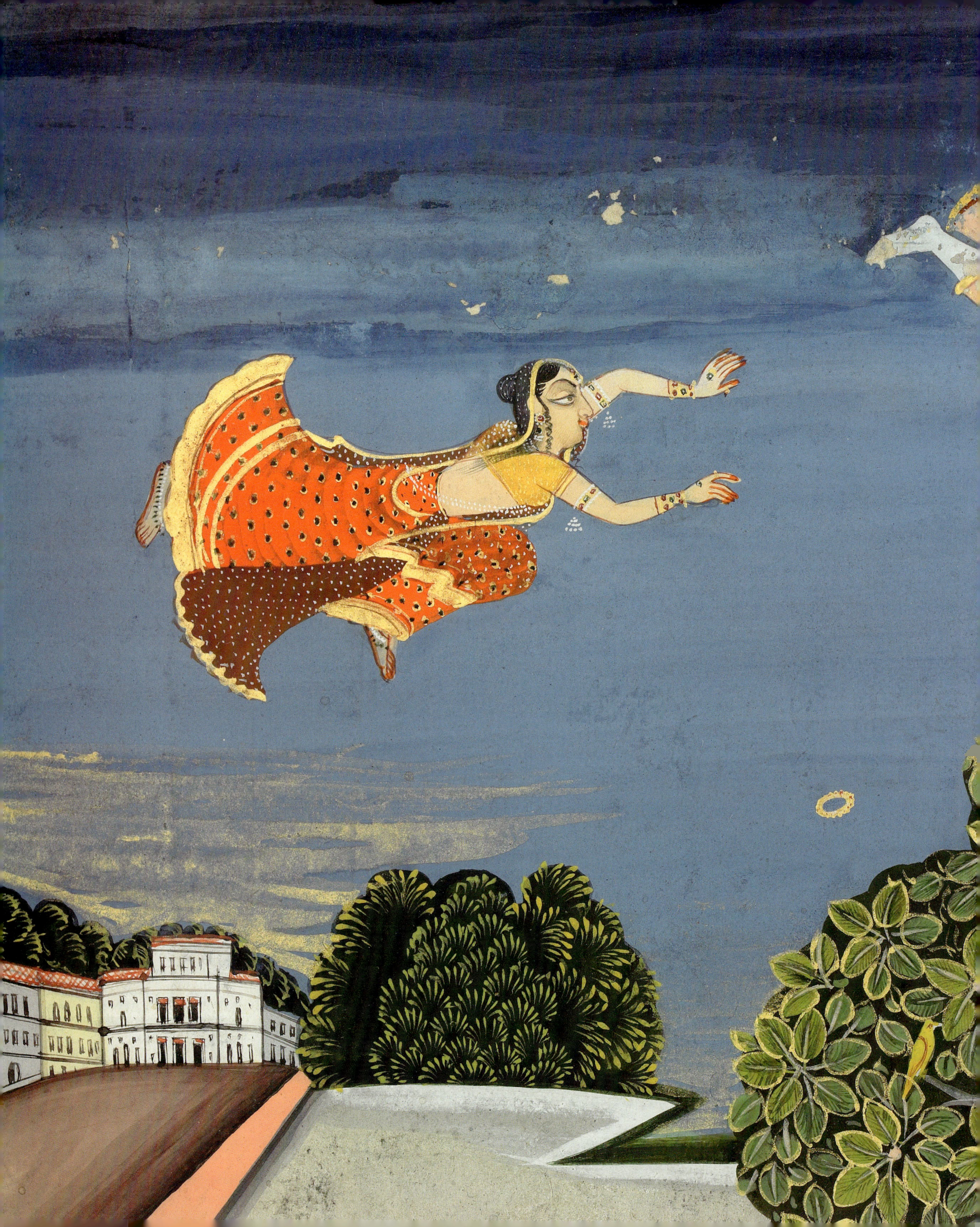

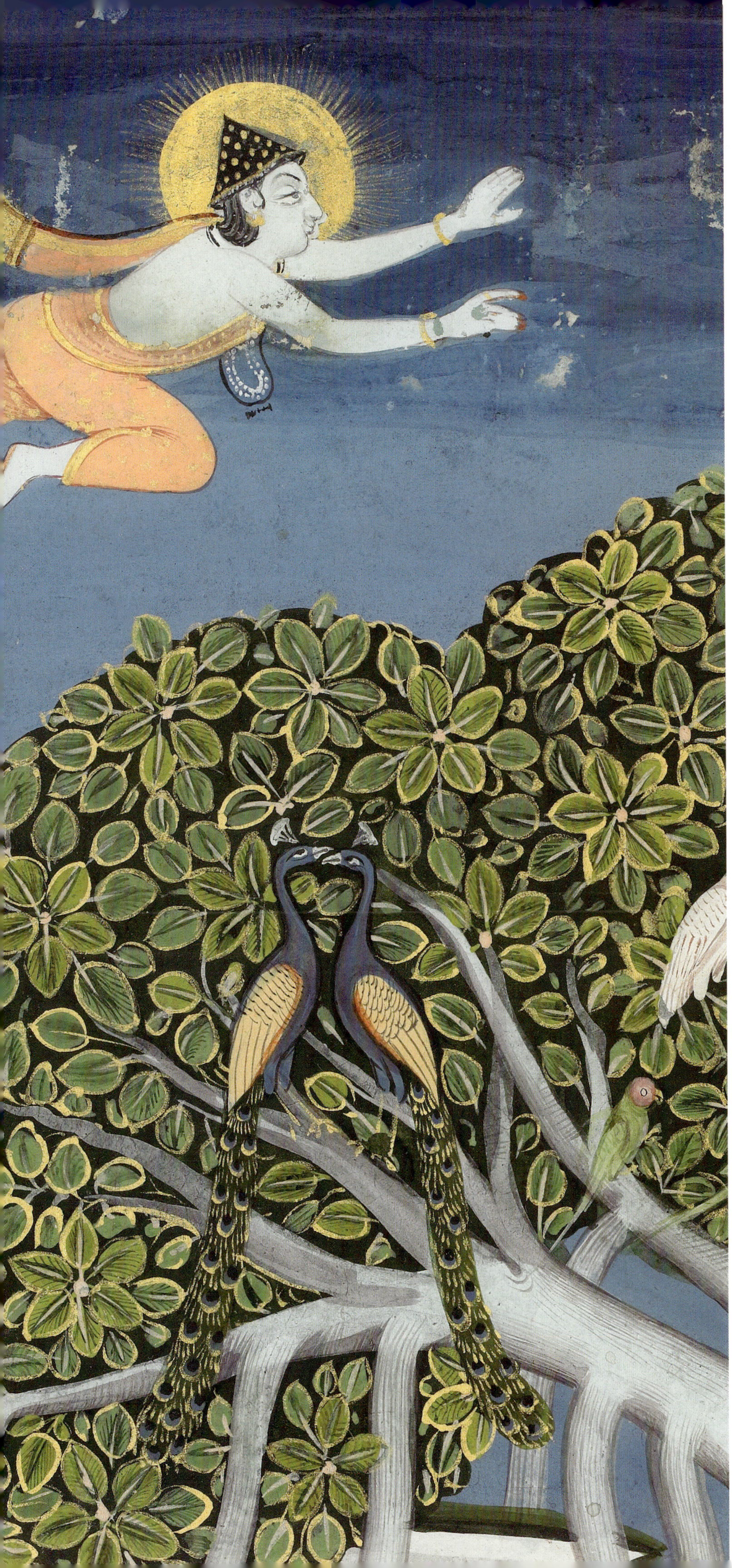

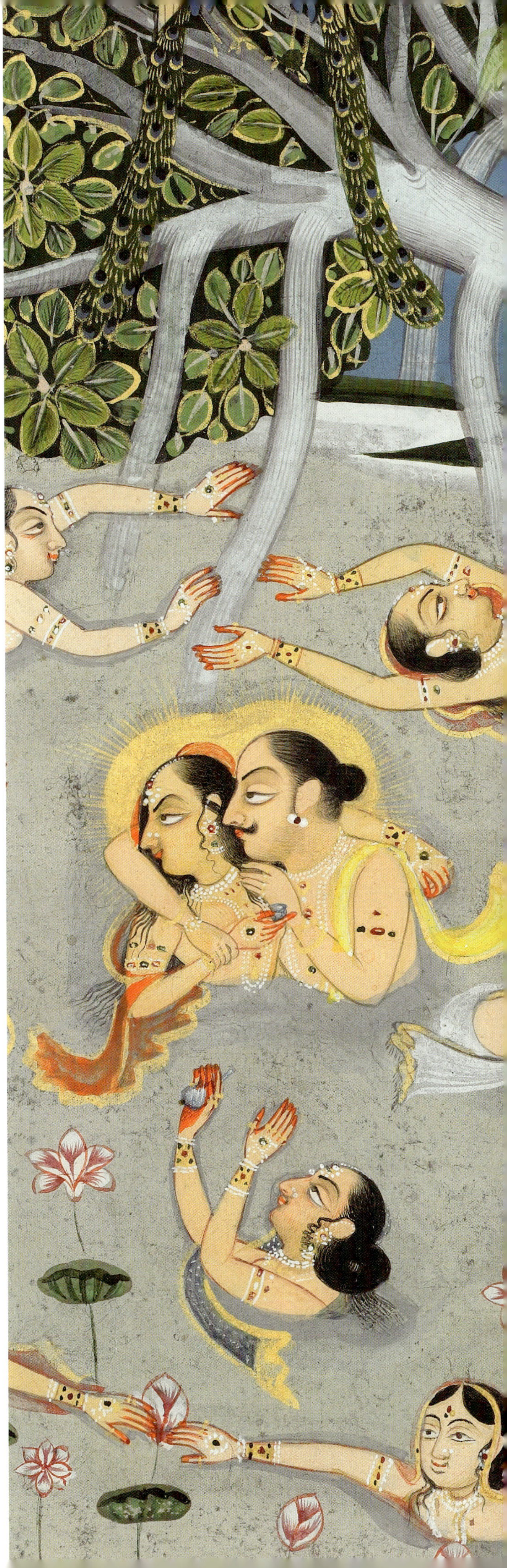

35

Prince Subuddhi in the Forest of Illusion

folio 35 from the *Suraj Prakash*
Amardas Bhatti, 1830; 23.3 x 38.6 cm
Mehrangarh Museum Trust

Granth suraj prakas ro
Da[khal] dholiya re kothar kalam amra ri
The book of the *Suraj Prakash*
Entered into the *dholiya* storeroom, the work of Amardas

In the *Suraj Prakash,* the greatest of the Rathore dynasty histories in verse, the poet Karnidan wrote of an ancestor so brave that even the gods were frightened of his courage. To test the king's bravery, the deity Shiva, in his fierce form Virbhadra, created a nightmarish forest:

> In the middle of a moonless night
> The king came to a river of red blood
> On both shores, fire raged like war cannons
> Causing broken skulls to shine like lotuses....[9]

The artist Amardas depicts Shiva's terrifying illusion with pictorial glee. Half-submerged in washes of translucent crimson, grunting demons ride bloated animal carcasses in the torrential river of blood. Grinning and roaring, brandishing snakes and skulls, they play Sindhu raga on femur flutes and *tamburas* strung with intestines. Above, fierce birds and winged heads spew fire and devour body parts snatched from the corpses bobbing and sinking like fish in the torrential river. At the painting's center stands King Subuddhi in a fresh white *jama,* heroically unruffled by the crackling gold flames of the midnight sky, the demon orchestra, and the twisted limbs of his dead horse. At right, enthroned within a flaming mandorla, Shiva views his illusion—and King Subuddhi's calm bravery—with delight. In recognition of the king's courage, Shiva promised divine assistance in any war. Because of this gift from Virbhadra, Subbuddhi's descendants were called the Vir Rathores.

Amardas based his depiction of the twelfth-century King Subuddhi on a seventeenth-century Jodhpur archetype. Subuddhi wears the turban and translucent *jama* (with saffron-dyed bodice) that Maharaja Jaswant Singh (reigned 1638–78) dons in cat. 6. Royal portraiture emerged fully in Jodhpur under Jaswant Singh, and his image in this text signals royal authority and links distant ancestors to more recent history. DD

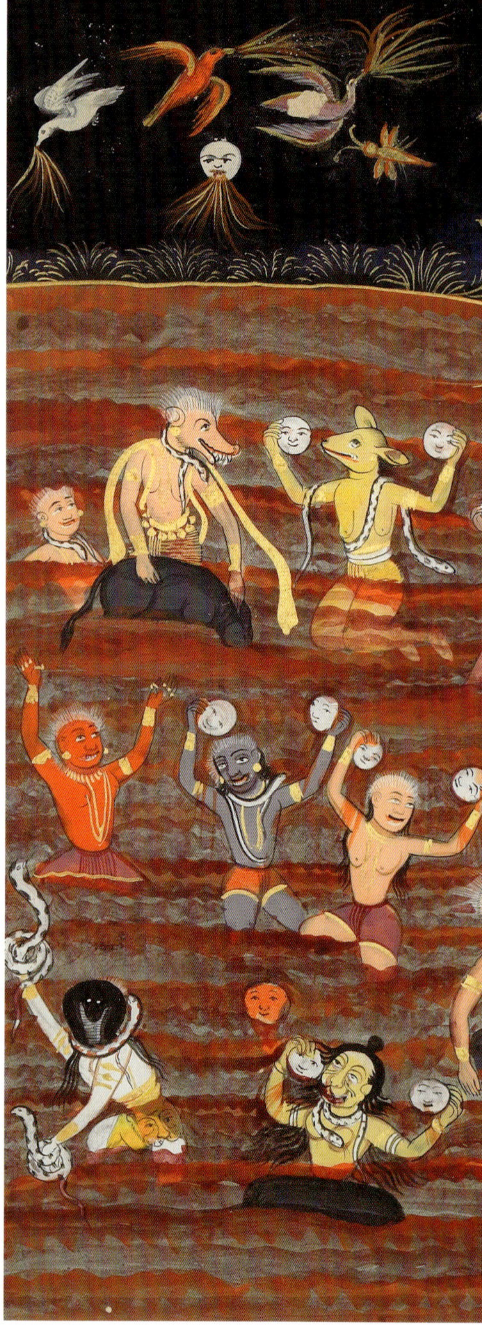

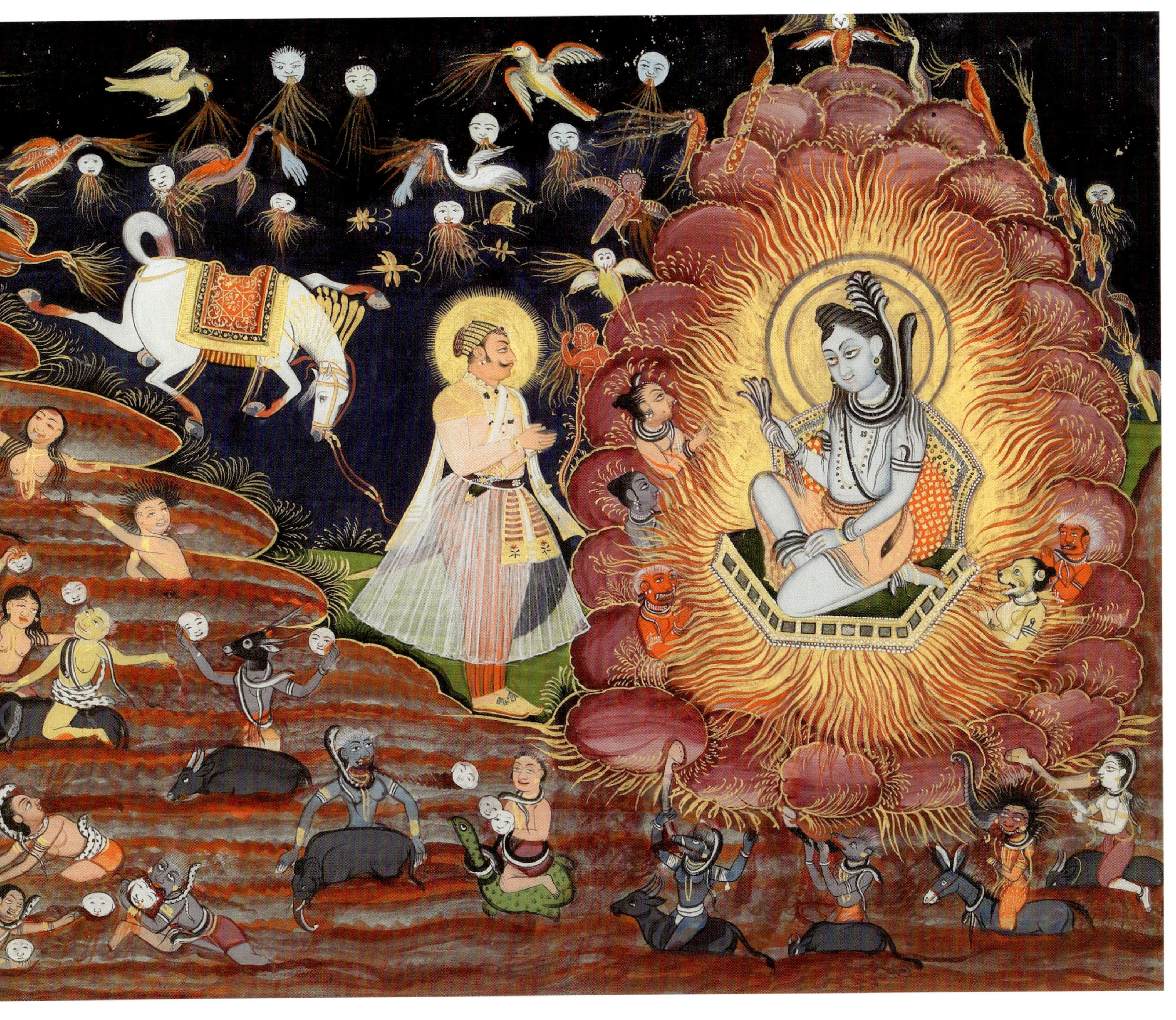

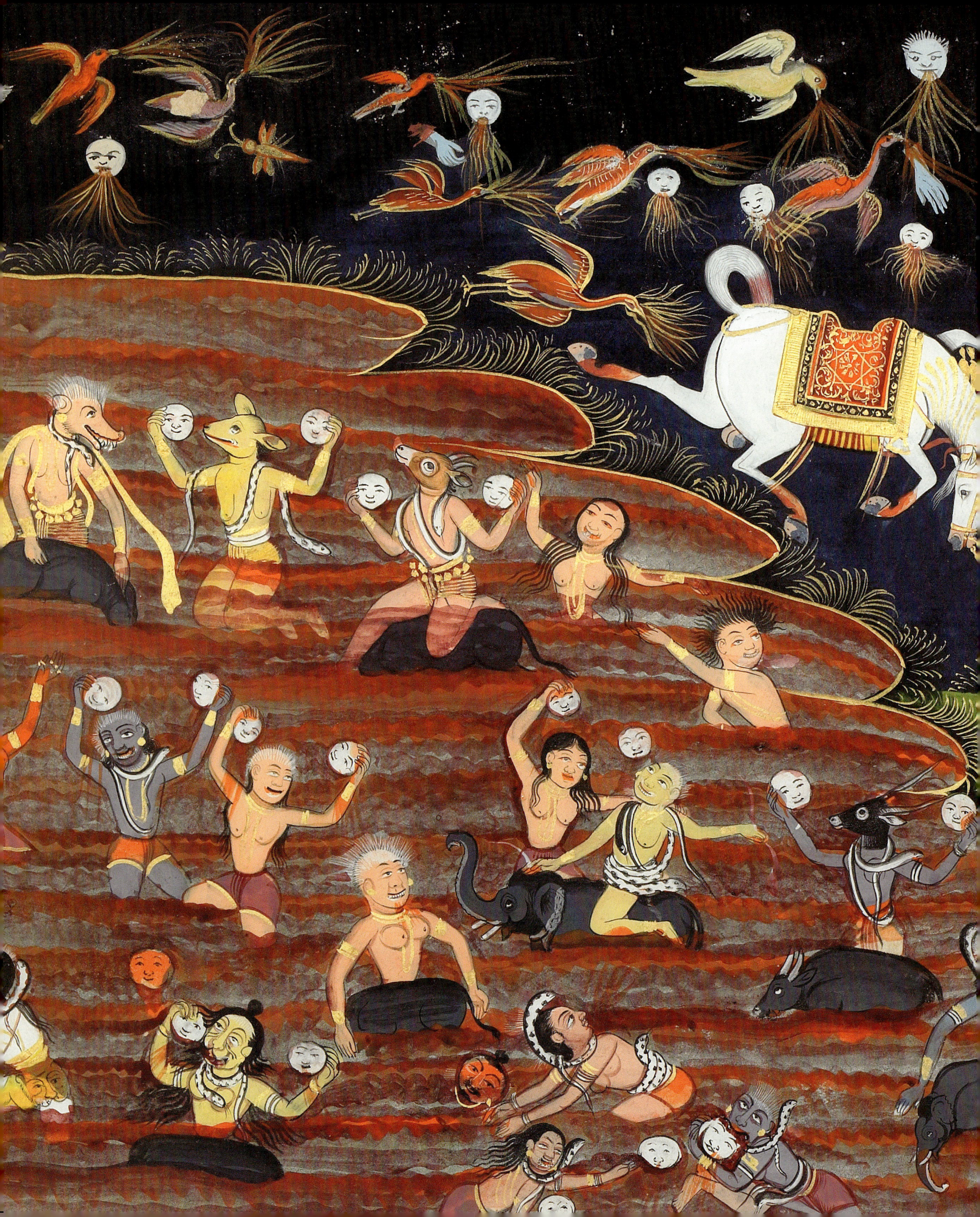

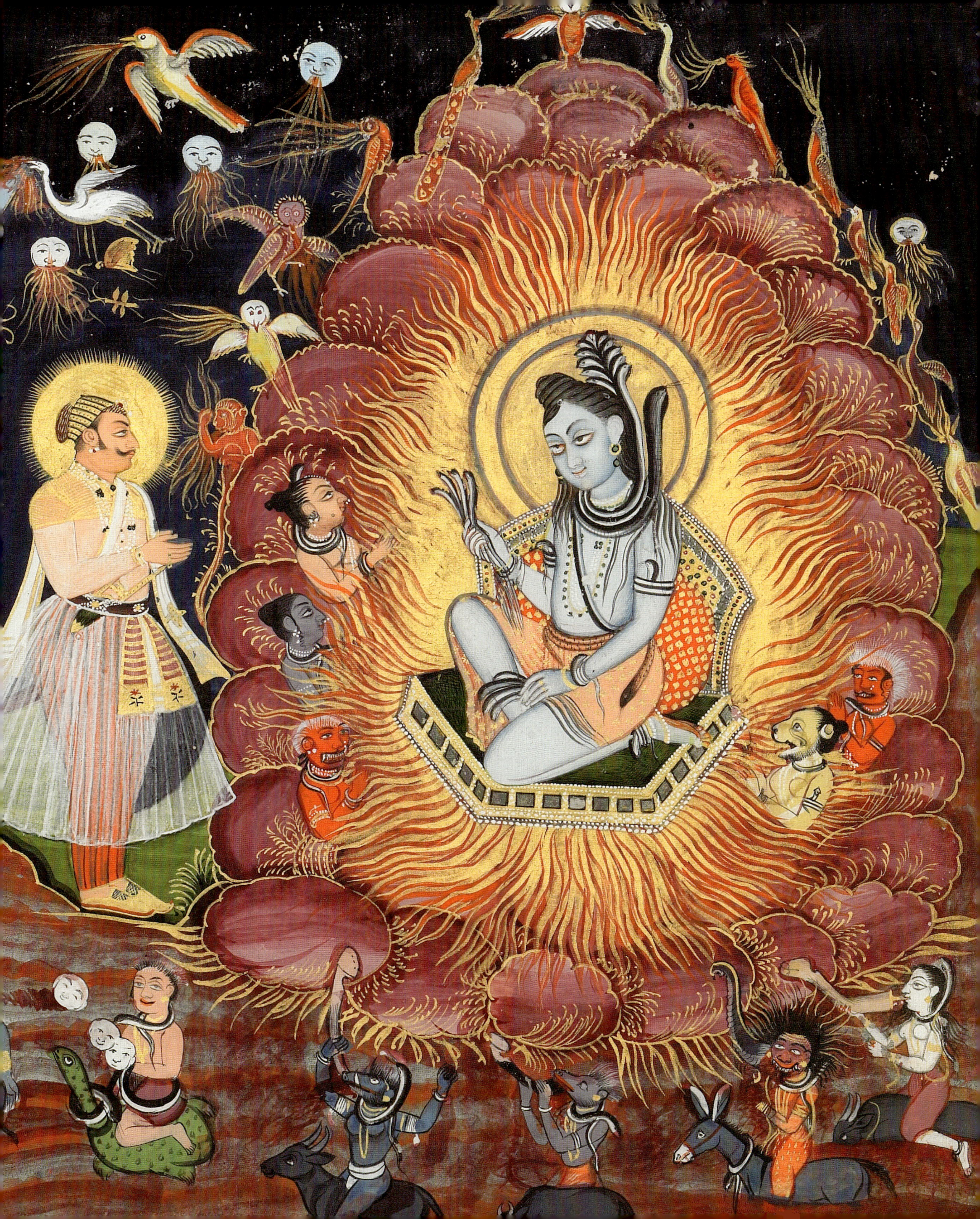

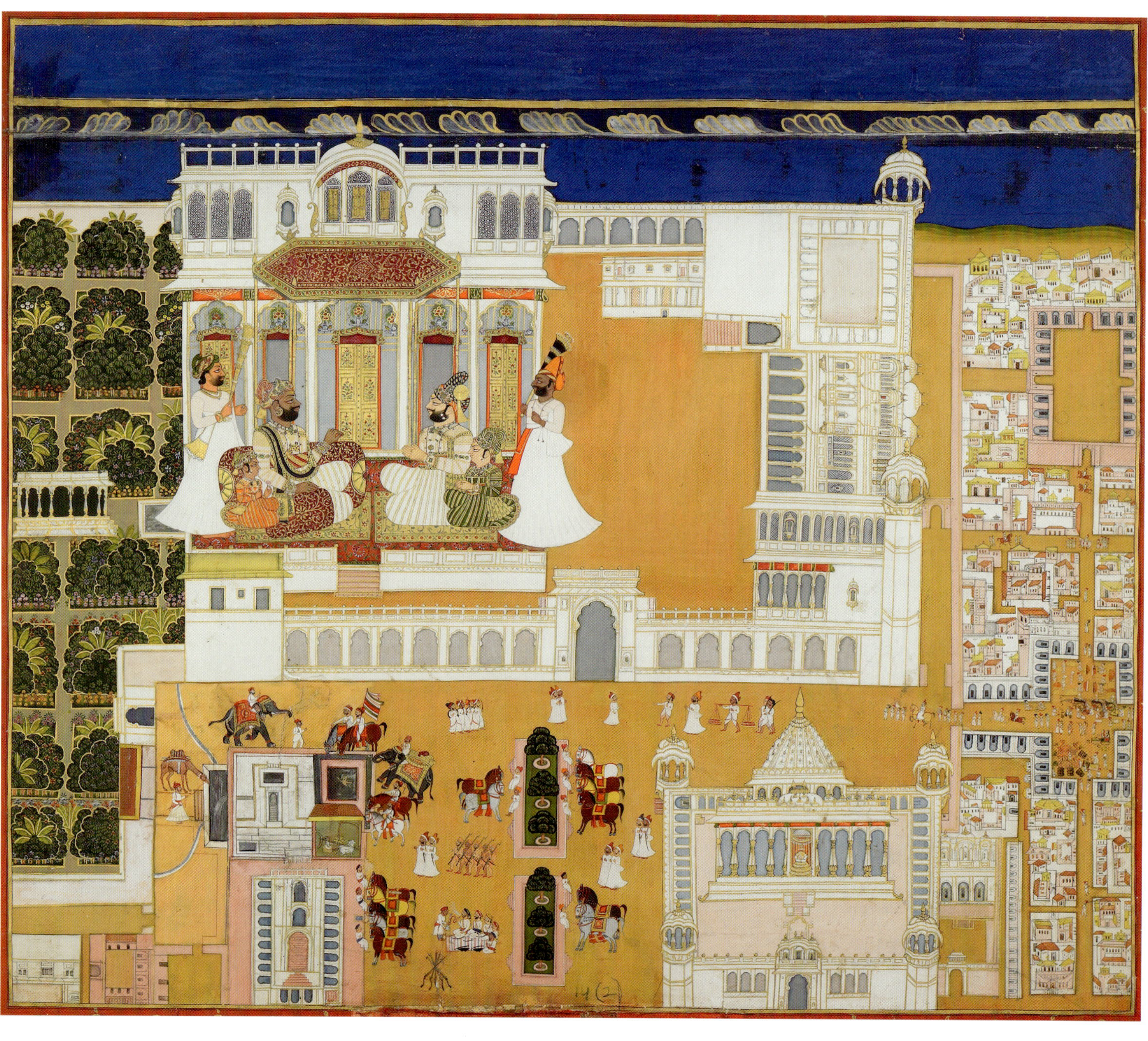

36

Maharaja Man Singh and Dev Nath at Mahamandir Haveli

Jodhpur, ca. 1810; 58.5 x 67.5 cm
Mehrangarh Museum Trust

[numbered] 14
Sri mahamandir ri sri devnathji maharaj
Da[khal] dholiya re kothar hajri sam[vat] 1887 ra Jeth mai
Glorious great temple of the glorious Dev Nathji Maharaja
Entered in the *dholiya* storeroom and inventory in Jyestha (May–June), 1830, 14

At the heart of this relatively large painting is an intimate meeting between Man Singh and his guru Dev Nath. Until his murder in 1815, Dev Nath was both a spiritual and political advisor to the maharaja.[10] Seated on the left with his young son Ladu Nath, the guru is rendered as an almost mirror image of the maharaja and his son, Prince Chattar Singh. In the logic of Rajput portraiture, this doubling indicates that the guru's status is equivalent to that of the king's. Located within his grand *haveli* (mansion) in the temple township of Mahamandir, Dev Nath appears as both spiritual preceptor and lord of his domain.

Construction on Mahamandir (great temple) began in the second year of Man Singh's reign. In building Mahamandir, the maharaja acknowledged Jallandharnath and his guru Dev Nath as powerful repositories of sacred power. The temple township, which ultimately included more than a thousand homes, a flourishing bazaar, and had the right to confer sanctuary, was an economic and strategic resource for the Naths.[11] It thus epitomizes the symbiotic relationship between the maharaja and the order, an alliance that worked to legitimize the king as the worthy recipient of divine grace as it transformed the Naths into a powerful and wealthy polity.

The painting ingeniously joins planimetric views with frontal and bird's-eye perspectives in its depiction of the temple township (see p. 162). The squares (*chauks*), main well, and ground plans of the buildings are drawn as if seen from above, while the guru's *haveli* is seen from the front. Residential dwellings are rendered simply in frontal perspective, while the temple and *haveli* are articulated with domes, pillars, and columns that quite accurately reveal their structures. Covered pavilions (*chatris*) at the temple's four corners are drawn in oblique perspective, rendered from a bird's-eye vantage point.

The rendering of the palace in elevation view transforms the structure into a stage for the maharaja's enactment of piety. With Man Singh and Dev Nath at its core, the complex represents both the king's power to build and his justification for building. The multiple perspectives can be read as a narrative. In the eyes of its patron, the civil elite who oversaw the financing or supervised the construction, the courtiers who attended its consecration ceremony, and the Naths who lived there, the planimetric views of streets and structures documented the town's foundations. The elevation views recorded its completion. Man Singh's power to allocate funds, authorize overseers, hire masons, and move populations is the implied link between the two perspectives. DD

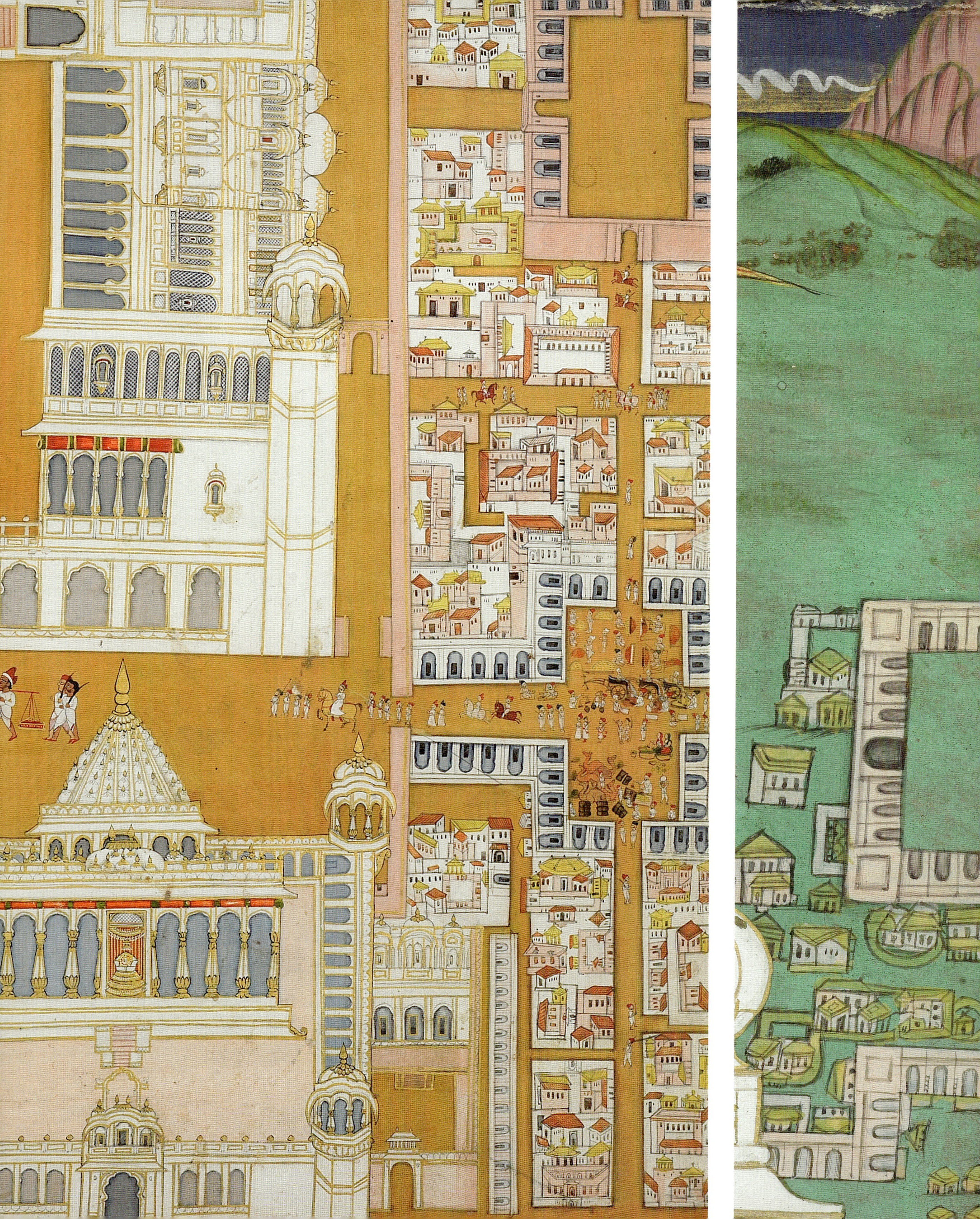

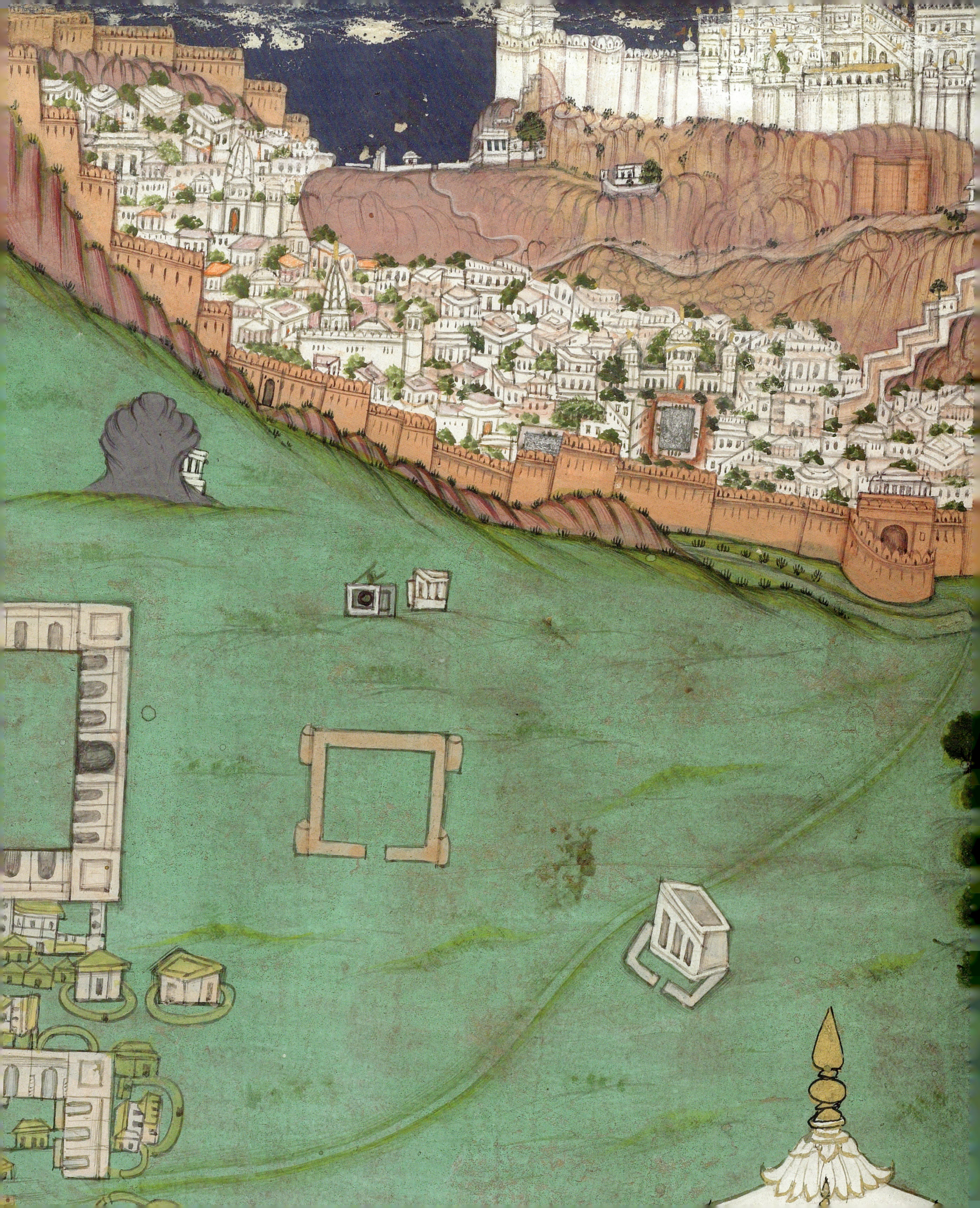

37

Jallandharnath Worship at Mahamandir

Raso and Shivdas Bhatti
Jodhpur, ca. 1812; 82 x 56 cm
Mehrangarh Museum Trust

The complete inscription appears in the reference catalogue.

Hundreds of paintings record Man Singh's intimate *darshan* of Jallandharnath. Here, Raso and Shivdas map Man Singh's devotion onto the larger landscape of the Mahamandir temple township.[12] Man Singh began constructing the Nath temple and its extensive walled town in the second year of his reign. By 1837, it was, in the words of the British East India Company surveyor A. H. E. Boileau, "too remarkable a place to be passed over without description."[13]

Boileau noted that the township and temple were located within "cannonshot" of Jodhpur city and Mehrangarh Fort, which are here depicted in the painting's upper right. The surveyor further noted that Mahamandir's spire was "conspicuous even from a very great distance on account of the dazzling whiteness of the fine marble lime with which it is covered; indeed the whole building as well is the same pure looking material." (The limewash is now gone; see fig. 1, p. 33.)

Although rendered in varying scales and from various perspectives, Mahamandir's dazzling white spire, baluster-columned porch, cloistered courtyard, and monumental gateway are realized with architectural accuracy. In contrast to their factual realization of the outer temple structure, the artists erased the wall separating the inner sanctum from the columned porch to make the ritual of worship clearly visible (in a compositional framework that recalls earlier paintings of Vijai Singh worshiping Krishna). (See fig. 4, p. 34.) Tellingly, the artists did not represent the marble *charan* (footprints) of Jallandharnath on the inner sanctum's altar (see cat. 36, detail, p. 162). Instead, they depicted Jallandharnath from a devotional perspective as fully present. Seated comfortably on a skirted throne—youthful, blue-skinned, and raising his hand in the gesture of teaching—the *mahasiddha* gazes into the eyes of Man Singh.

With his hands clasped in *anjali mudra,* Man Singh meets and returns the *mahasiddha's* attention. Guru Dev Nath stands directly behind Jallandharnath's throne, holding a peacock feather whisk (*morchal*). Both his proximity to Jallandharnath and the honor of bearing the *morchal* substantiate his status as Mahamandir's abbot and the royal preceptor. Dev Nath is flanked by three family members who will successively serve as abbots of Mahamandir: his brother Bhim Nath in white, his son Ladu Nath in red, and his nephew Lakshmi Nath in orange. These four Naths were the kingdom's most important power brokers during Man Singh's reign.[14]

Since Ladu Nath and Lakshmi Nath appear somewhat smaller here (and therefore younger) than they do in the Mahamandir worship scene dated 1815 (see fig. 3, p. 33), this painting is dated circa 1812. DD

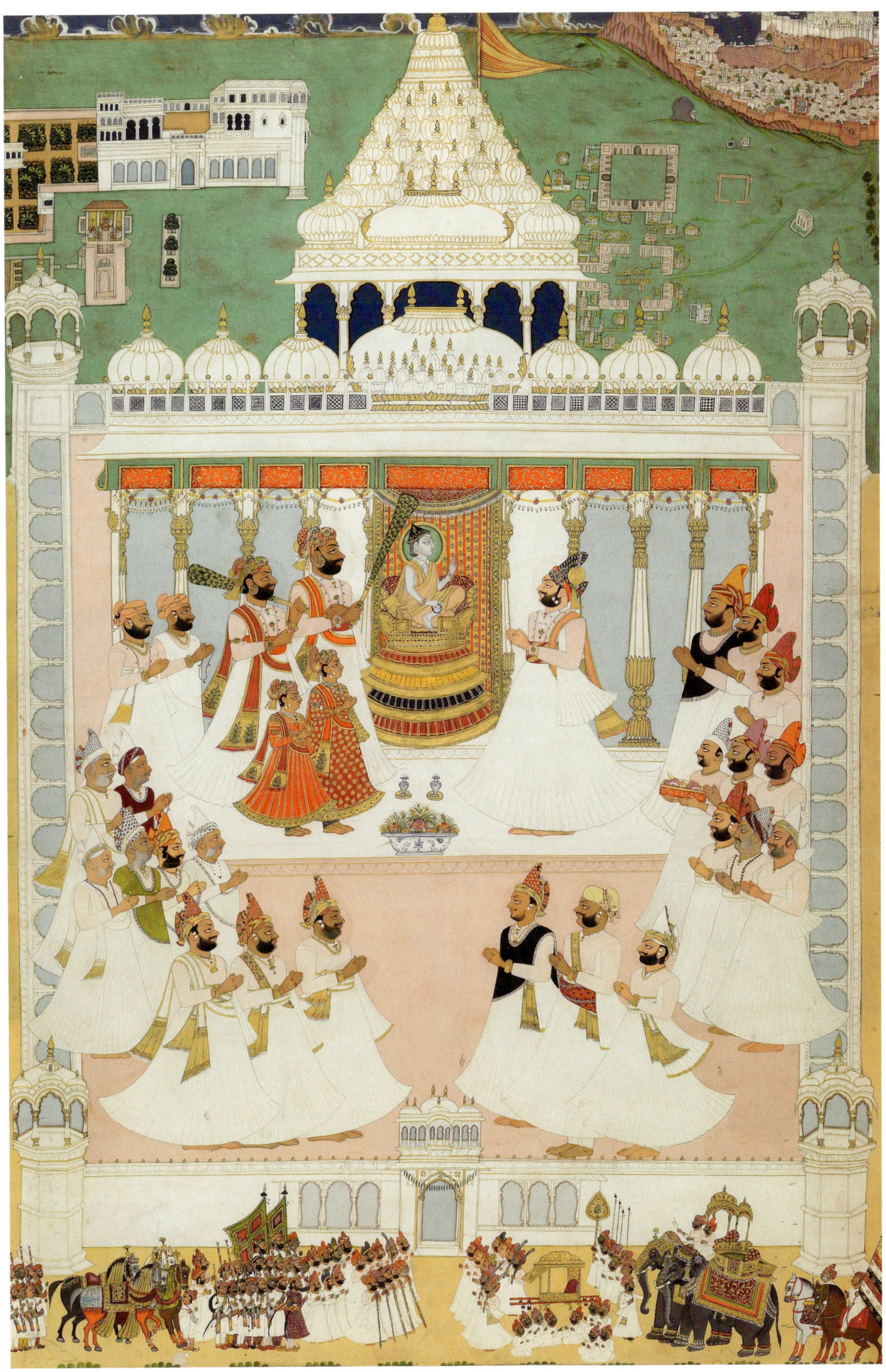

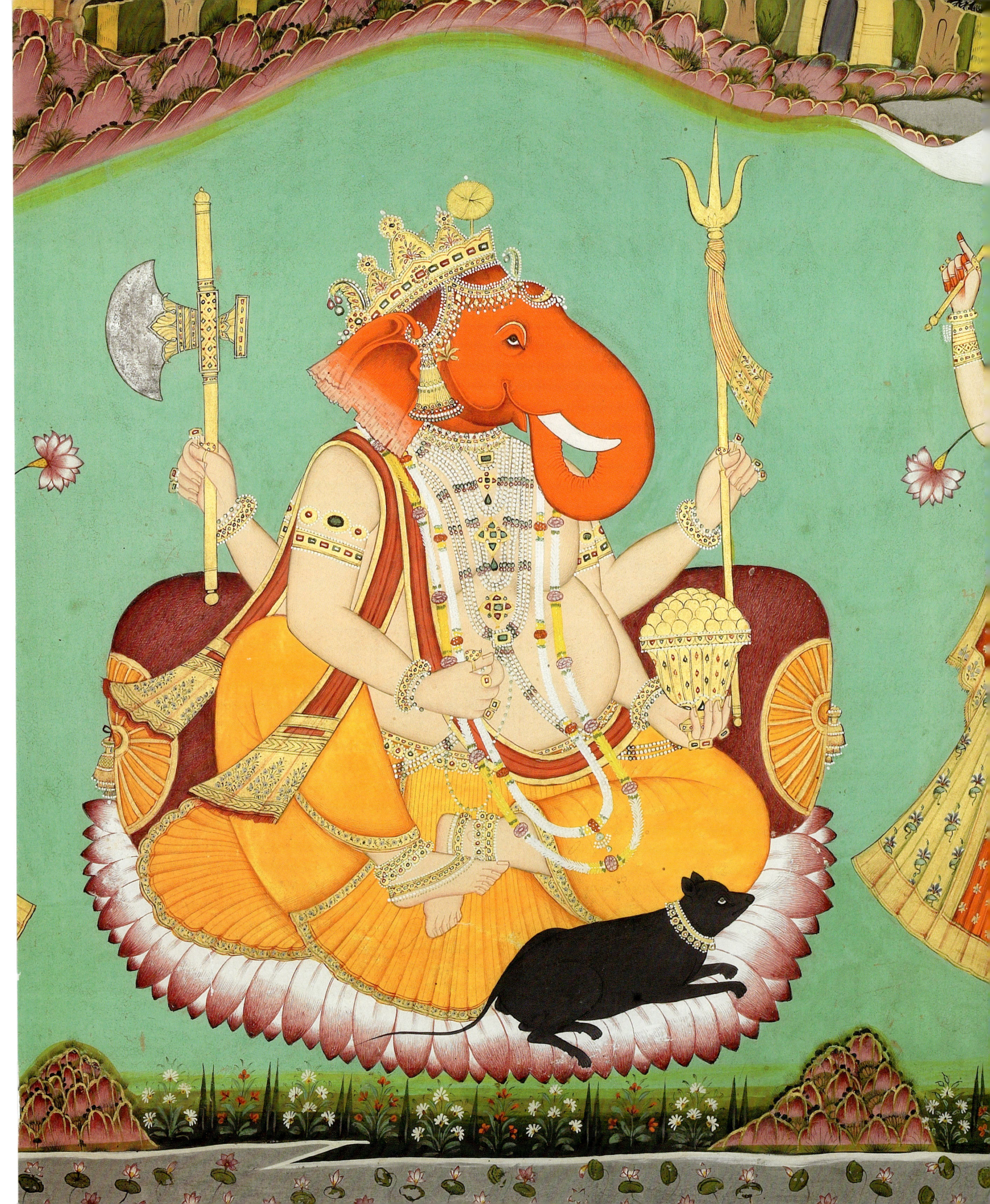

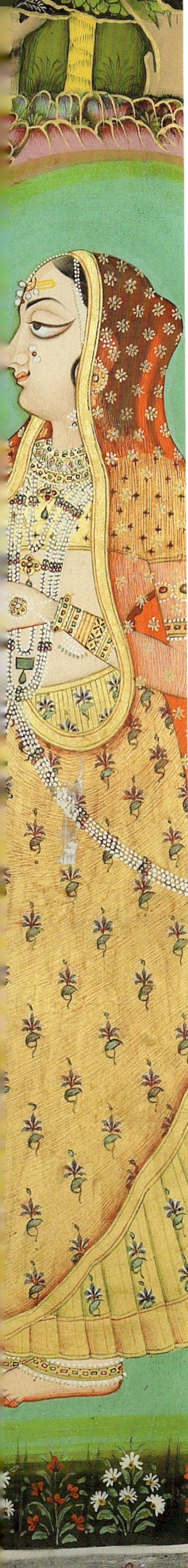

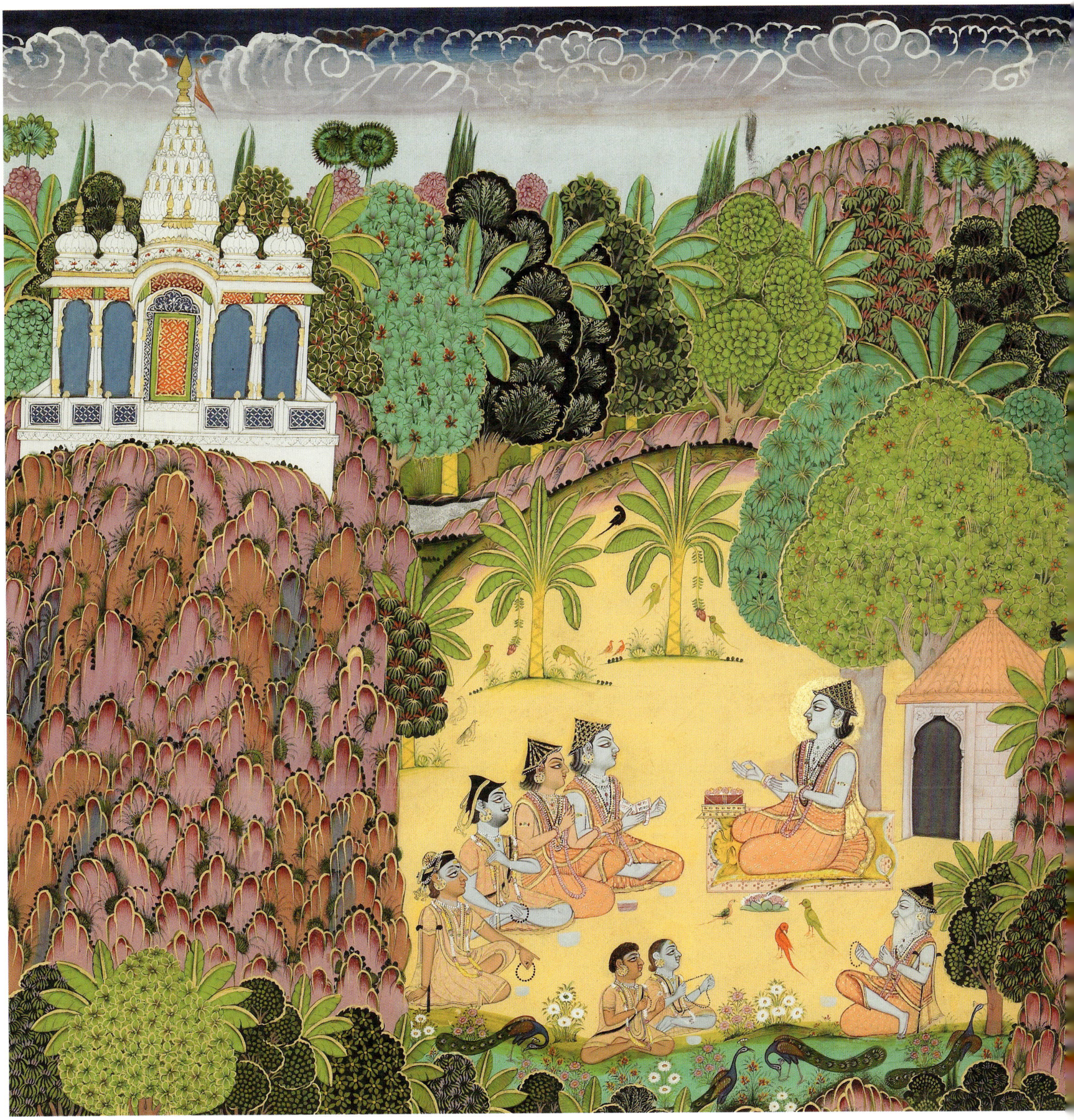

Cat. 39 Details

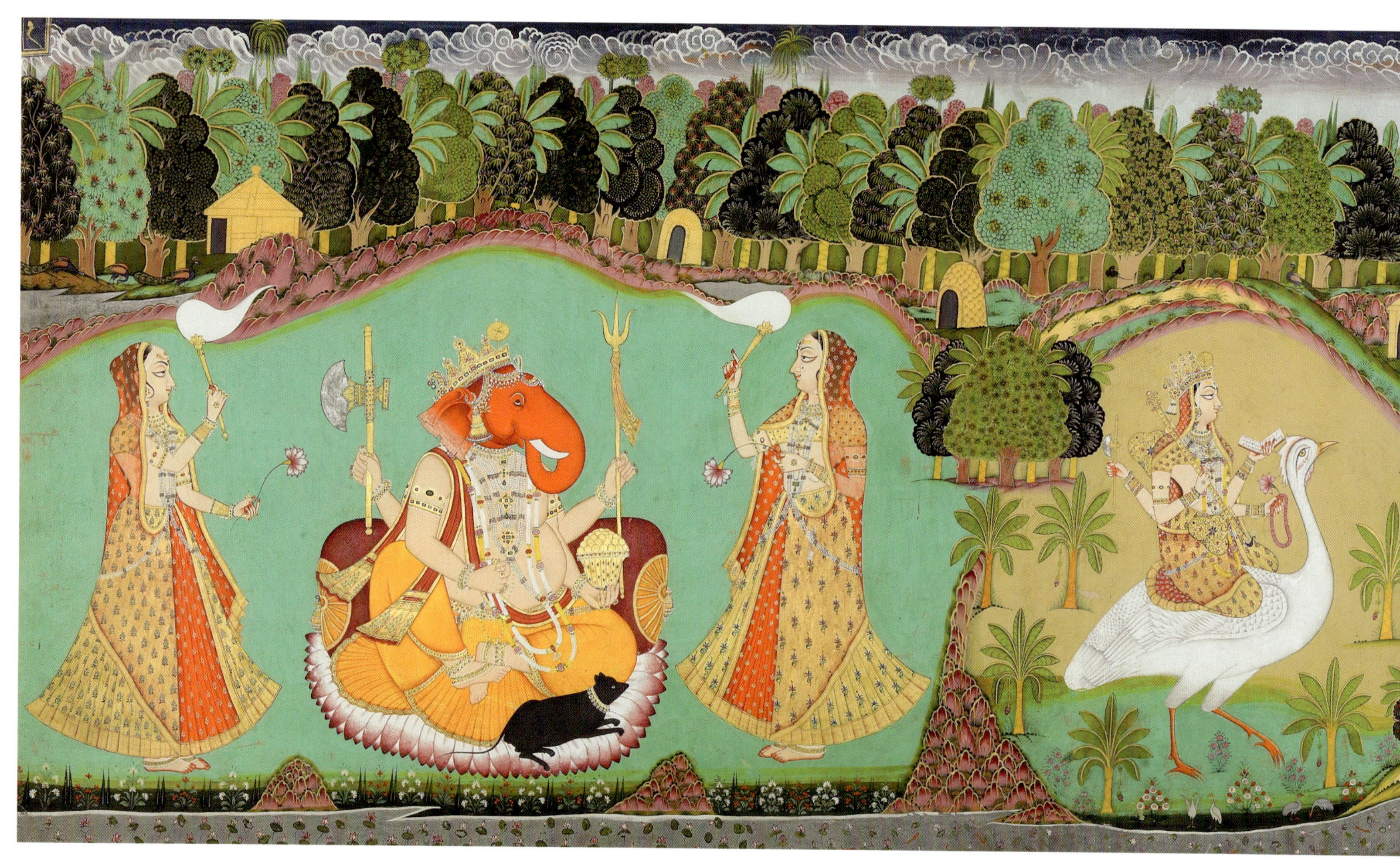

Ganesha, Saraswati, and Jallandharnath

Identified here as a copy of folio 1 from the *Nath Purana*[21]
Attributed to Amardas, ca. 1825; 47 x 123 cm
Mehrangarh Museum Trust

Numbered 1 in the upper left corner.
The complete inscription appears in the reference catalogue.

> At a gathering of many *siddha* deities on Guru peak at Girnar, Jallandharnath
> spoke of his greatness:
>> O Glorious Nath of the Three Worlds....Even Shiva and Vishnu do not
>> know its extent. Therefore, I will tell you. Once upon a time, I was formless
>> (*niranjan*) and eternal (*nirakar*) and I wished to create the world. Then five
>> deities appeared. I appeared first, then Shiva, then Devi, then Vishnu and
>> then Brahma.

Nath Purana[22]

At the folio's right, Jallandharnath sits calmly yet tautly erect within his idyllic
ashram at Girnar, a sacred mountain in Gujurat (see p. 169). Raising his hands in
the gesture of teaching, he gently smiles as he reveals that he created the cosmos.

The auspicious deities Ganesh (see p. 168) and Saraswati, who are regularly
depicted on the first folio of Hindu manuscripts, appear here in forest clearings
at the painting's left and center. Although the *Nath Purana* text does not begin by
invoking these gods, the expanded horizontal surface of the painting comfortably
permits their inclusion. The three divine vignettes are loosely united within a lush
landscape bordered by scalloped clouds and a silver river.

While other court painters, including Bulaki and Shivdas, meticulously shade
forms, this painting's softer style can be attributed to the artist Amardas. Only he
could have created the intimate ashram clearing with its air of contemplative
interaction. In their delicacy and ease of posture, the dhoti-clad ascetics can be
compared to his seated Jallandharnath (cat. 32). Crisp yet graceful contours in
delicate tones, occasionally softened by a translucent wash line on their outer
edge, also animate the iconic figures of the sweetly grinning Ganesh, his splendidly
handsome attendants, and the regal Saraswati.

Amardas achieves a level of detail here that is rare in Man Singh painting.
The dainty mottling of Ganesh's rippled ear and lapidary precision of his crown,
the grisaille feathers of Saraswati's swan and the floral arabesques ornamenting
her *vina*, the braided thatch roof of the ashram hut, and the soft smear of ash on
the disciples' foreheads are beautifully realized. Unique and unexpected passages
of color further reveal the subtlety of the atelier master's sensibility. Magenta,
salmon, and lilac deliciously (and deliriously) streak boulders. Chiffon *orhnis*
(shawls) rippling across golden garments transform floral motifs of crimson to
red and blue to lavender. Parrot-green and orange birds, magenta banana flowers,
blue peacocks, and the *siddhas*' black caps enliven the ashram's sandy clearing
while linking it to the bolder colors of the larger landscape. Gleaming surfaces,
punctuated by copious gold detailing, further indicate that the painting was skillfully
and repeatedly burnished during its production.[23] DD

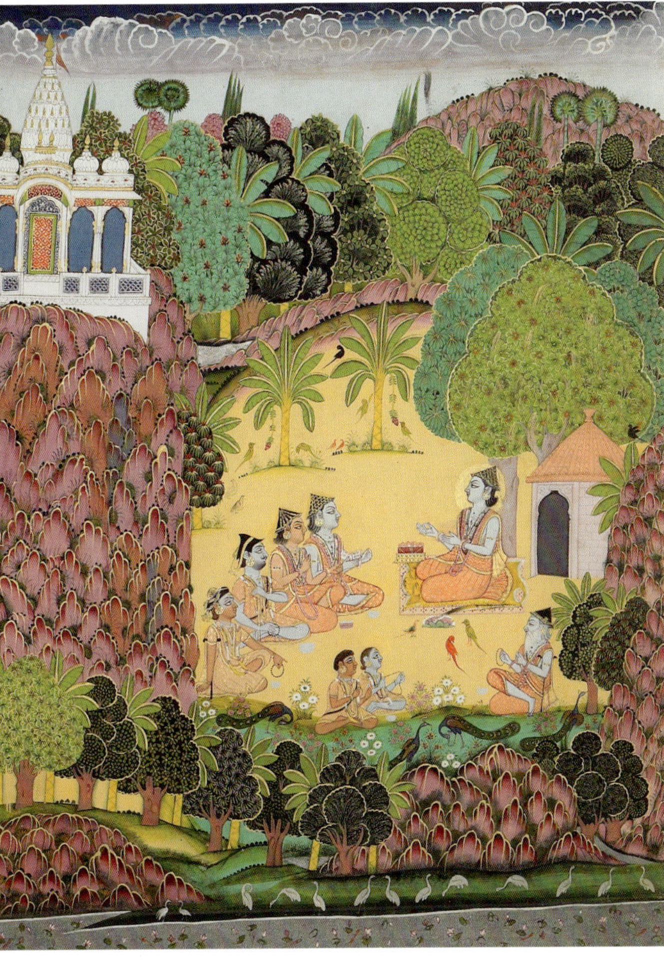

ORIGINS OF THE COSMOS

Since the emergence of the Nath religious tradition in the twelfth–thirteenth century, *mahasiddhas* (great perfected beings) have sought to reveal the mystery of existence. At the core of their teachings is the Absolute, a supreme, immeasurable, and transcendent essence that exists simultaneously with all creation. This profound conception, which has many names but is most often known as Brahman, is central to many Hindu philosophical and religious traditions.

South Asian artists rarely attempted to represent Brahman. Instead, they focused on depicting deities with knowable forms who served as accessible intermediaries or portals to the Absolute for worshipers. Man Singh's artists, however, rose to the challenge of conveying the undifferentiated and self-luminous Brahman. They evoked the Absolute with solid fields of shimmering gold pigment, creating paintings that were paradoxically both luxurious and immaterial. The abstraction epitomizes the atelier's aesthetic of the sublime.

Three Aspects of the Absolute

identified here as folio 1 from the *Nath Charit*[1]
Bulaki, 1823 (Samvat 1880); 47 x 123 cm
Mehrangarh Museum Trust

Numbered 1 on recto.
The complete inscription appears in the reference catalogue.

Sri nath charit
Da[khal] dholiya re kothar
Citara bulaki vagaire ra kiyo da
Glorious Nath Charit
Entered into the *dholiya* storeroom
The painter Bulaki and others made it

The artist Bulaki created three astonishingly minimal squares of shimmering metallic color to evoke the formless and eternal essence of the universe. On the left, an undifferentiated field of gold conveys the self-luminous Absolute. In the center panel, a Nath *siddha* hovering against a golden expanse represents the first manifestation of the cosmos into subtle form. On the right, a *siddha* exuding silvery light (*jyoti*) engenders the next level of cosmic matter and consciousness (see also pp. 176–77).

Both the subject matter of the painting—and its minimal and luminous aesthetic of the immaterial—are highly unusual. Although central to Hindu metaphysics, the Absolute is rarely represented in India's sacred art. Deities with comprehensible qualities and forms are far more visible in Hindu religious practice and visual culture. As foci of devotion, images of deities provide the primary portal to the ineffable for most Hindus. But Nath adepts (disciples who have been initiated by a Nath guru) seek to become gods themselves. Through hatha yoga practice, they become immortals by reintegrating their individual bodies with the Absolute. By disciplining their bodies (through postures and meditation), adepts gain the ability to move back and forth between this phenomenal world and supreme reality. Having experienced the Absolute, the great Nath *siddhas* reveal in their teachings its nature and the interrelationships among the transcendent essence, matter, and consciousness.

Man Singh's artists met the challenge of depicting an Absolute reality that is always defined by what it is not (without form, without origin, without color, etc.) by employing undifferentiated fields of gold pigment (see also cats. 41 and 42).[2] This solid gold plane, which appears throughout the cosmologies of the monumental manuscript corpus, appears to be an innovation of the Jodhpur atelier.[3] The square and rectangular golden panels might be transcriptions of the devotional practice of applying pigment or gilding to divine forms during worship; broad patches and small squares in metallic or primary colors adorn sacred boulders in Rajasthan's numerous roadside shrines.[4]

The choice of gold to evoke the divine essence reflects its value in Hindu traditions as the most pure of metals and in court traditions as a signifier of luxury. The silvery pigment, a tin alloy that offers the advantage of never tarnishing, has the shimmer of mercury, which Naths valued for its alchemical qualities and ingested for longevity. DD

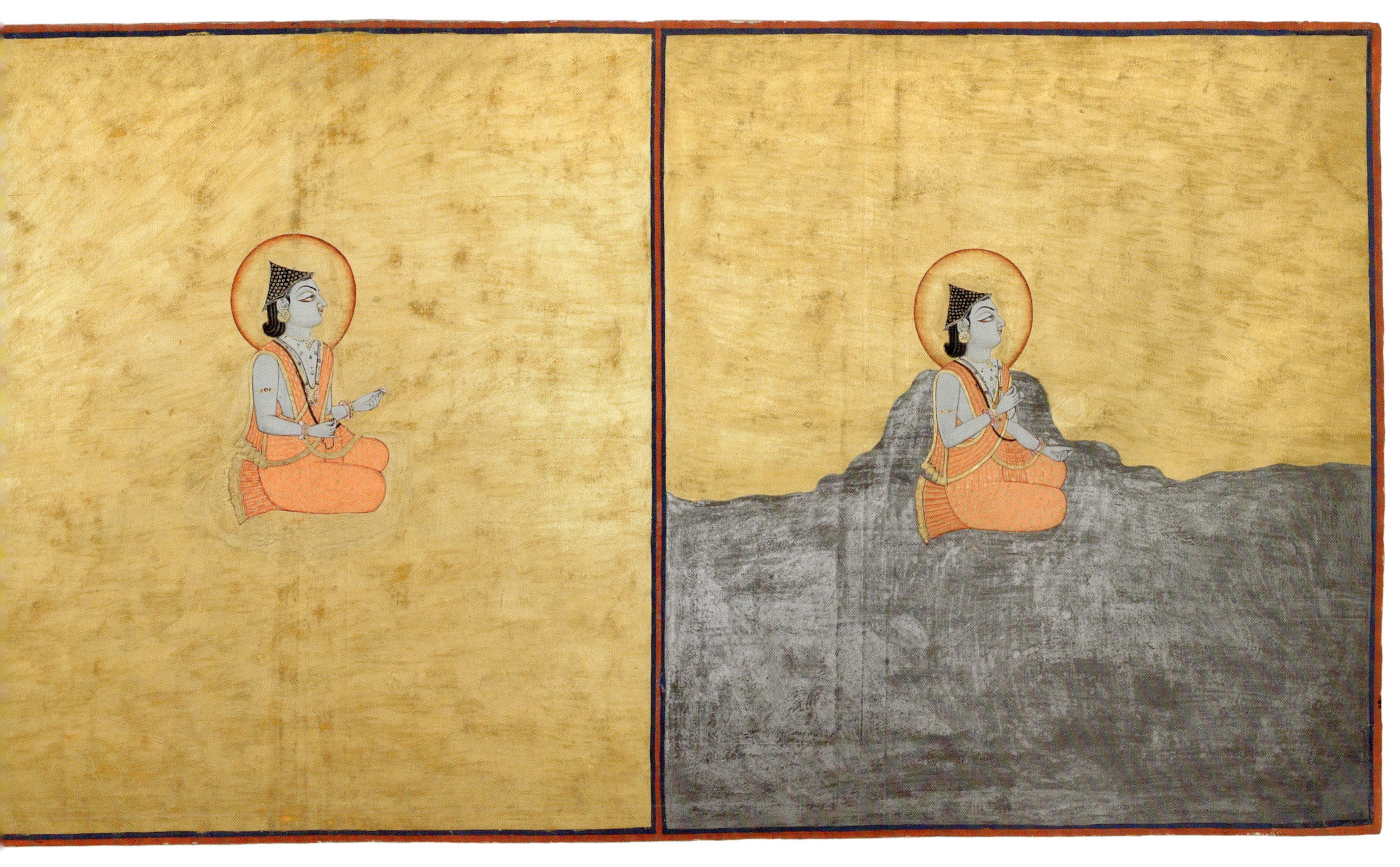

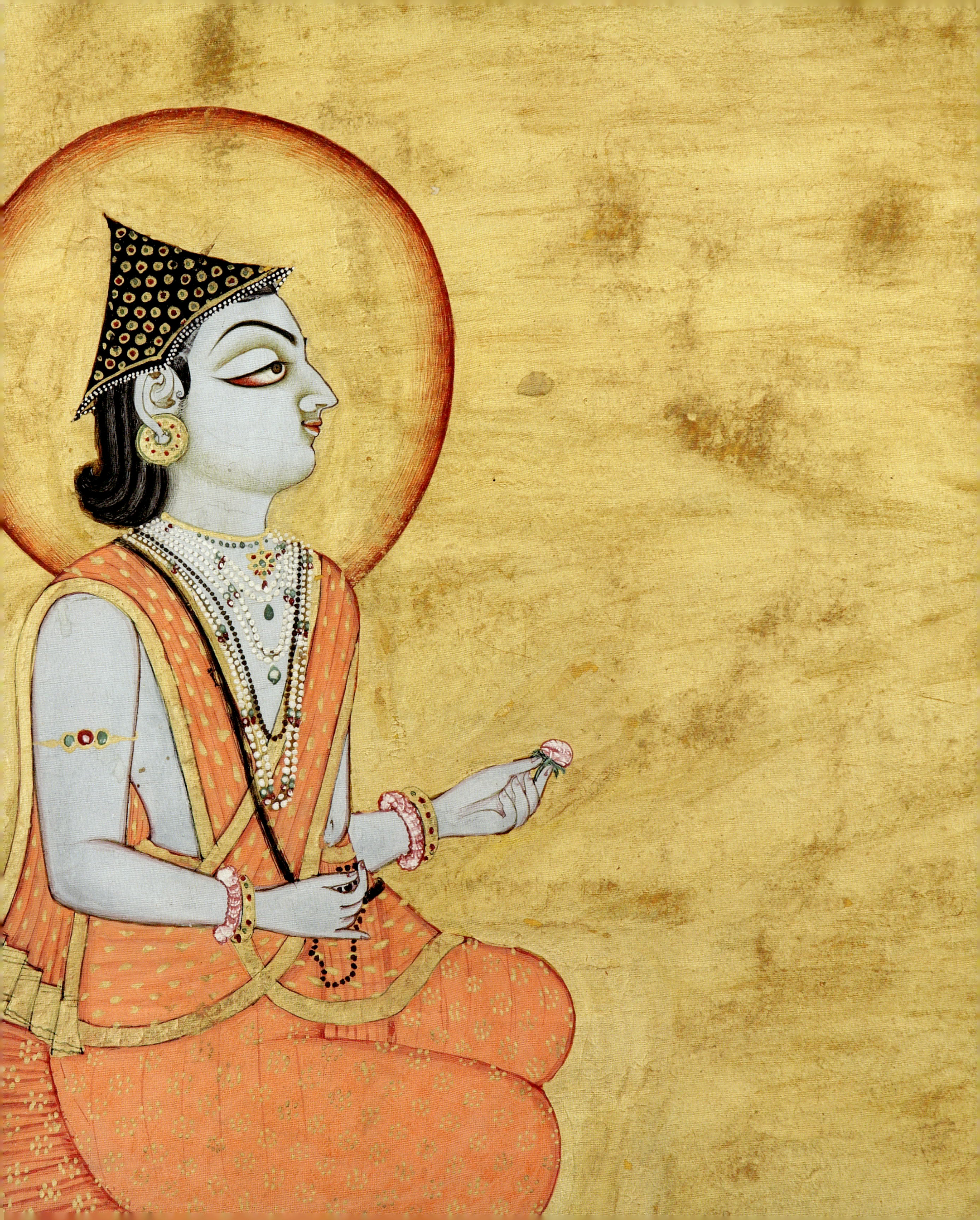

Cat. 40 Details

41

The Emergence of Spirit and Matter

folio 2 from the *Shiva Purana*
Attributed to Shivdas, ca. 1828; 47 x 126 cm
Mehrangarh Museum Trust

Numbered 2 on recto.
The complete inscription appears in the reference catalogue.

Sri siv puran
Da [khal] dholiya re kothar
Glorious Shiva Purana
Entered into the *dholiya* storeroom

The Hindu puranas (ancient treatises) are vast compendia of sacred knowledge, relating everything from myth and ritual to the nature of existence. In the *Shiva Purana*, the deity Brahma describes the transcendental nature of the Absolute:

> when the present world is not in existence, the Absolute (*Sat Brahman*) alone
> is present. It is incomprehensible to the mind [and] cannot be expressed
> by words. It has neither name nor color.... It is immeasurable, propless,
> unchanging, formless, without attributes, perceptible to Yogins, all-pervasive,
> and the sole cause of the universe.[5]

Luminous fields of gold evoke the ineffable Absolute in this painting. On the shimmering ground the bounded forms of deities, representing consecutive stages of cosmic evolution, hover in an appropriately mysterious fashion. The folio's center and right panels depict Consciousness (Purusha) and Matter (Prakriti) as resplendently crowned male and female deities. Their substantial forms, sloping chins, and heavily lidded, lotus-petal eyes typify the ideal body of the Man Singh atelier. The varying thickness and tonalities of the prominent contour outlining the figures, and the delicate shading of the faces in the central panel, exemplify the subtlety with which master artists modulated the period's somewhat ponderous figural conventions. While the painting is not inscribed with an artist's name, Shivdas' hand is suggested both by the solidity of the bodies and by small, finely realized details—a sense of connection between the two deities, red-limned halos radiating delicately incised rays, softly smiling coral lips, the wisp of down descending from Purusha's side curl, and the gold flame pattern on Prakriti's red skirt (see cat. 32). DD

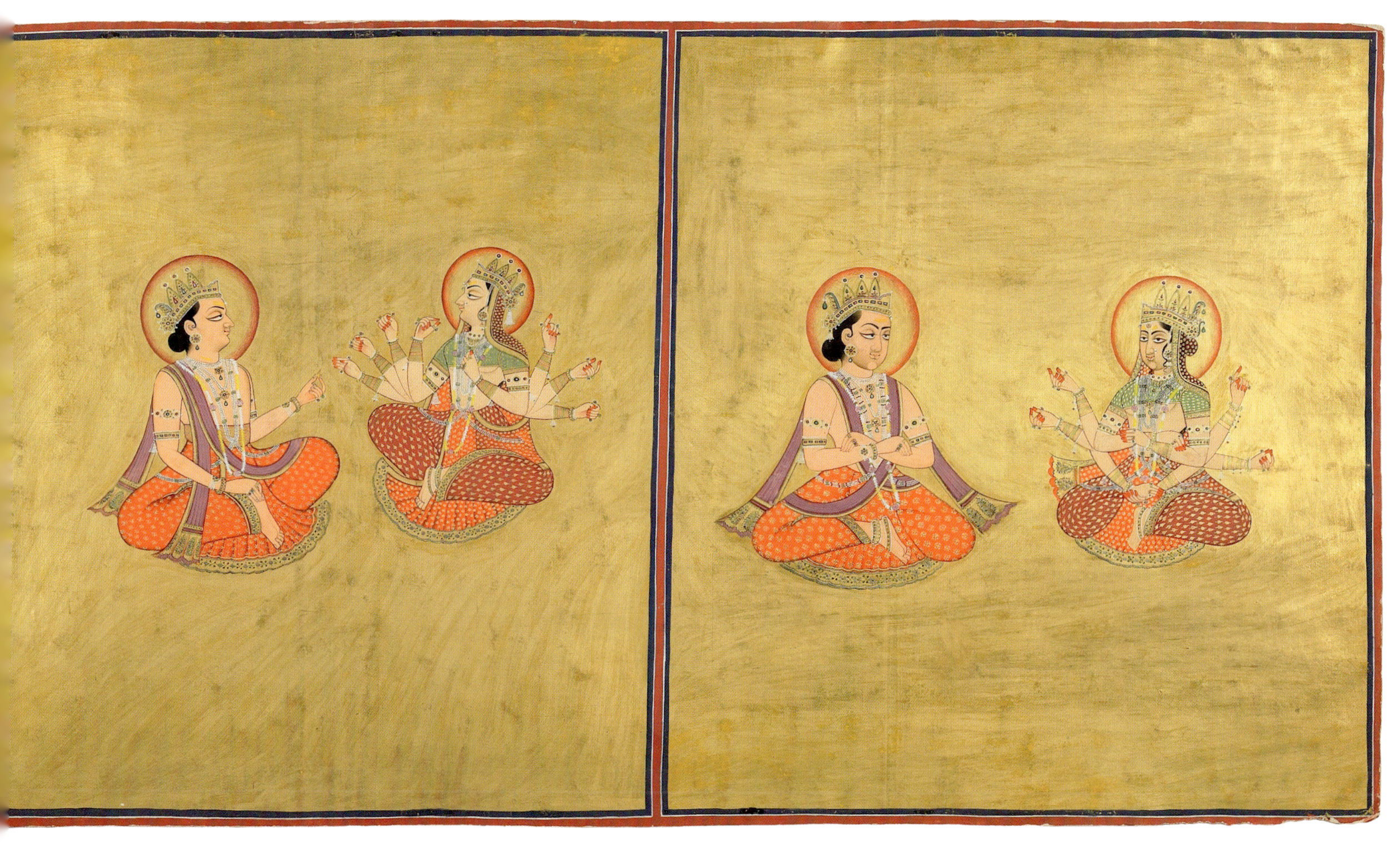

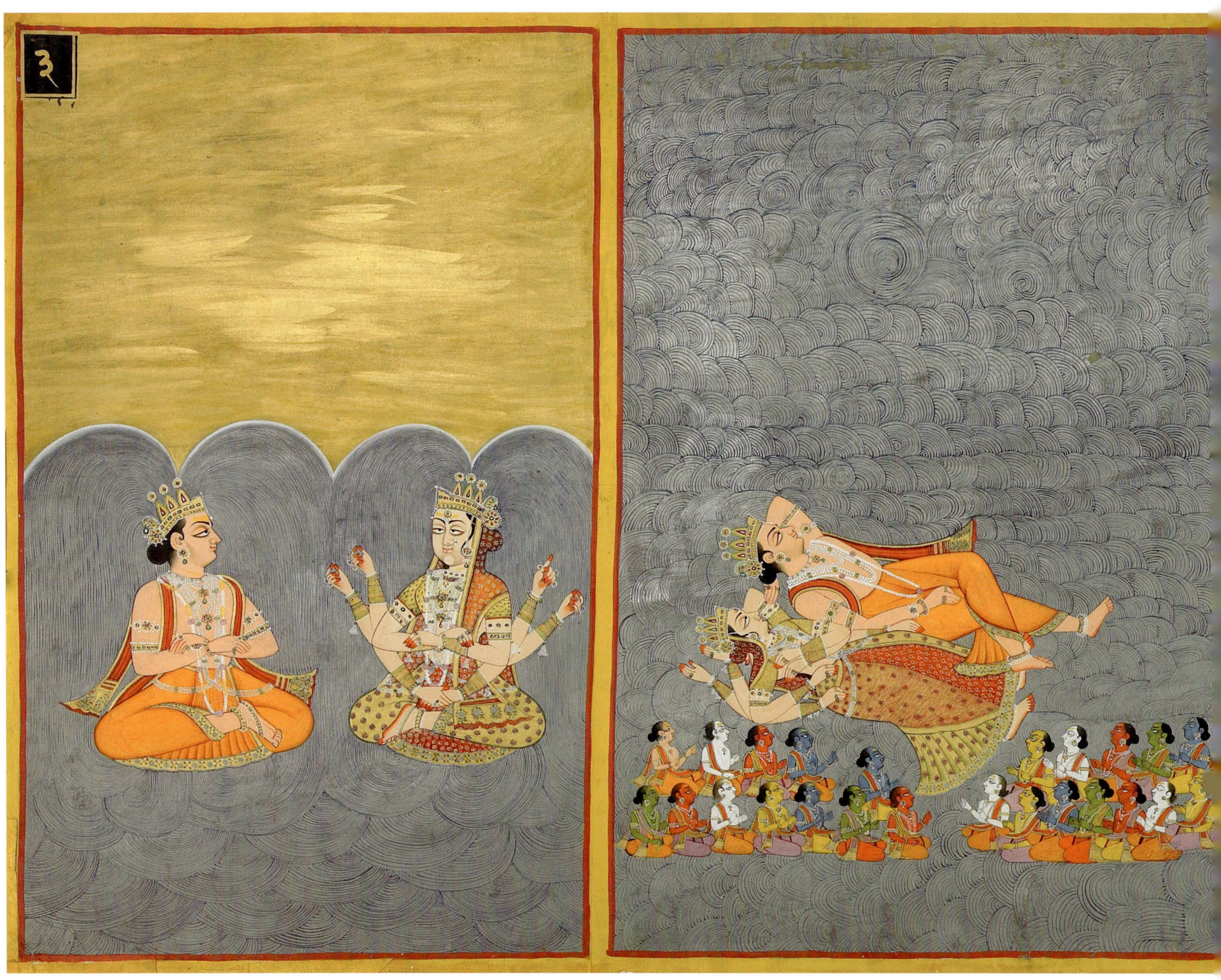

Cat. 42

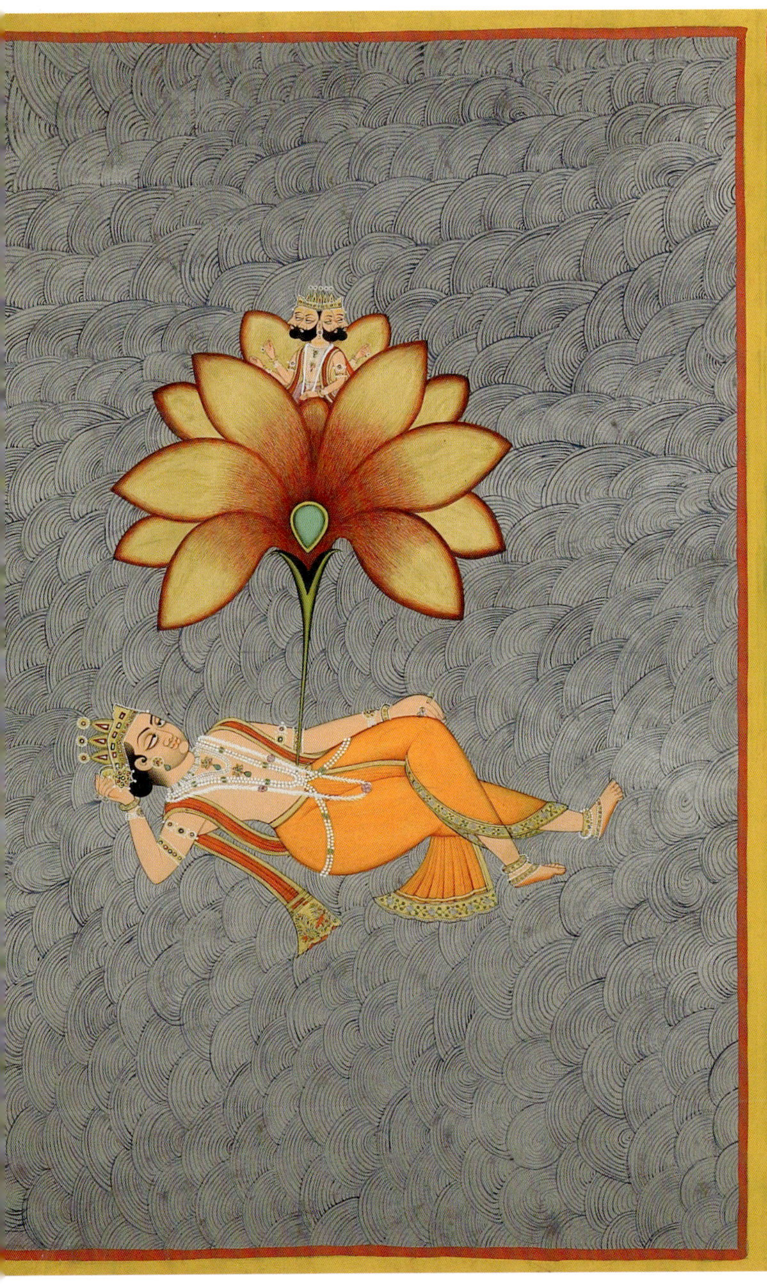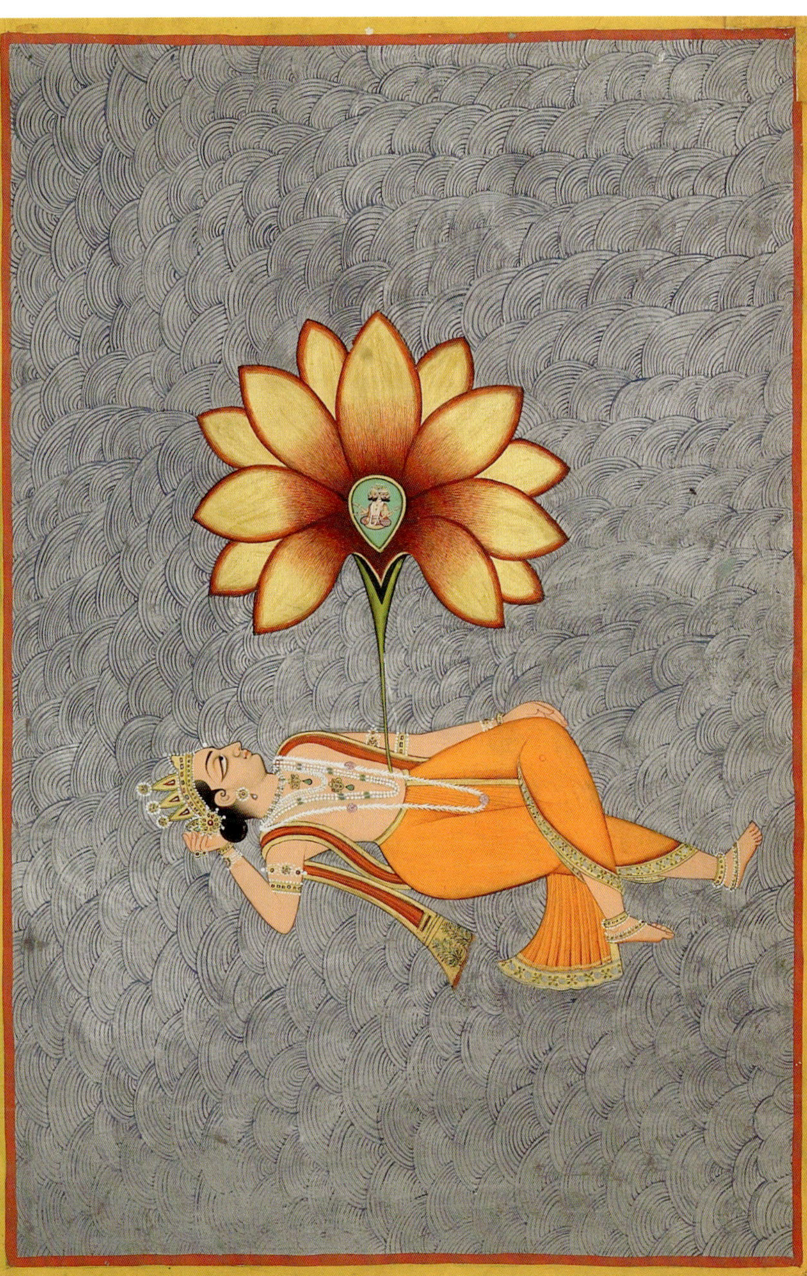

42

The Creation of the Cosmic Ocean and the Elements

folio 3 from the *Shiva Purana*
ca. 1828; 45.5 x 124 cm
Mehrangarh Museum Trust

Numbered 3 on recto.
The complete inscription appears in the reference catalogue.

The cosmos continues to emerge with dreamlike intensity in the *Shiva Purana's* third folio (see pp. 180–81). On the left, Conscience (Purusha) and Matter (Prakriti) manifest the next ground of creation, the cosmic waters (*narajal*). The artist imagines the sublime waters gushing smoothly and perfectly from the deities, gradually obscuring the Absolute above while pooling into waves below. In the next panel, Purusha and Prakriti recline upon the ocean's blue-scalloped whorls and produce the twenty-four elements (*tattvas*) essential to experience. Depicted in the painting as small multi-colored beings, the *tattvas* are matter, intelligence, ego, mind, the five senses, the five action organs (speech, prehension, movement, digestion, generation), the five subtle senses (sound, touch, sight, taste, smell), and the five great elements (the essences of ether, air, fire, water, earth).[6]

Cosmic evolution continues in the third panel, as the male and female deities merge into the sleeping Narayana (a form of Vishnu).[7] As Narayana sleeps, a magnificent lotus "with an endless stalk, a pericarp of brilliant hue…[and the luminosity] of ten million suns" comes forth from his navel (panel 3).[8] In contrast to Narayana's placid immobility, the lotus quivers into an extravagant bloom, its tear-shaped core appearing vivid green against the red-tinged petals. The god of creation, the four-headed deity Brahma, emerges from the splendid lotus in a state of utter bewilderment. Voicing the fundamental question of existence, Brahma asks, "Where have I come from? Who is [my] creator?"[9]

The *Shiva Purana* text then explains that Brahma was "deluded by illusion" and sought answers to his questions in the lotus, the only thing that he knew. He descended the endless stalk for a hundred years, seeking its base, then wandered among the lotus's upper reaches for another century. When his physical search didn't yield answers, the god began an interior journey. After twelve years of penance, Narayana appeared and revealed Shiva to be the ultimate cause of Brahma's—and indeed all—creation. DD

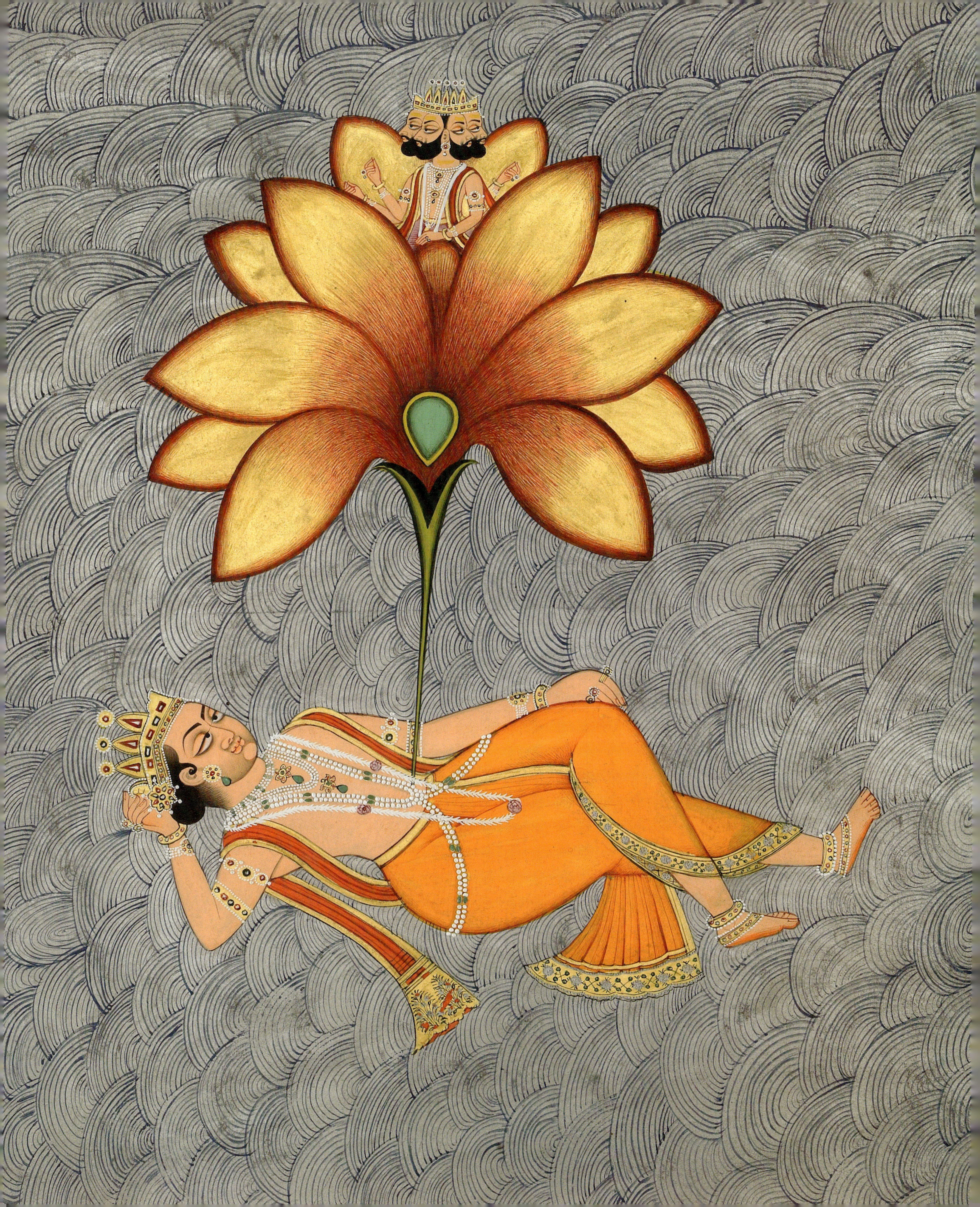

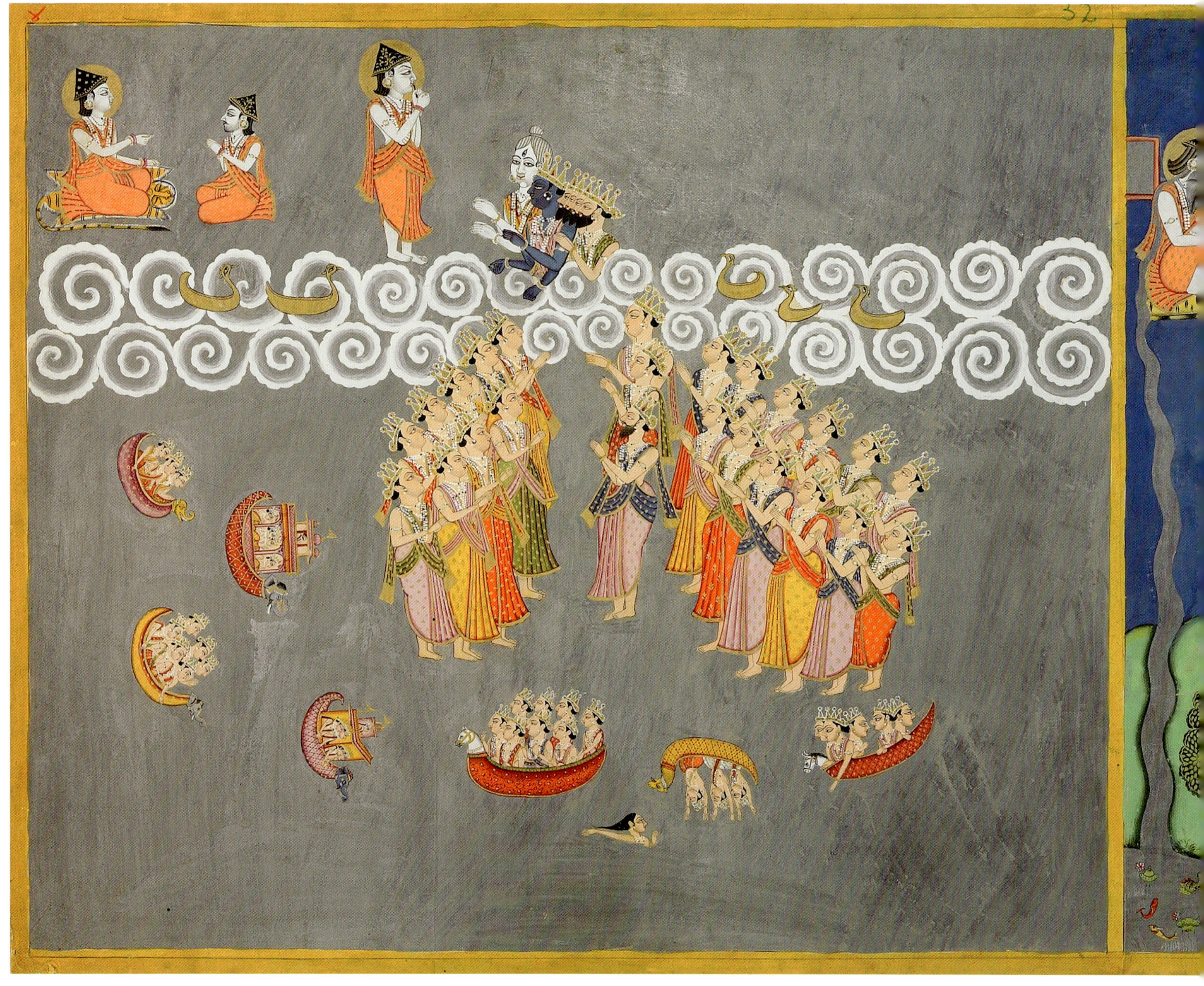

Cat. 43

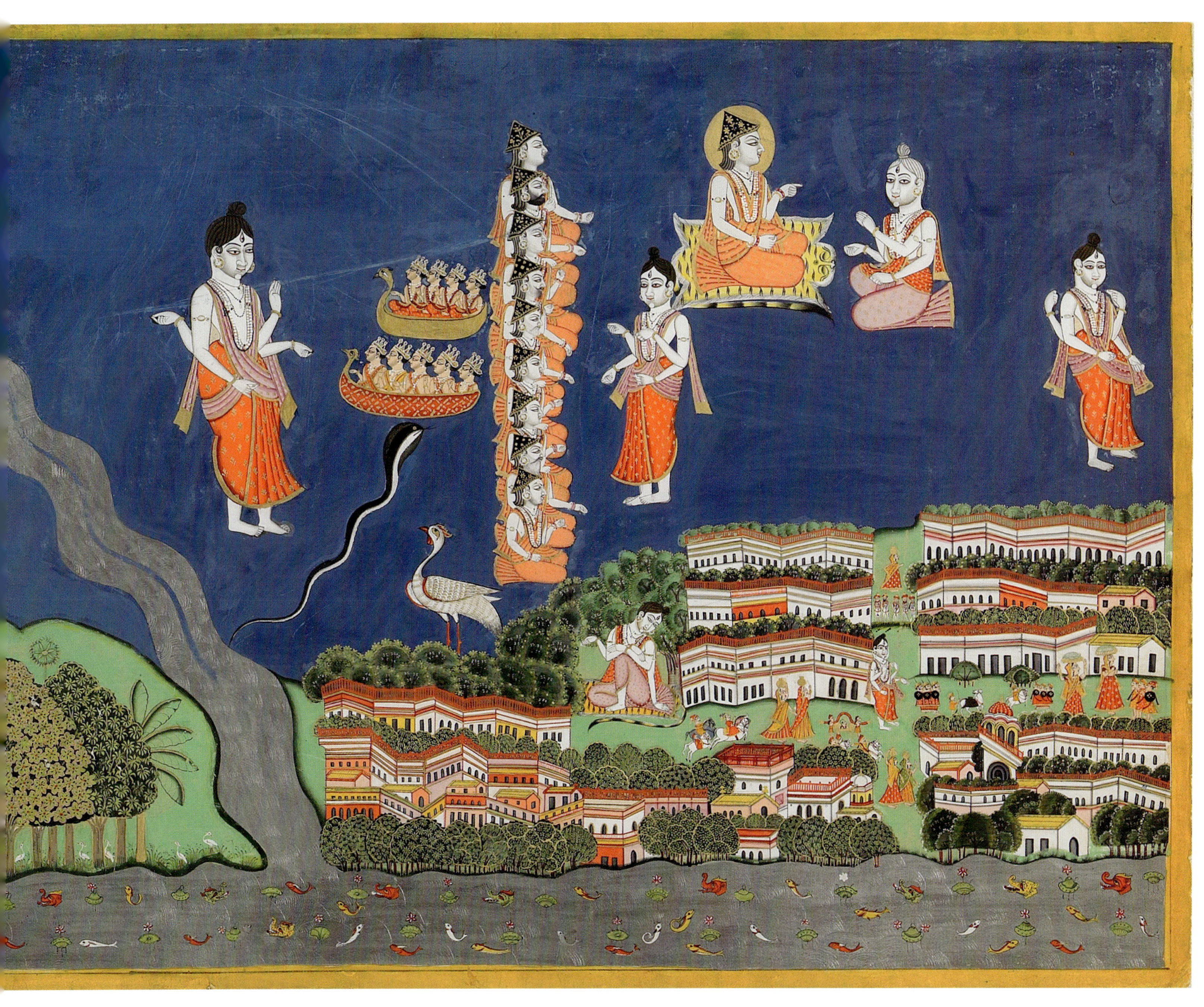

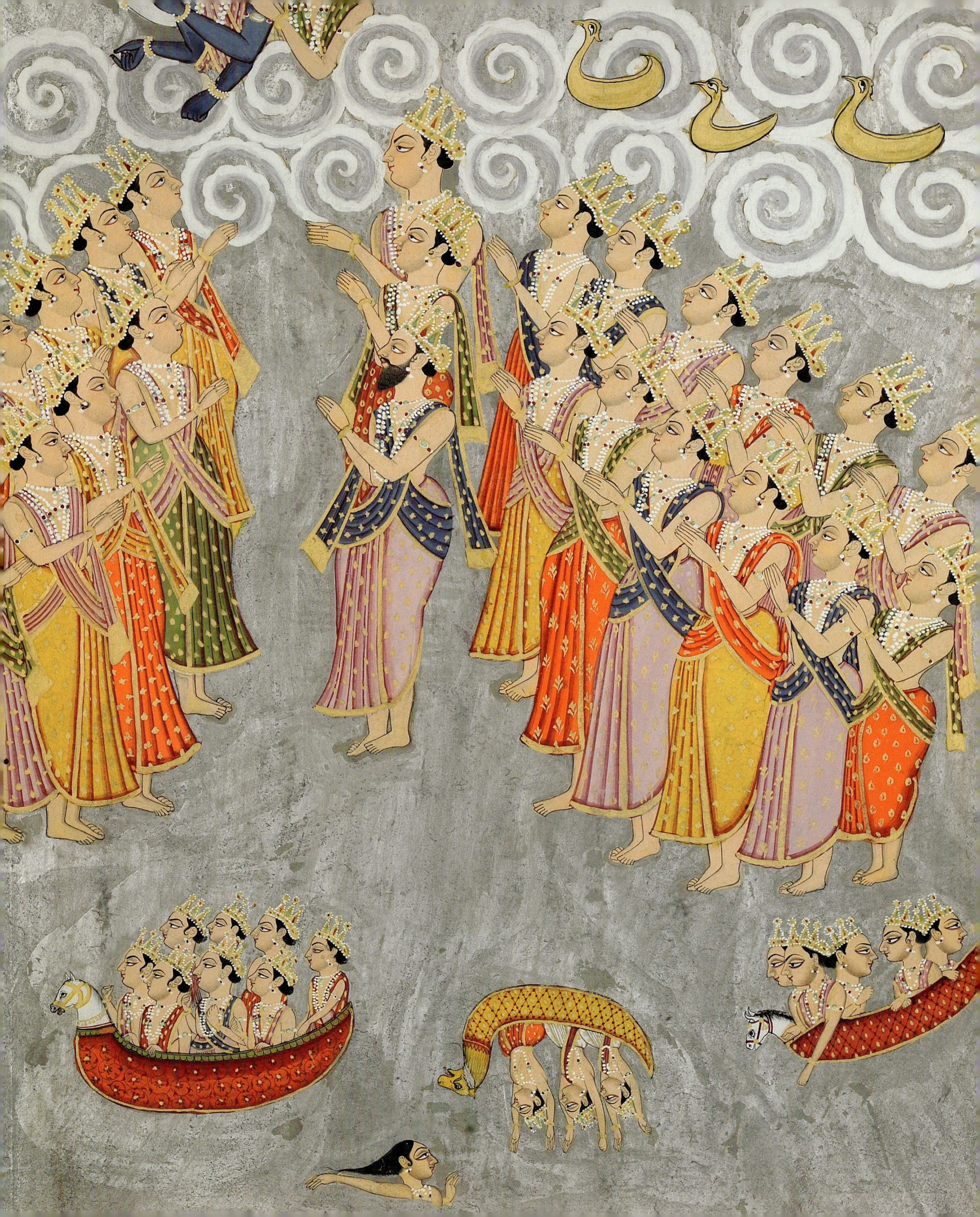

Nathji Creates the Earth's Sacred Waters

folio 4 from the *Nath Charit*
1823 (Samvat 1880); 47 x 123 cm
Mehrangarh Museum Trust

Numbered 4 in red by Reu.

sri nath carit
da [khal] dholiya re kothar
Glorious Nath Charit
Entered into the *dholiya* storeroom

Within the Nath Sampraday and, more broadly, the tantric orders, the Hindu gods are "long lived beings on subtle planes with extraordinary powers," but they are not fully mature spiritual beings like *siddhas*.[10] Therefore, many of the revelations in the *Nath Charit* are framed as discourses to the gods, who learn of the nature of being from the most subtle manifestation of the Absolute, Nathji himself. In the shimmering left panel (p. 184), above the white scalloped clouds, Nathji, in his anthropomorphic form, teaches Kala (Time, represented here as a Nath *siddha*). In his second appearance, Nathji blows the deer-horn whistle that is a characteristic element of Nath garb (seen more clearly in cat. 45) as he instructs the three great Hindu gods: Shiva, blue-skinned Vishnu, and four-headed Brahma. A number of lesser deities, however, are mystified by Nathi's all-pervasive light (*jyoti*). Overawed, the gods fall from the heavens as they try to swim in or row upon his radiance.[11]

In the right panel (p. 185), Nathji creates the Ganges, Yamuna, and Godavari rivers of the Indian subcontinent, which stream down to the earth. (The creation of the Ganges also is depicted in cat. 45.) Two small silver squares in this panel represent Nathji's other watery creations, the holy lake of Pushkar (Rajasthan) and all the world's oceans. Several encounters between Nathji and Shiva, who here doubts Nathji's primacy, are sandwiched into the blue sky above the earth. These encounters reiterate a common trope in Nath texts. A god challenges Nathji's omnipresence, then is awed by his omnipotence, and finally sits down for a discourse.[12]

The two panels juxtapose Nathji's silver light and the silver rivers to connect Nathji's cosmic radiance to the earth's sacred waters. This is no mean achievement. The equivalence between subtle and gross matter is central to Nath teachings. It provides the mechanism by which yogic adepts transmute their mortal bodies into immortal, perfected essences.[13] DD

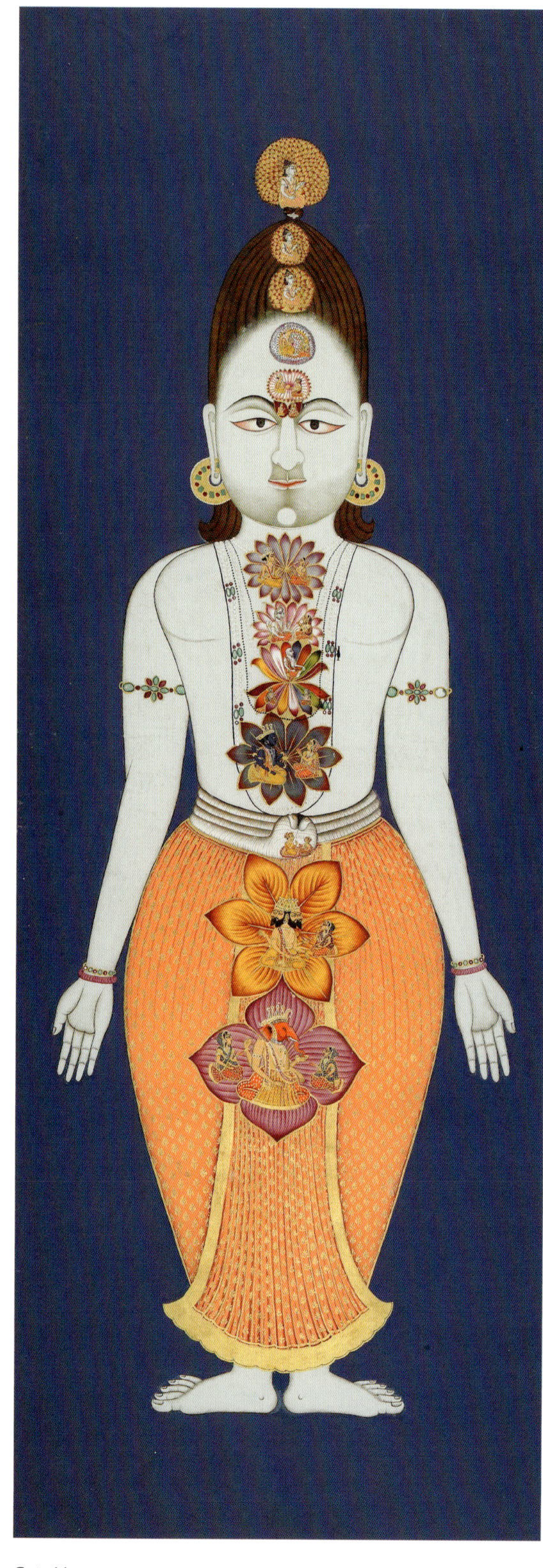

Cat. 44

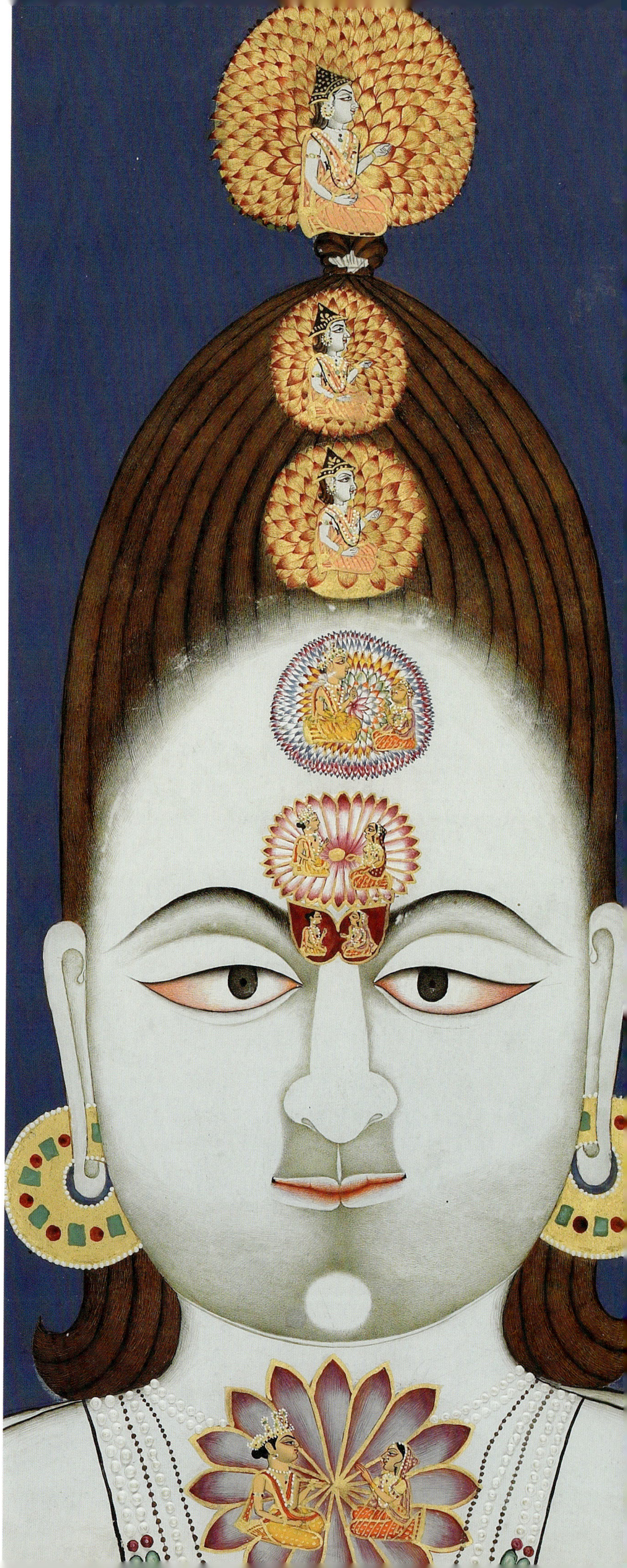

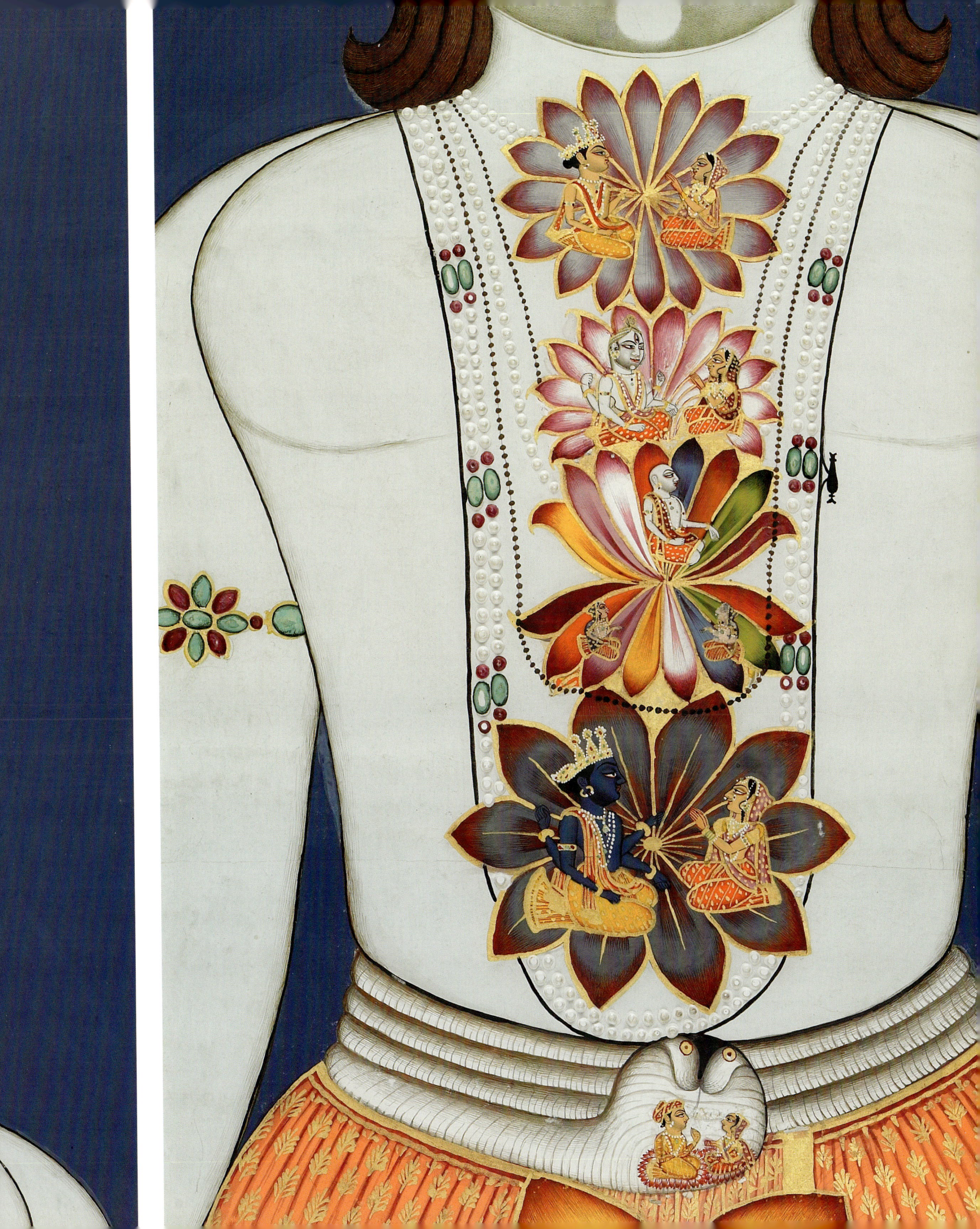

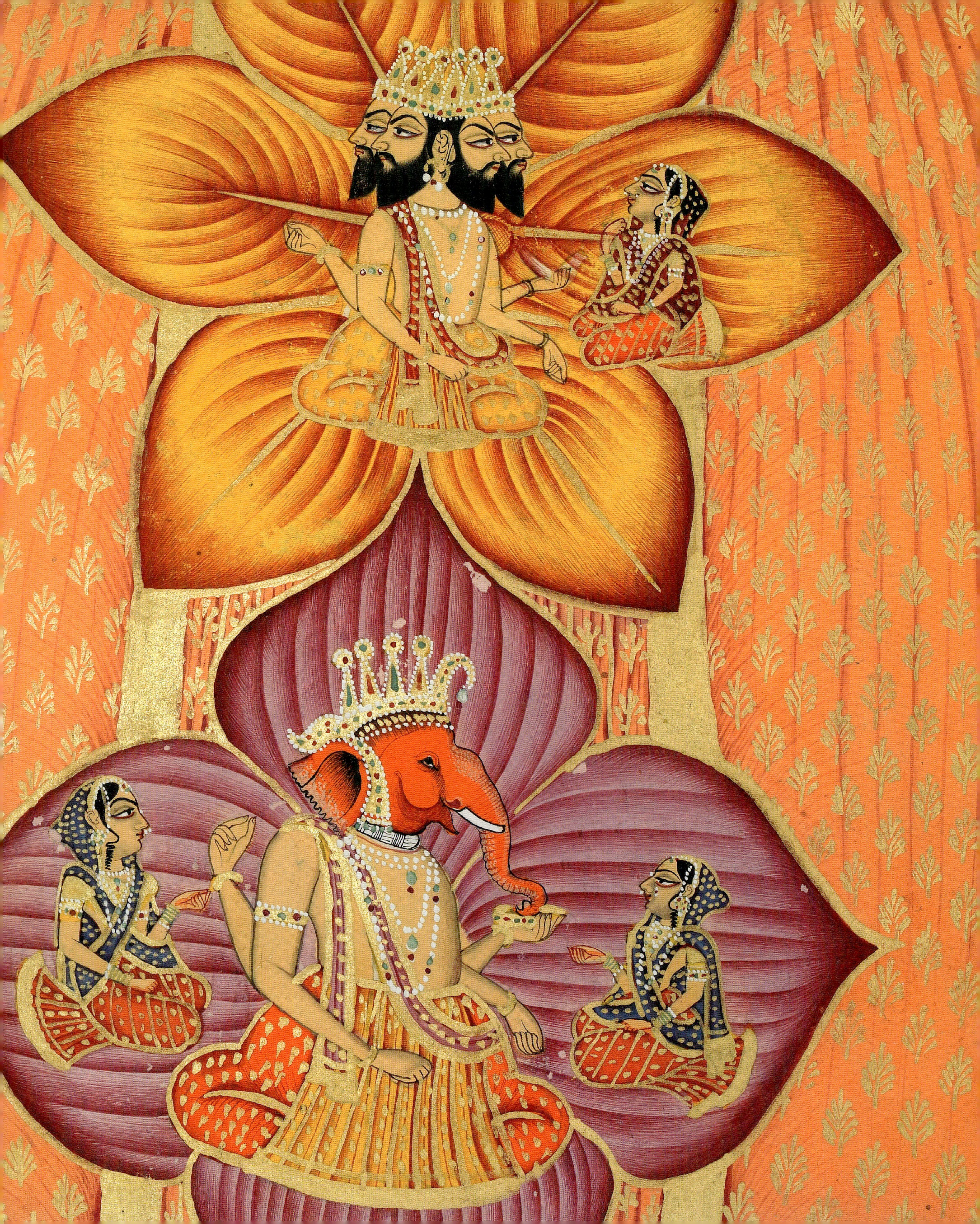

44

Chakras of the Subtle Body
folio 2 from the *Nath Charit*
Attributed to Bulaki, 1823 (Samvat 1880); 122 x 46 cm
Mehrangarh Museum Trust

Sri nath charit
Da[khal] dholiya re kothar
Glorious Nath Charit
Entered into the *dholiya* storeroom

Cartilage-piercing earrings, shoulder-length *jata* (dreadlocks), and saffron garb identify this massive figure as a Nath *siddha*. He stands in the yogic posture of *tadasana*, his eyes crossed in inward meditation and his body covered in pale blue ash (see pp. 188–89). Expansive curves delineate the broad shoulders, tapered waist, and wide hips of his fleshy body, while gleaming details—a gold-patterned dhoti with flowing pleats, jeweled ornaments, and luminous chakras (energy stations of the subtle body)—shimmer against a deeply saturated blue ground. The surreal intensity of the *siddha's* precisely shaded face and the schematic frontality of the body point to Bulaki as its artist.

Hatha yoga's emphasis upon knowing the body lies behind this imposing yet uncanny image, which depicts the subtle body (*sukshmasharira*)—the mediating space (mesocosm) between the Absolute (macrocosm) and the material body (microcosm). While important Hindu traditions (such as Advaita Vedanta) advocate knowledge of the self's equivalence with the cosmos as the means towards enlightenment, hatha yoga promises to transform the body into the universe. This process of perfection takes place within the subtle body, which yogic adepts mobilize through somatic purification, breath control, fixed postures, and meditation. Aware of the energy centers (chakras) of the subtle body, represented here as lotus blooms, adepts can awaken the *Kundalini-shakti* (female energy) that lies in a triple coil at the base of the spine and draw it upward in successive stages. As *Kundalini* pierces each chakra, gross matter transforms into subtler essence, reversing the natural tendency toward decay and death. With each transformation, the yogin reaches a higher plane of spiritual awareness and is able to control the gross matter associated with that energy center. In the early years of the twelve-year process, the adept learns to fly, see, and hear over great distances; in the middle years, he overcomes disease and becomes immortal; in the penultimate year, he experiences the oneness of the universal macrocosm with his own body; and in the twelfth year he becomes even greater than the gods.[14] The centrality of the subtle body in Nath metaphysics and practice is reflected in the folio's vertical orientation, which allows for its almost life-size representation. Indeed, amid the three hundred fifty-four horizontal monumental folios created during Man Singh's reign, the colossus—like the two subtle bodies depicted on the *Siddha Siddhanta Paddhati's* vertical pages—"stands out."[15]

Chakras are conceptualized somewhat differently in various yoga treatises, even those attributed to a single author such as Gorakhnath, and number anywhere from six to fourteen, but they are always arrayed in a vertical hierarchy. In this subtle body of fourteen chakras, the upper energy centers are the realms of Nath *mahasiddhas*, while the lower ones are identified with Hindu deities. DD

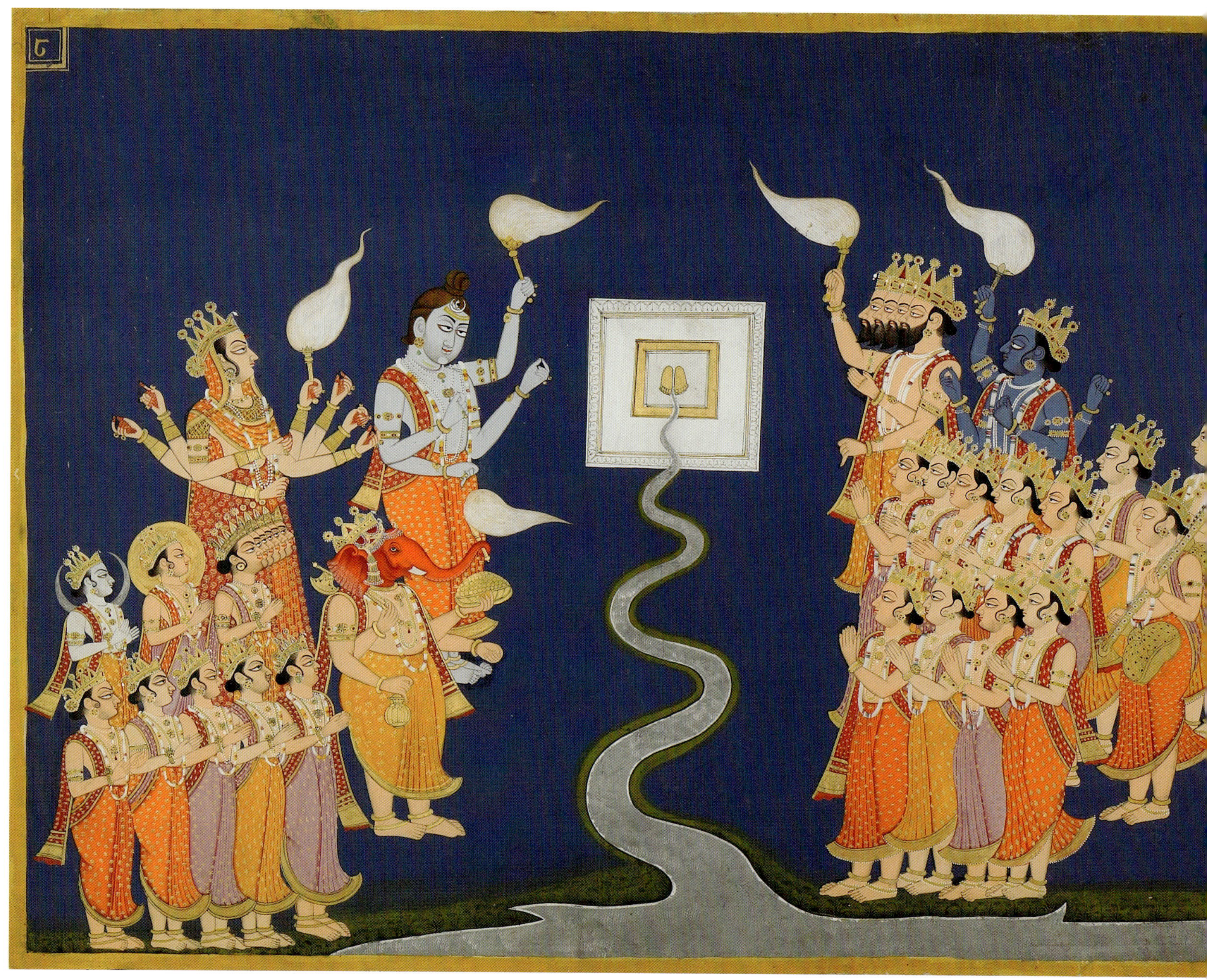

Cat. 45

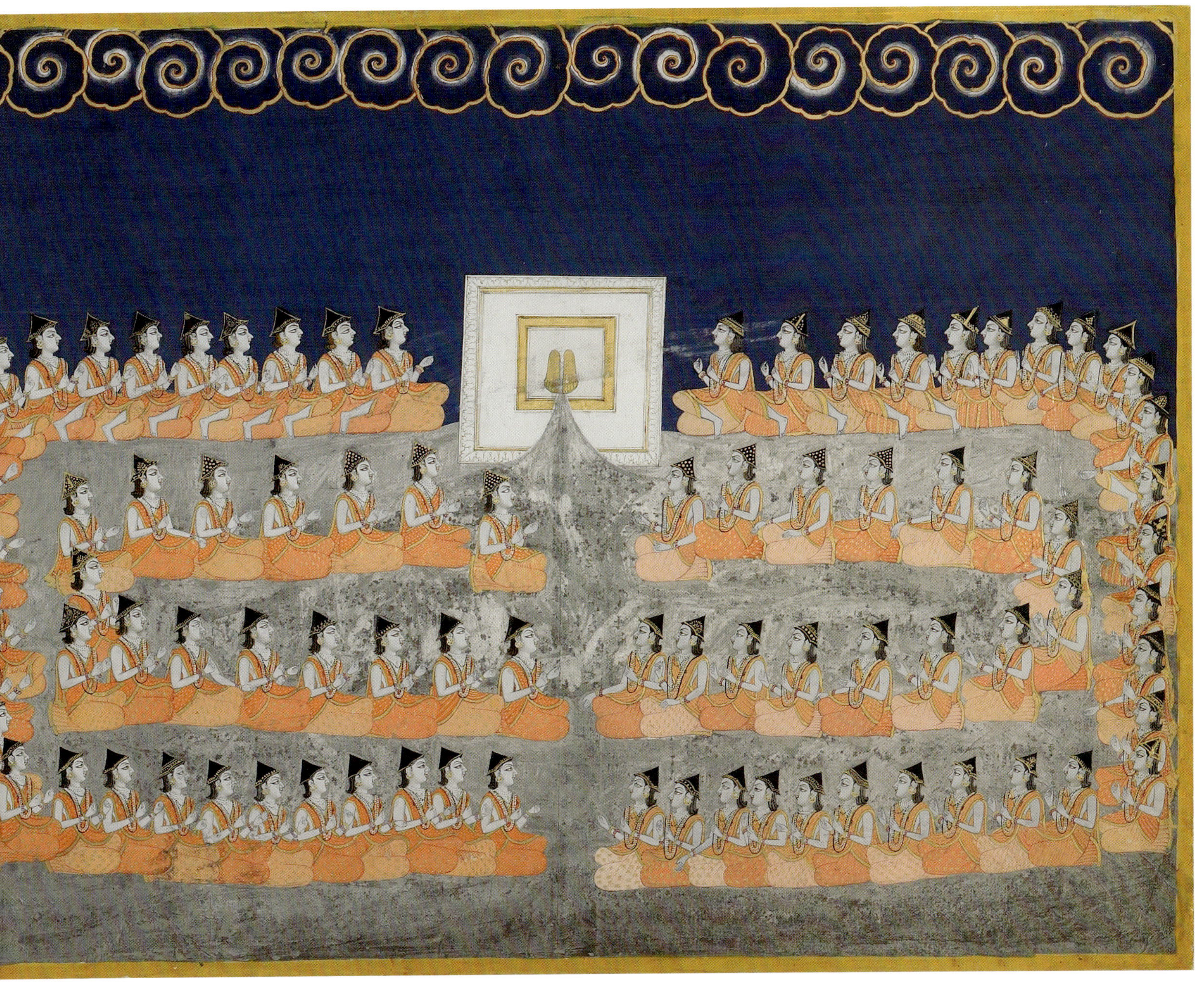

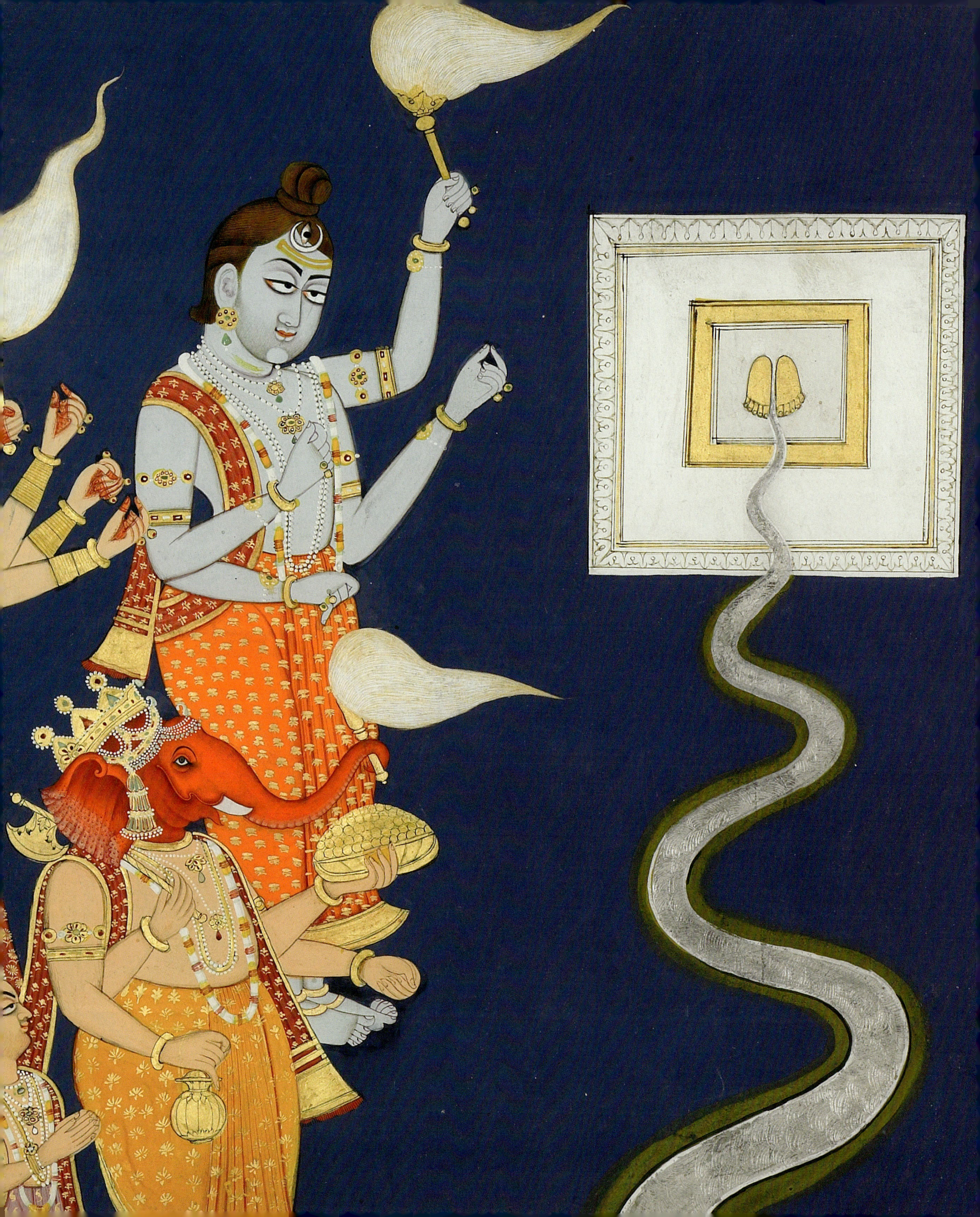

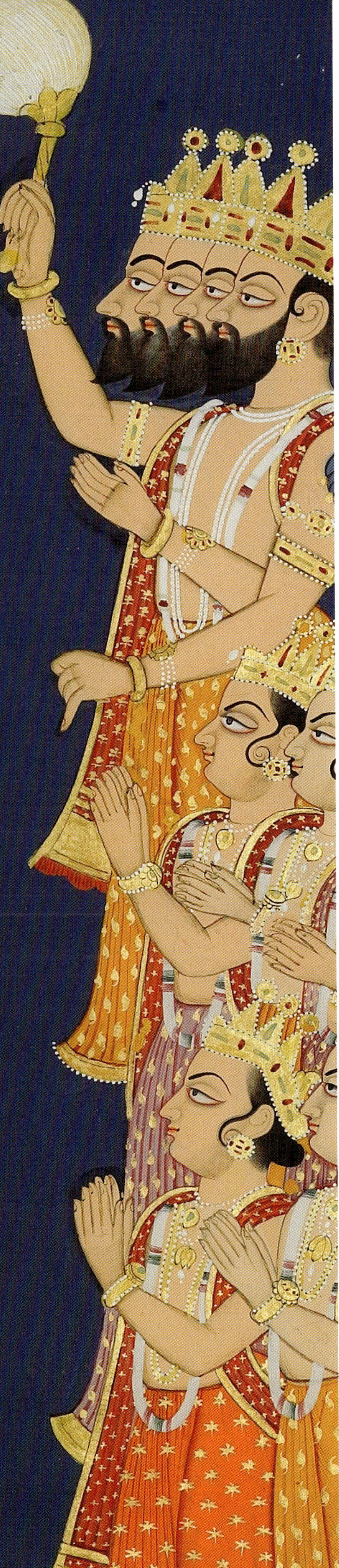

Nathji Creates the Ganges
folio 8 from the Nath Purana
Attributed to Shivdas, ca. 1825; 44.9 x 124.1 cm
Mehrangarh Museum Trust

Numbered 8 on recto.
The complete inscription appears in the reference catalogue.

Both the *Nath Purana* and the *Nath Charit* reveal that Nathji, a sublime manifestation of the cosmos, emerged on earth as the sacred river Ganges.[16] The *Nath* narratives thus displace the canonical Hindu account in which the sage Bhagiratha beseeches the goddess Ganga (Ganges) to descend to earth.[17] Here, Ganga's purifying waters emerge through the grace of Nathji, who is depicted, in both the left and right panels of the painting (see pp. 192–93), as footprints of light (*jyoti kundal*).[18]

On the left, a gathering of Hindu deities—including Shiva, Devi, Ganesha, Skanda, Surya (Sun), Chandra (Moon), Brahma, and Vishnu—worship Nathji's footprints within the universe's highest realm (*akasha mandala*).[19] In turn, Nathji blesses the gods with the sacred river, a sinuous, silver streak flowing from his golden footprints. Against the deep blue ground, the multiple gold borders of the platform create the illusion that the brilliant white square is expanding, perhaps evoking the gradual formation of the cosmos.[20] The right panel exploits the hypnotic potential of repetitive forms by depicting scores of seated Nath *siddhas*.[21]

During Man Singh's reign, poets, artists, and writers responded to their patron's devotion in their respective art forms. The resulting network of symbolic references constructed and, to some extent, reconceived the nature of Nath greatness.[22] The image of footprints in this painting drew upon an established sacred authority; footprints signifying holy presence had circulated within Buddhist, Jain, and Hindu devotional networks for millennia, and in Islamic and Nath contexts for centuries. Repeated references to the footprints in Jodhpur paintings and verse exemplify how a familiar symbol was reinterpreted as the representation of Nath grace. Here, the artist's rendering of Nathji's radiant footprints within a lotus-petal border on a white square recalls (and perhaps was inspired by) the carved marble slabs the maharaja installed in Nath shrines and temples. (See cat. 37 and fig. 32a, p. 281.) Such marble footprints instantiate the maharaja's verse: "I have become attached to the feet of Nath and will announce it to the world."[23] A contemporaneous court poem employs the motif of divine footprints as "proof" that Nathji bestowed the throne of Marwar upon Man Singh:

> [Nathji] produced a miracle in that difficult time,
> giving his proof one day at morningtide
> on the tenth day of the bright fortnight of Ashvin (September–October).
> His two beautiful footprints shone,
> On the fine-grained yellow stone…
> The king touched his forehead to those feet
> [Nathji] has come to meet the king.[24]

DD

MAPPING THE COSMOS

The paintings in this section are maps that draw upon the immense body of cosmographic conceptions that developed in South Asia over millennia. They illustrate texts that relate the metaphysical knowledge and legends of the Naths, a religious order whose adepts gained immortality and omniscience through the practice of hatha yoga. The paintings demonstrate how *mahasiddhas* (perfected Naths) situated themselves at the apex of the universe and how they visualized the equivalence of their bodies and the macrocosm. As cartographic representations of cosmic and metaphysical spaces, the folios meticulously establish spatial relationships between multiple worlds, celestial landmarks, divinities, and the human body.

With their glowing mineral pigments, abundant gilding, and elegant precision, the paintings transform the diagrammatic into the shimmering aesthetic of the court. Dramatic shifts from the gigantic to the miniature invoke the vastness of the cosmos. Formal strategies, including vibrating color harmonies and juxtaposed perspectives, convey its ineffable wonder.

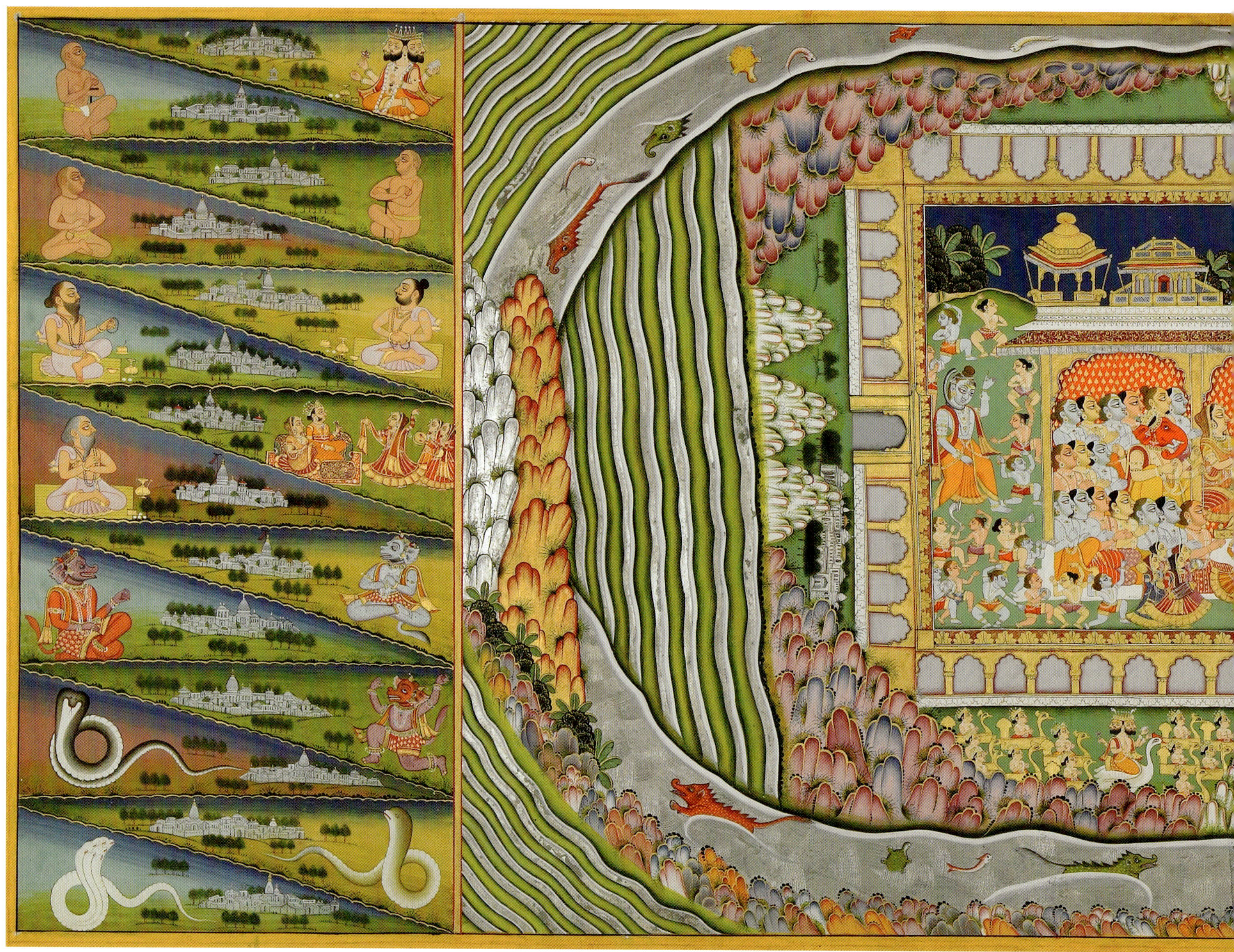

Cat. 46

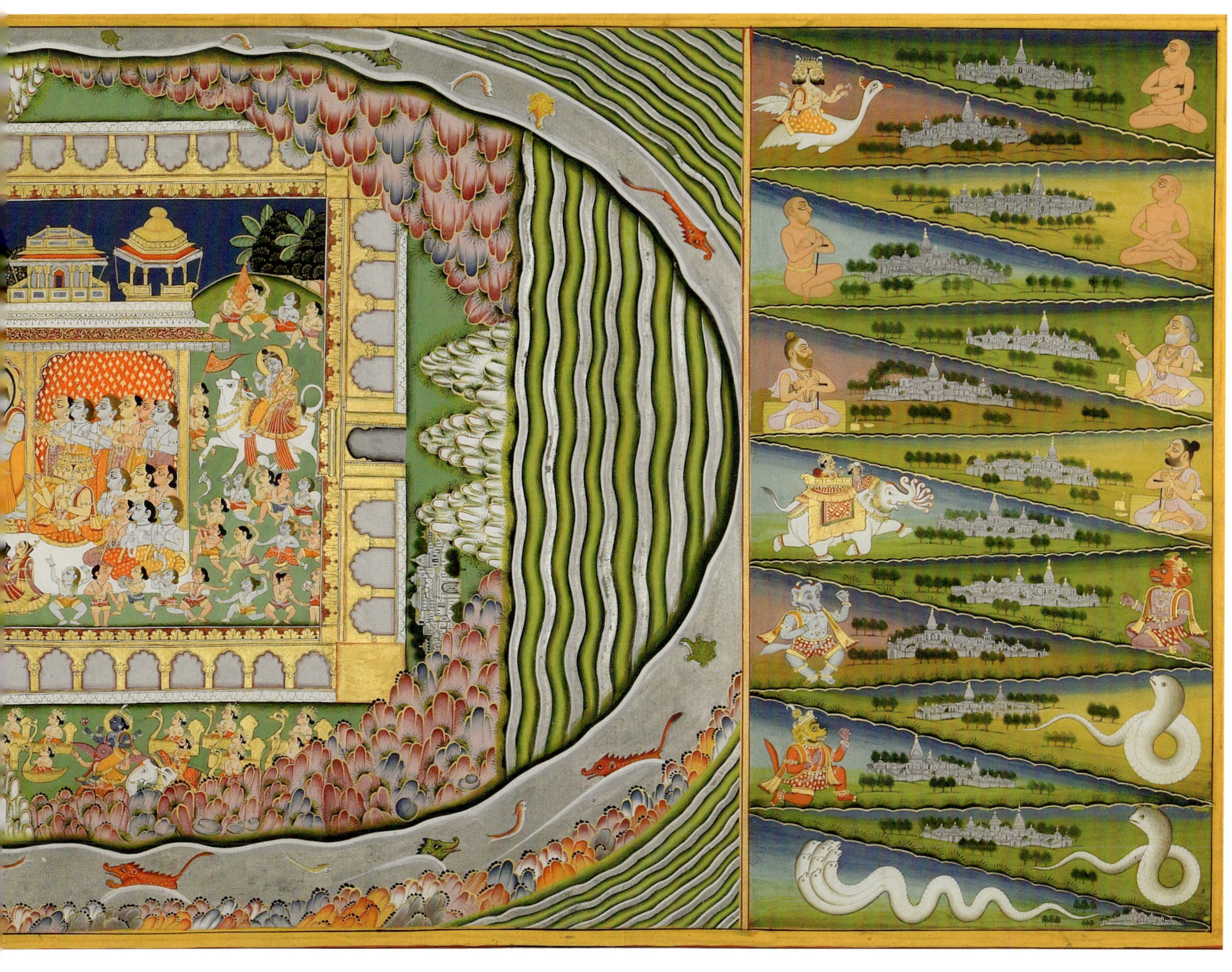

The Mandala of Shiva

folio 8 from the *Shiva Rahasya*
Jodhpur, 1827 (Samvat 1884); 46 x 121 cm
Mehrangarh Museum Trust

The complete inscription appears in the reference catalogue.

A mandala is a symbolic diagram of cosmic infrastructure. This mandala reveals Shiva to be the supreme deity at the center of the universe; the great god is depicted three times within his gold-walled palace (see pp. 198–99). To the left of the central pavilion, Shiva dances with his impish attendants (*ganas*). To the palace's right, Shiva and Parvati enter the pavilion, affectionately seated together on the bull Nandi. Within the palace, the divine couple, benevolently engaged in devotion, sustain the universe through their pious actions.[1] Together they worship a sandalwood paste-streaked lingam, an abstract form of Shiva himself, by placing white blossoms on the sacred form. Their attendants include their two sons, many-headed Skanda, and orange-colored Ganesha. The scene evokes a blissful and gentle form of Shiva on Mount Kailash, which was described in sacred texts as a focus for meditation:

> [On Kailash's summit] peopled by hosts of adepts, bards, celestial nymphs, and followers of Ganapati [Ganesha], there was the silent God, world teacher of moveable and immobile things,
>
> who is ever benevolent, ever blissful, an ocean of ambrosial compassion, white like camphor or jasmine, consisting of pure *sattva*, all-pervasive,
>
> space-clothed, lord of the destitute, master of yogins, beloved of yogins, upon whose topknot the Ganges splashes, who is adorned with locks of hair,
>
> besmeared with ashes, peaceful, wearing a garland of snakes and skulls, with three eyes, who is lord of the three realms, holding a trident,
>
> who is easily appeased, full of wisdom, bestower of the fruit of liberation, formless, fearless, undifferentiated, untainted....

> —*Mahanirvana Tantra*[2]

Two-dimensional mandalas are blueprints that map relationships between celestial landmarks and multiple worlds. Six continents and seven oceans—represented as green and silver ribbons—circle Shiva's palace atop the snowy peaks of Mount Kailash. The universe's seven heavens and seven underworlds, stacked in an unusual zigzag formation, flank the earth-island. But if mandalas are templates, this artist has boldly exceeded the boundaries of the diagrammatic to convey the wonder of the ineffable universe. He shifts vertiginously from the gigantic to the miniature, juxtaposes multiple perspectives, and employs an hallucinatory palette in which acid-green continents vibrate against silver oceans, crimson-tipped golden mountains glow, and mauve sunsets glimmer portentously. DD

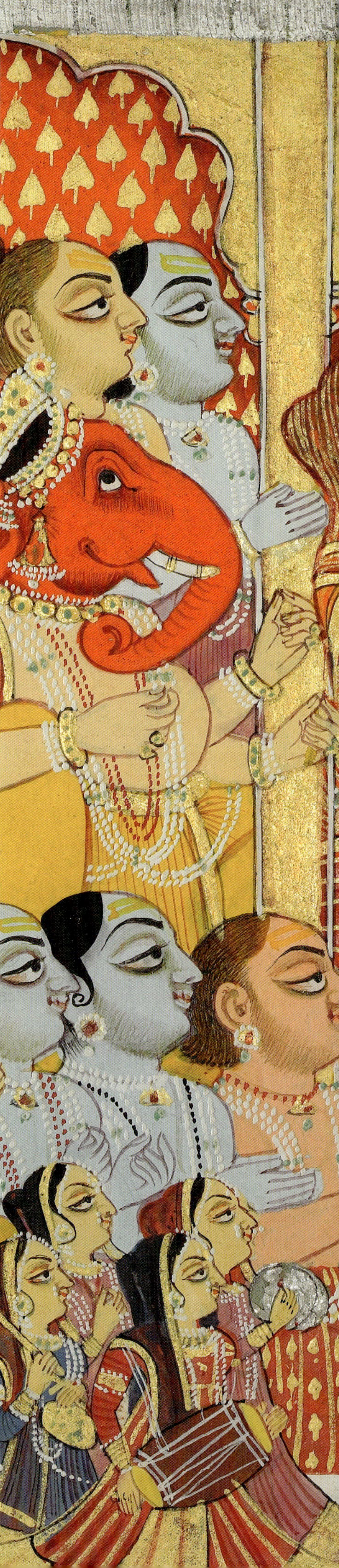

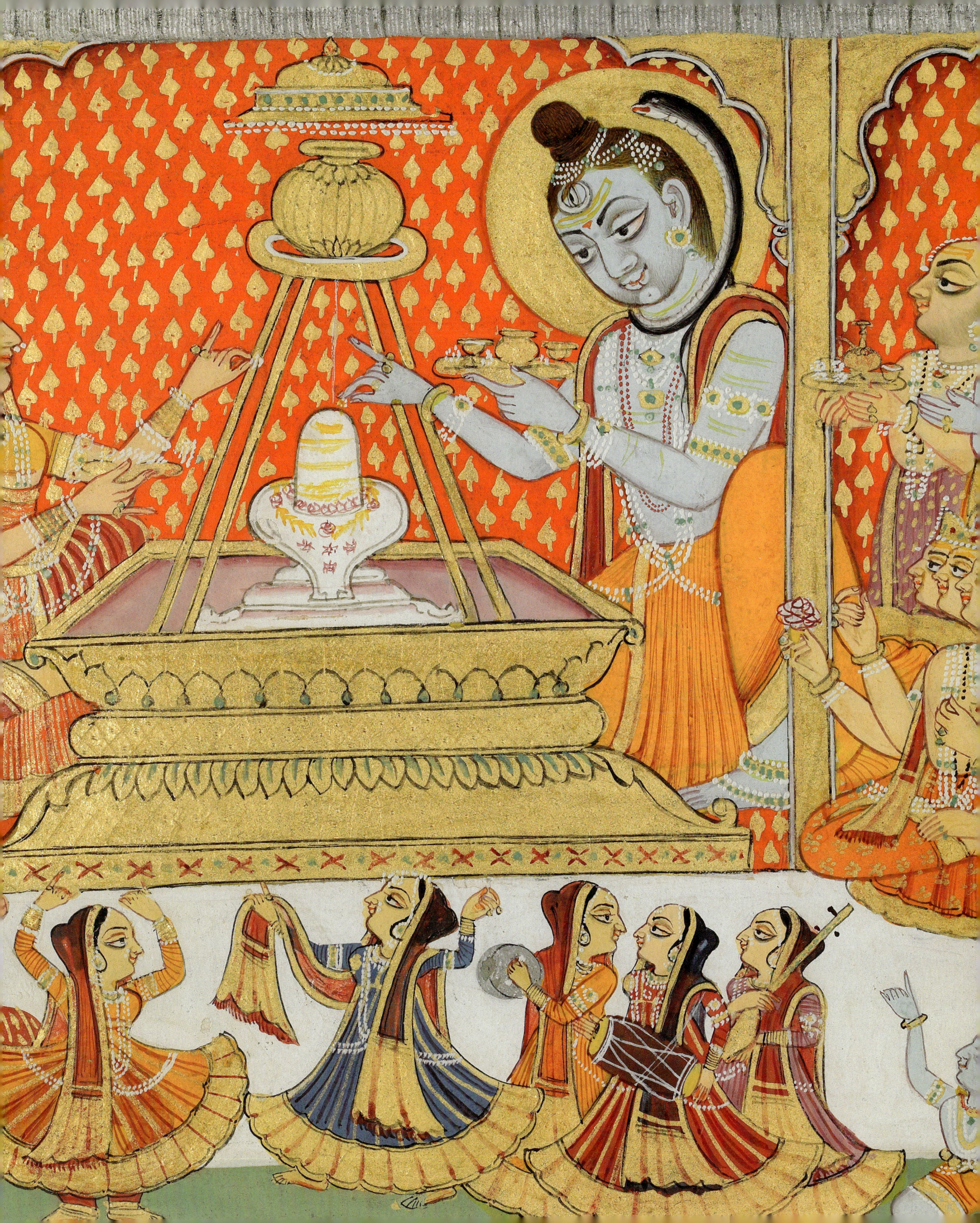

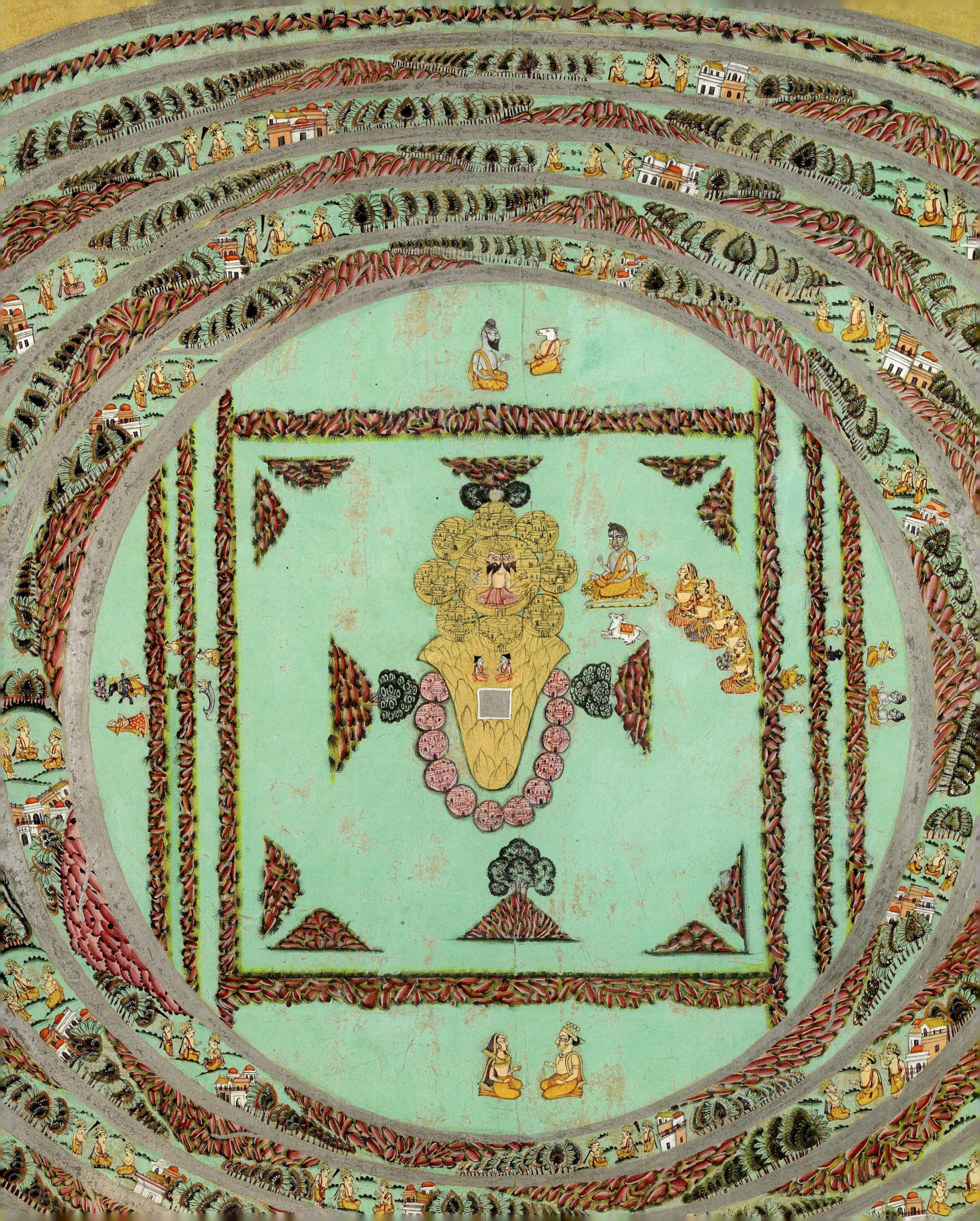

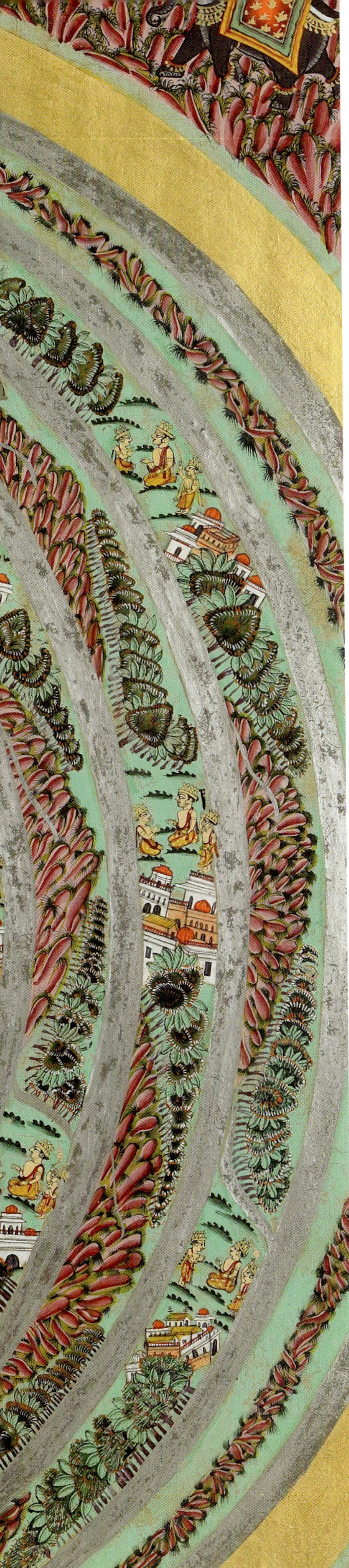

47

The Mandala of Great Ether (Mahakasha Mandala)

folio 7 from the Nath Purana
Attributed to Bulaki, ca. 1825; 46.9 x 129.9 cm
Mehrangarh Museum Trust

Numbered 7 on recto.
The complete inscription, accompanied by a chart,
appears in the reference catalogue.

Bulaki realizes the *Nath Charit's* mandala (map of the cosmos) from the dispassionate perspective of a celestial cartographer (see pp. 204–5). While he reduces the gigantic to the miniature with dry precision, the artist does not obscure cosmic geometry. Unlike the accessible world of Shiva at the center of the *Shiva Purana* mandala (cat. 46), here god and demons alike are reduced to symbols of the realms they inhabit.

The *Nath Charit* mandala combines two cosmographical conceptions: the horizontal world system in which concentric continents encircle an egg-shaped earth, and the vertical structure of netherworlds, human realms, and heavens. Bulaki fills the painting's prominent central panel with the horizontal realm of earth, the *bhumandal*. At its center, within a sacred space (*yantra*) comprised of tightly lobed crimson mountains, the vast Mount Meru appears as a diminutive inverted cone that serves as the dwelling for two Nath *mahasiddhas* and the great Hindu deity Brahma.[3]

On the left, the lowest heaven is the realm of the deity Indra, who is transported by the white elephant Airavata. Various sages and naked renunciants dwell in the next three heavens. Ascetics, their skin pale blue from smeared ash, converse with the four-headed deity Brahma in the fifth world. The penultimate heaven includes three celestial worlds, rendered from right to left as the floating sky-palaces of Krishna, Shiva, and Vishnu. On the right, the seven lower worlds of snakes, demons, and gods rise above *Sheshnag*, the serpent who bears the universe on his many heads.

Bulaki reserves his finest painting for the *mahasiddhas* Jallandharnath, Gorakhnath, Matsyendranath, and Kanerinath, who are flanked by the nine and eighteen Naths in the folio's upper right corner.[4] It is, in fact, Bulaki's distinctive rendering of the Naths (sharp-nosed profiles; gray, pageboy dreadlocks; red-tinged eyes) that enables the confident attribution of this painting to his hand. The celestial Naths preside over the realm of the great ether (*mahakasha* mandala), the most subtle, enduring, and supreme world in the cosmos, which Bulaki represents as a solid field of gold. DD

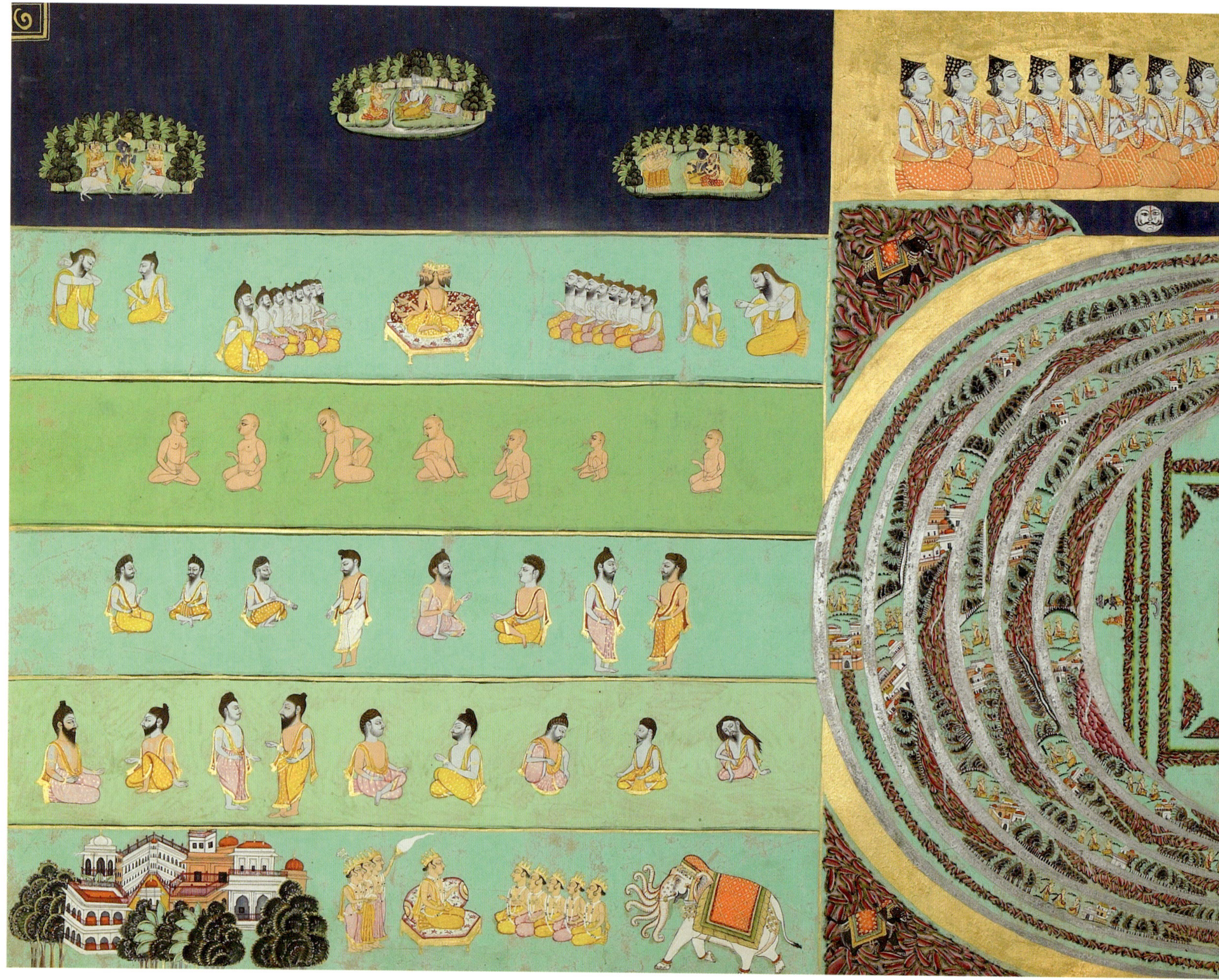

Cat. 47

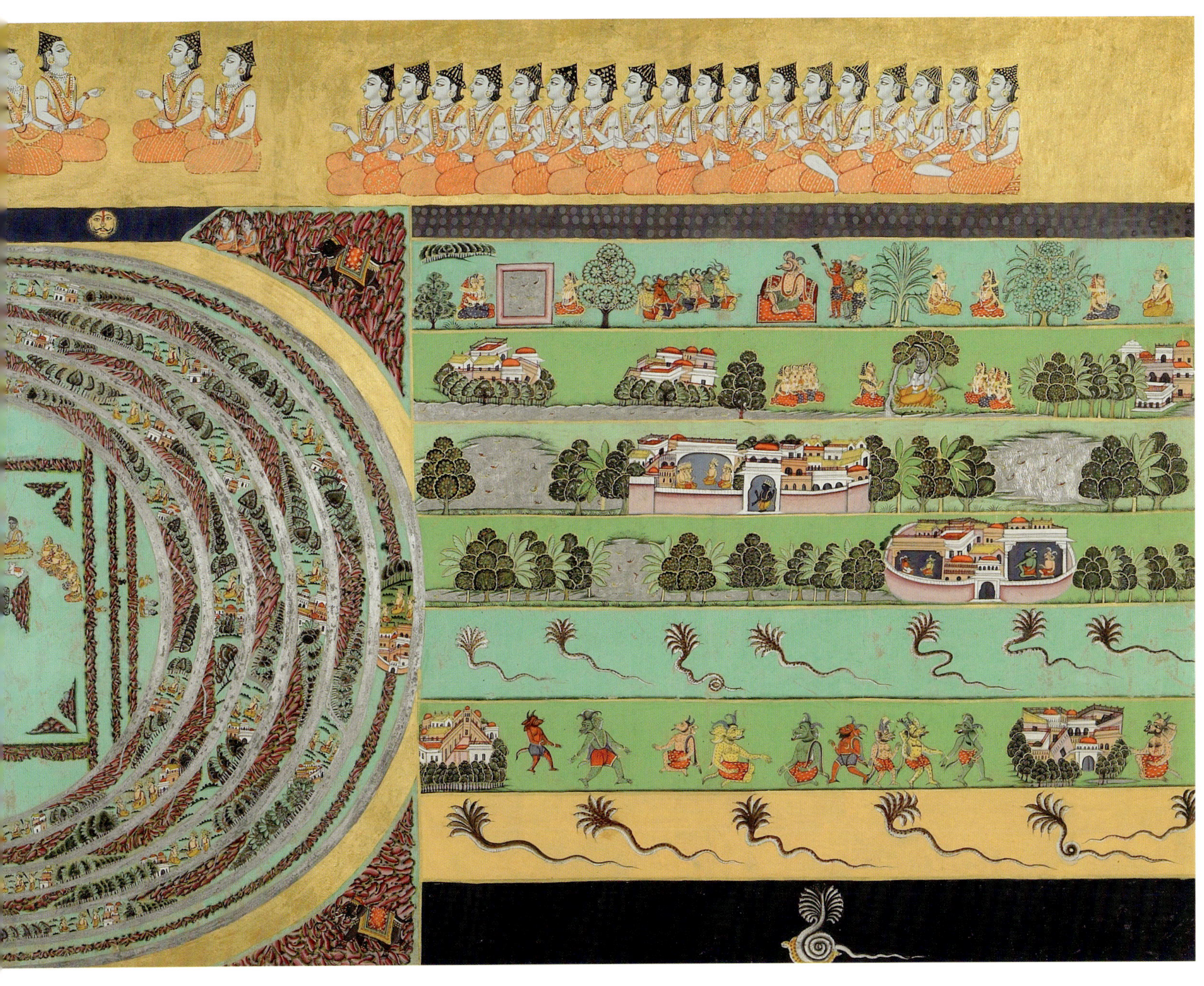

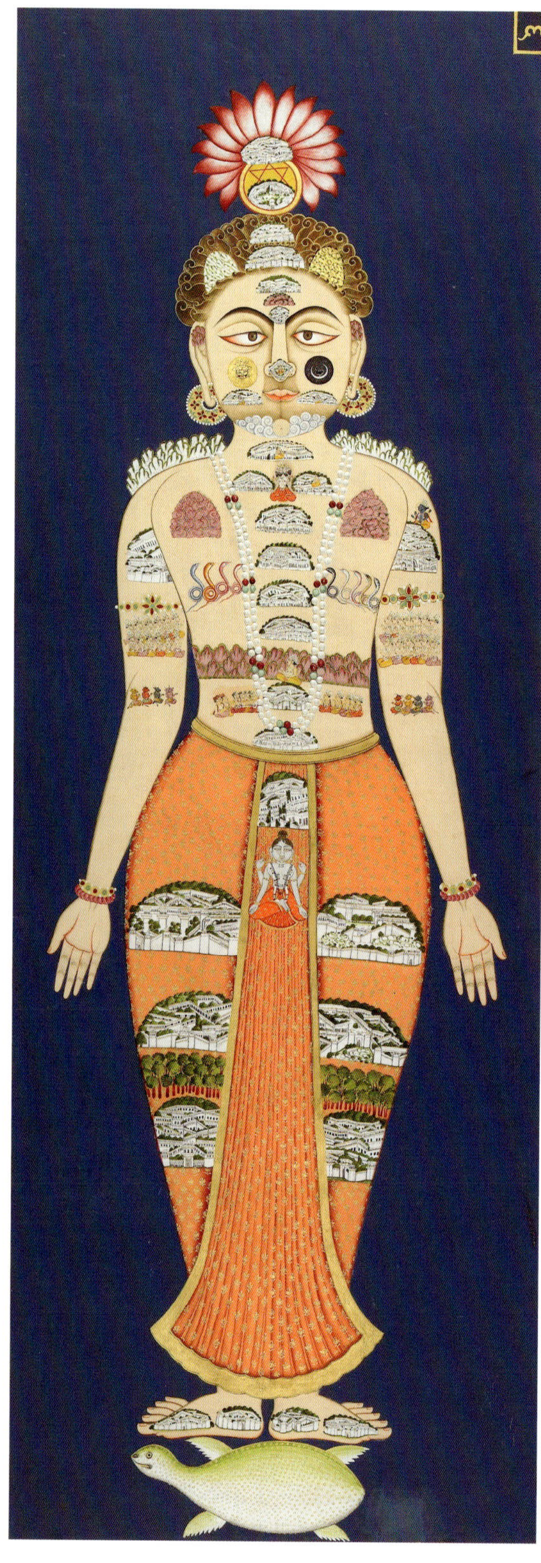

Cat. 48

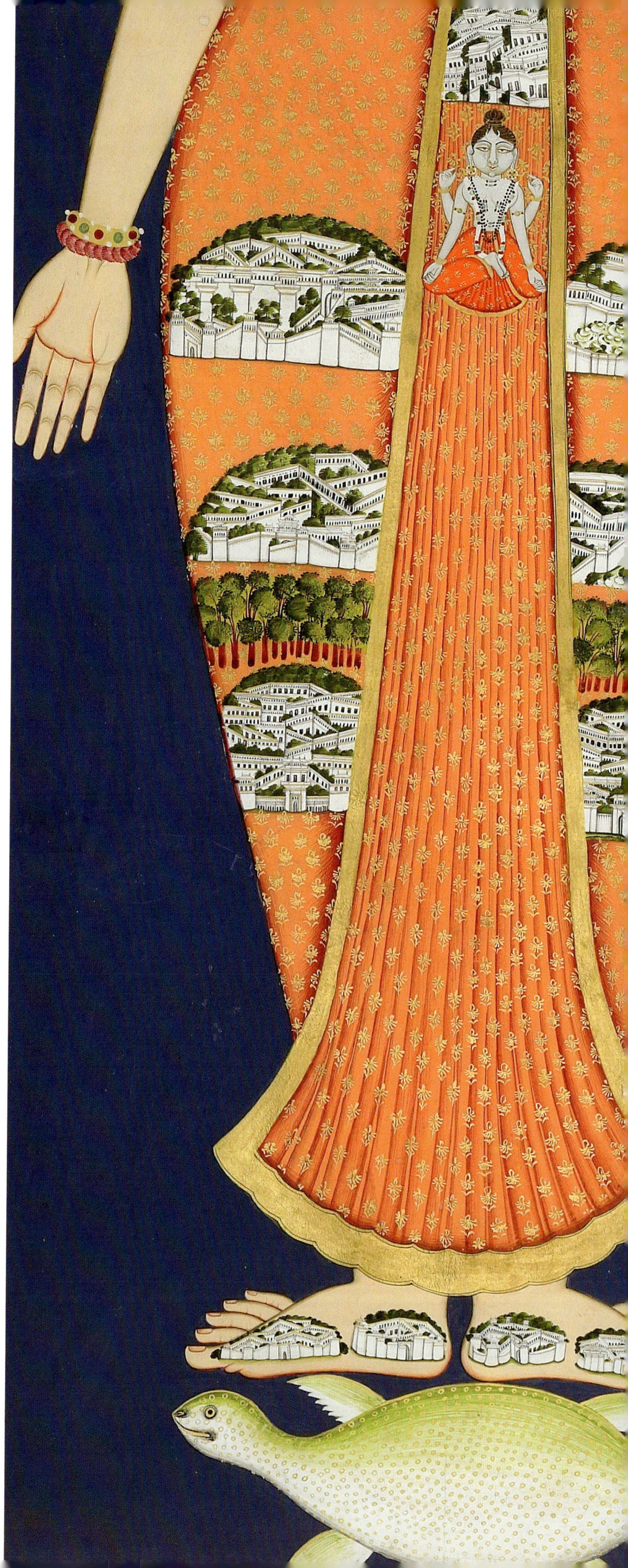

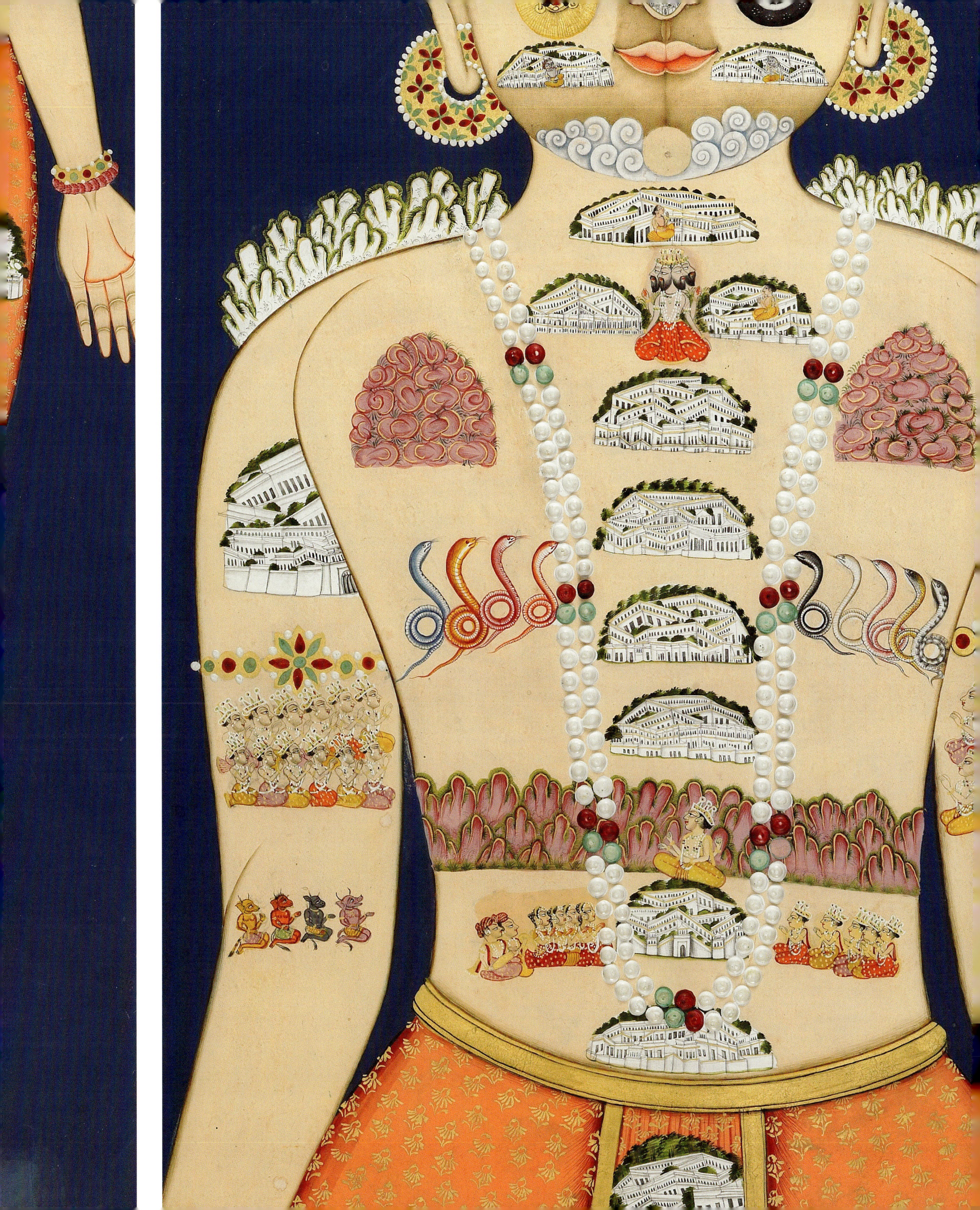

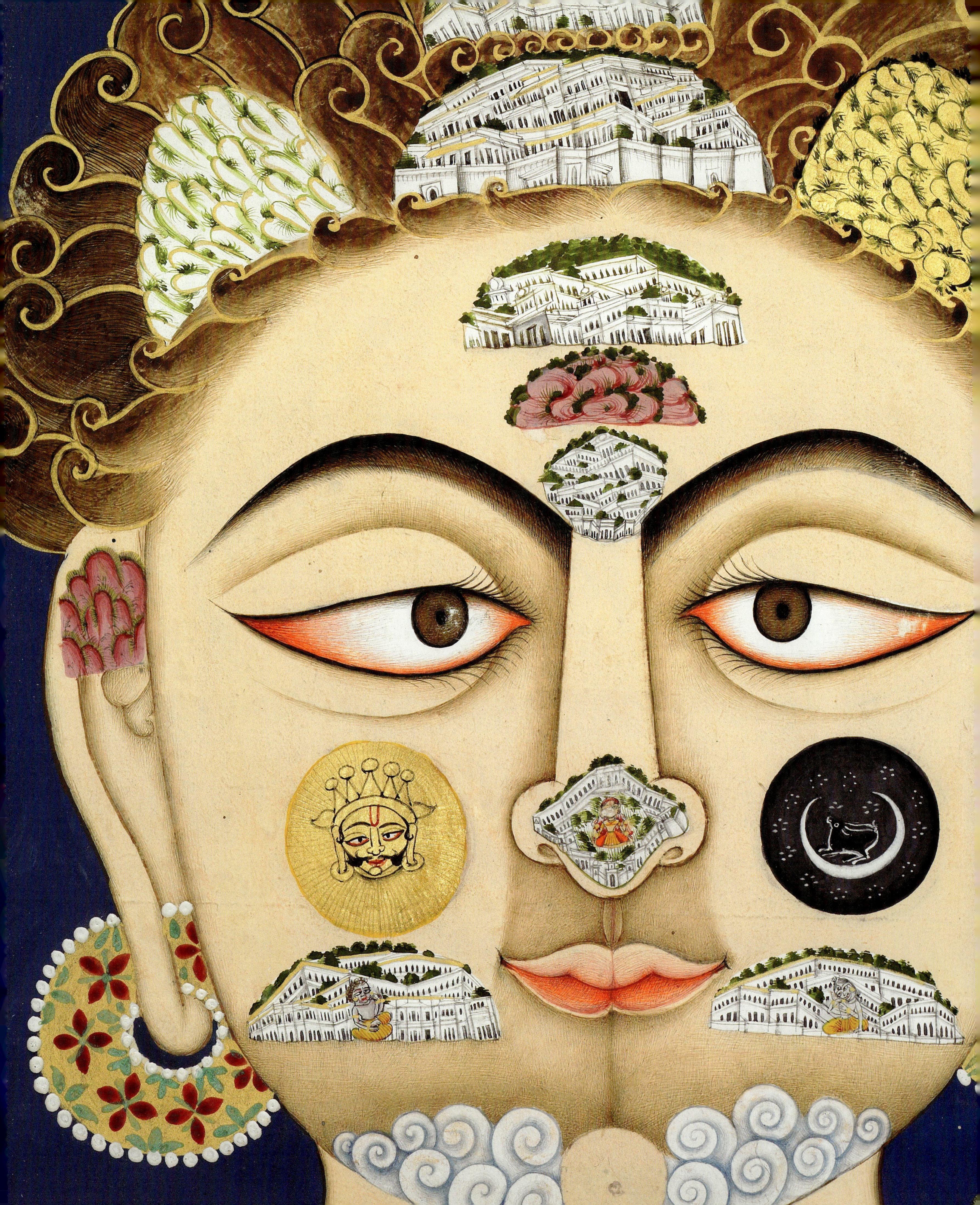

48

The Equivalence of Self and Universe

folio 6 from the *Siddha Siddhanta Paddhati*
"The Muslim Artist" (Bulaki), 1824 (Samvat 1881); 122 x 46 cm
Mehrangarh Museum Trust

The complete inscription appears in the reference catalogue.

> Within this body exist Mount Meru, the seven continents, lakes, oceans,
> mountains, plains, and the protectors of these plans. All beings embodied in
> the three worlds…exist in the body together with all their activities. He who
> knows all this is a yogin. There is no doubt about this.[5]

In the penultimate year of the twelve-year course of hatha yoga, a yogin becomes
a *siddha*, a perfected being who achieves an equivalence of self and universe
(see pp. 206–7).

With his eyes crossed in yogic meditation, this *siddha* experiences the bliss
of enlightenment. His body's expansive and fleshy contours incorporate a vast
cosmos, numerous deities, and all manner of creation. Following the text of the
Siddha Siddhanta Paddhati, the artist maps the universe's fourteen principal
worlds along the yogi's limbs in a vertical hierarchy. Four heavens (including the
siddha heaven) are located along his chest and head; three middle worlds are
situated at his lower torso; and seven underworlds nestle within his feet and amid
the folds of his orange *dhoti*. Seven additional worlds are placed along his
shoulders. Semi-divine snake gods and parti-color demons nestle in the crooks of
his elbows. His thighs support all the world's forests, and his ribs, shoulders, and
head bear the world's great mountains.

The Nath *siddha* appears huge in contrast to the minutely rendered interior
worlds—gleaming fortress-cities presided over by deities. Even his face becomes
enormous: in a dramatic (and witty) inversion of scale, the sun and moon (the *ha*
and *tha* of hatha yoga) become the Nath's cheeks, the clouds his beard, and
the mountains his ear hair.

Representing yogic insight is a paradoxical task. Nath doctrine maintains that
the equivalence of self with universe is beyond the comprehension of ordinary
individuals. Ultimate reality can be perceived only through the insight gained by
the physical and mental transformations wrought by yogic practice. Indeed, the
painting's multiple representational systems deny the beholder complete and
simultaneous vision. White palace cities, with perspectival walls that create the
painting's only areas of tangible depth, offer a transcendent vision of the worlds.
But these bird's-eye views, once grasped, are negated by the painting's emphatic
planarity. The surface's gleam, which was created by rubbing the verso of the
painting with a stone to fuse the pigments, emphasizes the flatness of the paper
support. Flatly painted deities, humans, and demons, rendered in crystalline
detail, seamlessly cohere with the burnished surface. In turn, the yogi's pearls
rendered in high relief call into question the materiality of the deities tucked
between its double strand. The image oscillates between surface and depth,
between materiality and illusion. By allowing only fleeting apprehension, the
painting situates the viewer as an imperfect witness to the omniscience of yogic
insight, but invokes the perfected yogin's profound comprehension of the
simultaneous coexistence of the Absolute and its myriad of emanations. DD

Three Yantras from the Meghmala

ca. 1825; 41.4 x 199.4 cm

Mehrangarh Museum Trust

On recto: white numbered 7, pink numbered 8, green numbered 9.

Yantras are composed of triangles, circles, and squares that map divine identity (i.e., the universe and its manifestation as a deity) as sacred geometry.[6] Deceptively simple in form, their shapes, points, and interstices house the yantra's primary deity (usually a goddess) and myriad divine attendants, existential planes, or ontological categories.[7] In principle, yantras are as numerous as the Hindu, Buddhist, and Jain gods combined, for they play a role in each religion's rituals. Generally, square enclosures (bearing "gates" at the cardinal directions) demarcate the sacred topos in which inverse triangles represent the goddess, upward pointing triangles represent gods, and their overlap represents the union of the two. A dot (*bindu*) at the yantra's center (and apex) represents the supreme reality.

Yantras usually serve as tools for meditation and realization of the self with a deity, although they can also harness supernatural powers for more worldly purposes. In either case, the deities are invoked within the yantra through rituals, such as the chanting of mantras. For the Nath *siddhas* who seek to perfect their bodies into the very fabric of the universe, the deities and their realms are levels of spiritual attainment that can be realized through the practice of yoga.

Made of both ephemeral and permanent materials, yantras usually take a purely geometric form. Some, however, include sacred syllables or anthropomorphic representations of deities.[8] Displaying the pictorial excess of the Man Singh monumental folios, these three yantras extend their cosmic fields into expansive landscapes (see pp. 210–11, 214–19). Conceived by a master colorist, each is dominated by the hue of its organizing yantra. The pink yantra expands into glowing mountains with boulders glazed in crimson, peach, and ochre; the celadon and chartreuse diagram opens out into verdant hills with fantastically slender and wispy trees; and the glassy white yantra is the underlying structure of a brilliantly lit mountain, blanketed in snow and speckled with lichens.[9] The warm red, pink, and orange hues of the deities' garments and the pale ash-covered complexions of the male gods alternately harmonize or contrast with the palette of each landscape, uniting the three through color harmonies.

The textual "key" to the three yantras has not yet been located, but we can understand them as variations on concepts represented on other Nath folios. For example, the *bindu* at the green yantra's center signifies the Ultimate Reality, which is depicted as a gold field in cats. 40 and 41. The overlapping triangles represent the male and female aspects of creation. These manifestations of the Absolute appear as enthroned multi-armed deities in the painting's central landscape and elsewhere as Prakriti and Purusha and Shiva and Parvati (cats. 42, 46). The cosmographic logic that structures the yantras underlies the mandalas (cats. 46, 47), the subtle body (cat. 44), and the macrocosmic body (cat. 48), for each is a two-dimensional diagram of the universe.

Although the paintings' figural conventions recall deities and *siddhas* by Bulaki, the faces exhibit marked differences in the shading. This factor, along with the sheer diversity of techniques—calligraphic delicacy, fields of saturated color, and areas of transparent wash—suggests that several artists worked together on the series. DD

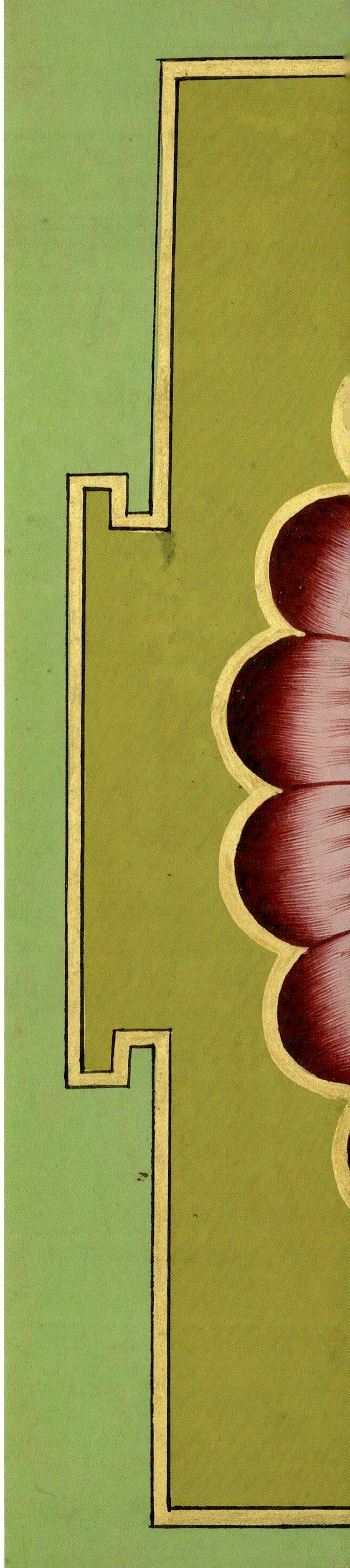

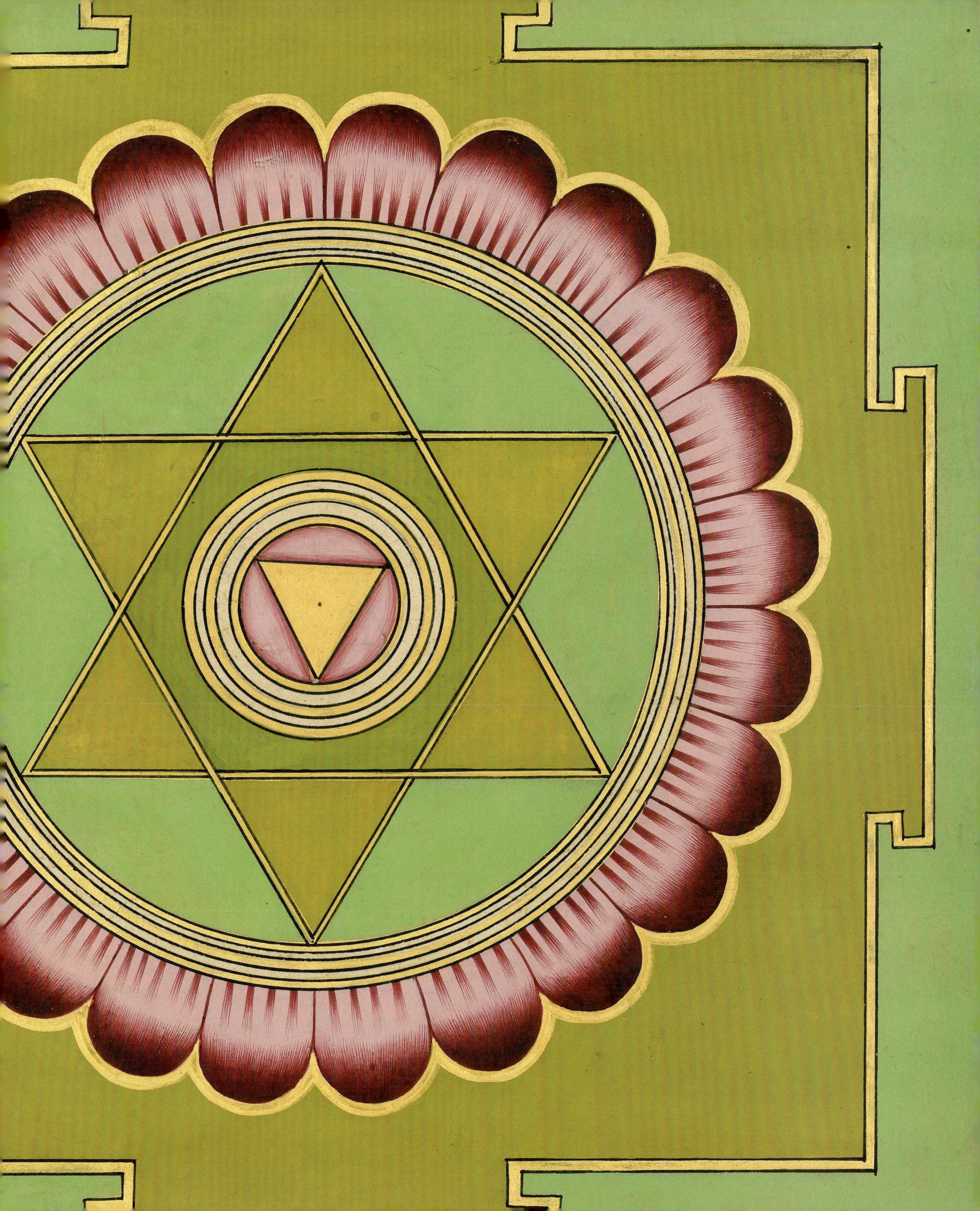

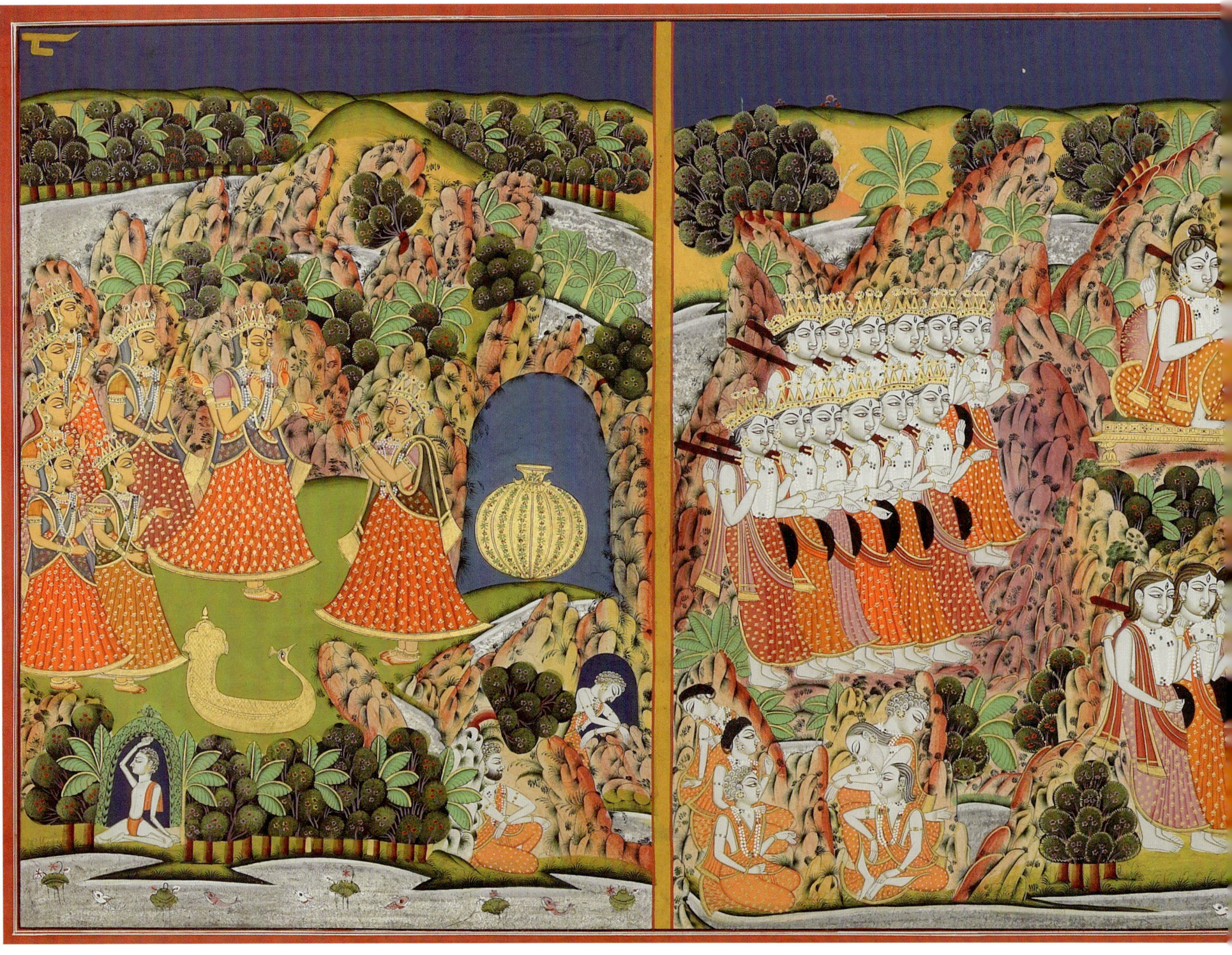

Cat. 49b

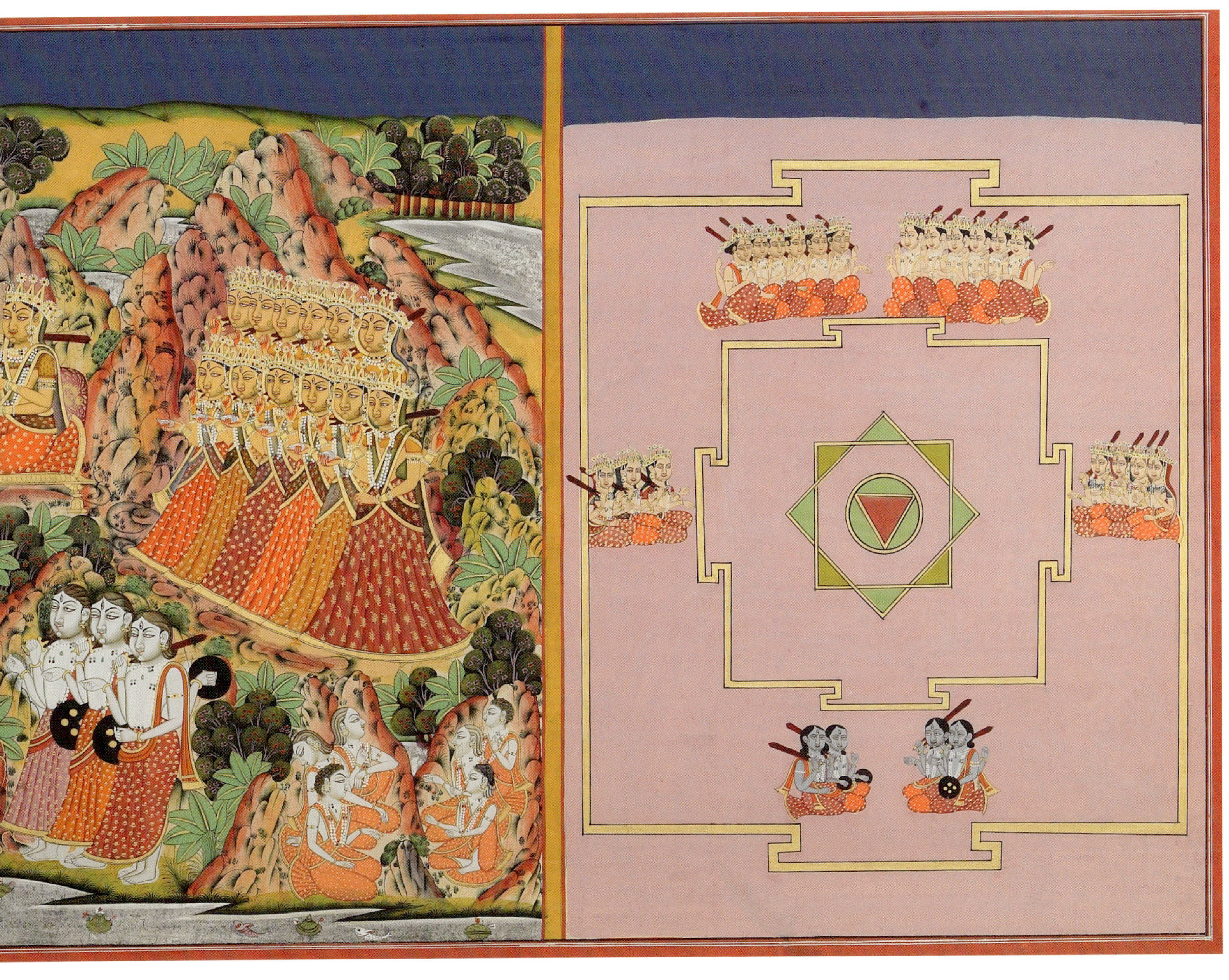

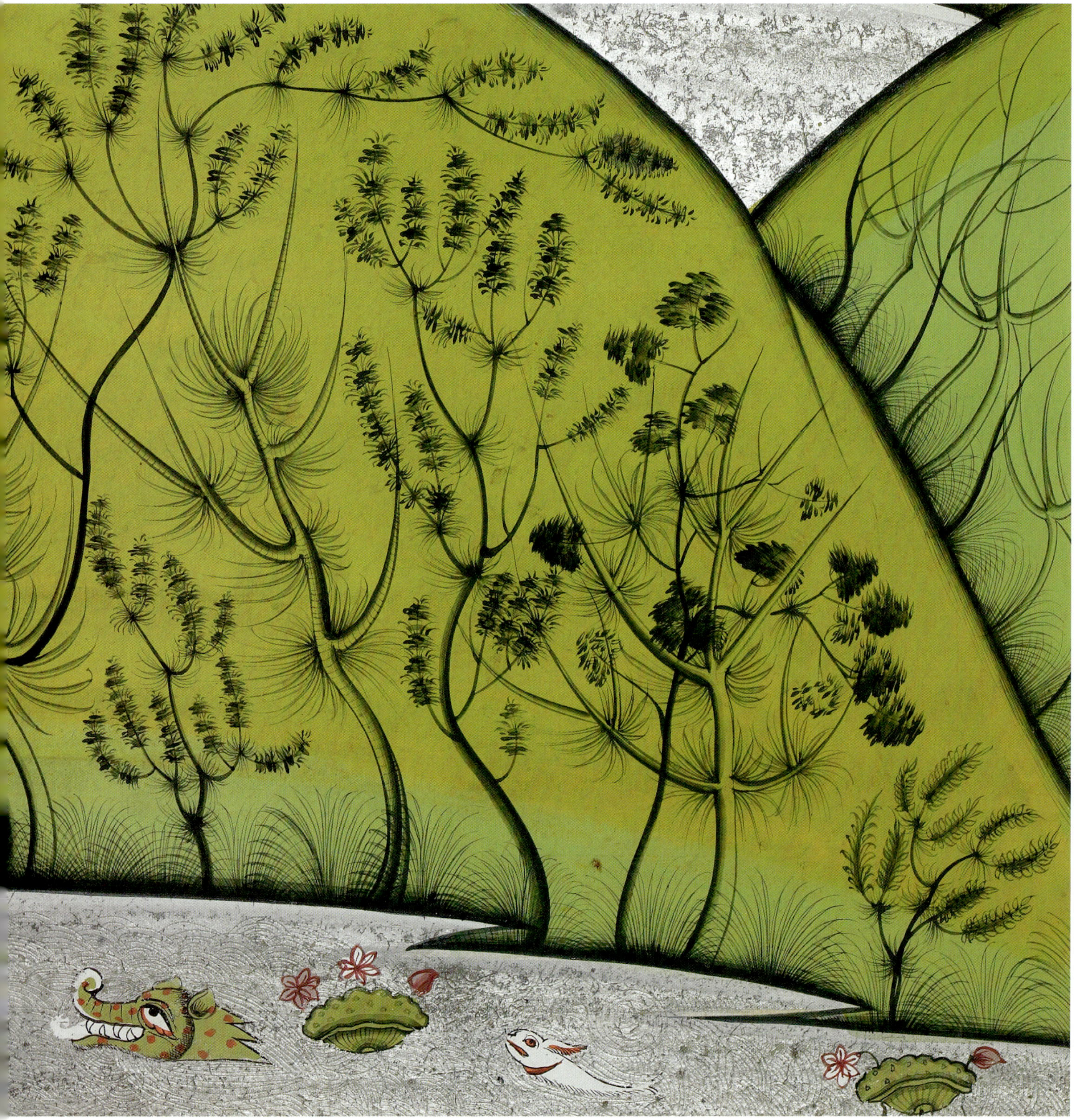

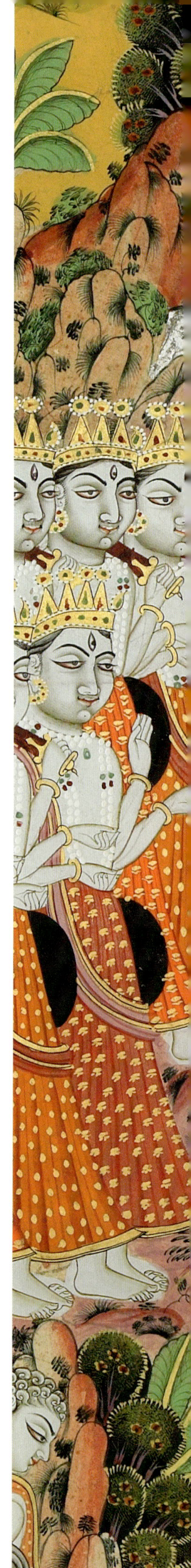

Cat. 49a Detail (above)

Cat. 49b Detail (left)

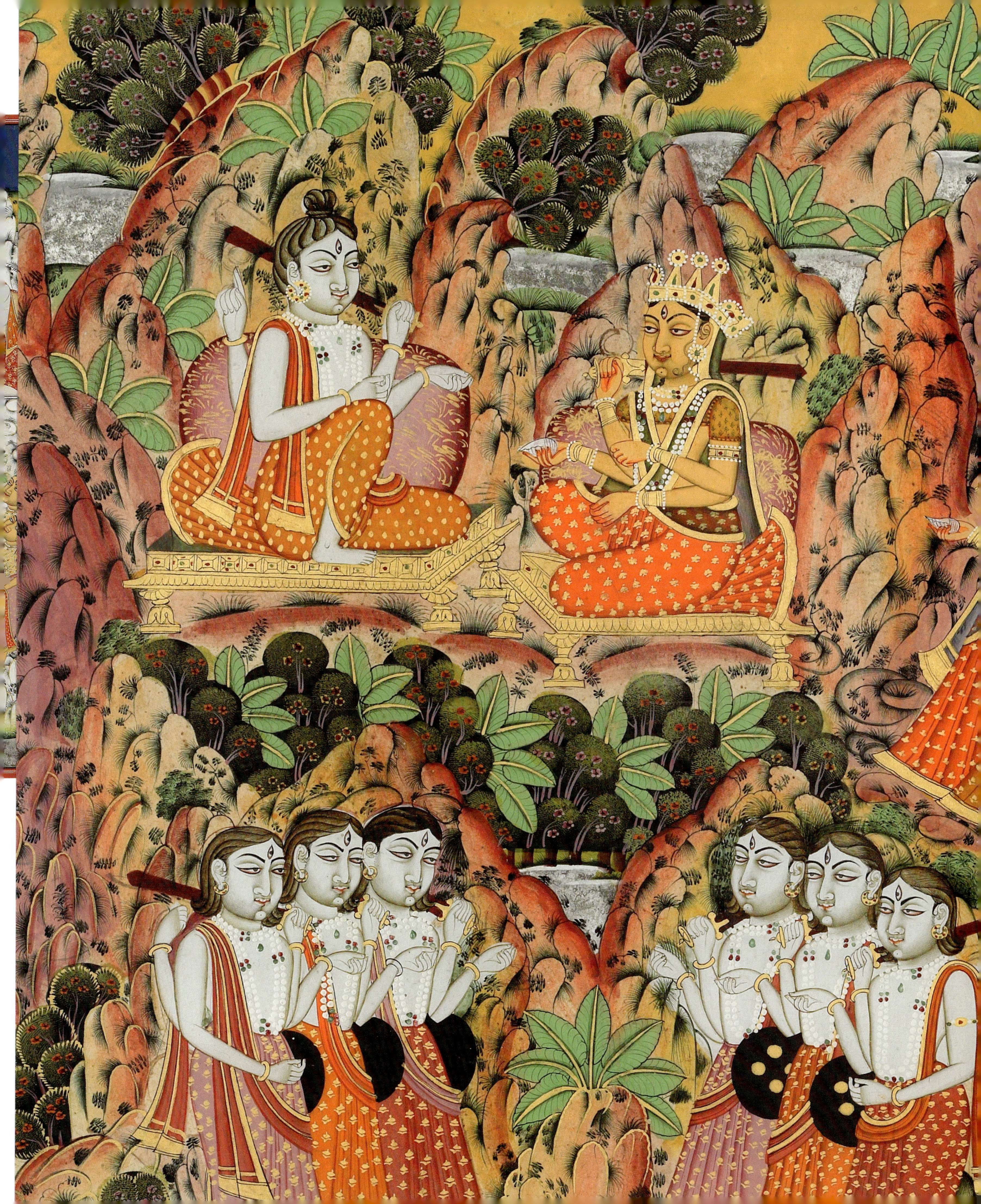

SACRED SITES AND COSMIC OCEANS

In the Indian religious landscape, the gods are omnipresent. Deities manifest on earth as mountains and sin-cleansing rivers, and also graciously dwell within temples and shrines. Equally charged with the divine are the hermitages (ashrams) where Nath yogins perfect their bodies to become gods. According to Nath metaphysics, the *mahasiddhas* (great perfected beings) even remain sentient in a higher realm when the universe is periodically destroyed.

These monumental manuscript folios depict magically lush groves, flashing silver rivers, fancifully colored peaks, and swirling oceans that convey the pervasive presence and power of *mahasiddhas* and the deity Shiva. Jodhpur artists intensified the otherworldly intensity of these sacred sites through reverberating color harmonies, surface shine, and the hypnotic repetition of motifs or patterns.

50

Shiva Temples

folio 28 from the *Shiva Rahasya*
1827 (Samvat 1884); 40.2 x 115.5 cm
Mehrangarh Museum Trust

sri siv rahasya sa[mvat] 1884 ra
pratham ams pano 28
da [khal] dholiya re kothar
glorious Shiva Rahasya of 1827
first section, page 28
entered in the *dholiya* storeroom

The *Shiva Rahasya* text maps a Shiva-centered universe through extended lists of sites where the great god is worshiped. Man Singh's atelier transformed those mechanical inventories into an ecstatic surfeit of piety in a sequence of ten folios depicting hundreds of shrines.[1] Each folio employs a variation on a grid-like composition, but all employ similar strategies of shine and color syncopation for optical effect. In the best folios, as here, the impact is visionary and pulsating, rather than worldly and three-dimensional (see pp. 224–25).

The artist employs three pictorial devices—geometric composition, shimmering optical effects, and hypnotic repetition—to convey the sublime energy generated by the universe's devotion to Shiva. Its serpentine, silver rivers provide a rigorous two-dimensional structure, which is syncopated by multi-colored temples. Cerulean blue, gleaming white, orange, pink, and yellow shrines create rhythms and counterpoints. Their variously shaped and recombined cupolas, enclosure walls, and textile hangings evoke the infinite diversity of a cosmos devoted to Shiva, rather than a mundane record of shrines on earth. The shrines are arrayed within three vertically stacked registers. The color progression, from bottom to top, of yellow green to pea green to aqua conceptually recalls the technique of atmospheric perspective, in which distant locations are tinged in bluer tones (e.g., fig. 8 in "Painting, Politics, and Devotion," p. 40). But here, the warm-to-cool sequence—like the soft thumbprint coronas behind each mountain and the dark green grass that softens the banks of the silver rivers—is an intellectual reference to space rather than a strategy to recreate depth on the surface of the page.

The otherworldly nature of the Nath texts reinforced the Jodhpur atelier's trend towards two-dimensional landscapes and imaginary architecture. The large format intensifies the aesthetic potential of shine, as lifting the folios for viewing caused light to flicker across the burnished surfaces. This folio is exemplary in that regard. Its snaking, silver rivers shimmer when viewed, lending the planar surface a motility that further animates the compositional grid. DD

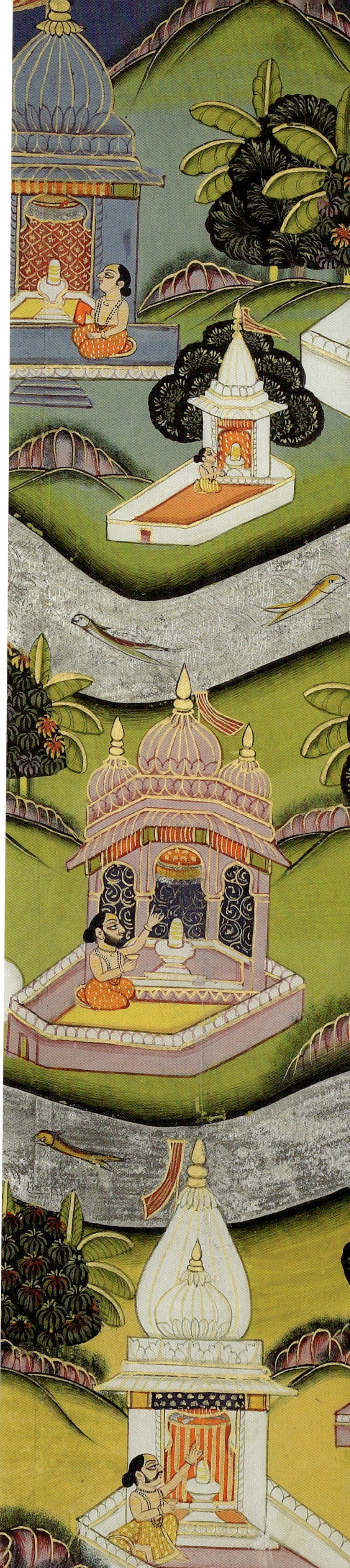

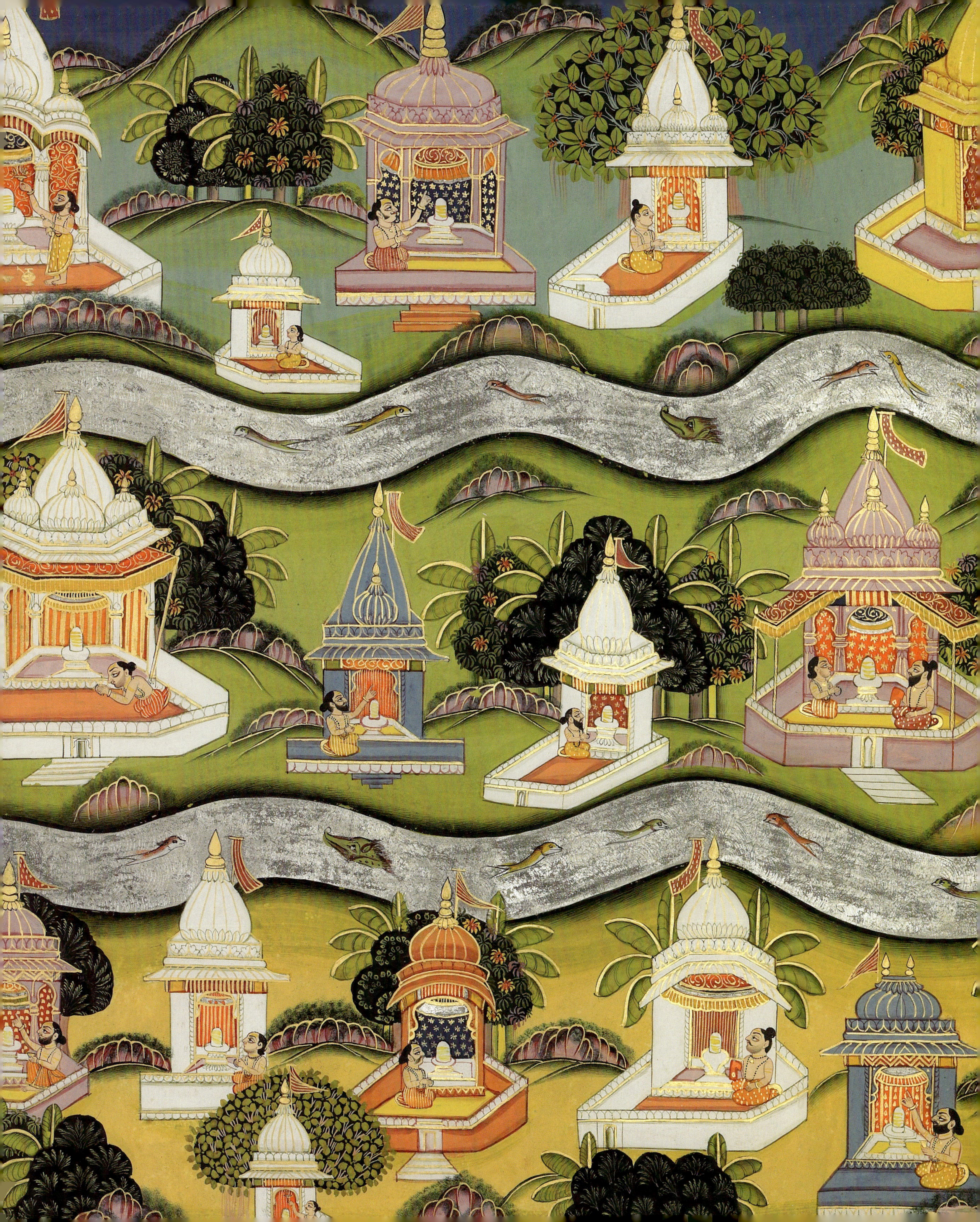

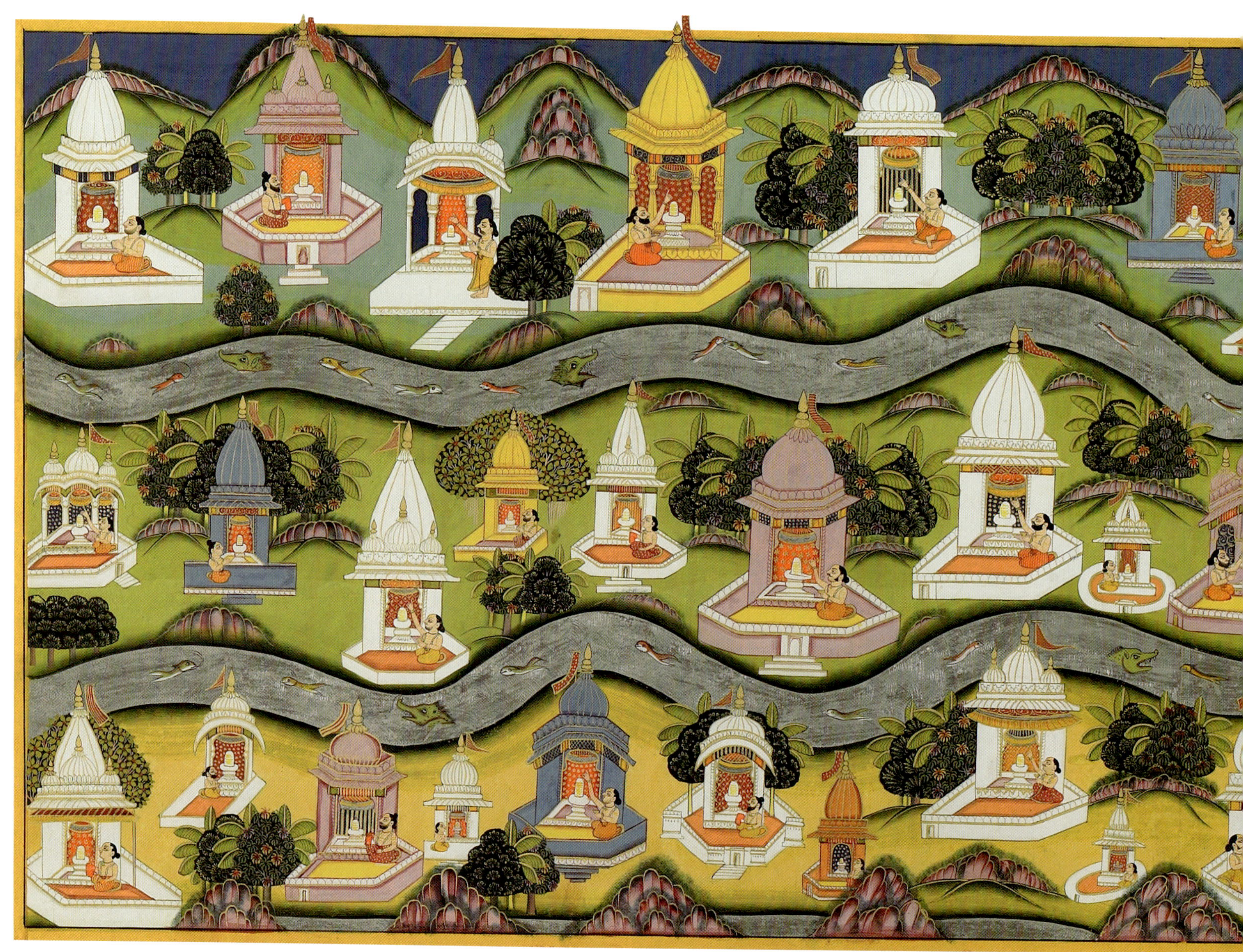

Cat. 50

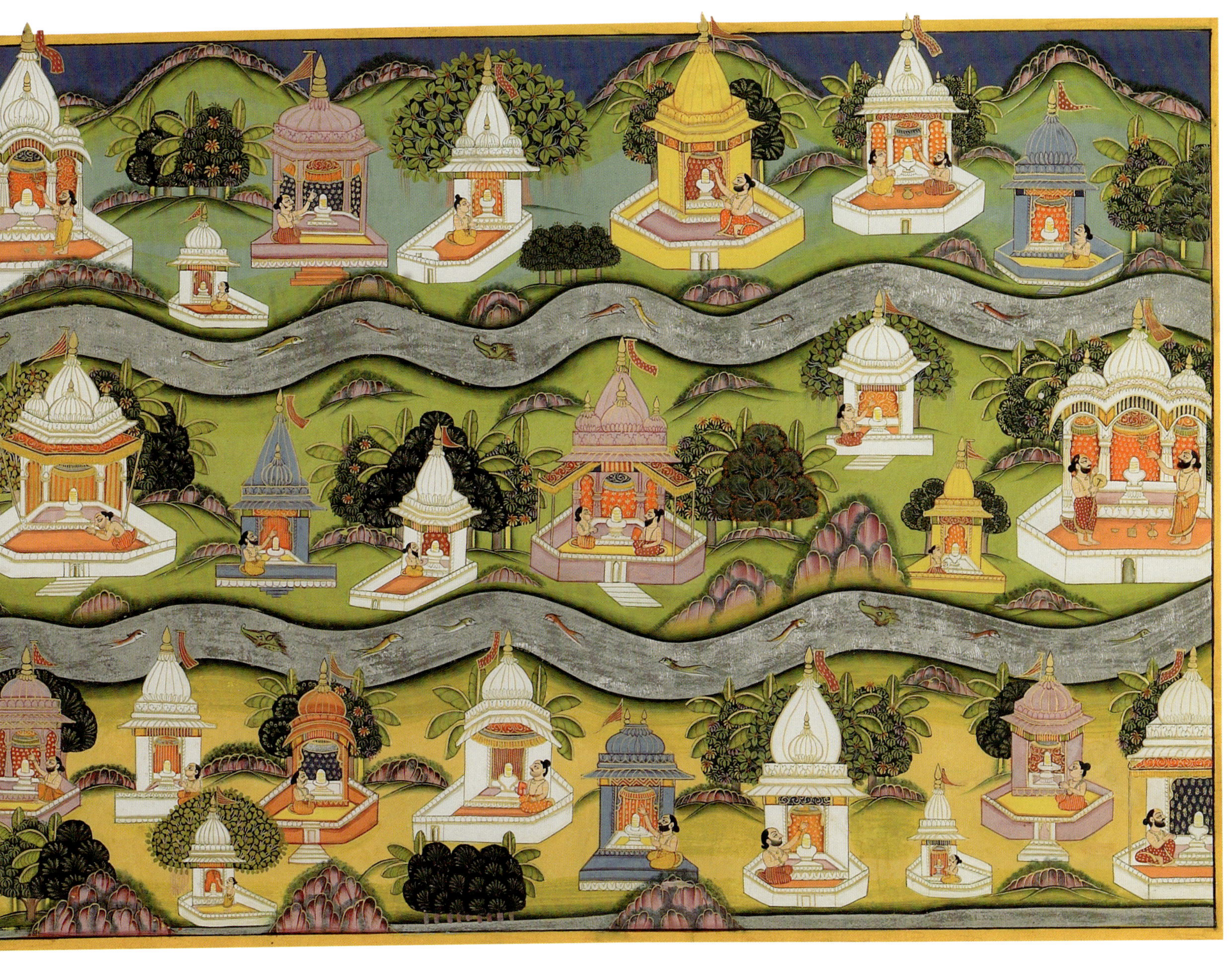

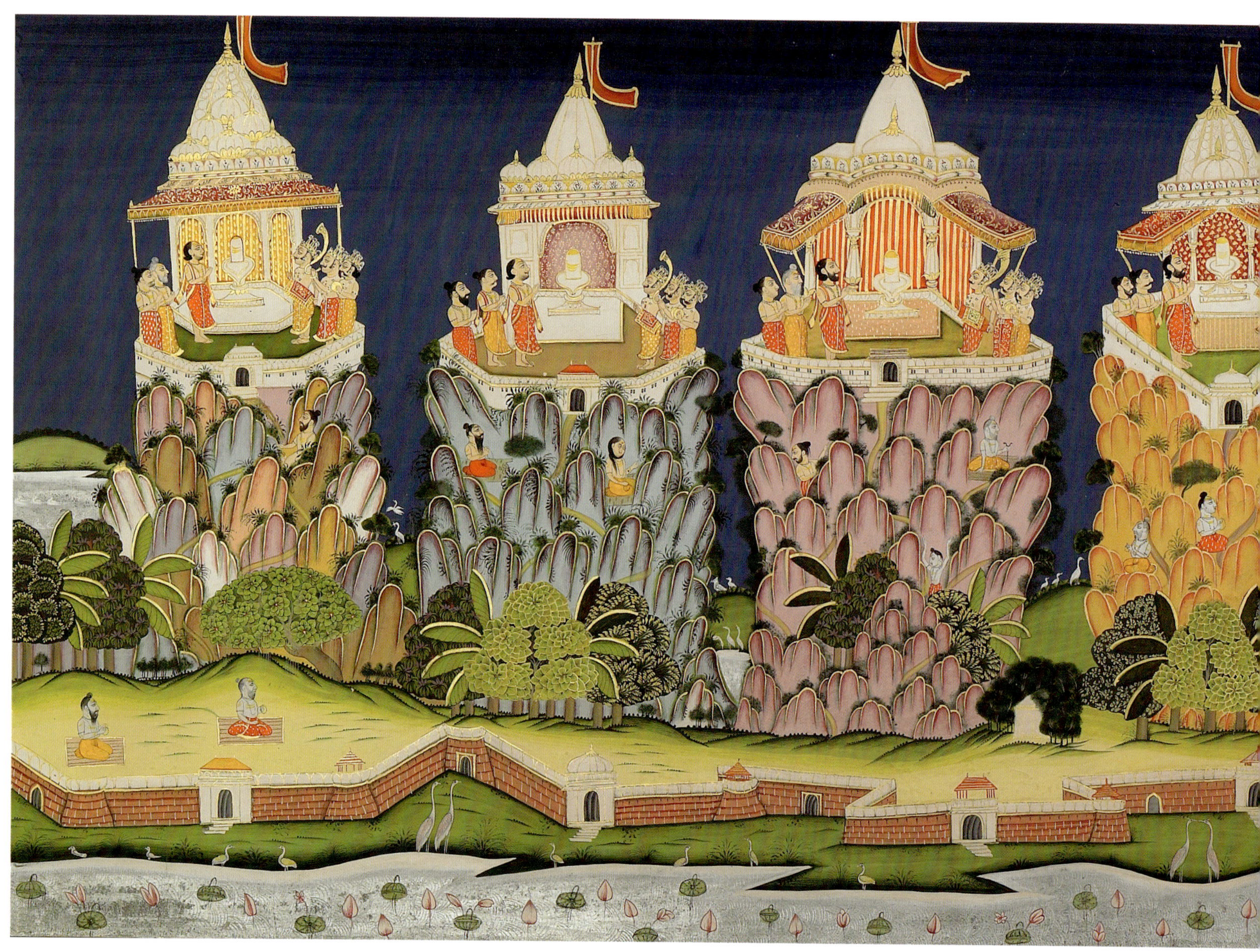

Cat. 51

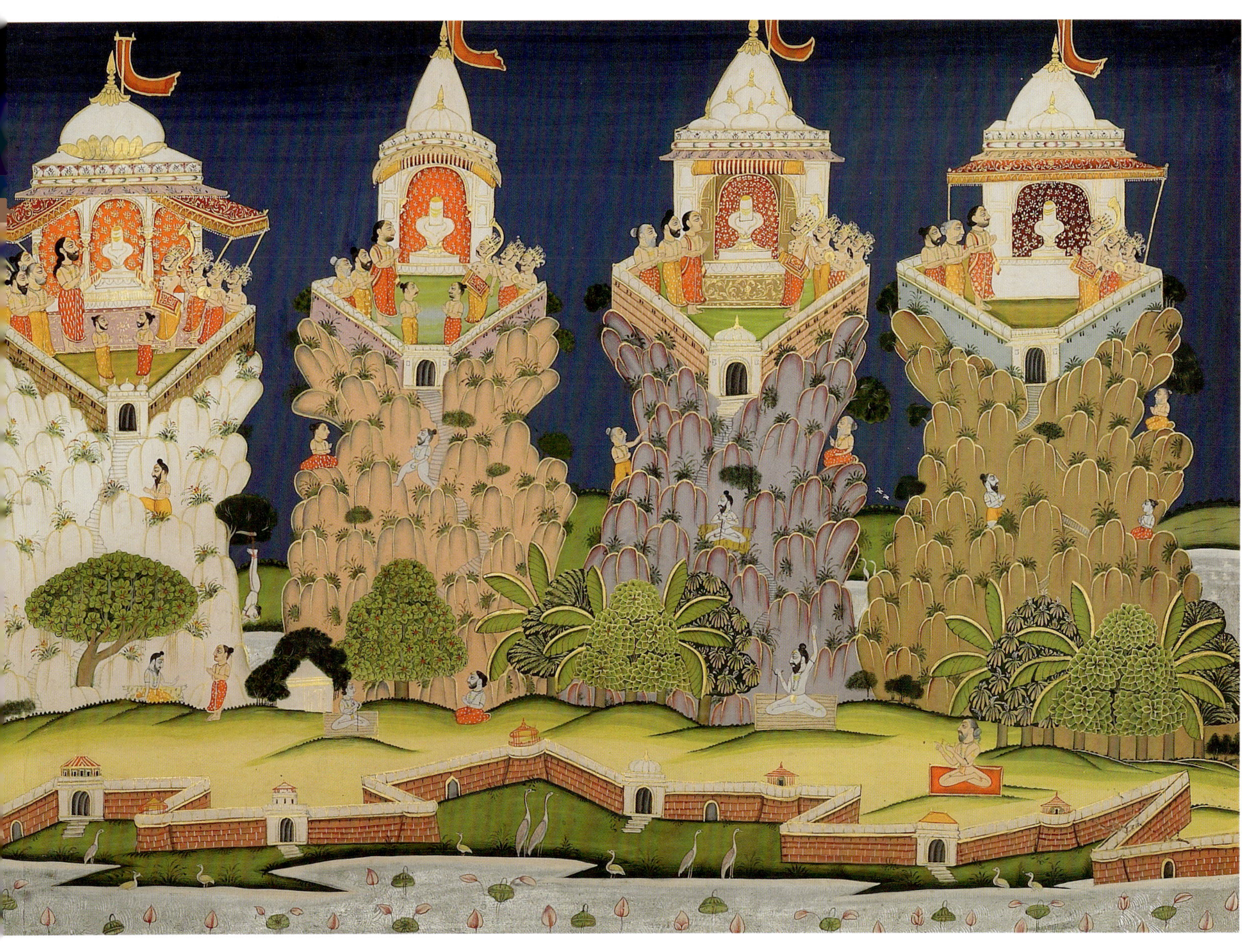

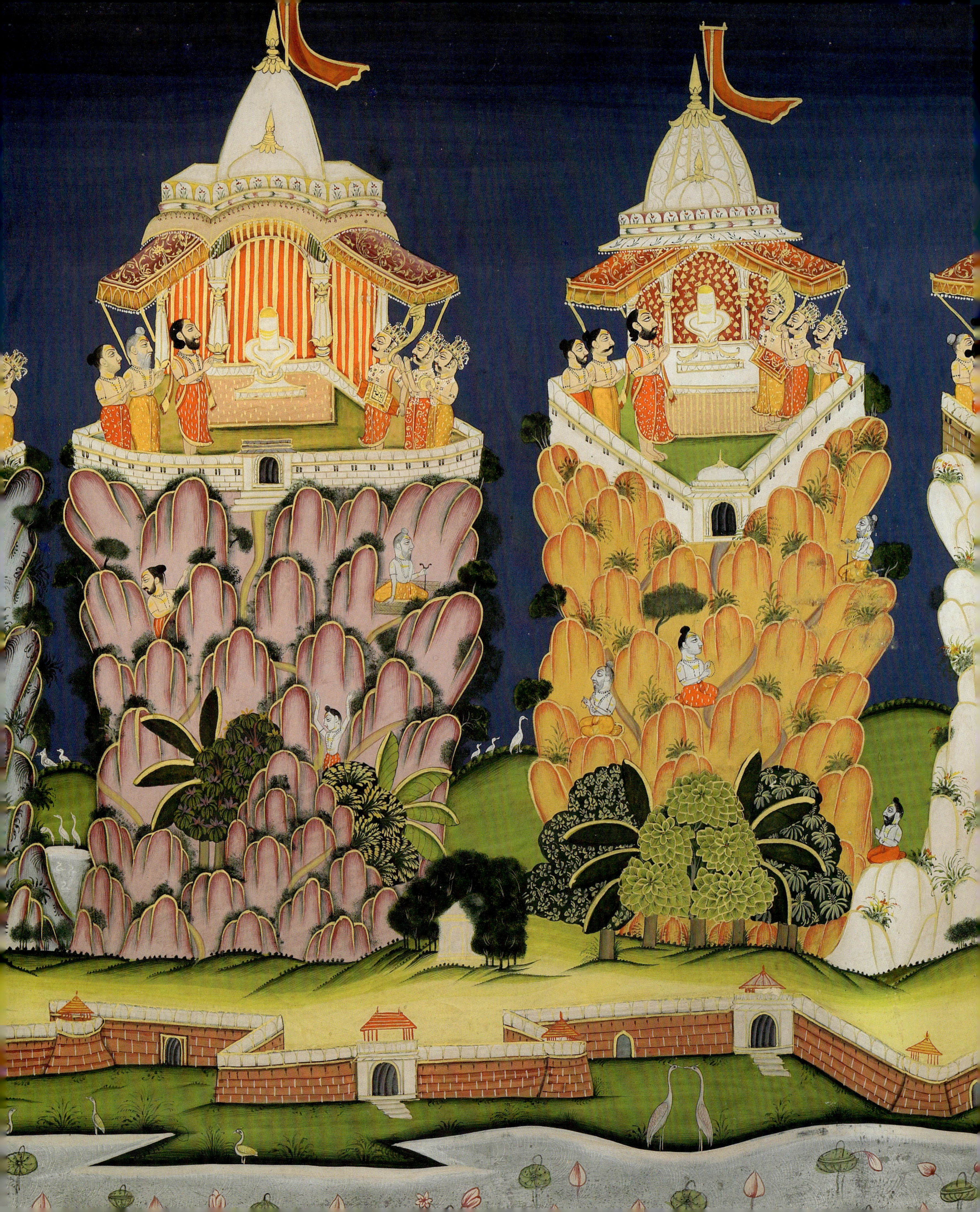

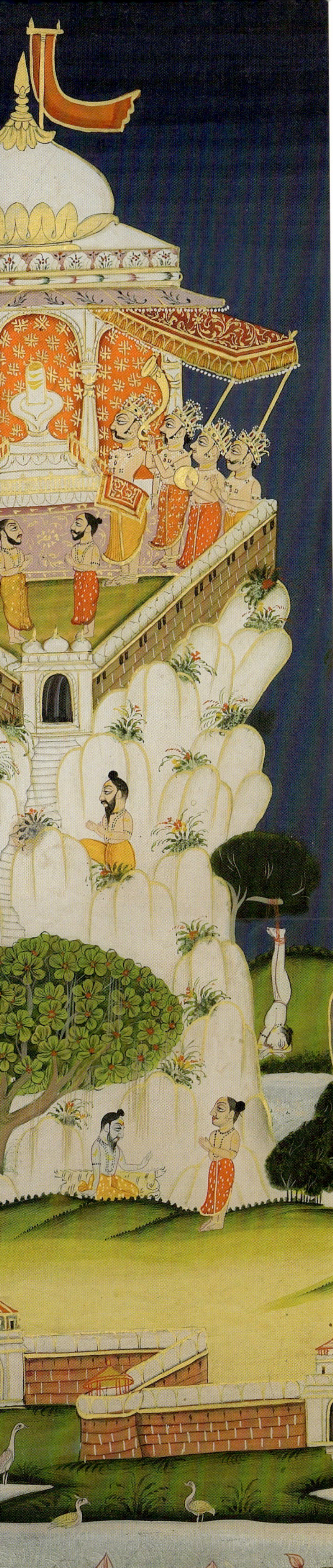

51

The Mountains of the Eight Directions

folio 17 from the *Shiva Rahasya*
1827 (Samvat 1884); 40.2 x 115.5 cm
Mehrangarh Museum Trust

The complete inscription appears in the reference catalogue.

Indian literary traditions characterize mountains as idyllic. From sacred Hindu texts to the refined court poems (*mahakavyas*) of classical Sanskrit and the vernacular folk tales of the Nath *siddhas*, they are described as:

> ...resplendent with various gems, covered with various trees and creepers, resounding with the songs of various birds,

> redolent with the fragrance of flowers from all the seasons, most delightful, fanned by plentiful cool, aromatic, slow breezes....[2]

The enchanted quality of *The Mountains of the Eight Directions* emerges through a magical palette. Peaks of sky blue, lavender, and pink are tempered by mountains in warmer hues of brown, salmon, and gold. Boulders, streaked in red or fuchsia and contoured in gold, glimmer. Their diverse colors poetically evoke literary descriptions of mountains as variously streaked with minerals, studded with gems, covered with snow, or speckled with the herbs of immortality.

If the painting lacks the refined forms and subtle shading seen in folios by Bulaki and Amardas, its colors and shapes are brilliantly conceived. The mountains' hues, for example, are repeated on the stone enclosure walls of each summit's temple, but they follow the pattern irregularly, so that new color reciprocities emerge. Horizontal rhythms are no less subtle. A deep-blue sky that quietly lightens toward the horizon anchors the artist's fresh interpretation of the river motif that appears at the bottom of so many monumental folios. The syncopated juxtaposition of jagged riverbank, sharply angled fortress wall, and gently rolling hills creates twisting, elongated forms that are silver, lime, rosy pink, and custard in color. Bright dashes of orange, red, green, white, and silver fuse the whole into an animated fabric (see pp. 226–27).

The painting's fantastic landscape maps the topographic hierarchy of sacred mountains in which gods dwell on summits and semi-divine beings, great sages, and enlightenment-seeking ascetics live on their flanks. Small white Shiva shrines with fluttering red flags perch atop the eight peaks. They manifest Shiva's presence in the form of lingams (a symbolic form of the deity).

Playful waterfowl, perky tufts of mountain grass, and schematically but affectionately rendered yogins—including one who performs penance by dangling upside-down from a tree—enhance the landscape's charm. DD

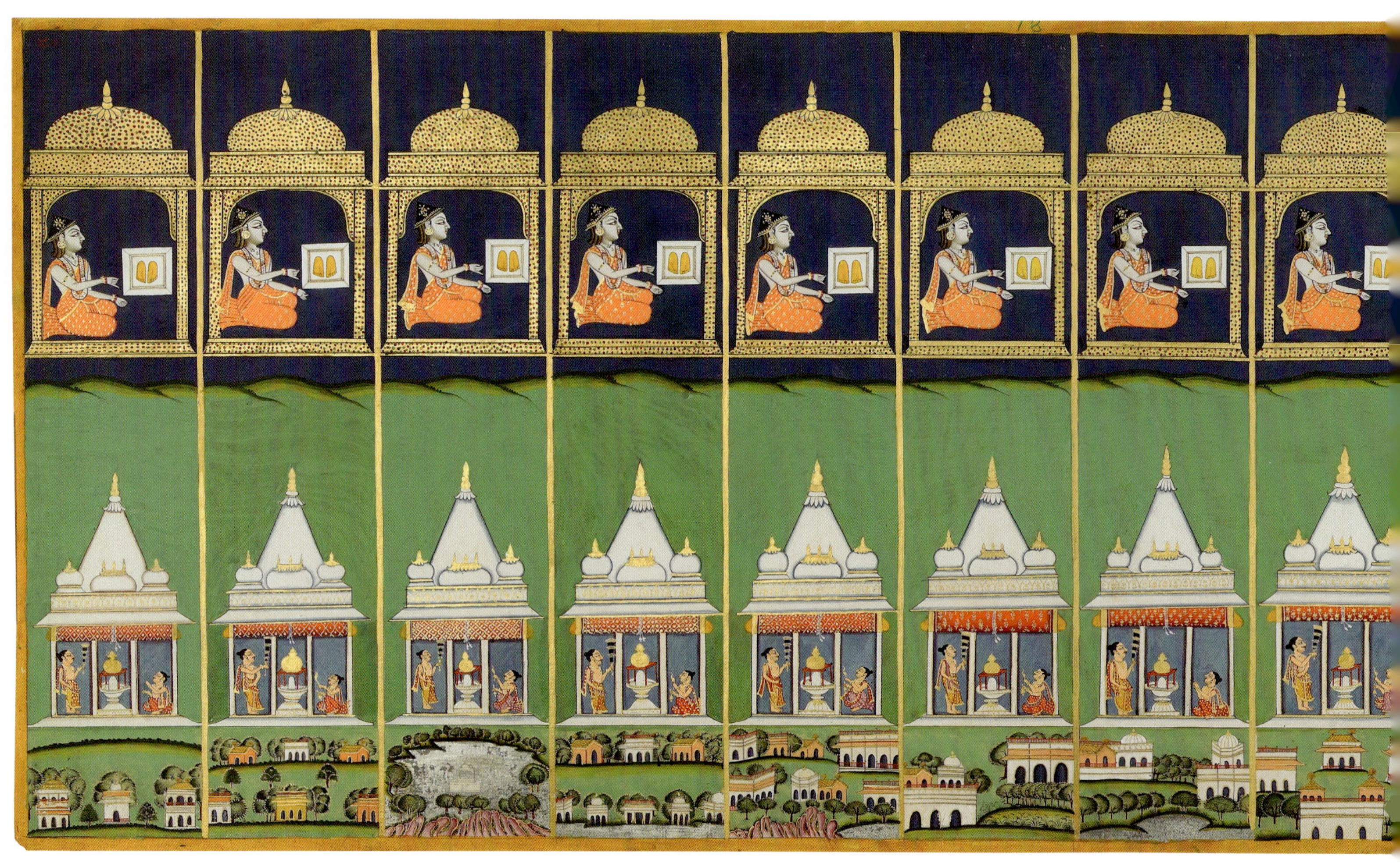

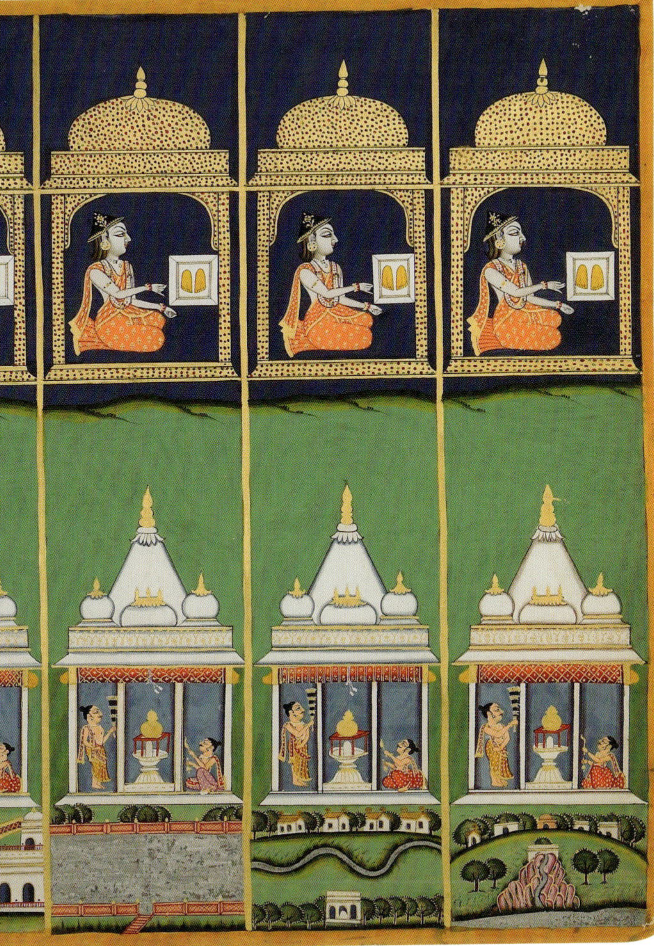

Twelve Light-form Manifestations of Nathji
folio 50 from the *Nath Charit*
1823 (Samvat 1880); 47 x 123 cm
Mehrangarh Museum Trust

Numbered 50 in red by Reu.

Sri nath charit
da [khal] dholiya re kothar
Glorious Nath Charit
Entered in the *dholiya* storeroom

In the folio's upper register, twelve Nath *siddhas*—recognizable from their triangular black hats, ash-white skin, and large, round earrings—worship in jewel-studded gold shrines. Replicated with strict precision (undoubtedly through the use of a stencil), the *siddhas* and the shrines hover ambiguously on the deep-blue ground that surrounds and pervades the temple structures. Each *siddha* raises his upper hand in the ritual gesture (*mudra*) that mobilizes subtle energies to dispel obstacles and meditates upon Nathji's footprints of light, a particularly sublime manifestation of the cosmic essence. (See also cat. 45 for Nathji's manifestation as light-form footprints before an assembly of the great Hindu gods.)

Human devotees worship in twelve temples set within the more prosaic landscapes of the lower register. These represent twelve particularly sacred Shiva temples on the subcontinent.[3] At these sites, Shiva conferred his eternal light and grace upon devotees by manifesting as light-form lingams (*jyotirlingams*).[4] The artist of this folio has not attempted to depict the appearance of India's Jyotirlingam Temples. Rather, he stresses their shared identity through architecture and conveys an earthly location by placing the temples among village dwellings, small mansions, water tanks, and lakes.

The artists of the illustrated *Nath Charit* and the *Shiva Rahasya* employed a variety of grids to represent and organize the many Shiva shrines enumerated in the texts. This folio combines two common strategies—the emphatic linear border and the less-overt landscape convention (here, the horizon line)—to organize the picture plane into twenty-four sacred sites. The relatively subtle horizontal division between upper and lower registers emphasizes the vertical connection between each subtle realm and a temple on earth. Indeed, all Nath ontology is based upon connections between subtle and gross manifestations, which provide the routes for human contact with and reintegration into the Absolute. DD

The Practice of Yoga

folio 5 from the *Siddha Siddhanta Paddhati*
Attributed to Bulaki, 1824 (Samvat 1881); 46 x 122 cm
Mehrangarh Museum Trust

The complete inscription appears in the reference catalogue.

> Very many Nath saddhus are praying, very many are meditating,
> having purified their hearts, very many hear and attain wisdom.
> Very many drink milk and eat fruit, very many live on air alone,
> in their hearts there is limitless sound yet silence appears on their faces.
> Varieties of clustered trees create dense cool shade,
> the pollen of the *mallika* is dear to the heart, the *ketaki* flower causes happiness.[5]

Bounded by a deep-blue sky punctuated by scalloped cloud clusters and a silver river teeming with lotuses and marine life, this celestial hermitage is dotted with groves, gardens, and rocky promontories (see pp. 234–35).[6] On the right, a fortress-city beneath its own patch of sky nestles improbably amid the hills. The walled white city, like those on the cosmic body of *Siddha Siddhanta Paddhati*, folio 6 (cat. 48), serves as the cartographic signifier of a celestial heaven. Great perfected beings (*mahasiddhas*) dwell in eternal bliss in celestial heavens, where they subsist on sweet ether and practice yoga.

The painting combines two environments associated with Nath *siddhas*—the mountain and the ashram. Here, Bulaki has composed the landscape's rolling hills and groves to isolate the nine great Naths in vignettes of idyllic seclusion. The *mahasiddha* at the far left meditates within a mountain cave, depicted as a pea-green hillock capped by pink boulders. Depicted frontally at the center, another perfected being compresses his nostril as he practices *pranayama* (breath control). Pairs of alert but tranquil animals listen to the sermon of a third *mahasiddha*.

The first six folios of the illustrated *Siddha Siddhanta Paddhati* correlate closely to the opening chapters of the twelfth- to thirteenth-century text. Attributed to the *mahasiddha* Gorakhnath, the *Siddha Siddhanta Paddhati* widely is recognized as the most clear and systematic exposition of Nath metaphysics and practice. Gorakhnath begins by presenting creation as a progressive devolution from the most subtle (i.e., the Absolute) to increasingly gross (*sthula*) forms of matter.[7] The sage then reveals the yogic body to be the hinge on which cosmic devolution can be reversed. Through the practice of hatha yoga, an adept mobilizes his subtle body (see cat. 44) to transform its gross, material "sheath" into the subtler stuff of the universe. This painting relates to a significant teaching that describes the most important of the fixed yoga postures (*asanas*) and charts a twelve-year schedule for the attainment of supernatural powers, immortality, and spiritual awareness. In the eleventh year of practice, for example, the *siddha* gains complete self-knowledge, i.e., the blissful awareness (*samadhi*) of the universe within himself and all beings. Knowing creation, *siddhas* develop great compassion and become more powerful than any of the contained (i.e., lower) orders of existence. They may intervene in any of the lower worlds (as Jallandharnath intervened in Man Singh's accession to the Jodhpur throne) or dwell in meditative bliss. The program culminates "in the twelfth year, [when the *siddha*] becomes a creator and destroyer like Shiva."[8] DD

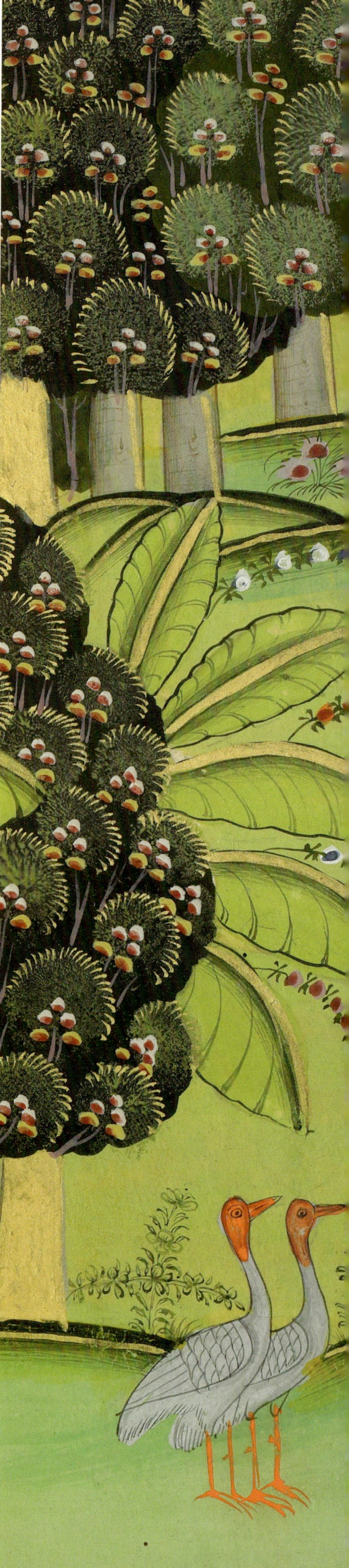

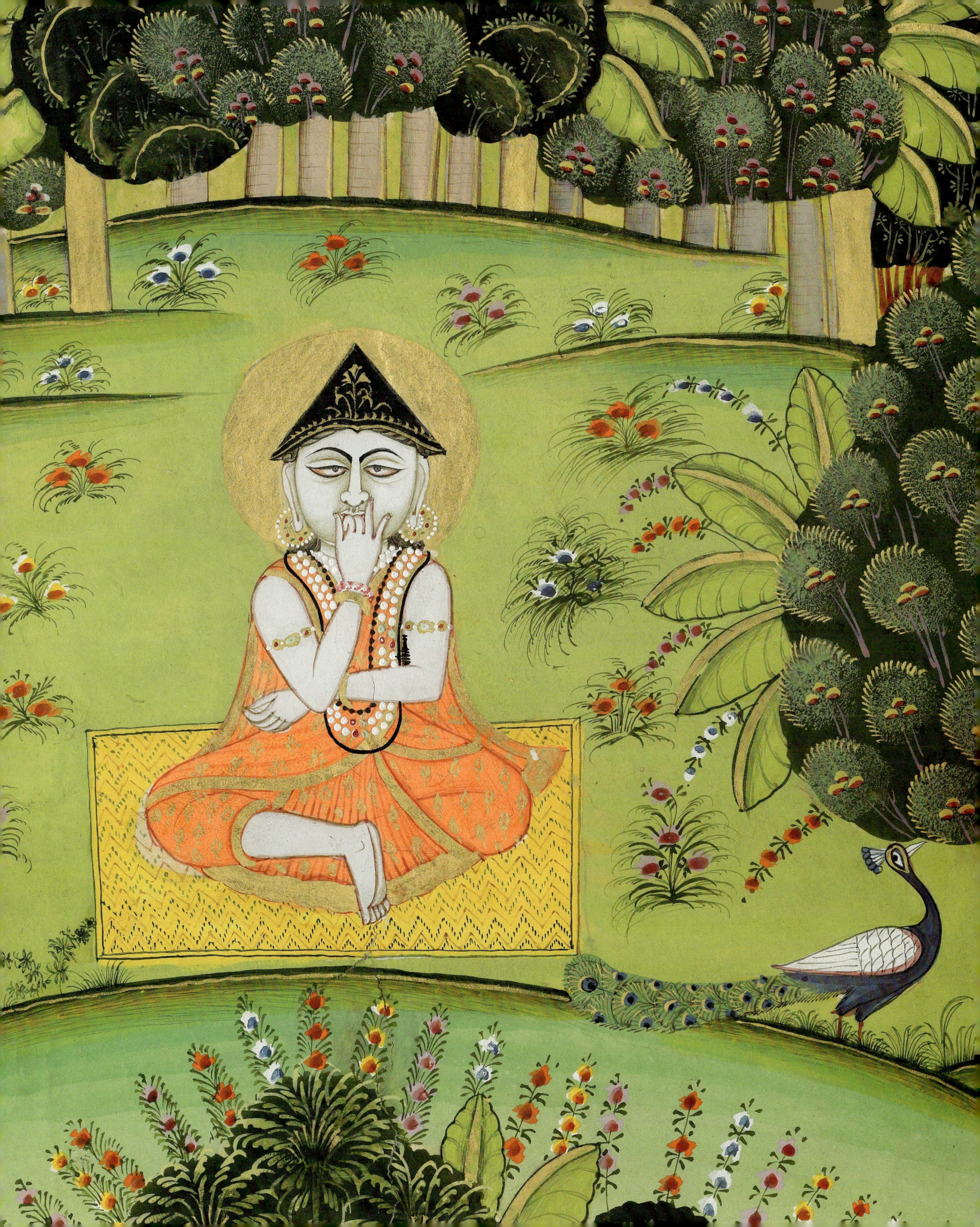

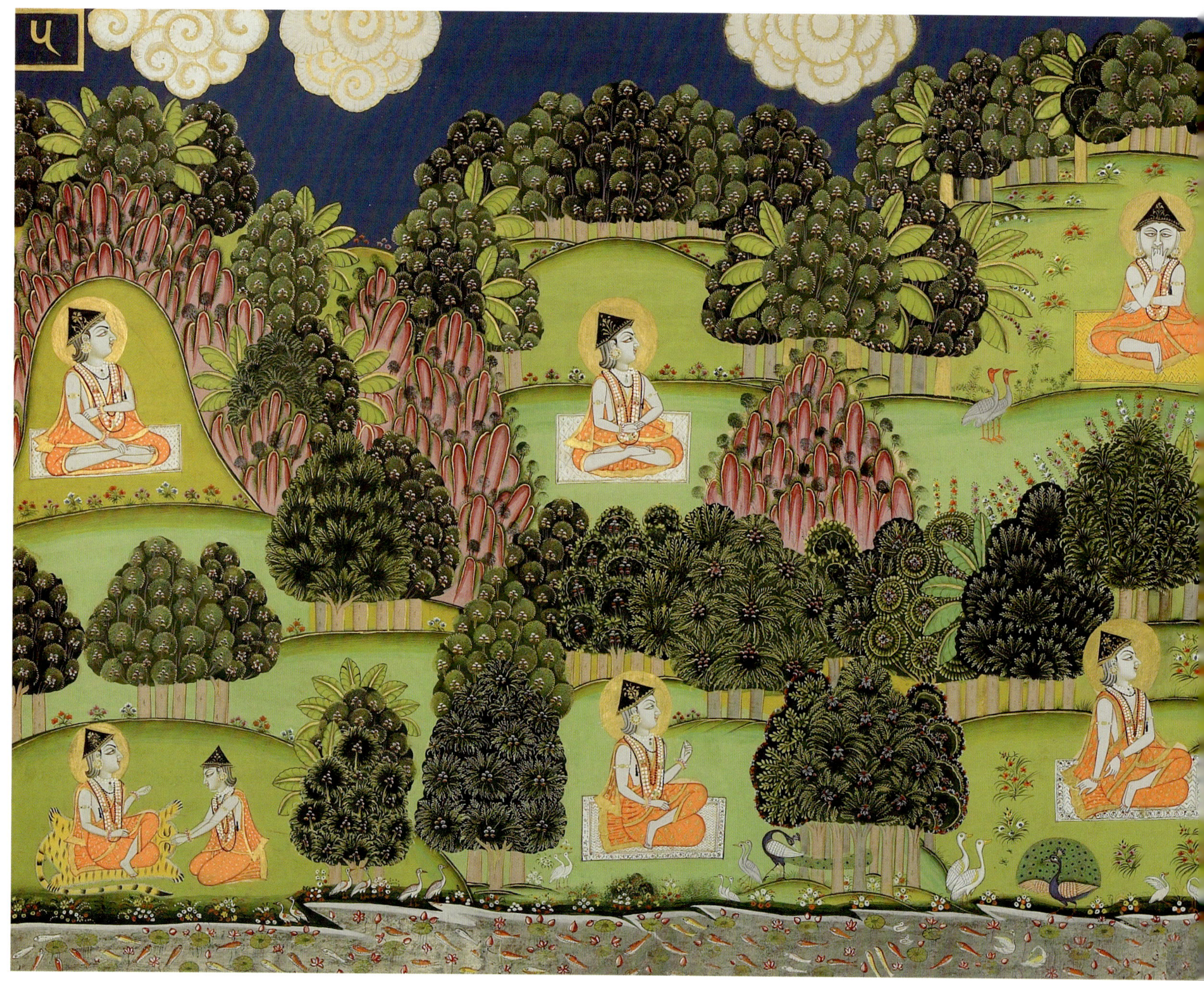

Cat. 53

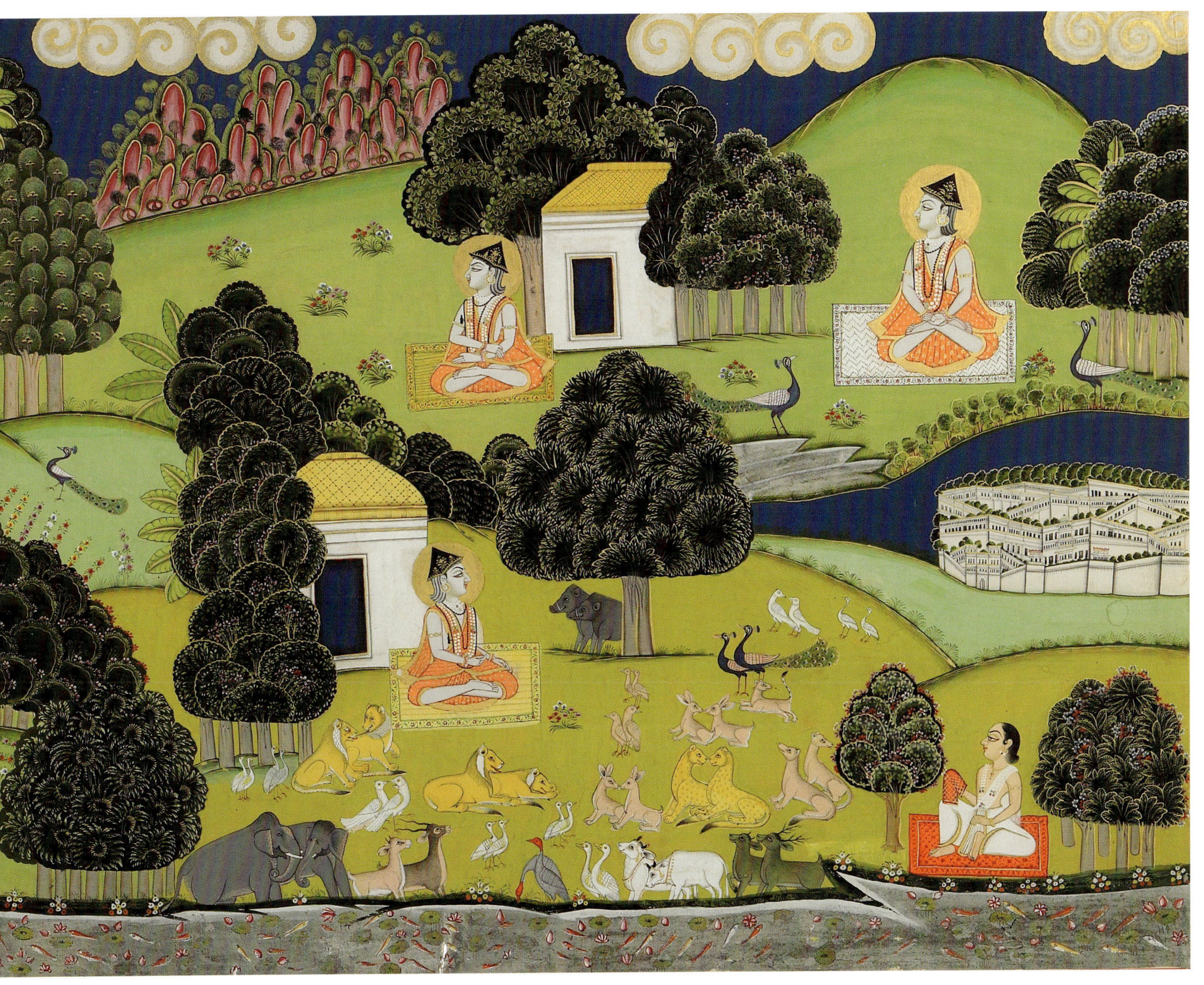

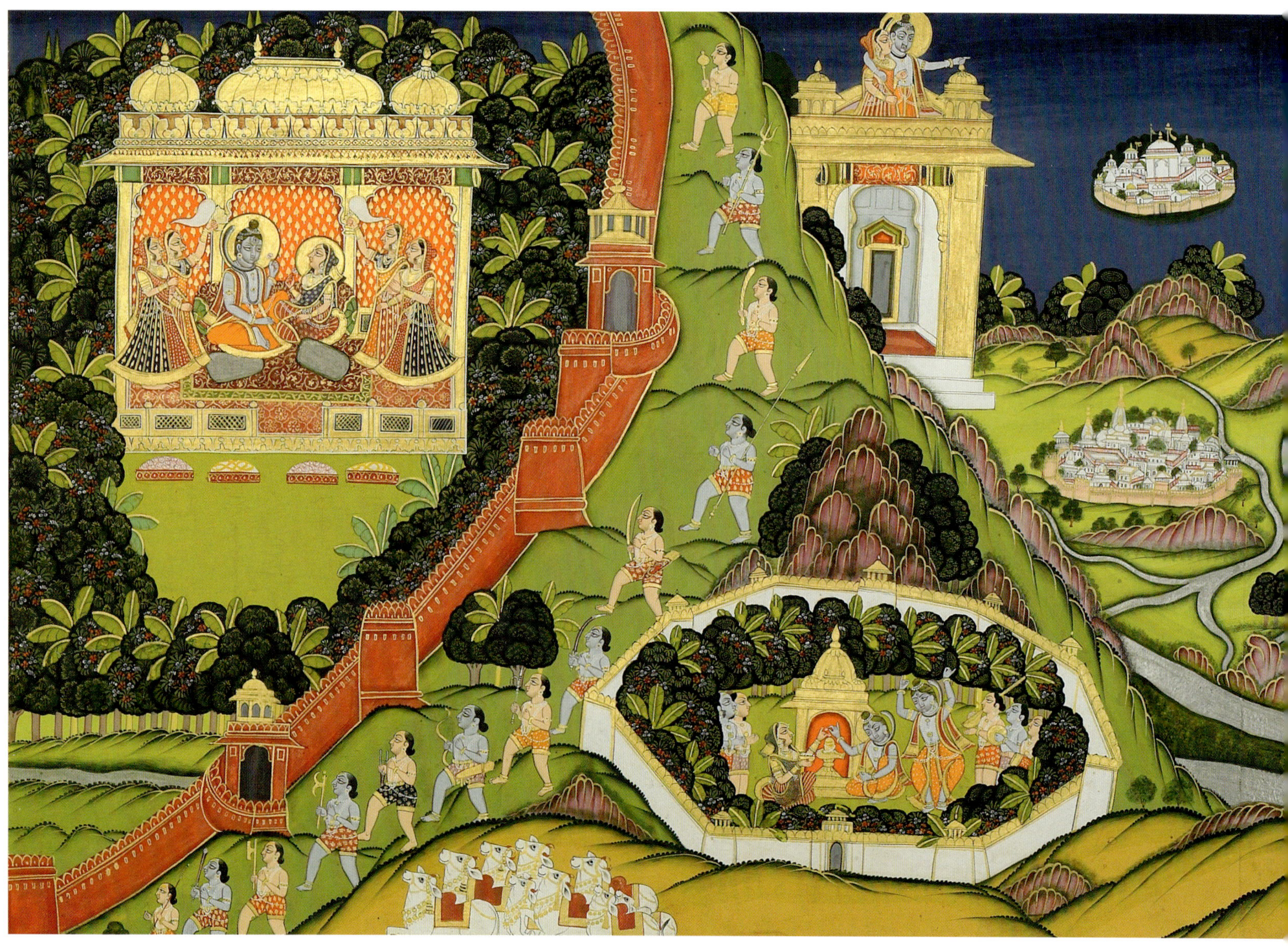

Cat. 54

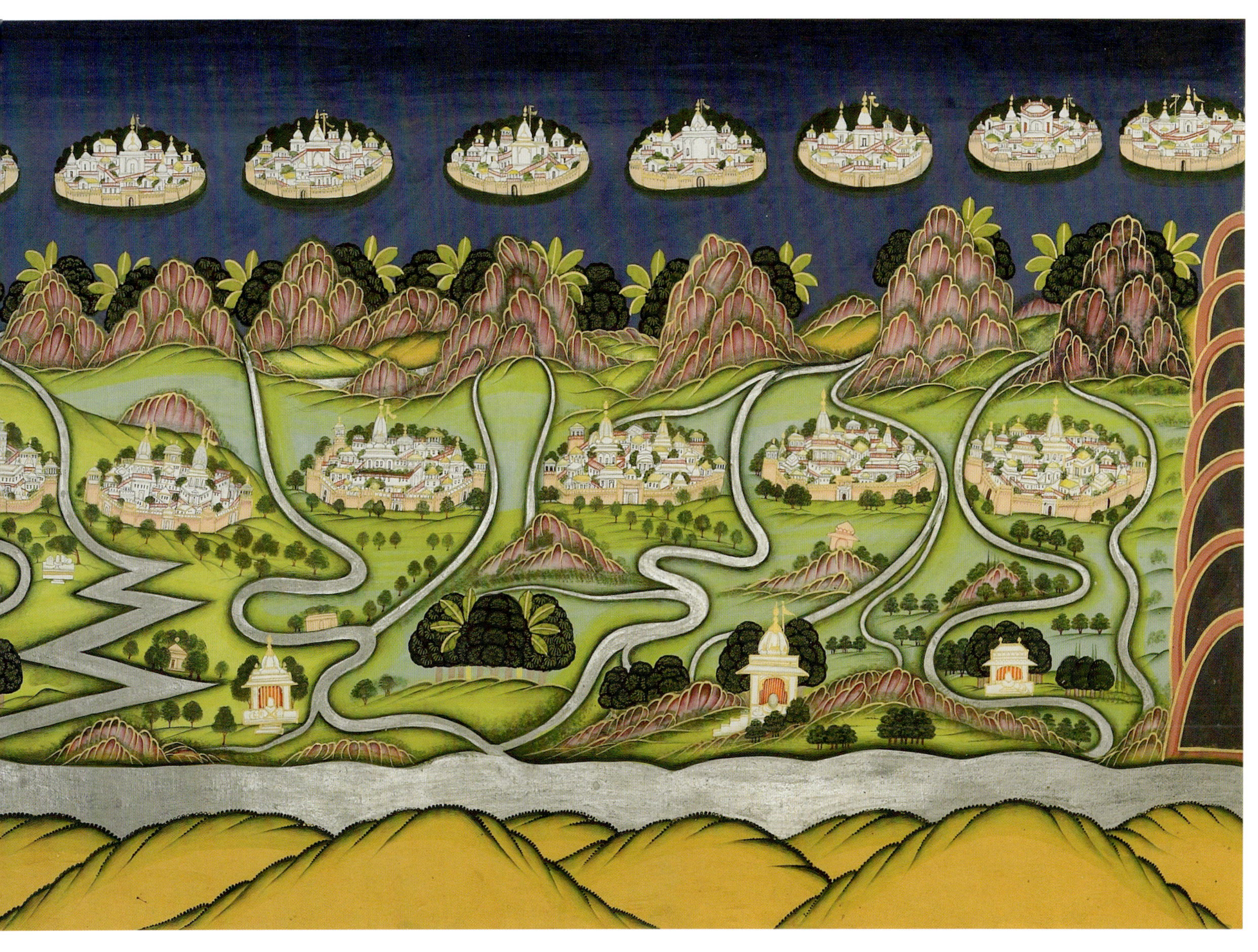

Shiva Reveals the Geography of the Three Worlds to Parvati

folio 13 from the *Shiva Rahasya*
Attributed to Vana Akhavat, 1827 (Samvat 1884); 40.4 x 115.6 cm
Mehrangarh Museum Trust

sri siv rahasya
pratham ams ri panau 13
da[khal] dholiya re kothar
glorious Shiva Rahasya
first section, page 13
entered into the *dholiya* storeroom

In the *Shiva Rahasya*, the great god Shiva describes the boundaries, mountains, and rivers of the three worlds.[9] He reveals this knowledge to the goddess Parvati from the terrace of a golden palace modestly tucked into the mountain on the folio's left (see pp. 236–37). Shiva drapes one arm companionably over Parvati's shoulders, an embrace that conveys the conjugal intimacy of husband and wife, and with his other arm gestures to the valley that unfolds below. The god thus begins to reveal a cartography in which the salient aspects of location are sacred mountains, Shiva shrines, and Shiva worship.[10] In this landscape, flashes of silver from coursing rivers that descend from rosy peaks enliven a horizontal terrain. Golden banners (presumably denoting Shiva temples) flutter above nine aerial and seven terrestrial cities, and smaller shrines with Shiva lingams dot the verdant valley.

Over the *Shiva Rahasya's* one hundred and one folios, court artists illustrated hundreds more Shiva shrines. While many are grouped within abstract grids, others are located atop and among mountains. Man Singh's artists apparently reveled in creating varied rock formations, which range from stubby pink knobs dusted with frowsy shrubs, as here, to icy lappets and candy-colored boulders. The omnipresence of these "lofty sites where divine beings make themselves visible" within the Man Singh manuscript corpus reflects their sacred resonance within Indian religious culture broadly and Nath tradition specifically.[11] The Rig Veda hymns of the second millennium B.C.E. personify mountains as supernatural beings. Some two thousand years later, mountains would be considered—across sectarian and religious boundaries—the homes of powerful semi-deities known as *siddhas*, an identity subsequently appropriated by the Nath religious order in the twelfth–thirteenth century.[12] Because they were associated with Nath *siddhas*, mountains came to be regarded as the ideal location for yogic adepts aspiring to perfection.

Mountains also are identified as the gods who dwell upon them. The *Nath Purana*, a text compiled for Man Singh, draws upon established traditions in connecting Nathji to Mount Girnar (cat. 39), Devi with Mandrachal, Brahma with Himalaya, Vishnu with Govardhan, and Shiva with Mount Kailash (cat. 46). Today, on the subcontinent, many peaks are still identified as divine Naths.[13] DD

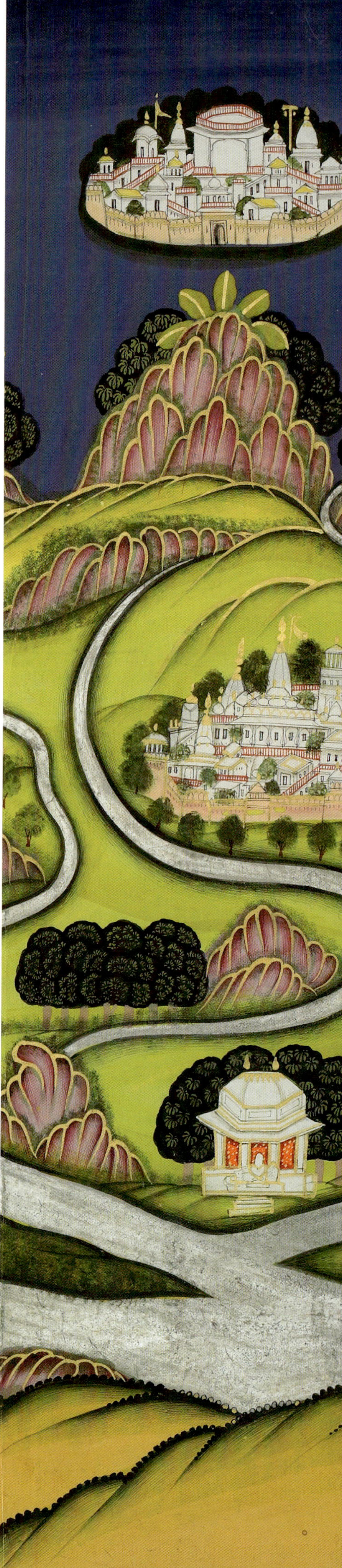

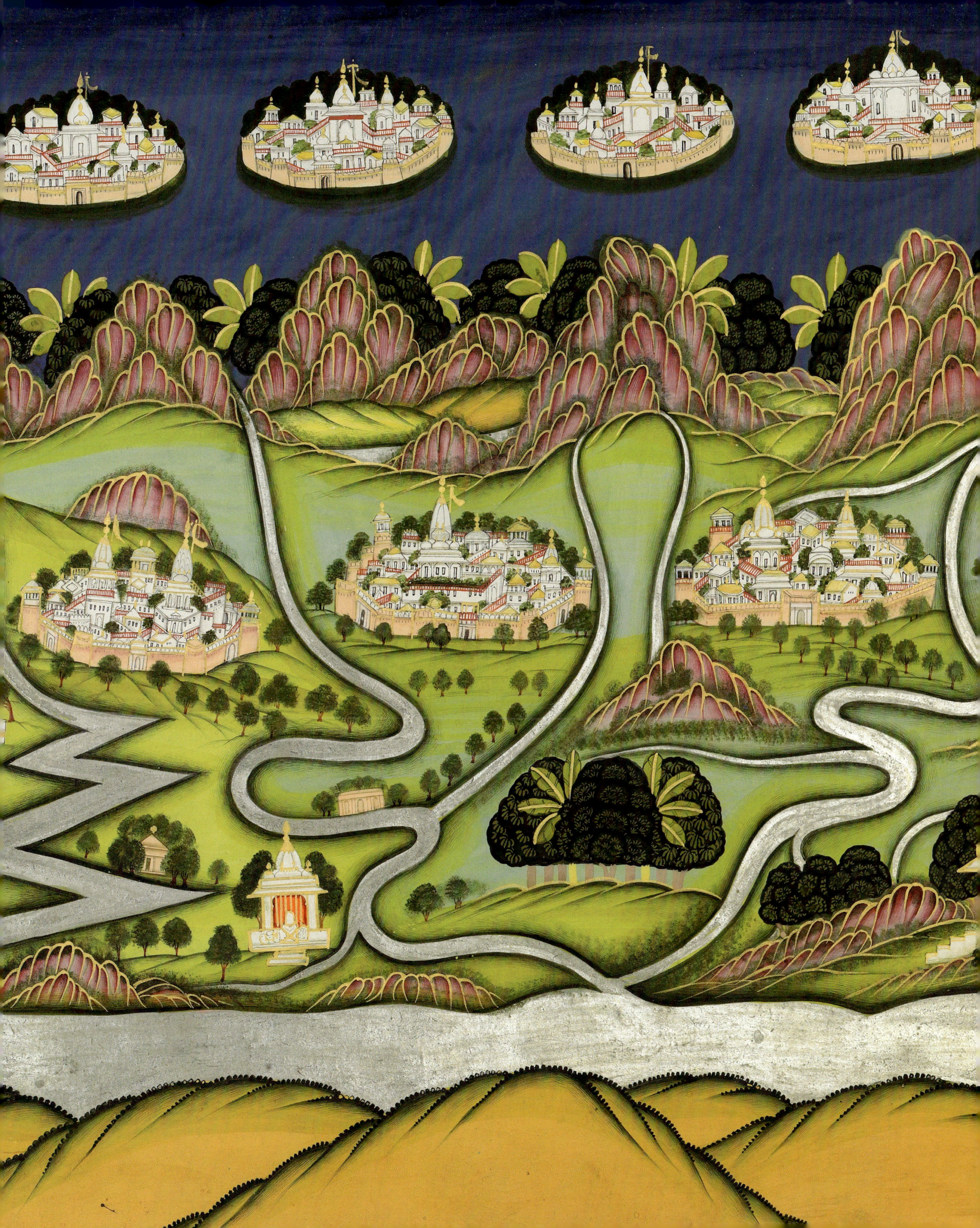

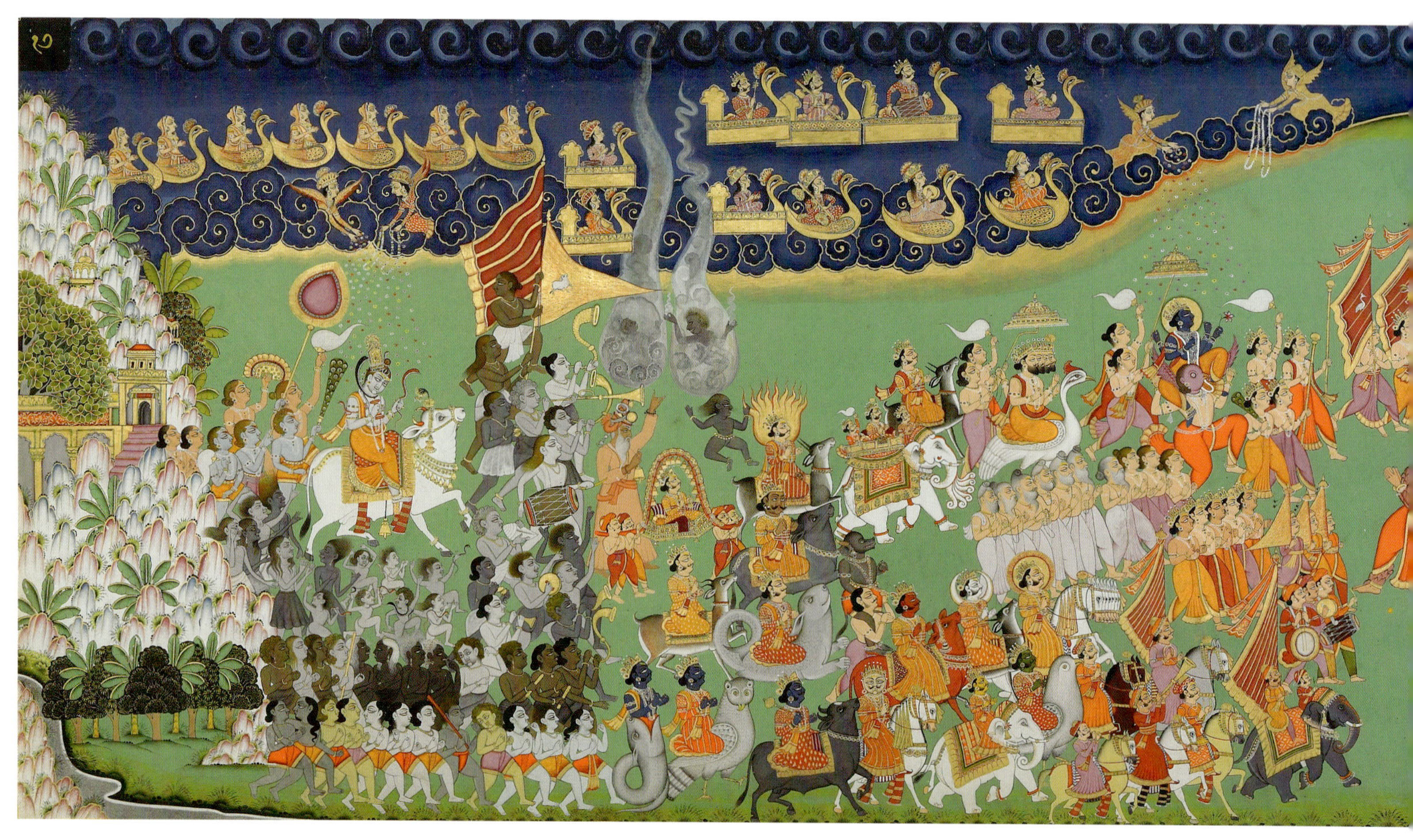

Shiva's Wedding Procession

folio 17 from the *Shiva Purana*
Vana Akhavat, ca. 1828; 46.3 x 124 cm
Mehrangarh Museum Trust

Numbered 17 in the upper left corner.
The complete inscription and a chart appear in the reference catalogue.

Sri siv puran
Da[khal] dholiya re kothar
Citarai vanai akhavat kino
Glorious Shiva Purana
Entered into the *dholiya* storeroom
Made by the painter Vana Akhavat

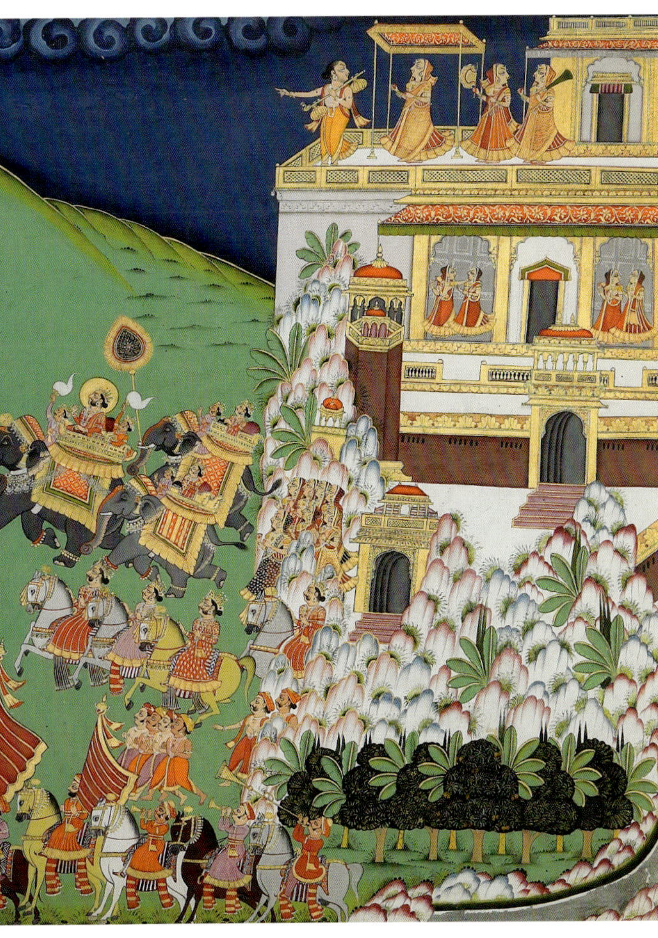

Passages of glorious painting—smoky-gray imps, animal vehicles elegantly realized in grisaille, and the animated contours delineating Shiva and his ghoulish friends—reveal Vana Akhavat to be one of the more accomplished artists in Man Singh's atelier. His masterpiece is this cheerful panorama, which represents the Himalayas as the personified deity Himavat and as a mountainous landscape crossed by a spectacular wedding procession (see pp. 242–43).

As the father of the bride, the personified mountain Himavat benevolently advances on an elephant from his mountain-palace on the painting's right. His envoy Parvat (literally, mountain), clad in rocky pink protrusions, steps forward to greet the *barat* (groom's procession) of Shiva. An A-list gathering of divinities—the great Hindu gods, the deities of the planets and directions, and the seven celestial sages (Ursa Major)—leads the glorious *barat*. Behind them, Shiva advances beneath a mist of heavenly flowers, smiling gently and tilting a bit on the bull he is riding, dazed from intoxication. He wears the golden headdress (*toran*) of a groom but otherwise remains the archetypal ascetic. His skin is white from the ashes of the cremation grounds, serpents adorn his body, and he is accompanied by his impishly cavorting but gruesomely deformed pals, the *ganas*.

Like all the puranas, the *Shiva Purana* includes not only cosmologies and cosmographies, but also myriad stories of the gods.[14] In these, mountains can become stages for the enactment of events, such as Shiva's wedding, which convey humanly comprehensible aspects of divinity. Himavat's wife, Mena, who eagerly watches the procession from the palace terrace at the painting's upper right, soon will faint, as she sees the future husband of her daughter, Parvati, for the first time. She is horrified that her daughter has chosen a snake-adorned, ash-strewn, crematorium-dwelling partner. When she regains consciousness, Mena loudly laments the ruin of her family's reputation, berates Parvati for trading gold for dross, and promises that when she finds the seven celestial sages who negotiated the marriage arrangements, she will rip out their beards! Only later, when Shiva manifests a supremely beneficent form, does Mena bless the marriage. The mythological narrative thus combines intimacy and reverence. It makes Shiva accessible even as it acknowledges the contradictory ascetic and erotic aspects of his persona.[15] DD

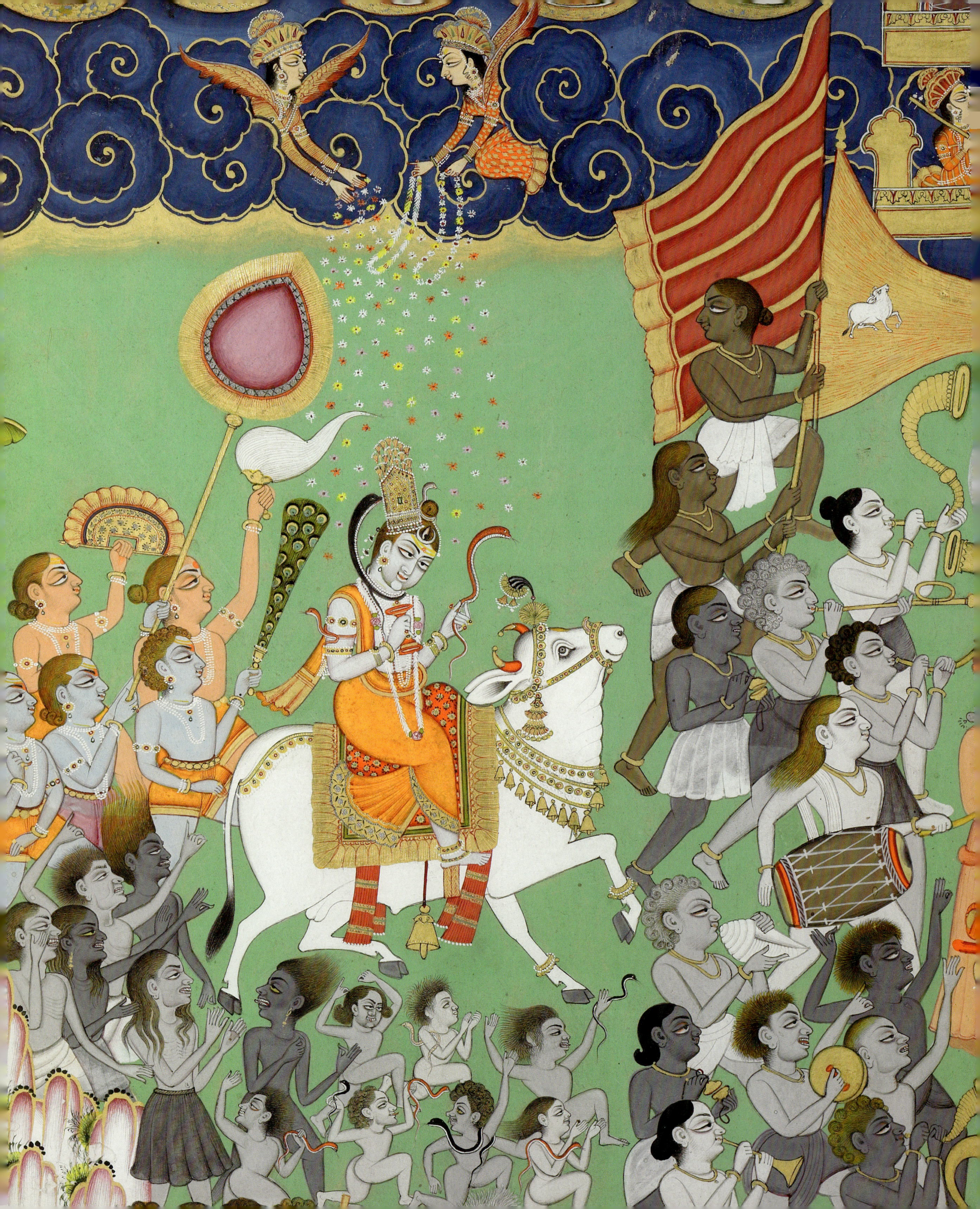

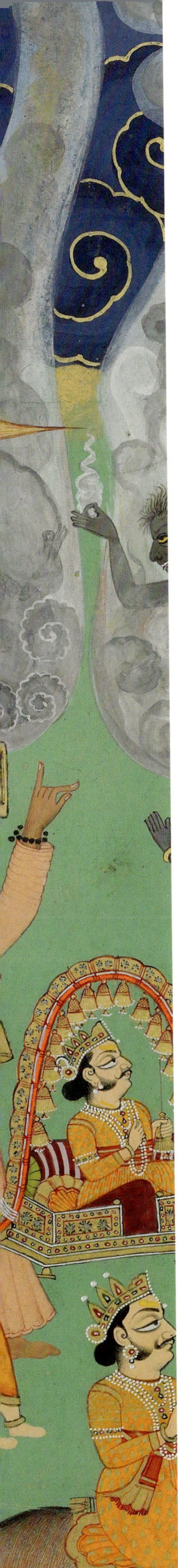

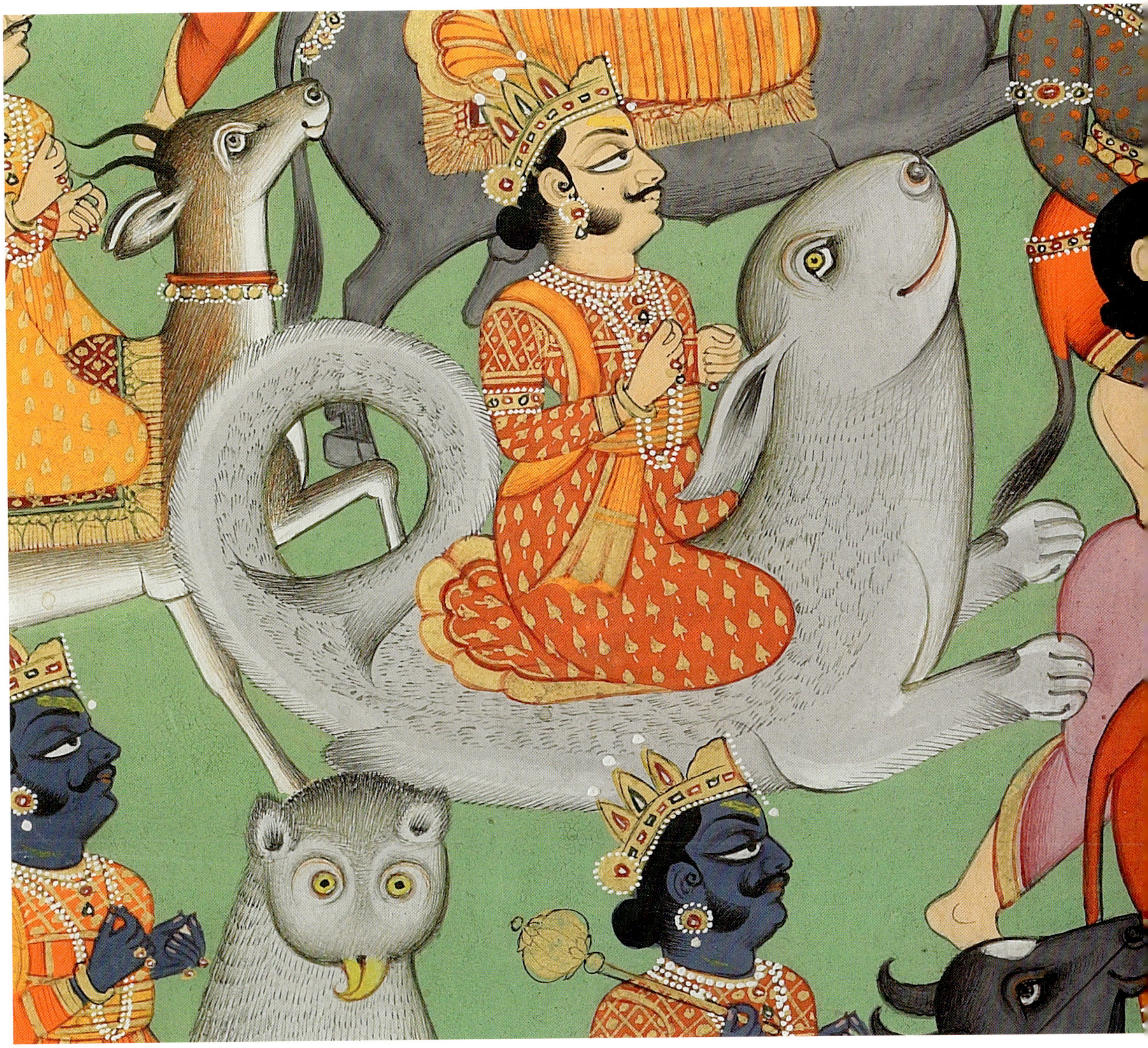

Cat. 55 Details

56a–g

Cosmic Oceans

seven folios from the *Nath Charit*
Attributed to Bulaki, 1823 (Samvat 1880); 44.1 x 118.2
Mehrangarh Museum Trust

The complete inscription appears in the reference catalogue.

The sublime intensity of seven paintings depicting vast cosmic oceans is paralleled by the enigma of their esoteric content. Against each field of saturated color, three seated Nath *mahasiddhas* raise one hand in the gesture of explication. Their iconography (jeweled *kundal* earrings, triangular black hat, halo, etc.) is absolutely consistent with Bulaki's other representations of *mahasiddhas*, but they are arranged here, perhaps meaningfully, in the inverted triangle that signifies the goddess in yantra diagrams (see cat. 49). The *mahasiddha* on the left sits astride the shoulders of an unusual antelope-riding figure—with the dreadlocks of an ascetic but curiously colored in acid-green—who does not appear in any other Jodhpur paintings.[16] Beneath the central *mahasiddha* on five of the folios are the symbols "om," fish, snake, swan, and tortoise, which have a wide range of associations in yogic traditions. In short, "om" is the ultimate sacred syllable; the *mahasiddha* Matsyendranath was born as a fish; the snake stands for the latent female energy (Kundalini Shakti) the yogin must awaken to achieve omniscience; the swan (*hamsa*) represents release from *samsara* (the cycle of rebirth) and is the vehicle of the goddess Saraswati; and the tortoise is the support of the earth.[17] The sixth folio bears a strange, soot-colored fellow, and the seventh folio is blank. All of the figures hover ambiguously above the rippling picture planes.

The slightly reverberating effect of the oceans arises not only from their expansive breadth but also from their swirling waters.[18] On close observation, the color fields separate into oblong orange swells and small breakers, coil snakelike into circular pink eddies, or take on the density of lobed gray boulders. One milk-white ocean is incised with waves of cobweb delicacy, while the other has a raised, rather chunky fish-scale pattern. And while most of the oceans display the precision that we associate with Bulaki, the tremulous whorls of the gray "om" ocean reveal a calligraphic virtuosity (pp. 252–53).

The dense symbolic language of these folios is consistent with that of yogic and tantric traditions, but the code will remain unbroken until the corresponding *Nath Charit* text is located.[19] While many of the painted folios in the *Nath Charit* and the *Nath Purana* can be correlated with portions of their texts, others bear subjects that the texts do not illuminate. Perhaps the illustrated and textual versions of the manuscripts were compiled simultaneously, with bards and pandits relating legends and cosmological conceptions to both writers and painters. It is worth noting that the *Nath Charit* and *Nath Purana* texts are composed in a workaday Marwari vernacular that differs from other, more carefully crafted, period compositions related to the Naths. Artists may have been assigned (or listened to) Nath stories to produce folios that were subsequently sequenced as manuscripts. Further study of these fascinating folios—including an analysis of the many earthy accounts of mischievous *mahasiddhas* drawn from the oral folk tradition—promises to yield important information about the circulation and compilation of Nath popular and esoteric knowledge under Man Singh's patronage. DD

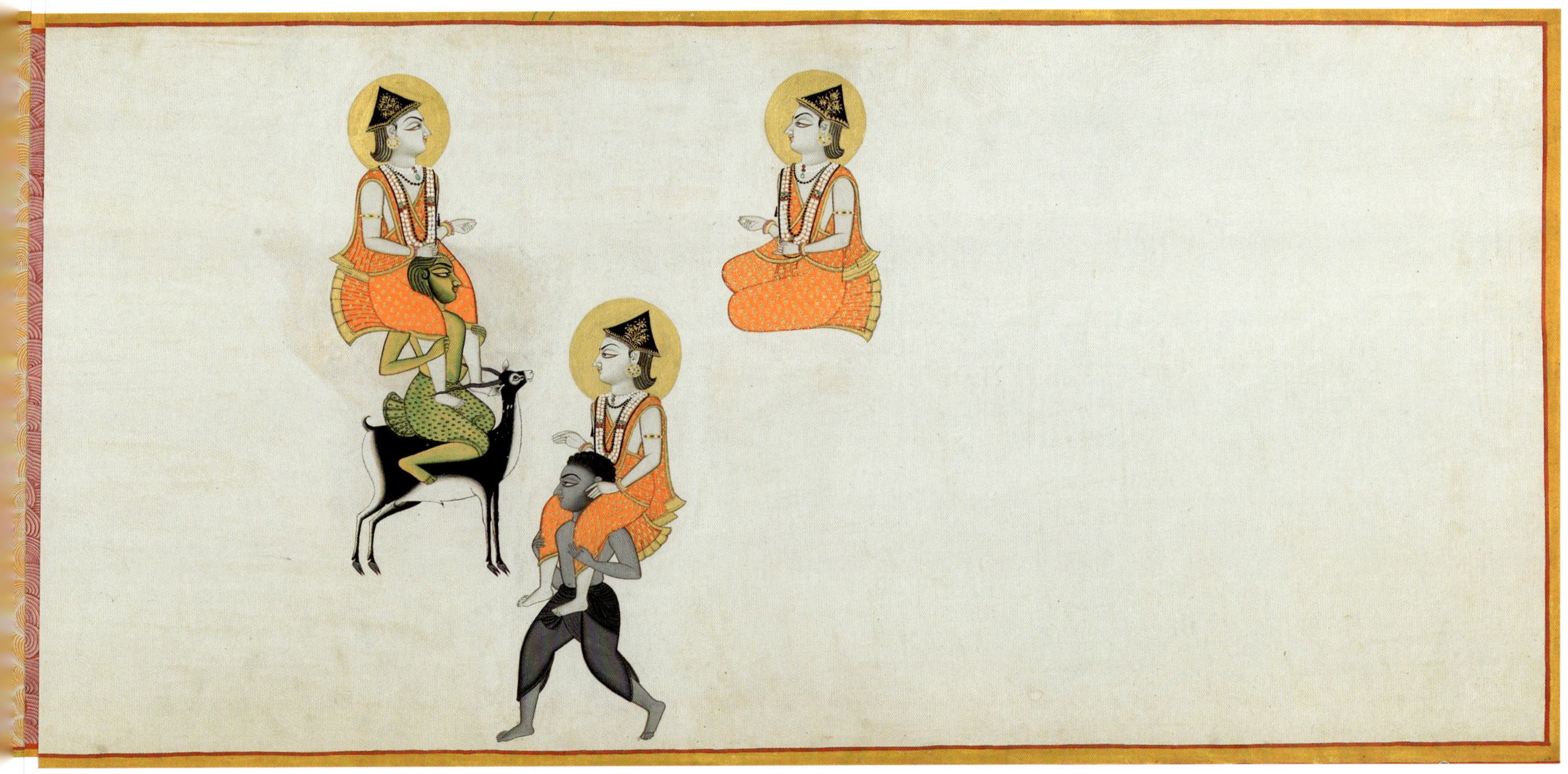

Cat. 56a

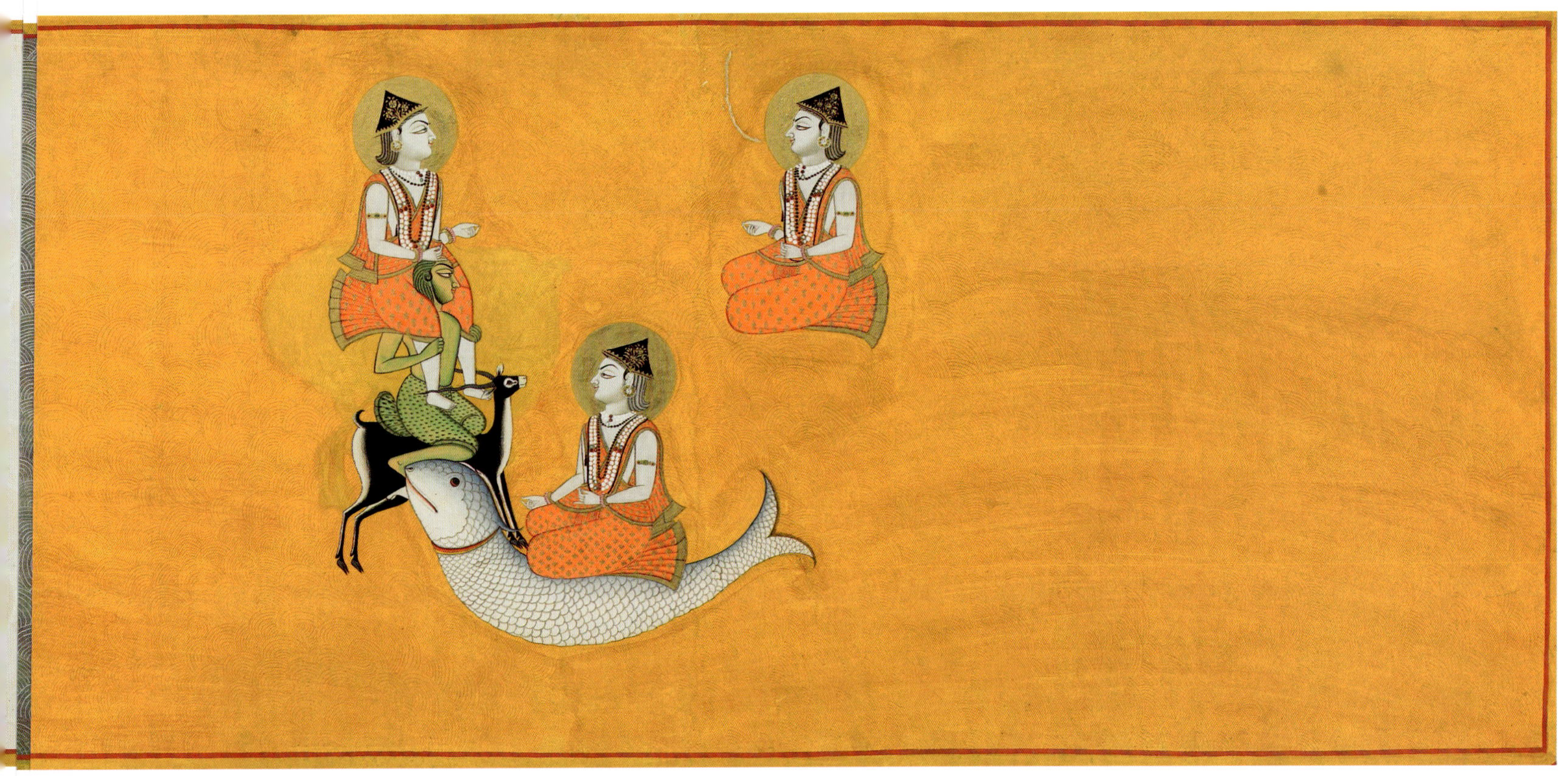

Cat. 56b

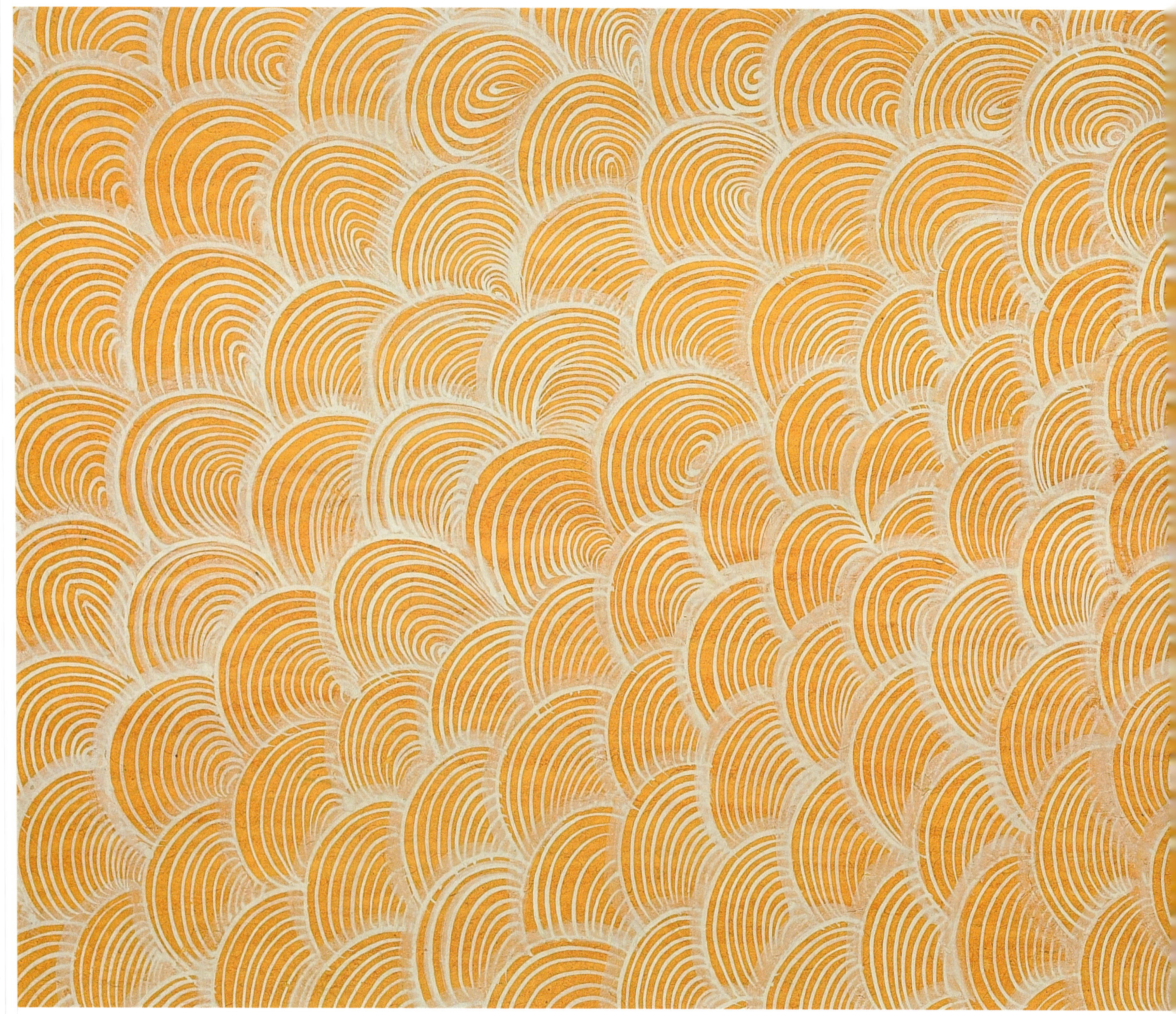

Cat. 56e Detail

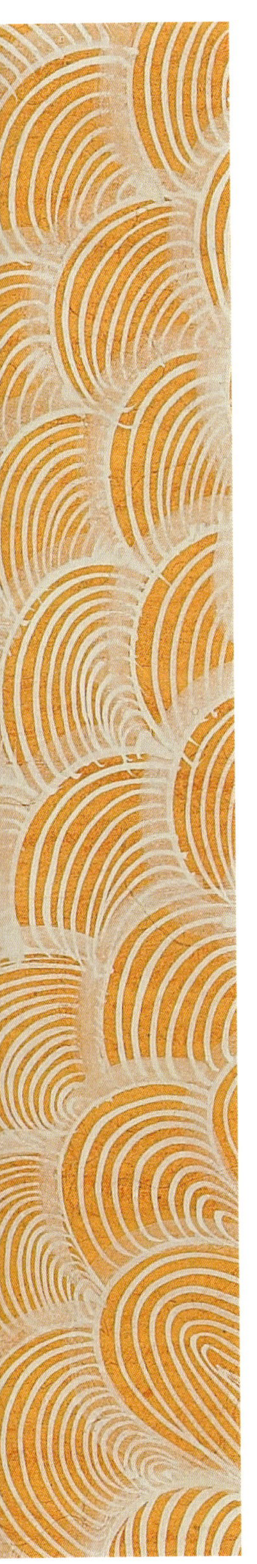

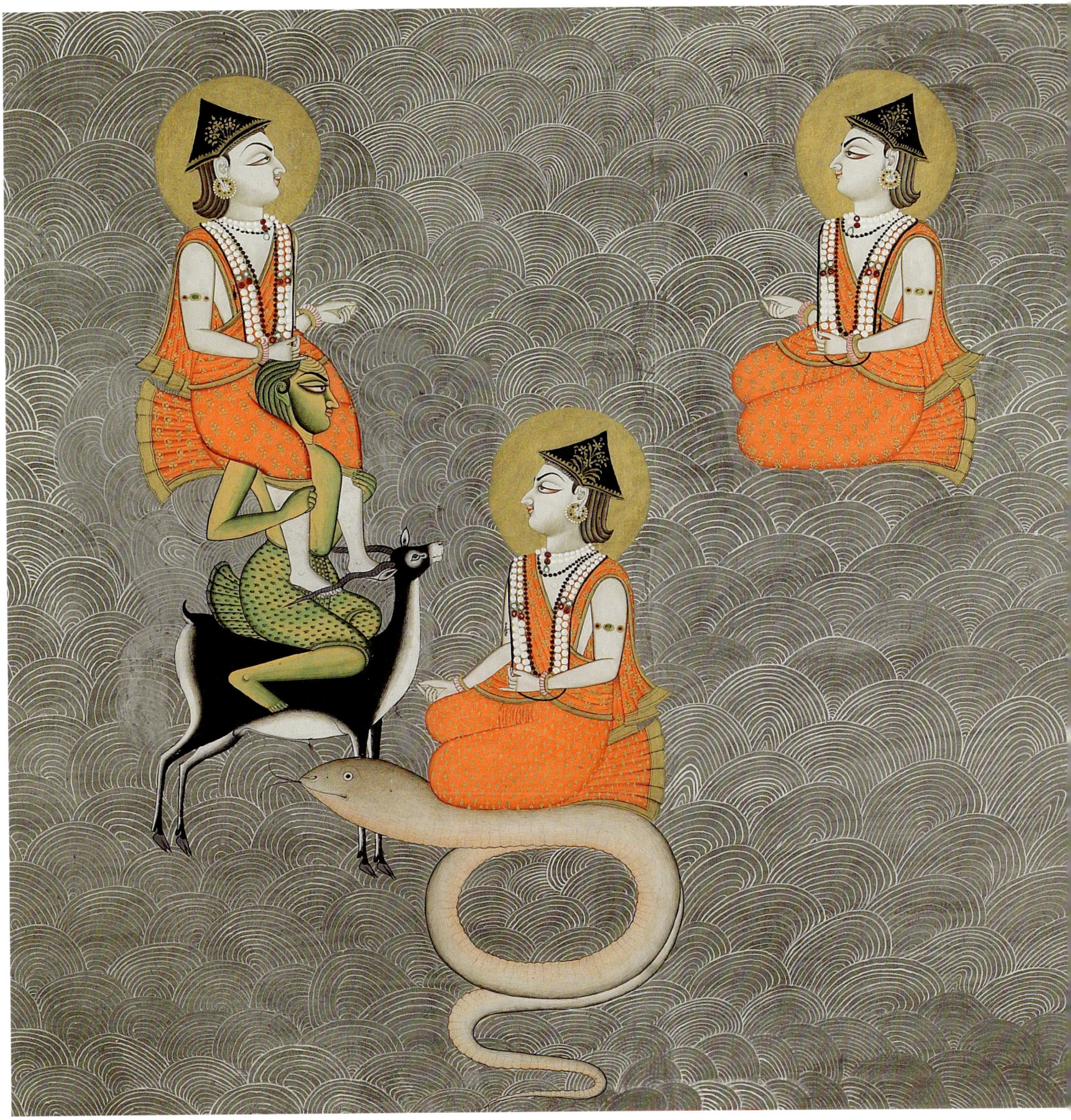

Cat. 56d Detail

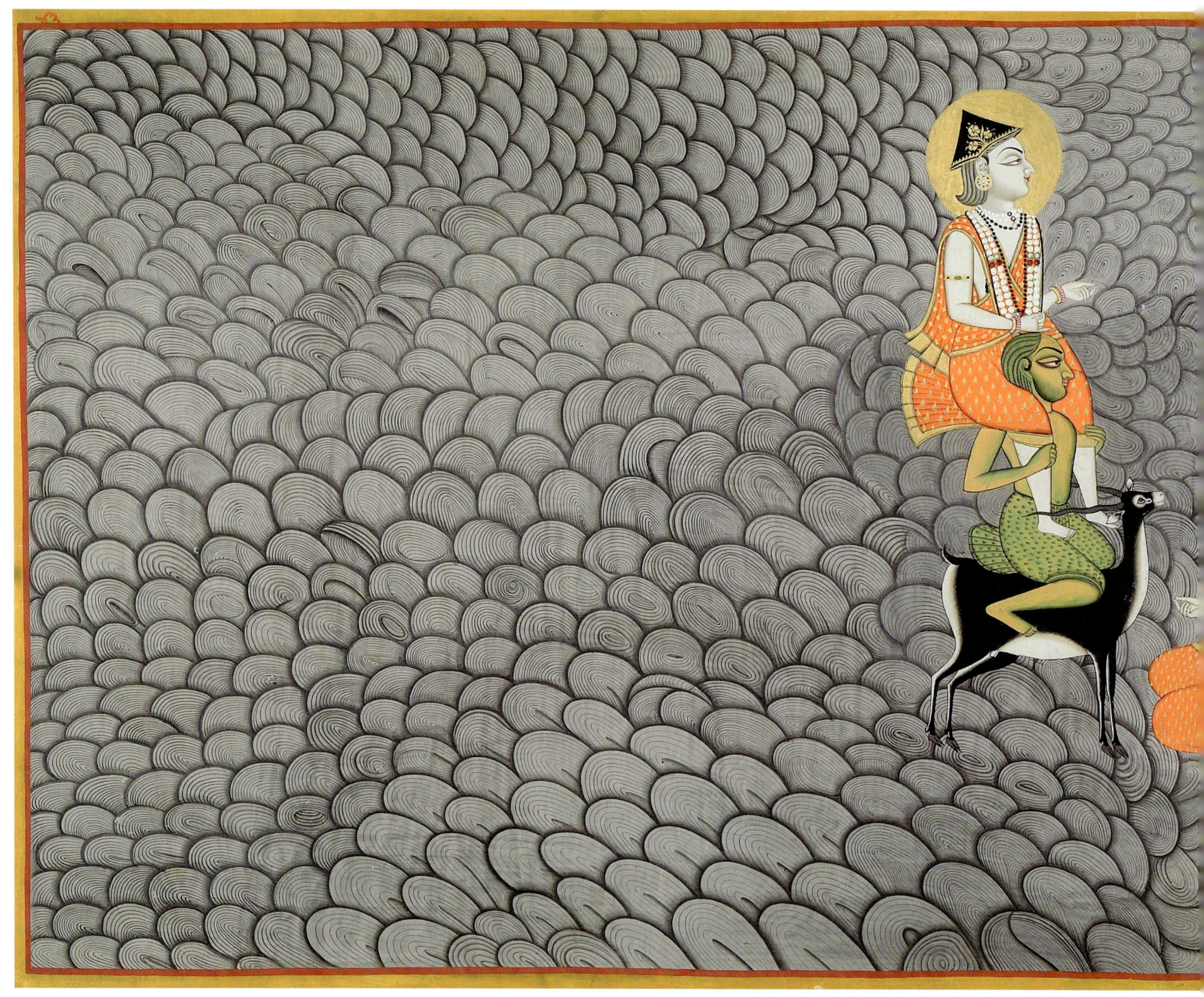

Cat. 56g

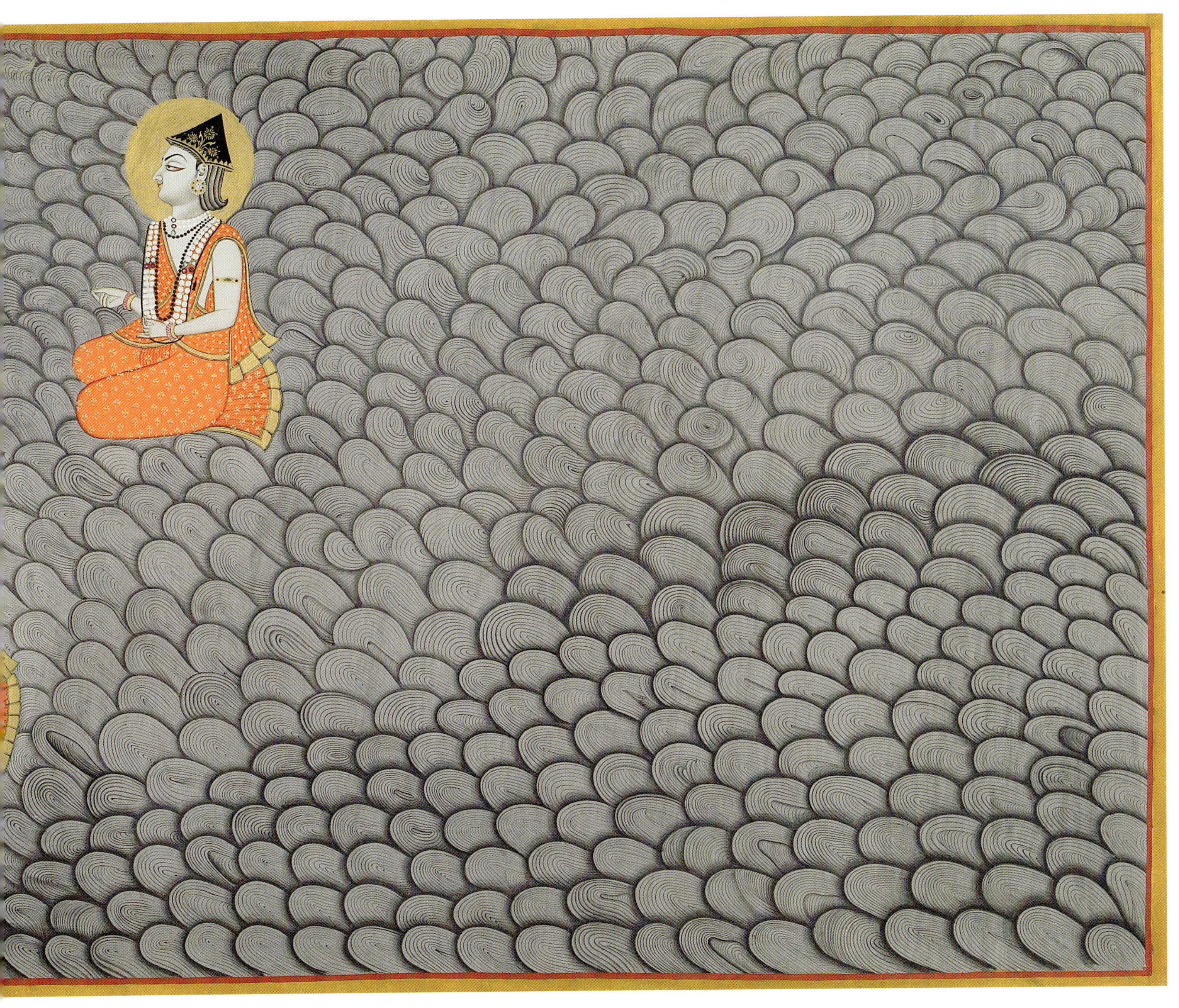

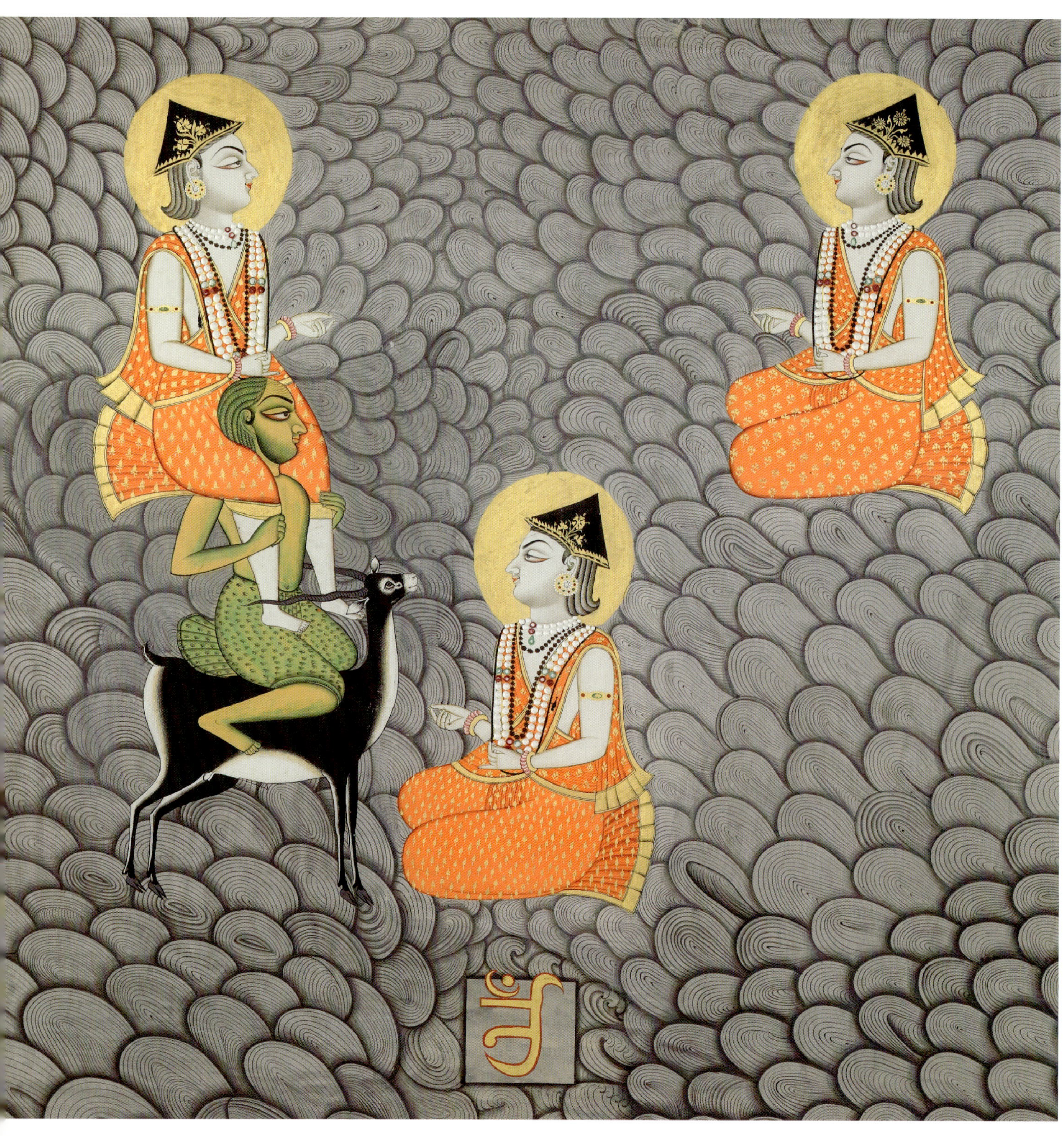

Cat. 56g Detail (above)

Cat. 56c Detail (left)

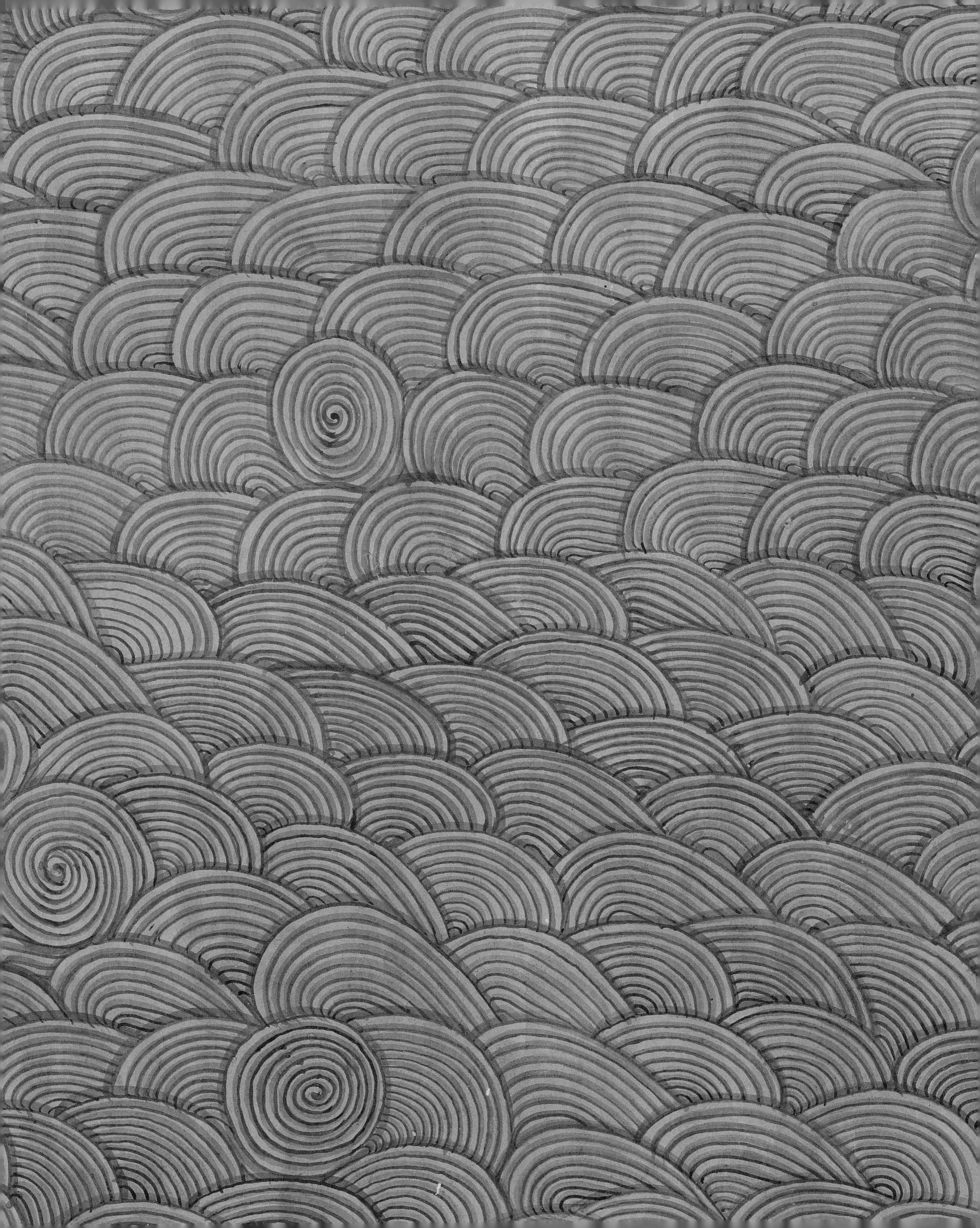

REFERENCE
CATALOGUE

The Origins of Jodhpur Court Painting

1

Page from a Ragamala Series: Gujari Ragini

Pali, Marwar, 1623 (Samvat 1680)
Opaque watercolor on paper; 15.9 x 20.3 cm
National Museum of India, New Delhi 83.209

2

Page from a Ragamala Series: Gunakali Ragini

Jodhpur, ca. 1640–50
Opaque watercolor on paper; 31.5 x 28.3 cm
San Diego Museum of Art, Edwin Binney 3rd Collection, 1990:895
Not in exhibition

3

Page from a Ragamala Series

Jodhpur, ca. 1660
Opaque watercolor on paper; 29.3 x 18.4 cm
National Museum of India, New Delhi, 54.58.28

4

Raja Sur (Suraj) Singh of Marwar

Bishan Das
Mughal, ca. 1595
Opaque watercolor and gold on paper; 38.7 x 25.6 cm
The Metropolitan Museum, New York, 55.121.10, f. 7r
Not in exhibition

shabih-i...raja surajsingh rathor, kar-i bishandas (Persian)
a portrait of the Rathore Raja Suraj Singh, painted by Bishan Das

This album leaf consists of additions and layers built up over more than a few decades. The original painting, defined by the tight, light green area surrounding Suraj Singh, was completed around the time of his succession to the throne of Marwar in 1595. The darker green section and the multi-layered borders were added when the original painting became part of an album produced for Mughal Emperor Shah Jahan in the second quarter of the seventeenth century. The painting is inscribed on the border in Shah Jahan's own handwriting as "a portrait of the Rathor Raja Suraj Singh, painted by Bishan Das," one of the preeminent artists who specialized in portraits and worked for Shah Jahan's predecessors, Akbar and Jahangir.[1]

During the reigns of Suraj Singh's son, Gaj Singh I (cat. 5), and grandson, Jaswant Singh I (cat. 6), Jodhpur court paintings began to incorporate Mughal elements, especially in portraiture, as the fashion moved away from the regional idiom of the early seventeenth century (see cats. 1 and 2). However, it is likely that the seeds of this different Mughal-related painting style were planted during Suraj Singh's time because of his intimate exposure to Mughal court life: "[N]ot unnaturally, a raja who is repeatedly depicted as a mere courtier in the presence of an overlord will eventually set up his own atelier of artists to provide pictures in which he is shown to be the focus of attention, and the wielder of power over his assembled nobles."[2] CG

5

Maharaja Gaj Singh I

Mughal, ca. 1630–38
Opaque watercolor and gold on paper; 26.5 x 16.5 cm
The British Museum, London, Add. 1920.9-17.013 (14)

The Rathore rajas Udai Singh, Suraj Singh (cat. 4), and Gaj Singh (cat. 5) all appear in imperial Mughal portraits. It is likely that they would have seen those finished Mughal paintings and have been familiar with the naturalism and polished technique of Mughal artists. The vivid resemblance in the Gaj Singh portrait was a catalyst for Rajput artists attempting to capture the Mughalized portraiture style in Marwar (cat. 6).

Three related drawings are evidence that the Mughal style increasingly was embraced by some of the artists in the Jodhpur atelier.[3] Two of them, fig. 5a and a *jharokha* portrait now in the National Museum of India, New Delhi,[4] are half-length bust portraits of Gaj Singh.[5] These two drawings are based on the same stencil, though they may have been modified: the heads are essentially similar, but the hands and lower areas are different. In fig. 5a, Gaj Singh is somewhat leaner than the rounded version in the collection of the National Museum. Both Rajput drawings are done with artistic finesse and a sure hand that captures the subtle variations in the turban and coat textiles and leaves the viewer with a compelling image of Gaj Singh himself. The third Rajput drawing,[6] also in New Delhi, is an almost exact duplicate of fig. 5a, but it is both less refined and more rigid; the decoration on the coat is abbreviated, and the folds on the sleeves seem almost unfinished. All three drawings were completed after Gaj Singh died in 1638, though the first two are probably from the mid-1600s and the third from later in the seventeenth century.

The naturalism so prevalent in Mughal painting (cats. 4 and 5) also is seen in a Jodhpur portrait of Gaj Singh's elder son, Amar Singh, born in 1613 (fig. 5b).[7] As a reward for his military service, Emperor Shah Jahan gave Amar Singh the principality of Nagaur in 1634 and the title rao in 1638.[8] Gaj Singh banished Amar Singh from the Jodhpur court in 1634, and Amar Singh's younger brother, Jaswant Singh (cat. 6), became ruler at their father's death in 1638. In 1644 Amar Singh disgraced the emperor and dishonored his Rathore heritage by assassinating the Mughal court paymaster/treasurer, Salabat Khan, during an

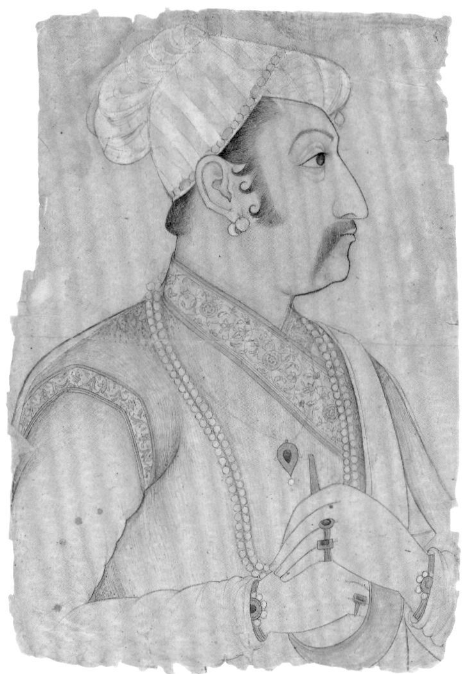

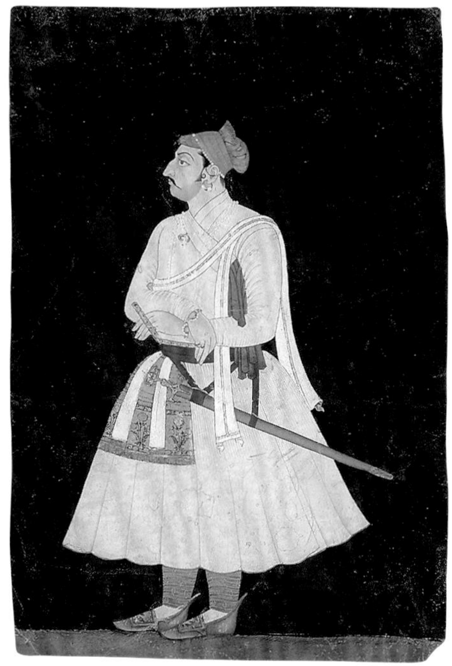

Fig. 5a Raja Gaj Singh of Marwar, Jodhpur, Rajasthan, 17th century, Smithsonian American Art Museum

Fig. 5b Rao Amar Singh of Jodhpur, Marwar, ca. 1640, San Diego Museum of Art, 1990:612

imperial assembly presided over by Shah Jahan. After this violent act and breach of security, court officials pounced on Amar Singh and he was killed.[9]

The painting of Rao Amar Singh exhibits both the Mughal taste for realism and the Rajput use of vivid color for drama and impact. The artist captures Amar Singh's likeness, particularly the facial resemblance between the father and son, including their prominent noses. The composition is closer, however, to Rajput sensibilities, which featured blocks of color, less shading, and the broad application of paint. CG

6

Maharaja Jaswant Singh I at a Music Performance during a Monsoon

Mughalized Rajasthani painting for a Marwar patron
Jodhpur, ca. 1670
Opaque watercolor on paper; 26.8 x 17.4 cm
Formerly in the Mewar Royal Collection
National Gallery of Victoria, Melbourne, Australia,
Felton Bequest, 1980 AS 28-1980

bahadur jaswant sang (Persian)
jasut sihaji raja bikaner ka ri chabi majal ki (Rajasthani)
the noble man Jaswant Singh
Raja Jaswant Singh of Bikaner

Translated by Andrew Topsfield

Gardens and garden design were important aspects of both Rajasthani and Mughal culture, and many elements of Mughal garden design were introduced into Rajput court gardens. Rathore rulers used controlled water channels, cusped fountain design, and regulated flower beds—essential elements of the Mughal model—to capture the gardens' essence in an arid, desert environment.[10]

A successful general, efficient administrator, and patron of artists,[11] Jaswant Singh had an intellectual side as well. He wrote a gazetteer, *Marwar ra Pargana ri Vigat*, describing the governing customs of Marwar, that is still an essential document for historians. He wrote his own commentary on the *Bhagavad Gita*, a central Hindu religious text in Sanskrit, a metaphysical treatise *Siddhant Bodh*, and texts on poetics, including the *Bhasha-bhushan*, that were illustrated by artists in Mewar.[12] He was also a patron of learning and literature, notably sponsoring the historian Muhata Nainsi, whose comprehensive historical treatise, *Khyat*, included local Marwar traditions and oral chronicles. CG

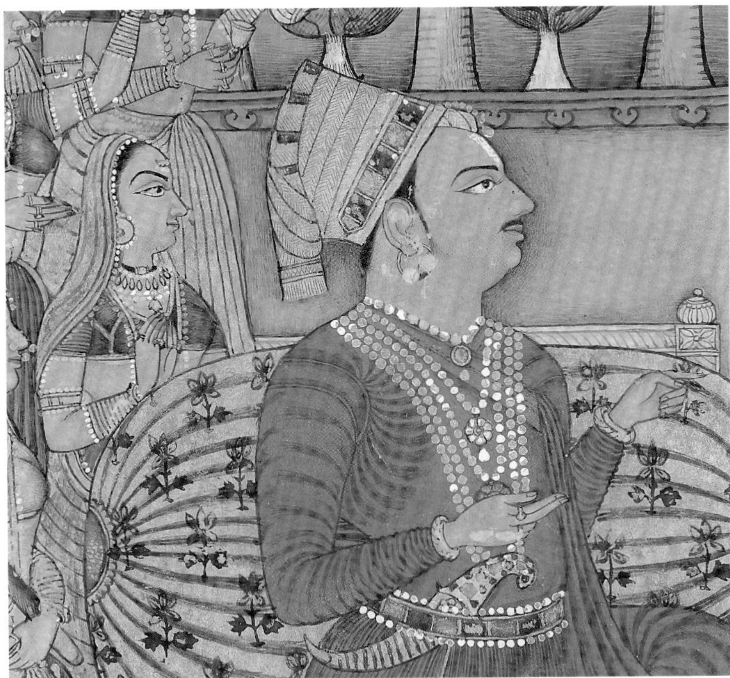

Cat. 7 Detail

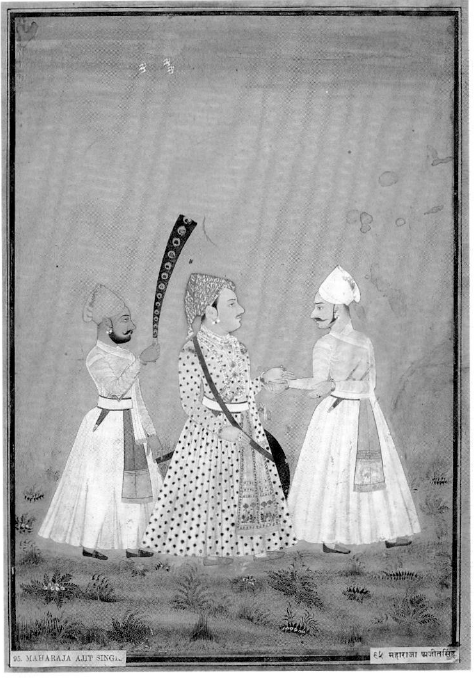

Fig. 7a Maharaja Ajit Singh and Prince Bakhat Singh, Udaipur, ca. 1723–24, Mehrangarh Museum Trust, RJS 1974

7

Evening Musical Festivities within a Garden

Jodhpur, ca. 1715
Opaque watercolor on paper; 40.6 x 30.5 cm
Mehrangarh Museum Trust, RJS 2060
Not in exhibition

Rajrajeshvar maharaj sri ajit singhji ri sabi
Da [khal] dholiya re kothar
Portrait of lord of king of kings, supreme king, glorious Ajit Singhji
Entered in the *dholiya* storeroom

Much of this garden picture reflects the painting style of Mewar, a state to the south, rather than Marwar. Contemporary paintings (circa 1720) from Udaipur in Mewar have decorative trees arranged in a similarly regimented pattern, an especially high or even no horizon, flat architectural elements, and similar idealized figure types.[13]

During Ajit Singh's youth, when he was banished from Jodhpur and continually evading Aurangzeb's army, among other enemies, he found shelter at Udaipur. In 1694, when he was fifteen years old, he married a local princess, cementing a political alliance between Jodhpur and Udaipur[14] It is reasonable to think that Udaipur painting and artists influenced his taste[15]; and a painting now in the Jodhpur royal collection, but clearly done in the Udaipur style, suggests that a least one artist from Udaipur painted in Jodhpur. Fig. 7a, circa 1723–24, is a portrait of Ajit Singh extending his hand in greeting to his second son, Bakhat Singh, who would later murder him. It is inscribed on the reverse in Marwari in the typical Jodhpur format:

rajarajeshwar maharajadhiraj maharaja sri ajit singhji ri tasvir,
da [khal] dholiya re kothar
Picture of lord of king of kings, supreme king of great kings, great, glorious king Ajit Singhji
Entered in the *dholiya* storeroom

Bakhat Singh and Ajit Singh might have been given the painting in Mewar. However, because it was inscribed in Jodhpur, has no Mewar inventory markings and features an intimate gesture between father and son, it likely was painted in Jodhpur by an artist from Mewar. Similar treatment of figures and ground cover can be found in Mewar paintings from the late seventeenth century.[16]

Bakhat Singh continued to be involved with Udaipur. In 1728, he donated Indrapura, a Marwar village under his control, to the esteemed holy site of Nathdwara, located in Mewar.[17] The land and revenue from farming and animal husbandry in the village supported the maintenance of the prominent Krishna shrine at Nathdwara, which was affiliated with the Mewar ruling house. CG

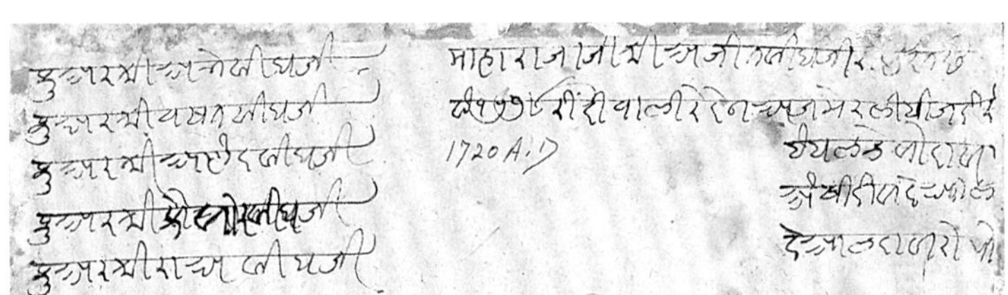

Cat. 8 Verso

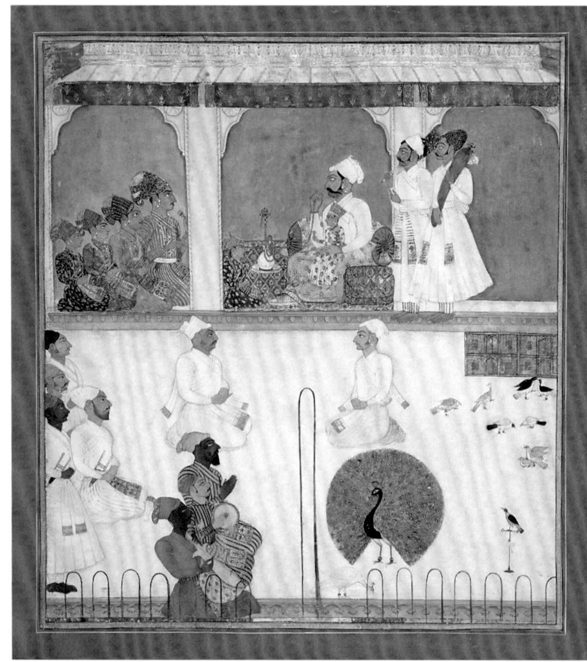

Fig. 8a The Sons of Maharaha Ajit Singh of Jodhpur, ca. 1720,
Philadelphia Museum of Art, 2004-149-47

8

Maharaja Ajit Singh and Sons during the Festival of Diwali
Jodhpur, 1721 (Samvat 1778)
Opaque watercolor and gold on paper; 33.8 x 25.3 cm
Harvard University Art Museums, Arthur M. Sackler Museum, Gift in gratitude
to John Coolidge, Gift of Leslie Cheek, Jr., Anonymous Fund in memory of
Henry Berg, Louise Haskell Daly, Alpheus Hyatt, Richard Norton Memorial
Funds and through the generosity of Albert H. Gordon and Emily Rauh
Pulitzer; formerly in the collection of Stuart Cary Welch, Jr., 1995.131

*Ku[nv]ar sri abhe singhji, ku[nv]ar sri vakhat singhji, ku[nv]ar sri anand singhji,
ku[nv]ar sri kisor singhji, u[nv]ar sri rai singhji*
Glorious Prince Abhai Singhji, glorious Prince Bakhat Singhji, glorious Prince
Anand Singhji, glorious Prince Kishor Singhji, glorious Prince Rai Singhji

maharaja sri ajit singhji ri surat che
1778 ri devali re den ajmer lidi jad ri
dhanyal keso das amvidas deal deal das ro po[18]
Portrait of supreme king, glorious Ajit Singhji, Diwali,
1721–22, when he conquered Ajmer
Dhandal Keso Das [and] Ambadas Deal, grandson of Deal Das

The image of Maharaja Ajit Singh performing puja (worship) to the goddess
(see p. 3) is another example of a Jodhpur artist incorporating elements of
Mughal taste. The raja's handsomely designed gold garment is almost indistin-
guishable from the one he wears in cat. 8, and the floor spreads used in both
paintings seem to match.[19] Both the Mughalized style and the long-established
traditional Rajput style of painting were prevalent in 1720s Jodhpur. The latter is
exemplified in a theatrical painting of a larger family gathering, featuring Ajit Singh
and his sons on a large terrace with retainers and other nobles (fig. 8a). Unlike
cat. 8 and the painting on p. 3, fig. 8a has strong, primary colors, more stylized
facial treatment, and uses white for drama and to isolate the main actors within
the complex composition. The Rajputs changed the Mughal interest in depth of
field into a flat pattern of shapes arranged in a straightforward manner. All three
paintings demonstrate the range of stylistic interest of the royal court artists Ajit
Singh patronized before his death in 1724. It is clear that subject matter did not
determine style: of the two paintings of Ajit Singh and his sons, cat. 8 is in a
Mughalized style, while fig. 8a is in a Rajput style. Choice of styles likely was
determined by the artist's talent, training, preference, and the desire of the patron.

Within a particular Rajasthani studio, new influences often accompanied the
arrival of an artist from a different state studio or occurred after artists trained in
the locally prevalent style saw paintings from other courts and then expanded
in new directions. The last line of the inscription refers to two of the figures in
white behind the raja. CG

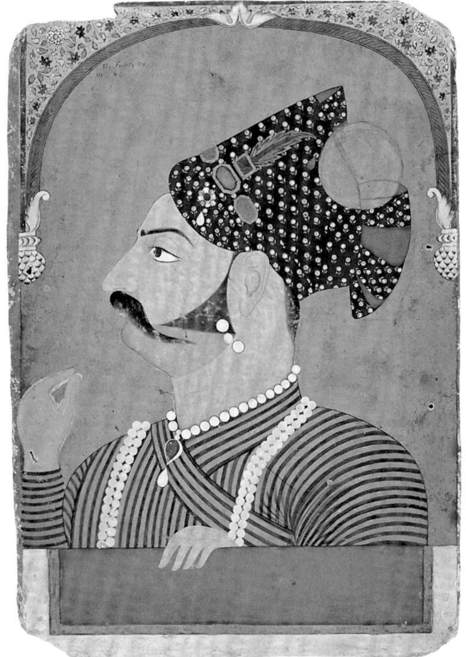

Cat. 9

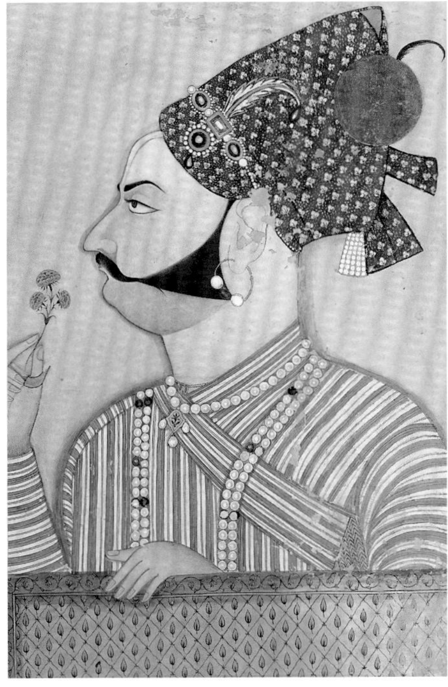

Fig. 9a Maharaja Vijai Singh, by Ajmal Khan, Marwar, ca. 1660–70, Mehrangarh Museum Trust, RJS 4825

9

Maharaja Bakhat Singh

Nagaur, ca. 1740
Opaque water color and gold on paper; 43.1 x 30.4 cm
National Gallery of Canada, Ottawa, Gift of Max Tanenbaum, Toronto, 1979.23597
Not in exhibition

raja sri bakhat singhji
glorious king Bakhat Singh

Because we know some of the dates of some of the Nagaur paintings and other related works, we can estimate how old Bakhat Singh was in each work. This *jharokha* portrait is one of four paintings of Bakhat Singh produced over a period of a decade or longer. The earliest is in the collection of Sir Howard Hodgkin and can be placed in the later 1720s–early 1730s;[20] Bakhat Singh appears to be the same age as he is in cats. 10, 11, and 12, approximately twenty-five to thirty years old. Two other *jharokha* paintings, circa 1740—cat. 9 and an unfinished drawing, the Ray portrait[21]—show Bakhat Singh slightly older, approximately the same age as in cat. 17.[22] A fourth *jharokha* work, in the Goenka collection[23] like the Hodgkin painting is entirely finished, but was produced a decade or so later, circa 1745. In the Goenka painting and cat. 18, Bakhat Singh is about the same age; in addition, in these two paintings, but not in any of the other *jharokha* images, cascading strands of pearls, perhaps wedding jewelry, hang from his dark-hued turban.

The four *jharokha* portraits, like the portable paintings from Nagaur (cats. 10–20), show that the artists in Bakhat Singh's atelier consciously depicted the maharaja as he aged between circa 1725 and 1752 (see Bakhat Singh chronology). In works produced by most Rajput ateliers, the ruler usually is shown in an ideal manner and in his prime, regardless of his age. This makes the Nagaur paintings particularly interesting, both artistically and historically.

Several other large *jharokha* paintings show the influence of the Bakhat Singh images: a circa 1750 painting of Rao Desalji (reigned 1718–41) from Kutch in Gujarat, where Bakhat Singh visited in 1751[24]; a large image (circa 1765–70) of Kumar Raj Singh of the neighboring Rathore state of Bikaner, which may provide evidence that one of the Bakhat Singh *jharokha* paintings was known to Bikaner rulers or artists and used in the Bikaner royal workshop as a model;[25] and a portrait of Vijai Singh, Bakhat Singh's heir (fig. 9a). CG

Royal Pastimes in the Gardens
at Nagaur Palace

10

Amusements on a Moonlit Water Terrace

Nagaur, ca. 1729–32
Opaque water color and gold on paper; 65 x 45.1 cm
Mehrangarh Museum Trust, RJS 1981

Rajrajeshwar maharajadhiraj maharaja sri bakhat singhji ri tasbir
Picture of lord of king of kings, supreme king of great kings, great king,
glorious Bakhat Singhji

Cypress trees are found in all the Bakhat Singh portraits from Nagaur, but usually
as part of a larger mix of vegetation. In this painting, seven tall cypress trees on
each side are used as the sole green element; separated by pink flowering
bushes, they provide a delightful and rhythmic decorative backdrop. This
cadenced design is balanced by two uniform rows of women holding offerings
of refreshments for the raja in their hands. The cypress tree was a favorite motif
of both the Mughals and the Rajputs.[1] In Islamic poetry, the cypress tree often
is used to symbolize the mystical yearning of the beloved for spiritual union with
God. Here, it may also convey order and devotion; bent slightly like the rows of the
attending women, the cypress trees seem focused on the royal couple. During
the reign of Maharaja Takhat Singh (1843–72), this painting was adapted with
an image of the new patron, Takhat Singh, replacing the one of Bakhat Singh.[2]

While a Rajput warrior usually is depicted with his trademark belongings—
sword, shield, dagger, or other military accoutrements—men usually removed
their weapons as they relaxed in the zenana; thus it is not surprising to find them
absent during this romantic interlude depicting Bakhat Singh. This is one of three
paintings in which we see actual physical contact between the raja and a woman.
Here, Bakhat Singh caresses his companion's thigh; in cat. 11, he embraces his
companion; and in cat. 19, a woman massages his foot.

The painter of cat. 10 has made a conscious effort to isolate the woman who
receives Bakhat Singh's affections.[3] She may represent a *nayika*, an idealized
heroine from Hindu literature. Another possibility is that she is one of his wives,
perhaps Bakhat Singh's second wife, Rani Chandrakunwar from Osian. They
married in 1718 when he was twelve, and she gave birth to his son and heir,
Vijai Singh, in 1729, around the time this painting was completed. She may be his
fourth wife, Rani Abhaikanwar, from Manhorpur (in Jaipur district), who became his
bride in 1729, or his fifth wife, Rani Swaropkanwar, a princess from neighboring
Jaisalmer, who married him in 1730.[4]

An atypical aspect of both this painting and cat. 11 is Bakhat Singh's turban:
the shape is conical rather than the rectangular form that was preferred in Marwar
during the first half of the eighteenth century and is featured in all the remaining
Bakhat Singh portraits from Nagaur (cats. 13–19).[5] Even portraits painted by
Jodhpur artists show Bakhat Singh with the rectangular turban.[6] Turban style was
a vital part of Rajput dress; it was used to distinguish clan allegiance, geographical

location, and patrimony, among other indicators. Both cats. 10 and 11 depict a
youthful raja and were probably painted after 1725, shortly after his brother, Abhai
Singh, gave him Nagaur as a reward for killing their father. Bakhat Singh's
departure from the usual Marwar turban style may have been an act of stylistic
independence, a way of visually proclaiming his rule over his own fiefdom. A less
likely reason, but one that should be considered, is that the conical turban may
have been preferred by the woman who shared his affection on that night, perhaps
because it came from her region of birth or was favored by her family.

This painting is not attributed to a specific artist; however, this portrait of
Bakhat Singh resembles the one in the triple portrait with Abhai Singh and Vijai
Singh (see p. 299, top left). Based on the depiction of Vijai Singh, who appears
to be three or four years old, the latter work can be dated circa 1732–33 and
helps place cat. 10 chronologically. CG

11

Celebration of Holi in a Garden Pavilion

Attributed here to the "Nagaur Master"
Nagaur, ca. 1729–32
Opaque watercolor and gold on paper; 45.1 x 62.2 cm (image)
Mehrangarh Museum Trust, RJS 2033

Rajrajeshvar maharajadhiraj maharaja sri bakhat singhji ri tasbir
Painting of lord of king of kings, supreme king of great kings,
supreme king, glorious Bakhat Singhji

Dakhal dholiya re kothar hajri sam[vat] 1885 ra savan sud 12 mandi
Entered in the *dholiya* storeroom and inventory on the twelfth day
of the light half of Shravan (July–August), 1828

The Holi scene in cat. 20 takes place in the same central area of the palace
compound depicted in cat. 11, but that work dates from approximately two
decades later, after the small pool was enlarged and the two small pavilions
were replaced by larger buildings. The grove of trees and the central *bangla*
(curved roof) viewing pavilion remained after the renovation. The pavilion is still
in place today at Nagaur (see fig. 20a, p. 274).

This portable painting clearly is related to some of the wall paintings still visible
in the Hadi Rani Mahal at Nagaur, which Bakhat Singh built for his personal
pleasure and private relaxation.[7] The composition and content of the portable
paintings presented in this catalogue confirm that the raja was also the patron of
the wall paintings at Nagaur and that they were completed during the same period.[8]

All except two of the women wear head scarves; the other two wear caps
like those seen in the wall paintings of the Hadi Rani Mahal. The rectangular
cap on the serving woman in the left pavilion is similar to the Chaghatay style
originated by the Mughals in the sixteenth century (fig. 11b).[9] In cat. 11, the woman
standing just above the one playing the orange double-headed drum wears a
conical cap similar to one in fig. 11a. Pairs of strollers embracing each other in
the left and right pavilions have distinct parallels in the Hadi Rani Mahal images.
In fact, all the compositional elements—the grove of trees, multiple pavilions, the
women outdoors, and the water—also are found in the wall paintings.

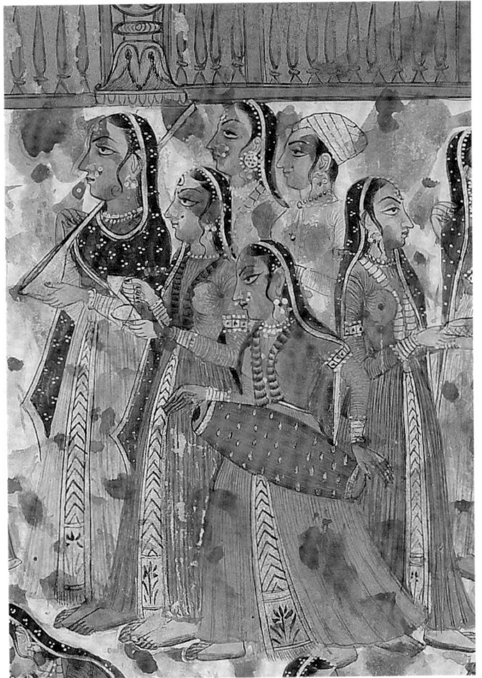

Cat. 11 Detail

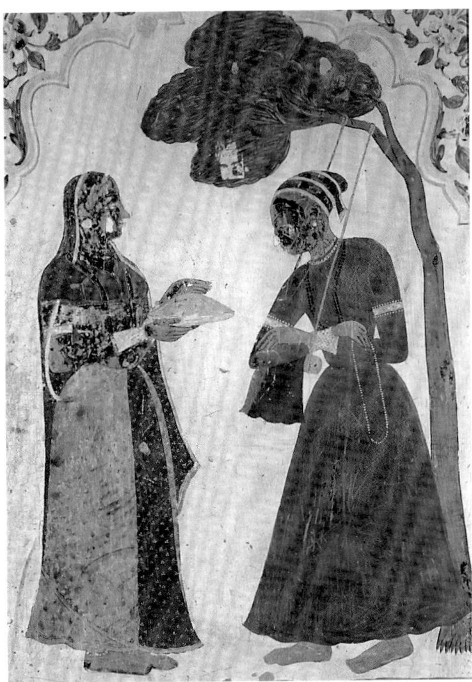

Fig. 11a Wall painting, Hadi Rani Mahal, Nagaur, ca. 1730–40

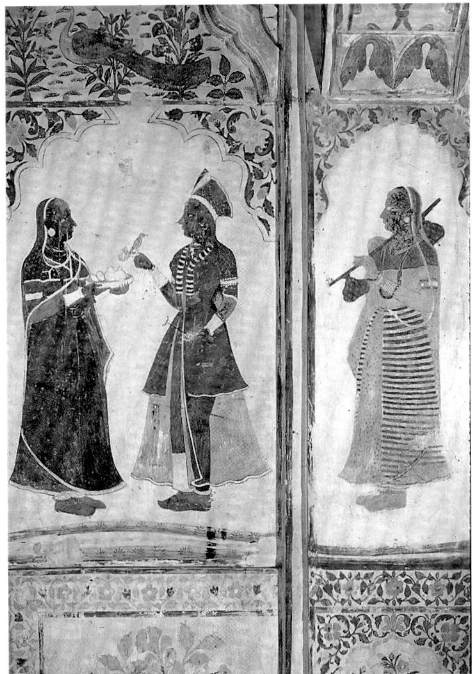

Fig. 11b Wall painting, Hadi Rani Mahal, Nagaur, ca. 1730–40

The artist of this painting, whom I call the "Nagaur Master," was influential for some time. He had a distinct, lyrical way of treating trees and birds, depicted somewhat large female figures, and used pink tones for his architectural borders. He also was responsible for cats. 12, 13, 16, and 18, painted for Bakhat Singh in the 1730s and 1740s, and his style can be seen in work done during the 1760s for Bakhat Singh's son and successor, Vijai Singh: the *Krishnalila* paintings (cats. 23–25) and a *Ram Charit* folio (cat. 26). CG

12

Maharaja Bakhat Singh Worshiping Krishna

Attributed here to the "Nagaur Master"
Nagaur, ca. 1730–35
Opaque watercolor on paper; 34 x 23 cm
Mehrangarh Museum Trust, RJS 1971

Maharajadhiraj maharaj sri bakhat singhji
Lord of king of kings, supreme king, glorious Bakhat Singhji

Dakhal dholiya re kothar hajri sam[vat] 1885 ra savan sud 12 budhvar
Entered in the *dholiya* storeroom and inventory on Wednesday, the twelfth day of the light half of Shravan (July–August), 1828

By the early eighteenth century, most Rajput Hindu courts in Rajasthan had perfected the *charbagh*, a quintessential Mughal garden form.[10] For the Rajputs, the precisely ordered garden indicated power and privilege and, by extension, association with the Mughals; it was also a way to impose order on the constantly encroaching and often uncontrollable desert. Water was a crucial element for any oasis, and we know that "in 1565–66, Khan-i-Jahan Hussain Quli Khan [Mughal Emperor Akbar's governor of Nagaur] made an addition to the fort by constructing 27 fountains and an artificial pond."[11] Today, remnants of two lotus-shaped fountains and water systems on the palace grounds are evidence of Bakhat Singh's outstanding engineering capabilities.

The Krishna temple at Nagaur was erected by Bakhat Singh over a mid-seventeenth century structure built by Amar Singh (see fig. 12a) and is still an

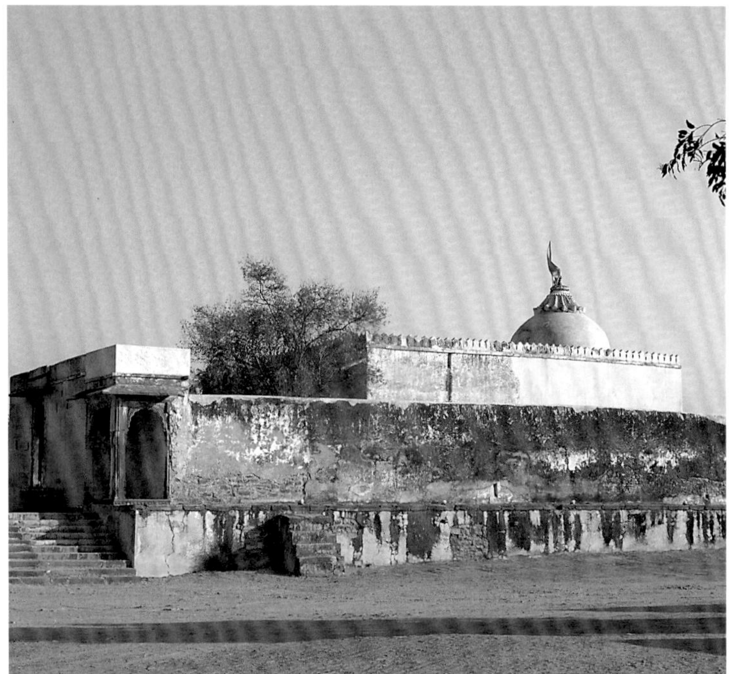

Fig. 12a Krishna Temple, Nagaur, ca. 1725–35

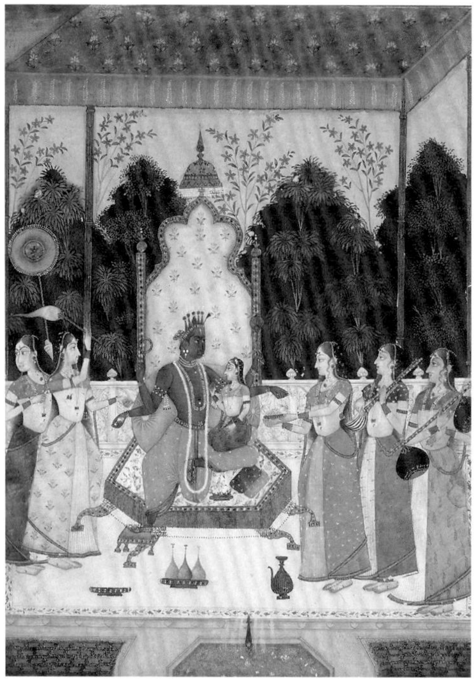

Fig. 12b Vishnu and Lakshmi, by Murad and Lupha, Bikaner, ca. 1710, Brooklyn Museum of Art, 1990.134

active religious site.[12] The temple complex has changed since this painting was completed. For example, in fig. 12a, the steps below the current wall originally led to the temple; now they are blocked by a wall. The large garden in the painting is no longer there, although its location is marked by a single tree.

Wall paintings depicting stories from the life of Krishna decorate the temple's interior rooms. One wall image of Krishna worship is similar in composition to this portable painting (cat. 12), including the multi-arched wall, carpet, canopy, and the deities being worshiped.[13] Since other Bakhat Singh paintings (cat. 13, 14, 15) are usually architecturally accurate, we can presume that the original arched wall depicted in the portable and wall paintings is correct, not the flat wall we see now. The temple's capitals and supporting beams retain the colors of the paintings.

The subject matter here and in the wall painting recalls a series of works from Bikaner, the adjacent Rathore state established in 1488 by Rao Bika, a descendant of the founder of Jodhpur, Rao Jodha. Ongoing cultural interchange between Bikaner and Jodhpur had existed for centuries; the two states were related dynasties.

In the mid-seventeenth century, Ali Reza of Delhi completed a painting of the spiritual vision of the Bikaner Raja Karan Singh (reigned 1631–74).[14] The story of Karan Singh's dream was renowned among all the Rathores. According to the legend, the Hindu god Vishnu and Lakshmi, his consort, enthroned in their celestial dwelling, visited Karan Singh in a dream. The subject became a popular one and was painted often by Bikaner court artists (fig. 12b),[15] including Ruknuddin in 1678.[16]

Unlike the Bikaner versions, cat. 12 represents not a dream but the deities themselves appearing to Bakhat Singh. Krishna and Radha are presented within a temple, perhaps the very Krishna sanctuary that existed in Nagaur during Bakhat Singh's time. While in the Bikaner versions Vishnu looks toward the viewer, in the Nagaur painting the divinities communicate directly with Bakhat Singh.

Bakhat Singh's ambition was growing, and visual identification with such mythic lore would have been a personal and political goal. In fact, in August 1733 the raja attacked Bikaner, marching with an army of fifteen thousand troops against his Rathore clansman, Maharaja Surjan Singh. Despite the fact that Abhai Singh sent additional troops from Jodhpur, Bakhat Singh suffered an embarrassing defeat and had to negotiate an unfavorable treaty.[17]

The "Nagaur Master" emphasizes Bakhat Singh's importance by depicting him larger than the nobles, musicians, dancers, and even the priests, and placing him at the center, framed by an arch. The trees and birds as well as the two tones of pink on the architectural elements are treated exactly the same as they are in cats. 11, 12, 16, and 18. In addition, the carefully and orderly painted garden and water elements in cat. 11 are related to the depiction of those same areas in cat. 12. CG

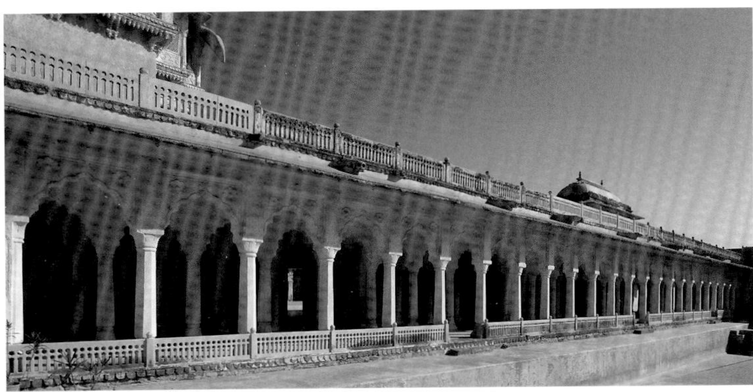

Fig. 13a Baradari, Nagaur, ca. 1725–35

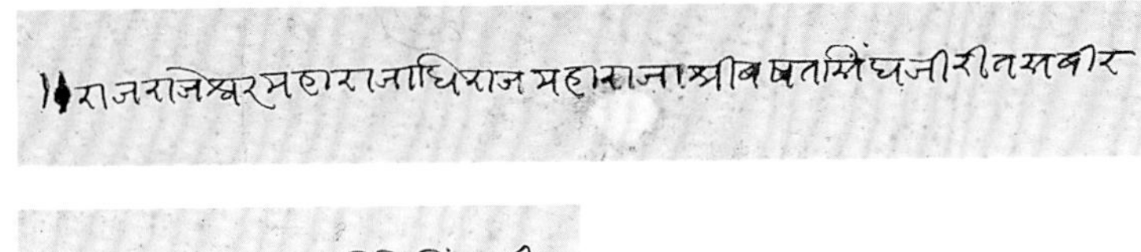

Cat. 13 Verso

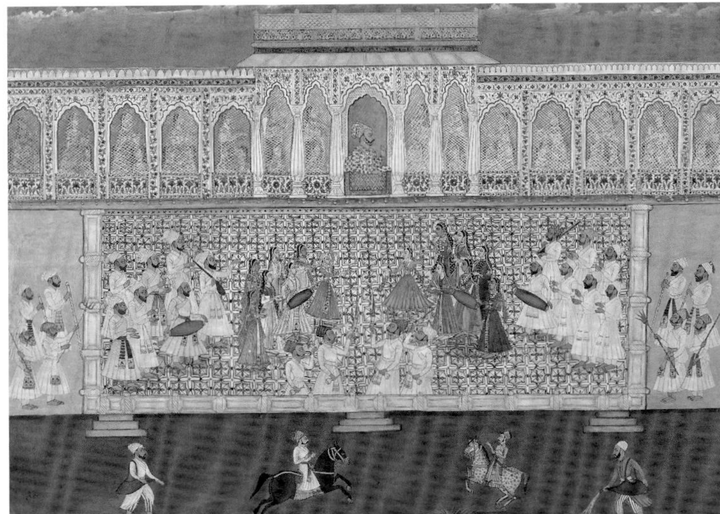

Fig. 13b Maharaja Bakhat Singh Viewing a Dance Performance, Nagaur, ca. 1736, Mehrangarh Museum Trust, RJS 2026

13

Musical Merriment for Maharaja Bakhat Singh and Prince Vijai Singh

Attributed here to the "Nagaur Master"
Nagaur, ca. 1736
Opaque watercolor and gold on paper; 43.5 x 61.3 cm
Mehrangarh Museum Trust, RJS 2028

Rajrajeshvar maharajadhiraj maharaja sri bakhat singhji ri tasbir
Painting of lord of king of kings, supreme king of great kings, supreme king, glorious Bakhat Singhji

Maharaj kanvar sri vijai singhji
Heir apparent Prince Vijai Singhji

The rhythmic pattern of partitioned gardens and a fountain pool reflect the importance of Mughal garden design. As one scholar has remarked, "codification of Mughal gardens by the time of Shah Jahan (reigned 1627–58) included walkways, garden pavilions, pools, channels of water, walls surrounding the gardens with towers at the corners, and waterfalls."[18] The expansive garden depicted in the painting, with its carefully tended plantings and pool, played a significant role in the life of the Nagaur palace; it is also featured in wall paintings decorating the Hadi Rani Mahal.

Cat. 13, along with a Hadi Rani Mahal wall painting and a photograph of the Nagaur palace today (fig. 13a), all feature the same cusped bracket arches and the juxtaposition of open, partially open, and enclosed spaces. The same recurring placement of the arches in the large *baradari* (hall) on the north side of the central courtyard in fig. 13a can be seen in the arches in the upper area of cat. 13. These *baradari* arches once were fashioned with *jali* (protective screens) similar to the pink ones in the painting, each displaying a different design.

The painter of cat. 13 is also the "Nagaur Master" (see cats. 11, 12, 16, and 18). The wispy trees and garden treatment are very similar to those in cats. 12 and 16, and the golden pattern on the orange textile sheltering Bakhat Singh is identical to those used on the canopies in cat. 11. Here, though, there are no signature birds inhabiting his customary trees, and the women's heads are slightly smaller, with pushed-in faces and sloped foreheads.

A Nagaur painting by different artists, but with a similar subject, depicts Bakhat Singh and the women of the zenana watching dancers and musicians, this time both male and female, performing on an open terrace (fig. 13b).[19] This work probably was produced by two different painters: the artist of the upper portion was very interested in architectural detail, used a pastel palette, and painted women with large heads. The lower third of the painting was done by a less-accomplished artist, who favored darker colors, such as the solid block of hunter green, and smaller, simply drawn figures.[20] CG

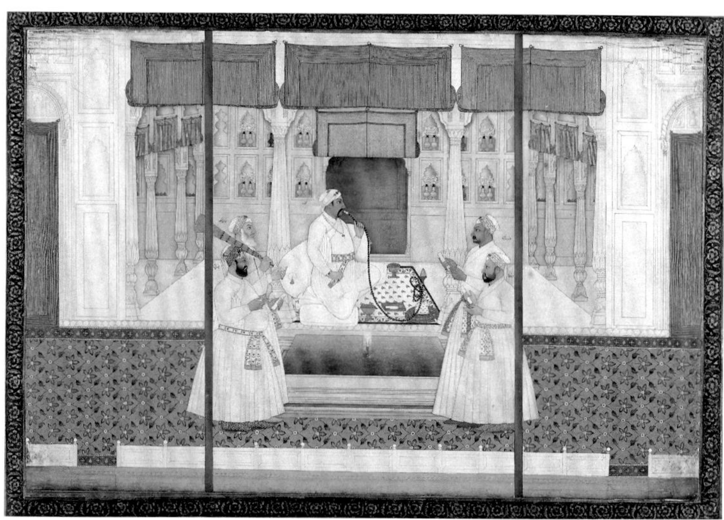

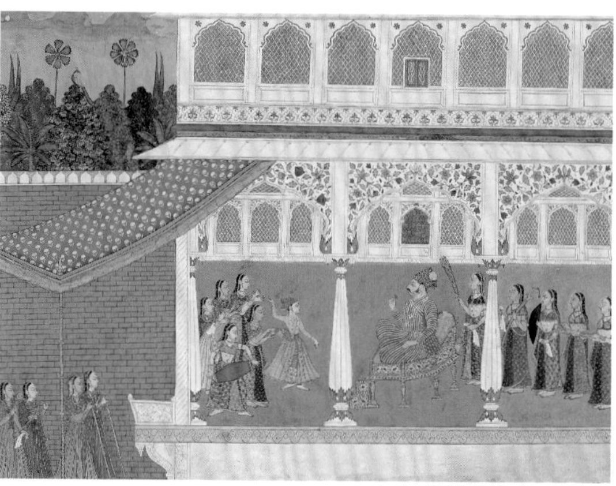

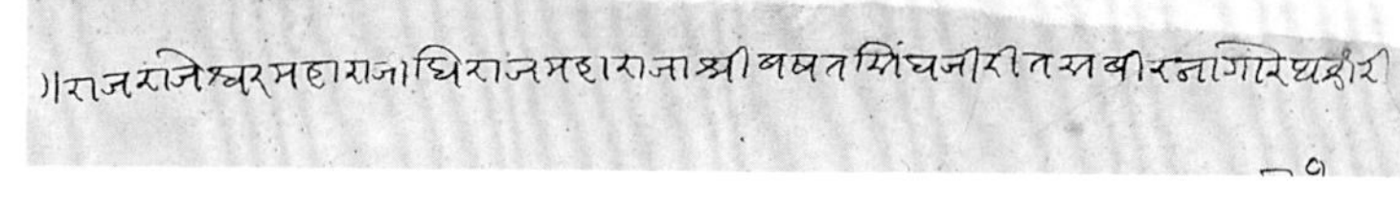

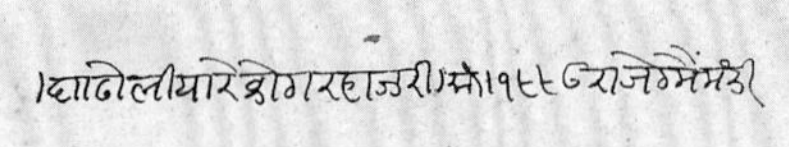

Fig. 14a The Emperor Muhammad Shah with Courtiers, India, ca. 1730–40, Bodleian Library, Ms. Douce Or. a. 3, f. 14r

Cat. 14 Detail (above) and verso (below)

14

Maharaja Bakhat Singh Watches a Dance Performance at the Bakhat Singh Mahal

Attributed here to "Artist 2"
Nagaur, ca. 1737
Opaque watercolor on paper; 44.5 x 63.8 cm
Mehrangarh Museum Trust, RJS 2610

[numbered] 31
Rajrajeshvar maharajadhiraj maharaja sri bakhat singhji ri tasbir nagare thaka ri
Painting of lord of king of kings, supreme king of great kings, great king, glorious Bakhat Singhji when in Nagaur

Da[khal] dholiya re kothar hajri sam[vat] 1887 ra jeth main mandi
Entered in the *dholiya* storeroom and inventory in Jeth (May–June), 1830, 31

The inscription on the reverse describes this work as a portrait of Bakhat Singh "when in Nagaur." Cat. 15 helps identify the location of this dance scene. The two paintings are companion pieces; they depict the same building, the Bakhat Singh Mahal (built by the raja during the first decade of his reign at Nagaur, 1725–35), viewed from different angles.[21] While cat. 15 shows the front (or north side) of the mahal, this work presents the east façade of the verandah before the addition of a later building with a viewing balcony. When the two paintings are placed next to each other, the garden walls and vegetation make a continual line. In addition, both have walls of pink-colored brick, identical second-story cusped arches with the same open-flower design in the corners, a red wooden

window decorated with gold sprigs in one of the *jali* screens, and pillars decorated at top and base with green acanthus leaves. The marble platform projecting from the left side of the base in cat. 14 is the same *jharokha* dais in cat. 15 and is also in Nagaur today (see fig. 15b, and fig. 5, p. 19).

Cat. 15 is dated 1737, and this work likely was completed around the same time and by the same artist, who I will call "Artist 2."[22] The treatment of the trees, unified palette, architectural details, and, perhaps most important, the proportions of the figures all point to the same hand.

Precedents for the composition of this painting and others in the Bakhat Singh group (cats. 17, 19) are found in Mughal images of the Muhammad Shah period (1719–48). The similarities to fig. 14a, a Mughal painting completed around 1730, include floral decoration of the pillars, the white color that dominates the painted surface, and the careful attention to the rendering of textile patterns. CG

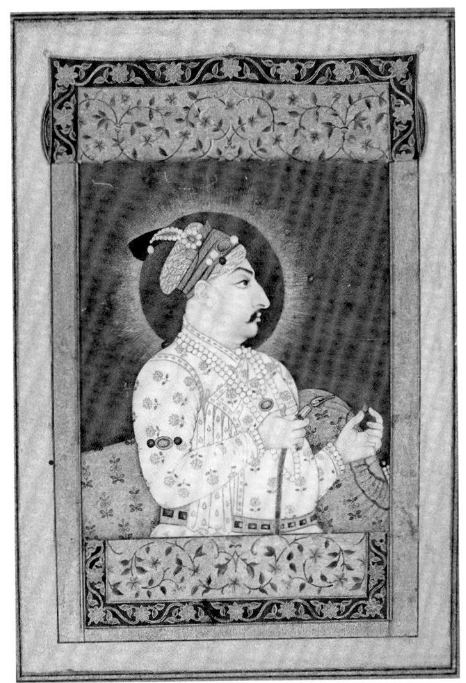

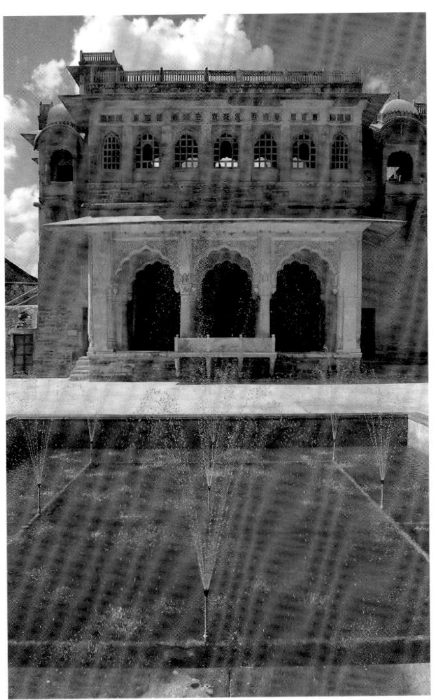

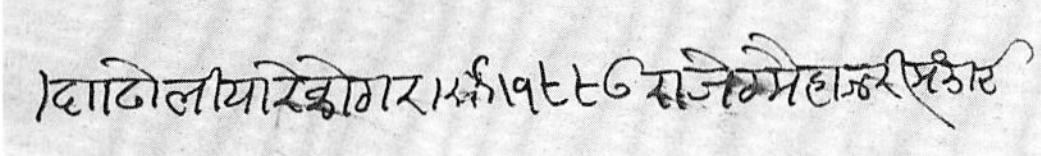

Fig. 15a Emperor Muhammad Shah at a Window, by Nidha Mal, ca. 1730, San Diego Museum of Art, 1990:376

Fig. 15b Bakhat Singh Mahal, Nagaur, ca. 1725–35

Cat. 15 Verso

15

Maharaja Bakhat Singh at the Jharokha Window of the Bakhat Singh Mahal

Attributed here to "Artist 2"
Nagaur, 1737 (Samvat 1794);
Opaque watercolor on paper; 62.9 x 43.8 cm
Mehrangarh Museum Trust, RJS 2031

[numbered] 30
Sri rajadhiraj sri bakhat singhji ri sabi rajmaihal mai birajiyan ri sammat 1794 jeth
Portrait of the glorious, king of great kings, glorious Bakhat Singhji seated
in the royal palace In Jeth (May–June), 1737

Da[khal] dholiya re kothar sam[vat]) 1887 ra jeth mai hajri mandai
Entered in the inventory and placed in the *dholiya* storeroom in Jeth
(May–June), 1830, 30

This painting shows that there was a clear relationship between imperial paintings
produced under the patronage of Mughal Emperor Muhammad Shah (reigned
1719–48) and paintings commissioned by Bakhat Singh at Nagaur. In both
cat. 15 and fig. 15a, Bakhat Singh and Muhammad Shah are surrounded by
sumptuous textiles—in their personal attire and in the window drapery.[23] Fig. 1
depicts Muhammad Shah at a *jharokha* window in his middle years, circa 1730.[24]
Portraits of Bakhat Singh place him within a semi-circular opening that provides
an interesting parallel to the halo symbol given to Muhammad Shah.[25] (See cats.
9, 14, 17, and fig. 13b on p. 267.)

Cat. 15 and fig. 15b both feature the north façade of the Bakhat Singh Mahal.
While the painting seems to depict a three-story building, the photograph demonstrates that the actual building has two stories. In the painting the artist has
expanded the mezzanine floor to convey the depth between the outside veranda
pillars and the interior *jharokha* window, thereby providing a higher level on which
the raja could sit, similar to the raised elevation of Mughal rulers in their *darbars*.[26]
In both the painting and the photograph, the upper story has seven arched
openings and the lower story has three larger ones.

The decorative treatment of the pillar capitals in the painting almost matches
that of the pillars on the actual building, though the bases are slightly different. In
both, the acanthus leaf decoration dominates the white stucco. The artist's interest
in factual accuracy extended to the inclusion of the marble viewing platform at the
base of the veranda, which is still in place at Nagaur (fig. 15b and fig. 5, p. 19). CG

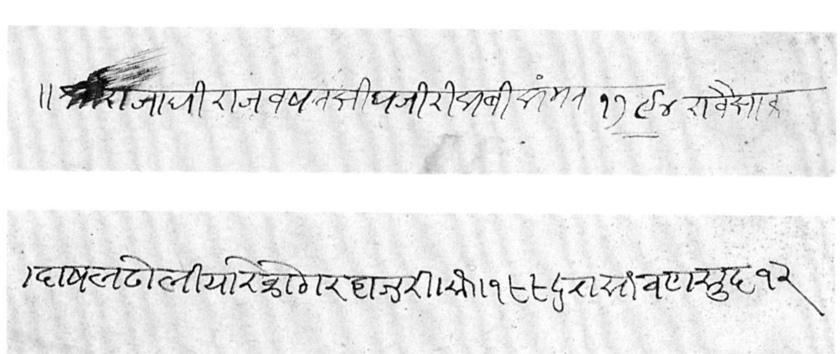

Cat. 16 Verso

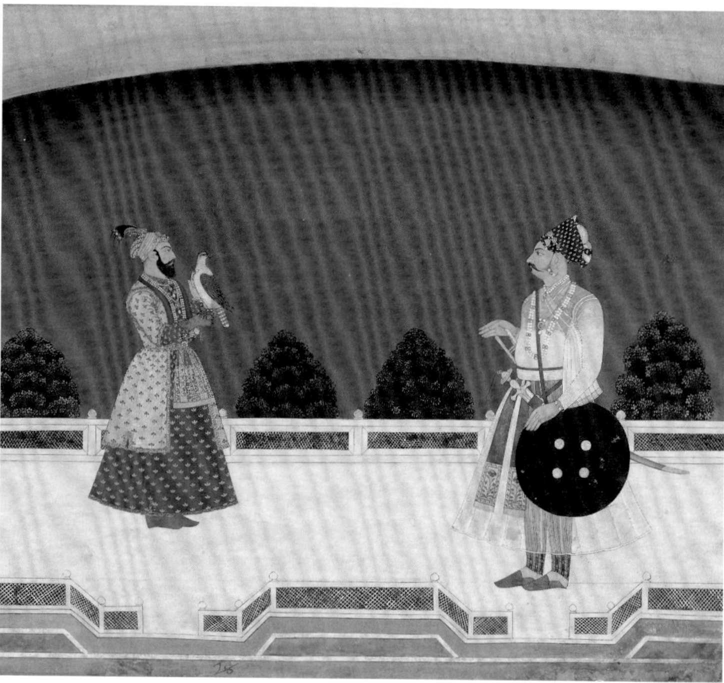

Fig. 16a Nawab Sher-i Jang before Maharaja Bakhat Singh, Jodhpur, ca. 1635–40, Mehrangarh Museum Trust, RJS 4230

16

Maharaja Bakhat Singh Delights in an Outdoor Musical Performance

Attributed here to the "Nagaur Master"
Nagaur, 1737 (Samvat 1794)
Opaque watercolor and gold on paper; 52.1 x 42.5 cm (image)
Mehrangarh Museum Trust, RJS 1991

Sri rajadhiraj vakhat singhji ri sabi sammat 1794 ra vaisak
Portrait of glorious, king of great kings Bakhat Singhji;
the month of Vaishakah (April–May), 1737

Dakhal dholiya re kothar hajri sam(vat) 1885 ra savan sud 12
Entered in the *dholiya* storeroom and inventory in Shravan (July–August), 1828

This painting, like cat. 15, is dated by inscription to 1737, the twelfth year of Bakhat Singh's reign. While the faces in both paintings show a man of about the same age with a two-day beard, the beginnings of a jowly chin, a high forehead, and hooded eyes, the manner in which they are painted suggests that two different artists are at work. In cat. 15, Bakhat Singh is painted with less intensity than he is in this work in which the figure has a solid presence. The colors of the face have been applied in a thin, delicate manner in cat. 15, while here the paint is thicker and the hue more intense. The artist of cat. 15 has relied heavily on white to unify the painting around the figure of the raja, while this artist has used the rounded hill to frame the raja's head and the one-point perspective of the trees to emphasize Bakhat Singh's central position. The

surface has been highly burnished, producing a lustrous finish.

With its fine technique; glossy, elegant finish; and recognizable compositional elements, this painting is very much like the work of the celebrated artist Dalchand, who worked in Jodhpur for Bakhat Singh's brother, Abhai Singh, during the 1720s.[27] Dalchand arrived there around 1724, the year that Abhai Singh returned from Delhi to assume the Jodhpur throne. In 1727, a decade before this work was produced, Dalchand painted a portrait of Abhai Singh.[28] Whether the artist visited Nagaur while he was in Jodhpur is unknown.[29] It is likely that Bakhat Singh was well aware of Dalchand because he visited Jodhpur while the artist was in residence there, circa 1724–27. It was around this time that the raja launched his Nagaur building projects, including the Hadi Rani Mahal and its wall paintings. While in Jodhpur, Dalchand may have taught his meticulously detailed and dramatic style to one or more of the artists who eventually moved to Nagaur to work for Bakhat Singh.[30]

This painting, more than any other, reflects Dalchand's influence and aesthetic in both painterly style and composition. The main figure is framed by a rounded hill, and the treatment of the sky is similar to the sky in Dalchand's dramatic equestrian portrait of Abhai Singh, circa 1725.[31] In cat. 16 and the equestrian portrait, the artist pays careful attention to the colorful textiles and the sophisticated combination of different textile patterns. In addition, the face of the figure holding the royal fan in the equestrian painting is remarkably similar in execution to that of Bakhat Singh in cat. 16, particularly the eyes and sideburns.

Whether he was Dalchand or a highly proficient and well-trained student, the painter I call the "Nagaur Master" worked in the royal ateliers for some time. The hand responsible for the colorful trees populated with cranes in this painting also produced the cranes and trees in cats. 11, 12, and 18 as well as artworks for Vijai Singh during the 1760s: the *Krishnalila* paintings (cats. 23–25) and a page from

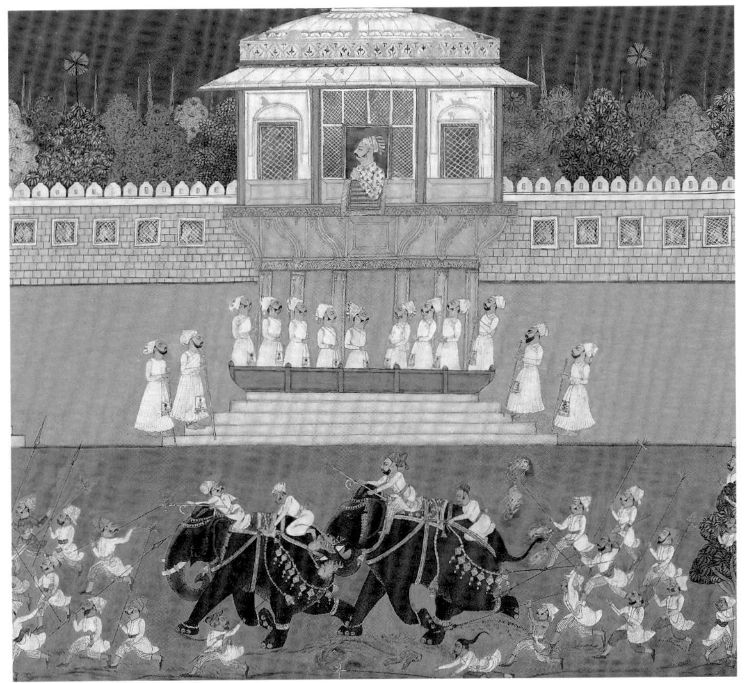

Cat. 17 Detail

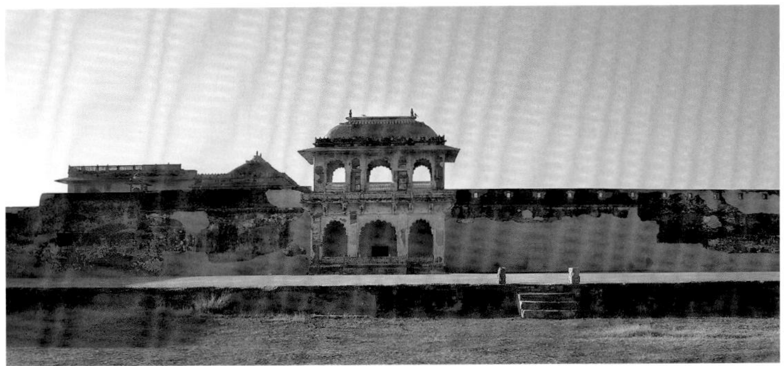

Fig. 17a Jharoka pavilion in the Diwani-l Am, Nagaur, ca. 1730–40.

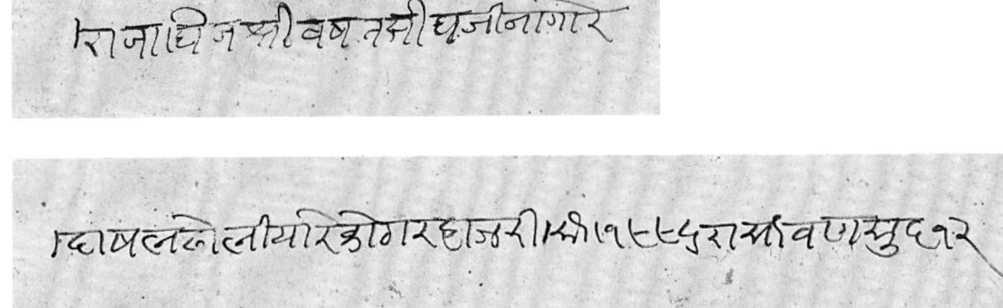

Cat. 17 Verso

the *Ramayana* (cat. 26). It was not unusual for a court painter's career to last thirty or forty years.

An intriguing painting, completed around the same time as cat. 16 but by a very different artist, depicts Bakhat Singh standing on a white terrace, offering his hand to a second figure holding a hawk (fig. 16a).[32] This work was painted by an artist from Jodhpur because it differs from other Bakhat Singh paintings done in the Nagaur style.[33] It is painted not in pastel colors but more intense hues, and lacks the emphasis on textile detail seen in the Nagaur works. Vegetation, in all of its variety and splendor, an important aspect of the Nagaur paintings, serves the more traditional role of background element in fig. 16a, which features stolid, recurring, almost identical trees. CG

17

Maharaja Bakhat Singh Watches Elephants Wreaking Havoc

Nagaur, ca. 1740
Opaque watercolor on paper; 45.1 x 64.1 cm
Mehrangarh Museum Trust, RJS 2032

Rajadhi[ra]j sri bakhat singhji nagare
King of great kings, glorious Bakhat Singhji of Nagaur

Dakhal dholiya re kothar hajri sam[vat] 1885 ra savan sud 12
Entered in the *dholiya* storeroom and inventory on the twelfth day
of the light half of Shravan (July–August), 1828

Specific geographic references and architectural verity play an integral part in the composition of this work, as they do in many of the Nagaur paintings. Because of their faithfulness to architectural detail, the Bakhat Singh Nagaur paintings also offer clues to structural elements that no longer exist. This painting accurately depicts the *jharokha* pavilion in the Diwan-i-Am; it also shows the now missing crenellations at the top of the wall. Below the crenellations, the windows of the zenana are clearly still in place. A large *charbagh* once flourished in the main courtyard behind the wall; the painting shows the tops of mature trees, including palms, cypress, and mango, in full bloom after the monsoon rains, conveying the fecundity of an abundant garden.[34]

A Muhammad Shah-period painting from around the same time relates closely in structure to cat. 17.[35] The compositional similarities between the imperial work and the Nagaur painting are striking. Both incorporate real-world subject matter

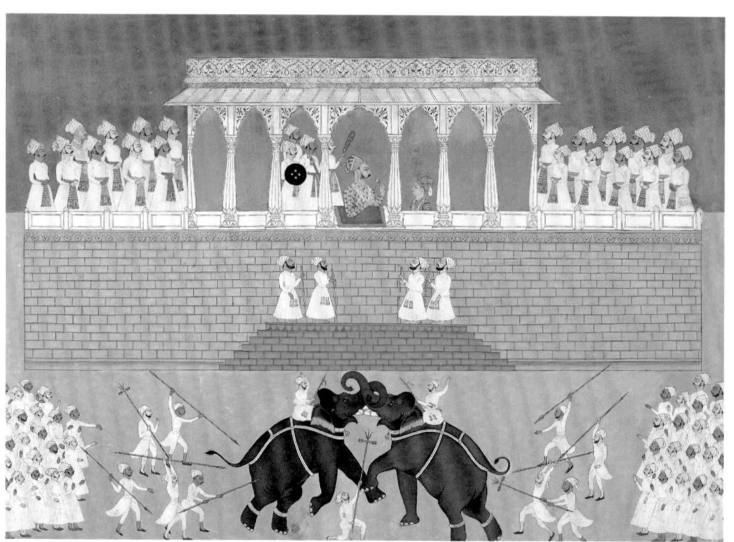

Fig. 17b Maharaja Bakhat Singh and Prince Vijai Singh Watch an Elephant Fight, Nagaur, ca. 1735, Mehrangarh Museum Trust, RJS 1992

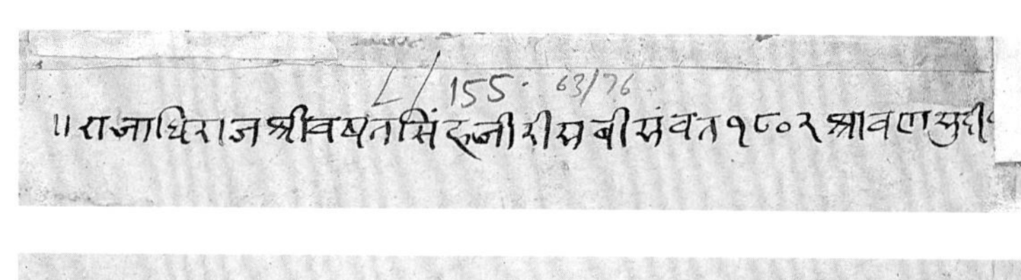

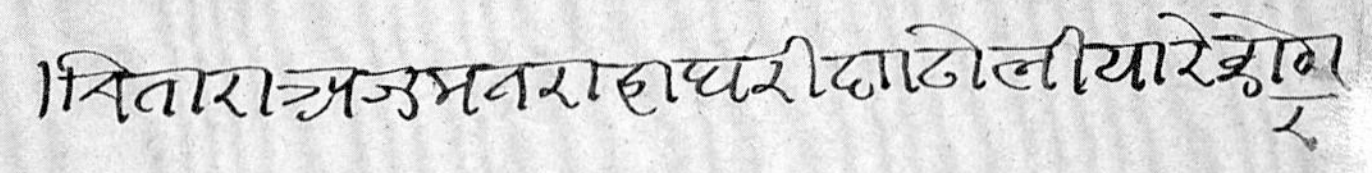

Fig. 18a Portrait of Bakhat Singh, verso, 1745. Mehrangarh Museum Trust, RJS 4813

and have a basic tripartite structure: a panel of trees and wall, a garden, and the lower register in which the main action occurs.

Another elephant painting (fig. 17b), one of the Bakhat Singh portable paintings, shows the raja's son, Vijai Singh (born 1729), accompanying him in the viewing pavilion.[36] Given that Vijay Singh appears to be about six years old—slightly younger than he is in cat. 13—fig. 17b can be dated to approximately 1735. If we compare Bakhat Singh's image in fig. 17b with the two paintings dated 1737 (cats. 15 and 16), we see that all three paintings are close chronologically.

The parade ground in fig. 17b resembles the Diwan-i-Am of cat. 17, but is farther from the private palace, although still within the fort's outer wall. The elevated arches of the viewing pavilion still exist, providing an optimum view of the parade ground and, in Bakhat Singh's time, protection from the sometimes dangerous entertainment below.

The display of wealth, royal power, and prerogative was intended to illustrate Bakhat Singh's growing military might. If my dating (circa 1740) for cat. 17 is correct, the painting was completed around the time of the seminal battle between Nagaur and Jaipur on May 28, 1741, at Gangwana, an expanse eleven miles northeast of Pushkar. Greatly outnumbered, the Rathore troops under Bakhat Singh's charge struck those of Sawai Jai Singh of Jaipur with such force and purpose that "like tigers upon a flock of sheep the battle lasted four hours before the Jaipur army fled."[37] In cats. 10–20, male-dominated activities—such as battles, hunts, *darbars*, and equestrian portraits—are extremely rare. Cats. 12 and 17 and fig. 17b are the only ones of the thirteen known Bakhat Singh portable paintings in which women are absent and the subject matter conforms to the male-dominated warrior compositions of innumerable other Rajput court artists. Perhaps this balance will change when, and if, additional Bakhat Singh portable paintings are discovered. CG

18

Maharaja Bakhat Singh Revels in a Pleasure Boat Ride

Attributed here to the "Nagaur Master"
Nagaur, ca. 1745–48
Opaque watercolor on paper; 43.2 x 61 cm (image)
Mehrangarh Museum Trust, RJS 2030

Rajadhiraj sri vakhat singhji
King of great kings, glorious Bakhat Singhji

Dakhal dholiya re kothar hajri sam[vat] 1885 ra savan sud 12
Entered in the *dholiya* storeroom and inventory on the twelfth day
of the light half of Shravan (July–August), 1828

This painting conveys the close relationship between the portable Bakhat Singh paintings and the wall paintings in the Krishna temple and the Hadi Rani Mahal at Nagaur (see cat. 11). For example, the women in the center of the pavilion closely resemble a pair in a mural at the Hadi Rani Mahal (see fig. 18b).

A potential inspiration for this painting may be the pavilions at the Ana Sagar Lake in Ajmer. Mughal Emperor Shah Jahan turned the lake into a splendid retreat, part of a large palace complex, finished in 1636. Surviving are four white marble pavilions that decorate the embankment.[38] Bakhat Singh would have been familiar with these lustrous ivory-colored structures since he traveled through Ajmer—the gateway from Nagaur to Delhi—a number of times. In July 1734, for example, he attended a conference at Hurda, just outside of Ajmer, where he met with the rulers of Jaipur and Mewar to forge an allegiance against the Marathas.[39]

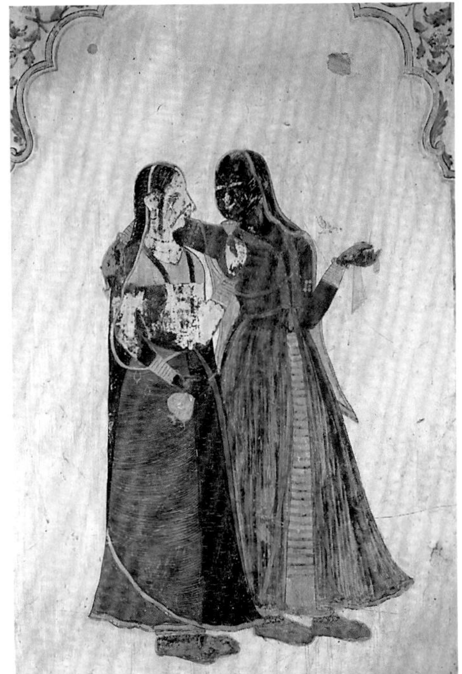

Fig. 18b Wall painting, Hadi Rani Mahal, Nagaur, ca. 1730–40

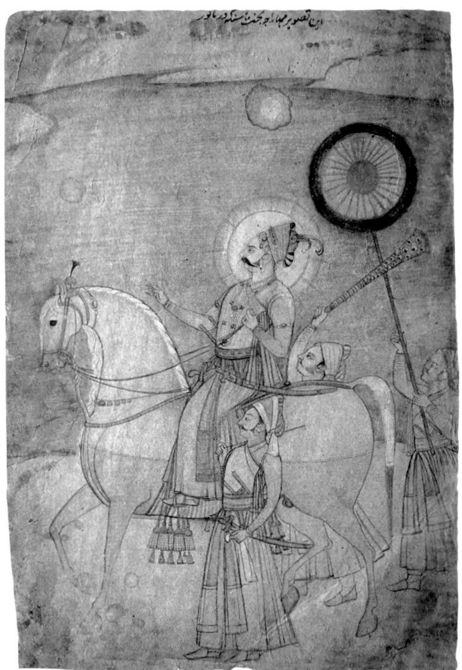

Fig. 18c Bakhat Singh Entering Nagaur, attributed here partially to Dalchand, Kishangarh, ca. 1745, Sven Gahlin collection

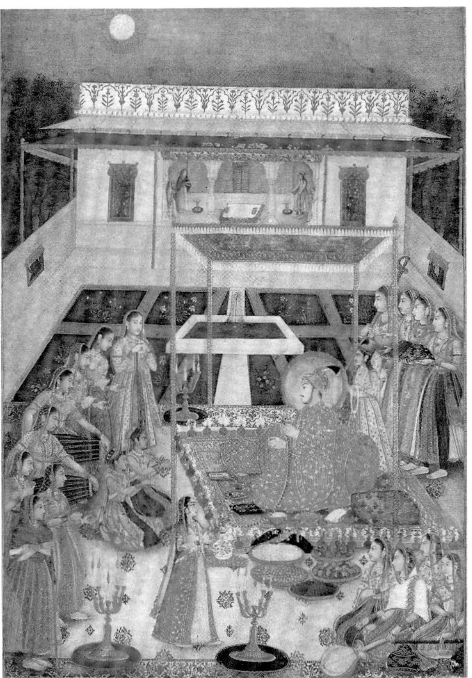

Fig. 19a Emperor Muhammad Shah on a Terrace at Night, Mughal dynasty, ca. 1720–25, Kasturbhai Lalbhai Collection, Ahmedabad

In all of the Nagaur portable paintings, Bakhat Singh establishes his supremacy through his position in the center or as the largest figure within the group. He orders the activities—dances, musical performances, water sports, and events with elephants—to begin. He is the active force; "thus on a purely representational level, the peripheries of these paintings were female, cooperative and physically identical, while their focal points were male, active and individualized."[40]

The "Nagaur Master" has accentuated the excitement of the scene below by populating the upper portion with abundant foliage, enlivened by cranes cavorting in the trees. The same ornamentation occurs in cats. 11–13, 16, 23–26.

A Jodhpur-style portrait of Bakhat Singh (see detail, p. 299, bottom, second from right) standing against a black hill fringed with a ridge of trees is dated 1745 on the verso (fig. 18a).[41] In both that portrait and cat. 18, Bakhat Singh's eyelids convey a weariness not apparent in other paintings, suggesting a date of 1745–48 for the latter work as well. Based on the facial features, the same date is likely for a drawing of an equestrian Bakhat Singh (fig. 18b).[42] While the horse and figure of the ruler are by an accomplished hand, the other figures were produced more quickly—perhaps because they were less important or because they were by a different artist altogether.

The drawing is in the Kishangarh style, which uses the *nim qalim* (colored drawing) technique; the horse, with its attenuated neck, is typical of this atelier. The horse and ruler are similar to an equestrian portrait of Abhai Singh painted by Dalchand about twenty years earlier.[43] In the late 1720s, some time after he left Jodhpur—and perhaps met Bakhat Singh—Dalchand went to Kishangarh, where his cousin, Kalayan Das, was working and his father, Bhawani Das, headed the painting studio until at least 1748.[44] This drawing might have been inspired by Dalchand's memories of an earlier time. CG

19

Maharaja Bakhat Singh and Zenana Women Savor the Moonlight Evening

Attributed here to Artist 3
Nagaur, ca. 1748–50
Opaque watercolor on paper; 45.4 x 63.5 cm
Mehrangarh Museum Trust, RJS 1987

Rajrajeshvar maharajadhiraj maharaja sri bakhat singhji ri tasbir
Painting of lord of king of kings, supreme king of great kings, supreme king, glorious Bakhat Singhji

Dakhal dholiya re kothar hajri sam[vat] 1885 ra savana sud 12 mandi
Entered in the *dholiya* storeroom and inventory in Shravan (July–August), 1828

The white clothes of the celebrants indicate that the festivities may be taking place during the Hindu festival of Sharad Purnima, when devotees dress in the color of the moon.[45] Moonlight and its attendant atmosphere create a sense of mystery and heightened emotions, perfectly capturing the raja's more personal moments with the women of the zenana. Terrace scenes of intimacy and seemingly private palace life appear periodically in Mughal paintings, beginning more than a hundred years before this Bakhat Singh painting (see fig. 1, p. 12).[46] The earlier Mughal examples are subtle in their sexual context, more intimate and refined. During Muhammad Shah's reign, which roughly coincided with Bakhat Singh's rule at Nagaur, moonlight scenes became quite popular in Mughal court painting (fig. 19a) and perhaps those works recalled the moonlight celebrated in Sharad Purnima.[47]

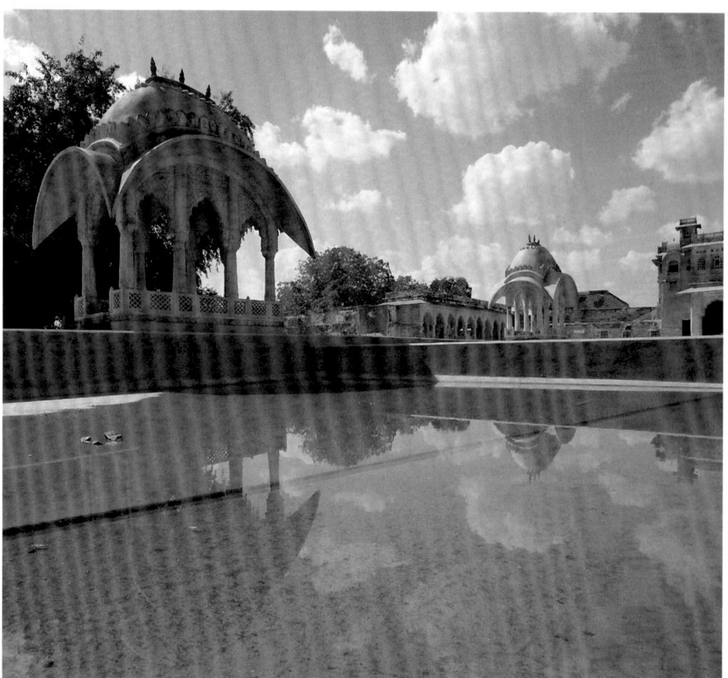

Fig. 20a Central courtyard and tank, Nagaur, ca. 1725–35

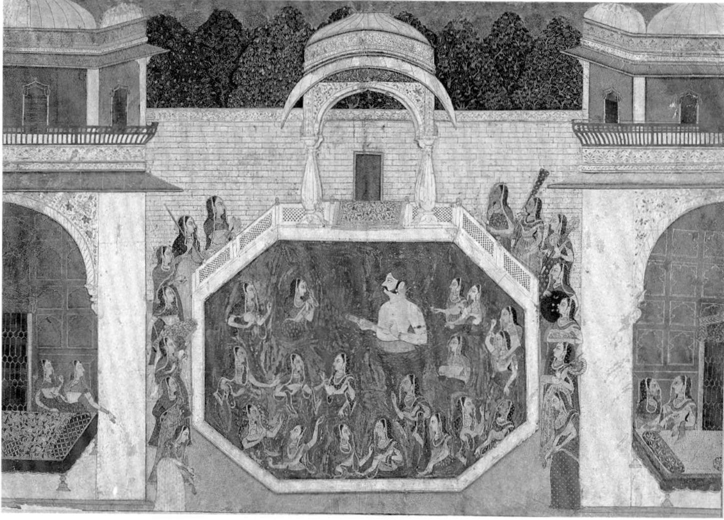

Fig. 20b Raja Vijai Singh Celebrates Holi at Nagaur, Jodhpur,
ca. 1760–70, Collection Howard Hodgkin

Bakhat Singh made numerous visits to the Mughal court, where he would
have seen and gained an appreciation for Muhammad Shah's paintings, including
moonlit love scenes,[48] an admiration he is likely to have shared, either verbally
or visually, with his own artists in Nagaur. A Mughal painting from about thirty
years earlier (fig. 19a) incorporates many of the same elements found in cat. 19.
The sexual connotations in these eighteenth-century paintings are much clearer,
the scenes more intimate, than they are in seventeenth-century works.

Cat. 19 can be dated to the late 1740s based on two other portraits of
Bakhat Singh: see detail, p. 299, bottom, second from right, dated 1745, and a
large double portrait of Bakhat Singh and his brother. The latter was painted by
a Jodhpur artist, most likely before the June 21, 1749, death of Abhai Singh.[49]
The double portrait previously has been dated circa 1751,[50] the year of Bakhat
Singh's accession to the Marwar throne, suggesting that he was the patron.
However, this author places the Mehrangarh work slightly earlier, circa 1748–50,
based on Bakhat Singh's younger facial features and the contrasting dress of
the two rulers. Abhai Singh wears a lavish gold turban and matching saffron-
colored top and skirt; he hands a flower garland to his younger brother. Bakhat
Singh is dressed less luxuriously, making it more likely that Abhai Singh was the
patron of the grand double portrait. Neither brother has a halo, often a sign of
hierarchy, but Abhai Singh's apparel is much finer and his gift is the gesture of a
ruler. Had Bakhat Singh commissioned this impressive work after he ascended
the throne in 1751, there likely would have been more equality in the dress of
the two men, and Bakhat Singh would have looked much older than he does
in the 1745 painting. CG

20

Maharaja Bakhat Singh Rejoices during Holi

Attributed here to "Artist 3"
Nagaur, ca. 1748–50
Opaque watercolor on paper; 44.1 x 65.1 cm
Mehrangarh Museum Trust, RJS 1986

Rajrajeshvar maharajadhiraj maharaja sri vakhat singhji ri tasbir
Painting of lord of king of kings, supreme king, glorious Bakhat Singhji

Da[khal] dholiya re kothar hajri sam[vat] 1885 ra savan sud 12
Entered in the *dholiya* storeroom and inventory in the month
of Shravan (July–August), 1828

Photographs of the central tank at Nagaur depict a rectangular pool with a *bangla*
(curved) pavilion on the long side (fig. 20a). The tank is flanked by two palaces
built by Bakhat Singh. The Abha Mahal is on the west side and the Bakhat Singh
Mahal is on the east (visible on the right side of fig. 20a). This is the same con-
figuration of buildings shown in the *Holi* painting. I propose that this central
courtyard is the location of cats. 20 and fig. 20b, although the pool now has a
rectangular shape. A significant number of Nagaur paintings completed between
1737 and 1760 include a large octagonal pool; see, for example, cat. 18. Nagaur
has seen many renovations in the more than two hundred fifty years since this
painting was produced; at some point, the shape of the pool must have changed
as well.[51]

A companion painting (fig. 20b) is in the collection of Howard Hodgkin.[52] We now can state that this striking painting was completed a generation after cat. 20; the male figure is Bakhat Singh's son, Maharaja Vijai Singh of Marwar (reigned 1752–92). While the two works are similar in composition, particularly the architectural elements, there are also enough differences to suggest the later date.[53] The facial features, notably the moustache and sideburns, and the turban style indicate that this work was painted a generation later than scholars previously thought.

Even the earliest images of Bakhat Singh (e.g., cats. 10 and 11) show an opening between the moustache and the sideburns; this was a fashion he borrowed from his father, Ajit Singh, and maintained throughout his life.[54] Images of Vijai Singh (see figs. 2 and 3, p. 23), however, show that he groomed his moustache to grow into his sideburns.[55] All of the known images of Vijai Singh depict him in this fashion (see figs. 20b and fig. 9a, p. 263).[56]

Fig. 20b features a higher horizon, only one type of flowering tree, strong white walls without decoration on the side buildings, no clouds, no pots of *Holi* water, and no funnels. Though the composition is beautifully balanced and architecture is emphasized, the painting lacks some of the elements found in cat. 20. CG

Gardens for Divine Play

21

Embroidered Canopy

Gujarat or north India, first quarter of the 18th century
Cotton; 364 x 352 cm (central rectangular panel),
364 x 112 cm (triangular side panels)
Mehrangarh Museum Trust, Jodhpur, TNT 37/76

Media

Base Fabric

Medium weight, plain weave cotton, white, quilted
Warp: cotton, single Z-spun, white
Weft: cotton, single Z-pun, white

Original Backing

A wide border of a satin weave, silk-warp/cotton-weft mashru fabric, patchworked
into a classic Mughal chevron pattern; the border encloses a field of a second
mashru fabric, deep reddish-pink, plain; both fabrics probably date from the
18th century

Modern Backing

Medium weight, plain weave cotton, mill-made, deep pink; medium weight,
plain weave cotton, striped pale orange and flesh pink

Frill

Thin plain-weave silk, pale yellow

Embroidery

Floss silk, twistless, multiple colors, worked in a chain stitch; metal thread, gilt
foil S-wrapped sparsely over core of pale yellow silk (metal-woven Mughal and
late Mughal velvets, sashes, and fabrics from Gujarat feature high-quality metal
threads with foil wrapped in the Z-direction over a silk core)

Tie Cords

Twisted bundles of thick cotton cord, individual cords dyed
in different colors, 18th century

The style and quality of the chain-stitch embroidery are of a type practiced by
the professional Mochi embroiderers of Kutch in Gujarat. Cobblers and leather-
workers by tradition, the Mochi are believed to have once exclusively embroidered
leather furnishings such as floormats and saddle covers, an art they trace to
neighboring Sindh, and later applied their skills to sturdy local fabrics of cotton
and silk. Their work was distinguished by an evenly laid chain stitch worked in
colored floss silks or metal thread with a hooked awl (*ari*), a smaller version of a
cobbler's awl and similar to a tambour or crochet hook. The fine point of the Mochi
awl permitted much finer work than was obtained with the tambour hook used
in Europe and west Asia. Embroiderers guided the *ari* using a tambour thimble

with a notch cut in the top. The embroidery generally was worked on fabrics of
plain cotton or satin-weave silk or mixed silk and cotton, which were stretched on
a frame. As remarkable as the quality and evenness of the stitch was its carefully
controlled directionality. Subtly varying the vertical, horizontal, and diagonal placement of the silk stitches allowed the Indian embroiderer to evoke a multitude of
hues from the play of light on a palette that rarely exceeded two shades of crimson,
two of blue-green, and perhaps a white, yellow, or purple.

Gujarat's chain-stitch quilts, coverlets, and bed hangings became, in the
seventeenth and eighteenth centuries, one of India's best-known exports to Europe.
During this period, European markets also imported dye-painted chintz furnishings
from the Coromandel coast of south India. Indian craftsmen from both regions
were at the peak of their technical mastery and creative power. Often, the dye-
painted and embroidered versions were so similar that English patrons sometimes
referred to the latter as "worked chintz," and included both types in a coordinated
set of room furnishings that comprised wall hangings, bed curtains with valances
and coverlets, chair and cushion covers, and small carpets for placing around the
bed. European merchants and agents ensured that Indian embroiderers and dye
painters adapted their designs to suit prevalent English, French, or Dutch taste.

At the same time, in both Gujarat and on the Coromandel coast, there was
an extensive parallel production of tent panels, canopies, hangings, and floor
spreads, which were supplied to Mughal and regional Indian courts. Once again,
design and pattern for these dye-painted and embroidered local furnishings
crossed from one genre to the other. The Jodhpur tents reveal that two entirely
different styles of pattern on textiles were produced at the same workshop. While
the canopy presented here recalls the boldness and vigor of decorative designs
from the Sultanate Deccan, most of the other related tents in the Mehrangarh
collection are decorated with the more refined and naturalistic floral forms of
high Mughal design dominant in northern India. It is likely that the two styles
were produced for two different clients in two different regions but in this case
found their way to the same court.

Little is known of the precise location and organization of the professional
Gujarati workshops that produced these embroidered tents. European travelers,
however, mentioned Cambay in Kutch as the source of the finest qualities of
chain-stitch work during the Mughal period. Another Gujarati urban center that
was a likely site for professional embroidery workshops at that time is Patan,
mentioned in the records of the East India Company.[1] More generally, the presence of well-known textile manufactories at Ahmedabad and Surat suggests
that elaborate embroideries were produced there as well. The imperial Mughal
karkhana (workshop) at Ahmedabad, for instance, was renowned for its exclusive
embroidered velvets and furnishings, although we cannot be certain if it sustained
a lineage of traditional masters from the Mochi community. Whether this canopy
or the other tent panels in the Mehrangarh collection were produced at a Gujarati
center or at court workshops further north is less clear. As yet, little is known of the
extent to which the art of Mochi embroidery spread to centers beyond Gujarat in the
late medieval period. It is reasonable to presume that dedicated court workshops
in the imperial cities of Agra, Lahore, and Delhi and, later, in other provincial capitals,
would have offered the highest levels of patronage to the craft.

There is little evidence about when and how this group of embroidered
tents reached Jodhpur, but there are two possibilities. One relates to the reign
of Maharaja Abhai Singh (circa 1724–49), the other to the taking of the Jodhpur
throne by his brother and rival Bakhat Singh, ruler of Nagaur, in circa 1751. Abhai

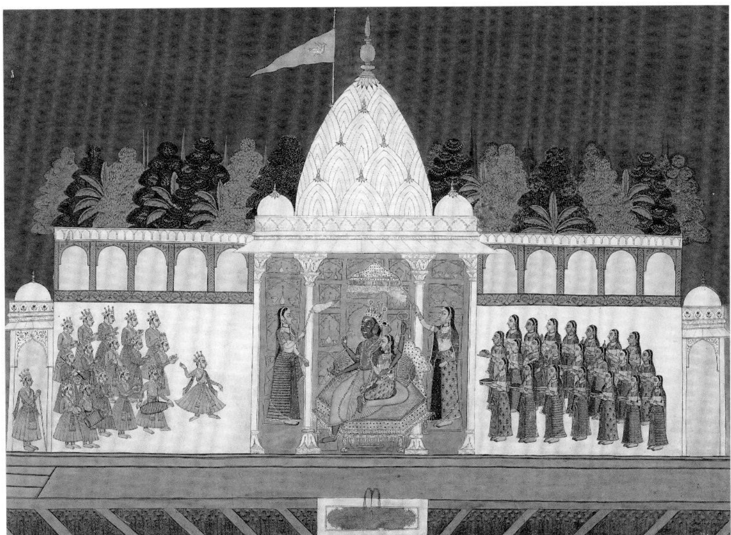

Fig. 22a Vishnu and Lakshmi, Nagaur, ca. 1755–60, 44.5 x 62.5 cm, Mehrangarh Museum Trust, RJS 1821

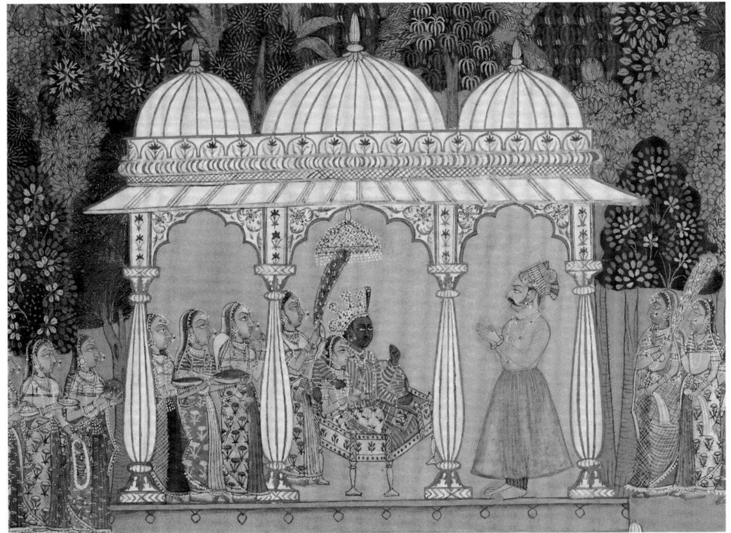

Fig. 22b Detail, Vishnu and Lakshmi, Jodhpur or Nagaur, ca. 1755, 62.2 x 43.8 cm. Mehrangarh Museum Trust, RJS 1819.

Singh was also the Mughal *subahdar* (governor) of Gujarat during the second quarter of the eighteenth century. Some believe that these textiles were part of the loot from Abhai Singh's historic siege of Ahmedabad, the capital of Gujarat, in circa 1730. Bakhat Singh played a major role in the siege and, as a reward, was given Patan to rule by Abhai Singh. No clear evidence for this, however, has come to light. An alternative possibility is that these tents were among the many that *bahis* (local written records) say came to Jodhpur from the royal stores of Nagaur when Bakhat Singh defeated Abhai Singh's son Ram Singh and declared himself ruler of Jodhpur. Bakhat Singh, who had ruled Nagaur since circa 1725, allied himself closely with the Mughal emperor Muhammad Shah and his successor, Ahmad Shah. It is possible then that this group of Mughal tents reached Jodhpur via Nagaur.

The material quality of this canopy and its companions at Mehrangarh opens up other questions regarding their provenance and date. Their chain-stitch work is more open and tentative compared to the extremely controlled craftsmanship seen in the finer Mughal examples dating from the second half of the seventeenth century. This robustness would seem appropriate for large-scale, architectural textiles whose patterns were meant to be read only from a certain distance. It might also suggest that the work belongs not to the Mochi masters of Gujarat but to derivative streams of production that, by this time, had moved farther north. The use of metal thread for the embroidery on these tents distinguishes them from the classical Gujarati examples worked purely in silk. Most significant, perhaps, is the physical difference in the metal thread used here compared to the seventeenth- and eighteenth-century courtly textiles from Gujarat. It is possible, therefore, that this group of tents was produced at a court workshop in northern India. RJ

22

Vishnu and Lakshmi in their Heavenly Palace
Nagaur, ca. 1755–60
Opaque watercolor on paper; 44.5 x 62.2 (image)
Mehrangarh Museum Trust, RJS 1822

Numbered 91 on verso.

This celestial palace painting and its two companions, fig. 22a (above) and p. 23 of "Maharaja Vijai Singh and the Epic Landscape," once were thought to be part of a *Bhagavata Purana* series commissioned circa 1775 by Vijai Singh. (For folios from this series, see figs. 6 and 7, pp. 27, 28, and fig. 46a, p. 291.) We now can place them as a separate group, which was completed earlier in Vijai Singh's reign.[2]

Vishnu and Lakshmi (p. 23 and fig. 22b) is a bold composition; the artist devotes half the space to a rectangular pool. One might be tempted to identify the supplicant at this Vishnu devotional performance, a single man dressed in yellow, as Bakhat Singh because of his moustache and beard. In fact, he is a generic figure, similar to the male villagers in the *Krishna Lila* paintings (cats. 23–25) produced about a decade later during Vijai Singh's reign (1752–93).

The artist represented the realm of the divine as a verdant environment with a variety of trees, many bursting with flowers. These celestial gardens form the backdrop for the devotions taking place in both paintings. A row of pink- and orange-tipped "fantasy" trees repeat the colors of the women's garments in both paintings and add a bit of whimsy. The trees in fig. 22a, however, are less energetic, playing the more restricted role of a background curtain. CG

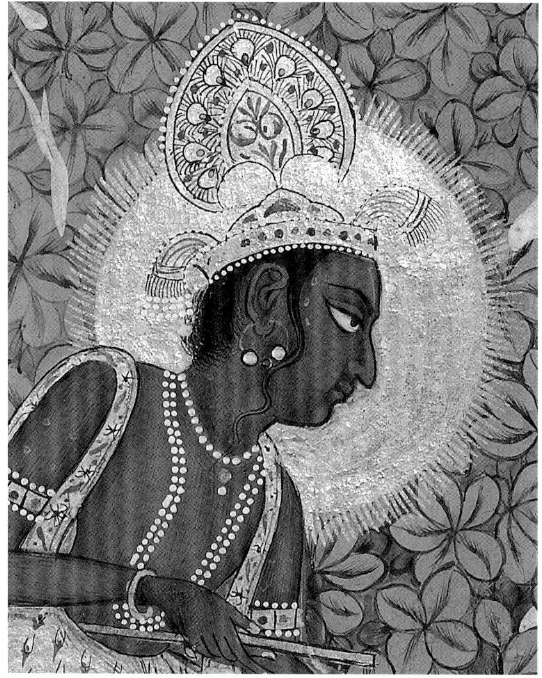

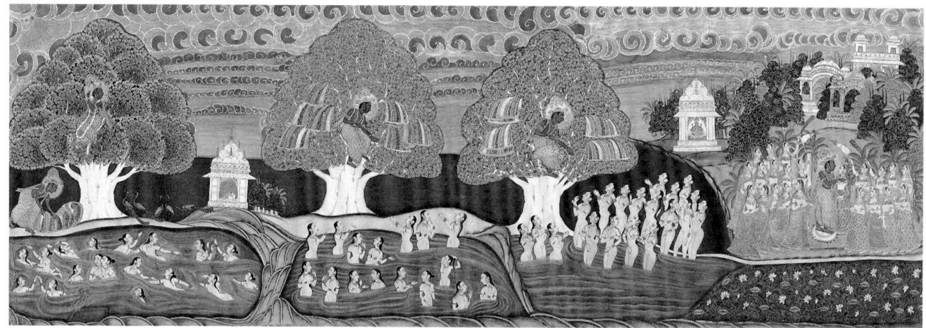

Fig. 23b Detail, Krishna Steals the Gopis' Clothes

Fig. 23a Krishna Steals the Gopis' Clothes, Jodhpur, ca. 1785, 63.5 x 136.5 cm, Mehrangarh Museum Trust, RJS 2153

23

24

The Gopis Leave the Village to Meet Krishna

folio 1 from the *Krishna Lila*
Jodhpur, ca. 1765
Opaque watercolor and gold on paper; 63.5 x 136.5 cm
Mehrangarh Museum Trust, RJS 2157

Sri krishnalila
Da[khal] dholiya rai kothar
Glorious Krishna Lila
Entered in the *dholiya* storeroom

Similar in size to a *Krishna Lila* folio, fig. 23a was inscribed on the verso during the reign of Man Singh (1803–43) as the clothes-stealing episode of the *Krishna Lila* (*sri krishna lila vastra haran*) and placed in the *dholiya* storeroom (*dakhal dholiya re kothar*). While the inscription reveals that the painting was understood in the early nineteenth-century as a *Krishna Lila* manuscript folio, its unusual "pearl-strand" border pattern (of gold circles with red centers) implies it was originally produced as a single painting. In contrast, the 1765 *Krishna Lila* folios have unadorned gold borders. The larger size of Krishna and the gopis (they are almost twice the height of the *Krishna Lila* series figures), the different style of the figures, and the gold scalloped clouds further indicate that the painting is not contemporaneous with the seven-folio *Krishna Lila* of ca. 1765. A marked resemblance between the halo and profile face of the "clothes-stealing" Krishna (see fig. 23b) with the Vishnu of the *Durga Charit's* second folio (see fig. 7, p. 28) suggests that this work was created closer to 1785. DD

Krishna Frolics with the Gopi Girls

folio 2 from the *Krishna Lila*
Jodhpur, ca. 1765
Opaque watercolor and gold on paper; 63.5 x 136.5 cm
Mehrangarh Museum Trust, RJS 2149

Sri krishnalila
Da[khal] dholiya rai kothar
Glorious Krishna Lila
Entered in the *dholiya* storeroom

25

The Gopis Search for Krishna
folio 4 from the *Krishna Lila*
Jodhpur, ca. 1765
Opaque watercolor and gold on paper; 63.5 x 136.5 cm
Mehrangarh Museum Trust, RJS 2150

Sri krishnalila
Da[khal] dholiya rai kothar
Glorious Krishna Lila
Entered in the *dholiya* storeroom

26

Monkeys and Bears in the Kishkindha Forest
from the *Ramcharitmanas* of Tulsidas (1532–1623)
Jodhpur, ca. 1775
Opaque watercolor and gold on paper; 64 x 130 cm
Courtesy of Mehrangarh Museum Trust, RJS 2532

Sri ram carit
Dakhal dholiya re kothar
Glorious Ram Charit
Entered in the *dholiya* storeroom

27

Death of Vali; Rama and Lakshmana Wait Out the Monsoon
from the *Ramcharitmanas* of Tulsidas (1532–1623)
Jodhpur, ca. 1775
Opaque watercolor on paper; 62.7 x 134.5 cm
Courtesy of Mehrangarh Museum Trust, RJS 2534

Sri ram carit
Da[khal] dholiya rai kothar
Glorious Ram Charit
Entered in the *dholiya* storeroom

28

Rama's Army Crosses the Ocean to Lanka
from the *Ramcharitmanas* of Tulsidas (1532–1623)
Jodhpur, ca. 1775
Opaque watercolor on paper; 63 x 125.8 cm
Courtesy of Mehrangarh Museum Trust, RJS 2548

Sri ram carit
Dakhal dholiya re kothar
Glorious Ram Charit
Entered in the *dholiya* storeroom

29

Sarayu Palace
from the *Ramcharitmanas* of Tulsidas (1532–1623)
Jodhpur, ca. 1775
Opaque watercolor on paper; 60.9 x 128.2 cm
Courtesy of Mehrangarh Museum Trust, RJS 2594

Sri ram carit
Da[khal] dholiya re kothar
Glorious Ram Charit
Entered in the *dholiya* storeroom

30

Sage Markandeya's Ashram and the Milky Ocean
folio 5 from the *Durga Charit*
Attributed to the "Durga Master"
Jodhpur, ca. 1780–90
Opaque watercolor and gold on paper; 48.3 x 129.5 cm
Courtesy of the Mehrangarh Museum Trust, RJS 1700

Numbered 5 on recto.
Rshi ra asram mai raja phirtan thakan ek vaishya dekhiyo tarai raja vaishya ne
puchiyo tarai vaishya kayo samadhi maro nanv chai maro vero beta ne lugayan
uro lino ne mane kad danon su dukhi thako van me ayo hamai raja ne vaishya
donu jana rshi kane gaya rshi devi ri katha kevai che
Da [khal] dholiya re kothar
A king saw a merchant wandering in a sage's ashram. The king asked the merchant
[his identity] and the merchant said, "My name is Samadhi. My son stole my money
and forced me away. Therefore I felt sorrow and came to the forest." Together the
king and the merchant went toward the sage. The sage told the story of the goddess.
Entered in the *dholiya* storeroom

Maharaja Man Singh and the Naths

The Rajtilak Darbar of Maharaja Man Singh

Amardas Bhatti, ca. 1804
Opaque watercolor and gold on paper; 74 x 80 cm
Courtesy of Mehrangarh Museum Trust, RJS 4770

Raj rajeswar maharajadhiraj maharaja man singhji rajtilak
Citara amar das ra hath ri
Da[khal] dholiya re kothar

The coronation of lord of king of kings,
supreme king of great kings, Maharaja Man Singhji
From the hand of the painter Amardas
Entered into the *dholiya* storeroom

Previously published in Rosemary Crill, *Marwar Painting: A History of the Jodhpur Style* (1999), fig. 99.

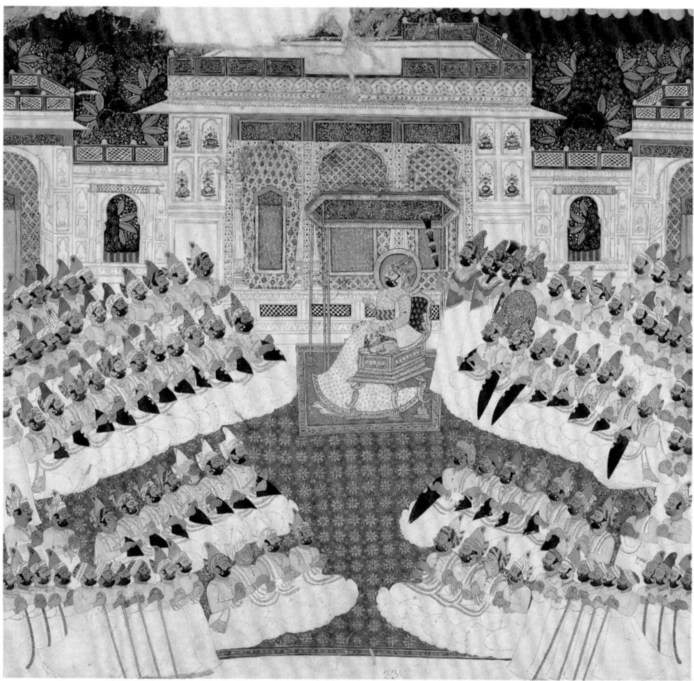

Fig. 31a The Sire Darbar of Maharaja Man Singh, by Dana, Jodhpur, ca. 1830, 53 x 73 cm, Mehrangarh Museum Trust, RJS 4769

In addition to *The Rajtilak Darbar*, four other *sire* (special) *darbar* paintings of Man Singh's complete court are extant in the Mehrangarh collection.[1] Painted by Amardas and his son Dana, each work presents the maharaja on a lion throne with a full complement of courtiers, although some depict palace settings less grand than the one in *The Rajtilak Darbar*. Although few in number given Man Singh's forty-year reign, their rather large size (approximately 70 x 50 cm) indicates that he valued the periodic, if ephemeral, reconciliations with his noblemen.

Within the Rajput state, the *darbar* was the central institution of political integration for the maharaja and his kinsmen. In the *darbar*, the maharaja exchanged honors and gifts with the nobility, who were required to attend on a schedule set by customary agreement. The ritual articulated the participants' rank and prestige through insignia, dress, and the subjects' positions and postures. Protocol dictated that the maharaja, wearing royal insignia, sit upon a throne (or cushions) in the center of the assembly. The noblemen's portraits recorded not only their attendance (i.e., allegiance), but their genealogical connection to the king because hereditary seats established during the seventeenth century located the nobles in ranked proximity to the royal center.[2] In addition, dress codes and the custom of adopting the ruler's turban style expressed loyalty and deference, and ensured a visual solidarity among the courtiers. The *darbar's* customs and rituals thus can be understood as a set of motivated practices that perpetually re-established the king's distribution of authority to his kinsmen, the hereditary nobility. Within their own domains (*thikanas*) and with their own subordinates, the nobility replicated the ritual on a smaller scale.

Both rulers and nobles documented these events with a visual rhetoric that was eminently clear to court audiences. As participants in the royal *darbar*, they enacted its elaborate rituals. And as patrons of *darbar* painting, they understood the events' translation into the visual realm. Noble viewers would have grasped how *darbar* paintings emphasized hereditary kinship bonds rather than shifting levels of influence and power. The formal "class pictures" of their day, representations of royal assemblies also did not depict the transitory honors—such as the right to an intimate greeting at the start of each *darbar*—granted by maharajas to favored noblemen. Courtiers would have been able to appreciate the historic specificity of each painting because an assortment of sumptuary laws, royal gifts, and festival traditions determined the apparel they wore at court gatherings. Thus, the identical gold garb worn by the noblemen in the coronation painting is not Amardas' conceit, but rather his attentive recording of a royal mandate.[3] DD

Jallandharnath and Maharaja Man Singh on Diwali

Shivdas Bhatti, ca. 1820–before July 1825
Opaque watercolor and gold on paper; 50 x 33 cm
Mehrangarh Museum Trust, RJS 4050

Da[khal] dholiya re kothar 1882 savan sud 11
Kalam citara sivdas ri
Entered into the *dholiya* storeroom on the eleventh day
of the bright half of Shravan (July–August), 1825
The work of the painter Shivdas

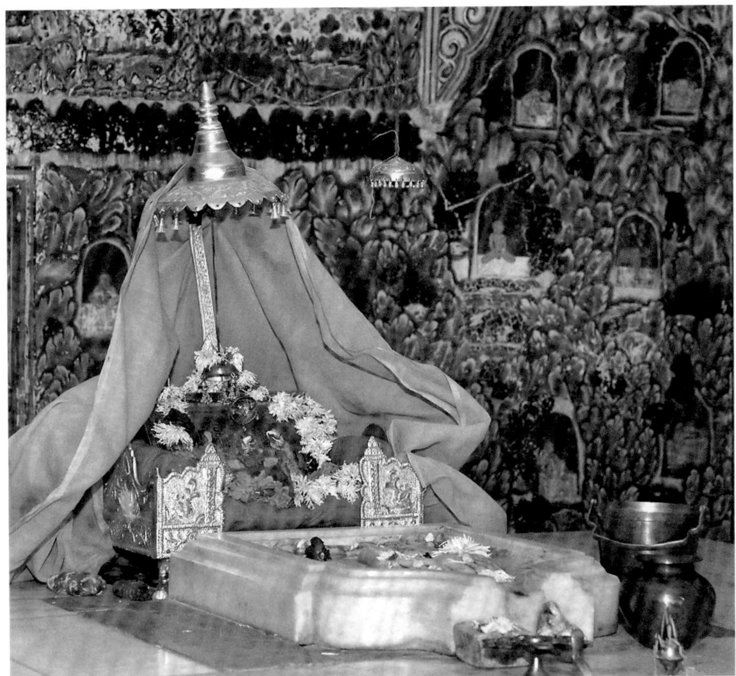

Fig. 32a Udaimandir Altar, Jodhpur (2005).

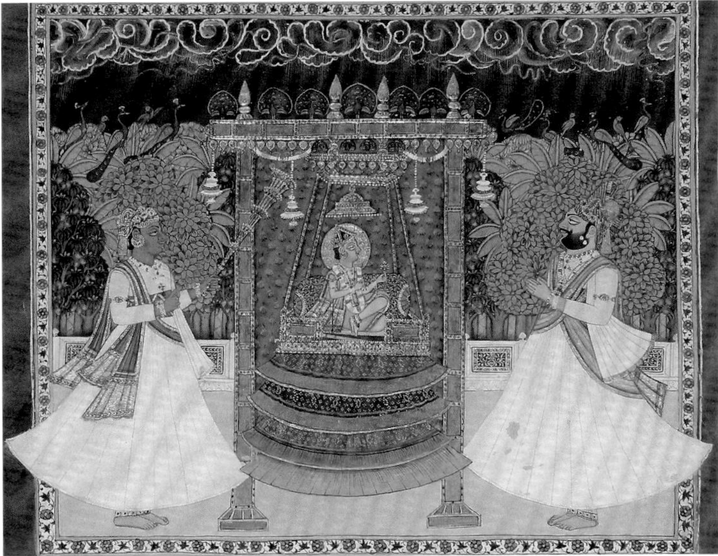

Fig. 32b Maharaja Man Singh and Ladu Nath Worshiping Jallandharnath, by Raso, Jodhpur, ca. 1826 to before July/August, 1828, 40 x 33 cm. Mehrangarh Museum Trust, RJS 4024

Previously published in Debra Diamond, "Court Painting and Yogic Metaphysics in Nineteenth-Century Jodhpur," in *Court Painting In Rajasthan* (2000), fig. 2 (p. 141); Debra Diamond, "The Cartography of Power," in *Arts of Mughal India: Studies in Honour of Robert Skelton* (2004), fig. 4.

Paintings reveal how strongly the sensibilities and practices of the Vallabha Sampraday—the religious community of Man Singh's grandfather, Maharaja Vijai Singh—colored Nath devotion during Man Singh's reign. Previously, Nath shrines did not include figural imagery, and figurative paintings were not considered vehicles of worship. Nor did Nath verse employ the romantic sensibility (*shringar rasa*) of *bhakti* devotionalism.[4] "Nathism" in the Jodhpur court, therefore, must be understood as a particular socio-historical manifestation of an evolving tradition.

Court records indicate that Man Singh—or attendants acting on his behalf—performed *chitra darshan* (picture seeing) and *chitra seva* (picture service) on an almost daily basis.[5] The Hindi/Rajasthani terms (and the practices they describe) originated with the Vallabha Sampraday (see "Maharaja Vijai Singh and the Epic Landscape"). Their appearance in Man Singh's court records reveal that the *mahasiddha* was understood to inhabit painted images during worship. The paintings in these rituals were undoubtedly those that depict the maharaja, with his hands raised in the gesture of respect, worshiping the enthroned Jallandharnath; in fact, one remains today on the altar of Udaimandir (fig. 32a).[6] Propped up on a small silver throne beneath a silver umbrella (at the head of a marble slab carved with Jallandharnath's footprints), the Udaimandir painting is barely visible beneath flower garlands and daubs of ritual paste. Its composition is more clearly reiterated in a work by the artist Raso (fig. 32b), one of scores—perhaps hundreds—of paintings that depict Man Singh and a Nath priest standing on either side of Jallandharnath, who is always represented in profile facing the maharaja.[7]

These devotional images follow the compositional conventions of the *chitra darshan* paintings made for Vijai Singh (see fig. 4 in "Maharaja Vijai Singh and the Epic Landscape," p. 24). There is, however, one significant exception. In the devotional paintings of Krishna, the god is always represented frontally, with his eyes wide open to engage and return the gaze of the devotee/viewer of the painting. In contrast, Jallandharnath is always represented in profile. This shift from frontal to profile visage conveys an intimate and exclusive relationship between the *mahasiddha* and the maharaja.[8]

Man Singh, whose early years were spent in a Vallabha milieu, wrote poems that expressed his fervent desire for Jallandharnath's *darshan*. A similar sensibility imbues Raso's *chitra darshan* painting (fig. 32b).[9] The powerful, intimidating and vulgar *mahasiddha* of popular lore (see "Painting, Politics, and Devotion under Maharaja Man Singh, 1803–43") is transformed in the painting into a benign blue-complexioned child on a swing decorated with peacocks (commonly associated with Krishna). Crackling lightning and the cries of peacocks, two common tropes in devotional poems to Krishna, contribute to the mood of passionate devotion.

The archival inscription on the painting's verso notes that it "was brought by Raso's hand from Mahamandir," which indicates that the Nath priests gave paintings by court artists as gifts to the maharaja.[10] Perhaps the painting, which includes a portrait of Ladu Nath, the nineteen-year-old guru, was a farewell memento. In 1828, Ladu Nath went on pilgrimage to Mount Girnar in Gujarat (and died from illness before he could return to Jodhpur). DD

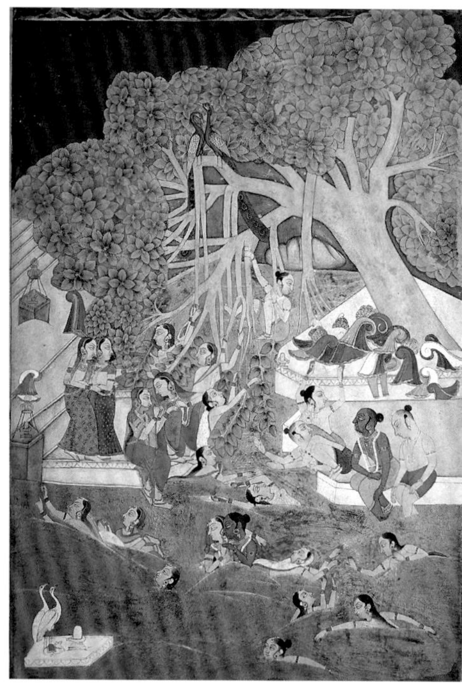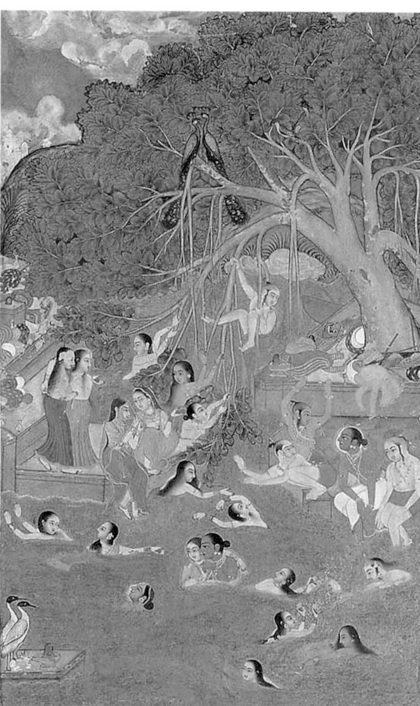

33

Jallandharnath at Jalore

Amardas Bhatti, ca. 1805–10
Opaque watercolor and gold on paper; 29 x 39 cm
Mehrangarh Museum Trust, RJS 4126

[numbered] 31
Da[khal] dholiya re kothar
Citara amardas ra hath ri
Entered into the *dholiya* storeroom
From the hand of the painter Amardas, 31

Previously published in Rosemary Crill, *Marwar Painting: A History of the Jodhpur Style* (1999), fig. 124.

34

Jallandharnath and Princess Padmini Fly over King Padam's Palace

folio 19 from the *Suraj Prakash*
Amardas Bhatti, 1830 (Samvat 1887)
Opaque watercolor and gold on paper; 23.3 x 38.6 cm
Mehrangarh Museum Trust, RJS 1644

Granth suraj prakash ro
Da[khal] dholiya re kothar ka[lam] amari
The book of the *Suraj Prakash*
Entered into the *dholiya* storeroom, the work of Amardas

Amardas, the workshop supervisor of the *Suraj Prakash*, painted many of its seventy folios. The heavily shaded faces with small eyes and the emphatic pictorial quotations in this folio reveal the master's hand.[11] Here, and throughout Amardas' oeuvre, we find ample evidence that his references to visual motifs in other paintings created meaningful allusions for visually literate audiences.

To emphasize King Padam's beauty, Amardas appropriated the popular motif of the blue-skinned god Krishna sporting in the Yamuna River. Comparing the Padam painting with one of Krishna, also from Jodhpur, we see that the two have a common archetype, a painting from the Bundi court (a kingdom southeast of Jodhpur).[12] (See figs. 34a and b.) In all three works, a similarly placed blue banyan tree arches over a silver bathing pool; Krishna/Padam embraces a woman beneath a pair of peacocks; two cranes alight upon a Shiva lingam shrine at the painting's lower border; and many of the swimmers' postures are identical, such as the woman in the center who raises her hands above her head as she floats on her back. The halo behind Padam's consort does not appear in Bundi images of Radha (Krishna's beloved), nor do queens have haloes in Jodhpur paintings. However, a preparatory drawing (circa 1815) by Jodhpur court artist depicts Radha, Krishna's divine lover, with a halo.[13] Amardas' depiction of the double halo strongly suggests that he changed the Padam narrative by twice referring to Krishna via traditions from Bundi and Jodhpur painting.

Fragmented compositions such as *Princess Padmini Espies King Padam* have been generally understood as markers of a decline in Rajput court painting during the nineteenth century. Amardas' layered references to Krishna, however, signal an aesthetic that pointedly mobilizes heterogeneous sources. Art criticism is not part of the rich literary tradition of the Rajput courts, but numerous texts on poetics address the repetition of literary motifs. Although the terms of poetic analysis cannot be directly applied to painting, they do provide insight into a parallel aesthetic sensibility. Treatises on poetry typically discuss the mechanisms and advantages of reworking long-established equivalences, such as "lotus-like eyes." By reiterating the convention, a poet evokes a chain of associations for a literate audience, whose memories enhance the verse's aesthetic impact. A poet's ability to nuance an established equivalence was recognized as a marker of a skillful command of the literary tradition. In this light, Amardas' ingenious modifications of already-established motifs can be read as an invitation for the court to delight in both the painting's visual allusions and the painter's skill. DD

35

Prince Subuddhi in the Forest of Illusion

folio 35 from the *Suraj Prakash*
Amardas Bhatti, 1830 (Samvat 1887)
Opaque watercolor and gold on paper; 23.3 x 38.6 cm
Mehrangarh Museum Trust, RJS 1660

Granth suraj prakas ro
Da[khal] dholiya re kothar kalam Amra ri
The book of the *Suraj Prakash*
Entered into the *dholiya* storeroom, the work of Amardas

Previously published in Rosemary Crill, *Marwar Painting: A History of the Jodhpur Style* (1999), fig. 134.

> In the middle of a moonless night
> The king came to a river of red blood
> On both shores, fire raged like war cannons
> Causing broken skulls to shine like lotuses....
>
> On countless boats of buffalo carcasses
> Evil spirits dance.
> Severed heads laugh,
> Fire spits from their mouths....
>
> The *dakinis* ride, grunting
> with loud and fearful sounds.

> Hordes of headless demons, each with [the] power of many men,
> Explode like fireworks....
>
> From many dismembered elephants
> [*Dakinis*] play on *mridangam*-drum hooves,
> femur-bone flutes, conch shell [trumpet] skulls,
> And keep *tal* [rhythm] with the elephant ears in their hands.
>
> Lifting horse legs and bodies,
> Making bridges from small bones,
> Plucking ferocious strings of intestines,
> They make many tamburas....
>
> On dismembered heads of elephants,
> They beat drumsticks of tusks.
> They play on *bheri* drums of elephant trunks,
> They dance and sing Sindhu raga....
>
> 64 Yoginis and 52 forms of Bhairava
> dancing, drunken, and intoxicated,
> Many headless bodies arising and dancing
> They keep the raga's time perfectly....
>
> The land, trees, mountains, and sky were afire
> Nothing but fire could be seen
> Seeing the flame the horse's heart felt fright
> And he fell onto the ground, his soul departed....
>
> Even then the king was not at all afraid.
> Seeing, he felt enjoyment in his heart, and laughed.
> Virbhadra recognized his bravery and called the king to the hill of the dead.

Karnidan's *Suraj Prakash* (1731) extols fifty-eight ancestral generations of his patron, Maharaja Abhai Singh (reigned 1724–49). Multiple nineteenth-century copies in the royal library, as well as Man Singh's gift of a *Suraj Prakash* manuscript to Colonel James Tod in 1820, attest to the continued popularity of Karnidan's text during Man Singh's reign.[14]

The pictorial cycle selectively illustrates episodes from the voluminous text. Two-thirds of its folios (forty-seven of its seventy paintings) depict the narratives of a single, relatively obscure generation in the dynasty's past.[15] These minor ancestors were the thirteen sons of King Punja of Kanauj. In the twelfth century, Kanauj was the capital of the powerful Gahadvala dynasty of northeast India, and it is likely that Rathores served its kings as generals and governors. In the fifteenth century, the Rathores migrated west and established their kingdom in Marwar. Rathore dynastic histories subsequently incorporated the Gahadavala kings as direct ancestors.

Karnidan's verses dramatically and fluently convey the wondrous events, miracles, flying princesses, terrifying demons, and ferocious battles that marked the reigns of King Punja's sons. Uniting these fantastic narratives are the boons from deities, Naths, and holy men that each son received after performing a heroic deed. The stories were clearly mobilized to prefigure Man Singh's grace from the *mahasiddha* Jallandharnath and to legitimate his redefined conception of sovereignty. DD

36

Maharaja Man Singh and Dev Nath at Mahamandir Haveli

Jodhpur, ca. 1810
Opaque watercolor and gold on paper; 67.5 x 58.5 cm
Mehrangarh Museum Trust, RJS 2024

[numbered] 14
Sri mahamandir ri sri devnathji maharaj
Da[khal] dholiya re kothar hajri sam[vat] 1887 ra jeth mai
Glorious great temple of the glorious Dev Nathji Maharaja
Entered in the *dholiya* storeroom in Jyestha (May–June) 1830, 14

Previously published in Rosemary Crill, *Marwar Painting: A History of the Jodhpur Style* (1999), fig. 92; Debra Diamond, "The Cartography of Power," in *Arts of Mughal India: Studies in Honour of Robert Skelton* (2004), fig. 1.

Three topographical overviews of the Mahamandir township, circa 1810–15, survive from Man Singh's atelier: two in the Mehrangarh collection (this work and cat. 35) and a third in the Philadelphia Museum of Art (see fig. 2, p. 33). In each, the temple and *haveli* are represented with an architectural fidelity familiar from the Bakhat Singh Nagaur paintings of a century earlier (see, for example, the reference catalogue entries for cats. 13 and 15). However, the surrounding Mahamandir suburbs are realized in the cartographic fashion (pp. 162–63) that was employed for city maps and plans, which endows them with a different geographic and historical density.

Man Singh, the Nath elite, and the administrative class were demonstrably familiar with secular cartography. Correspondence regarding Nath temple construction alone indicates that the maharaja looked over plans, appointed or removed construction overseers (*kamdars*) and their assistants, offered his opinion on specific renovations, approved continuing construction at Mahamandir, and received requests to build or renovate Nath temples or monasteries in various parts of India.[16]

Although plans drawn for the Jodhpur court have not been located, a cache of maps and plans made for the Amber capital of the neighboring kingdom (Jaipur) similarly integrate planimetric and elevation views.[17] Residential dwellings drawn with geometric precision entirely from above, which appear to the right of the temple tower in this painting, are closely related to schematics in eighteenth-century Jaipur construction drawings.[18] Likewise, the convention for a simple dwelling employed in the previous entry—a triangular roof atop a square with a single rectangular door and one or two windows—appears regularly in Jaipur city plans. In their reference to the descriptive and documentary, the town plan allusions invoke both Mahamandir's material reality and its ongoing construction, which continued at least through the late 1820s.

The cartographic logic that structures the three Mahamandir paintings is further revealed in their consistent orientation. In each, the palace is located in the upper left and the temple in the lower right. Although each building is enlarged when

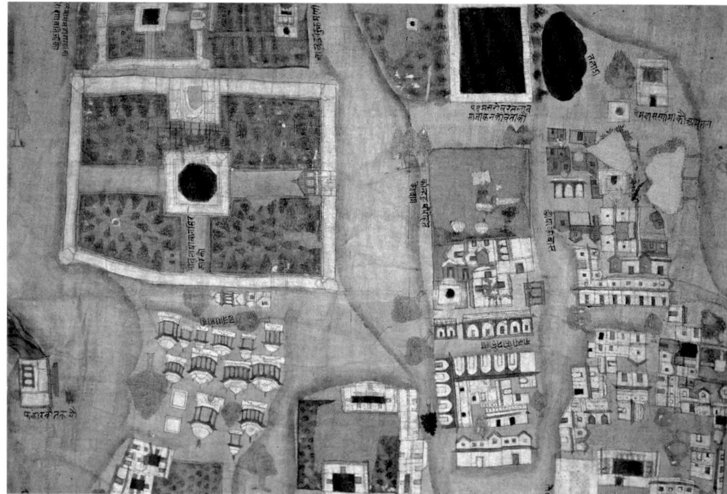

Fig. 36a Detail, Map of Amber, Rajasthan, Amber, ca. 1711.
National Museum of India, New Delhi 56.92.4

it becomes the site of significant action, their unvarying placement alludes to the logic of the town plan. Situated on either side of the main gate (which, like the bastion wall, is not represented in these paintings), the townships' two largest buildings announced the dual lordship of *mahasiddha* and sectarian order over Mahamandir.

Paintings from numerous Rajput courts include mapping conventions, which are sometimes stylistic and at other times refer to specific sites. In the Mahamandir paintings, a consistent orientation, the high degree of architectural fidelity, and the geometric rendering of the suburbs are cartographic references to the township. More than generic conventions, the cartographic citations invite us to consider how these paintings were understood by their makers and viewers.[19] The motivations for any particular artist's adaptations across genres (including maps) are complex and may include expedience as well as the construction of meaning. Nonetheless, the probable involvement of Man Singh's artists in the township's planning, their definite engagement in its wall painting, and their awareness of its significance to their patrons (the maharaja and the Nath elite) strongly suggest that court painters cited the town plans to remind court and sectarian viewers of the freshness, importance, and magnitude of Mahamandir's ongoing construction. DD

37

Jallandharnath Worship at Mahamandir
Raso and Shivdas Bhatti
Jodhpur, ca. 1812
Opaque watercolor and gold on paper; 82 x 56 cm
Mehrangarh Museum Trust, RJS 2005

[numbered] 12
Sri mahamandir ra bhivi ri
Da [khal] dholiya re kothar
Kalam citara rasa ne shivdas ri
Inside the glorious Mahamandir
Entered in the *dholiya* storeroom
The work of the artists Raso and Shivdas, 12

From 1804–15, Man Singh regularly traveled in a large procession from the Jodhpur fort to visit his guru at Mahamandir.[20] Every Monday, as the maharaja advanced on an elephant behind the royal standard, musicians beat large drums to announce his progress. Just as Mahamandir's gleaming spire was "conspicuous from even a great distance,"[21] the din and pageantry of the royal processions made the maharaja's devotion visible and audible to the city's populace on a weekly basis. But once the retinue reached Mahamandir, Man Singh's drummers ceased their beating and the maharaja left his soldiers and weapons outside the *haveli* (mansion) in a show of respect to his guru.

The trappings of a halted procession appear in each of the three topographical paintings of Mahamandir (cats. 36, 37, and fig. 3, p. 33). The animals gathered at the well to drink, dispersed soldiers, and stacked muskets outside the palace in *Maharaja Man Singh and Dev Nath at Mahamandir Haveli* (cat. 36) convey the quiet, respectful disarming of royal presence before a spiritual superior. The genre scenes outside the two temple worship paintings are grander. Caparisoned horses and elephants, palanquins, banners, and troops announce the prestige of both the Nath elite and the maharaja.

The three paintings share compositional strategies with the rich and diverse corpus of pilgrimage maps produced in northwest India during this period. Jain and Hindu pilgrimage maps typically combine plan and elevation views for locative clarity and often depict the elephant entourages of prestigious devotees.[22] While the Mahamandir paintings are not directly based, to my knowledge, on existing pilgrimage maps, it is likely that their compositional similarities to the pilgrimage genre would have triggered viewers' understanding that the paintings represented sacred sites. DD

38

Maharaja Man Singh Celebrates Gangaur at Nijmandir
Satidas
Jodhpur, March–April 1820 (Samvat 1877)
Opaque watercolor and gold on paper; 65 x 49 cm
Mehrangarh Museum Trust, RJS 2007

Upper right
Sri ayasji ra sarup
The form of glorious Ayasji [a title for Man Singh's Nath gurus]

Upper central
Raj rajesvar maharajadhiraj sri man singhji
Lord of king of kings, supreme king of great kings, the glorious Man Singhji

Right
Ra[thore] surtan singh simbhu singhot patai nimbaj
Chun [davat] rav prithiraj durjan singhot patai kilanput
Rathore Surjan Singh of Neemaj, son of Shambhu Singh
Chandawat Rao Prithviraj of Kalyanpur, son of Surjan Singh

Left
Ra[thore] salam singh savai singhot patai pokaran
Ra[thore] syamkaran karnidanot
Rathore Salim Singh of Pokhran, son of Sawai Singh
Rathore Shyam Karan, son of Karni

Bottom center
Samvat 1877 ra chait sud 5 sri gavar ra uchav ri asvari gulab sagar padhariti
Da [khal] dholiya re kothar tasbir citare satidas kivi
The Gangaur festival of the 5th of the bright half of Chait (March–April), 1820; arrived at Gulab Sagar on horseback
Entered in the *dholiya* storeroom; painting made by the painter Satidas

39

Ganesha, Saraswati, and Jallandharnath
Identified here as a copy of folio 1 from the *Nath Purana*[23]
Attributed to Amardas, ca. 1825
Opaque watercolor and gold on paper; 47 x 123 cm
Mehrangarh Museum Trust, RJS 2398

Numbered 1 on recto.

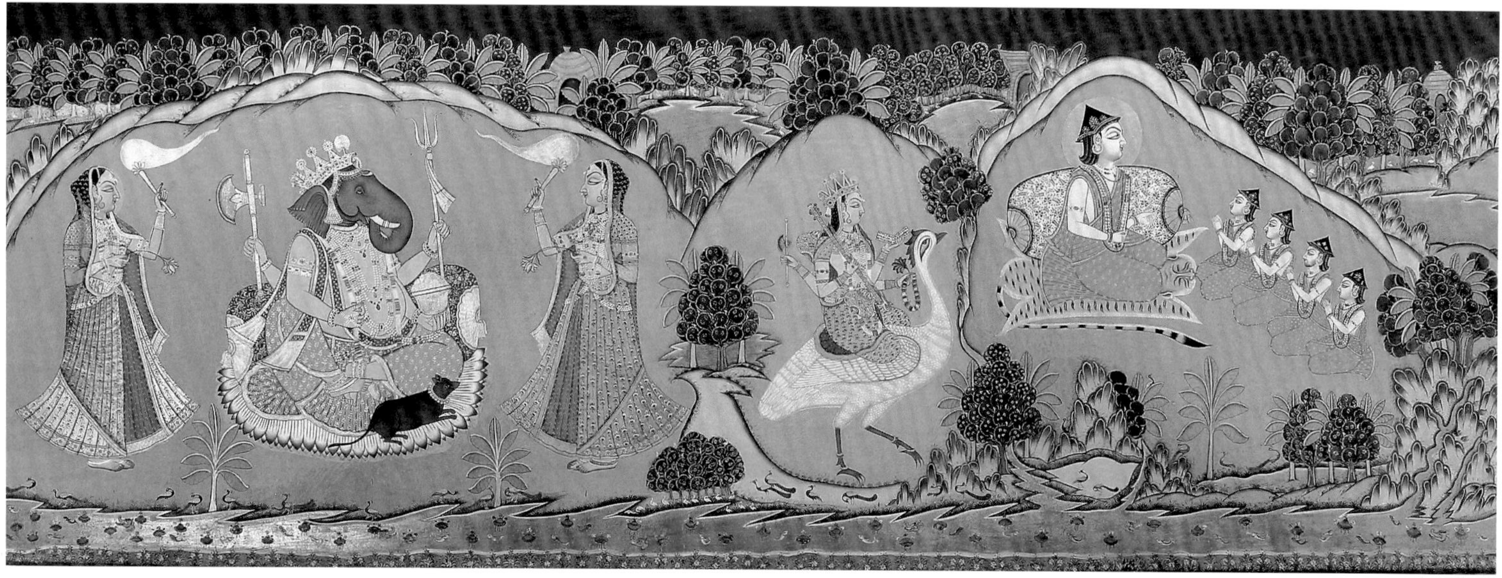

Fig. 39a Ganesha, Saraswati, and Trilok Srinath, identified here as folio 1 from the *Nath Purana*, Bulaki and others, Jodhpur, ca. 1825, 47 x 123 cm, Mehrangarh Museum Trust, RJS 2426

sri nath puran

sri jallandharnathji sanpathai

da[khal] dholiya re kothar

1 Sri saraswati devi

2 Sri ganeshji siddhi buddhi shakti samjukt virajman hai

3 Srinathji siddha .sabha samjukt virajman hai.

Srinath samhita nam mahajog shashtra jin rai anusar citra karaya

Raivatchal parvat vishai sri siddh sabha samjukt

Sri kanerinathji mahatma puchai hai

Sri nathji uttar sambhashan karai hai

Glorious Nath Purana

Glorious Jallandharnath and his community of perfected beings

Entered in the *dholiya* storeroom

1 Glorious goddess Saraswati

2 Glorious Ganeshji seated with his divine consorts, Siddhi and Buddhi

3 Glorious Nathji seated together with an assembly

The picture was made according to the great yoga treatise that is named the Srinath Samhita. On Raivatchal [Girnar] mountain the glorious community of perfected beings gathered. After Glorious Kanerinath asked a question to the great soul, Glorious Nathji answered.

Previously published in Rosemary Crill, *Marwar Painting: A History of the Jodhpur Style* (1999), fig. 123.

I propose that Amardas' *Ganesha, Saraswati, and Jallandharnath* (cat. 39) is a copy of the first folio (fig. 39a) of the complete illustrated *Nath Purana* manuscript in the Mehrangarh Museum Trust collection. Bulaki's compositionally and iconographically similar folio also depicts Ganesh, Saraswati, and Nathji framed within three hillocks on a rolling landscape. On the painting's back, the archivist inscribed the words *Sri Nath Puran* and identified its artists as "Bulaki and others." Bulaki,

also known as "the Muslim painter," had a distinctive style.[24] His signature characteristics (e.g., porcelain-white Nath face with airbrush-smooth shading, elongated crimson eye, oversize bolster pillow) support the reliability of the Bulaki attribution of this work. Paintings in this style recur throughout the manuscript.

Faced with the conundrum of duplicate folios inscribed "sri nath puran"— and aware that archival titles and recto numerals on the *Nath Purana* and *Nath Charit* can be unreliable—Reu had earlier classified the Bulaki painting as the *Nath Charit's* first folio.[25] This solution is unsatisfying. It addresses neither the uncanny similarity of the two paintings in *Nath Purana* nor the curious appearance of the deities Ganesha and Saraswati, who are not mentioned at the beginning of either text or represented on the first folios of any other Man Singh-period monumental manuscripts.

The discovery of a monumental manuscript folio in the Jaipur collection of Vyakul Acharya sheds new light on the duplicate paintings. The Acharya painting closely duplicates the fifth folio of the *Siddha Siddhanta Paddhati* (cat. 50), a monumental manuscript by Bulaki. The "Ganesha" and "Acharya" pairs thus exhibit an intriguing similarity: one folio in each pair is inscribed to Bulaki; the other folio in each pair can be attributed by its softer style to Amardas.

It follows then that the Bulaki "Ganesha" is the *Nath Purana's* first folio and that the Amardas' painting is a duplicate. More broadly, we learn from the existence of the duplicates that master compositions were kept within the royal workshop for various artists to consult since the (Hindu) Amardas and the (Muslim) Bulaki did not belong to the same family. Almost everything else about the duplicates remains a mystery. Why doesn't the name of Amardas, who was one of the workshop's great masters, appear on any monumental manuscript inscriptions? Did he create these two paintings to try his hand at the genre? Was he perhaps showing off his skills in relation to Bulaki, another leading painting in the royal atelier? Most intriguingly, are these the only remaining examples of once complete, but now dispersed, manuscripts? DD

The Origins of the Cosmos

40

Three Aspects of the Absolute
identified here as folio 1 from the *Nath Charit*[1]
Bulaki, 1823 (Samvat 1880)
Opaque watercolor and gold on paper; 47 x 123 cm
Mehrangarh Museum Trust, RJS 2399

Numbered 1 on recto.

Sri nath carit
Da[khal] dholiya re kothar
Citara bulaki vagaire ra kiyo da
Glorious Nath Charit
Entered in the *dholiya* storeroom
The painter Bulaki and others made it

Left
Pratham sri adi anadi niranjan nirakar jyotih svarup nath [numbered]*1*
First there is the glorious Nath, whose nature is self-effulgent and
without beginning, limit, form, or blemish, 1

Center
Anand murtirvan nath
Bliss-form Nath

Right
Pachai kitarak jug parvat jal vishaini ra lanban kasan kiyo jin vastai jalandhar
Isa nam ri prasiddh hui jyonai hi koi gorakhnath kahai hai nirgun rupvan huvo
citran vastai [numbered] 3
Then after many eons, Jallandhar sat down and created vast waters. Thus, he
is renowned as lord and as Gorakhnath. The third picture [represents] this form
without attributes.

41

The Emergence of Spirit and Matter
folio 2 from the *Shiva Purana*
Attributed to Shivdas, ca. 1828
Opaque watercolor and gold on paper; 47 x 126 cm
Mehrangarh Museum Trust, RJS 2599

Numbered 2 on recto.

Sri siv puran
Da [khal] dholiya re kothar
Glorious Shiva Purana
Entered into the *dholiya* storeroom

Left
Nirgun nirakar svayam jyoti param brahm sadashiv
Without attributes or form, the self-effulgent absolute
Brahman [is called] Sadashiva

Center
Nirgun brahm sun prakrti purush naranari rup ri utpanni shrshti rai adi chai
At the beginning of creation, the male and female forms of Prakriti and
Purusha emerge from the Brahman without qualities

Right
Prakrti purush donun tapasya karai
Prakriti and Purusha together practice austerities

॥अथमश्रीआदिअनादिनिरंजननिराकारज्योतिःस्वरूपनाथ॥
२

Cat. 40 Verso, left

॥वढैकितरकजुगपर्यंतजलविषेनिरालंबएकासनकियोजिणवासैजालंधर
इसानामरीषसिद्धझुई ज्यांनैद्रीकेईगोरक्षनाथकदेदैनिर्गुलसंतैसगुणंझवासिण रूपवान
वासै३

Cat. 40 Verso, right

निर्गुणनिराकारस्वयंज्योतिपरंबह्लसदाशिव

Cat. 41 Verso, left

निर्गुलीबुल सुंप्रकृतिपुरुषनरनारीरूपरीउत्पत्रिसष्टिरैआदिषे

Cat. 41 Verso, center

प्रकृतिपुरुषदोनूंतयस्याकरै

Cat. 41 Verso, right

42

The Creation of the Cosmic Ocean and the Elements
folio 3 from the *Shiva Purana*
ca. 1828
Opaque watercolor and gold on paper; 45.5 x 124 cm
Mehrangarh Museum Trust, RJS 2600

Numbered 3 in the upper left corner.

Sri siv puran
Da [khal] dholiya re kothar
The Glorious Shiva Purana
Entered into the *dholiya* storeroom

Left
Prakriti purusha dona rai tapasya kartan sharir sun apraman jal utpann huva tike jal naranari sun utpana tin nara isa nam kahaya.
Purusha and Prakriti together perform austerities. From the heat generated by austerities, water emerges from their bodies; they are called Lord Nara from the water having arisen.

Center left
Narana mai jal tin vishai prakriti purush donan sayan kiyo tinsun purush narayan kahaya nai prakriti narayani kahai narayan narayani rai sambandh sun chois tattva upana

Both Prakriti and Purusha are lying on the waters; Purusha is called Narayan and Prakriti is called Narayani; twenty-four elements emerge from the two together.

Center right
Tattvan samet narayan narayani ek huva keval sri narayan rup jal mein suta tinnari nabhi su kamal utpano kamal mein brahmaji utpana
Narayan, Narayani, and the elements became one in the form of glorious Narayan lying on the water. A lotus emerged from his navel and from the lotus emerged Brahma.

Right
Brahmaji vichar kino hun kun kavasun ayo mhari utpanni karan hua lokun hun kamal mai upjiyo tomharo utpanni karan pin kamal mai gusiyun vichar kamal ri daandi mein brahmaji utarta huva
Brahma thought, "Where did I come from? Who is my creator? I was born from a lotus, so perhaps my creator will also be in the lotus." Thinking in this way, Brahma descended the stem of the lotus.

Cat. 42 Verso, left

Cat. 42 Verso, center right

Cat. 42 Verso, center left

Cat. 42 Verso, right

43

Nathji Creates the Earth's Sacred Waters
folio 4 from the *Nath Charit*
1823 (Samvat 1880)
Opaque watercolor and gold on paper; 47 x 123 cm
Mehrangarh Museum Trust, RJS 2429

Numbered 4 in red by Reu.

sri nath carit
da [khal] dholiya re kothar
glorious Nath Charit
Entered in the *dholiya* storeroom

44

Chakras of the Subtle Body
folio 2 from the *Nath Charit*
Attributed to Bulaki, 1823 (Samvat 1880)
Opaque watercolor and gold on paper; 46 x 122 cm
Mehrangarh Museum Trust, RJS 2427

Sri nath carit
Da[khal] dholiya re kothar
Glorious Nath Charit
Entered into the *dholiya* storeroom

The yogic adept stands firmly upon splayed feet, his spine taut, arms extended down, and palms facing forward. His face, too, is symmetrical, with features almost mathematically arranged upon a central vertical axis. The schema of the yogic body was unknown in Jodhpur court painting prior to Man Singh's reign. It appears in full-size on folios 4 (fig. 44b) and 6 (cat. 48) of the *Siddha Siddhanta Paddhati*, and in smaller scale on folios 1 and 3. The corpus includes no archetype for the yogic body's diagrammatic frontality, for Jodhpur court painters depicted figures in profile with three-quarter torsos and, less often, three-quarter profiles. (For a Vijai Singh-period example of the latter, see cat. 22, p. 103.)

Bulaki undoubtedly adopted the esoteric and detailed iconography of the stations from a yogic source. A roughly painted and lightly colored watercolor drawing of the chakras (fig. 44a) indicates the type of source material that he may have consulted. Given to Man Singh as a gift, the didactic diagram is brushed directly onto untreated paper and the *siddha's* garment, jewels, and chakras are

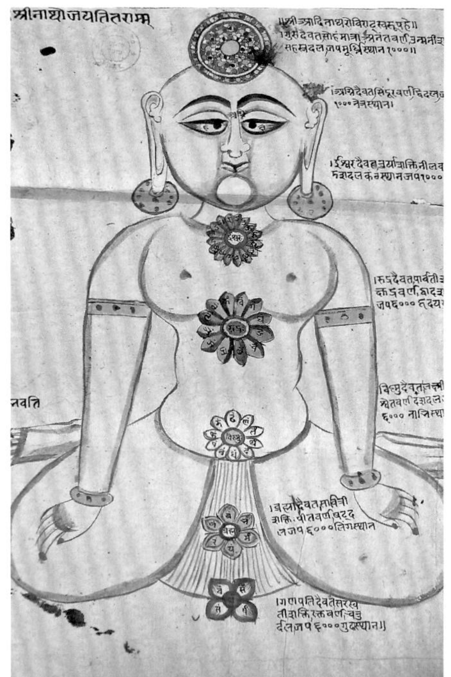
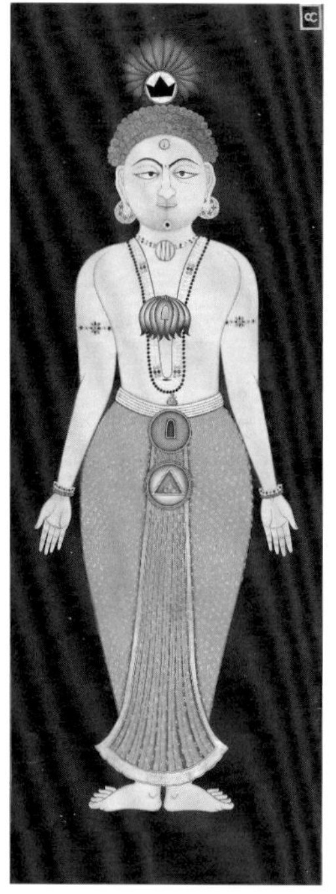

Fig. 44a Adinath Virat Swarup, Manmoi (Rajasthan?), n.d.
Pustak Prakash Library, Jodhpur, no. 1450.1283

Fig. 44b *Chakras of the Subtle Body*, folio 4 from the *Siddha Siddhanta Paddhati*. Jodhpur, 1824 (s. 1881), 122 x 46 cm. Mehrangarh Museum Trust, RJS 2376.

Cat. 45 Verso, left

reduced to their simplest signifying components. The chakra florets, for example, concisely convey the information essential to yogic knowledge: location in the body, number and color of petals, presiding deities, and correlated sacred syllables. Where the didactic drawing contains perfunctory symbols—such as the inscription *gan*, an abbreviation for Ganapati or Ganesha—the monumental folios bear a richly elaborated, iconographically complete deity. Each lush lotus flower is a shimmering focus of attention, which suggests both their yogic importance and Man Singh's conspicuous piety. DD

45

Nathji Creates the Ganges
folio 8 from the *Nath Purana*
Attributed to Shivdas, ca. 1825
Opaque watercolor and gold on paper; 44.9 x 124.1 cm
Mehrangarh Museum Trust, RJS 2405 0

Numbered 8 on recto.
Sri nath charit
Da [khal] dholiya re kothar
Glorious Nath Charit
Entered in the *dholiya* storeroom

Left

Pachai ek samai samast devagan samjukt shiva shakti sri nath charan ri akash mandal mai upasana karta huva jad sri nath kamana puran vastai ganga pragat kini su jalandhri ganga isa nam sun prasiddh hai, 1
When one time all the gods joined with Shiva and Shakti worshiped the footprints of Glorious Nath in the realm of ether, then Ganga was produced because of the desire of Sri Nath and Jalandhri became renowned as the deity Ganga, 1

Right

Pachai nathas siddh varg pragat huva so un ganga rai vishai aasankar sri caran upasana kar jo gampa sa karta huva min matsyendra goraksh adi caturasi samkhya. 2
Then the group of *siddhas* become manifest and they sat in postures and worshiped the glorious footprints and the group, which included Mina, Matsyendra, and Gorakh, numbered eighty-four, 2

Mapping the Cosmos

46

The Mandala of Shiva
folio 8 from the *Shiva Rahasya*
Jodhpur, 1827 (Samvat 1884)
Opaque watercolor and gold on paper; 46 x 121 cm
Mehrangarh Museum Trust, RJS 2714

Sri siv rahasya
pratham ans pano 8
Da [khal] dholiya re kothar
The glorious Shiva Rahasya
First section, page 8
Entered into the *dholiya* storeroom

Previously published in Rosemary Crill, *Marwar Painting: A History of the Jodhpur Style* (1999), fig. 129.

Several of the *Shiva Rahasya* mandala's more decorative elements are strikingly unusual. Most mandalas and cosmic diagrams are structured symmetrically upon geometric ground plans. In this regard, the ornamental continent-and-ocean ribbons in the mandala's corners and the triangular heavens are surprising. Certainly the mandala bears no relationship to the only extant earlier (circa 1775) Jodhpur painting of the seven island-worlds and oceans (see fig. 46a). The striking folio 66 of the *Bhagavata Purana* manuscript commissioned by Maharaja Vijai Singh represents the Hindu conception of an egg-shaped universe comprised of seven concentric island-continents and oceans. Here the artist has focused on a pie-slice wedge of land and sea rings. The painting's unusual composition and its earthy palette bear a remarkable resemblance to a folio, undoubtedly from another *Bhagavata Purana* manuscript, provisionally attributed by B. N. Goswamy to Datia or Orchha.[1] As yet, no one has discovered a visual source for the *Shiva Rahasya* mandala, and it cannot be determined at this stage whether its idiosyncrasy emerges from the artist's imaginative interpretation of a text or from a now-lost esoteric drawing provided by a Nath adept. DD

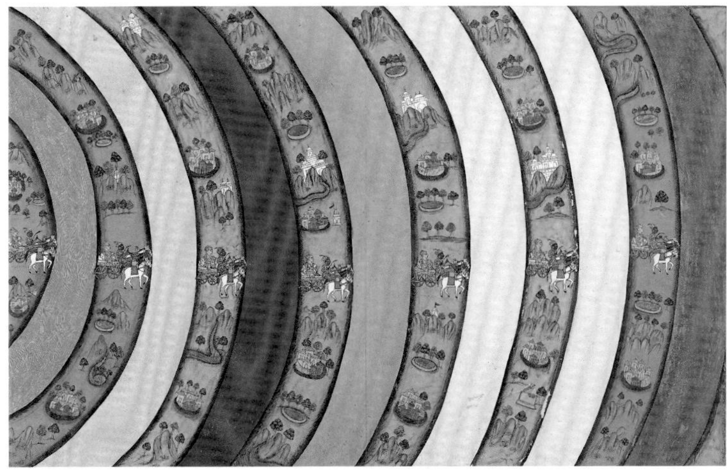

Fig. 46a Detail, *The Seven Continents and Seven Oceans*, folio 66 from the *Bhagavata Purana*, Jodhpur, ca. 1775, 68 x 49 cm. Mehrangarh Museum Trust, RJS 1817.

47

The Mandala of Great Ether (Mahakasha Mandala)
folio 7 from the *Nath Purana*
Attributed to Bulaki, ca. 1825
Opaque watercolor and gold on paper; 46.9 x 129.9 cm
Mehrangarh Museum Trust, RJS 2404

Numbered 7 on recto.

Bulaki maps the cosmos onto an irregular grid, which begins at the lower-right corner with the tortoise-serpent support of the universe, continues up through seven netherworlds, turns sharply left to the central panel of the oval island-continent *bhulok*, dips down to the lower-left corner to depict the first in a series of increasingly more ethereal heavens, and then finishes, after a sharp turn back to the right, with the rectangular gold realm where the Nath *mahasiddhas* dwell at the apex of the universe (see p. 292). Bulaki's overtly uneven distribution and zigzag progression of heavens is surprising because mandalas typically are laid out with bilateral symmetry. Although no explanation is proffered in the gloss on the painting's back, the mandala's underlying structure appears to be the swastika, an ancient symbol of the auspicious. (Entry continues on pp. 292–93.) DD

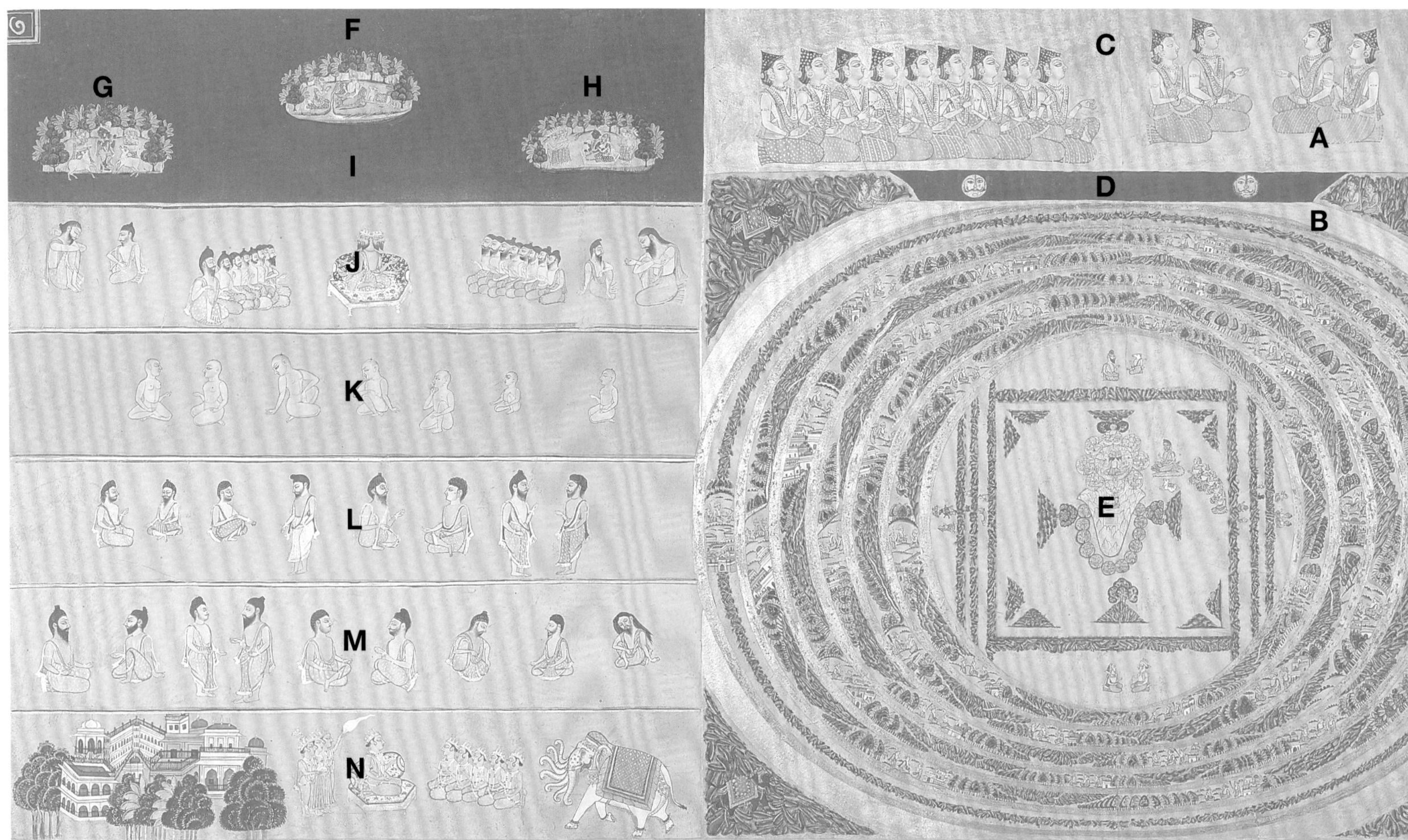

Cat. 47

The letters on this chart correspond to inscriptions on the painting's verso:

A   *Sri nath charit*
    Glorious Nath Charit

B   *Da [khal] dholiya re kothar*
    Entered in the *dholiya* storeroom

C   *[numbered] 1 Mahakakash mandal rai shikhar main sri nathji navanath
    ashtadash shishyan samjukt... svarup sun virajai hai. sri jallandharnath
    (1) sri gorakshnath (2) sri kanerinath (3) sri matsyendranath (4).*
    1: On the peak of the realm (mandala) of great ether, Sri Nath, the Nine
    Naths, and the eighteen disciples are together: 1, Glorious Jallandharnath,
    2, Glorious Gorakhnath, 3, Glorious Kanerinath, and 4, Glorious
    Matsyendranath.

D   *[numbered] 6[?] Bhuvarlok*
    6[?]: the world of air

E   *[numbered] 7[?] Bhulok bhumandal dvip samudra parvat nadiyan khand
    nagar gram vanavasti vanaspati lokalok diggaj sumeru gir gandh madan
    adi sthit deva viharasthan adi samjukt hai*
    7[?]: In the Bhu mandala of the earth, there are islands, oceans, mountains,
    rivers, towns, cities, forest dwellings, forests, the mountains Lokalok, Meru,
    Gir Gandh, Madan and other places that the gods enjoy.

F   *[numbered] 2: Jin rai adhobhag mahakailas sthan jin rai vishai param shiv
    para shakti samjukt virajai hai.*
    2: Supreme Shiva and Supreme Shakti are together in the
    great abode of Kailash.

G   *[numbered] 3: Pakhti golok jin vishai radha krishna*
    3: Close by are Krishna and Radha in Golok

H   *[numbered on left] 4: Jin rai adho bhag vaikunth sthan jin vishai
    sri lakshmi narayan*
    4: Lakshmi and Narayan dwell in Vaikuntha

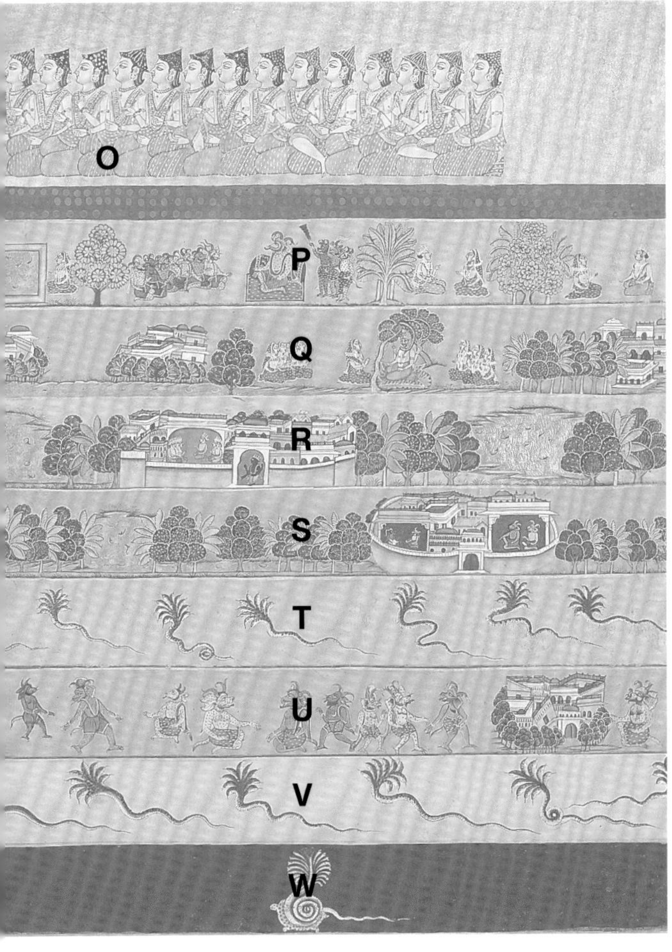

Cat. 47 Verso, E, F, G, H, and I

I *[numbered on left] 5: Sri nath agya sun brahma shrshti svi hai so tin lok*
   caturdash bhuvan nirman kiya
   5, Commanded by glorious Nath, Brahma made the three worlds
   and the fourteen worlds

J *Pratham Satyalok*

K *Taplok*

L *Janlok*

M *Maharlok*

N *Svarlok*

O *[numbered] 9? Bhulok sun hethai patal lok upar tircha thaka naraklok*
   9?, The underworlds are under the earth and to the side of the underworld

P *Atal*

Q *Vital*

R *Sutal*

S *Rasatal*

T *Talatal*

U *Rasatal*

V *Patal*

W *Sheshnag Kurma (Snake and Tortoise)[2]*

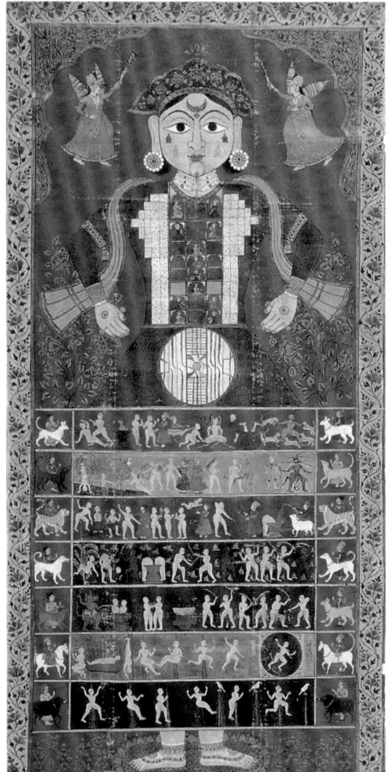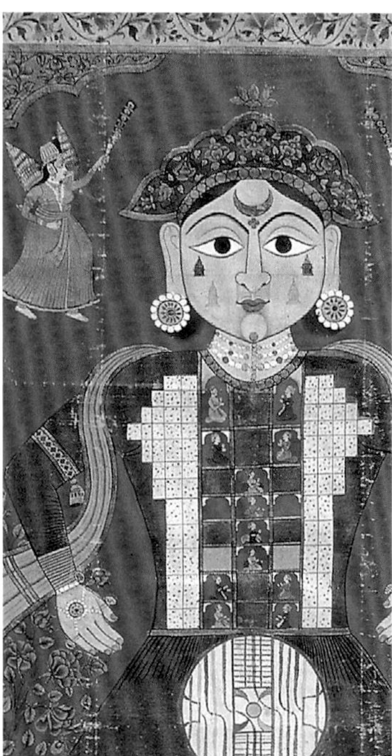

Fig. 48a Cosmic Man (*Lokapurusha*), Bikaner, Rajasthan, ca. 1775. Paul F. Walter Collection

48

The Equivalence of Self and Universe
folio 6 from the *Siddha Siddhanta Paddhati*
"The Muslim Artist" (Bulaki), 1824 (Samvat 1881)
Opaque watercolor and gold on paper; 122 x 46 cm
Mehrangarh Museum Trust, RJS 2378

Numbered 6 on recto.

Sri sidh sidhant padhati 1881 ra
da [khal] dholiya re kothar
Sri siddha siddhanta paddhati of 1824
Entered in the *dholiya* storeroom

Previously published in Debra Diamond, "Court Painting and Yogic Metaphysics in Nineteenth-Century Jodhpur," in Andrew Topsfield, ed., *Court Painting in Rajasthan* (2000), fig. 1 (p. 140).

To represent metaphysical and cosmographic concepts that were new to court painting, Man Singh's artists sorted through and selected visual source material from diverse court genres and vernacular painting traditions.

The cosmic body of folio 6 was adapted from an archetype of the anthropomorphic universe that circulated widely among Jains in northwest India. A typical Jain *lokapurusha* (world-man; see fig. 48a) depicts a hierarchical universe of fourteen worlds with demonic underworlds located in the lower body and heavens for enlightened beings positioned at its apex. While Bulaki transformed the peopled

Jain worlds into white palace-cities, he reproduced the Jain archetype's circular head, crossed lotus-eyes, arched brows that continue into a line around the nose's tip and nostrils, and small, pursed mouth above a "mango-stone" chin. These are, arguably, well-established visual conventions but particularities of shading attest a stronger connection between the *Siddha Siddhanta Paddhati* figure and the Jain *lokapurusha*. The connection is most clearly visible in the distinctive abstraction of the shaded area between nose and lips, which is crisply bisected by a pale philtrum and bordered by an equally pale contour along the upper lip's curved rim. Moreover, the Nath *siddha's* curls suggest a second, unassimilated borrowing from the Jain iconographic tradition: while painted Jain *lokapurushas* wear crowns, Jinas (in both painting and sculpture) usually are depicted with snail-shell curls. The Jodhpur artist, however, has altered stance and garb to transform the *lokapurusha* into a Nath *siddha*.[3]

Several factors contributed to the availability and adaptability of the Jain archetype. Jains and Naths long interacted at pilgrimage sites such as Girnar in Gujarat and Abu in Rajasthan, where artists may have produced *lokapurushas* for both communities. Alternately, since ties between Girnar and Jodhpur were strong, a Jain archetype could have been brought directly from the holy mountain peaks to Man Singh's court. Finally, Jodhpur court artists may have worked from locally produced Jain paintings because the city had a thriving Jain community. Court artists or members of their families may even have painted the Jain image that provided the source for this citation.[4]

Notably, Man Singh's artist declined to appropriate another cosmic conception that circulated widely in Rajasthan during this period. The verses of the *Bhagavad Gita*, which powerfully convey the awesome equivalence of the Hindu deity Vishnu with the universe, inspired many paintings of the god's monumental body filled with minute worlds. However, those works are not cartographic. The rare Vaishnava paintings that carefully represent the locations of the worlds emerge within tantric milieus. Like the Nath *siddha* of folio 6, they depict the cosmic man according to the pictorial schemata that were developed most fully for Jain patrons. They range in size from a monumental Vaishnava *lokapurusha* on cloth to smaller paintings on paper.[5] DD

49

Three Yantras from the Meghmala
ca. 1825
Opaque watercolor and gold on paper; 41.4 x 199.4 cm
Mehrangarh Museum Trust
White numbered 7, RJS 2502
Pink numbered 8, RJS 2504
Green numbered 9, RJS 2503

Numbered in the upper left corners.

Sacred Sites and Cosmic Oceans

50

Shiva Temples
folio 28 from the *Shiva Rahasya*
1827 (Samvat 1884)
Opaque watercolor and gold on paper; 40.2 x 115.5 cm
Mehrangarh Museum Trust, RJS 2734

sri siv rahasya sa[mvat] 1884 ra
pratham ams pano 28
da [khal] dholiya re kothar
glorious Shiva Rahasya of 1827
first section, page 28
entered in the *dholiya* storeroom

51

The Mountains of the Eight Directions
folio 17 from the *Shiva Rahasya*
1827 (Samvat 1884)
Opaque watercolor and gold on paper; 40.2 x 115.5 cm
Mehrangarh Museum Trust, RJS 2729

Sri siv rahasya sam[vat] 1884 ra
pratham ams ro pano 17
Da[khal] dholiya re kothar
Glorious Shiva Rahasya of 1827
First section, page 17
Entered in the *dholiya* storeroom

52

Twelve Light-form Manifestations of Nathji
folio 50 from the *Nath Charit*
1823 (Samvat 1880)
Opaque watercolor and gold on paper; 123 x 47 cm
Mehrangarh Museum Trust, RJS 2475

Numbered 50 in red by Reu.
Sri nath charit
da [khal] dholiya re kothar
Glorious Nath Charit
Entered in the *dholiya* storeroom

53

The Practice of Yoga
folio 5 from the *Siddha Siddhanta Paddhati*
Attributed to Bulaki, 1824 (Samvat 1881)
Opaque watercolor and gold on paper; 122 x 46 cm
Mehrangarh Museum Trust, RJS 2377

Numbered 5 on recto.
Sri sidh sidhant padhati 1881 ra
Dakhal dholiya re kothar
Glorious Siddha Siddhanta Paddhati of 1824
Entered in the *dholiya* storeroom

54

Shiva Reveals the Geography of the Three Worlds to Parvati
folio 13 from the *Shiva Rahasya*
Attributed to Vana Akhavat,* 1827 (Samvat 1884)
Opaque watercolor and gold on paper; 40.4 x 115.6 cm
Mehrangarh Museum Trust, RJS 2719

sri siv rahasya
pratham ams ri panau 13
da[khal] dholiya re kothar
glorious Shiva Rahasya
first section, page 13
entered into the *dholiya* storeroom

*Attributed to Vana Akhavat by comparison to *Shiva Purana*, folios 31 and 76 (Mehrangarh Museum Trust, RJS 2628, 2673), both of which are inscribed *citarai vanai akhavat kino.*

Shiva's pointing gesture can be understood as the margin between pictorial sources adopted from two different traditions. While the palaces on the left rely on the conventions of Jodhpur court painting, the disposition of rivers across the plains recall extant terrain maps of mountainous Kashmir and the Himalayan foothills.[1] In these maps, cartographers charted the jagged paths of rivers from above and depicted mountains, dwellings, and trees in elevation view, as in a Hardwar to Tibet route map from the collection of the City Palace, Jaipur; other Kashmiri maps from this period employ silver paint to color the rivers.[2] While no such maps have yet been located in the Jodhpur archives, it is likely that artists had access to this genre of imagery.[3] We know that Rajput rulers collected and commissioned maps and that Man Singh had texts from all over India and Nepal brought to his library. A letter to the maharaja from the otherwise unknown Ganesh Nath, for example, asks Man Singh to construct a resting place for Naths traveling on pilgrimage to Kedarnath and Badrinath. Man Singh, who took every Nath request seriously (and seems to have never turned one down), may have indeed consulted a map when he considered Ganesh Nath's suggestion.[4] When the maharaja patronized

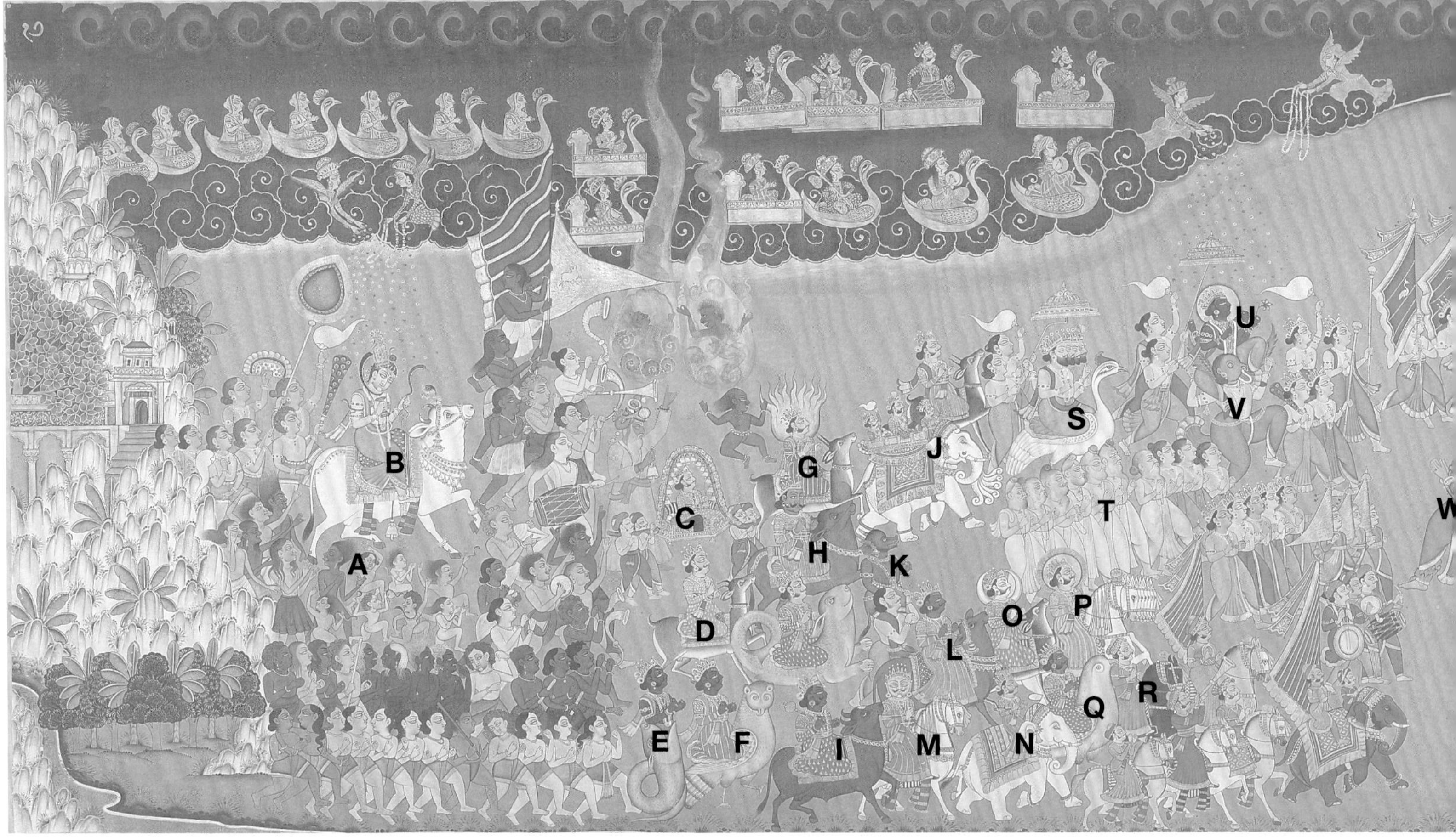

Cat. 55

temple reconstruction, he also consulted building plans, and several Man Singh-period paintings draw closely upon local city maps, as well as plans of distant cities (see pp. 162–63).[5] Indeed, it strains credulity that a painter who lived in the midst of a relatively flat desert could have devised this composition from the observation of nature; the more plausible source is a map from a mountainous region.

I have gone on this lengthy digression for two reasons. One, it reveals how Jodhpur artists created imagery for new subjects, which had not been previously illustrated in court painting, by citing and juxtaposing motifs from various genres of painting. Two, it offers a perspective on how court audiences may have responded to this painting. The viewing expectations engendered by topographical maps, which imply a studied and observed connection to an anterior reality, are different from those of other pictorial genres. The citation of this mapping convention connects sites on earth with those of celestial worlds and may have lent the authority of the real and the concrete to the artist's representation of Shiva's realm. DD

55

Shiva's Wedding Procession
folio 17 from the *Shiva Purana*
Vana Akhavat, ca. 1828
Opaque watercolor and gold on paper; 46.3 x 124 cm
Mehrangarh Museum Trust, RJS 2612

Numbered 17 in the upper left corner.

Sri siv puran
Da[khal] dholiya re kothar
Citarai vanai akhavat kino
Glorious Shiva Purana
Entered into the *dholiya* storeroom
Made by the painter Vana Akhavat

[numbered] 1 Kailas parvat sun siv ri jan chadi agai anek bhant rup kiyan gan
bhuta dik nrtya karai gavai vadiya bajave seva karai hai

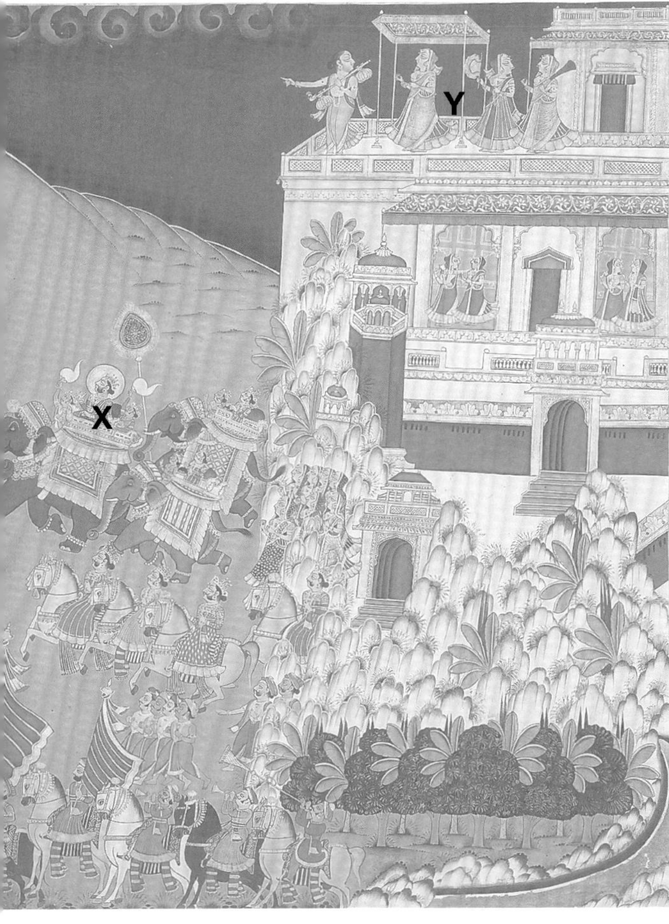

In *Shiva's Wedding Procession*, the painter Vana Akhavat's primary concern is to create the sense of a jubilant wedding procession. He eschews the cardinal orientation and many of the symbols that identify sculpted deities on temple architecture.[6] Nonetheless, many of the gods can be identified from their vehicles, skin color, and their loose groupings in space.[7] Tentative identifications are accompanied by a question mark. DD

A Ganas
B Shiva

Directional Deities
C Kubera (north)
D Vayu (northwest)
E Varuna (west)
F Nairrti? (southwest)
G Agni (southeast)
H Ishana (northeast)
I Yama (south)
J Indra (east)

Planetary Deities
K Lunar nodes? (Rahu and Ketu)
L Mars (Mangala)
M Venus? (Shukra)
N Jupiter (Brihaspati)
O Moon (Chandra)
P Sun (Surya)
Q Mercury (Budha)
R Saturn? (Shani)

S Brahma
T Seven Celestial Sages
U Vishnu
V Garuda
W Parvat
X Himavat
Y Menaka and Sage Narada

The wedding procession begins from Mount Kailash. Different types of imps and spirits dance, sing, play instruments, and attend [Shiva], 1

[numbered] 2 Agai brahma vishnu adi indra dik dikpal navgraha gan gandharv apsara adi jani prayam karai nai sanmukh himachal ro dut parvat takid karai hai Vishnu, Indra, the deities of the directions, the gods of the planets, and celestial beings journey toward Himavat, whose envoy Parvat waits to receive them, 2

[numbered] 3 Himachal apro parvar bandhav linam sanmukh jan ro samelan karan ayo nai himachal rai mahalan upar ubhi rani menaka naradji nai puchai hai mharo janvai kiso rupvan hai so vatavo anukram sun avata janiyan nai to naradji vatavai jina ro rup aishvarya dekh ne mainaka jani hai isa janiyan ro hi mukhya hai tarai to mharo janvai ati sundar husi jin vastai mhari putri bhalan tapasya kari Himavat, with family and friends, receives the wedding party. Himavat's wife, Queen Menaka, standing atop Himavat's palace, asks Narada about the appearance of her son-in-law. Narada describes the guests in sequence. Upon seeing the beauty of the illustrious guests, Menaka thinks "since the wedding party is this beautiful then its leader, for whom my daughter completed arduous austerities, will surely be very handsome," 3

Previously published in Rosemary Crill, *Marwar Painting* (1999), fig. 131.

56a–g

Cosmic Oceans

seven folios from the *Nath Charit;* attributed to Bulaki, 1823 (Samvat 1880)
Opaque watercolor and gold on paper; 44.1 x 118.2
Mehrangarh Museum Trust
RJS 2468, f. 43 (gray, om)
RJS 2469, f. 44 (marigold)
RJS 2470, f. 45 (pink, swan)
RJS 2471, f. 46 (white, tortoise)
RJS 2472, f. 47 (gray, snake)
RJS 2473, f. 48 (orange)
RJS 2474, f. 49 (white, gray man)

Numbered 43–49 in red by Reu.
Sri nath charit
Da[khal] dholiya re kothar
Glorious Nath Charit
Entered in the *dholiya* storeroom

Marwar Rulers

Rao Jodha	1453–89
Rao Satal	1489–92
Rao Suja	1492–1515
Rao Ganga	1515–32
Rao Maldeo	1532–62
Rao Chandrasen	1562–81
Rao Rai Singh	1582–83
Mota Raja Udai Singh	1583–95
Raja Sur Singh	1595–1619
Maharaja Gaj Singh	1619–38
Maharaja Jaswant Singh	1638–78
Maharaja Ajit Singh	1707–24
Maharaja Abhai Singh	1724–49
Maharaja Ram Singh	1749–51
Maharaja Bakhat Singh	1751–52
Maharaja Vijai Singh	1752–93
Maharaja Bhim Singh	1793–1803
Maharaja Man Singh	1803–43
Maharaja Takhat Singh	1843–73
Maharaja Jaswant Singh II	1873–95
Maharaja Sardar Singh	1895–1911
Maharaja Sumer Singh	1911–18
Maharaja Ummed Singh	1918–1947
Maharaja Hanuwant Singh	1947–52
Maharaja Gaj Singh II	1953–

Maharaja Bakhat Singh Chronology

Although most Rajput portraits do not represent rulers as they age, Nagaur court artists were encouraged by their patron to convey Bakhat Singh as he grew older over time. Thus, through these portraits, arranged chronologically over a span of thirty-six years, we can observe Bakhat Singh's actual progression from youth to middle age.

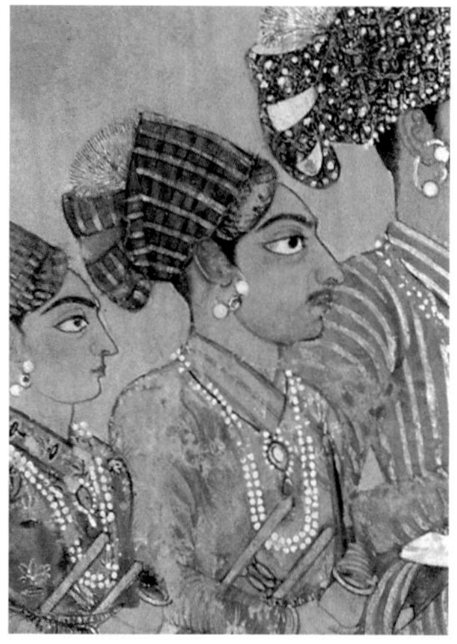

Ca. 1715–18

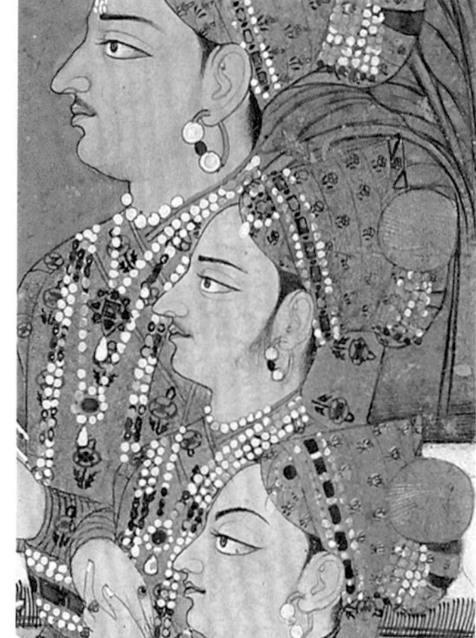

Dated 1721

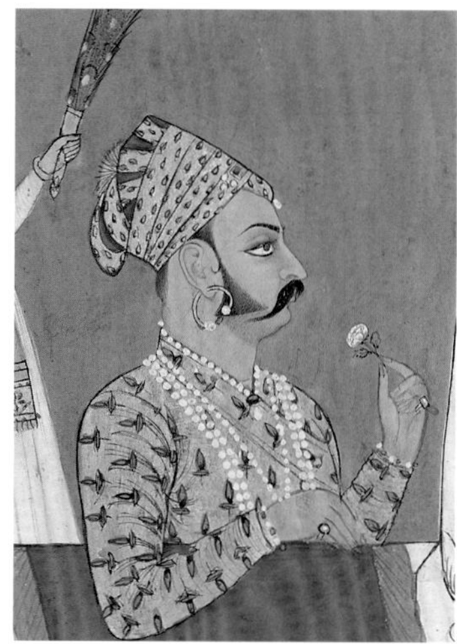

Ca. 1735

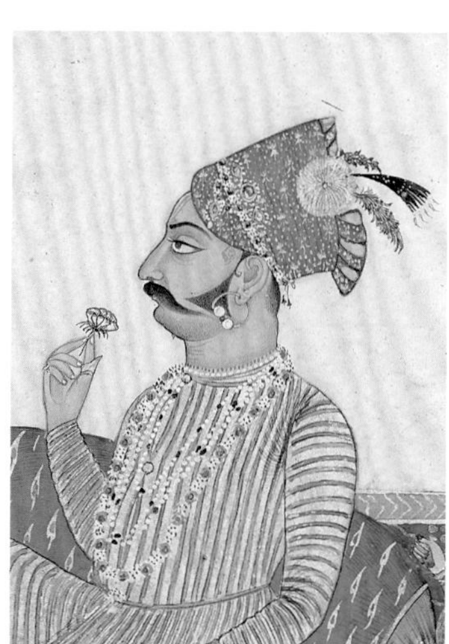

Ca. 1736

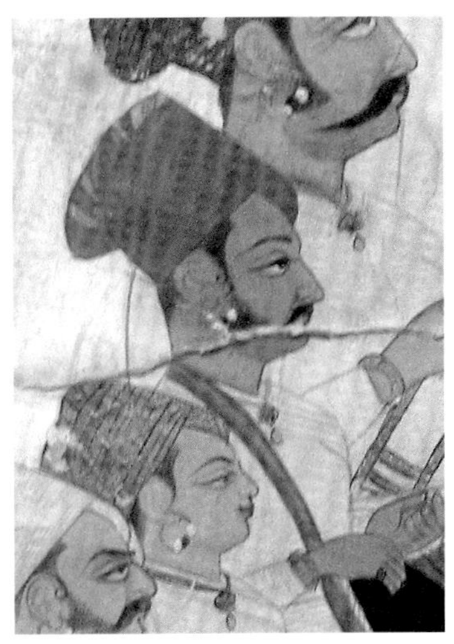

Ca. 1722

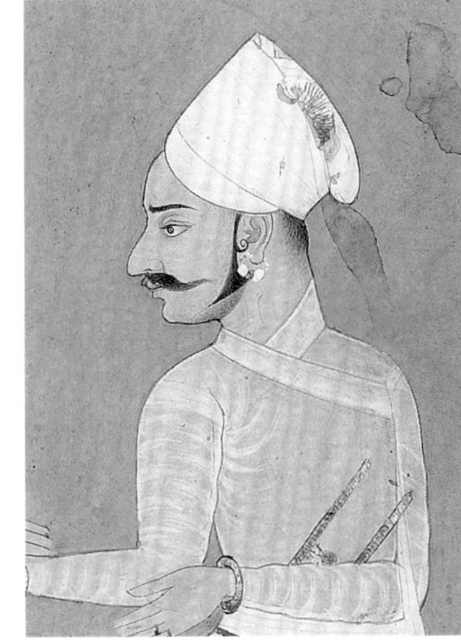

Ca. 1724

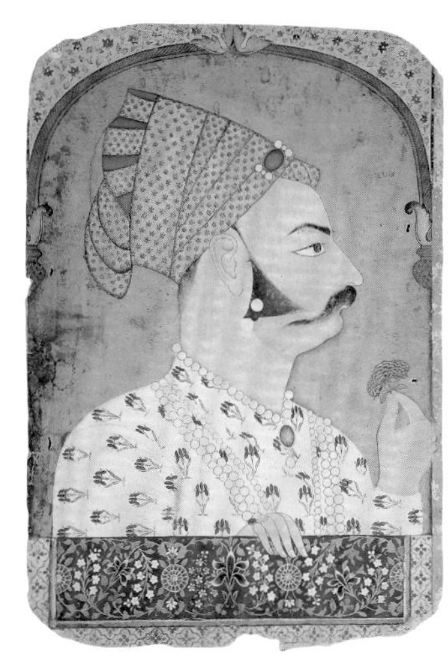

Ca. 1730

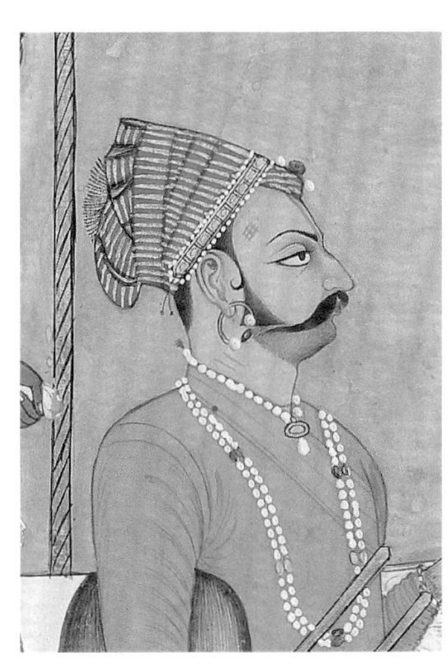

Ca. 1732

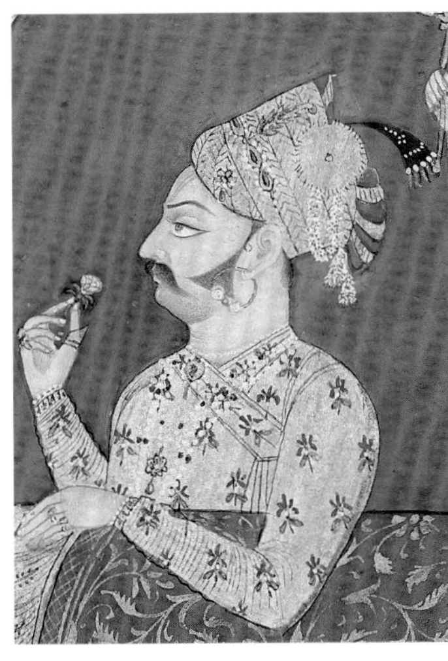

Dated 1737

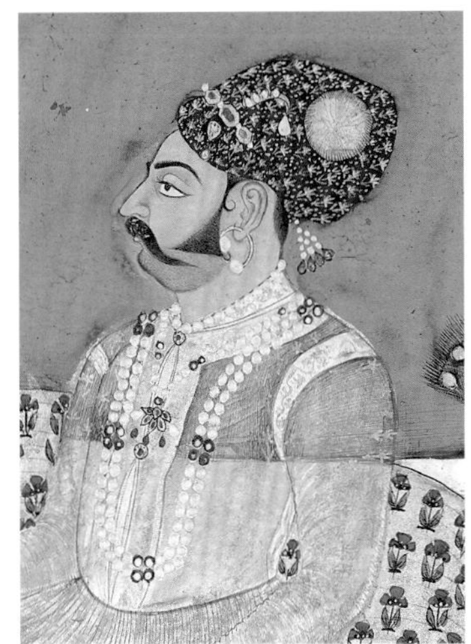

Dated 1737

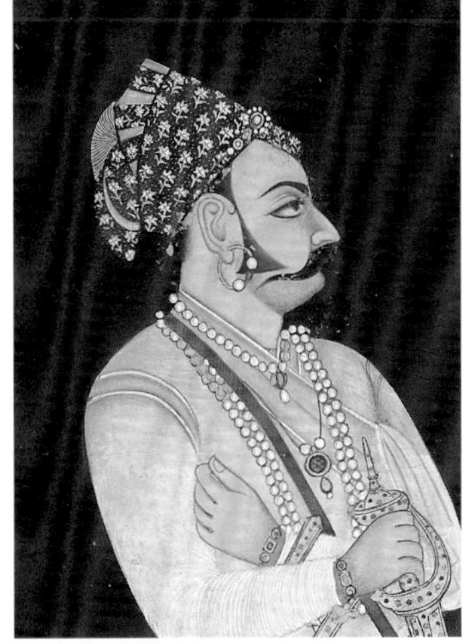

Dated 1745

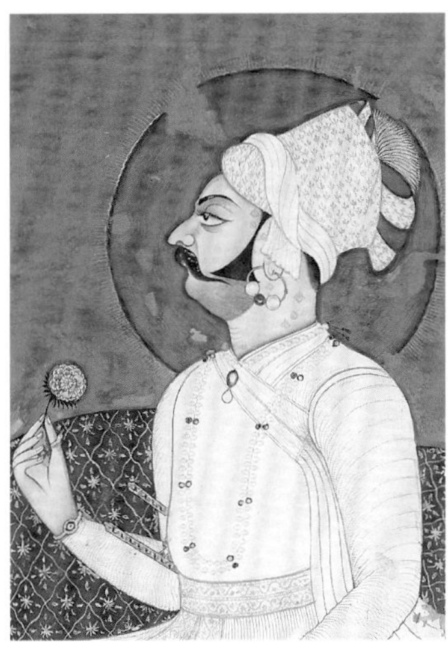

Ca. 1751

Notes to the Essays

The Rathores of Jodhpur–Marwar

1. Among these pursuits are water management, girls' education, and brain-trauma education.

2. According to the Rathore bards, the clan descended from Jai Chand of Kanauj, the cousin and rival of the famous medieval leader Prithviraj Chauhan. Both these rulers were defeated by Afghan invaders at the end of the twelfth century, a catastrophe that led to the disruption and migration of the early Rajput clans. The Rathores came to Pali, in Marwar, in what is now central Rajasthan. It is claimed that they were invited to settle there to protect Brahmin villages against cattle-rustling local tribes. The story may have a whiff of legend, but the protection of the priestly caste is a traditional Rajput role. Their success in Pali was the basis of their expanding power in the region.

3. Annie Besant and Bhagvan Das, *The Bhagvad-Gita* (Delhi: Anmol Publication, 1986), 18: 43, In Marwari, it is commonly recited as "Man, swami seva, desh bhakti, maryada, dan virta, sharangati, bal, rajrang, kshetraseva, dharmaseva" (honor, loyalty, patriotism, propriety, generosity, braviding, providing sanctuary, service of the people, protection of social order [are the duties of Rajput rulers]).

4. Indeed, *rajputai*, which refers to acts of bravery, inflects the meaning of Rajput (Sanskrit, son of a king).

5. Bards (*charans*) accompanied Rajputs on military campaigns and recited verses such as these prior to battles in order to inspire valor and instill values. Poem translated by Karni Singh Jasol.

6. They identified with Devi because the goddess had been created from the combined power of the gods to destroy evil, exemplified in this verse from the *Devi Mahatmya*: "O Durga, (when) called to mind, you take away fear from every creature…. O you who destroy poverty, misery, and fear, who other than you is always tender-minded, in order to work benefits for all? Thomas B. Coburn, *Encountering the Goddess: A Translation of the Devi-Mahatmya and a Study of Its Interpretation* (Albany: State University of New York Press, 1991), verse 4.16, p. 50.

7. "…gods create a beautiful goddess in order to combat the forces of evil." Vidya Dehejia, *Devi: The Great Goddess* (Sackler Gallery, 1999), p. 16.

8. They built temples and shrines, inside and outside the kingdom; patronized religious festivals; supported Brahmins, holymen, and religious communities; and commissioned devotional literature, poetry, and paintings.

9. These devotional bonds also strengthened connections beyond the borders of Marwar, as demonstrated by the transregional Vaishnava relationships cultivated by Maharaja Vijai Singh (see "Maharaja Vijai Singh and the Epic Landscape").

10. Gopalnarayan Bahura, "Contribution of Marwar to Sanskrit," *Studies in Marwar History*, ed. N. S. Bhati (Chopasni, Jodhpur: Rajasthani Shodh Sansthan, 1979), 33–35. See also n.9, p. 306.

11. *Meher* is a Rajasthani word for the sun. It is likely that the name was chosen to honor the sun from which the Rathores were understood to descend.

12. Natural outcroppings surround and protect the land at the base of the fort. The town that sprang up at its base was named Jodhpur, meaning Jodha's city.

Becoming Rajput

1. B. Chattopadhyay uses the phrase "Rajputization" in "Origin of the Rajputs" in B. Chattopadhyay, *The Making of Early Medieval India* (Delhi: Oxford University Press, 1997), 59.

2. Chattopadhyay (p. 81) discusses this aspect of a wide range of terms for ruling elites, beginning in about the twelfth century.

3. D. Kolff, *Naukar, Rajput and Sepoy: The Ethnohistory of the Military Labor Market in Hindustan, 1450–1850* (Cambridge University Press, 1990), 196–97.

4. Ibid.

5. See James Tod, *Annals and Antiquities of Rajasthan* (New Delhi: Oriental Books Reprint Corporation, 1983 [1829, 1832]), vol. 1, 68–105.

6. For a bibliography on the topic, see J. N. Asopa, *Origin of the Rajputs* (Delhi, India: Bharatiya Publishing House, 1976). Nationalist evocations—either of the Rajputs as ancestors of the Vedic past or as glorious defenders of a Hindu tradition—inform the more chauvinist historical narratives. British Romantic orientalism, however, takes a remarkably similar line in its racialized view of caste and its search for ancient, authentic peoples. Tod's *Annals* is the quintessential statement of this position, and it is not coincidental that it has fed this historical view of the Rajputs.

7. Chattopadhyay, 76–78.

8. See n.2, "The Rathores of Jodhpur–Marwar."

9. Kolff's treatment of the development of the Rajput lineages out of the military labor market in India is especially helpful in understanding this process. See chap. 3, "The Rajput of Pre-Mughal North India," 71–116.

10. An important example of the politically transformative power of marriage is the story of how the Rathore princess Hansa Bai was introduced into the Mewar house. Rao Chunda of Marwar (r. 1384–1428) proposed that his daughter marry the son of Rana Lakha of Mewar, Prince Chunda. The proposal arrived when Prince Chunda was away from court, and his father the rana jokingly rebuffed the offer to allow his son to respond to the proposal from such a young and lovely princess. From an abundant sense of honor, however, Prince Chunda rejected the offer of marriage because his father had done so, even though that was in jest. To prevent an insult to the Rathores, Rana Lakha married Hansa Bai and asked his son to renounce all claims to the throne in the event that she bore a son. Such was the power of the marriage alliance, and the sense of honor between houses, that it overtook the rightful birthright by primogeniture within the Mewar court. Prince Chunda was given a high position in the court as a result of his loyalty to the rana, but the increasing Rathore influence in Mewar after the marriage, and the ambitions that Hansa Bai harbored for her son, Mokal, brought the Mewari Chunda into conflict with the Rathores. Chunda drove the Rathore Rao Jodha out of his capital of Mandor for a time and brought about a crisis in Marwari–Mewari relationships.

11. Richard D. Saran and Norman P. Ziegler, *The Mertiyo Rathors of Merto, Rajasthan: Select translations bearing on the history of a Rajput family, 1462–1660* (Ann Arbor: University of Michigan, Centers for South and Southeast Asian Studies, 2001), vol. 1, 58–59.

12. Tod, vol. 1, 107–72. For a full examination of the structure of the Rajput court, see also R. K. Saxena, *Rajput Nobility: A Study of 18th Century Rajputana (1761–1818 AD)* (New Delhi: S. Chand & Co., 1996) and A. C. Lyall, *Asiatic*

Studies: Religious and Social (London: John Murray, 1882). All refer to the system as *primer inter pares*.

13. For the history of the founding of Jodhpur, see Tod, vol. 2, 9–18; R. Hooja, *A History of Rajasthan* (New Delhi: Rupa & Co., 2006).

14. G. D. Sharma, *Rajput Polity: A Study of Politics and Administration in the State of Marwar, 1638–1749* (New Delhi: Manohar, 1977), 5.

15. J. R. Richards, *The Mughal Empire.* The New Cambridge History of India (Cambridge University Press, 1993), 29–57.

16. S. Bayly, "The 'Brahman Raj' c. 1700–1830," in *Caste, Society and Politics in India from the Eighteenth Century to the Modern Age* (Cambridge University Press, 1999), 64–96.

17. See Richards, *The Mughal Empire;* Kolff, pp. 19–20; and the work in Stewart Gordon's volume on robes and robing as political acts. S. Gordon, ed., *Robes of Honour: Khilat in Pre-colonial and Colonial India* (Oxford University Press, 2003).

18. Hooja, 589–96; G. D. Sharma, 47–59; Tod, vol. 2, 36–48.

19. G. D. Sharma, 52.

20. Shah Jahan's father was Jahangir, and his mother was a Rathore Rajput.

21. Jaswant Singh was a defeated ruler and therefore could not have had legitimate status within the court. Sharma, 56.

22. Hooja, 592. Contemporaneous European travelers in the Mughal Empire also report this story.

Rathore and Mughal Interactions

1. Joan Cummins, *Indian Painting from Cave Temples to the Colonial Period* (Boston: MFA Publications, 2006), 70, pl. 32.

2. Frances H. Taft "Honor and Alliance: Reconsidering Mughal-Rajput Marriages" in *The Idea of Rajasthan: Explorations in Regional Identity*, ed. Karine Schomer, Joan L. Erdman, Deryck O. Lodrick, and Lloyd I. Rudolph (New Delhi: Manohar, 1994), vol. II, 226; Abu'l Fazl Allami, *Akbar-Nama*, trans. H. Beveridge, (Delhi: Rare Books, 1972), vol. 2, 305; Mohammad Haleem Siddiqui, *History of Nagaur* (Jodhpur: Maharaja Man Singh Prakash, 2001), 82 (Traslated for this project by Shagupta Parekh and Anand Kumar Dwivedi).

3. Rosemary Crill, *Marwar Painting: A History of the Jodhpur Style* (Mumbai: India Book House Limited, 1999), figs.1, 2, 9, 10, 16, 19, 21–24. The luminous surface of these later seventeenth-century paintings was achieved through the burnishing (rubbing with a hard stone such as agate) of the pigments from the reverse side.

4. Marriage alliances between the Hindus of Jodhpur and Muslim rulers in Nagaur were not uncommon. Raja Maldev of Jodhpur (r. 1531–83) gave a daughter to a Nagaur Muslim ruler in the early sixteenth century, and Raja Udai Singh (r. 1583–94) continued the practice by giving one of his daughters to Mohammad Daulat Khan of Nagaur (Taft, 225, and Norman P. Ziegler, "Evolution of the Rathor State of Marvar: Horses, Structural Change and Warfare," in *The Idea of Rajasthan*, vol. II, 197). Another Nagaur Hindu/Muslim marriage occurred when a Hindu princess, the daughter of Amar Singh, ruler of Nagaur, was married to Sulaiman Shikoh, grandson of the Mughal emperor Shah Jahan (Taft, 223–24).

5. M. A. Chaghtai, "Nagaur * –A Forgotten Kingdom," *Bulletin of the Deccan College Research Institute*, part 2, nos. 1–2 (November 1940), 166; Siddiqui, 3. The complex occupies thirty-six acres and includes four major palace buildings along with sixty additional buildings, including bath houses, verandahs, temples, queens quarters, reception halls, and stables.

6. Chaghtai, 182–83. On p. 170, Chaghtai notes that for Indian Muslims Nagaur was second only to Ajmer as an important Muslim center. Nagaur's importance was due to two eminent Muslim saints who were associated with the city, Qadi Hamidu 'd-Din and Shaykh Hamidu 'd-Din, both of whom died in the thirteenth century and were followers of the eminent Mu'inu 'd-Din Chishti.

7. *The Cambridge History of India: Turks and Afghans*, ed. Lt. Colonel Sir Wolseley Haig (Delhi: S. Chand & Co, 1965), vol. III, 622; Chaghtai, 182–83; H. Goetz, "The Nagaur School of Rajput Painting (18th century)," *Artibus Asiae XII* (1949), 89–90; Siddiqui, 29.

8. Siddiqui, 83; Catherine B. Asher, *Architecture of Mughal India* (New Delhi: Foundation Books, 1995), 76.

9. Chaghtai, 181; *The Cambridge History of India: The Mughal Period*, planned by Lt. Colonel Sir Wolseley Haig, ed. Sir Richard Burn (Delhi: S. Chand & Co., 1963), vol. IV, 102; Abu'l Fazl, vol. 2, 517. During the 1570 trip Akbar stayed in Nagaur for fifty days, during which the formal submission of Jodhpur was performed by Chandra Sen, son of Raja Maldev of Jodhpur. At the same time Akbar solidified the Marwar–Mughal connection by taking two Rathore princesses into his zenana. Two illustrations of Akbar's visit to Nagaur are included in the Victoria and Albert copy of Abu'l Fazl's *Akbarnama* (IS 2-1896). Folio 81 depicts Akbar being received by the governor of Nagaur. Folio 82 is the purification of the Kular Talao (tank) at Nagaur and includes the fort in the background and the dredging of the tank in the foreground. I am grateful to Rosemary Crill for this information.

10. See n.9 regarding Abu'l Fazl's description of Akbar's visit. Shaykh Mubarak Nagawri was a distinguished Islamic and Sufi scholar, particularly revered by members of the mystical aspect of Islam. Along with Shaykh Salim Chishti, Nagawri directed Akbar toward more openly tolerant and spiritual religious thinking.

11. Siddiqui, 88.

12. See Crill, 18, for a dated Samvat 1646 (1589) drawing of Ganesha and Parvati done in Nagaur by the artist Dayala. Reproduced in Stuart Cary Welch, *Indian Drawings and Painted Sketches* (New York: Asia Society, 1976), no. 1.

13. I am grateful to Vinod Kanoria, Robert Skelton, Rosemary Crill, Debra Diamond, and Rajeshwari Shah for their assistance with these two images.

14. Amina Okada, *Indian Miniatures of the Mughal Court* (New York: Harry N. Abrams, 1992), 183, pl. 217.

15. Mark Zebrowski, *Deccani Painting* (London: Sotheby Publications, 1983), 145, pl. XVII. Paintings from the central region of the Indian peninsula, an area known as the Deccan, were particularly fanciful in subject matter and used a palette composed primarily of pinks, oranges, mauves, and grays.

16. Milo Cleveland Beach and Ebba Koch, *King of the World: The Padshahnama, an Imperial Mughal Manuscript from the Royal Library, Windsor Castle* (London: Azimuth Editions, 1997), figs. 43, 45; Zebrowski, particularly fig. 92 and also figs 98, 99.

17. See n.12 above and n.7 (p. 311) in the reference catalogue entries for "Origins of Jodhpur Court Painting."

18. Crill, figs. 16, 18, 21–24.

19. W. E. Begley and Z. A. Desai, *The Shah Jahan Nama of 'Inayat Khan* (Delhi: Oxford University Press, 1990), 314–16; Siddiqui, 90–92. Amar Singh's remains were taken to Nagaur and placed in the Amar Singh Chhatri, which is still maintained and visited today.

20. Rai Singh's sister married Shah Jahan's grandson, Sulaiman Shikoh, in 1655, further cementing the relationship between Nagaur and the Mughal court (Siddiqui, 98–99; Taft, 223–24).

21. Siddiqui, 111.

22. Deccan stylistic aspects in Jodhpur painting first appeared during the reign of Jaswant Singh (1638–78), cat. 6. Whether any artists were working in Nagaur for Indar Singh is unknown, as no paintings can be positively attributed to Indar Singh's studio. In fig. 3, we see some Deccan elements, particularly the palette. Yet perhaps further aspects of the Deccan style were introduced to Nagaur during Indar Singh's reign and remained in the artists' repertoire, visible in paintings from the second quarter of the eighteenth century produced for Bakhat Singh.

23. Haig and Burn, vol. IV, 247. Aurangzeb moved to the Muslim enclave of Ajmer, considered by the Mughals to be the "gateway to Rajasthan," so he could be physically closer to Marwar to quell any Rajput opposition.

24. Francis Robinson, *The Mughal Emperors and the Islamic Dynasties of India, Iran and Central Asia, 1206–1925* (London: Thames & Hudson, 2007), 161. It is not known if this condition met with much success; it could not have been well received by the Hindu Rathores.

25. Siddiqui, 117.

26. Robinson, 161; H. M. Elliot and John Dowson, *The History of India as Told by Its Own Historians* (Allahabad: Kitab Mahal, 1877), vol. 7, 159 and 298. Aurangzeb, who came to the Mughal throne after murdering his three brothers, was ruthless in his treatment of Jodhpur, ordering the burning of the fields of crops surrounding the city and even burning women and infants. Hindus were excluded from holding public office. Rather than subduing anger, Aurangzeb's actions fueled further revolt by the Rathores and other Rajput allies.

27. Elliot and Dowson, vol. 7, 187.

28. G. D. Sharma, *India Polity: A Study of Politics and Administration of the State of Marwar, 1638–1749* (New Delhi: Manohar, 1977), 234. Nagaur was confirmed as Ajit Singh's holding by Emperor Farrykshiyar (r. 1713–19) in February 1717. The acceptance of the right of Ajit Singh to rule over Nagaur (as opposed to Indar Singh, who headed a junior branch of the clan) was a significant factor in the consolidation of the Rathore power and territory. Under Ajit Singh, Marwar territory was as large geographically as it had been during the mid-seventeenth century, the height of its power.

29. G. D. Sharma, 240.

30. Ibid, 248.

31. Ibid, 248–49; Sixty-seven individuals—wives, concubines, mistresses, and servants—immolated themselves on Ajit Singh's funeral pyre; Siddiqui, 181. In 1751, Bakhat Singh also ordered someone to blind two of his younger brothers, Ratan Singh and Rup Singh; shortly afterward, the brothers committed suicide.

32. See G. D. Sharma, 240–41, and Bhargava, 164, for information regarding Abhai Singh's promise to give Nagaur to Bakhat Singh and a letter from Abhai Singh instructing Bakhat Singh to kill their father. See Bhargava, 165, regarding the illicit affair. Rima Hooja, *A History of Rajasthan* (New Delhi: Rupa Co., 2006), 708, has suggested that Ajit Singh fell out of favor at the Mughal court and there was a suggestion from the Mughals that he be removed. The very important Rajput ruler Raja Sawai Jai Singh of Amber, who was close to Abhai Singh, also is rumored to have promoted the removal of Ajit Singh in order to further the Rajput position with the Mughals. Bakhat Singh "acted at the written command (in a letter) from Prince Abhay Singh." G. D. Sharma (p. 240) reiterates that the emperor was not happy with and distrusted Ajit Singh because of his alliance with former powers at the Mughal court, the Sayyids. Emperor Muhammad Shah conveyed to Abhai Singh, to whom he had become close, that it would be in the best interest for Abhai Singh's ancestral lands if he killed his father. After this discussion, a letter with Abhai Singh's signature was secretly sent to Bakhat Singh, instructing him to perform the heinous deed.

33. James Tod, *Annals and Antiquities of Rajasthan*, (London: Routledge & Kegan Paul, 1960), vol. 1, 562. Abhai Singh did not leave Delhi to return to Jodhpur until July. He traveled out of his way, via Mathura, where he stopped to marry the daughter of Maharaja Jai Singh of Jaipur on August 1, 1724. The wedding further fueled the rumor that Jai Singh had been part of the plot to kill Ajit Singh (see preceding note); G. D. Sharma, 248–49.

34. Tod, vol. 1, 562. Abhai Singh died in Ajmer on June 19, 1749. The last rites were performed in nearby Pushkar, where there is still a *chatri* (marker) for him.

35. According to custom, the Rathore ruler of the Marwar sub-state of Bagri was the noble who normally conferred the title on the Jodhpur raja and elevated him to his new ruling position.

36. Crill, figs. 37–43. For a Udaipur painting exhibiting a time of rare Rajput harmony amid shifting alliances, see Gerd Kreisel et al., *Rajasthan: Land der Konige* (Stuttgart: Linden Museum, 1995), 156, fig. 138, showing the equestrian procession of Raja Abhai Singh of Jodhpur, Rana Sangram Singh of Mewar, Raja Jai Singh of Jaipur, and the Rathore noble Durga Das.

37. G. D. Sharma, 249, 252.

38. B. D. Chattopadhyaya, "The Emergence of the Rajputs as Historical Process in Early Medieval Rajasthan," in *The Idea of Rajasthan*, vol. II, 175–76. Nagaur was given to Bakhat Singh by his brother Abhai Singh as a prebendal domain. This type of land is not inheritable but is granted by a ruler to a person in return for services to the state, one of the reasons for the conjecture that Bakhat Singh killed his father at his brother's request. Rajasthan personal estates are mentioned as early as the tenth century so his award was not unusual, just not timely since Nagaur was not under Abhai Singh's control. In essence the grant meant that Bakhat Singh had Abhai Singh's permission to invade Nagaur and if he succeeded in wresting it from Indar Singh, he could retain it as his fiefdom.

39. Tod, vol. 1, 590. He was an intrepid soldier, liberal in his thinking, and also a poet who loved literature (Hooja, 713).

40. Sarkar, 191–97. Bakhat Singh had been ruling Nagaur for twenty-four years and felt he was entitled to the throne, particularly since Ram Singh was not popular with the Marwar ruling establishment. He was "insufferably arrogant and at the age of twenty, steeped in immoral and unhealthy vice." D. Singh, 104.

41.   Tod, vol. II, 89; vol. I, p. 589. As Tod writes, "it was therefore resolved to punish one crime [the murder of Ajit Singh] by the commission of another [the killing of Bakhat Singh]." Bakhat Singh died in September 1752. He was cremated and a cenotaph called *Booro Dewul* (Shrine of Evil) is still near Malpura.

42.   Siddiqui, 185; Tod, vol. 1, 589. There are other ideas regarding Bakhat Singh's death, namely, that he died of cholera (Sarkar, vol. 1, 199), but most historians favor the poisoned coat theory.

43.   Singh, 101. With its ornate gold ceiling and walls, it is the fort's grandest room. Much of Abhai Singh's building was made possible by the wealth acquired after conquests in Gujarat, particularly the commercially rich metropolis of Ahmedabad.

44.   For additional imperial works completed between 1720 and 1740, see Stuart C. Welch, *The Art of Mughal India* (New York: Asia Society, 1963), no. 77, and Karl Khandalavala, *Paintings of Bygone Years* (Bombay: Vakils, Feffer and Simons Limited, 1991), plate III; Terence McInerney, "Mughal Painting during the Reign of Muhammad Shah," in Barbara Schmitz, *After the Great Mughals: Painting in Delhi and the Regional Courts in the 18th and 19th Centuries* (Mumbai: Marg, 2002), fig. 5.

45.   Inscriptions on the verso of two magnificent paintings in Jodhpur, circa 1724–25, mention that the painter is "the Delhi artist, Dal Chand." Crill, 66, figs. 37, 38.

46.   Abhai Singh was at the court in Delhi in 1723 and left for Jodhpur in July 1724.

47.   A painting in the National Museum of India, New Delhi (51.205), which can be attributed to Bhawani Das while he was still in Delhi (prior to 1719), shows a style and composition that would influence his son in his circa 1725 palace scene for Abhai Singh (fig. 4). See Mohinder Singh Randhawa and Doris Schreier Randhawa, *Kishangarh Painting* (Bombay: Vakils, Feffer & Simons Limited, 1980), plate XIV; Vijay Kumar Mathur, *Marvels of Kishangarh Painings from the Collection of the National Museum, New Delhi* (Delhi: Bharatia Kala Prakashan, 2000), pl. 1.

48.   Crill, fig. 37; see fig. 14a, entry for cat. 14; Welch, 1963, no. 77, and Khandalavala, pl. III; McInerney, fig. 5; See entry for cat. 15. Also compare Crill, fig. 38, an equestrian portrait of Abhai Singh with fig. 1 in McInerney.

49.   McInerney, fig. 6; see cat. 14, fig. 14a, and cat. 19, fig. 19a.

50.   See Stuart Cary Welch, *India: Art and Culture 1300–1900* (New York, Metropolitan Museum of Art, 1985) 254–45, no. 165, for a magnificent mid-seventeenth century silk velvet Mughal tent still in the royal holdings. See also cat. 21.

51.   Crill, figs. 39 and 40. Faiyaz Ali Khan, "The Painters of Kishangarh," *Roopa-lekha* 51, nos. 1–2 (1979–80), 65, states that Dalchand was in Kishangarh by 1726. The dated 1727 Jodhpur Abhai Singh portrait (Crill, fig. 39) would appear to contradict that 1726 date unless Dalchand painted the Abhai Singh portraits after he left Jodhpur and arrived in Kishangarh, which this author thinks is unlikely.

52.   Crill, 115, n.28. In 1726, Dalchand's father received ninety rupees a month, while his cousin, the artist Kalayandas, received thirty-five rupees a month. Faiyaz Ali Khan, 65.

53.   Khan, 65; Navina Haidar, assistant curator, Department of Islamic Art, Metropolitan Museum of Art, personal conversation, 2007. There is a difference of opinion on when Bhawani Das left Kishangarh, but he was there

54.   at the same time as Dalchand in the late 1720s.

54.   Crill, figs. 43, 46, 47.

55.   For a Jodhpur painting of Abhai Singh (labeled incorrectly Bakhat Singh) by a Dalchand-trained artist and in the floral, Mughal-inspired style associated with Bakhat Singh's artists, see Christie's London, *Art of the Islamic and Indian Worlds*, October 23, 2007, lot. 323.

56.   Goetz (1949), 91, has suggested that Bakhat Singh destroyed much of the earlier structures in order to construct his more magnificent, Mughal-style buildings.

57.   Catherine B. Asher and Cynthia Talbot, *India Before Europe* (Cambridge University Press, 2006), 91–92. The white lime plaster on fifteenth- and early sixteenth-century Gujarat buildings was translated by the Mughals into white marble for their buildings.

58.   Goetz; Y. K. Shukla, "Fresco Paintings in the Nagaur Fort," in *Roopa-Lekha* XLI, nos. 1–2 (1972), 95–100; Y. K. Shukla, *Wall Paintings of Rajasthan: Jaipur, Galta, Kota, Nagaur* (Ahmedabad: L. D. Institute of Indology, 1980), figs. 23–28.

59.   When Goetz wrote his article in 1949, he speculated (p. 94) that though he was not aware of any portable paintings in the same style as the Bakhat Singh wall paintings, similar works on paper, more carefully executed than the wall paintings, would be discovered. He was certainly correct; see cats. 10–20. Goetz incorrectly attributes several portable paintings to Nagaur, including a *Ragamala* series now in the British Library (Toby Falk and Mildred Archer, *Indian Miniatures in the India Office Library* [London: Sotheby Parke Bernet, 1971] no. 426), but in fact these paintings are from other ateliers. Goetz (1949), 97, fig. 4, for example, is a portrait of Ram Singh of Amber, ca. 1680 (see Catherine Glynn, "Evidence of Royal Painting for the Amber Court," *Artibus Asiae* LVI, nos. 1–2, [1996], 67–93).

60.   Cummins, pls. 65, 66, 69, 77, 88, and 89. In the early part of the eighteenth century, Udaipur painters, like those at Nagaur, often incorporated actual architecture and specific hunting grounds or other explicit locales in their paintings, but this was not the norm for most Rajput paintings. Topsfield (2002), figs. 107, 110, 111, 113a, 136–42.

61.   It was clear from the Nagaur Garden Workshop, January 30–February 3, 2006, attended by historians of garden design, a water specialist, and art and architectural historians from around the world that this attention to authenticity would assist scholarship in fields as varied and interrelated as conservation, landscaping and garden design, contemporary flora, and water systems.

62.   For more about the connection between the Bakhat Singh paintings and the imperial artworks produced during the reign of Muhammed Shah, see cats. 14, 15, 17, and 19; see also n.44 for references to Mughal paintings dated 1720–30.

63.   The depiction of hunts was meant to commemorate kingly heroism and was also an occasion to display wealth in horse trappings and other equestrian paraphernalia. The Rajput ruler was expected to have superior martial and equestrian abilities, symbols of his capacity to protect his kingdom and the subjects under his control. Knowing that Bakhat Singh was a excellent warrior and ruler, it is all the more surprising not to have hunting paintings from his atelier. There are paintings of Bakhat Singh amid an assembly of nobles, but these were done after his accession to the Jodhpur throne in

1751. See B. N. Goswamy and A. Dallapiccola, *A Place Apart: Painting in Kutch 1720–1820* (Delhi: Oxford University Press, 1983), 75, pl. VI.

64. Ziegler, 193–94. Jodhpur artists painted several equestrian images of Ajit Singh and Abhai Singh, but no similar portraits of Bakhat Singh were produced while he ruled Nagaur. Crill, 30, states that it was during Ajit Singh's reign that complex processional scenes and hunts were produced in Jodhpur for the first time.

65. Francis Brunel, *Splendour of Indian Miniatures* (Delhi, n.d.), no. 51; Rani Kalayankumar was from Lunwara in Gujarat, and Rani Rupkumar was from Nimabaj, a Marwar *thikana* near Ajmer. Mahendra Singh Nagar, *Ranimangar Bhado ki Bahi* (Jodhpur: Maharaja Man Singh Research Institute, 2002), 59–60. Fig. 18c in the reference catalogue entry for cat. 18 is an earlier equestrian portrait of Bakhat Singh but in the Kishangarh style rather than the Nagaur style, perhaps partially by Dalchand or a Kishangarh artist trained by him.

66. Perhaps, in time, additional Nagaur portable paintings with popular texts as their subject matter will emerge. The permanent wall paintings in the Hadi Rani show women of the zenana enjoying themselves in the palace grounds, the gardens, and the nearby countryside. These are also themes of some *Ragamala* paintings, but the wall paintings are not organized in such a manner as to be interpreted as *Ragamala* images. Paintings of religious themes such as the *Bhagavata Purana* and *Krishnalila* are in the Krishna temple located inside the fort walls.

Maharaja Vijai Singh and the Epic Landscape, 1752–93

1. Vijai Singh's coronation took place on January 31, 1753. G. R. Parihar, *Marwar and the Marathas, 1724-1843* (Jodhpur: Hindi Sahitya Mandir, 1968), 76.

2. Hermann Goetz, "The Nagaur School of Painting (18th Century)," *Ars Orientalis* 1 (Freer Gallery of Art and University of Michigan, 1954), 98.

3. The relationship between the Mughal and the local styles also shaped the development of Jodhpur court painting in the eighteenth century. Imperial aesthetics reached Jodhpur both indirectly through the Nagaur school and directly through Mughal-trained artists who arrived in Jodhpur during the first half of the century. Terence McInerney has noted the increasing coalescence of Mughal and local styles in the Marwar court after 1750. Darielle Mason et al., *Intimate Worlds: Indian Paintings from the Alvin O. Bellak Collection* (Philadelphia Museum of Art, 2001), 126.

4. See cats. 13 and cat. 17, fig. 17b.

5. The palaces of Ahhichatragarh Fort are set within extensive gardens that reach their peak only in late summer, during and briefly after the yearly monsoon. James Westcoat, conversation with the author, May 2007.

6. An inscription on the reverse of the painting identifies the artist as "Fazl, son of the artist Abdullah." The maharaja's slenderness and youth suggest that the portrait was painted early in his reign, when he was twenty-three to twenty-five years old. For other portraits of Vijai Singh, see reference catalogue entry cat. 9, fig. 9a, and cat. 20, fig. 20b. A *jharokha* portrait appears in Rosemary Crill, "The Thakurs of Ghanerao as Patrons of Painting," in Andrew Topsfield, ed., *Court Painting in Rajasthan* (Mumbai: Marg, 2000), 100, no. 9.

7. *Maharaja Bakhat Singh and Prince Vijai Singh.* Attributed to Fazl, Jodhpur or Nagaur, 1751–52. Opaque watercolor and gold on paper, 24.9 x 34.3 cm. Mehrangarh Museum Trust, RJS 4215.

8. Catherine Glynn observes that the delicate shading of Vishnu's face, the relatively elongated figures of the attendants, and architectural elements strongly suggest that these paintings were produced shortly after Bakhat Singh's death. Compare also the parterre garden structures, floral textiles, carpet patterns, treatment of trees, and delicate architectural decoration of this series to Bakhat Singh-period paintings.

9. These are scenes of Vaikhuntha heaven, which is depicted in its cosmic location on a nineteenth-century mandala, cat. 46.

10. Visual evidence of stylistic exchange suggests the exchange of paintings and the movement of artists between the two Rathore courts, a topic for further study in the storerooms and archives of Jodhpur and Bikaner; see cat. 12, fig. 12b.

11. The terrace of a palace with an arched colonnade is similar to buildings in the Nagaur paintings; see entries for cats. 12, 13, and 17, which also show the tripartite horizontal compositions.

12. The painting (Mehrangarh Museum Trust, RJS 78-76) is inscribed *kalam nagaur se chitara kayam*. Rosemary Crill, *Marwar Painting: A History of the Jodhpur Style* (Mumbia: India Book House, Ltd. in association with Mehrangarh Publishers, 1999), fig. 74.

13. A painting in the collection of Howard Hodgkins, which Catherine Glynn has identified as Vijai Singh bathing in a palace tank at Nagaur, demonstrates how artists' employment of stencils to create new paintings encouraged the continuity of style across reigns. See fig. 20b, p. 274.

14. Vijai Singh's first return to his secure former home occurred in the second year of his reign, when the armies of his cousin Ram Singh (allied with Maratha forces) attacked Marwar. During the ensuing civil war over control of the throne, Vijai Singh was besieged at Nagaur for fourteen months, while the Rathore kinsmen who supported his cause were similarly hemmed in at Jodhpur. The young maharaja only returned to Jodhpur in January 1756, after a peace accord with the Marathas was reached. Parihar, 80–88.

15. Molly Aitken, "The Practiced Eye: Styles and Allusions in Mewar Painting." Ph. D. dissertation, Columbia University, 2000, *passim*.

16. It would be fruitful, for example, to examine whether the maharaja's patronage of his father's atelier formed part of a continued engagement with a broader Nagaur network of relations that included advisors, administrators, and servants. And if so, how did the Nagaur circle interact with other factions at the court?

17. The Vallabha Sampraday further understands Krishna to be "the supreme absolute truth from which all other deities, including Vishnu, evolve." Edwin F. Bryant, *Krishna: The Beautiful Legend of God: Srimad Bhagavata Purana, Book X* (London: Penguin Books, 2003), xiii.

18. Chopasni village is located just outside the city of Jodhpur. Mahendra Singh Naggar notes that the shrine is popularly known as Gosain Temple. Personal conversation with the author, February 25, 2007.

19. Udairam's career, which lasted approximately forty years, from 1770 to 1810, spanned the reigns of Vijai Singh, Bhim Singh (1793–1803), and Man Singh (1804–43). His oeuvre includes two other paintings of Vijai Singh worshiping at Chopasni (Mehrangarh Museum Trust, RJS 2048—reproduced in Crill,

(1999), fig. 74—and RJS 2057). A similarly composed work—which features Udairam's somewhat flat and insubstantial figures and depicts Maharaja Bhim Singh worshiping Krishna (RJS 4992)—also can be attributed stylistically to this artist. Indeed, Udairam retains some of these compositional elements in his devotional paintings of Man Singh worshiping Jallandharnath; see fig. 5, p. 35, and RJS 4206, reproduced in Crill (1999), fig. 126.

20. The Vallabha order believes that Krishna manifests himself completely in paintings as well as sculptures, while most Hindu devotional traditions understand gods to appear only in three-dimensional forms. Woodman Taylor, "Picture Practice: Painting Programs, Manuscript Production, and Liturgical Performances at the Kotah Royal Palace," in Stuart Cary Welch, ed., *Gods, Kings, and Tigers: The Art of Kotah* (Munich and New York: Prestl, 1997), 61–72.

21. Another pictorial convention typical of *chitra darshan* paintings is the depiction of priests and worshipers, who would have stood directly in front of the deity, in profile on either side of the cult image. See, for example, "The Worship of Shri Nathji on Sharat Purnima in the Nijamandira of the Shri Nathji Mandira at Nathadwara," in Joseph Dye III, *The Arts of India: Virginia Museum of Fine Arts* (Richmond: Virginia Museum of Fine Arts, 2001), figs. 103 and 106.

22. Dr. Pema Ram, *Jodhpur Maharaja Vijai Singhji par Valabh Sampradaya ka Prabhav* (Rajasthan History Congress Series, vol. IX, Kota Session), 22–29. Vijai Singh's correspondence with other Rajput rulers indicates his enthusiasm for the spread of Vaishnavism; his interest or attendance at Vallabha festivals in various Rajput kingdoms; and he is addressed in at least one letter (from Kishangarh) as a great Vaishnava devotee (*vaishnavaseviparambhagavat*). G. N. Sharma, *A Bibliography of Medieval Rajasthan: Social and Cultural* (Agra: Lakshmi Narain Agarwal, 1965), 22 and 120. Vijai Singh also provided and maintained forces of up to five hundred troops to protect Nathadwara. Norbert Peabody, *Hindu Kingship and Polity in Precolonial India* (Cambridge University Press, 2003), 72. The Vallabha religious orientation shared by the Rajput rulers undoubtedly also worked to cement the diplomatic alliances that played such a dominant role in Rajput politics in the second half of the eighteenth century.

23. The most renowned royal devotee of Krishna in this period was Maharaja Sawant Singh of Kishangarh (r. 1748–64), who wrote *bhakti* verse under the pen name Nagaridas. Vijai Singh collected Nagaridas' verses and was in correspondence with the Kishangarh court. During the eighteenth century, moreover, paintings of Krishna as a playful child or romantic youth (two *bhakti* archetypes) were produced in almost every Rajput court. See for example, Joseph Dye III, *The Arts of India: Virginia Museum of Fine Arts* (Richmond: Virginia Museum of Fine Arts, 2001), figs. 102, 111, 120, 123.

24. The Pustak Prakash Library in Mehrangarh Fort Museum includes numerous Vallabha poems, such as verses by Nagaridas (see n.25), and religious treatises from the eighteenth century; it is likely that many of these were brought into the royal library by Vijai Singh. *A Catalogue of Hindi and Rajasthani Manuscripts in Maharaja Mansingh Pustak Prakash at Fort Jodhpur, Part I* (Jodhpur Fort: Mehrangarh Museum Trust, 1981), 148–62.

25. It previously was catalogued as a manuscript of the Man Singh (1803–43) period by Bisheshwarnath Reu, *The Story of Srimad Bhagavata (10th chapter) and Notes on its Paintings* (Jodhpur: Sardar Museum, 1947).

26. Taylor, *passim.*

27. The *Bhagavata Purana* (which includes the *Raslila*) offers release from *samsara* (rebirth) to devotees who approach it with the proper devotional attitude. Bryant, p. xxxii.

28. The *Ram Charit* folios relate to the preeminent Hindi telling of Valmiki's Sanskrit epic, the *Ramayana*, which is dated to approximately 200 B.C.E. The illustrated manuscripts were first catalogued by Bisheshwarnath Reu in *Ramayana ka Katha* (Jodhpur: Sardar Museum, 1934), *The Story of Gajendramoksha and Notes on its Paintings* (Jodhpur: Sardar Museum, 1936), and *Abstract of the Story and Notes on the Paintings of the Durga Charit* (Jodhpur: Sardar Museum, 1946).

29. I am grateful to Rajeshwari Shah for suggesting that the manuscript is an illustrated *Ramcharitmanas* because of its verso inscription (*Sri ramcharit*) and the subject matter of folios 88–91. Three incomplete *Ramcharitmanas* texts (nos. 211, 212, and 213) are extant in the Pustak Prakash Library, which houses the manuscript collection of the Jodhpur royal family. Philip Lutgendorf has noted that royal patronage of the *Ramcharitmanas* emerges as a significant factor across northern Indian in the second half of the eighteenth century. Philip Lutgendorf, *The Life of a Text: Performing the Ramcaritmanas of Tulsidas* (Berkeley: University of California Press, 1991), p. 135.

30. The stylistically similar four-folio *Gajendra Moksha* also can be dated to circa 1775.

31. These scenes do not appear in illustrated *Ramayanas* from other Rajput courts. Note also that the *Ram Charit* paintings do not depict the tragic episodes, which Tulsidas omits from his text, of the Sanskrit *Ramayana's* last book: Sita is not banished and Rama does not die. Lutgendorf, *The Life of a Text*, p. 28, n.61.

32. Lutgendorf, *The Life of a Text,* 371.

33. For the devotional emphasis on Rama and Sita in Ayodhya, see Philip Lutgendorf, "The secret life of Ramchandra of Ayodhya" in *Many Ramayanas: The Diversity of the Narrative Tradition in South Asia*, ed. Paula Richman (Berkeley: University of California Press, 1991), 220–21; and Ronald Stuart Macgregor, "The *Dhyanmanjari* of Agradas," in *Bhakti in Current Research 1979–1982*, ed. Monika Thiel-Horstmann (Berlin: Dietrich Reimer, 1983) 237–44. For the spread of *Ramrajya* as a "validating model of temporal authority" for Hindu rulers in the eighteenth and nineteenth century, see Lutgendorf, *The Life of a Text,* 134.

34. *Bhagavan*, which means lord, is a common appellation for Krishna; the *Bhagavat Purana* was composed sometime between the fourth and the thirteenth century, with many western scholars favoring a ninth- to thirteenth-century date. The most popular of the puranas, it offers those who hear its verses liberation from *samsara* at the time of death. Bryant, xxxi.

35. The shift in size, as well as the periodic appearance of text bars on the recto of folios, may indicate that two *Bhagavata Purana* manuscripts were later combined. A thorough study of this intriguing manuscript is required. Reu, *The Story of the Shrimad Bhagavata*, attributed seventy-one paintings to the manuscript and noted that various folios were missing. We believe that the refined style of the three paintings (fig. 3, cat. 22, and fig. 22a, p. 277) identified by Reu as the illustrated manuscript's opening folios were in fact painted in the early 1760s; six other folios with similar measurements exhibit

a looser style more consistent with paintings from the following decade.

36. The scene depicts the narrative of Vrikasura, whose devotion Shiva has rewarded with a boon. Unfortunately, the boon Vrikasura desires is Shiva's wife Parvati. Vishnu steps in to help Shiva out of this conundrum—for gods cannot take back the promise of a boon—and tricks the lustful Vrikasura into cutting off his own head. After this clever feat, the gods assemble in praise of Vishnu.

37. Other folios with text bars are reproduced in B. N. Goswamy, *Essence of Indian Art* (San Francisco: Asian Art Museum of San Francisco, 1986), fig. 185, and Crill (1999), fig. 82.

38. Reu was the first to date the manuscript to Man Singh's reign (1803–43) in *Ramayana ka Katha* (Jodhpur: Sardar Museum, 1934). Similarly dated folios are published in Crill (1999), figs. 127 and 130; Goswamy (1986), figs. 108 and 114 (details); and D. Diamond, "Court Painting and Yogic Metaphysics in Nineteenth-Century Jodhpur," in *Court Painting of Rajasthan*, ed. Andrew Topsfield (2000), fig. 9.

39. See especially Rosemary Crill, *A History of the Jodhpur Style* (Bombay: Popular Press, 1999), fig. 127, and Goswamy (1986), figs. 108 and 114.

40. Hermann Goetz, *Art and Architecture of Bikaner* (Oxford: Bruno Cassirer, 1950), first noted these visual similarities between paintings from the politically connected and geographically adjacent kingdoms whose ruling classes both belong to the Rathore clan. Further research of both royal collections promises to yield a more definitive outline of the Bikaner–Jodhpur artistic exchange—and the role of Nagaur within it—throughout the eighteenth and early nineteenth century.

41. Gulab Rai was a *khawas* (companion of a ruler) before she was formally granted the higher *pasban* status in 1766. Rima Hooja, *A History of Rajasthan* (New Delhi: Rupa and Company, 2006), p. 717.

42. The thakurs of Pali, Asop, and Pokhran, whose sons later challenged Man Singh's sovereignty, were the ringleaders of the assassination plot. Brijeshkumar Singh, ed., *Maharaja Sri Vijai Singhji ri Khyat* (Jodhpur: Rajasthan Oriental Research Institute, 1997), 9.

Painting, Politics, and Devotion under Maharaja Man Singh, 1803–43

1. These challenges came from many sources: numerous Rathore noblemen, Dhonkal Singh (a pretender to the throne), several Rajput kings, Maratha armies, the Afghan general Amir Khan, and the British East India Company. Dhonkal Singh (1804–1851) was born after the death of his father, Maharaja Bhim Singh, in 1803.

2. Jodhpur paintings from this period—particularly those exhibiting disjointed compositions, flat surfaces, or idealized portraits of the maharaja with Naths instead of kinsmen—are typically interpreted, when they are not ignored, as reflections of weak or autocratic rule. The model of the weak nineteenth-century ruler emerges from Colonel James Tod's seminal history of the Rajput kingdoms, *Annals and Antiquities of Rajasthan* (1829–32). According to Tod, Man Singh exemplified the degraded Rajput king for—despite his intelligence, noble bearing, and the blood of an ancient and great race running through his veins—he was mentally unstable and weakly allowed devious Nath priests and non-Rajput administrators to dominate the government. James Tod, *Annals and Antiquities of Rajasthan, or the Central and Western Rajpoot States of India* (New Delhi: Oriental Books Reprint Corporation, 1983), vol. II, pp. 119, 122, 563. For a full historiography of late nineteenth-century Jodhpur painting, see Debra Diamond, "Politics and Poetics" (Ph.D. diss., Columbia University, 2000), chap. 2. For more on Tod's biases and pervasive impact, see Norbert Peabody, "Tod's Rajast'han and the Boundaries of Imperial Rule in 19th-century India," *Modern Asian Studies* 30, no. 1 (1996), 185–220; Ronald Inden, *Imagining India* (Oxford: Basil Blackwell, 1990), 172–76; and Jason Freitag, "The Power that Protects You: James Tod, Historiography, and the Rajput Ideal" (Ph. D. diss., Columbia University, 2001).

3. Jalore is located eighty-five miles south of Jodhpur.

4. *Jallandhar Charit* (Stories of Jallandhar), quoted in Bhagvatilal Sharma, *Sri Jalandharnath-Pith* (Jalore, Rajasthan: Sri Bhairunathji ka Akhara, 1995), 150.

5. The faction of nobles who most strongly supported Bhim Singh, and therefore had the most to lose upon Man Singh's accession, was headed by the powerful *thakur* (nobleman) of Pokhran, Sawai Singh (d. 1808). In the summer of 1803, these nobles were scattered in their estates around Marwar, unable to gather quickly enough to promote a more amenable successor.

6. The relative erasure of the Naths in scholarship is partly the legacy of Orientalism, which privileged Sanskritic and Brahmanical Hindu traditions. For more on the social, political, and economic roles of Naths, see David Lorenzen, "Warrior Ascetics in Indian History," *Journal of the American Oriental Society* 98 (1978), 68–70; Dirk H. A. Kolff, *Naukar Rajput and Sepoy: The Ethnohistory of the Military Labour Market in Hindustan, 1450–1850* (Cambridge University Press, 1990), 74–85; David Gordon White, *The Alchemical Body: Siddha Traditions in Medieval India* (University of Chicago Press, 1996), epilogue, 335–52.

7. The narratives repeatedly reveal that determining whether wandering yogins were enlightened beings, well-meaning disciples, or scoundrels was a judgment call with dire or miraculous consequences.

8. For example, Prithvinarayan Shah, an eighteenth-century prince of Gurkha (i.e., Gorakh), unified Nepal with the help of the Nath holyman Bhagvatnath. In legend, Bhagvatnath has become firmly identified with the *mahasiddha* Gorakhnath. White (1996), 310–11, 343.

9. It was also the last great instance of royal patronage for the Nath order. For recent Nath involvement with politics, at the time of the destruction of Babri Masjid in 1992, see White (1996), 346–48.

10. Since these powers included healing and the ability to repel locusts, at least one Nath lived in every village in Marwar. Both Hindus and Muslims sought boons (such as sons) at the many small Nath shrines that dotted the countryside.

11. The appellation *siddha* refers to adepts associated with several tantric orders. The *Nath siddhas* were particularly connected to the alchemists of the *Rasa Siddha* tradition: both propose interrelated and concrete practices that enable humans to attain *siddha* status. White (1996), 2–3.

12. Naths are also a householder caste in Rajasthan.

13. After the *mahasiddha* Gorakhnath systematized hatha yoga as a practice for mortals to become gods in the twelfth–thirteenth century, Naths organized into twelve religious orders (*panths*). Nath spiritual lineages were head-quartered at monasteries throughout the subcontinent.

14. Nath shrines also were erected within Mehrangarh Fort and Nath temples were commissioned for each of Marwar's districts. B. Sharma (1995), 209.

15. For example, Dev Nath brokered a reconciliation between Man Singh and Maharaja Surat Singh of Bikaner in 1813, an event depicted in a painting by Shivdas (Mehrangarh Museum Trust, RJS 2023).

16. Dev Nath's provision of funds to Man Singh during the 1803 siege (Padmaja Sharma, *Maharaja Mansingh of Jodhpur and His Times* [Agra: Shiva Lal Agarwala and Company, 1972], 41) and the ease with which the Jalore Naths reconstituted themselves as an elite polity within Man Singh's kingdom suggests that they were, like many eighteenth-century monastic orders, engaged in economic and political realms broader than monastic oversight. William Pinch has noted that monastics in this period "speculated in real estate and...acted as merchants, bankers, and most importantly, soldiers." *Peasants and Monks in British India* (Berkeley: University of California Press, 1996), 24.

17. Nath status within the caste hierarchy was not equal to that of the twice-born castes, such as Brahmins or Rajputs.

18. *Sri Ayasji Maharaj Agya Furmayi*. Undated, but circulated sometime after 1805, the *firman* is housed among the Nath correspondence to Maharaja Man Singh in the collection of the Rajasthan Oriental Research Institute in Bikaner. It states that Dev Nath was descended from a Jailsamer Bhatti Rajput who migrated to Jalore in the seventeenth century. Jallandharnath commanded him to marry and blessed his descendents. Similarly, the injunction against widow remarriage points to Nath desire for higher social status. Lakshmi Nath sent an armed force to kill a widowed relative and her intended in 1841, stating that respected Naths, like Rajput nobles and Brahmins, should not enter into such marriages. Daniel Gold, "The Instability of the King: Magical Insanity and the Yogis' Power in the Politics of Jodhpur, 1803–1843," in *Bhakti Religion in North India: Community Identity and Political Action* (Albany: State University of New York Press, 1995), 126. By forbidding widows to remarry, the Nath elite brought their family practices in line with Brahmin and Rajput social conventions.

19. For an extended discussion of Jodhpur portraiture and its role in the construction of royal, noble, Jain, and Nath elites in the seventeenth–nineteenth century, see Debra Diamond, "The Politics and Aesthetics of Citation: Nath Painting in Jodhpur, 1803–43," (Ph.D. diss., Columbia University, 2000), chap. 3, "Portraiture and the Aesthetics of Rule." Portraits of the Rathore nobility—which became particularly prevalent during Maharaja Vijai Singh's reign as the nobles demanded increased autonomy—are reproduced in Rosemary Crill, *Marwar Painting: A History of the Jodhpur Style* (Mumbai: India Book House Ltd. in association with Mehrangarh Publishers, 1999), *passim*.

20. It bears an unusually explicit verso inscription dating the depicted ritual to the first year (Samvat 1860) of Man Singh's reign. Udairam's delicate handling of hue, pattern, and line further supports this date. Warm indigos and deep greens balance a palette of pink, salmon, cream, and white. A rather fluid contour line in medium gray integrates the figures within the shallow architectural space. The marble base of the shrine, for example, has the same light quality as the maharaja's white costume. The restrained contours, along with small patterns that break up large fields of color and beards that end in wispy strands mitigate the hard-edged geometries that often freeze individuals into isolated icons in Man Singh-period paintings.

21. Scholars of religion invariably designate saffron (in Hindi, *gerua*) as the color of sacred Hindu garb. While the hues that Jodhpur artists employ might be more accurately described as dark peach or salmon pink, I will continue to use saffron to emphasize its sacred connotation.

22. Their sons are Ladu Nath (b. 1809) and Prince Chhattar Singh (b. 1803). Within the pictorial logic of Rajput painting, the similarity in appearance and garb announces that Dev Nath partakes of the bodily substance and authority of the king. The guru's gold-bordered scarf (*dupatta*), jewel-encrusted *kundal* earrings, and elaborate turban ornament were, in all likelihood, royal gifts. Rajput rulers commonly distributed gold-bordered shawls in the acts of ceremonial exchange that accompanied assemblies, holidays, or special events such as birthdays. A letter from Pir Iccha Nath to Man Singh thanking him for a gift of anklets, *kundal* earrings, a gold *palki*, and gold coin indicates that Man Singh distributed Nath earrings along with other marks of his favor, dated Samvat 1879 (1832) *Chaitr Vadi* 14, Rajasthan Oriental Research Institute, Nath correspondence to Maharaja Man Singh. The lavish ruby-, emerald-, and pearl-encrusted ornament in Dev Nath's turban—and especially its similarity to one often worn by the maharaja—assert its status as a royal gift. Only those authorized by the state could display the differentially distributed honorific gifts that conferred rank and status. For a list of Jodhpur honorifics (*lawazma*), see Ram Prasad Vyas, *The Role of Nobility in Marwar, 1800–1873 A.D.* (Jodhpur: University of Jodhpur, 1969), 179.

23. There are neither records (*bahis*) detailing the protocols of Nath *darbars* nor first-hand descriptions from the British, who were rigorously denied contact with the Nath gurus. Reports on Nath *darbars* by Lt. Boileau, who traveled through Jodhpur in 1835 and was otherwise an excellent observer, were based on hearsay, but he noted that Lakshmi Nath—Bhim Nath's son, the abbot of Mahamandir from 1828 to 1843—"assuming the airs of a prince... [has] a considerable number of attendants in durbar, and a party of guards in the ante-room and outer court." A. H. E. Boileau, *Narrative Tour through the Western States of Rajwara* (Calcutta: Baptist Mission Press, 1837), 137.

24. The implausibility of anyone other than a Nath commissioning images of Nath *darbars* and the dispersal of all extant Nath *darbar* paintings (suggesting that they never entered the royal collection) point toward sectarian patronage of these works. Other Nath commissions are listed in "Monumental Manuscripts at the Jodhpur Court," n.8. Man Singh's court artists could have easily produced *darbar* paintings for the Naths, just as they depicted the *darbars* of Man Singh's Rathore kinsmen. For the latter, see Crill (1999), figs. 101 and 102.

25. The bards (individually named in recto inscriptions) sit on elephants that attest not only to Ladu Nath's generosity but their reputation as guardians of truth. Whether given as a gift or provided for the ceremony, the elephant symbolized the prestige of both its donor and its recipient.

26. Man Singh's poet laureate (*kaviraj*) Bankidas appears at the upper right. For *charan* verses honoring Naths, see Bhagvatilal Sharma, *Sri Jalandharnath-Pith* (Jalore, Rajasthan: Sri Bhairunathji ka Akhara, 1995), *passim*. It is also possible that *charans* wrote a fair number of the fifteen thousand to twenty thousand poems expressing devotion to the Naths that are attributed to Man Singh.

27. Hermann Goetz, "The Marwar School of Rajput Painting," *Bulletin of the Baroda Museum and Picture Gallery* 5, no. 1 (1947), 43–54.

28. Goetz (1947), 52.

29. Nagaur artists first exploited the glistening potential of a tin alloy during the early eighteenth century in depictions of Raja Bakhat Singh's water-palaces at Nagaur (cats. 10, 16, 18). Tanks of silver water also feature prominently in Vijai Singh-period paintings of celestial palaces (see fig. 2, p. 23 and cat. 29). Tin alloy enlivened and organized riverine landscapes in the first monumental Jodhpur manuscript, the *Krishna Lila* of ca. 1760 (cats. 22–24).

30. Because artists generally went unnamed and iconography remained the same for long periods of time, the individual and historically contingent contributions of artists often cannot be determined.

31. A genealogical chart for this family, which includes painters at Maharaja Takhat Singh's court, appears in Crill (1999), 178–79.

32. Unlike orthodox Shaiva traditions (Shaiva Siddhanta), which propose ritual worship of the deity and therefore employ icons (*murtis*) or other visual representations, Nath practice is one of internal meditation and bodily transformation. Prior to their ascension in Jodhpur, there is scant evidence that Naths had much use for or interest in painted images: gurus transmit teachings directly to their disciples and yogic practice requires no external visual supports. In contrast to Hindu devotional traditions that exalt deities with form and characteristics, the Naths understand the Supreme Absolute as an infinite and formless entity. Nath shrines, which are foci of divine immanence, typically were marked with simple mounds or indexical traces of interred *siddhas*—usually the imprint of a holy man's feet in stone, or a yogi's hearth fire kept burning for centuries after his death.

33. Illustrated Nath hagiographies have not been located, but Nath legends that were significant to other sectarian traditions entered, at least occasionally, the realm of the visual. Wellcome Library's "composite manuscript" (ORMS Hindi 371), which was produced in 1715 in the main center of the Dadupanthi order, in Naraina, Rajasthan, includes twenty-three simple drawings relating to Naths among its two hundred fifty-six folios. Illustrated manuscripts of the life story (*Janam Sakhi*) of Sikhism's founder, Guru Nanak, often depict his legendary meeting with the *mahasiddha* Gorakhnath. Tushuru Bindu Gode, "Siddhas and Sikhs: Encounters from Sikh Hagiographies," in Rob Linrothe, ed., *Holy Madness: Portraits of Tantric Siddhas* (New York: Rubin Museum of Art, 2006), 156–63, fig. 9.1.

34. Dana demonstrated a controlled mastery of diverse representational modes almost equal to that of his father, although his oeuvre became increasingly restricted to two-dimensional patterning during the reign of Maharaja Takhat Singh (1843–73).

35. See "Monumental Manuscripts at the Jodhpur Court" and the reference catalogue entry for cat. 39, p. 285.

36. A Bulaki painting with a small image of Jallandharnath (Mehrangarh Museum Trust, RJS 4138) is an exception that depicts the *mahasiddha* with less tidy curls.

37. See "Monumental Manuscripts at the Jodhpur Court."

38. Gold (p. 126) reports that they acted as urban enforcers within the capital and the British detail their plundering of the countryside outside Jodhpur. Major Alves reports that Bhim Nath's "plundering parties committed depradations in Marwar territory to within a few miles of the capital." Cons. 24 July 1839, *Marwar Precis: Containing a General History of the Relations with Marwar* (Calcutta: Foreign Department Press, 1874), 44.

39. A Bikaner painting of 1809 depicts the young Dhonkal Singh seated on the lap of Maharaja Surat Singh (r. 1787–1828). Hermann Goetz, *The Art and Architecture of Bikaner State* (Oxford: Bruno Cassirer, 1948), fig. 82.

40. Inderaj Singhvi, the general who had brought Man Singh to Jodhpur in 1803, was a member of the Jain administrative elite. He became the kingdom's chief administrator upon Man Singh's accession. The *thakurs* of Auwa and Asop hired the Afghan mercenary Amir Khan to assassinate the pair. After the murders, Man Singh abdicated the throne and went into retreat. His son Chattar Singh ruled from 1815 until his death from illness in 1818. Man Singh returned to the throne after the three-year interregnum on March 27, 1818. Vyas (1969), 50–54.

41. Vyas, 69–78, 90–93; Tod (1983), vol. II, 122; Cons. 24 July 1839, no. 33, in *Marwar Precis*, 53.

42. Tension between the Brahmin priests of the Vallabha community and the Nath yogins, recorded at various moments throughout Man Singh's reign, also must have continued to simmer in this period. For specific examples of Vallabha-Nath conflict in Jodhpur, see Diamond (2000), chap. 2, "To Celebrate the Copy." For the broader conflict between *bhakti* devotionalism and yogins, see William R. Pinch, *Warrior Ascetics and Indian Empires* (Cambridge University Press, 2006), 194–230.

43. Lakshmi Nath "has aroused not only the spirit of the Rajpoots but even of the Brahmins against him. He was in the habit of seizing and carrying off the daughters and wives of both classes." In one incident, the Mahamandir abbot sent a band of twenty-five armed men to "storm a *thakur's haveli* and kidnap a girl." Major Alves to the secretary to Governor General Macnaughten, p. 39. *Foreign Political* 14 (November 26, 1832), National Archives at New Delhi.

44. I am grateful to Thakur Nahar Singh Jasol for relating this song to me. Discontent with the Naths appears also in historical records and Marwar folk tales.

45. The treaty was established during Man Singh's interregnum. Although Charles Metcalfe believed that "Chutur Singh kept his father under restraint" during this period, he conveniently "presumed [the son had] the consent of his father" when he signed the treaty. Cons. 6 February 1818, no. 102, in *Marwar Precis*, 2.

46. Colonel Sutherland complained that Lakshminath "was more inaccessible in his sanctuary in Mahamunder [sic] than even the regent ranees [sic] of this country in their purdas [sic]." Cons. 24 July 1839, no. 33, in *Marwar Precis*, 53.

47. Colonel Sutherland to the secretary to Government Maddock, paragraph 5, January 28, 1842, in *Foreign Political* 28, no. 22 (February 28, 1842), National Archives of India.

48. The *thakurs* say that "the Maharaja is their Dunnee [*dhani*, master] and they cannot act in opposition to his known will." Colonel Ludlow to Colonel Sutherland, letter no. 15, paragraph 17, January 28, 1842, in *Foreign Political* 28, no. 22 (February 28, 1842), National Archives of India.

49. Kaviraja Shyamaldas, *Vir Vinod*, vol. 2 (Delhi: Motilal Banarsidass, 1986), 872.

50. It was said that the Naths threatened to commit suicide if Man Singh cut their annuities, a sin that would have fallen upon the maharaja. Man Singh explained to the British that he looked "more to salvation [while others cared] more about the affairs of the world." Cons. 24 July 1839, no. 33, in *Marwar*

Precis, 57. For Nath suicide threats, see the same report, p. 57; letter no. 15, paragraph 16, January 28, 1842, in *Foreign Political* 28, no. 22 (February 28, 1842), National Archives of India; and Shyamaldas, 874.

51.   Cons. 28 February 1841, nos. 22–23, in *Marwar Precis,* 114.

52.   Shyamaldas, 873.

53.   For more on Girnar, see cat. 39.

54.   He lived as a "faqir, eating only one pera, chandaloi vegetable, and…yogurt" each day. Shyamaldas, 873.

55.   Shyamaldas, 874.

Monumental Manuscripts at the Jodhpur Court

1.   The corpus remains remarkably intact and in excellent condition today; it is now housed in the Umaid Bhavan Palace in Jodhpur. Several dispersed folios (see codicology at end of chapter) reveal that the corpus was originally larger. I do not include in this group the four important manuscripts of smaller dimensions. The 68-folio *Bhagavata Purana* and the *Panchtantra* fables (more than 400 folios) were produced during the Vijai Singh period; the Marwar romance, *Dhola and Maru* (121 folios), and the dynastic history *Suraj Prakash* (70 folios) were created during Man Singh's reign. Both small and monumental manuscripts were first described by B. N. Reu in a series of pamphlets printed for the Sardar Government Museum, Jodhpur, from the 1920s to the 1940s. Reu correlated images to the text or offered readings of less clearly identifiable images; unfortunately he did not distinguish between the two methodologies.

2.   The next largest manuscript folios, at approximately 63 x 83 cm, comprise the spectacular *Siege of Lanka* series painted in eighteenth-century Guler, but the *Ramayana* is incomplete and the format was only used once. For large paintings on cloth, see Stuart Cary Welch et al., *Gods, Kings, and Tigers: The Art of Kotah* (Munich: Prestel, 1997), fig. 65; Amit Ambalal, *Krishna as Srinathji* (Ahmedabad: Mapin Publishers, 1987), *passim*. For large Mewar paintings, see Andrew Topsfield, *Court Painting at Udaipur: Art under the patronage of the Maharanas of Mewar* (Switzerland: Artibus Asiae Publishers and Museum Rietberg, 2001), *passim*, and Joanna Williams et al., *Kingdom of the Sun: Indian Court and Village Art from the Princely State of Mewar* (San Francisco: Asian Art Museum of San Francisco, 2007), *passim*.

3.   After Maharaja Ummed Singh (r. 1918–47) lent the court's illustrated manuscripts to Jodhpur's Sardar Museum, scholar B. N. Reu took on the massive task of cataloguing the folios. From 1924 to 1947, Reu dated the manuscripts and identified, measured, and numbered the folios.

4.   A painting of equal size (fig. 23b, p. 278), which depicts Krishna stealing the gopis' clothes, was attributed by Reu to the *Krishna Lila* series. However, the scale of the figures and style of painting is markedly different, and therefore I have excluded it from the set.

5.   The four folios of the *Gajendra Moksha*, which were painted by *Ram Charit* artists in roughly the same period (1775–80), do not reveal anything additional about the workshop process.

6.   Archival information is more abundant for Man Singh's reign, and several manuscripts from this period name workshop supervisors.

7.   Vishakha N. Desai suggests that the production process for verse specific illustrations in the Mewar atelier began with "an erudite intermediary" interpreting texts for artists. Vishaka Desai, "From Illustrations to Icons: The Changing Context of the Mewar Rasikapriya Paintings in Mewar," ed. B. N. Goswamy, *Indian Painting, Essays in Honour of Karl J. Khandalavala* (New Delhi: Lalit Kala Academy: 1995), 97–127, p. 99.

8.   We can surmise that the maharaja was the patron because these manuscripts remain in the royal collection and because of the project's overall scale. It seems less likely that the Nath elite commissioned them as gifts for the maharaja, although other extant paintings indicate Nath patronage of court painters; these include wall paintings at the Jodhpur Nath temples (at which construction was overseen by Naths), Nath *darbar* paintings (see fig. 6 in "Painting, Politics, and Devotion under Maharaja Man Singh, 1803–43"), portrait series, a monumental procession scene (Rosemary Crill, *Marwar Painting: A History of the Jodhpur Style* [Mumbai: India Book House Limited, 1999], fig. 97), and a devotional painting inscribed *sri mahamandir su ayi haste citara raso* (brought from Mahamandir by the painter Raso), see fig. 32b, p. 281).

9.   Several dispersed folios (listed in the codicology) reveal that the monumental corpus was originally larger.

10.   Small paintings entered the storeroom in a slightly different fashion. The archivist often noted the date of entry—apparently, the paintings arrived in batches because many of them bear the same date—and sporadically described the subject, dated the depicted event, or named the artist. Paintings produced or collected during earlier reigns also were entered into the storeroom. Man Singh established the *dholiya* storeroom to house original drafts of correspondence in 1823, as part of an administrative reorganization to suppress intrigue and graft. It was located in what is today the Turban Gallery of the Merhangarh Fort Museum. The manuscript texts were housed separately in the Pustak Prakash Library established by Man Singh in 1805.

11.   See p. 37 in "Painting, Politics, and Devotion" for a list of the painters.

12.   Moreover, the gold numerals vary; some are enclosed in gold-ruled cartouches on blue grounds, while others are painted directly onto the artwork.

13.   Illustrated *Shiva Puranas* were produced in the courts of the Punjab Hills, although there is no clear evidence that these were known in Jodhpur. See, for example, B. N. Goswamy and Eberhard Fischer, *Pahari Masters: Court Painters of Northern India* (Switzerland: Artibus Asiae Publishers Supplementum XXXVIII and Museum Rietberg, Zurich, 1992), figs. 166–67, 170, 192.

14.   Images of *mahasiddhas* and mandalas appear prominently in Tibetan Buddhist and Nepalese art, but we have found no evidence that the Jodhpur images are directly related. For Himalayan imagery, see Rob Linrothe, *Holy Madness: Portraits of Tantric Siddhas* (New York: Rubin Museum of Art, 2006), *passim*.

15.   For the holyman archetype, see Debra Diamond, "By the Grace of Jalandranath: Politics and Painting in Jodhpur," in Linrothe, 144–55.

16.   It is unlikely that any painter would have been fluent enough in Sanskrit to translate esoteric texts; certainly the Muslim supervisor of the Sanskrit *Siddha Siddhanta Paddhati* would not have known that language. Even those texts written in the local language, Marwari, include esoteric concepts—cosmogonies and cosmographies—that would have required the input

of a learned Nath. The input of Nath pandits can be further surmised from iconographic corrections; evidence of such overpainting is on the seven *Nath Charit* folios depicting cosmic oceans (cat. 56).

17. See fig. 44a, p. 290.

18. Maps are addressed in the reference catalogue entries for cats. 35 and 49, and Jain painting is discussed in the reference catalogue entry for cat. 47.

19. See, for example, fig. 39a, p. 286 and cat. 36. Others include *Vane* (Vana Akhavat) *vagera*, *Shiva Purana*, f. 64, Mehrangarh Museum Trust, RJS 2661; *citarai mahesh donon danai rai kino* (made by the painters Mahesh and Dana together), *Shiva Purana*, f. 21, Mehrangarh Museum Trust, RJS 2618.

20. It is not known why Bulaki was referred to as the "Muslim artist," or for that matter, why a *Shiva Purana* folio is attributed to the "Hindu artist."

21. Now in the Ajit Mookerjee Collection of the National Museum of India, the *khaka* is reproduced in Ajit Mookerjee and Madhu Khanna, *The Tantric Way: Art, Science, Ritual* (Boston: New York Graphic Society, 1977), 151. It depicts a vertical *siddha* body (similar to that of cats. 45 and 47) with *nadis* (yogic channels). *Nadis* are mentioned in the *Siddha Siddhanta Paddhati* text but are not illustrated in the Mehrangarh manuscript.

22. See reference catalogue entry for cat. 39.

23. On the whole, most seventeenth- and eighteenth-century Jodhpur paintings are quite small. With average dimensions of 30 x 38 cm, they were designed to be held in the hand and enjoyed from an intimate distance. A painting from the Punjab Hill court of Guler captures the intimacy of such viewing. An enthroned raja beholds a small red-bordered painting, sharing his experience only with the artist standing behind the throne. Goswamy and Fischer, fig. 117.

24. Repeatedly interspersed within the texts is the promise of salvation to those who recite or listen to their words.

25. Jyotindra Jain, *Picture Showmen: Insights into the Narrative Tradition in Indian Art* (Mumbai: Marg Publications, 1988), *passim*. We may also note instances of picture storytelling in northern Indian courts.

26. John Seyller. *The Adventures of Hamza: Painting and Storytelling in Mughal India* (Washington, D.C.: Freer Gallery of Art and Arthur M. Sackler Gallery, Smithsonian Institution, 2002), 32–43, discusses how the *Hamzanama* paintings on cloth were presented at the imperial court of Akbar (r. 1556–1605).

27. Karl Khandalavala, *Pahari Miniature Painting* (Bombay: The New Book Company, 1958), 127–47.

28. All dimensions are approximations since folios vary in size by up to 2 cm.

29. The division into the two manuscripts here follows Reu's separation of the ninety-nine folios into two groups, with the exception of Amardas' copy of *Nath Purana*, folio 1, which Reu had identified as the first folio of the *Nath Charit*, in *Nath Charitra ki Katha* (Jodhpur: Sardar Museum, 1937); see reference catalogue entry to cat. 39.

30. The first forty paintings relate to the text's first chapter (*amsh*); the next sixteen relate to the second chapter; the final forty-five relate to the third chapter. B. N. Reu, *Shivrahasya ka Katha* (Jodhpur: Sardar Museum, 1934).

31. Crill (1999), p. 145, discusses the appearance of patronymics on a cache of erotic paintings.

32. I am grateful to David Gordon White for this information.

Notes to the catalogue

The Origins of Jodhpur Court Painting

1. In paintings of this subject in other *Ragamala* series, the woman represents a Gujarati tribeswoman dressed in a skirt of leaves. Klaus Ebeling, *Ragamala Painting* (Basil: Ravi Kumar, 1973), 207, 254.

2. Ananda K. Coomaraswamy, *Catalogue of the Indian Collections in the Museum of Fine Arts, Boston*: Part V, *Rajput Painting* (Cambridge, Mass.: Harvard University Press, 1926), 42.

3. With its riches from trade, Pali became a thriving and profitable commercial center for traders, merchants, and landowners.

4. Kumar Sangram Singh, "An early *Ragamala* MS from Pali (Marwar) dated 1623 A.D.," *Lalit Kala* 7 (1960), 76–81, reproduces the colophon and illustrates nine leaves. The colophon lists the completion date as Samvat 1680 (November 21, 1623); the scribe/artist as Pandit Virji; and three patrons, Gopal Das, his son Bithal Das, and Gopal Das's brother, Mohan Das. Gopal Das ruled Pali from 1583 to his death in 1606, so his inclusion is posthumous; his son, born in 1582, ruled from 1606 to 1657. Discussed in Ebeling, 165–66, no. 218. Crill, 18 and 20, reproduces two pages, *Kedar Ragini* and *Lalit Ragini*; Andrew Topsfield, ed., *Court Painting in Rajasthan* (Mumbai: Marg, 2000), 4, reproduces *Todi Ragini*.

5. This particular *Ragamala* series, unlike the Pali series represented by cat. 1, does not have a place or a patron name.

6. Other leaves—identified within brackets—are published in Ebeling, pl. C20 [*Desakh*] and p. 183 [*Sindhu/Nata*]; Ernst and Rose Lenore Waldschmidt, *Miniatures of Musical Inspiration in the Collection of the Berlin Museum of Indian Art, Part II* (Berlin: Museum für Indische Kunst, 1975), 284 [*Asavari*]; Christie's London, *Fine Islamic and Indian Manuscripts and Miniatures*, May 5, 1977, lot. 116 [*Bilaval*], also reproduced in Toby Falk, *Indian Painting: Mughal and Rajput and a Sultanate Manuscript* (London: P & D Colnaghi & Co. Ltd., 1978), no. 82; Sotheby Parke-Bernet, New York, *Fine Oriental Miniatures and Manuscripts, Islamic Works of Art, and 19th Century Paintings*, December 15, 1978, lot. 56 [*Setamallar*], also reproduced in *Pratapaditya Pal, Court Paintings of India: 16th–19th Centuries* (New York: Navin Kumar, 1983), pl. R7; Christie's London, *Important Islamic, Indian, Himalayan and South-East Asian Art*, April 24, 1990, lot. 55 [*Pacham*]; Crill, fig. 8 [*Gaurmallar*], also reproduced in Francesca Galloway, *Treasures from India* (London, 2006), no. 21. Ebeling notes that there are pages in the Goenka collection [*Kanada*] and the Madame Kumar collection [*Bangalo*]. Two more pages, *Sarang Ragini* and *Todi Ragini*, are in other private collections.

7. Joachim Bautze, "An Illustrated Dhola-Maru Manuscript from Nagaur," in T. S. Maxwell, ed., *Eastern Approaches: Essays on Asian Art and Archaeology* (Delhi: Oxford University Press, 1992), 176–86, figs. 64–70. Before 1650, most Marwar paintings were either *Ragamala* subjects or versions of the local romance of Dhola and Maru, the star-crossed lovers who used a camel to escape and be together.

8. Some Mughal elements are found in seventeenth-century paintings from Datia, Bikaner, Mewar, and Amber: Darielle Mason, *Intimate Worlds: Indian Paintings from the Alvin O. Bellak Collection* (Philadelphia Museum of Art, 2001), nos., 16, 18, 20; Andrew Topsfield, ed., *In the Realm of Gods and Kings: Art of India* (London: Philip Wilson, 2004), nos. 43, 54–58, 157–62, 170; Catherine Glynn and Ellen Smart, "A Mughal Icon Re-examined," *Artibus Asiae*, LVII, nos. 1/2 (1997), 5–15.

9. Leela Shiveshwarkar, *The Pictures of the Chaurapanchasika: A Sanskrit Love Lyric* (Delhi: National Museum of India, 1967). See also Mason, nos. 7–9, 11, 12. The style takes its name from this manuscript but also includes other manuscripts, such as an *Aranyaka Purana*, a *Bhagavata Purana*, and a *Mahapurana* (see Mason, 46, for further discussion). The other pre-Mughal style that is closely related is the Delhi/Agra *Bhagavata Purana*; see Mason, cats. 7–9 and the post-Mughal Issarda *Bhagavata Purana*.

10. Coomaraswamy, 96.

11. Ebeling, 124, from the *Ragamala* series named the "Gem Palace series," after the establishment that originally sold many of the leaves.

12. Ebeling, pls. C31, 46, 89, 210, and 218.

13. See cat. 6, for additional discussion of the Deccan influence on Marwar painting.

14. Another school of thought relates such luminous *Ragamala* paintings to an awareness of painting in the neighboring state of Sirohi to the south. Crill, 26, and figs. 11 and 12.

15. John Guy and Deborah Swallow, eds., *Arts of India: 1550–1900* (London: Victoria and Albert Museum, 1990), 78; see Vishakha N. Desai, *Life at Court: Art for India's Rulers, 16th–19th Centuries* (Boston: Museum of Fine Arts, Boston, 1985), no. 11, for a portrait completed in the last year of his reign; Beach and Koch, no. 5 and p. 161, no. 6 and p. 163, no. 9 and p. 165, no. 37 and pp. 198–90, no. 38 and pp. 200–1.

16. For a clear explanation of Mughal rankings, see Bamber Gascoigne, *The Great Mughals* (New York: Dorset Press, 1971), 105.

17. G. D. Sharma, 33.

18. Gopal Das, whose name is mentioned in the colophon of the Pali *Ragamala* (cat. 1), accompanied Suraj Singh as part of the Rathore contingent fighting with Jahangir's imperial forces at the battle of Mandav (Madhya Pradesh), where Gopal Das died in 1606. Kumar Sangram Singh, 79.

19. After he ascended to the throne in 1595 he was awarded a *mansab* (ranking position) of 2,000 zat/2,000 sawar (for a clear explanation of zat and sawar, see Gascoigne, 105). When he died in 1619, his *mansab* was a very reputable 5,000 zat/5,000 sawar, reflecting the Mughal court's continued appreciation. G. D. Sharma, 39.

20. Most of his service was in the Deccan, a vast area in the middle of the Indian peninsula, south and east of Marwar.

21. Bithal Das, a patron of the Pali manuscript, cat. 1, served with Gaj Singh in the Deccan battle against Malik Ambar in 1621. Crill, 20, 22; Kumar Sangram Singh, 79.

22. Dhananjaya Singh, *The House of Marwar* (New Delhi: Lustre Press Ltd., 1994), 83.

23. Ibid, 82. His ranking at his death was 5,000 zat and 5,000 sawar, one of the highest ranks for a Rajput at that time. For a detailed explanation of zat and sawar, see Gascoigne, 105.

24. Begley and Desai, 220.

25. Thackson, 1999, 378; Singh, 82.

26. The portrait is listed in Norah Titley, *Miniatures from Persian Manuscripts in the British Library and the British Museum* (London: British Museum, 1977), 163, no. 32 of item 395, and reproduced in Gavin Hambly, *Cities of Mughal India* (New York: G. P. Putnam's Sons, 1968), no. 51. Other pages from the same album are reproduced in Andrew Topsfield, *Paintings from Mughal India* (Oxford: Bodleian Library, 2008), no. 7, where the album is identified as mid- to late seventeenth century, and Andrew Topsfield, *In the Realm of Gods and Kings* (London: Philip Wilson, 2004), 326, no. 144.

27. Beach and Koch, no. 10 and pp. 168–69; nos. 19, 25, 32 and pp. 190–91; figs. 142, 143, p. 218, fig. 146, p. 219, fig. 167, p. 226.

28. Reproduced in Andrew Topsfield, *Paintings from Rajasthan in the National Gallery of Victoria* (Melbourne: National Gallery of Victoria, 1980), no. 12; Milo Cleveland Beach, *Mughal and Rajput Painting* (Cambridge University Press, 1992), fig. 94; Crill, fig. 26; Topsfield (2000), 5, fig. 4.

29. Primogeniture was still in place when India became independent in 1947, and self-governing principalities were abolished. See also D. Singh, 83.

30. For other Mughalized images of Jaswant Singh, see Christie's, London, *Important Islamic and Indian Manuscripts,* April 29, 1979, lot. 83; Linda Leach, *Indian Miniature Paintings and Drawings: The Cleveland Museum of Art Catalogue of Oriental Art* (Cleveland Museum of Art, 1986), no. 88; Sotheby's, New York, *The Heeramaneck Collection of Indian Sculpture, Paintings and Textiles,* November 2, 1988, lot. 64; Crill, figs. 21–24. For imperial Mughal *darbar* paintings including Jaswant Singh, see Beach and Koch, 222, app. M and N.

31. "[D]uring the reign of Shah Jahan (r. 1627–58), Jaswant Singh (r. 1638–78) remained outside of Marwar for thirteen years out of his total reign (during Shah Jahan's rule) of 20 years [1638–58]. It is significant to note that almost every second year Jaswant Singh was granted an increment in his *mansab* (ranking)." Also, "the grant of a *mansab* of 4,000 zat/4,000 sawar was significant in itself as no other Rathor ruler before [Jaswant] had been given that rank at the time of succession." When Jaswant Singh died in 1678, his *mansab* was an extraordinary 7,000 zat/7,000 sawar. G. D. Sharma, 52, 41. For a clear definition of Mughal ranking, see Gascoigne, 105.

32. Jaswant Singh received an imperial directive dated June 25, 1645, to appear at court in Lahore; he likely would have seen the Shalimar gardens, as they had been completed by that time. Begley and Desai, 325.

33. For Deccan paintings with a similar use of color, see Zebrowski, pls. XVI, XVII, and XXI.

34. See Crill, fig. 35, for a Mughalized garden painting produced between the Jaswant Singh painting (1670, see cat. 6) and this Ajit Singh work. Both fig. 35 and the Ajit Singh garden scene share the extensive use of white, which provides a visual focus for the primary subject and also relieves the intensity of the strong colors.

35. Abdul Rehman, professor, and Shama Anbrine, lecturer, Department of Architecture, University of Engineering and Technology, Lahore, Unity and Diversity of Mughal Garden Experiences, lecture at the Dumbarton Oaks Garden conference, Washington, D.C., May 2007.

36. See Crill, figs. 30, 31, for paintings in this Rajput style dated 1722 and 1718.

37. This gave Ajit Singh prominence at the Mughal court where he, and perhaps his sons, would have been exposed to Mughal court paintings. Bakhat Singh would have been thirteen years old at Farrukh Siyar's death in 1719, old enough to have absorbed various aspects of court culture. Another daughter of Ajit Singh was married to Sawai Jai Singh of Amber in November 1719, providing contact with a Rajput court that had a history of Mughalized painting (see Glynn, 1996 and 2000, and Glynn and Smart) that the Jodhpur princes, especially Bakhat Singh, could experience. In addition to the exalted title, Ajit Singh received the village of Raisina as a *jagir* (land whose profit went to the owner). The village was in close proximity to the imperial court since it was only a few miles away from Shahjahanabad and Mughal Delhi. Two centuries later, it became the site of the British capital of New Delhi.

38. A *mansab* (rank) of 2,000 zat/2,000 sawar was given to Bakhat Singh at the death of Farrukh Siyar. Sharma, 235.

39. He died on November 28. He had been posted there in 1672, after serving as governor of Gujarat in 1670–71, to take up a new appointment as governor of the Mughal outpost in the northwest territory. Visheshwar Sarup Bhargava, *Marwar and the Mughal Emperors: A.D. 1526–1748* (Delhi: Munshiram Manoharlal, 1966), 110.

40. In fact, the Mughal emperor Aurangzeb took possession of the Rathore's holdings before the baby Ajit and his Rathore guardians could reach Marwar. Aurangzeb moved to Ajmer to be closer to Jodhpur. Haig and Burn, 247.

41. The years in exile produce an extraordinary hunger for power in Ajit Singh. He is described as sly, avaricious, and involved in many betrayals and intrigues. D. Singh, 25.

42. Ibid, 95. There is a folk saying that translates loosely as "all Rajput childless kings die with pregnant wives and the posthumous offspring are always male!"

43. In addition to painters, Ajit Singh invited scholars and poets to his court. Like Jaswant Singh before him (see cat. 6), the maharaja also composed several literary works. Hooja, 709.

44. Ajit Singh had been appointed governor of Ajmer on October 22, 1719, but he was removed from this post in May 1721. The festival of Diwali takes place in the month of Asvin (October–November); thus, as the inscription states, the family made the trip to Ajmer, but it was after Ajit Singh's dismissal. Bhargava, 161, 164.

45. Mason, no. 50. Ellen Smart has noted that the turbans, with their round discs, are those worn at festivities, such as Diwali.

46. D. Singh, 104. Ahmad Shah ruled the Mughal empire from 1748–54.

47. Published in Alice N. Heeramaneck, *Masterpieces of Indian Painting from the Former Collections of Nasli M. Heeramaneck* (Italy: Alice N. Heeramaneck, 1984), pl. 81; Pratapaditya Pal, *Divine Images, Human Visions: The Max Tanenbaum Collection of South Asian and Himalayan Art* (Ottawa: National Gallery of Canada, 1997), 147, no. 125. See cat. 15 for additional information on *jharokha* images.

48. A similar portrait of Bakhat Singh holding a pink rose is reproduced in Mason, no. 51.

49. There is no decoration on the textile at the bottom of the painting, no earring to support the hanging pearls, and no decoration on the turban disk (see cat. 8). In addition, the hand on the ledge of the window is treated in a summary fashion and the pinched fingers hold nothing—all of which suggest that the painting is unfinished.

50. For further information on *jharokha* presentation, see Gascoigne, 144–45.

51. Heeramaneck, pls. 81 and 82; Topsfield and Beach, 72, fig. 4; Simon Ray,

52. Crill, fig. 70. There are published portraits that have been described as images of Bakhat Singh, but in this author's opinion they have been misidentified. A portrait identified as Bakhat Singh is reproduced in Amy G. Poster, *Realms of Heroism: Indian Paintings at the Brooklyn Museum* (New York: Hudson Hills Press, 1994), no. 152, although it bears only a small resemblance to him. Poster also refers to a Bakhat Singh *darbar* in R. E. Lewis, *Indian Paintings and Drawings,* exhibition brochure (San Francisco: R. E. Lewis, 1969), no. 42, but it is a later Bikaner or Jaiselmer *darbar,* and the figure does not resemble the Bakhat Singh depicted in the identified portraits. Also the reference in *Realms of Heroism* to Coomaraswamy, 1926, pl. CXVII, is not to an image of Bakhat Singh but another noble. An inscription on a Kotah processional painting reproduced in Stuart Cary Welch, ed., *Gods, Kings, and Tigers: The Art of Kotah* (Munich: Prestel-Verlag, 1997), no. 36, mentions that Maharaja Bakhat Singh is part of the retinue. The face does not resemble that of the Marwar/Nagaur Bakhat Singh, however, and the figure wears a Mewar-style turban, not the usual Marwar style.

Royal Pastimes in the Gardens at Nagaur Palace

1. Elizabeth Moynihan, ed., *The Moonlight Garden: New Discoveries at the Taj Mahal* (Washington, D.C.: Arthur M. Sackler Gallery, 2000), 30–31.

2. In cat. 15, Bakhat Singh also wears a flower garland intertwined in his turban as he appears on the *jharokha* (balcony) of his palace.

3. Another example can be found in cat. 20, which could be Dutch or Chinese in origin.

4. Topsfield (2002), fig. 136. The palace at Bikaner also has decorative delft tiles dating from the eighteenth century. I am grateful to Andrew Topsfield for information concerning the Bikaner palace.

5. Crill, fig. 44. Our knowledge of Rajput garden structure and forms is limited, but the use of the palanquin image here raises the question of whether a homology was deliberately designed to evoke kingship.

6. In those paintings the octagonal shape has become a pool, not a terrace.

7. Karni Singh Jasol, curator, Mehrangarh Fort Museum, contributed important information to this entry.

8. Karni Singh Jasol, personal communication to the author, December 2007.

9. Both the Christian prints and the Chaghatay hats were filtered into Rajput painting through late sixteenth- and early seventeenth-century Mughal paintings. Okada (1992), figs. 106, 191, and especially 226. See also reference catalogue cat. 11.

10. The arabesque design on this carpet is similar to the carpet in cat. 16, a painting also attributed to the "Nagaur Master."

11. Karni Singh Jasol, personal communication to the author, 2007.

12. This mark also is displayed prominently on his forehead in other Nagaur portraits, announcing his association with Vishnu.

13. In the desert culture of Nagaur, the monsoon was more than just a season; it was considered an announcement or harbinger of life. Many rituals and festivities took place during the monsoon months, overtly or subliminally celebrating water as the substance of life.

14. For an oversized Mughal painting with a predominance of white completed during the life of Muhammad Azim Mirza, Azim us-Shan Bahadur (died 1712), third son of emperor Bahadur Shah, see Robert Skelton, et al., *The Indian Heritage: Court Life & Arts under Mughal Rule* (London: St. Martins Press, 1982), no. 83. For Muhammad Shah paintings, see Welch (1963), no. 77; Khandalavala, pl. III; McInerney (2002), 17, fig. 4. Many of the Muhammmad Shah zenana paintings also prominently feature gardens.

15. Some Rajput family scenes do show familiarity (Amina Okada, *Pouvoir et Desir: miniatures indiennes du San Diego Museum of Art* [Paris: Paris-Musees, 2002], no. 5), usually expressed through holding and touching between adult and child. For a contemporary garden portrait of Bakhat Singh in the Jodhpur style, see Goswamy (1999), fig. 137.

16. Here we can glimpse an expansive space where women had freedom of movement because men were absent. (See cat. 17 and fig. 13b.)

17. Gold or yellow (*goguli*) is considered to be a sacred color, a gift from the holy cow. The symbolism relates to the nature of divine light. Desmond Peter Lazaro, *Materials, Methods & Symbolism in the Pichhvai Painting Tradition of Rajasthan* (Ahmedabad, India: Mapin Publishing, 2005), 55. The placement of the building's opening, oriented toward the southeast, allows for the maximum benefit from cool summer breezes as well as the warm winter sun.

18. Asher and Talbot, 159 and 161. Whether Bakhat Singh, like many other nobles, owned ships or invested in their cargoes or supported the production of trade exports is unknown, but his familiarity with Gujarat and his organizational skill make this kind of entrepreneurial activity a distinct possibility.

19. Siddiqui, 155; Nagar, 59. During that visit, Bakhat Singh married the daughter of Jam Lakha of Nawargarh, ruler of the area of Kutch in northwestern Gujarat. After the marriage, she became Rani Tejkanwar, Bakhat Singh's sixth wife. Marriages between Gujarati Mulsim rulers and Hindu Rajput women also took place. Asher and Talbot, 91. Another visit to Kutch by Bakhat Singh, this time as raja of Marwar in 1751, was documented by his painters; see Goswamy and Dallapiccola, 75, pl. VI. Goswamy and Dallapiccola also reproduce portraits of Jam Lakha, frontispiece and pls. III, IV.

20. Siddiqui, 156. The Marathas came from the western central area of India, Maharashtra. During the eighteenth century, armies of Marathas invaded Rajasthan and northern India in an attempt to displace the Rajput rulers and the Mughals. At times they were successful, but they always extracted tribute, even when negotiating retreats.

21. Muslim men were prohibited from wearing silk against the skin. Bakhat Singh, though not a Muslim, still would have been attracted to this type of luxurious cloth.

22. Catherine B. Asher, "A Ray from the Sun: Mughal Ideology and the Visual Construction of the Divine," in Matthew T. Kapstein, ed., *The Presence of Light: Divine Radiance and Religious Experience* (Chicago and London: University of Chicago Press, 2004), 177–78.

23. The inscription on the reverse identifies the building as "the royal palace" and gives a date of 1737. Bakhat Singh was born in 1706.

24. By 1737, he had eight official wives, but probably also a number of concubines. Nagar, 59.

25. Note that the raja was the patron of the painting, so the inclusion of high spirits on the part of the women may be exaggeration.

Indian and Islamic Works of Art (London: Simon Ray, 2003), 94–95, no. 42; Crill, fig. 67.

26. Perhaps, in fact, this painting commemorated the completion of the palace.
    It is one of three palaces built by Bakhat Singh at Nagaur; the other two
    are the Abha Mahal and the Hadi Rani Mahal. G. H. R Tillotson, "Nagaur
    Architecture," draft paper prepared for the Mehrangarh Trust, 2007. Much
    of the architecture reflects Bakhat Singh's visits to Gujarat, particularly
    Ahmedabad, where he would have seen exquisite carving and tasteful
    use of detail.

27. Architectural elements include the same cusped arches with open flower
    elements in the corners, rope motifs running down columns, and *jali*
    screens. G. H. R. Tillotson, *The Rajput Palaces: The Development of an
    Architectural Style, 1450–1750* (New Haven: Yale University Press, 1987),
    137, 139; Antonio Martinelli and George Michell, *Princely Rajasthan:
    Rajput Palaces and Mansions* (New York: Vendome Press, 2004), 188.

28. Priyaleen Singh, "Historic Gardens: Rationale for Conservation in the
    Indian Context," Nagaur Garden Conservation Workshop, Nagaur, January
    28–February 1, 2006. The plants in the Nagaur paintings—including holly-
    hock, daisies, poppies, carnations, marigolds, zinnia, and mango trees—all
    have holistic qualities; sacred, aromatic, or cosmetic.

29. Elliot and Dowson, vol. VIII, 52.

30. See cats. 11, 12, 13, and 18 for additional information about the
    "Nagaur Master."

31. Catherine wheels—fireworks in the form of a flat coil that spins when lit—
    were used to control the elephants.

32. The figures and the trees are similar to work done by the Ajmer/Sawar artist
    Pemji later in the eighteenth century. See Stuart Cary Welch, *A Flower from
    Every Meadow: Indian Paintings from American Collections* (New York: Asia
    Society, 1973), 37, no. 14; Ehnbom, no. 57; Okada (2002), no. 15. See
    Christie's South Kensington, *Indian and Islamic Works of Art*, October 26,
    2007, lot. 41, for another Pemji-style painting. The scene also relates to a
    painting in the David Collection in which the raja is identified as Ajit Singh.
    Kjeld von Folsach, *Art from the World of Islam in the David Collection*
    (Copenhagen: Kjeld von Folsach, 2001), no. 80, and Kjeld von Folsach,
    For the Privileged Few (Copenhagen: The David Collection and Louisiana
    Museum of Art, 2007), 207, no. 120. However, the figure does not resemble
    Ajit Singh of Marwar.

33. An inscription on the reverse identifies the figure in the *jarokha* window as
    "Rajadhiraj Sri Bakhat Singhji of Nagaur." This painting is the only one among
    the group of thirteen known Nagaur Bakhat Singh paintings to identify the
    raja within his fiefdom.

34. Sarkar, 177.

35. The soldiers symbolize the power and duty of the raja to build, maintain,
    and protect waterworks in the midst of a desert. A similar patterning of
    rifles also appears in cat. 29.

36. Siddiqui, 82–83. This visit by Akbar to Nagaur took place in 1570. Abu'l
    Fazl, vol. 2, 517. See "Rathore and Mughal Interactions," n.9, p. 301.

37. They are known as the Kaydani, the Geelani, and the Shams (renamed
    Shukr). Haig and Burn, 102. Mughal Emperor Akbar also constructed a
    fountain with seventeen jets, which is still in existence.

38. See cat. 11, 12, 13, and 16 for further information about the "Nagaur Master."

39. Moynihan, 30–31.

40. July and August are more typical months for rain in India so the depiction of

cloud formations is unusual, though these clouds are not the dark, menacing
forms normally associated with the summer monsoon. For a similar painting
dated 1737–38 of Muhammad Shah celebrating Holi with his zenana women,
see Andrew Topsfield, *Paintings from Mughal India* (Oxford: Bodleian
Library, 2008), 109, pl. 50.

41. The pattern on the white ground cover is seen again in the carpet in cat.
    22 and the early portrait of Vijai Singh as maharaja (fig. 2 on p. 23) and is
    similar to a textile seen in cat. 19 and the magnificent tent in cat. 21. It may
    represent embroidery acquired by Bakhat Singh when he was governor
    of Gujarat. In any case, its use in multiple paintings indicates a particular
    regard for this type of textile.

Gardens for Divine Play

1. Velvet tents, such as the great tent exhibited in the Metropolitan Museum
   of Art's India exhibition, are also in the Mehrangarh collection. Stuart Cary
   Welch, *India: Art and Culture 1300–1900* (New York: The Metropolitan
   Museum of Art and Holt, Rinehart and Winston, 1985), cat. 165

2. An early version of this style of floral pattern appears on a Mughal floorspread from Masulipatnam in the Deccani sultanate of Golconda; see
   detail of floorspread, circa 1630, in Ellen S. Smart and Daniel J. Walker,
   *Pride of the Princes: Indian Art of the Mughal Era in the Cincinnati Art
   Museum* (Cincinnati Art Museum, 1985), fig. 65.

3. See, for example, "Maharana Sangram Singh of Mewar as a Romantic
   Hero, Mewar, circa 1720–30," in Joan Cummins, *Indian Painting* (Boston:
   MFA Publications, 2006), p. 133, pl. 72.

4. See cat. 12 for a discussion on a related Nagaur painting and a Bikaner
   model with similar subject matter.

5. See fig. 13a, p. 267, for a photograph of the veranda at Nagaur.

6. As in the Bakhat Singh zenana paintings, no males are present.

7. The carpet design is less refined in cat. 22 than it is in cat. 20.

8. The *Raslila* verses constitute the tenth canto of the *Bhagavata Purana*.
   The translations of the verses cited in cats. 23, 24, and 25 are from Edwin
   F. Bryant, *Krishna: The Beautiful Legend of God: Srimad Bhagavata Purana,
   Book X* (London: Penguin Books, 2003).

9. Edwin F. Bryant, introduction to *Krishna: The Beautiful Legend of God*, p. xxx.

10. Tulsidas titled his work the *Ramcharitmanas* (Holy Lake of the Acts of Rama),
    although it is commonly referred to as the Tulsi *Ramayana* or the *Manas*.

11. With the exception of illustrated animal-centered texts, such as the Kishkindha
    book of the *Ramayana*, the *Panchtantra*, and the *Kalila wa Dimna*, paintings
    without human figures are rare in Indian painting. For *Ramayana* landscapes
    that focus exclusively on frolicking bears and monkeys, see *Ramayana:
    Pahari Paintings*, ed. Roy C. Craven, Jr. (Bombay: Marg Publications, 1990),
    pp. 93 and 94 (Shangri folios) and p. 13 f(Guler, ca. 1720).

12. For example, Vidya Dehejia observes that the consistent topographical
    alignment of palaces is a feature of the Jagat Singh *Ramayana* of Mewar.
    "The Treatment of Narrative in Jagat Singh's '*Ramayana*': A Preliminary
    Study," *Artibus Asiae* 56, nos. 3/4 (1996), 306–7.

13. Ibid, 306.

14. *Ramcharitmanas* 1.146, quoted in Philip Lutgendorf, *The Life of a Text:*

Performing the Ramcaritmanas of Tulsidas (Berkeley: University of California Press, 1991), 226.

15. This longing, known as *viraha*, was felt to be especially intense during the rainy season, in which lovers traditionally reunite.

16. For numerous Vaishnava traditions that emerged in the late medieval/early modern period, such as the Ramnandis and the Gaudiya Vaishnavas, the epic quest of Rama is less important than the joyous union of the divine couple. Meditating upon Rama and Sita's time together, either before or after the forest exile, constitutes the highest form of devotion and leads towards salvation.

17. Lutgendorf, *Life of a Text,* 134, 371.

18. Valmiki's Sanskrit epic, the *Ramayana*, is dated to approximately 200 B.C.E.

19. Most illustrated versions of the *Ramcharitmanas* were and are depicted by village artists for popular consumption. One notable exception is the lavish illuminated manuscript commissioned in 1783 by Raja Udit Narayan Singh (1783–1835) of Banaras/Varanasi. Since Tulsidas completed his composition in Varanasi in the sixteenth century, the city has been the epicenter of *Ramcharitmanas* exposition, performance, and devotion. Lutgendorf, *Life of a Text,* 135.

20. The Sanskrit composition, which dates from roughly the sixth century, has been and remains one of India's most prominent Hindu texts. Thomas B. Coburn, *Encountering the Goddess: A Translation of the Devi Mahatmya and a Study of Its Interpretation* (Albany: State University of New York Press, 1991), 1.

21. King Samadhi had lost his realm to a foreign king and treacherous kinsmen; the merchant's family had stolen his wealth and turned him out.

22. This illusion, the goddess Mahamaya or Yoganidra, is so powerful and pervasive that she even constitutes the yogic sleep of the supreme deity Vishnu. Verses 1.34–46 in Coburn (1991), 35–36.

Maharaja Man Singh and the Naths

1. By tradition, the thakur of Bagri applies the coronation *tilak* and invests the maharaja with the sword of office. R. P. Vyas. *The Role of the Nobility in Marwar* (New Delhi: Jain Brothers, 1969), 175.

2. After Maharaja Bhim Singh's sudden death in 1803, the general Inderaj spirited Man Singh from Jalore to Jodhpur before the Rathore nobility could choose a successor more to their liking. Outmaneuvered, the nobles accepted Man Singh's succession and attended the formal coronation. But dissension arose even at the *rajtilak* ceremony because Man Singh had erased Bhim Singh's name from the recitation of Marwar's successive rulers. Later that same year, a posthumous son was born to Bhim Singh. Man Singh contested the boy's paternity and refused to abdicate. The powerful "Pokhran faction" left Jodhpur in protest. Vyas, 26–27.

3. Bhagvatilal Sharma, *Sri Jalandharnath-Pith.* (Jalore, Rajasthan: Sri Bhairunathji ka, Akhara 1995), 152.

4. Ibid, 148.

5. From Man Singh's "Jallandhar Charit," quoted in B. Sharma, 150.

6. Composed in 1739 by Karnidan for Maharaja Abhai Singh and highly esteemed for its poetic fluency, the vast compendium of regnal biographies and geneaological lists traces the history of the Jodhpur dynasty from the Rathore clan's divine origins through the early eighteenth century. The illustrated manuscript contains seventy unbound folios; archival inscriptions comprise the only text. The colophon on the back of the first folio names Amardas as the workshop supervisor (*da [khal] dholiya re kothar kalam chitara amar ri*). Other *Suraj Prakash* folios are published in Debra Diamond, "By the Grace of Jalandranath: Politics and Painting in Jodhpur," in *Holy Madness: Portraits of Tantric Masters* (New York: Rubin Museum of Art, 2006), figs. 1 and 2. Diamond "Poetics and Politics of Citation," in Panikkar, Shivaji et al., *Towards a New Art History: Studies in Indian Art* (New Delhi: D. K. Printworlds (P) Ltd., 2003), fig. 32. Rosemary Crill, *Marwar Painting: A History of the Jodhpur Style* (Mumbai: India Book House Ltd. in association with Mehrangarh Publishers, 1999), fig. 134.

7. Two painted scrolls depicting dynastic narratives from the Mewar court are extant: Victoria and Albert Museum, IS 07965; The New York Public Library, Indian MS 89, reproduced in Joanna Williams, *Kingdom of the Sun: Indian Court and Village Art from the Princely State of Mewar* (San Francisco: Asian Art Museum), fig. 20.

8. The manuscript received water damage on its upper margin at an unspecified date, and the figures of the Nath and princess have been repainted (almost certainly during Singh's reign).

9. Karnidan, *Kavya Karnidanji Charan Krit: Suraj Prakash.* 3 vols., ed. Sitaram Lalas (Jodhpur: Rajasthan Oriental Research Institute, 1962), 144–45. Trans. by D. Diamond.

10. The Jain administrator and general Inderaj Singhvi, who lifted the siege of Jalore and brought Man Singh to Jodhpur in 1803, was the maharaja's other chief advisor until he was assassinated, along with Dev Nath, in 1815.

11. A. H. E. Boileau, *Narrative Tour through the Western States of Rajwara* (Calcutta: Baptist Mission Press, 1837), 135.

12 This is one of several Man Singh-period paintings in the Mehrangarh Museum Trust collection that bear an ascription to two artists.

13. Boileau, 135.

14. The four Naths also are depicted worshiping together in the Philadelphia Museum of Art's *Maharaja Man Singh of Jodhpur Visits the Mahamandir* (see fig. 2 in "Painting, Politics, and Devotion under Maharaja Man Singh, 1803–43").

15. Gangaur celebrates the departure of Gauri, a manifestation of the goddess Parvati, who heads the home of her future husband, the great god Shiva.

16. Nij Mandir, the smallest of the three Nath temples in Jodhpur, was constructed for Surat Nath, one of the younger brothers of Ayas Dev Nath. It is adjacent to the Gulab Sagar, a large freshwater tank built by Gulab Rai, the consort of Maharaja Vijai Singh (see p. 29). The painting faithfully records the location of the temple by the tank as well as the pavilion above the walled temple's main gate and directly in front of the inner sanctum's domed roof; recent reconstruction has replaced the tall platforms represented on either side of the dome.

17. The *pradhan* attested all grants of lands and villages made by the court; by hereditary right, the position was held by the thakur of Pokhran. Vyas, 175.

18. Nij Mandir was Surat Nath's temple. The other three Naths were the principal members of the Nath elite after Dev Nath's murder in 1815.

19. The strange bedfellows that politics engender include the elite Naths seated

on the upper terrace. Bhim Nath had supported the faction that assassinated his brother Dev Nath. Man Singh apparently forgave Bhim Nath, but Dev Nath's son, Ladu Nath, never reconciled with his uncle. Until Ladu Nath left the kingdom in disgust in 1828, the two Naths vigorously promoted competing policies (in their roles as advisors to the king) and their forces skirmished on several occasions.

20. He also had the administrators who supported Prince Chattar Singh put to death. Vyas, 58–62.

21. The painting's identification is discussed in the related reference catalogue entry, pp. 285–286.

22. The *mahasiddha* is referred to as Jallandharnath in the verso inscription, but as Trilok Srinath (Glorious Nath of the Three Worlds) in the *Nath Purana* text, Pustak Prakash Library, Ms. 1723, p.1.

23. Typically, the most beautifully painted monumental folios exhibit the highest level of burnishing. Some hastily painted folios in the *Shiva Purana* have hardly been burnished, if at all.

Origins of the Cosmos

1. Although it is numbered 1, Reu catalogued this painting as *Nath Charit*, f. 2.; its reattribution is discussed in the reference catalogue entry to cat. 39, pp. 285–86.

2. *Nath Charit*, f. 5 (Mehrangarh Museum Trust, RJS 2430), and *Siddha Siddhanta Paddhati*, f. 1 (RJS 2373). *Nath Purana* ff. 6 (RJS 2403) and 20 (RJS 2417) employ the unbounded gold plane to depict a subtle (non-physical) manifestation of the Absolute.

3. In north Indian court painting, the closest precedents are the gleaming gold ovals that represent the cosmic egg (*brahmananda*). These appear in small folios from illustrated *Bhagavata Purana* manuscripts from the Punjab Hills but there is no evidence they were known to the Jodhpur atelier. See, for example, T. Richard Blurton, *Hindu Art* (London: British Museum Press, 1992), fig. 127; B. N. Goswamy, *Essence of Indian Art* (San Francisco: Asian Art Museum, 1986), fig. 200.

4. See Priya Mookerjee, *Pathway Icons: The Wayside Art of India* (London: Thames and Hudson, 1987), *passim*.

5. Verses 8, 9, and 12, chapter 6, *The Siva-Purana: Ancient Indian Tradition and Mythology Series*. Translated by a Board of Scholars (Delhi: Motilal Banarsidass, 1977), 195.

6. The evolutionary theory of the *tattvas* is one of the most influential teachings of the philosophical *Samkhya* school. See George Feuerstein, *Tantra: The Path of Ecstasy* (Boston: Shambhala Publications, 1998) for a glossed list of an ontological model of thirty-six *tattvas*, pp. 62–66.

7. Narayana/Vishnu sleeping on the cosmic waters is a bold re-appropriation of a canonical cosmological model (stated, for example, throughout the *Mahabharata*) that is central to texts explicating Vishnu's supreme power. Within the *Shiva Purana*, Vishnu's role in creation is located within a larger frame that extols Shiva as the motivating force behind the universe. This strategy is typical of the aggregate nature of Hindu cosmologies, which accumulate and reframe, rather than discard, potentially competing or contradictory narratives. For the reinscription of Vishnu's awakening from

his yogic sleep as the Goddess's activity in the *Devi Mahatmya*, see cat. 39, and Thomas B. Coburn, *Encountering the Goddess: A Translation of the Devi Mahatmya and a Study of Its Interpretation* (Albany: State University of New York Press, 1991), 22.

8. Verses 2 and 3, chapter 7, *The Siva Purana*, 199.

9. From the verso inscription on panel 3; see reference catalogue entry (pp. 288–89) for complete translation.

10. Feurstein, 70.

11. One can follow the thematic trajectory of Jodhpur painting over a century through representations of animal-prow boats on silver waters. The motif appears first as Bakhat Singh's pleasure boat in a painting depicting royal pleasure at Nagaur palace (see cat. 18). In the *Ramcharitmanas* commissioned by the ardent Vaishnavite Vijai Singh, the boats are rowed on the silver waters of a heavenly palace for the delight of Rama (cat. 26). During Man Singh's reign, the animal-prow boat was turned upside down to convey metaphorically the ineffable and awesome power of Nath *mahasiddhas* in the celestial realm.

12. Since Nath teachings emerged from and within a religious landscape of competing philosophical and religious traditions, they often relate encounters between Naths and divine, semi-divine, and human doubters, who are eventually convinced of Nath primacy.

13. Nath alchemists draw upon these same homologies to convert base metals into gold. See David Gordon White, *The Alchemical Body: Siddha Traditions in Medieval India* (Chicago: University of Chicago Press, 1996), *passim*.

14. *Siddhsiddhantapaddhanti*, ed. Ramlal Srivastav (Gorakhpur, U. P.: Gorakhnath Mandir, 1981), verses 3.35–41.

15. The *Siddha Siddhanta Paddhati* vertical bodies are illustrated in cat. 48 and fig. 44b, p. 290.

16. Shiva, Vishnu, and Goddess traditions each conceive of their deity as the center of the universe. Similarly, the Nath texts written in Jodhpur during Man Singh's reign situate the transcendent entity Nathji as the font of the universe.

17. Depicted in the Mewar *Bhagavata Purana*, f. 24, reproduced in Vidya Dehejia, (1996), 303–24, fig. 10.

18. As early as the first century C.E., the Buddha's presence was evoked in stone carvings that represented the imprint of his feet. For more on sacred footprints, see Kathryn H. Selig Brown, *Eternal Presence: Handprints and Footprints in Buddhist Art* (New York: Katonah Museum of Art, 2004), *passim*.

19. See cat. 47 for a cosmograph that locates the *akasha mandala* at the apex of the universe.

20. Although the Nath cosmologies articulate the formation of the universe, no sectarian or aesthetic texts describe these paintings.

21. The multitude contains only eighty-one figures, but the artist was undoubtedly instructed to represent eighty-four Naths. In both Hindu and Buddhist traditions, the important sets of Nath *mahasiddhas* number 9, 18, and 84.

22. See the reference catalogue entry for cat. 32, pp. 280–81.

23. B. Sharma, (1995), 137.

24. The "difficult time" in the verse's first line refers to the siege of Jalore Fort, discussed in "Painting, Politics, and Devotion under Maharaja Man Singh, 1803–43." David Gordon White, "Yoga and Political Power Among the Nath Siddhas of North India," n.37 from the *Jallandhar Charit*, 7, quoted in B. Sharma (1995), 155. Trans. David Gordon White.

Mapping the Cosmos

1. The *Shiva Rahasya's* thirteenth folio, cat. 54 also depicts the sweetly domestic activities of Shiva and Parvati in their celestial abode.
2. The *Mahanirvana Tantra*, verses 1.5–9, quoted in George Feurstein, *Tantra: The Path of Ecstasy* (Boston and London: Shambhala, 1998), 73.
3. Over millennia, various conceptions of the cosmos were aggregated in Hindu treatises and puranas; Meru often is described as an inverted cone.
4. From the late twelfth–thirteenth century, the emergent *Nath Sampraday* listed and classified Naths and *siddhas* (perfected beings from Buddhist or other Hindu ascetic traditions) into subsets of nine, eighteen, and eighty-four Naths. See David Gordon White, *The Alchemical Body: Siddha Traditions in Medieval India* (Chicago: University of Chicago Press, 1996), 90–101.
5. Verses 2.1, 2.4–5 from a seventeenth-century hatha yoga treatise, the *Shiva Samhita*, in George Feurstein, *Tantra: The Path of Ecstasy* (Boston and London: Shambhala Publications, 1998), 61.
6. The fourth yantra from the Meghmala is reproduced as fig. 2, p. 45.
7. Ontological categories represented within yantras include the *tattvas*, which are represented in anthropomorphic form as twenty-four deities on the third folio of the *Shiva Purana* (cat. 42).
8. Pictorial yantras blur into the category of mandalas, which share a similar structural logic and role within tantric ritual, but they are relatively rare. For other pictorial yantras, including a Jain yantra, see figs. 94, 95, and 104 in Jackie Menzies, *Goddess Divine Energy* (Sydney: Art Gallery of New South Wales, 2006). See also Dehejia, *Devi: The Great Goddess* (Washington, D.C.: Arthur M. Sackler Gallery, 1999), fig. 26.
9. The use of translucent washes appears only here and on red mountains that cover the walls of the inner sanctum at Udaimandir.

Sacred Sites and Cosmic Oceans

1. Folios 22–31. Shrine grids also are employed in *Nath Charit*, ff. 50 and 54, and *Shiva Purana*, ff. 78–84.
2. From a description of Mount Kailash in the *Mahanirvana Tantra*, quoted in Feurstein, *Tantra*, 73: 1.1–2.
3. The twelve *Jyotirlingam* Temples that Shiva describes to Parvati are Kedara, Omkara, Vidyanatha, Ghusrinesha, Naganatha, Mahakala, Bhimesha, Tryambaka, Vishvesha, Shrishaila, Gokarnesh, and Rameshvaia. *Sri Sivarahasyan*, TMSSM Library, Thanjavur, 1985. ed. Swaminatha Atreya.
4. Advanced adepts see these *jyotirlingams* as columns of fire, although they appear to the uninitiated as stone pillars.
5. A description of Mount Kailash in the "Nath Chandrika" by Man Singh's courtier and poet Uttamchand Bhandari, quoted from Narayan Singh Bhatti, *Parampara* 92 (1989), 14.
6. A painting identical in size and composition, also numbered five on the recto in its upper left corner, is in the collection of Vyakul Acharya (Jaipur, Rajasthan). For a discussion of "duplicate" folios, see the reference catalogue entry for cat. 39.
7. Although the all-pervasive Absolute and the myriad forms of matter and being are simultaneous, Gorakhnath explains them as consecutive events for the sake of unenlightened listeners.
8. *Siddha Siddhanta Paddhati*, 5.41
9. B. N. Reu refers to Shiva's three palaces as the Chandrakanth, which is represented within a red fortress wall; the Vaidurya, which is depicted as a small temple where Shiva and Parvati worship a lingam; and the golden Hirak Mahal. *Shivrahasya ka Katha* (Jodhpur: Sardar Museum, 1934).
10. Shiva, of course, is worshiped in his world (Shivalok), but the *Shiva Rahasya* further reveals that he also is worshiped by the deities Brahma and Vishnu (in their respective worlds of Brahmalok and Vishnulok, f. 14), various other Hindu gods (ff. 15 and 16), and the mountains (f. 17).
11. The quote is from the fifteenth-century *Shankaravijaya of Anandgiri*, cited in David Gordon White, "Yoga and Political Power among the Nath Siddhas of North India," in Peter Flügel and Gustaaf Houtman, eds., *Asceticism and Power in South and Southeast Asia* (Abingdon, U.K.: Routledge, 2009).
12. A cult of mountain-identified demigods called Naths or *siddhas* existed at least a thousand years before the advent of the historical Nath Sampraday in the twelfth–thirteenth century. White (1996), pp. 2–3.
13. White, "Yoga and Political Power," pp. 15–16. Mountains in Maharashtra, Himachal Pradesh, Rajasthan, and Nepal remain identified with Divine Naths. Jallandharnath is the Kalaschal Mountain at Jalore, where Prince Man Singh grew up.
14. Indeed, most of the folios in the illustrated *Shiva Purana* depict Shiva's exploits and encounters with other deities.
15. All of the major Hindu deities encompass contradictions for they are transcendental, all-pervasive, and omnipotent forces as well as divine agents who engage in activities (like marriage) that mirror human actions. To his devotees, Shiva is simultaneously the sublime force behind all creation, the archetypal ascetic, the vanquisher of demons, the lord of dance, and the loving husband of the goddess Parvati.
16. Known on the subcontinent as a black buck, the male has ringed horns with a moderate spiral twist.
17. For the tortoise as the support of the universe see cats. 47 and 48; for Saraswati's vehicle, see cat. 39.
18. In Indian art, water with a basket-weave pattern is a well-established abstraction that appears as early as the sixth-century Ajanta fresco depicting the *Purna Avadana*. In addition to its many appearances in the Jodhpur corpus (e.g., cat. 25), it appears first in north Indian painting representing the Yamuna River in the 1525–40 *Bhagavata Purana*; see Darielle Mason et al, *Intimate Worlds: Indian Paintings from the Alvin O, Bellak Collection* (Philadelphia Museum of Art, 2001), 46. In Paharai painting, the pattern often was employed to represent cosmic waters; see B. N. Goswamy, *Essence of Indian Art* (San Francisco: Asian Art Museum, 1986), figs. 112, 174, and 203.
19. The prose text, like that of the *Nath Purana,* was compiled during Man Singh's reign; multiple copies of each are housed in the Pustak Prakash Library. In the absence of critical editions, we examined two manuscripts, neither of which contained text that could be tied to these paintings.

Notes to the reference catalogue

The Origins of Jodhpur Court Painting

1. For information on Bishan Das and other works by him, see Asok Kumar Das, "Bishandas: Unequalled in His Age in Taking Likenesses," *Mughal Masters: Further Studies* (Mumbai: Marg, 1998), 112–33. The Berlin image mentioned in the catalogue entry is reproduced in plate 3 of this article.

2. Crill, 37. For the role of portraiture in Mughal painting, see Gascoigne, 150–51.

3. An often-published painted portrait of Gaj Singh and Mirza Raja Jai Singh of Amber is an example of the Mughalized style in Amber, another Rajput atelier. See Crill, fig. 17, and Glynn and Smart.

4. Desai, no. 27 (formerly in the Khajanchi Collection), museum number 63.1789. The *jharokha* theme is repeated in the portrait of Gaj Singh's great-grandson, Bakhat Singh, cat. 15. See Gascoigne, 144–45, for more information about the symbolism of the *jharokha* appearance.

5. These Gaj Singh paintings are a Rajput variation of Mughal head-and-shoulder images; for the Mughal prototypes, see Andrew Topsfield and Milo Cleveland Beach, *Indian Paintings from the Collection of Howard Hodgkin* (New York: Thames and Hudson, 1991), 45, no. 12; Guy and Swallow, figure 89. An alabaster relief *jharokha* portrait of Shah Jahan is published in Jorge Flores and Nuno Vassallo e Silva, *Goa and the Great Mughal* (Lisbon: Calouste Gulbenkian Foundation, 2004), 146.

6. Crill, fig. 19.

7. An inscription on the reverse identifies the figure as "Sri Rao Amar Singhji." Portraits of the renegade Amar Singh are extremely rare. After his death in Agra, Amar Singh was cremated on the banks of the Yamuna. The two queens that had accompanied him to Agra committed *sati* (burned themselves with their husband), while three other wives performed the burning rite in Nagaur. Around Amar Singh's *chatri* in Nagaur are eight other shrines dedicated to his wives and sons.

8. Amar Singh had ruled Nagaur earlier; Emperor Jahangir gave it to him in 1626, but took it back in 1627. Nagaur was Mughal-owned land (*khalsa*) so the emperors were able to dispose of it as they chose. Mughal sources relate these two different dates for the gifts, but James Tod, vol. 11, 34, states that both awards were given by Shah Jahan in 1634, when Amar Singh was disowned and expelled from court by his father; see Siddiqui, *History of Nagaur*, 88–89. One of Amar Singh's most important roles was to help the Mughal forces quell the rebellion of Raja Jagat Singh of Pathankot in 1639.

9. Begley and Desai, 314–16; Singh, 83–85; Tod, vol. II, 34–35; Siddiqui, 90–91.

10. Cat. 6 is related to a similar composition, painted around the same time, of Raja Jagat Singh of Kotah in a garden, Kotah, ca. 1670; see Stuart Cary Welch, *India: Art and Culture: 1300–1900* (New York: Metropolitan Museum of Art, 1985), 358, no. 241. Kotah is a Rajput state to the southeast of Marwar. Jagat Singh of Kotah also may have ordered his painting as a result of his awareness of the Mughal Taj Mahal and the Shalimar gardens projects.

11. Toward the end of his life, Jaswant Singh went to Peshawar, accompanied by four artists: Karim, son of Ghasi; Natho, son of Gayo; Narayandas, son of Bagha Devara; and Nago, son of Vago Devara. Crill, 48.

12. Crill, 44. Andrew Topsfield, *Court Painting at Udaipur: Art Under the Patronage of the Maharanas of Mewar* (Zurich: Eberhard Fischer, 2002), 97. Hooja, 597.

13. Topsfield (2002), figs. 114 and 115.

14. Crill, 59.

15. Andrew Topsfield has suggested that the Ajit Singh family portrait at the Philadelphia Museum of Art (see fig. 8a) also has strong affinities with early eighteenth-century Mewar painting.

16. Topsfield (2002), figs. 95, 98, 99. Throughout the first quarter of the eighteenth century, there were ongoing relations between Ajit Singh and the Mewar court; even one of Ajit Singh's daughters was married to Prince Pratap Singh of Mewar. Hooja, 707.

17. Siddiqui, 186. In addition, Bakhat Singh is mentioned in an inscription and is included in a Mewar painting dated 1750 of Maharana Jagat Singh II hunting wild boar and tiger (V. P. Dwivedi, "Some Inscribed and dated Rajasthan Miniatures in the Collection of the State Museum, Lucknow," *Journal of the Indian Society of Oriental Art*, New Series, vol. VIII, (1976–77), 49–50, pls. XIX, 1 and 1b). Bakhat Singh's son, Vijai, was married to Jagat Singh's daughter.

18. Karni Singh was instrumental in the translation of this inscription.

19. The floor spread can be seen in another painting of Ajit Singh, circa 1719–20, (Crill, fig. 32), which is also done in a Mughalized style. For more on the family gathering, see Mason, no. 50. Another Rajput-style family gathering is in the L. D. Institute of Indology, Ahmedabad, 87.16 (unpublished, but fig. 3 in the Bakhat Singh chronology is a detail of the Ahmedabad painting).

20. Heeramaneck, pl. 81; Sotheby's New York, November 2, 1988, lot. 63; Topsfield and Beach, no. 26; Gian Giuseppe Filippe, *Indian Miniatures and Paintings from the 16th to the 19th Century: The Collection of Howard Hodgkin* (Milan: Electra, 1997), no. 36.

21. Ray, 94–95, no. 42.

22. A portrait of Bakhat Singh receiving a noble on a terrace, also circa 1740, is illustrated in B. N. Goswamy, *Painted Visions: The Goenka Collection of Indian Paintings* (New Delhi: Lalit Kala Akademi, 1999), no. 137, and Crill, fig. 69. Bakhat Singh appears to be the same age as he is in cat. 9. This author has not seen the inscription on the reverse, but Goswamy has interpreted a date of Vikram Samvat 1831 (1774), which is likely an inspection date. The style of this Goenka painting of Bakhat Singh is a hybrid—not the delicate, pastel style of Nagaur (cat. 10–20), but also not as dependent on the primary colors, stylization of figures, and dark outline as seen in Jodhpur painting of the same time. See Crill, figs. 55, 58, and 59.

23. Topsfield and Beach, 72, fig. 4; Crill, fig. 67.

24. B. N. Goswamy and A. L. Dallapiccola, *A Place Apart: Painting in Kutch, 1720–1820* (Delhi: Oxford University Press, 1983), pl. II.

25. Heeramaneck, pl. 85 (also reproduced in Pal, 1983), 256, no. R41.

Royal Pastimes in the Gardens at Nagaur Palace

1. Ebba Koch, "Mughal Garden Types and Rajput Responses," Nagaur Garden Conservation Workshop, Nagaur, India, January 28–February 1, 2006. Post-1700 Rajput gardens are quite similar to Mughal gardens; both contain cross-axial designs with water sources, such as fountains, pools, and areas lined with water channels.

2. Unpublished, Mehrangarh Museum Trust, RJS 2806.

3. Most Bakhat Singh paintings do not show a distinguishable hierarchy among the women, but in reality some of the zenana women had more power than others. This may be indicated in compositions that single out certain women, such as cat. 11 and 19.

4. Nagar, 60.

5. In cat. 12, he wears a skull-cap similar to that used during religious worship; in cat. 20, he is bare-headed; and in cat. 9, he wears the usual rectangular turban.

6. Crill, figs. 68–71.

7. The Hadi Rani Mahal is actually two joined buildings, an entranceway and a palace. It is the only three-story structure in the current Nagaur fort compound. The building faces the central square and lies between the Bakhat Singh Mahal and a large *baradari* (hall with pillars), which connects to the Abha Mahal. The Hadi Rani Mahal was built by Bakhat Singh (Gilles Tillotson, Mehrangarh Trust draft document, 2007) as part of his extensive building program for Nagaur. The walls are covered with floral decoration and paintings; women are featured in scenes of dancing, singing, enjoying the countryside, bathing, and other pleasurable activities; the absence of male figures is notable. The size and scale of these paintings devoted to women enjoying life in the palace and gardens is unique. At Bundi, another large-scale wall-painting program from approximately the same time period featured Krishna-related paintings and scenes showing the far more typical male activities of hunting and processions.

8. For more images of the wall paintings, see Goetz (1949), 89–98; Y. K. Shukla, "Fresco Paintings in the Nagaur Fort," *Roopa-Lekha* XLI, nos. 1–2 (1972), 95–100. Shukla, *Wall Paintings of Rajasthan: Jaipur, Galta, Kota, Nagaur* (Ahmedabad: L. D. Institute of Indology, 1980), figs. 23–28. Mira Seth, *Wall Paintings of Rajasthan* (New Delhi: National Museum of India, 2003), figs. 219, 221–25. One scholar has suggested that in Mewar and Jaipur "paintings of rajas enjoying pastimes such as sitting on a throne, listening to musicians, watching the moon, playing holi, enjoying games of *chaupar*, smoking *huqqas* were probably provided to the zenana rather than purchased by its women." Molly Emma Aitken, "Pardah and Portrayal: Rajput Women as Subjects, Patrons and Collectors," *Artibus Asiae* LXII, no. 2 (2002), 253. Perhaps Bakhat Singh's patronage of the portable and wall paintings also were intended as gifts to various individuals in the zenana or to the zenana as a whole.

9. This hat may be an image appropriated from Mughal court painting for Nagaur imagery; it may be a style adopted generally by Nagaur royal women as a Mughal court fashion; or it may indicate that its wearers, like Chaghtay hat wearers in the Mughal court, were zenana officials and administrators. For Mughal paintings featuring this type of cap, see Okada (1992), figs. 106, 191, and especially 226.

10. Long before the advent of Islam in India, however, lush gardens played an

11. Siddiqui, 83. Although Jodhpur was conquered by Akbar in 1562–63, Rajput Rathores continued to rule with Akbar's consent. Nagaur, on the other hand, had an Islamic governor during the late sixteenth and early seventeenth centuries, who was appointed directly by the Mughal emperor.

12. Muhata Nansi, *Marwar ra Pargana ri Vigat* (Marwar Chronicles), ed. Fateh Singh (Jodhpur: Rajasthan Oriental Research Institute, 1968), 580.

13. The faces of Krishna and Radha have been repainted.

14. Karl Khandalavala, Moti Chandra, and Pramod Chandra, *Miniature Paintings from the Sri Motichand Khanjanchi Collection* (New Delhi: Lalit Kala Akademi, 1960), 49, pl. E.

15. Daniel Ehnbom, *Indian Miniatures: The Ehrenfeld Collection* (New York: Hudson Hills Press, 1985), no. 66; Poster, 157, no. 117; Hermann Goetz, *The Art and Architecture of Bikaner State* (Oxford: Bruno Cassier, 1950), fig. 79.

16. Now in the Rietberg Museum, Zurich, Switzerland. Published in Sotheby's London, *Oriental Manuscripts and Miniatures*, April 23, 1997, lot. 12; Colnaghi, no. 60.

17. Siddiqui, 156–57. Bakhat Singh and his brother, Abhai Singh, demanded that Bikaner pay them for their military losses of food and equipment. Surjan Singh and his son Zorwar Singh refused to do so, and the two brothers had to settle with a pact that the Bikaner army would not follow them back to Jodhpur and Nagaur to seek revenge.

18. Koch (2006).

19. The dimensions of fig. 13b are 43.1 x 61.3 cm. It is inscribed on the reverse in Rajasthani: *Rajeshvar Maharajadhiraj Maharaj Sri Bakhat Singhji ri tasbir* (Picture of king of kings, supreme king of great kings, great king, glorious Bakhat Singhji). Mehrangarh Museum Trust, RJS 2026.

20. The continuity of cultural tradition from the time of the two Nagaur paintings well into the nineteenth century is illustrated by a photograph of a *nautch* (dance and music presentation) in a palace courtyard taken by Charles Shepherd during a visit to Jaipur in the 1860s. In the photograph *chiks* shield the zenana women while all the men—nobles, musicians, and even young boys—watch the sole female dancer with pleasure. See Naveen Patnaik, *A Second Paradise: Indian Courtly Life 1590–1947* (New York: Doubleday, 1985), 34, fig, 2; E. Jaiwant Paul, *Gloire des Princes, Louange des Dieux* (Paris: Réunion des musées nationaux, 2003), 133.

21. Asher and Talbot (p. 200) have pointed out that Shah Jahan's palace in Delhi, Shahajahanabad, "reflects an almost slavish sense of flattering the ruler…. Shah Jahan's palace, like his painting, was artfully contrived to highlight the Mughal ruler's status." For Bakhat Singh, Nagaur and the buildings that he constructed there, along with his paintings, became his personal monument.

22. An interesting omission in the Bakhat Singh paintings with musicians is the absence of a horn or trumpet player. In other Rajput paintings, men take on that role; however, that is not the case in the Bakhat Singh paintings, even those where male musicians are present (e.g., cat. 12 and fig. 13b in the reference catalogue entry for cat. 13). Royal patronage of musicians continues today; the celebrated sarod player Ustad Ali Akbar Khan is a current Rathore court musician.

23. R. K. Tandan, *Indian Miniature Painting: 16th through 19th centuries*

(Bangalore: Natesan Publishers, 1982), fig. 60, is a Muhammad Shah *jharokha* painting by an artist from Bikaner. The Bikaner artist adopted the painting now in the San Diego Museum of Art, or one very similar to it, as his model. The appearance of similar *jharokha* paintings in Nagaur and Bikaner illustrates how images and associated styles traveled from one locale to another, which, in the case of *jharokha* paintings, also carried political content and concepts related to royal authority. Compare cat. 15 with Topsfield (2002), fig. 132, a *jharokha* painting of Rana Sangram Singh of Mewar, ca. 1725–30, which may have served as a Rajput model.

24. The entry for cat. 5 discusses several earlier seventeenth-century Mughal *darshan* images.

25. For information on the nimbus/halo in Mughal painting, see Gascoigne, 152–53.

26. Molly Emma Aitken, personal communication to the author, 2007. The mezzanine contains a beautiful painted ceiling with an interlocking floral and geometric design, and it retains much of its original opulent gilding.

27. Crill, 66–72, figs. 37–40. A painting inscribed "Rai Dalchand" is illustrated in Topsfield (2004), 326, no. 144. A portrait of "Rai Dalchand" by the Lucknow artist Mohan Singh is in the British Library; Toby Falk and Mildred Archer, *Indian Miniatures in the India Office Library* (London: Sotheby Parke Bernet, 1981), no. 287. It is this author's opinion, along with that of Navina Haidar (associate curator, Department of Islamic Art, Metropolitan Museum of Art; personal communication to the author, 2007) that Rai Dalchand is not the same artist who worked for Abhai Singh in Jodhpur. The Jodhpur paintings with inscriptions that mention his name do not refer to him as "Rai"; in addition, the style of the painting illustrated in Topsfield and the Dalchand works (Crill, figs. 37–40) from Jodhpur are not even closely related. Two vibrant flower paintings may be part of Dalchand's oeuvre: (a) a carnation-type plant (Barbara Schmitz and Ziyaud-Din A. Desai, *Mughal and Persian Paintings and Illustrated Manuscripts in the Raza Library, Rampur* [New Delhi: Indira Gandhi National Centre for the Arts, 2006], acc. no. 33 verso, 72, pl. 153); (b) A poppy plant (Stuart Cary Welch, *India: Art and Culture 1300–1900* [New York: Metropolitan Museum of Art, 1985], 370, pl. 248). According to Schmitz, the Rampur painting is signed "Dal Chand" and if that attribution is correct, then the poppy painting probably can be assigned to him as well (Navina Haidar, 2007).

28. Crill, fig. 39.

29. Navina Haidar (2007) has suggested that he was in Kishangarh in 1726. Faiyaz Ali Khan also states that Dalchand was in Kishangarh in 1726; see Faiyaz Ali Khan, "The Painters of Kishangarh," *Roopa Lekha* LI, nos. 1–2 (New Delhi, 1979–80), 65. However, given the 1727 date of the Jodhpur-style portrait of Abhai Singh, we may have to amend Dalchand's 1726 presence in Kishangarh, unless he returned to Jodhpur to paint the 1727 portrait.

30. Bakhat Singh may have found a local Nagaur artist and brought him to Jodhpur for training. We know from a mid-seventeenth century *Dhola Maru* manuscript that artists existed in Nagaur (see cat. 5. n.7). Further research into the records and archives of the royal Rathore families, now stored in the Bikaner Palace and in the Rajasthan State Archives in Bikaner, may hold answers to some of these questions.

31. Crill, fig. 38. I am grateful to Navina Haidar for alerting me to two equestrian paintings in the Metropolitan Museum of Art that have been attributed to

Dalchand, 2002.349 and 2002.411.

32. An inscription on the reverse of fig. 2 reads: *Maharajadhiraj sri bakhat singhji ri sabi nawab sherjang sri hazur maihajar. da[khal] dholiya re kothar hajari sam 1885 ra savan sud 12.* (Image of supreme king of great kings, glorious Bakhat Singh. Nawab Sher [i] jang [is] in the presence of Sri Hazur [his glorious highness Bakhat Singh]. Entered into the *dholiya* storeroom, 1828 the month of Shravan [July–August]). Andrew Topsfield (personal communication to the author, 2008) has suggested that the nawab may be one of the Kalhora chiefs from Sindh, a group that came to power in the mid-eighteenth century. The title Sher-i Jang (Lion of battle) is an honorific, not a full name. When Vijai Singh of Jodhpur invaded Sindh later in the eighteenth century, he was defeated by a certain Sher-i Jang Mir Fateh Khan Mankani. The man with Bakhat Singh is perhaps part of the Sindh hierarchy.

33. There is a discrepancy in size between the two figures. Debra Diamond has suggested that the figure on the left was traced from a different painting, which might account for the figure's smaller size.

34. A series of elephant wall panels is still visible in the entrance vestibule to the Hadi Rani Mahal. Stylistically slightly later in date than cat. 17, they never-theless reveal a thematic continuity with the portable paintings. The slightly later date is suggested by the crude, unrefined faces of the *mahouts* (elephant drivers) and because the landscape in the wall painting is more abbreviated than it is in cat. 17.

35. A young prince, perhaps Ahmad Shah (1725–1754) practicing archery; inscribed: work of Nidha Mal, ca. 1740–45, Indian Museum, Calcutta, 340/286, 25.8 x 41.2 cm; published: B. N. Goswamy, *Rasa: les neuf visages de l'art indien* (Paris: Ministere des Relations Exterieures Association Francaise d'Action Artistique, 1986), no. 171; Goswamy, *Essence of India Art* (San Francisco: Asian Art Museum of San Francisco, 1986), no. 6; McInerney (2002), 28, fig. 12. Ahmad Shah was the son and successor of Muhammad Shah. Nidha Mal also painted the Muhammad Shah *jharokah* portrait (see fig. 15a, p. 269).

36. *Maharaja Bakhat Singh and Prince Vijai Singh watch an elephant fight*, Nagaur, ca. 1735, 44.2 x 62.3 cm. Inscribed: *Rajrajeshvar Maharajadhiraj Maharaj Sri Bakhat Singhji ri tasbir* (Picture of lord of king of kings, supreme king of great kings, supreme king, glorious Bakhat Singhji) *hathi ladave* (he ordered the elephant fight) *Maharaj Kanvar Sri Vijai Singhji* (Supreme king, Prince Vijai Singh) *Da(khal) dholiya re kothar hajri sam(vat) 1885 ra savan sud* 12 (Entered in the *dholiya* storeroom and inventory, 1828, the twelfth day in the light half of Shravana [July–August]), Mehrangarh Museum Trust, RJS 1992. The inscription tells us that the elephant entertainment was requested by Bakhat Singh, giving us some insight into court practices. Perhaps the event was organized to teach Vijai Singh about manly pursuits, just as the entertainment in cat. 13 may have taught the young prince about music and dance. Interestingly, an elephant fight representation also occupies the lower third of the Victoria and Albert *Akbar Nama* page (f. 81) in which Akbar is welcomed to Nagaur by the governor (see "Rathore and Mughal Interactions," n.9, p. 301).

37. Jadunath Sarkar, *Fall of the Mughal Empire*, vol. 1 (New Delhi: Orient Longman Ltd., 1971), 174–76.

38. Catherine Asher, *The New Cambridge History of India I*, no. 4: *Architecture of Mughal India* (Cambridge University Press, 1995), 174.

39. Siddiqui, 158; G. D. Sharma, 272.

40. Aitken, 268. Bakhat Singh appears non-aggressive in his paintings, yet the records show that he was militarily belligerent, continually attempting to expand his territories and waging war upon his neighbors.

41. Cited in Crill, 98, n.68; see p. 299, bottom, second from right. The inscription on the reverse reads: *Rajadhiraj sri vakhat singhji ri sabi samvat 1802 savan sudi. Chitara ajmat ra hath ri dha[khal]dadholiya re kothar....* (Portrait of king of great kings, glorious Bakhat Singhji, on the light half of Shravan [July–August], 1745, by the hand of [the artist] Ajmat, placed in the *dholiya* storeroom. Signature elements of the Jodhpur style include a flat background, intense colors rather than pastels, and a less-polished, stiffer treatment of the figure. Crill (p. 92) states that "it is difficult, if possible at all, to distinguish paintings done for Bakhat Singh at Nagaur from those done when he was ruler of Jodhpur." However, that was written before the discovery of the Bakhat Singh paintings represented here, and with this new material, we now can clearly identify the Nagaur style.

42. Reproduced in Terence McInerney and Howard Hodgkin, *Indian Drawing* (London: Arts Council of Great Britain, 1983), no. 15. On the front is an inscription in Persian: *in taswir-i maharaj bakhat singh dar Nagaur* (picture of Bakhat Singh in Nagaur). On the verso is another inscription, in Rajasthani: *asabi maharajdhiraj maharaj sri bakhat singhi ri chhe* ([this] is an image of supreme king of great kings, supreme king, glorious Bakhat Singh).

43. Crill, fig. 38. For Kishangarh-style horses, see Topsfield (2004), fig. 65.

44. "Rathore and Mughal Interactions," p. 16.

45. Sharad Purnima occurs during the full moon of the winter month of Asvina (September–October). It is believed that during the festival, the Hindu moon god Chandra showers the earth with *amrit* (elixir or spiritual nectar). A special mixture of milk, rice, and sugar, prepared and offered to Krishna, is kept outdoors all night so that it may absorb the *amrit* falling from the moon. (Perhaps that is the white mixture in one of the bowls on the white cloth in the painting.) The next morning it is consumed by devotees and temple worshipers.

46. For example, a painting of royal lovers, probably Shah Shuja and a favorite wife, by the imperial artist Bal Chand is dated 1633. Stuart Cary Welch, *Imperial Mughal Painting* (New York: George Braziller, 1978), pl. 35.

47. A later Muhammad Shah work (ca. 1740) in the Jaipur collection is based on fig. 19a, the earlier Lalbhai composition; see Goswamy, 1986, no. 57.

48. For example, in January 1748 Muhammad Shah summoned Bakhat Singh to Delhi. Siddiqui, 166. For examples of Muhammad Shah paintings, see Welch (1963), no. 77; Khandalavala, pl. III; McInerney (2002), 17, fig. 4.

49. Crill, fig. 70.

50. Crill, 92 and fig. 70.

51. According to most participants at the 2006 Nagaur Garden Conservation Workshop (see n.1, above), further archaeological work at the site will uncover an octagonal footprint.

52. Filippe, no. 19, where it is identified as "A Maharaja bathing, Jodhpur, ca. 1720."

53. There is no inscription to help with the identification of the protagonist in fig. 20b. I am grateful to Andrew Topsfield of the Ashmolean Museum for confirming the absence of any inscription on the reverse of the painting.

54. Crill, figs. 29–32, 34, 36 and pp. 298–99.

55. Crill, figs. 67–72, 73–76. Bhanwar Singh of Mehrangarh Fort was particularly helpful regarding the distinction between Bakhat Singh and Vijai Singh.

56. Crill, figs. 73–76. In the Hodgkin work, Vijai Singh wears a tall turban similar to one in an unpublished painting in the Mehrangarh collection, RJS 1975.

Gardens for Divine Play (pages 276–79)

1. Rosemary Crill, *Indian Embroidery* (New Delhi: V&A Publications for Prakash Book Depot, 1999), 8.

2. Crill, 106; a page from the *Bhagavata Purana* series is illustrated as fig. 82. See B. N. Goswamy, *Essence of Indian Art* (San Francisco: Asian Art Museum of San Francisco, 1986), fig. 185, for another *Bhagavata Purana* page.

Maharaja Man Singh and the Naths (pages 280–86)

1. Mehrangarh Museum Trust, RJS 4767, 4768, 4769, and 2076.

2. Although the kinship connections date from 1459, the seats were formalized in the seventeenth century, when *darbar* rituals were codified.

3. Rajput courtiers tied their turbans in the ruler's style and wore *jamas* of prescribed width and length when attending court. Textile patterns and colors were also associated with rituals, seasons, and royal events; for example, the maharaja distributed turban lengths with a "five gold *mohur*" pattern on the accession of a nobleman. Within these strictures, resistance could be also expressed. A. H. E. Boileau notes that disaffected thakurs attending Man Singh's *darbars* in the 1830s adhered to the "regulation patterns" concerning *jama* width and length, but had the garments sewn from coarse cloth rather than fine cottons and silks. Boileau (1837), 123.

4. David Gordon White observes, moreover, that Man Singh-period texts construct Nath appearances on earth in a manner that is more consistent with the Vaishnava conception of Vishnu's avatars than with earlier Nath tradition. (Personal conversation, June 2007).

5. For example, "In the second hour of the afternoon, Man Singh gave *darshan* and *seva* to the painting, then rode on horseback through the Lakshman and Jai gates to Gol [a colony near Talhatee]." Haqiqat Bahi, Samvat 1882 [1825] *Shravan Vadi* 5, Rajasthan State Archives, Bikaner.

6. The painting is reproduced in Rob Linrothe, *Holy Madness: Portraits of Tantric Siddhas* (New York: Rubin Museum of Art, 2006), fig. 8.5.

7. Devotional paintings of Jallandharnath and Man Singh are widely scattered, which suggests that they were given as gifts or were part of the now-dispersed collections of the Nath elite.

8. Paintings that depict a Nath (without Man Singh) worshiping Jallandharnath feature the *mahasiddha* and a guru gazing into each other's eyes.

9. Ladu Nath is depicted with a full beard on p. 36, which can be dated no later than 1828, the year of his death. Because of Ladu Nath's more youthful appearance in the Raso painting, it must have been painted earlier, perhaps 1826–27, and then placed in the storeroom, per the archivist's inscription, in 1828.

10. For other evidence that artists in the royal atelier created paintings for the

Nath elite, see "Painting, Politics, and Devotion under Maharaja Man Singh, 1803–43."

11. Amardas often employed a heavily shaded, small-eyed, egg-shaped head that draws upon the Bundi court style. Bundi paintings must have been in the Jodhpur court collection for study by artists. Rosemary Crill, *Marwar Painting: A History of the Jodhpur Style* (Mumbai: India Book House Ltd./Mehrangarh Publishers, 1999), p. 143 and figs. 116–19.

12. In the second half of the eighteenth century, Bundi painters produced numerous versions of Krishna sporting in the Yamuna with the cowherd girls. The Jodhpur copy suggests that fig. 34b on p. 282 or a closely related Bundi painting entered the Jodhpur royal collection. It is more than plausible that Amardas had access to a Bundi archetype; the Jodhpur court collected Bundi paintings as evidenced by one (Mehrangarh Museum Trust, RJS 2145, dated circa 1760) that remains in the royal collection today, which depicts Krishna and Radha in another setting.

13. *Krishna Lifts Mount Govardhan*, drawing for a *Bhagavat Purana*, Jodhpur, ca. 1815, 29 x 19 cm, black ink and opaque watercolor on paper, reproduced in Subhash Kapoor and Aaron Friedman, *Soul of the Artist: Drawings by Indian Masters from the Seventeenth, Eighteenth, and Nineteenth Centuries* (New York: Art of the Past, 1997), fig. 22.

14. See n.9, p. 315, for source of verses. Tod lists numerous manuscripts that he consulted when writing his Marwar annals, but cites the *Suraj Prakash* as the only gifted manuscript from Man Singh. James Tod, *Annals and Antiquities of Rjasthan* (New Delhi: Oriental Books Reprint Corporation, 1983), vol. II, p. 3. (original book published 1929–32).

15. The princes of this generation receive scant or no mention in less encyclopedic dynastic histories.

16. Letters to Man Singh from Ladu Nath (37.1); Nandraval (52.13, 16); Jhau Nath (70.4); Ragu Nath (30.1); Amar Nath (31.1–2); Lakshmi Nath (70.7, Samvat 1889 [1832 Samvat.]); Ganesh Nath (32.1); Yogeshvar Ridmal (34.3); Brindavan Gosain and Mundi Jeetmal (36.1); and Yogi Vasti Nath (66.5e), stored in the Nath/Man Singh Correspondence bundle at the Rajasthan Oriental Research Institute, Bikaner.

17. While Amber/Jaipur city plans survive in the greatest numbers, Schwartzberg has observed that secular plans of cities and towns produced elsewhere in Rajasthan between the seventeenth and nineteenth centuries generally portray important non-linear features in frontal perspective and employ planimetric perspective for streets, canals, tanks, etc., in the same manner as the Amber/Jaipur maps. Joseph Schwartzberg, *The History of Cartography: Traditional Islamic and South Asian Societies*, ed. J. B. Harley and David Woodward (University of Chicago Press, 1992), 446.

18. See, for example, Schwartzberg (1992), fig. 17.52 and Diamond (2004), figs. 5 and 6; Gole (1989), figs. 91–92.

19. It is likely that some of the atelier's painters were also the producers of the court's maps and plans. The Amber Palace Bhojan Shala wall paintings were adapted from town plan drawings. Rosa Maria Cimino, *Wall Paintings of Rajasthan: Amber and Jaiper* (New Delhi: Ayran Books International), 57–66. See also Gole (1989) pp. 170–73. Molly Aitken (personal conversation, November 2007) notes that Jaipur records indicate that court artists were asked to produce maps. Similar Jodhpur records have not yet been located, although a certain Motiram (who may or may not have been the painter Motiram) completed construction drawings of a Varanasi temple for Maharaja Man Singh.

20. Daniel Gold, "The Rise and Fall of Yogis' Power: Jodhpur 1803–1843," *Estudios de Asia y Africa,* January 1992, 10.

21. Boileau, 135.

22. See, for example, the Shatrunjaya *pata* reproduced in Jan Van Alphen et al., *Steps to Liberation: 2,500 Years of Jain Art and Religion* (Antwerp: Etnografisch Museum Antwerpen, 2000), fig. 54.

23. Crill, fig. 123. Following B. N. Reu (*Nath Charitra ki Katha*. Jodhpur: Sardar Museum, 1937), the folio is erroneously identified as the *Nath Charit's* first folio and ascribed to Bulaki and others.

24. The "Muslim artist's" identification as Bulaki is discussed in "Painting, Politics, and Devotion," pp. 38–39.

25. The court archivist noted *Nath Charit* or *Nath Purana* on the verso of many but not all folios; similarly, artists included numerals in the upper left corner of many but not all of the paintings. To further complicate matters, when painted numbers are present, their appearance (gold numerals on blue squares, yellow numerals on red bordered squares, etc.) varies without discernable pattern.

Origins of the Cosmos

1. Reu catalogued this unnumbered painting as *Nath Charit* folio 2.

Mapping the Cosmos

1   B. N. Goswamy and Caron Smith, *Domains of Wonder: Selected Masterworks of Indian Painting* (San Diego Museum of Art, 2005), fig. 24.

2. The idea that the supporting world is a tortoise is rooted in the *Brahmanas* (mid-1st millennium B.C.E.) but elaborated in later puranas, particularly the *Markandeya Purana.*

3. In contrast to the Jain *lokapurusha's* ordinary clothes and arms-akimbo stance, the monumental Nath wears the saffron dhoti of a holy man and stands with his arms stretched down, i.e., in the yogic posture named *tadasana.*

4. The artist-family is a nexus in a patronage network that traverses class and religion. This role is broadly accepted as the reason for centuries of iconographic overlap and syncretism in Buddhist, Jain, and Hindu temple sculptural programs.

5. A superb cosmic body on cloth, which was painted circa 1740 in Mewar, measures 296 x 256 cm, is published in *Pantheon of the Gods: Art from India and Southeast Asia* (New York: Carleton Rochell Asian Art, 2007), fig. 12. A smaller cosmic body, probably from Jaipur, is illustrated in Philip Rawson, *Tantra: The Indian Cult of Ecstasy* (New York: Thames and Hudson, 1987), fig. 48. Both depict the cosmic man within the *brahmananda* (egg-shaped world composed of seven continents and oceans).

Sacred Sites and Cosmic Oceans

1.   Schwartzberg (1992) 409–14.

2.   Hardwar to Tibet route map reproduced in Susan Gole, *Indian Maps
      from the Earliest Times to the Advent of European Surveys* (New Delhi:
      Manohar, 1989), fig. 22; for silver-painted rivers in a Kashmiri map, *see*
      Gole (1989), fig. 51.

3.   For maps from Indian royal collections, see Schwartzberg, pp. 425–69, and
      Gole, *passim*. The extensive extant royal collection of Jaipur is discussed
      in Chandramani Singh, "Early Eighteenth-Century Painted City Maps on
      Cloth," *Facets of Indian Art: A Symposium Held at the Victoria and Albert
      Museum on 26, 27, 28 April and May 1, 1882* (London: Victoria and Albert
      Museum, 1986). The collection of the Ravat of Devgarh, Nahar Singh,
      includes unpublished maps.

4.   Man Singh's involvement in the construction of Nath temples in Arunachal,
      Varanasi, and Brindavan is revealed in the following letters: Man Singh
      from Ganesh Nath (32.1); Yogeshvar Ridmal (34.3); Brindavan Gosain and
      Munshi Jitmal (36.1); Yogi Vasti Nath (66.5e). Rajasthan Oriental Research
      Institute, Bikaner.

5.   For urban plans, see entries for cats. 34 and 35. Man Singh-period paintings
      of Hardwar (Mehrangarh Museum Trust, RJS 2020) and Kanauj (Mehrangarh
      Museum Trust, RJS 2114) extensively list place names, which indicates the
      artists' reliance upon maps.

6.   Most iconographic studies of the Hindu planetary and directional deities
      are based upon temple programs. The location of sculptures of deities on
      temple architecture, as well their vehicles and accessories, provide the
      basis for their identification.

7.   I am grateful to Stephanie Rozman for her identification of the divine *barat*
      based on the following sources: Stephen Markel, *Origins of the Indian
      Planetary Deities* (Lewiston, N.Y.: The Edwin Mellen Press, 1995); David
      Pingree, "Indian Planetary Images and the Tradition of Astral Magic," *Journal
      of the Warburg and Cortauld Institutes* 52 (1989), 1–13; Corinna Wessels–
      Mevissen, *The Gods of the Directions in Ancient India: Origin and Early
      Development in Art and Literature (until 1000 A.D.)* (Berlin: Dietrich Reimer
      Verlag, 2001).

Bibliography

Agarwal, Madhu Prasad. *Marwar ki Chitrakala*. New Delhi: Radha Publications, 1993.

Agarwal, Ram Avatar. *Marwar Murals*. Delhi: Agam Prakashan, 1997.

Aitken, Molly. "The Practiced Eye: Styles and Allusions in Mewar Painting." Ph.D. diss., Columbia University, 2000.

Allami, Abu'l Fazl. *Akbar-Nama*, vol. 2. Translated by H. Beveridge. Delhi: Rare Books, 1972.

Ambalal, Amit. *Krishna as Srinathji*. Ahmedabad: Mapin Publishers, 1987.

Andhare, Shridhar. "Monumental Jain Painting." In *The Peaceful Liberators: Jain Art from India*, edited by Pratapaditya Pal. Los Angeles County Museum of Art, 1995.

Asher, Catherine B. *Architecture of Mughal India*. The New Cambridge History of India, part 1, vol. 4. Cambridge University Press, 1995.

——, and Cynthia Talbot, *India Before Europe*. Cambridge University Press, 2006.

Asopa, J. N. *Origin of the Rajputs*. Delhi, India: Bharatiya Publishing House, 1976.

Banerjea, Akshaya Kumar. *Philosophy of Gorakhnath with Goraksha-Vacana-Sangraha*. Delhi: Motilal Banarsidass, 1988.

Bayly, C. A. Rulers, *Townsmen and Bazaars: North Indian Society in the Age of British Expansion, 1770–1870*. Cambridge University Press, 1982.

Bayly, S. "The 'Brahman Raj' c. 1700–1830." In *Caste, Society and Politics in India from the Eighteenth Century to the Modern Age*. Cambridge University Press, 1999.

Beach, Milo Cleveland. "The Context of Rajput Painting." *Ars Orientalis* 10 (1975): 11–18.

——. *Mughal and Rajput Painting*. The New Cambridge History of India, part 1, vol. 3. Cambridge University Press, 1992.

——, and Ebba Koch. *King of the World: The Padshahnama, an Imperial Mughal Manuscript from the Royal Library, Windsor Castle*. London: Azimuth, 1997.

Begley, W. E., and Z. A. Desai. *The Shah Jahan Nama of 'Inayat Khan*. Delhi: Oxford University Press, 1990.

Bharati, Agehananda. *The Tantric Tradition*. London: Hillary House, 1965.

Bhargava, Visheshwar Sarup. *Marwar and the Mughal Emperors: A.D. 1526–1748*. Delhi: Munshiram Manoharlal, 1966.

Bhati, Narayan Singh, ed. *Maharaja Man Singh ri Khyat*. Jodhpur: Oriental Research Institute, 1972.

——. *Studies in Marwar History*. Chopasni, Rajasthan: Rajasthani Shodh Sansthan, 1979.

——, ed. *A Catalogue of Manuscripts in Maharaja Mansingh Pustak Prakash* I (Hindi and Rajasthani Manuscripts); II (Sanskrit and Prakrit Manuscripts). Jodhpur: Maharaja Mansingh Pustak Prakash, 1981.

——, ed. *Maharaja Man Singh: The Mystic Monarch of Marwar*. Jodhpur: Maharaja Mansingh Pustak Prakash, 1991.

——. "Nath Chandrika." *Parampara* 92. Chaupasni, Jodhpur: Rajasthan Shodh Sansthan, 1989.

Boileau, A. H. E. *Narrative Tour through the Western States of Rajwara*. Calcutta: Baptist Mission Press, 1837.

Briggs, G. W. *Gorakhnath and the Kanphata Yogis*. Delhi: Motilal Banarsidas, 1989.

Bryant, Edwin F. *Krishna: The Beautiful Legend of God: Srimad Bhagavata Purana, Book X*, translated and with an introduction and notes by Edwin F. Bryant. London: Penguin Books, 2003

Caillat, Collette, and Ravi Kumar. *The Jain Cosmology*. Basel: Harmony Books, 1981.

Chaghtai, M. A. "Nagaur*–A Forgotten Kingdom." *Bulletin of the Deccan College Research Institute*, part 2, nos. 1–2 (November 1940).

Chattopadhyaya, B. D. "The Emergence of the Rajputs as Historical Process in Early Medieval Rajasthan." In *The Idea of Rajasthan: Explorations in Regional Identity*, vol. 2, edited by Karine Schomer, Joan L. Erdman, Deryck O. Lodrick, and Lloyd I. Rudolph. New Delhi: Manohar, 1994.

——. "Origin of the Rajputs." In *The Making of Early Medieval India*. Delhi: Oxford University Press, 1997.

Coburn, Thomas B. *Encountering the Goddess: A Translation of the Devi-Mahatmya and a Study of Its Interpretation*. Albany: State University of New York Press, 1991.

Cohen, Bernard S. "The Role of the Gosains in the Economy of Eighteenth and Nineteenth Century Upper India." *Indian Economic and Social History Review* 1 (1964): 175–82.

Crill, Rosemary. *Marwar Painting: A History of the Jodhpur Style*. Mumbai: India Book House Ltd. in association with Mehrangarh Publishers, 1999.

Cummins, Joan. *Indian Painting from Cave Temples to the Colonial Period.* Boston: MFA Publications, 2006.

Dasgupta, Shashibhusan. *Obscure Religious Cults.* Calcutta: K. L. Mukhopadhyay, 1976.

Dave, R. K. *Society and Culture of Marwar.* Jodhpur: Books Treasure, 1995.

Dehejia, Vidya. "The Treatment of Narrative in Jagat Singh's 'Ramayana': A Preliminary Study." *Artibus Asiae* 56, nos. 3/4 (1996): 303–24.

——. *Devi: The Great Goddess.* Washington, D.C.: Arthur M. Sackler Gallery, 1999.

——. "Yoga as a Key to Understanding the Sculpted Body." In *Representing the Body: Gender Issues in Indian Art*, edited by Vidya Dehejia. New Delhi: Kali for Women, 1997.

Desai, Vishakha. *Life at Court: Art for India's Rulers, 16th–19th Centuries.* Boston: Museum of Fine Arts, 1985.

——. "Timeless Symbols: Royal Portraits from Rajasthan." In *The Idea of Rajasthan: Explorations in Regional Identity*, edited by Karine Schomer, Joan L. Erdman, Deryck O. Lodrick, and Lloyd I. Rudolph. New Delhi: American Institute of Indian Studies, 1994.

——. "From Illustrations to Icons: The Changing Context of the Mewar Rasikapriya Paintings in Mewar." In *Indian Painting, Essays in Honour of Karl J. Khandalavala*, edited by B. N. Goswamy. New Delhi: Lalit Kala Academy: 1995.

Dhadich, Ramprasad. *Maharaja Man Singh (Jodhpur): Vyaktitva evam Krtitva.* Jodhpur: Rajasthani Shoch Sansthan Chaupasni, 1972.

Diamond, Debra. "By the Grace of Jalandranath: Politics and Painting in Jodhpur." In *Holy Madness: Portraits of Tantric Masters*. Exhibition catalogue. New York: Rubin Museum of Art, 2006.

——. "The Cartography of Power." In *Arts of Mughal India: Studies in Honour of Robert Skelton*. India: Mapin Publishing, 2004.

——. "The Poetics and Politics of Citation." In *Towards a New Art History: Studies in Indian Art*, edited by Shivaji Panikkar, Parul Dave Mukherji, and Deeptha Achar. New Delhi: D. K. Printworld, 2003.

——. "Court Painting and Yogic Metaphysics in Nineteenth-Century Jodhpur." In *Court Painting of Rajasthan*, edited by Andrew Topsfield. Mumbai: Marg Publications, 2000.

——. "The Aesthetics and Politics of Citation: Nath Painting in Jodhpur, 1804–1843." Ph.D. diss., Columbia University, 2000.

Dirks, Nicholas. *The Hollow Crown: Ethnohistory of an Indian Kingdom.* Cambridge University Press, 1987.

Dvivedi, Hazariprasad. *Natha Sampradaya.* Varanasi: Naiveda Niketan, 1950.

Ebeling, Klaus. *Ragamala Painting.* Basel: Ravi Kumar, 1973.

Ehnbom, Daniel. *Indian Miniatures: The Ehrenfeld Collection.* New York: Hudson Hills Press, 1985.

——, and Andrew Topsfield. *Indian Miniature Painting.* London: Spink and Son, 1987.

Elliot, H. M., and John Dowson. *The History of India as Told by Its Own Historians*, vols. 7 and 8. Allahabad: Kitab Mahal, 1877.

Erskine, Major K. D. *Rajputana Gazetteers: The Western Rajputana States Residency and the Bikaner Agency.* Gugraon, Haryana: Vintage Books, 1992.

Filippe, Gian Giuseppe. *Indian Miniatures and Paintings from the 16th to the 19th Century: The Collection of Howard Hodgkin.* Milan: Electra, 1997.

Flores, Jorge, and Nuno Vassallo e Silva. *Goa and the Great Mughal.* Lisbon: Calouste Gulbenkian Foundation, 2004.

Folsach, Kjeld von. *Art from the World of Islam in the David Collection.* Copenhagen: Kjeld von Folsach, 2001.

——, *For the Privileged Few.* Copenhagen: The David Collection and Louisiana Museum of Art, 2007.

Freitag, Jason. "The Power that Protects You: James Tod, Historiography, and the Rajput Ideal." Ph.D. diss., Columbia University, in progress.

Feurstein, Georg. *Tantra: The Path of Ecstasy.* Boston and London: Shambhala, 1998.

Gascoigne, Bamber. *The Great Mughals.* New York: Dorset Press, 1971.

Glynn, Catherine. "Evidence of Royal Painting for the Amber Court." *Artibus Asiae* LVI, nos. 1–2 (1996).

——, and Ellen Smart. "A Mughal Icon Re-examined." *Artibus Asiae* LVII, nos. 1/2 (1997).

Goetz, Hermann. "The Marwar School of Rajput Painting." *Bulletin of the Baroda Museum and Picture Gallery* 5, no. 1 (1947): 43–54.

——. "The Nagaur School of Rajput Painting (18th century)." *Artibus Asiae* XII (1949).

——. *The Art and Architecture of Bikaner State.* Oxford: Bruno Cassirer, 1950.

———. "Marwar, with some Paintings of Jodhpur from Kumar Sangram Singh." *Marg* 11, no. 2 (1958): 42–49.

———, and Y. K. Shukla. "Fresco Paintings in the Nagaur Fort." *Roopa-Lekha* XLI, nos. 1 & 2 (1972).

Gold, Ann Gordzons. "The Once and Future Yogi: Sentiments and Signs in the Tale of a Renouncer-King." *Journal of Asian Studies* 48, no. 4 (1989): 770–86.

———. *A Carnival of Parting: The Tales of Bhartrhari and King Gopi Chand as Sung and Told by Madhu Natisar Nath of Ghatiyali, Rajasthan.* Berkeley: University of California Press, 1992.

Gold, Daniel, and Ann Gordzons Gold. "The Fate of the Householder Nath." *History of Religions* 24, no. 2 (1984): 113–32.

Gold, Daniel. "Clan and Lineage among the Sants: Seed, Service, Substance." In *The Sants: Studies in a Devotional Tradition of India*, edited by Karine Schomer and W. H. McLeod. Delhi: Motilal Banarsidass, 1987.

———. *Comprehending the Guru: Toward a Grammar of Religious Perception.* American Academy of Religion Academy Series, edited by Carl A. Raschke. Atlanta: Scholars Press, 1988.

———. "The Rise and Fall of Yogis' Power: Jodhpur 1803–1843." *Estudios de Asia y Africa*, January 1992.

———. "The Instability of the King: Magical Insanity and the Yogis' Power in the Politics of Jodhpur, 1803–1843." In *Bhakti Religion in North India: Community Identity and Political Action*. Albany: State University of New York Press, 1995.

Gole, Susan. *Indian Maps from the Earliest Times to the Advent of European Surveys.* New Delhi: Manohar, 1989.

Gordon, Stewart. *Marathas, Marauders and State Formation in Eighteenth-Century India.* Delhi: Oxford University Press, 1994.

———, ed. *Robes of Honour: Khilat in Pre-colonial and Colonial India.* Oxford University Press, 2003.

Goswamy, B. N. [Brijnath]. *Rasa: les neuf visages de l'art indien.* Paris: Ministere des relations exterieures and Association Francaise d'Action Artistique, 1986.

———. *Essence of Indian Art.* San Francisco: Asian Art Museum of San Francisco, 1986.

———. *Painted Visions: The Goenka Collection of Indian Paintings.* New Delhi: Lalit Kala Akademi, 1999.

———, and Anna Dallapiccola. *A Place Apart: Painting in Kutch, 1720–1820.* Delhi: Oxford University Press, 1983.

———, and Caron Smith. *Domains of Wonder: Selected Masterworks of Indian Painting.* San Diego Museum of Art, 2006.

Haig, Lt. Col. Sir Wolseley Haig, and Sir Richard Burn. *The Cambridge History of India: The Mughal Period*, vol. 4. Delhi: S. Chand & Co., 1963.

Haig, Lt. Col. Sir Wolseley Haig. *The Cambridge History of India: Turks and Afghans*, vol. 3. Delhi: S. Chand & Co., 1965.

Hooja, R. *A History of Rajasthan.* New Delhi: Rupa & Co., 2006.

The Idea of Rajasthan: Explorations in Regional Identity. Edited by Karine Schomer, Joan L. Erdman, Deryck O. Lodrick, and Lloyd I. Rudolph. 2 vols. New Delhi: Manohar, 1994.

Jain, M. S. *Rajasthan Through the Ages: A Comprehensive History of Rajasthan, 1761–1949*, vol. 3. Bikaner: Rajasthan State Archives, 1996.

Jain, Jyotindra, ed. *Picture Showmen: Insights into the Narrative Tradition in Indian Art.* Bombay: Marg Publications, 1998.

Joshi, Rajendra. "Feudal Bonds." In *Folk, Faith and Feudalism*, edited by N. K. Singhi and Rajendra Joshi. Jaipur: Institute of Rajasthan Studies, 1995.

Kapoor, Subhash, and Aaron Freedman. *Soul of the Artist: Drawings by Indian Masters from the Seventeenth, Eighteenth and Nineteenth Centuries.* New York: Art of the Past, 1997.

Karnidan. *Kaviya Karnidanji Charan Krit: Suraj Prakash.* 3 vols. Edited by Sitaram Lalas. Jodhpur: Rajasthan Oriental Research Institute, 1962.

Kathuria, Ramdev. *Life in the Courts of Rajasthan During the Eighteenth Century.* New Delhi: S. Chand & Co., 1987.

Khan, Amir, and Busawan Lal (Naeeb-Moonshee to the Nuwab), eds. *Memoirs of the Puthan Soldier of Fortune, the Nuwab Ameer-Ood-Doulah Mohummund Ameer Khan, Chief of Seronj, Tonk, Rampoora, Neemahera, and Other Places in Hindoostan.* Calcutta: G. H. Huttmann, Military Orphan Press, 1832.

Khandalavala, Karl. *Paintings of Bygone Years.* Bombay: Vakils, Feffer and Simons Limited, 1991.

Koch, Ebba. *Mughal Garden Types and Rajput Responses.* Talk at the Nagaur Garden Conservation Workshop, January 28–February 1, 2006, Ahhichatagarh Fort, Nagaur.

Kolff, Dirk. "Sannyasi Trader-Soldiers." *The Indian Economic and Social History Review* 6, no. 4 (1969): 213–18.

———. *Naukar, Rajput and Sepoy: The Ethnohistory of the Military Labour Market in Hindustan, 1450–1850.* Cambridge University Press, 1990.

Kuhnel, Ernst, and Hermann Goetz. *Indische Buchmalereien: Aus dem Jahangir-Album der Staatsbibliothek zu Berlin.* Berlin: Scarabaeus-Verlag, 1924.

Leach, Linda. *Mughal and Other Indian Paintings from the Chester Beatty Library.* 2 vols. London: Scorpion Cavendish, 1995.

——. *Indian Miniature Paintings and Drawings: The Cleveland Museum of Art Catalogue of Oriental Art,* vol. I. Cleveland Museum of Art, 1986.

Lorenzen, David. "Warrior Ascetics in Indian History." *Journal of the American Oriental Society* 98, no. 1 (1978): 61–75.

Losty, J. P. "The Thousand Petals of Bliss." *FMR* IV, no. 17 (1985).

Lutgendorf, Philip. *The Life of a Text: Performing the Ramcaritmanas of Tulsidas.* Berkeley: University of California Press, 1991.

Lyall, A. C. *Asiatic Studies: Religious and Social.* London: John Murray, 1882.

Mallik, Kalyani, ed. *Siddha Siddhanti Paddhati and Other Works of Nath Yogis.* Poona, India: Poona Oriental Book House, 1954.

Markel, Stephen. *Origins of the Indian Planetary Deities,* Lewiston, N.Y.: The Edwin Mellen Press, 1995.

Marwar Precis: Containing a General History of the Relations with Marwar. Calcutta: Foreign Department Press, 1874.

Martinelli, Antonio, and George Michell. *Princely Rajasthan: Rajput Palaces and Mansions.* New York: Vendome Press, 2004.

Mason, Darielle. *Intimate Worlds: Indian Paintings from the Alvin O. Bellak Collection.* Philadelphia Museum of Art, 2001.

McInerney, Terence. "Mughal Painting during the Reign of Muhammad Shah." In *After the Great Mughals: Painting in Delhi and the Regional Courts in the 18th and 19th Centuries,* edited by Barbara Schmitz. Mumbai: Marg, 2002.

Metcalfe, Thomas R. *Ideologies of the Raj. The New Cambridge History of India* 3, no. 4, edited by Gordon Johnson. Cambridge University Press, 1994.

Mookerjee, Ajit, and Madhu Khanna. *The Tantric Way: Art, Science, Ritual.* Boston: New York Graphic Society, 1977.

Moynihan, Elizabeth, ed. *The Moonlight Garden: New Discoveries at the Taj Mahal.* Washington, D.C.: Arthur M. Sackler Gallery, 2000.

Nagar, Mahendra Singh. *Ranimangar Bhado ki Bahi.* Jodhpur: Maharaja Man Singh Research Institute 2002.

Nansi, Muhata. *Marwar ra Pargana ri Vigat* [Marwar Chronicles], edited by Fateh Singh. Jodhpur: Rajasthan Oriental Research Institute, 1968.

Okada, Amina. *Indian Miniatures of the Mughal Court.* New York: Harry N. Abrams, 1992.

Pal, Pratapaditya. *Court Paintings of India: 16th–19th Centuries.* New York: Navin Kumar, 1983.

——. *The Peaceful Liberators: Jain Art from India.* Los Angeles County Museum of Art, 1995.

Parihar, G. R. *Marwar and the Marathas, 1724–1843.* Jodhpur: Hindi Sahitya Mandir, 1968.

Patnaik, Naveen. *A Second Paradise: Indian Courtly Life 1590–1947.* New York: Doubleday, 1985.

Paul, E. Jaiwant. *Gloire des Princes, Louange des Dieux.* Paris: Réunion des musées nationaux, 2003.

Peabody, Norbert. *Hindu Kingship and Polity in Precolonial India.* Cambridge University Press, 2003.

Pinch, William R. *Warrior Ascetics and Indian Empires.* Cambridge University Press, 2006.

——. *Peasants and Monks in British India.* Berkeley: University of California Press, 1996.

Pingree, David. "Indian Planetary Images and the Tradition of Astral Magic." *Journal of the Warburg and Cortauld Institutes* 52 (1989): 1–13.

Prabhakar, Manohar. *A Critical Study of Rajasthani Literature.* Jaipur: Panchsheel Prakashan, 1976.

Rawson, Philip. *Tantra: The Indian Cult of Ecstasy.* New York: Thames and Hudson, 1987.

Rehman, Abdul, and Shama Anbrine. Unity and Diversity of Mughal Garden Experiences. Talk at the Dumbarton Oaks Garden Conference, May 2007, Washington, D.C.

Reu, Bisheshwar Nath. *Abstract of the Story and the Notes on the Paintings of Suraj Prakash.* Jodhpur: Sardar Museum, 1924.

——. *Shivrahasya ka katha.* Jodhpur: Sardar Museum, 1934.

——. *Siddha Siddhanta Paddhati.* Jodhpur: Sardar Museum, 1935.

——. *Srimadbhagavat.* Jodhpur: Sardar Museum, 1935.

———. *The Story of Gajendramoksha and Notes on its Paintings*. Jodhpur: Sardar Musum, 1936.

———. *Nath Charitra ki Katha*. Jodhpur: Sardar Museum, 1937.

———. *Glories of Marwar and the Glorious Rathors*. Jodhpur: Archaeological Department and Sumer Public Library, 1943.

———. *The Story of Srimad Bhagavata (10th chapter) and Notes on its Paintings*. Jodhpur: Sardar Museum, 1947.

Richards, J. F., ed. *Kingship and Authority in South Asia*. Madison: University of Wisconsin Press, 1981.

———. *The Mughal Empire*. The New Cambridge History of India. Cambridge University Press, 1993.

Robin, Jeffrey, ed. *People, Princes and Paramount Power: Society and Politics in the Indian Princely States*. Delhi: Oxford University Press, 1978.

Robinson, Francis. *The Mughal Emperors and the Islamic Dynasties of India, Iran and Central Asia, 1206–1925*. London: Thames & Hudson, 2007.

Sarkar, Jadunath. *Fall of the Mughal Empire*. 4 vols. New Delhi: Orient Longman Ltd., 1971.

Saxena, R. K. *Rajput Nobility: A Study of 18th Century Rajputana (1761–1818 AD)*. New Delhi: S. Chand & Co., 1996.

Schwartzberg, Joseph. *The History of Cartography: Traditional Islamic and South Asian Societies*. The History of Cartography, vol. 1, book 1, edited by J. B. Harley and David Woodward. University of Chicago Press, 1992.

Seth, Mira. *Wall Paintings of Rajasthan*. New Delhi: National Museum of India, 2003.

Sharma, Bhagvatilal. *Sri Jalandharnath-Pith*. Jalore, Rajasthan: Sri Bhairunathji ka Akhara, 1995.

Sharma, G. D. *Rajput Polity: A Study of Politics and Administration in the State of Marwar, 1638–1749*. New Delhi: Manohar, 1977.

Sharma, G. N., ed. *The Historians and Sources of History of Rajasthan*. Jaipur: University of Rajasthan, 1990.

Sharma, Padmaja. *Maharaja Mansingh of Jodhpur and His Times*. Agra: Shiva Lal Agarwala and Company, 1972.

Shukla, Y. K. "Fresco Paintings in the Nagaur Fort." *Roopa-Lekha* XLI, nos. 1–2 (1972).

Shyamaldas, Kaviraja. *Vir Vinod*. Delhi: Motilal Banarsidas, 1986.

Siddiqui, Mohammad Haleem. *History of Nagaur*. Jodhpur: Maharaja Man Singh Pushtak Prakash, 2001. Translated from Hindi for this project by Shagufta Parekh and Anand Kumar Dwivedi.

Singh, Brijeshkumar, ed. *Maharaja Vijai Singhji ri Khyat*, Jodhpur: Rajasthan Oriental Research Institute, 1997.

Singh, Chandramani. "Early Eighteenth-Century Painted City Maps on Cloth." In *Facets of Indian Art: A Symposium Held at the Victoria and Albert Museum on 26, 27, 28 April and May 1, 1882*. London: Victoria and Albert Museum, 1986.

Singh, Munshi Hardyal. *The Castes of Marwar, Being the Census Report of 1891*. Jodhpur: Books Treasure, 1990.

Singh, Dhananjaya. *The House of Marwar*. New Delhi: Lustre Press Ltd., 1994.

Singh, Kumar Sangram. "An early Ragamala MS from Pali (Marwar) dated 1623 A.D." *Lalit Kala* 7 (1960).

Singh, Priyaleen. *Historic Gardens: Rationale for Conservation in the Indian Context*. Talk at the Nagaur Garden Conservation Workshop, January 28–February 1, 2006.

Singh, Zabar. *The East India Company and Marwar, 1803–1857*. Jaipur: Unique Traders, n.d.

The Siva-Purana: Ancient Indian Tradition and Mythology Series. 3 vols. Translated by a Board of Scholars. Delhi: Motilal Banarsidass, 1977.

Skelton, Robert. *Rajasthani Temple Hangings of the Krishna Cult*. New York: American Federation of the Arts, 1973.

Smart, Ellen S., and Daniel J. Walker. *Pride of the Princes: Indian Art of the Mughal Era in the Cincinnati Art Museum*. Cincinnati Art Museum, 1985.

Smith, John D. "An Introduction to the Language of the Historical Documents from Rajasthan." *Modern Asian Studies* 9, no. 4 (1975): 433–64.

Snell, Rupert. *The Hindi Classical Tradition: A Braj Bhasa Reader*. Delhi: Heritage Publishers, 1992.

Srivastav, Ramlal, ed. *Siddhsiddhantapaddhanti*. Gorakhpur, Uttar Pradesh, India.: Gorakhnath Mandir, 1981.

Stewart, Susan. *On Longing: Narratives of the Miniature, the Gigantic, the Souvenir, the Collection*. Durham: Duke University Press, 1993.

Taft, Frances H. "Honor and Alliance: Reconsidering Mughal-Rajput Marriages." In *The Idea of Rajasthan: Explorations in Regional Identity*, vol. 2, edited by Karine Schomer, Joan L. Erdman, Deryck O. Lodrick, and Lloyd I. Rudolph. New Delhi: Manohar, 1994.

Taylor, Woodman. "Picture Practice: Painting Programs, Manuscript Production and Liturgical Performances at the Kotah Royal Palace." In *Gods, Kings and Tigers: The Art of Kotah*, edited by Stuart Cary Welch. New York: Asia Society, 1997.

Thackson, Wheeler M., trans. and ed. *The Jahangirnama: Memoirs of Jahangir, Emperor of India*. New York: Oxford University Press, 1999.

Thiel-Horstmann, Monika. "On the Dual Identity of Nagas." In *Divine Devotion: Bhakti Traditions from the Regions of India, Studies in Honour of Charlotte Vaudeville*, edited by Diana Eck and Francoise Mallison. Groningen: Egbert Forsten, 1991.

Tillotson, G. H. R. *The Rajput Palaces: Development of an Architectural Style, 1450–1750*. New Haven: Yale University Press, 1987.

———. Nagaur Architecture. Draft paper prepared for the Mehrangarh Trust, 2007.

Tod, James. *Annals and Antiquities of Rajasthan, or the Central and Western Rajpoot States of India*. 2 vols. [1829, 1832] Reprint, London: Routledge & Kegan Paul, 1957, 1960; New Delhi: Oriental Books Reprint Corporation, 1983.

Topsfield, Andrew. *Paintings from Rajasthan in the National Gallery of Victoria*. Melbourne: National Gallery of Victoria, 1980.

———, ed. *Court Painting in Rajasthan*. Mumbai: Marg Publications, 2000.

———. *Court Painting at Udaipur: Art Under the Patronage of the Maharanas of Mewar*. Zurich: Eberhard Fischer, 2002.

———, ed. *In the Realm of Gods and Kings: Art of India*. London: Philip Wilson, 2004.

———, and Milo Cleveland Beach. *Indian Paintings and Drawings from the Collection of Howard Hodgkin*. New York: Thames and Hudson, 1991.

van der Veer, Peter. *Gods on Earth: The Management of Religious Experience and Identity in a North Indian Pilgrimage Centre*. London: Athlone Press, 1988.

Vashista, V. K. *Rajputana Agency, 1832–1858: A Study of the Relations with the State of Rajputana*. Jaipur: Alekh Publishers, 1978.

Vyas, Ram Prasad. *Role of the Nobility in Marwar, 1800–1872*. New Delhi: Jain Brothers, 1969.

———. *British Policy Towards Princely States of India*. Jodhpur: Rajasthan-Vidya Prakashan, 1991.

Waldschmidt, Ernst and Rose Lenore. *Miniatures of Musical Inspiration in the Collection of the Berlin Museum of Indian Art*. Berlin: Museum für Indische Kunst, 1975.

Welch, Stuart Cary. *The Art of Mughal India*. New York: Asia Society, 1963.

———. *A Flower from Every Meadow: Indian Paintings from American Collections*. New York: Asia Society, 1973.

———. *India: Art and Culture: 1300–1900*. New York: Metropolitan Museum of Art, 1985.

Wessels-Mevissen, Corinna. *The Gods of the Directions in Ancient India: Origin and Early Development in Art and Literature (until 1000 A.D.)* Berlin: Dietrich Reimer Verlag, 2001.

White, David Gordon. "The Wonders of Sri Mastnath." In *Religions of India in Practice*, edited by Donald S. Lopez, Jr. Princeton University Press, 1995.

———. *The Alchemical Body: Siddha Traditions in Medieval India*. Chicago: University of Chicago Press, 1996.

———, ed. *Tantra in Practice*. Princeton Readings in Religion. Princeton and Oxford: Princeton University Press, 2000.

———. *Kiss of the Yogini*. Chicago: University of Chicago Press, 2006.

———. "Yogic and Political Power Among the Nath Siddhas of North India." In *Asceticism and Power in Asia*, edited by Peter Flügel and Gustaaf Hartmann. London: Routledge, forthcoming.

Zebrowski, Mark. *Deccani Painting*. London: Sotheby Publications, 1983.

Ziegler, Norman. "Action and Power in Rajasthani Culture: A Social History of Rajputs of Middle Period Rajasthan." Ph.D. diss. University of Chicago, 1973.

———. "Marvari Historical Chronicles: Sources for the Social and Cultural History of Rajasthan." *Journal of Indian Economic and Social History* 13 (1976): 219–50.

———. "Some Notes on Rajput Loyalties during the Mughal Period." In *Kingship and Authority in South Asia*, edited by J. F. Richards. Madison: University of Wisconsin Press, 1981.

———. "Evolution of the Rathor State of Marvar: Horses, Structural Change and Warfare." In *In The Idea of Rajasthan: Explorations in Regional Identity*, vol. 2, edited by Karine Schomer, Joan L. Erdman, Deryck O. Lodrick, and Lloyd I. Rudolph. New Delhi: American Institute of Indian Studies, 1994.

———. "The Seventeenth-Century Chronicles of Marvara: A Study in the Evolution and Use of Oral Traditions in Western India." In *The Invention of Tradition*, edited by Eric Hobsbawm and Terence Ranger. Cambridge University Press, 1992.

Archival Sources

India Office Library, British Library, London. Board's Collections (1828–37).

National Archives of India, New Delhi. Foreign Political Consultations (1810–1844); Foreign Secret Consultations (1810–1844).

Pustak Prakash Library, Mehrangarh Fort, Jodhpur. *Adinath Virat Svarup* gr. no. 1450.1283

Rajasthan State Archives, Bikaner. Bundle of seventy-two letters from Naths to Maharaja Man Singh; *Haqiqat Bahi* (daily court records), v.s. 1882, 1825 c.e.

Glossary

Amsh | Portion or section

Arti | The circling of a lamp in front of an object of devotion

Asana | Yoga posture

Ayasji | Respectful title for Man Singh's Nath gurus

Bhagavata Purana | The sacred Hindu text that narrates the life of the deity Krishna, composed between the ninth and thirteenth centuries

Bhakti | Devotion

Bikaner | Rajput kingdom north of Marwar

Brahma | A Hindu deity

Brahman | Formless and eternal Absolute Reality

Charan | Bard

Charan, Kundal, Paduka | Sacred footprints

Charbagh | Four-part garden

Chatri | Covered pavilion

Chitra darshan | The worship of paintings in which deities are manifest

Chitra seva | Devotion and service to a deity manifest in a painting

Dakini | In Hinduism, wrathful female acolytes of the goddess

Darbar | Royal assembly

Darshan | Worship; the mutual gaze between devotee and deity

Deccan | Plateau region of central India

Devanagari | The script of Sanskrit and other regional languages, including Hindi and Marwari

Dholiya re kothar | The painting storeroom (*kothar*) at Mehrangarh Fort that was established by Maharaja Man Singh (reigned 1803–43); the space, which is now the Turban Gallery, may have earlier housed *dhol* (drums) or *dholiya* (cots).

Dhoti | Unstitched cloth garment worn by men

Diwali | The Hindu festival of lights

Gajendra Moksha | An important episode from the *Bhagavata Purana* in which the elephant Gajendra receives Vishnu's grace and liberation (*moksha*)

Ganga | The river Ganges in northern India and the name of the goddess who personifies the river

Gopi | Female cowherd

Gorakhnath | A Nath *mahasiddha* and historical founder of the Nath order in the twelfth–thirteenth century

Gosain | Priest

Guru | Spiritual guide or teacher

Hamsa | Alternately translated as goose and swan, it is the vehicle of the goddess Saraswati and a symbol of the passage from the world of *samsara*

Hatha Yoga | The yoga of violent exertion; revealed in the twelfth–thirteenth century by Gorakhnath.

Himalaya | Mountain range and the deity Himavat

Jallandharnath | A Nath *mahasiddha*

Jama | Long robe or overgarment

Jharokha | Overhanging balcony with arched opening

Jyoti (Sanskrit) | Light

Jyoti(h) svarup | Self-effulgent, i.e., innately luminous

Jumna (Sanskrit: Yamuna) | Second river of the Gangetic plane

Kailash | Himalyan peak, located on the Tibetan plateau, where Shiva dwells

Khalsa | Land belonging to the emperor or king

Krishna | Hindu deity, commonly known as an avatar of Vishnu and also considered by the Vallabha Sampraday as the ultimate deity (with Vishnu as his avatar)

Krishna Lila | Marwari term for the *Raslila*, the tenth canto of the *Bhagavata Purana*

Kshatriya | Warrior class/caste of the Hindu social order

Kundal or mudra | The thick hoop earrings of Nath ascetics worn through the cartilege of the upper ear (see also *charan*)

Lila | Spontaneous and pure play, an effortless expression of the nature of Hindu deities

Linga | Primary manifestation of the deity Shiva; the main object of worship in a Shiva temple

Mahal | Palace

Maharaja | Great king

Mahasiddha | Great perfected being

Mala | Garland or rosary

Mandala | A symbolic diagram of the cosmos; often used as support for meditation on or identification with deities

Mansab | Mughal measure of status and position marked by numerical rank and title

Mantra | Sacred syllables or incantation

Moksha | Release or liberation

Mudra | Sign or ritualized hand gesture (see also *kundal*)

Murti | Sculpture of deity consecrated for Hindu worship

Nath (Sanskrit: Natha, meaning lord) | A member of the Nath yogic order; a householder community in Rajasthan that is devoted to the Nath *mahasiddhas* (see srinathji)

Nath Sampraday | The yoga order founded by Gorakhnath in the twelfth–thirteenth century

Nirgun (Sanskrit: nirguna, meaning without qualities) | Without quantifiable attributes

Om | Sacred syllable

Puja | The Hindu ritual of worshiping a deity

Purana (Sanskrit: that which took place previously) | A sacred Hindu text. The puranas are a vast repository of lore, each of which includes cosmologies, sectarian theologies, narratives of gods, kings, and devotees, religious rites and philosophical arguments

Raga | Indian musical mode that expresses a particular time of day, season, or mood

Ragamala | A series of thirty-six or forty-two ragas with poetic texts illustrated by Indian painters

Raja | King

Rajput | Hindu ruling clans in northwest and central India of the *kshatriya* caste

Rajrajeshwar (Hindi, Marwari) | Lord of king of kings

Ramcharitmanas | Tulsidas' sixteenth-century Sanskrit *Ramayana* written in a vernacular Hindi

Ramrajya | The reign of the Hindu deity Rama, a period of peace and prosperity

Rani | Queen

Rao | Title for a king or a noble

Ras | Kirshna's circle dance with the village women of Braj

Rathore | Rajput dynasty that ruled the kingdoms of Marwar, Bikaner, and Jaisalmer

Rudraksha | Dark berry of the *Elaeocarpus ganitrus* tree that is strung on rosaries worn by Shiva and his devotees

Sampraday | Teaching tradition; religious community

Samsara | The cycle of birth, death, and rebirth

Samvat, vikram samvat | Indian era beginning in 57 B.C.E. that is employed in Marwar painting inscriptions

Saraswati | Goddess of learning and music

Shaiva (adjective) | Accepting Shiva as supreme

Siddha | A perfected being; a respectful term for Nath yogins

Srinathji | Glorious lord; a title for enlightened immortal Naths and deities, especially the Krishna worshiped by devotees of the Vallabha Sampraday

Tambura | A stringed instrument that is plucked like a lute

Tantra | Esoteric texts and practices that activate spiritual power and the attainment of union with Absolute Reality

Tapas | Ascetic practices that generate supernormal heat or power

Tilak | Mark of auspiciousness or devotion

Upanishads | Philosophical texts of the late Vedic period (circa 600 B.C.E.)

Vaikuntha | The heavenly realm of Vishnu

Vaishnava (adjective) | Accepting Vishnu as supreme

Vallabh Sampraday | Krishna *bhakti* religious order based upon the teachings of Vallabha (1479–1531)

Vedas | Oldest preserved literatures of India

Yantra | Geometric ritual diagram

Yogin (Sanskrit), jogi (Hindi, Marwari) | One who practices yoga

Zenana | The women's area in Rajput and Mughal palaces

Contributors

Three authors are co-curators of the exhibition *Garden and Cosmos: The Royal Paintings of Jodhpur:*

Dr. Debra Diamond is associate curator of South and Southeast Asian Art, Freer Gallery of Art and Arthur M. Sackler Gallery, Smithsonian Institution

Karni Singh Jasol is curator of the Mehrangarh Fort Museum, Jodhpur, India

Dr. Catherine Glynn is an independent scholar and curator, and a lecturer at Northwestern University and the University of California, Los Angeles

Dr. Jason Freitag is assistant professor of history at Ithaca College

Rahul Jain, textile historian, currently is cataloguing the textile collection of the Mehrangarh Museum Trust

Photo Credits

Mehrangarh Museum Trust (MMT)

Paintings from the Mehrangarh collection are reproduced courtesy of MMT. All MMT paintings are opaque watercolor and gold on paper unless otherwise noted in the reference catalogue. Photography of the MMT and Marwar locations are by Neil Greentree, except as noted below.

p. 12

Fig. 1. Zenana scene (*The Women of the Harem*), Mughal, northern India, ca. 1625–30, 23.5 x 15.8 cm. Museum of Fine Arts, Boston, gift of John Goelet, 66.149.

p. 16

Fig. 4. *Maharaja Abhai Singh Watching a Dance Performance*, by Dalchand, Jodhpur, 1725. Photo courtesy of Mehrangarh Museum Trust, RJS 24 (28).

p. 33

Fig. 3. *Maharaja Man Singh Visits Mahamandir*, ascribed to Bulaki, Jodhpur, 1815, opaque watercolor and gold on paper, 52.2 x 76.3 cm. Philadelphia Museum of Art: Alvin O. Bellak Collection, 2000-91-1. Photo by Lynn Rosenthal. Published in Darielle Mason, *Intimate Worlds: Indian Paintings from the Alvin O. Bellak Collection* (Philadelphia Museum of Art, 2001), fig. 77.

p. 36

Fig. 6. *Ladu Nath in Darbar Honoring Bards*, Jodhpur, ca. 1827–28, opaque watercolor and gold on paper, 44.5.x 61 cm. Kumar Sangram Singh Collection, no. 44.

p. 40

Fig. 8. *Maharaja Man Singh in a Mehfil*, Jodhpur, ca. 1829, 50.8 x 38.1 cm. Kumar Sangram Singh Collection, no. 99.

p. 53

Page from a Ragamala Series: Gujari Ragini, 1623, National Museum of India, New Delhi, 83.209.

p. 55

Page from a Ragamala Series: Gunakali Ragini, ca. 1640–50, San Diego Museum of Art, Edwin Binney 3rd Collection, 1990:895. Not in exhibition.

p. 57

Page from a Ragamala Series, ca. 1660, National Museum of India, New Delhi, 54.58.28.

p. 59

Raja Sur (Suraj) Singh of Marwar, by Bishan Das, ca. 1595, The Metropolitan Museum of Art, Purchase, Rogers Fund and the Kevorkian Foundation Gift, 1955, 55.121.10, f. 7r. Image © The Metropolitan Museum of Art, New York. Not in exhibition.

p. 61

Maharaja Gaj Singh I, ca. 1630–38, British Museum, London, Add. 1920.9-17.013 (14). © Copyright the Trustees of the British Museum.

p. 63

Maharaja Jaswant Singh Listening to Music, ca. 1660 [dated here ca. 1670], 26.8 x 17.4 cm, National Gallery of Victoria, Melbourne, Australia, Felton Bequest, 1980 AS 28-1980.

pp. 66 and 298 (detail, top right)

Maharaja Ajit Singh and Sons during the Festival of Diwali, 1721, Harvard University Art Museums, Arthur M. Sackler Museum, Gift in gratitude to John Coolidge, Gift of Leslie Cheek, Jr., Anonymous Fund in memory of Henry Berg, Louise Haskell Daly, Alpheus Hyatt, Richard Norton Memorial Funds and through the generosity of Albert H. Gordon and Emily Rauh Pulitzer; formerly in the collection of Stuart Cary Welch, Jr., 1995.131. Photo: Imaging Department, © President and Fellows of Harvard College.

p. 69

Maharaja Bakhat Singh, ca. 1740, National Gallery of Canada, Ottawa, Gift of Max Tanenbaum, Toronto, 1979.23597.

p. 260

Fig. 5a. *Raja Gaj Singh of Marwar*, Jodhpur, 17th century, opaque watercolor and ink on paper; 28.2 x 19.9 cm. Long-term loan from the Smithsonian American Art Museum; gift of John Gellatly.

Fig. 5b. *Rao Amar Singh of Jodhpur*, Marwar, ca. 1650 [dated here 1640], 30.7 x 20 cm. San Diego Museum of Art, Edwin Binney 3rd Collection, 1990:612.

pp. 262 (fig. 8a) and 298 (detail, top left)

The Sons of Maharaja Ajit Singh of Jodhpur, Marwar, ca. 1720, opaque watercolor and gold on paper, 39.1 x 35.6 cm. Philadelphia Museum of Art: Alvin O. Bellak Collection, 2004-149-47. Photo by Lynn Rosenthal.

p. 265

Figs. 11a, 11b. Hadi Rani Mahal. Photo courtesy Mehrangarh Museum Trust.

p. 266

Fig. 12a. Krishna Temple, Nagaur. Photo by Catherine Glynn.

Fig. 12b. *Vishnu and Lakshmi,* by Murad and Lupha, Bikaner, ca. 1710. Brooklyn Museum of Art, 1990.134.

p. 268

Fig. 14a. *The Emperor Muhammad Shah with Courtiers*, India, 16th–18th century [dated here ca. 1730–40], opaque watercolor on paper, 41 x 34.4 cm. Bodleian Library, Oxford University, MS. Douce Or. a.3, f. 14r.

p. 269

Fig. 15a. *Emperor Muhammad Shah at a Window*, by Nidha Mal, Delhi, late Mughal, ca. 1730, opaque watercolor and gold on paper, 12.4 cm x 8.5 cm. San Diego Museum of Art, Edwin Binney 3rd Collection, 1990:376.

p. 273

Fig. 18b. Hadi Rani Mahal, Nagaur. Photo courtesy Mehrangarh Museum Trust.

Fig. 18c. *Maharaja Bakhat Singh Entering Nagaur*, attributed here partially to Dalchand, Kishangarh, ca. 1745. Sven Gahlin Collection.

Fig. 19a. *Emperor Muhammad Shah on a Terrace at Night*, Mughal dynasty, ca. 1720–25. Kasturbhai Lalbhai Collection, Ahmedabad.

p. 274

Fig. 20b. *Raja Vijai Singh Celebrates Holi at Nagaur*, ca. 1760–70. Collection Howard Hodgkin. Photo by Prudence Cuming Associates, London.

p. 282

Fig. 34a. *Water Sport of Krishna*, Marwar, early 18th century, 30.5 x 21 cm (without border). The Trustees, Chhatrapati Shivaji Maharaj Vastu Sangrahalaya (formerly Prince of Wales Museum of Western India), Mumbai, 52.23.

Fig. 34b. *Water Sport of Krishna*, Rajasthani, Bundi, 1760–70, 24.6 x 17 cm (without border). The Trustees, Chhatrapati Shivaji Maharaj Vastu Sangrahalaya (formerly Prince of Wales Museum of Western India), Mumbai, 52.20.

p. 284

Fig. 36a. Detail, Map of Amber, Rajasthan, Amber, ca. 1711, ink and paint on cloth, 64.5 x 66. 1 cm. National Museum of India, New Delhi, 56.92.4.

p. 290

Fig. 44a. *Adinath Virat Swarup*, Manmoi (Rajasthan?), n.d., watercolor and ink on paper, 23 x 36 cm. Pustak Prakash Library, Jodhpur, no. 1450.1283. Photo by Debra Diamond.

p. 294

Fig. 48a. *Cosmic Man (Lokapurusha)*, Bikaner, Rajasthan, ca. 1775, opaque watercolor on cloth, 132.1 x 63.5 cm. Paul F. Walter Collection. Published in Pratapaditya Pal, *The Peaceful Liberators: Jain Art from India* (Los Angeles County Museum of Art, 1995), no. 103A.

p. 298

(bottom left) Detail, *Maharaja Bakhat Singh and Prince Vijai Singh Watch an Elephant Fight*, Nagaur, ca. 1735, Mehrangarh Museum Trust, RJS 1992.

(bottom right) Cat. 17, detail, *Maharaja Bakhat Singh Watches Elephants Wreaking Havoc*, ca. 1740, Mehrangarh Museum Trust, RJS 2032.

p. 299

(top left) Detail, *Darbar of Ajit Singh of Ghanerao*, Rajasthan, Ghanerao style, ca. 1722, Lalbhai Dalpatbhai Museum, Ahmedabad, 87.16.

(top, second from left) Detail, *Maharaja Ajit Singh and Prince Bakhat Singh*, by Udaipur, Jodhpur, ca. 1723–24, Mehrangarh Museum Trust, RJS 1974.

(top, second from right) Detail, *Maharaja Bakhat Singh*, Nagaur, ca. 1730, Collection Howard Hodgkin.

(top, right) Detail, *Bakhat Singh Conversing with Maharaja Abhai Singh, Who Holds His Nephew, Vijai Singh*, Jodhpur, ca. 1732, Mehrangarh Museum Trust, RJS 4833.

(bottom left) Cat. 12, detail, *Maharaja Bakhat Singh Worshipping Krishna*, Jodhpur, ca. 1730–35, Mehrangarh Museum Trust, RJS 1971.

(bottom, second from left) Cat. 15, detail, *Maharaja Bakhat Singh at the Jharokha Window of the Bakhat Singh Mahal*, Jodhpur, 1737, Mehrangarh Museum Trust, RJS 2031.

(bottom, second from right) Detail, *Maharaja Bakhat Singh*, Jodhpur, 1745, Mehrangarh Museum Trust, RJS 4813.

(bottom, right) Detail, *Prince Vijai Singh and Maharaja Bakhat Singh*, Jodhpur, ca. 1751, Mehrangarh Museum Trust, RJS 4215

Index

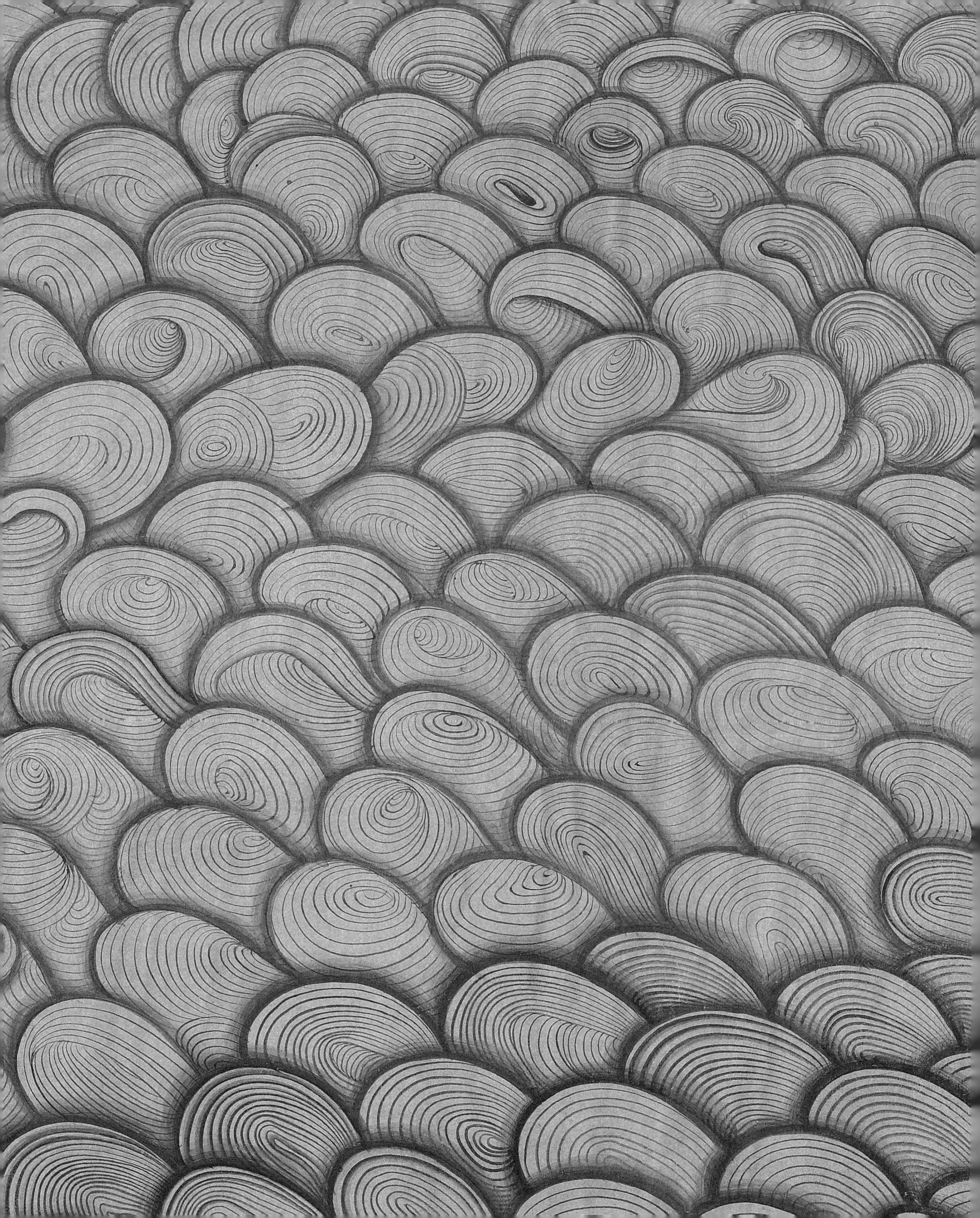

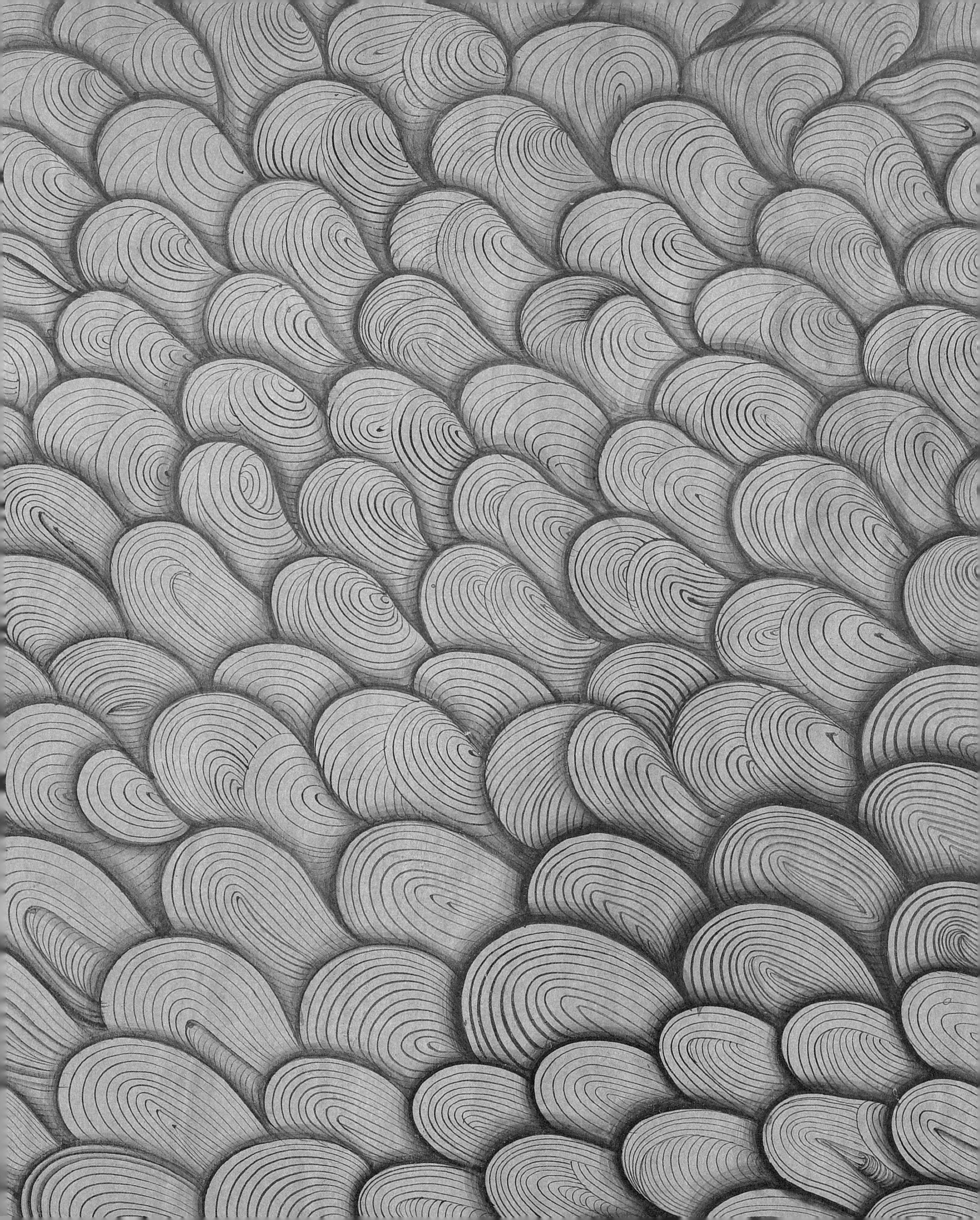

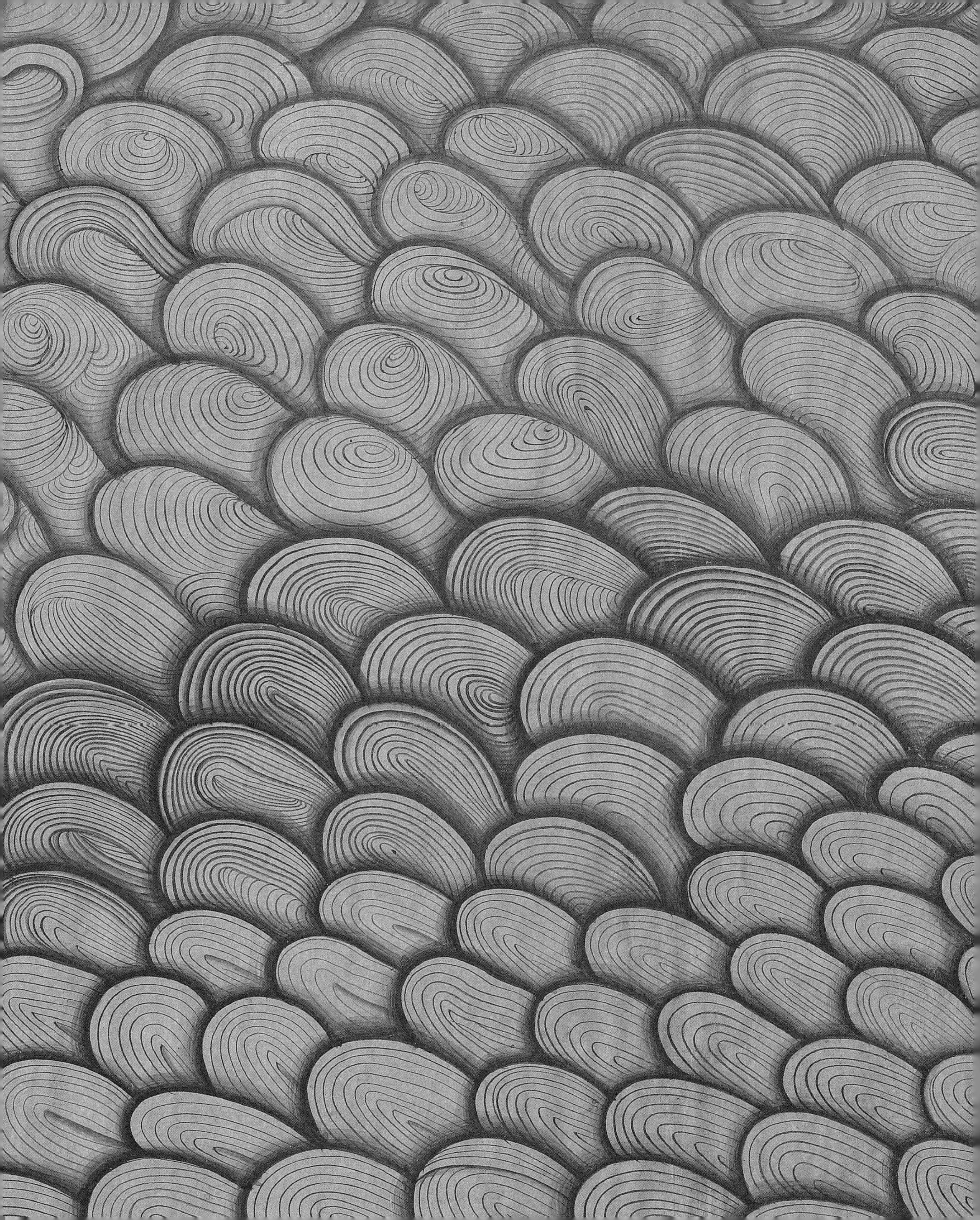

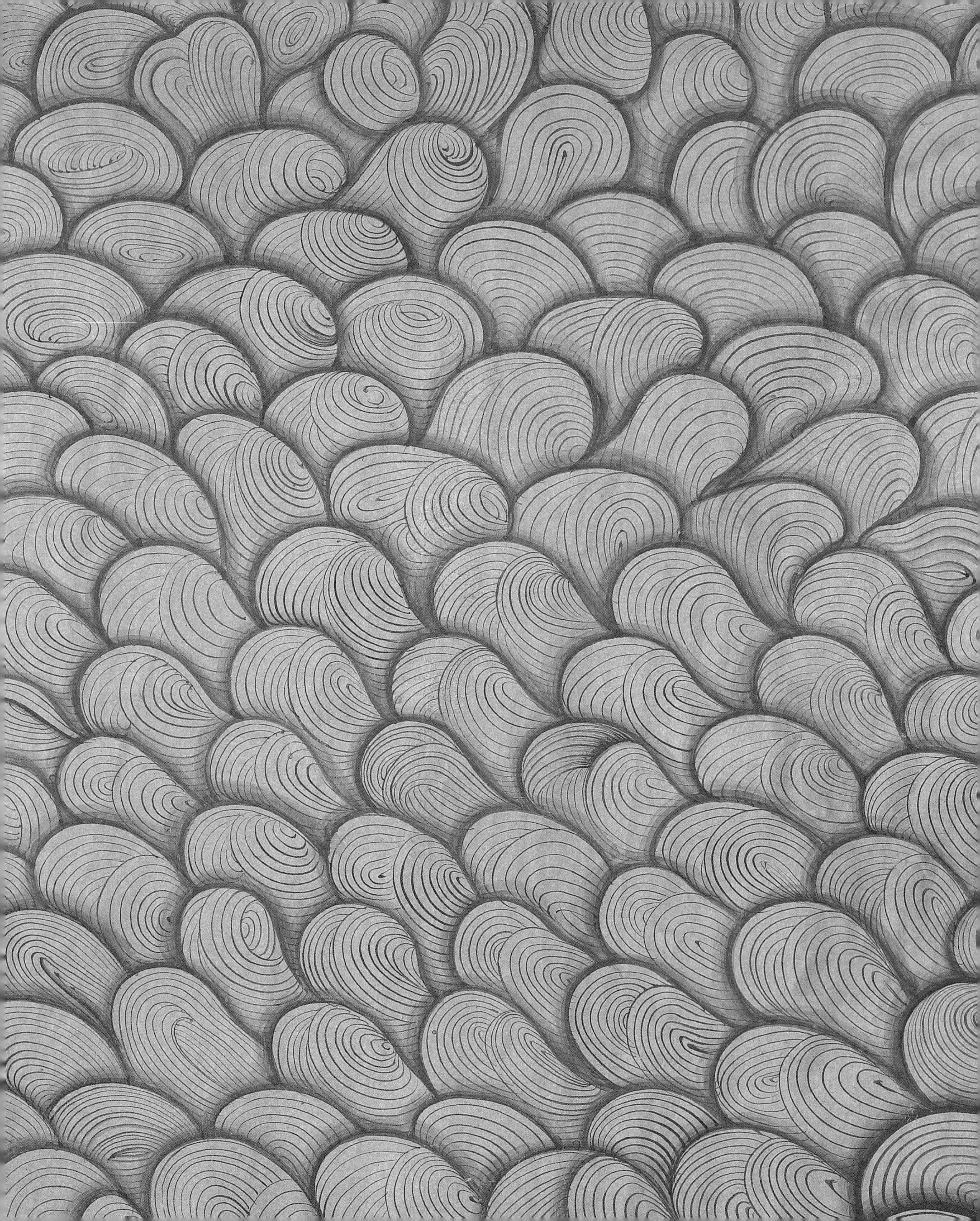